Beginning C

From Beginner to Pro

Sixth Edition

German Gonzalez-Morris
Ivor Horton

Apress®

Beginning C: From Beginner to Pro

German Gonzalez-Morris
Santiago, Chile

Ivor Horton
STRATFORD UPON AVON, UK

ISBN-13 (pbk): 978-1-4842-5975-7
https://doi.org/10.1007/978-1-4842-5976-4

ISBN-13 (electronic): 978-1-4842-5976-4

Managing Director, Apress Media LLC: Welmoed Spahr
Acquisitions Editor: Steve Anglin
Development Editor: Matthew Moodie
Coordinating Editor: Mark Powers

Cover designed by eStudioCalamar

Cover image designed by Freepik (www.freepik.com)

Distributed to the book trade worldwide by Apress Media, LLC, 1 New York Plaza, New York, NY 10004, U.S.A. Phone 1-800-SPRINGER, fax (201) 348-4505, e-mail orders-ny@springer-sbm.com, or visit www.springeronline.com. Apress Media, LLC is a California LLC and the sole member (owner) is Springer Science + Business Media Finance Inc (SSBM Finance Inc). SSBM Finance Inc is a **Delaware** corporation.

For information on translations, please e-mail editorial@apress.com; for reprint, paperback, or audio rights, please email bookpermissions@springernature.com.

Apress titles may be purchased in bulk for academic, corporate, or promotional use. eBook versions and licenses are also available for most titles. For more information, reference our Print and eBook Bulk Sales web page at http://www.apress.com/bulk-sales.

Any source code or other supplementary material referenced by the author in this book is available to readers on GitHub via the book's product page, located at www.apress.com/9781484259757. For more detailed information, please visit http://www.apress.com/source-code.

Printed on acid-free paper

To my parents, Germán and Felicia

—German Gonzalez-Morris

For my daughter, Dany

—Ivor Horton

Table of Contents

About the Authors

German Gonzalez-Morris is a software architect/engineer working with C/C++, Java, and different application containers, in particular, with WebLogic Server. He has developed different applications including JEE/Spring/Python. His areas also include OOP, Java/JEE, Python, design patterns, algorithms, Spring Core/MVC/Security, and microservices. German has worked in performance messaging, Restful API, and transactional systems. For more, see www.linkedin.com/in/german-gonzalez-morris.

Ivor Horton is self-employed in consultancy and writes programming tutorials. He worked for IBM for many years and holds a bachelor's degree, with honors, in mathematics. Ivor's experience at IBM includes programming in most languages (like assembler and high-level languages) on a variety of machines, real-time programming, and designing and implementing real-time closed-loop industrial control systems. He has extensive experience teaching programming to engineers and scientists (Fortran, PL/1, APL, etc.). Ivor is an expert in mechanical, process, and electronic CAD systems; mechanical CAM systems; and DNC/CNC systems.

About the Technical Reviewer

Michael Thomas has worked in software development for more than 20 years as an individual contributor, team lead, program manager, and vice president of engineering. Michael has more than 10 years of experience working with mobile devices. His current focus is in the medical sector, using mobile devices to accelerate information transfer between patients and healthcare providers.

Acknowledgments

I want to thank my family—my parents, Germán and Felicia Morris, for giving me education opportunities and support; Patricia Cruces, my partner, for her infinite patience and love; and my sons, Raimundo and Gregorio, for their happiness and inspiration.

I value the support and opportunity given to me by the complete Apress team, Steve Anglin and Mark Powers, and thank them for their guidance and advice. I also thank Michael Thomas, the technical reviewer, for his important feedback, suggestions, and corrections.

Thanks to my friends and colleagues for their understanding, perceptions, and recommendations on completing ideas in the book: Ariel Aguayo, Carlos Hasan, and Daniel Lagos.

Introduction

Welcome to *Beginning C: From Beginner to Pro*, Sixth Edition. With this book, you can become a competent C programmer using the latest version of the C language. In many ways, C is an ideal language with which to learn programming. It's very compact, so there isn't a lot of syntax to learn before you can write real applications. In spite of its conciseness, it's extremely powerful and is used by professionals in many different areas. The power of C is such that it can be applied at all levels, from developing device drivers and operating system components to creating large-scale applications. A relatively new area for C is in application development for mobile phones.

C compilers are available for virtually every kind of computer, so when you've learned C, you'll be equipped to program in just about any context. Once you know C, you have an excellent base from which you can build an understanding of the object-oriented C++.

My objective in this book is to minimize what I think are the three main hurdles the aspiring programmer must face: coming to grips with the jargon that pervades every programming language, understanding how to use the language elements (as opposed to merely knowing what they are), and appreciating how the language is applied in a practical context.

Jargon is an invaluable and virtually indispensable means of communication for the expert professional as well as the competent amateur, so it can't be avoided. My approach is to ensure that you understand the jargon and get comfortable using it in context. In this way, you'll be able to more effectively use the documentation that comes along with the typical programming product and also feel comfortable reading and learning from the literature that surrounds most programming languages.

Comprehending the syntax and effects of the language elements is obviously an essential part of learning C, but appreciating how the language features work and how they are used is equally important. Rather than just using code fragments, I provide you with practical working examples in each chapter that show how the language features can be applied to specific problems. These examples provide a basis for you to experiment and see the effects of changing the code.

Your understanding of programming in context needs to go beyond the mechanics of applying individual language elements. To help you gain this understanding, I conclude most chapters with a more complex program that applies what you've learned in the chapter. These programs will help you gain the competence and confidence to develop your own applications and provide you with insight into how you can apply language elements in combination and on a larger scale. Most important, they'll give you an idea of what's involved in designing real programs and managing real code.

It's important to realize a few things that are true for learning any programming language. First, there is quite a lot to learn, but this means you'll gain a greater sense of satisfaction when you've mastered it. Second, it's great fun, so you really will enjoy it. Third, you can only learn programming by doing it, and this book helps you along the way. Finally, it's certain you will make a lot of mistakes and get frustrated from time to time during the learning process. When you think you are completely stuck, you just need to be persistent. You will eventually experience that eureka moment and realize it wasn't as difficult as you thought.

How to Use This Book

Because I believe in the hands-on approach, you'll write your first programs almost immediately. Every chapter has several complete programs that put theory into practice, and these are key to the book. You should type in and run all the examples that appear in the text because the very act of typing them in is a tremendous memory aid. You should also attempt all the exercises that appear at the end of each chapter. When you get a program to work for the first time—particularly when you're trying to solve your own problems—you'll find that the great sense of accomplishment and progress makes it all worthwhile.

The pace is gentle at the start, but you'll gain momentum as you get further into the subject. Each chapter covers quite a lot of ground, so take your time and make sure you understand everything before moving on. Experimenting with the code and trying out your own ideas are important parts of the learning process. Try modifying the programs and see what else you can make them do—that's when it gets really interesting. And don't be afraid to try things out—if you don't understand how something works, just type in a few variations and see what happens. It doesn't matter if it's wrong. You'll find you often learn a lot from getting it wrong. A good approach is to read each chapter through, get an idea of its scope, and then go back and work through all the examples.

You might find some of the end-of-chapter programs quite difficult. Don't worry if it's not all completely clear on the first try. There are bound to be bits that you find hard to understand at first because they often apply what you've learned to rather complicated problems. If you really get stuck, you can skip the end-of-chapter exercises, move on to the next chapter, and come back to them later. You can even go through the entire book without worrying about them. However, if you can complete the exercises, it shows you are making real progress.

Who This Book Is For

Beginning C, Sixth Edition is designed to teach you how to write useful programs in C as quickly and easily as possible. By the end of *Beginning C*, you'll have a thorough grounding in programming the C language. This is a tutorial for those of you who've done a little bit of programming before, understand the concepts behind it, and want to further your knowledge by learning C. However, no previous programming knowledge on your part is assumed, so if you're a newcomer to programming, the book will still work for you.

What You Need to Use This Book

To use this book, you'll need a computer with a C compiler and library installed, so you can execute the examples, and a program text editor for preparing your source code files. The compiler you use should provide good support for the current international standard for the C language, C17 (ISO/IEC 9899:2018), which is a bug fix version for C11, commonly referred to as C17 or C18. You'll also need an editor for creating and modifying your code. You can use any plain text editor such as Notepad or vi to create your source program files. However, you'll get along better if your editor is designed for editing C code.

I can suggest two sources for a suitable C compiler, both of which are freeware:

- The GNU C compiler, GCC, is available from www.gnu.org and supports a variety of operating system environments.

- The Pelles C compiler for Microsoft Windows is downloadable from www.smorgasbordet.com/pellesc/ and includes an excellent integrated development environment (IDE).

Conventions Used

I use a number of different styles of text and layout in the book to help differentiate between the different kinds of information. For the most part, their meanings will be obvious. Program code will appear like this:

```
int main(void)
{   printf("Beginning C\n");
    return 0;
}
```

When a code fragment is a modified version of a previous instance, I occasionally show the lines that have changed in bold type like this:

```
int main(void)
{
  printf("Beginning C by Ivor Horton\n");
    return 0;
}
```

When code appears in the text, it has a different typestyle that looks like this: double.

I'll use different types of "brackets" in the program code. They aren't interchangeable, and their differences are very important. I'll refer to the symbols ( ) as parentheses, the symbols { } as braces, and the symbols [ ] as square brackets.

Important new words in the text are shown in italic *like this*.

CHAPTER 1

Programming in C

C is a powerful and compact computer language that allows you to write programs that specify exactly what you want your computer to do. You're in charge: you create a program, which is just a set of instructions, and your computer will follow them.

Programming in C isn't difficult, as you're about to find out. I'm going to teach you all the fundamentals of C programming in an enjoyable and easy-to-understand way, and by the end of this chapter, you'll have written your first few C programs. It's as easy as that!

In this chapter, you'll learn

- What the C language standard is

- What the standard library is

- How to create C programs

- How C programs are organized

- How to write your own program to display text on the screen

The C Language

C is remarkably flexible. It has been used for developing just about everything you can imagine by way of a computer program, from accounting applications to word processing and from games to operating systems. It is not only the basis for more advanced languages, such as C++, it is also used currently for developing mobile phone apps in the form of Objective C. *Objective C* is standard C with a thin veneer of object-oriented programming capability added and too many new devices/microcontrollers, such as Raspberry Pi and Arduino. C is easy to learn because of its compactness. Thus, C is an ideal first language if you have ambitions to be a programmer. You'll acquire sufficient knowledge for practical application development quickly and easily.

The C language is defined by an international standard, and the latest is currently defined by the C17 (ISO/IEC 9899:2018), which is a bug fix version for C11 more than new features (for instance, it deprecates ATOMIC_VAR_INIT). The current standard is commonly referred to as C17 or C18—the informal names of this version. This occurs because it was finished in 2017, but published in 2018. It is known that GCC uses C17 as a parameter to target this new version. Nevertheless, the aforementioned is not declared in the standard, and the language that I describe in this book conforms to C17 or can be considered C11 with several solved issues. You need to be aware that some elements of the language as defined by C17 are optional. This implies that a C compiler that conforms to the C17 standard may not implement everything in the standard. (A *compiler* is just a program that converts your program written in terms you understand into

© German Gonzalez-Morris and Ivor Horton 2020
G. Gonzalez-Morris and I. Horton, *Beginning C*, https://doi.org/10.1007/978-1-4842-5976-4_1

a form your computer understands.) I will identify any language feature in the book that is optional so far as C17 is concerned, just so you are aware that it is possible that your compiler may not support it. We will use C11/C17 as a synonym in the book.

It is also possible that a C17 compiler may not implement all of the language features mandated by the C17 standard; in particular, only the newest compilers have C11/C17 compatibility at 100 percent. It takes time to implement new language capabilities, so compiler developers will often take an incremental approach to implementing them. This provides another reason why a program may not work. Having said that, I can confirm from my own experience that the most common reason for things not working in a C program, at least 99.9 percent of the time, is that a mistake has been made.

The Standard Library

The *standard library* for C is also specified within the C17 standard. The standard library defines constants, symbols, and functions that you frequently need when writing a C program. It also provides some optional extensions to the basic C language. Machine-dependent facilities such as input and output for your computer are implemented by the standard library in a machine-independent form. This means that you write data to a disk file in C in the same way on your PC as you would on any other kind of computer, even though the underlying hardware processes are quite different. The standard functionality that the library contains includes capabilities that most programmers are likely to need, such as processing text strings or math calculations. This saves you an enormous amount of effort that would be required to implement such things yourself.

The standard library is specified in a set of standard files called *header files*. Header files always have names with the extension .h. To make a particular set of standard features available in your C program file, you just include the appropriate standard header file in a way that I'll explain later in this chapter. Every program you write will make use of the standard library. A summary of the header files that make up the standard library is in Appendix E.

At the beginning, there was the C POSIX library that implemented many features for ANSI C. One of those libraries is pthreads that today is obsolete and implemented in the standard library. Other POSIX libraries (ISO/IEC 9945 (POSIX)) are in the road map for C2x for future releases.

Learning C

If you are completely new to programming, there are some aspects of C that you do not need to learn, at least not the first time around. These are capabilities that are quite specialized or used relatively infrequently. I have put all these together in Chapter 14 so you will learn about them when you are comfortable with the rest.

Although the code for all the examples is available via the **Download Source Code** link located at www.apress.com/9781484259757, I recommend that you type in all the examples in the book, even when they are very simple. Keying stuff in makes it less likely that you will forget things later. Don't be afraid to experiment with the code. Making mistakes is very educational in programming. The more mistakes you make early on, the more you are likely to learn.

Creating C Programs

There are four fundamental stages, or processes, in the creation of any C program:

- Editing
- Compiling
- Linking
- Executing

You'll soon know all these processes like the back of your hand because you'll be carrying them out so often. First, I'll explain what each process is and how it contributes to the development of your C program.

Editing

Editing is the process of creating and modifying C source code—the name given to the program instructions you write. Some C compilers come with a specific editor program that provides a lot of assistance in managing your programs. In fact, an editor often provides a complete environment for writing, managing, developing, and testing your programs. This is sometimes called an *integrated development environment* (IDE).

You can also use a general-purpose text editor to create your source files, but the editor must store the code as plain text without any extra formatting data embedded in it. Don't use a word processor such as Microsoft Word; word processors aren't suitable for producing program code because of the extra formatting information they store along with the text. In general, if you have a compiler system with an editor included, it will provide a lot of features that make it easier to write and organize your source programs. There will usually be automatic facilities for laying out the program text appropriately and color highlighting for important language elements, which not only makes your code more readable but also provides a clear indicator when you make errors when keying in such words.

If you're working with Linux, the most common text editor is the Vim editor. Alternately, you might prefer to use the GNU Emacs editor. With Microsoft Windows, you could use one of the many freeware and shareware programming editors. These will often provide help in ensuring your code is correct, with syntax highlighting and autoindenting. There is also a version of Emacs for Microsoft Windows. The vi and Vim editors from the UNIX environment are available for Windows too, and you could even use Notepad++ (http://notepad-plus-plus.org/).

Of course, you can also purchase one of the professionally created programming development environments that support C, such as those from JetBrains or Microsoft(there is a free Community Edition), in which case you will have very extensive editing capabilities. Before parting with your cash though, it's a good idea to check that the level of C that is supported conforms to the current C standard, C17. With some of the products out there that are primarily aimed at C++ developers, C has been left behind somewhat.

Compiling

The *compiler* converts your source code into machine language and detects and reports errors in the compilation process. The input to this stage is the file you produce during your editing, which is usually referred to as a *source file*.

The compiler can detect a wide range of errors that are due to invalid or unrecognized program code, as well as structural errors where, for example, part of a program can never be executed. The output from the compiler is known as *object code,* and it is stored in files called *object files*, which usually have names with the extension .obj in the Microsoft Windows environment or .o in the Linux/UNIX environment. The compiler can detect several different kinds of errors during the translation process, and most of these will prevent the object file from being created.

The result of a successful compilation is a file with the same name as that used for the source file, but with the .o or .obj extension.

If you're working in UNIX, at the command line, the standard command to compile your C programs will be cc (or the GNU's Not UNIX [GNU] compiler, which is .gcc). You can use it like this:

```
cc -c myprog.c
```

where myprog.c is the name of the source file that contains the program you want to compile. Note that if you omit the -c flag, your program will automatically be linked as well. The result of a successful compilation will be an object file.

Most C compilers will have a standard compile option, whether it's from the command line (such as `cc myprog.c`) or a menu option from within an IDE (where you'll find a Compile menu option). Compiling from within an IDE is generally much easier than using the command line.

Compilation is a two-stage process. The first stage is called the *preprocessing phase*, during which your code may be modified or added to, and the second stage is the actual *compilation* that generates the object code (this second stage does assembly underneath; GCC and other compilers have options for these steps, but most of the time, it is not necessary). Your source file can include preprocessing *macros*, which you use to add to or modify the C program statements. Don't worry if this doesn't make complete sense now. It will come together for you as the book progresses.

Linking

The *linker* combines the object modules generated by the compiler from source code files, adds required code modules from the standard library supplied as part of C, and welds everything into an executable whole. The linker also detects and reports errors, for example, if part of your program is missing or a nonexistent library component is referenced.

In practice, a program of any significant size will consist of several source code files, from which the compiler generates object files that need to be linked. A large program may be difficult to write in one working session, and it may be impossible to work with as a single file. By breaking it up into a number of smaller source files that each provide a coherent part of what the complete program does, you can make the development of the program a lot easier. The source files can be compiled separately, which makes eliminating simple typographical errors a bit easier. Furthermore, the whole program can usually be developed incrementally. The set of source files that make up the program will usually be integrated under a *project name*, which is used to refer to the whole program.

Program libraries support and extend the C language by providing routines to carry out operations that aren't part of the language. For example, libraries contain routines that support operations such as performing input and output, calculating a square root, comparing two character strings, or obtaining date and time information.

A failure during the linking phase means that once again you have to go back and edit your source code. Success, on the other hand, will produce an executable file, but this does not necessarily mean that your program works correctly. In a Microsoft Windows environment, the executable file will have an `.exe` extension; in UNIX, there will be no such extension, but the file will be of an executable type. Many IDEs have a *build option*, which will compile and link your program in a single operation.

Executing

The execution stage is where you run your program, having completed all the previous processes successfully. Unfortunately, this stage can also generate a wide variety of error conditions that can include producing the wrong output, just sitting there and doing nothing, or perhaps crashing your computer for good measure. In all cases, it's back to the editing process to check your source code.

Now for the good news: This is also the stage where if your program works, you get to see your computer doing exactly what you told it to do! In UNIX and Linux, you can just enter the name of the file that has been compiled and linked to execute the program. In most IDEs, you'll find an appropriate menu command that allows you to run or execute your compiled program. This Run or Execute option may have a menu of its own, or you may find it under the Compile menu option. In Windows, you can run the `.exe` file for your program as you would any other executable.

The processes of editing, compiling, linking, and executing are essentially the same for developing programs in any environment and with any compiled language. Figure 1-1 summarizes how you would typically pass through processes as you create your own C programs.

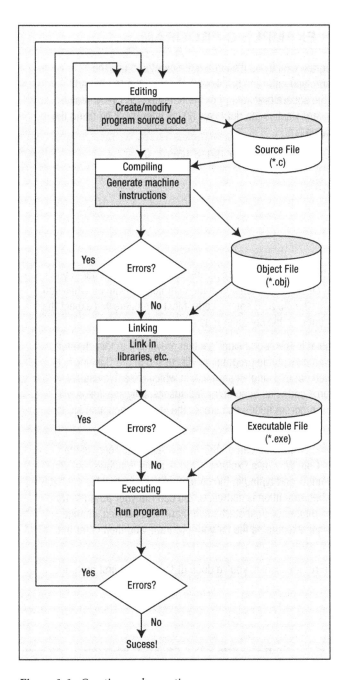

Figure 1-1. *Creating and executing a program*

Creating Your First Program

We'll step through the processes of creating a simple C program, from entering the program source code to executing it. Don't worry if what you type doesn't mean much to you at this stage—I'll explain everything as we go along.

5

TRY IT OUT: AN EXAMPLE C PROGRAM

Run your editor and type in the following program exactly as it's written. Be careful to use the punctuation exactly as you see here. Make sure you enter the brackets that are on the fourth and last lines as braces—the curly ones { }, not the square brackets [ ] or the parentheses ( )—it really does matter. Also, make sure you put the forward slashes the right way (/), as later you'll be using the backslash (\) as well. Don't forget the semicolon (;):

```
/* Program 1.1 Your Very First C Program - Displaying Hello World */
#include <stdio.h>

int main(void)
{
  printf("Hello world!");
  return 0;
}
```

When you've entered the source code, save the program as hello.c. You can use whatever name you like instead of hello, but the extension must be .c. This extension is the common convention when you write C programs and identifies the contents of the file as C source code. Most compilers will expect the source file to have the extension .c, and if it doesn't, the compiler may refuse to process it.

Next, you'll compile your program as I described in the "Compiling" section previously in this chapter and then link the pieces necessary to create an executable program, as discussed in the "Linking" section. Compiling and linking are often carried out in a single operation, in which case it is usually described as a *build operation*. When the source code has been compiled successfully, the linker will add code from the standard libraries that your program needs and create the single executable file for your program.

Finally, you can execute your program. Remember that you can do this in several ways. There is the usual method of double-clicking the .exe file from Windows Explorer if you're using Windows, but you will be better off opening a command-line window and typing in the command to execute it because the window showing the output will disappear when execution is complete. You can run your program from the command line in all operating system environments. Just start a command-line session, change the current directory to the one that contains the executable file for your program, and then enter the program name to run it.

If everything worked without producing any error messages, you've done it! This is your first program, and you should see the following output:

```
Hello world!
```

Editing Your First Program

You could try altering the same program to display something else. For example, you could edit the program to read like this:

```
/* Program 1.2 Your Second C Program */
#include<stdio.h>

int main(void)
{
  printf("\"If at first you don't succeed, try, try, try again!\"");
  return 0;
}
```

The output from this version will be

```
        "If at first you don't succeed, try, try, try again!"
```

The \" sequence that appears at the beginning and end of the text to be displayed is called an *escape sequence*, and there are several different escape sequences. Here, \" is a special way of including a double quote in the text to be output. This is necessary because double quotes (the straight kind, not curly quotes) are used to indicate where a character string begins and ends. The escape sequences cause a double quote to appear at the beginning and end of the output. If you didn't use the escape sequences, not only would the double quote characters not appear in the output but the program would not compile. You'll learn all about escape sequences in the "Control Characters" section later in this chapter.

You can try recompiling the program, relinking it, and running it again once you have altered the source code. With a following wind and a bit of luck, you have now edited your first program. You've written a program using the editor, edited it, and compiled, linked, and executed it.

Dealing with Errors

To err is human, so there's no need to be embarrassed about making mistakes. Fortunately, computers don't generally make mistakes, and they're actually very good at indicating where we've slipped up. Sooner or later, your compiler is going to present you with a list (sometimes a list that's longer than you want) of the mistakes that are in your source code. You'll usually get an indication of the statements that are in error. When this happens, you must return to the editing stage, find out what's wrong with the incorrect code, and fix it.

Keep in mind that one error can result in error messages for subsequent statements that may actually be correct. This usually happens with statements that refer to something that is supposed to be defined by a statement containing an error. Of course, if a statement that defines something has an error, then what was supposed to be defined won't be.

Let's step through what happens when your source code is incorrect by creating an error in your program. Edit your second program example, removing the semicolon (;) at the end of the line with printf() in it, as shown here:

```
/* Program 1.2 Your Second C Program */
#include<stdio.h>
```

```
int main(void)
{
  printf("\"If at first you don't succeed, try, try, try again!\"")
  return 0;
}
```

If you now try to compile this program, you'll see an error message that will vary slightly depending on which compiler you're using. A typical error message is as follows:

```
Syntax error : expected ';' but found 'return'
HELLO.C - 1 error(s), 0 warning(s)
```

Here, the compiler is able to determine precisely what the error is and where. There really should be a semicolon at the end of that printf() line. As you start writing your own programs, you'll probably get a lot of errors during compilation that are caused by simple punctuation mistakes. It's so easy to forget a comma or a bracket or to just press the wrong key. Don't worry about this; a lot of experienced programmers make exactly the same mistakes—even after years of practice.

As I said earlier, just one mistake can sometimes result in a whole stream of abuse from your compiler, as it throws you a multitude of different things that it doesn't like. Don't get put off by the number of errors reported. After you consider the messages carefully, the basic approach is to go back and edit your source code to fix at least the first error, because that may have triggered other errors, and ignore the errors you can't understand. Then have another go at compiling the source file. With luck, you'll get fewer errors the next time around.

To correct your example program, just go back to your editor and reenter the semicolon. Recompile, check for any other errors, and your program is fit to be run again.

Dissecting a Simple Program

Now that you've written and compiled your first program, let's go through another that's very similar and see what the individual lines of code do. Have a look at this program:

```
/* Program 1.3 Another Simple C Program - Displaying a Quotation */
#include <stdio.h>

int main(void)
{
  printf("Beware the Ides of March!");
  return 0;
}
```

This is virtually identical to your first program. Even so, the practice is good, so use your editor to enter this example and see what happens when you compile and run it. If you type it in accurately, compile it, and run it, you should get the following output:

```
Beware the Id.es of March!
```

Comments

Look at the first line of code in the preceding example:

```
/* Program 1.3 Another Simple C Program - Displaying a Quotation */
```

This isn't actually part of the program code, in that it isn't telling the computer to do anything. It's simply a *comment*, and it's there to remind you, or someone else reading your code, what the program does. Anything between /* and */ is treated as a comment. As soon as your compiler finds /* in your source file, it will simply ignore anything that follows (even if the text looks like program code) until it finds a matching */ that marks the end of the comment. This may be on the same line, or it can be several lines further on. If you forget to include the matching */, everything following /* will be ignored. Here's how you could use a single comment to identify the author of the code and to assert your copyright:

```
/*
 * Written by Ivor Horton
 * Copyright 2012
 */
```

You can also embellish comments to make them stand out:

```
/*****************************************
 * This is a very important comment      *
 * so please read this.                  *
 *****************************************/
```

You can add a comment at the end of a line of code using a different notation, like this:

```
  printf("Beware the Ides of March!");        // This line displays a quotation
```

Everything following two forward slashes on a line is ignored by the compiler. This form of comment is less cluttered than the previous notation, especially when the comment is on a single line.

You should try to get into the habit of documenting your programs, using comments as you go along. Your programs will, of course, work without comments, but when you write longer programs, you may not remember what they do or how they work. Put in enough comments to ensure that a month from now you (and any other programmer) can understand the aim of the program and how it works.

Let's add some more comments to the program:

```
/* Program 1.3 Another Simple C Program - Displaying a Quotation */
#include <stdio.h>              // This is a preprocessor directive

int main(void)                  // This identifies the function main()
{                               // This marks the beginning of main()
  printf("Beware the Ides of March!");  // This line outputs a quotation
  return 0;                     // This returns control to the operating system
}                               // This marks the end of main()
```

You can see that using comments can be a very useful way of explaining what's going on in the program. You can place comments wherever you want in your program, and you can use them to explain the general objectives of the code as well as the specifics of how the code works.

Preprocessing Directives

Look at the following line of code:

```
#include <stdio.h>              // This is a preprocessor directive
```

This is not strictly part of the executable program, but it is essential in this case—in fact, the program won't work without it. The symbol # indicates this is a *preprocessing directive*, which is an instruction to your compiler to do something before compiling the source code. The compiler handles these directives during an initial preprocessing phase before the compilation process starts. There are quite a few preprocessing directives, and there are usually some at the beginning of the program source file, but they can be anywhere.

In this case, the compiler is instructed to "include" in your program the contents of the file with the name stdio.h. This file is called a *header file*, because it's usually included at the head of a program source file. In this case, the header file defines information about some of the functions that are provided by the standard C library; but, in general, header files specify information that the compiler uses to integrate any predefined functions or other global objects within a program. You'll be creating your own header files for use with your programs. In this case, because you're using the printf() function from the standard library, you have to include the stdio.h header file. This is because stdio.h contains the information that the compiler needs to understand what printf() means, as well as other functions that deal with input and output. As such, its name, stdio, is short for *standard input/output*. All header files in C have file names with the extension .h. You'll use other standard header files later in the book.

▪ **Note**   Header file names are case sensitive on some systems, so you should always write them in lowercase in #include directives.

Every C compiler that conforms to the C11 standard will have a set of standard header files supplied with it. These header files primarily contain declarations relating to standard library functions and macros that are available with C. Although all C compilers that conform with the standard will support the same basic set of capabilities and will have the same set of mandatory standard header files available, there are standard header files that are optional, and in some cases extra library functions can be provided with a particular compiler that may not be available with other compilers that will typically provide functionality specific to the type of computer on which the compiler runs.

▪ **Note**   All the standard header files are listed in Appendix E.

Defining the main() Function

The next five statements define the function main():

```
int main(void)              // This identifies the function main()
{                           // This marks the beginning of main()
  printf("Beware the Ides of March!");  // This line outputs a quotation
  return 0;                 // This returns control to the operating system
}                           // This marks the end of main()
```

A *function* is just a named block of code between braces that carries out some specific set of operations. Every C program consists of one or more functions, and every C program must contain a function called main()—the reason being that a program always starts execution from the beginning of this function. So imagine that you've created, compiled, and linked a file called progname.exe. When you execute this program, the operating system executes the function main() for the program.

The first line of the definition for the function main() is as follows:

```
int main(void)                 // This identifies the function main()
```

This defines the start of main(). Notice that there is *no* semicolon at the end of the line. The first line identifying this as the function main() has the word int at the beginning. What appears here defines the type of value to be returned by the function, and the word int signifies that main() returns an integer value. The integer value that is returned when the execution of main() ends represents a code that is returned to the operating system that indicates the program state. You end execution of main() and specify the value to be returned in this statement:

```
return 0;                      // This returns control to the operating system
```

This is a return statement that ends execution of main() and returns the value 0 to the operating system. You return a zero value from main() to indicate that the program terminated normally; a nonzero value would indicate an abnormal return, which means things did not proceed as they should have when the program ended.

The parentheses that immediately follow the name of the function main enclose a definition of what information is to be transferred to main() when it starts executing. In this example, there's the word void between the parentheses, and this signifies that no data can be transferred to main(). Later, you'll see how data are transferred to main() and to other functions in a program.

The main() function can call other functions, which in turn may call further functions, and so on. For every function that's called, you have the opportunity to pass some information to it within the parentheses that follow its name. A function will stop execution when a return statement in the body of the function is reached, and control will then transfer to the calling function (or the operating system in the case of the function main()). In general, you define a function so that either it does return a value or it does not. When a function does return a value, the value is always of a specific type. In the case of main(), the value that is returned is of type int, which is an integer.

Keywords

In C, a *keyword* is a word with special significance, so you must not use keywords for any other purpose in your program. For this reason, keywords are also referred to as *reserved words*. In the preceding example, int is a keyword, and void and return are also keywords. C has several keywords, and you'll become familiar with more of them as you learn more of the language. You'll find a complete list of C keywords in Appendix C.

The Body of a Function

The general structure of the function main() is illustrated in Figure 1-2.

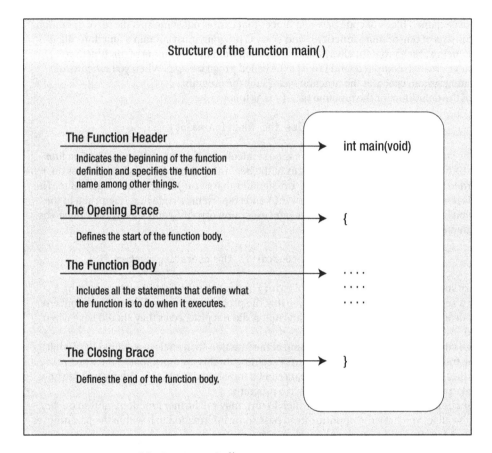

Figure 1-2. *Structure of the function* main()

The function body is the bit between the opening and closing braces that follows the line where the function name appears. The function body contains all the statements that define what the function does. The example main() function has a very simple function body consisting of just two statements:

```
{                               // This marks the beginning of main()
  printf("Beware the Ides of March!");   // This line outputs a quotation
  return 0;                     // This returns control to the operating system
}                               // This marks the end of main()
```

Every function must have a body, although the body can be empty and just consist of the opening and closing braces without any statements between them. In this case, the function will do nothing.

You may wonder what use a function that does nothing is. Actually, this can be very useful when you're developing a program that will have many functions. You can declare the set of (empty) functions that you think you'll need to write to solve the problem at hand, which should give you an idea of the programming that needs to be done, and then gradually create the program code for each function. This technique helps you to build your program in a logical and incremental manner.

■ **Note**   You can see that I've aligned the braces one below the other in Program 1.3 and indented the statements between them. I've done this to make it clear where the block of statements that the braces enclose starts and finishes. Statements between braces are usually indented by a fixed amount—usually two or more spaces—so that the braces stand out. This is good programming style, because it allows the statements within a block to be readily identified.

There are other styles for arranging braces in code, for example:

```c
int main(void)  {
  printf("Beware the Ides of March!");     // This line outputs a quotation
  return 0;

}
```

■ **Tip**   With whatever style you use to arrange your source code, the most important thing is to apply it consistently.

Outputting Information

The body of the main() function in the example includes a statement that calls the printf() function:

```c
  printf("Beware the Ides of March!");   // This line outputs a quotation
```

As I've said, printf() is a standard library function, and it outputs information to the command line (actually the *standard output stream*, which is the command line by default) based on what appears between the parentheses that immediately follow the function name. In this case, the call to the function displays the simple piece of Shakespearean advice that appears between the double quotes; a string of characters between double quotes like this is called a *string literal*. Notice that this line *does* end with a semicolon.

Function Arguments

Items enclosed between the parentheses following a function name, as with the printf() function in the previous statement, are called *arguments*, and they specify data that are to be passed to the function. When there is more than one argument to a function, they must be separated by commas.

In the previous example, the argument to the function is the text string between double quotes. If you don't like the quotation that is specified here, you could display something else by simply including your own choice of words enclosed within double quotes inside the parentheses. For instance, you might prefer a line from *Macbeth*:

```c
  printf("Out, damned Spot! Out I say!");
```

Try using this in the example. When you've modified the source code, you need to compile and link the program again before executing it.

> ■ **Note** As with all executable statements in C (as opposed to defining or directive statements), the `printf()` line must have a semicolon at the end. A very common error when you first start programming in C is to forget the semicolon.

Control Characters

You could alter the program to display two sentences on separate lines using a single `printf()` statement. Try typing in the following code:

```
// Program 1.4 Another Simple C Program - Displaying a Quotation
#include <stdio.h>

int main(void)
{
  printf("My formula for success?\nRise early, work late, strike oil.\n");
  return 0;
}
```

The output from this program looks like this:

```
My formula for success?
Rise early, work late, strike oil.
```

Look at the `printf()` statement. After the first sentence and at the end of the text, you've inserted the characters \n. The combination \n is another escape sequence that represents a newline character. This causes the output cursor to move to the next line, so any subsequent output will start on a new line.

The backslash (\) is always of special significance in a text string because it indicates the start of an escape sequence. The character following the backslash indicates what character the escape sequence represents. In the case of \n, it's n for newline, but there are plenty of other possibilities. Because a backslash itself is of special significance, you need a way to specify a backslash in a text string. To do this, you simply use two backslashes: \\.

Type in the following program:

```
// Program 1.5 Another Simple C Program - Displaying Great Quotations
#include <stdio.h>

int main(void)
{
  printf("\"It is a wise father that knows his own child.\"\nShakespeare\n");
  return 0;
}
```

The output displays the following text:

```
"It is a wise father that knows his own child."
Shakespeare
```

The double quotes are output because you use escape sequences for them in the string. Shakespeare appears on the next line because there is a \n escape sequence following the \".

You can use the \a escape sequence in an output string to sound a beep to signal something interesting or important. Enter and run the following program:

```
// Program 1.6 A Simple C Program - Important
#include <stdio.h>

int main(void)
{
  printf("Be careful!!\n\a");
  return 0;
}
```

The output of this program is sound and vision. Listen closely, and you should hear the beep through the speaker in your computer.

```
Be careful!!
```

The \a sequence represents the "bell" character. Table 1-1 shows all the escape sequences that you can use.

Table 1-1. *Escape Sequences*

Escape sequence	Description
\n	Represents a newline character
\r	Represents a carriage return
\b	Represents a backspace
\f	Represents a form-feed character
\t	Represents a horizontal tab
\v	Represents a vertical tab
\a	Inserts a bell (alert) character
\?	Inserts a question mark (?)
\"	Inserts a double quote (")
\'	Inserts a single quote (')
\\	Inserts a backslash (\)

Try displaying different lines of text on the screen and alter the spacing within that text. You can put words on different lines using \n, and you can use \t to space the text. You'll get a lot more practice with these as you progress through the book.

Trigraph Sequences

In general, you can use a question mark directly in a string. The \? escape sequence only exists because there are nine special sequences of characters called trigraph sequences that are three-character sequences for representing each of the characters #, [,], \, ^, ~, \, {, and }:

??= converts to #	??(converts to [	??) converts to]
??/ converts to \	??< converts to {	??> converts to }
??' converts to ^	??! converts to |	??- converts to ~

These are there for when it is necessary to write C code in the International Organization for Standardization (ISO) invariant code set, which does not have these characters. This is unlikely to apply to you. You can completely forget about all this unless you want to write a statement such as

```
printf("What??!\n");
```

The output produced by this statement will be

```
What|
```

The trigraph ??! will be converted to |. To get the output you intended, you need to write the statement as

```
printf("What?\?!\n");
```

Now the trigraph sequence does not appear because the second question mark is specified by its escape sequence. Your compiler may well issue a warning when you use a trigraph sequence because usually it is unintended. In modern compilers, such as GCC, a warning would be in the output, avoiding the wrong trigraph misinterpretation, and also can be forced with argument –Wtrigraphs:

```
program1_08.c:7:15: warning: trigraph ??! ignored, use -trigraphs to enable [-Wtrigraphs]
```

The Preprocessor

In the example, I explained how you use a preprocessing directive to include the contents of a header file into your source file. The preprocessing phase of compilation can do much more than this. As well as directives, your source file can contain macros. A *macro* is an instruction to the preprocessor to add to or modify the C statements in the program. A macro can be something as simple as defining a symbol, such as INCHES_PER_FOOT to be replaced by 12 wherever the symbol appears. The directive to do this is

```
#define INCHES_PER_FOOT 12
```

With this directive at the beginning of your source file, wherever INCHES_PER_FOOT appears in the code, it will be replaced by 12, for example:

```
printf("There are %d inches in a foot.\n", INCHES_PER_FOOT);
```

After preprocessing, this statement will be

```
printf("There are %d inches in a foot.\n", 12);
```

INCHES_PER_FOOT no longer appears because the symbol has been replaced by the string specified in the #define directive. This will happen for every instance of the symbol in the source file.

A macro can also be quite complicated, with significant amounts of code being added to a source file depending on specified conditions. I won't go into this further here. I will discuss preprocessor macros in detail in Chapter 13. You will meet some macros before that, and I'll explain them in context when they appear.

Developing Programs in C

The process for developing a program in C may not be obvious if you've never written a program before. It's very similar to many other situations in life where it just isn't clear how you're going to achieve your objective when you first start out. Normally you begin with a rough idea of what you want to achieve, but you need to translate this into a more precise specification of what you want. Once you've reached this more precise specification, you can work out the series of steps that will lead to your final objective. Having the idea that you want to build a house just isn't enough. You need to know what kind of house you want, how large it's going to be, what kinds of materials you have to build it with, and where you want to build it. You will also want to know how long it's going to take and the likely cost. This kind of detailed planning is also necessary when you want to write a program. Let's go through the basic steps that you need to follow when you're writing a program. The house analogy is useful, so I'll work with it for a while.

Understanding the Problem

The first step is to get a clear idea of what you want to do. It would be lunacy to start building your house before you had established what facilities it should provide: how many bedrooms, how many bathrooms, how big it's going to be, and so on. All these things affect the cost in terms of materials and the work involved in building the house. Generally it comes down to a compromise that best meets your needs within the constraints of the money, the workforce, and the time that's available for you to complete the project.

It's the same with developing a program of any size. Even for a relatively straightforward problem, you need to know what kind of input to expect, how the input is to be processed, and what kind of output is required—and how it's going to look. The input could be entered with the keyboard, but it might also involve data from a disk file or information obtained over a telephone line or a network. The output could simply be displayed on the screen, or it could be printed; perhaps it might involve writing a new disk file updating an existing file.

For more complex programs, you'll need to look at many more aspects of what the program is going to do. A clear definition of the problem that your program is going to solve is an essential part of understanding the resources and effort that are going to be needed for the creation of a finished product. Considering these details also forces you to establish whether the project is actually feasible. A lack of precision and detail in the specifications for a new program has often resulted in a project taking much longer and costing much more than planned. There are many instances of projects being abandoned for this reason.

Detailed Design

To get the house built, you'll need detailed plans. These plans enable the construction workers to do their jobs, and the plans describe in detail how the house will go together—the dimensions, the materials to use, and so on. You'll also need a plan of what is to be done and when. For example, you'll want the foundation dug before the walls are built, so the plan must involve segmenting the work into manageable units to be performed in a logical sequence.

It's the same with a program. You need to specify what the program does by dividing it into a set of well-defined and manageable chunks that are reasonably self-contained. You also need to detail the way in which these chunks connect, as well as what information each chunk will need when it executes. This will enable you to develop the logic of each chunk relatively independently from the rest of the program. If you treat a large program as one huge process that you try to code as a single chunk, chances are that you'll never get it to work.

Implementation

Given the detailed design of a house, the work can begin. Each group of construction workers will need to complete its part of the project at the right time. Each stage will need to be inspected to check that it's been done properly before the next stage begins. Omitting these checks could easily result in the whole house collapsing.

Of course, if a program is large and you are writing it all yourself, you'll write the source code one unit at a time. As one part is completed, you can write the code for the next. Each part will be based on the detailed design specifications, and you'll verify that each piece works, as much as you can, before proceeding. In this way, you'll gradually progress to a fully working program that does everything you originally intended.

A large programming project usually involves a team of programmers. The project is divided into relatively self-contained units that can be allocated among the members of the team. This allows several units of code to be developed concurrently. The interface between one unit of code and the rest of the program must be precisely defined if the units are going to connect together as a whole.

Testing

The house is complete, but there are a lot of things that need to be tested: the drainage, the water and electricity supplies, the heating, and so on. Any one of these areas can have problems that the contractors need to go back and fix. This is sometimes an iterative process, in which problems with one aspect of the house can be the cause of things going wrong somewhere else.

The mechanism with a program is similar. Each of your program *modules*—the pieces that make up your program—will need to be tested individually. When they don't work properly, you need to debug them. *Debugging* is the process of finding and correcting errors in your program. This term is said to have originated in the days when finding the errors in a program involved tracing where the information went and how it was processed inside the computer by using the circuit diagram for the machine. The story goes that in one instance it was discovered that a computer program error was caused by an insect shorting part of a circuit in the computer. The problem was caused by a bug. Subsequently, the term *bug* was used to refer to any error in a program.

With a simple program, you can often find an error simply by inspecting the code. In general, though, the process of debugging usually involves using a debugger that inserts code temporarily for working out what happened when things go wrong. This includes breakpoints where execution pauses to allow you to inspect values in your code. You can also step through a program a statement at a time. If you don't have a debugger, you can add extra program code to produce output that will enable you to check what the sequence of events is and what intermediate values are produced when a program executes. With a large program, you'll also need to test the program modules in combination because, although the individual modules may work, there's no guarantee that they'll work together! The jargon for this phase of program development is *integration testing*.

Functions and Modular Programming

The word *function* has appeared a few times so far in this chapter with reference to main(), printf(), function body, and so on. Let's explore what functions are in a little more depth and why they're important.

Most programming languages, including C, provide a way of breaking up a program into segments, each of which can be written more or less independently of the others. In C, these segments are called *functions*. The program code in the body of one function is insulated from that of other functions (although they are called functions, this is an imperative/procedural and not functional language). A function will have a specific interface to the outside world in terms of how information is transferred to it and how results generated by the function are transmitted back from it. This interface is specified in the first line of the function, where the function name appears.

Figure 1-3 shows a simple example of a program to analyze baseball scores that is composed of four functions.

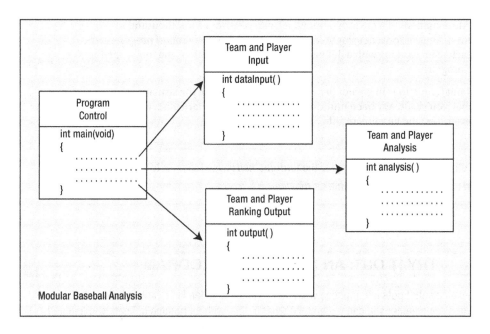

Figure 1-3. *Modular programming*

Each of the four functions does a specific, well-defined job. Overall control of the sequence of operations in the program is managed by one module, main(). There is a function to read and check the input data and another function to do the analysis. Once the data have been read and analyzed, a fourth function has the task of outputting the team and player rankings.

Segmenting a program into manageable chunks is a very important aspect to programming, so let's go over the reasons for doing this:

- It allows each function to be written and tested separately. This greatly simplifies the process of getting the total program to work.

- Several separate functions are easier to handle and understand than one huge function.

- Libraries are just sets of functions that people tend to use all the time. Because they've been prewritten and pretested, you know that they work, so you can use them without worrying about their code details. This will accelerate your program development by allowing you to concentrate on your own code, and it's a fundamental part of the philosophy of C. The richness of the libraries greatly amplifies the power of the language.

- You can accumulate your own libraries of functions that are applicable to the sort of programs that you're interested in. If you find yourself writing a particular function frequently, you can write a generalized version of it to suit your needs and build this into your own library. Then, whenever you need to use that particular function, you can simply use your library version.

- In the development of large programs, which can vary from a few thousand to millions of lines of code, development can be undertaken by teams of programmers, with each team working with a defined subgroup of the functions that make up the whole program.

You'll learn about C functions in greater detail in Chapter 8. Because the structure of a C program is inherently functional, you've already been introduced to one of the standard library functions in one of this chapter's earliest examples: the function printf().

■ **Note**   In some other programming languages, the term *method* is used to refer to a self-contained unit of code. Thus, *method* means essentially the same as *function*.

TRY IT OUT: AN EXAMPLE C PROGRAM

You can try an example that puts into practice what you've learned so far. First, have a look at the following code and see whether you can understand what it does without running it. Then type it in and compile, link, and run it and see what happens:

```c
// Program 1.7 A longer program
#include <stdio.h>                    // Include the header file for input and output

int main(void)
{
  printf("Hi there!\n\n\nThis program is a bit");
  printf(" longer than the others.");
  printf("\nBut really it's only more text.\n\n\n\a\a");
  printf("Hey, wait a minute!! What was that???\n\n");
  printf("\t1.\tA bird?\n");
```

```
    printf("\t2.\tA plane?\n");
    printf("\t3.\tA control character?\n");
    printf("\n\t\t\b\bAnd how will this look when it prints out?\n\n");
    return 0;
}
```

The output will be as follows:

```
Hi there!

This program is a bit longer than the others.
But really it's only more text.

Hey, wait a minute!! What was that???
        1.      A bird?
        2.      A plane?
        3.      A control character?

And how will this look when it prints out?
```

How It Works

The program looks a little bit complicated, but this is only because the text strings between parentheses include a lot of escape sequences. Each text string is bounded by a pair of double quotes. The program is just a succession of calls to the printf() function, and it demonstrates that output to the screen is controlled by what you pass to the printf() function.

You include the stdio.h file from the standard library through a preprocessing directive:

```
#include <stdio.h>                  // Include the header file for input and output
```

You can see that this is a preprocessing directive because it begins with #. The stdio.h file provides the definitions you need to be able to use the printf() function.

You then define the start of the function main() and specify that it returns an integer value with this line:

```
int main(void)
```

The void keyword between the parentheses indicates that no information is passed to the main() function. The opening brace on the next line indicates that the body of the function follows:

```
{
```

The next statement calls the standard library function printf() to output Hi there! to your display screen, followed by two blank lines and the phrase This program is a bit:

```
printf("Hi there!\n\n\nThis program is a bit");
```

The two blank lines are produced by the three \n escape sequences. Each of these starts a new line when the characters are written to the display. The first ends the line containing Hi there!, and the next two produce the two empty lines. The text This program is a bit appears on the fourth line of output. You can see that this one line of code produces a total of four lines of output on the screen.

The line of output produced by the next `printf()` starts at the character position immediately following the last character in the previous output. This outputs `longer than the others` with a space as the first output character:

```
printf(" longer than the others.");
```

This output will simply continue where the last line left off, following the `t` in `bit`. This means that you really do need the space at the beginning of the text; otherwise, the computer will display `This program is a bitlonger than the others`, which isn't what you want.

The next statement starts its output on a new line immediately following the previous line because of the `\n` at the beginning of the text string between the double quotes:

```
printf("\nBut really it's only more text.\n\n\n\a\a");
```

It displays the text and adds two empty lines (because of the three `\n` escape sequences) and beeps. The next output will start at the beginning of the line that follows the second empty line.

The next output is produced by the following statement:

```
printf("Hey, wait a minute!! What was that???\n\n");
```

This outputs the text and then leaves one empty line. The next output will be on the line following the empty line.

Each of the next three statements inserts a tab, displays a number, inserts another tab followed by some text, and ends with a new line. This is useful for making your output easier to read:

```
printf("\t1.\tA bird?\n");
printf("\t2.\tA plane?\n");
printf("\t3.\tA control character?\n");
```

This produces three numbered lines of output.

The next statement initially outputs a newline character, so that there will be an empty line following the previous output. Two tabs are then sent to the command line followed by two backspaces, which moves you back two spaces from the last tab position. Finally, the text is output followed by two newline characters:

```
printf("\n\t\t\b\bAnd how will this look when it prints out?\n\n");
```

The last statement in the body of the function is

```
return 0;
```

This ends execution of `main()` and returns 0 to the operating system.

The closing brace marks the end of the function body:

```
}
```

▓ **Note**   The precise effect of tabs and backspaces in the output can vary between compilers.

Common Mistakes

Mistakes are a fact of life. When you write a computer program in C, the compiler must convert your source code to machine code. To do this, your code must have a precise meaning, so there are very strict rules governing how you use the language. Leave out a comma where one is expected or add a semicolon where you shouldn't and the compiler won't be able to translate your program into machine code.

You'll be surprised just how easy it is to introduce typographical errors into your program, even after years of practice. If you're lucky, these errors will be picked up when you compile or link your program. If you're really unlucky, they can result in your program apparently working fine but producing some intermittent erratic behavior. You can end up spending a lot of time tracking these errors down.

Of course, it's not only typographical errors that cause problems. You'll often find that your detailed implementation is just not right. Where you're dealing with complicated decisions in your program, it's easy to get the logic wrong. Your program may be quite accurate from a language point of view, and it may compile and run without a problem, but it won't produce the right answers. These kinds of errors can be the most difficult to find.

Points to Remember

It would be a good idea to review what you've gleaned from your first program. You can do this by looking at the overview of the important points in Figure 1-4.

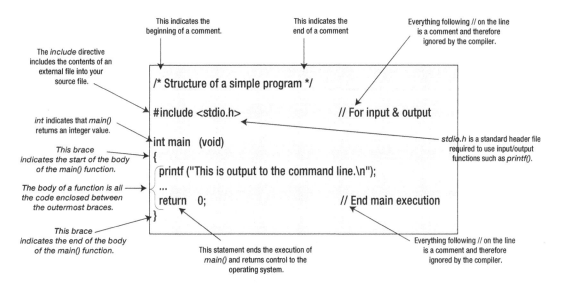

Figure 1-4. *Elements of a simple program*

Summary

You've reached the end of the first chapter, and you've already written a few programs in C. We've covered quite a lot of ground, but at a fairly gentle pace. The aim of this chapter was to introduce a few basic ideas rather than teach you a lot about the C programming language. You should now be confident about editing, compiling, and running your programs. You probably have only a vague idea about how to construct a C program at this point. It will become much clearer when you've learned a bit more about C and have written some programs with more meat to them.

In the next chapter, you'll move on to more complicated things than just producing text output using the printf() function. You'll manipulate information and get some rather more interesting results. And by the way, the printf() function does a whole lot more than just display text strings—as you'll see soon.

EXERCISES

The following exercises enable you to try out what you've learned in this chapter. If you get stuck, look back over the chapter for help. If you're still stuck, you can download the solutions from the Source Code/Download section of the Apress website (www.apress.com), but that really should be a last resort.

Exercise 1-1. Write a program that will output your name and address using a separate printf() statement for each line of output.

Exercise 1-2. Modify your solution for the previous exercise so that it produces all the output using only one printf() statement.

Exercise 1-3. Write a program to output the following text exactly as it appears here:

```
"It's freezing in here," he said coldly.
```

CHAPTER 2

First Steps in Programming

By now you're probably eager to create programs that allow your computer to really interact with the outside world. You don't just want programs that work as glorified typewriters, displaying fixed information that you included in the program code, and indeed there's a whole world of programming that goes beyond that. Ideally, you want to be able to enter data from the keyboard and have the program squirrel it away somewhere. This would make the program much more versatile. Your pcrogram would be able to access and manipulate these data, and it would be able to work with different data values each time you execute it. This idea of entering different information each time you run a program is what makes programming useful. A place to store an item of data that can vary in a program is not altogether surprisingly called a *variable*, and this is what this chapter covers.

In this chapter, you'll learn

- How memory is used and what variables are

- How you calculate in C

- What different types of variables there are and what you use them for

- What casting is and when you need to use it

- How to write a program that calculates the height of a tree—any tree

Memory in Your Computer

I'll explain first how the computer stores the data that's processed in your program. To understand this, you need to know a little bit about memory in your computer, so before you start your first program, let's take a quick tour of your computer's memory.

The instructions that make up your program, and the data that it acts upon, have to be stored somewhere that's instantly accessible while your computer is executing that program. When your program is running, the program instructions and data are stored in the *main memory* or the *random access memory* (RAM) of the machine. RAM is volatile storage. When you switch off your PC, the contents of RAM are lost. Your PC has permanent storage in the form of one or more disk drives (or solid-state drive, SSD). Anything you want to keep when a program finishes executing needs to be printed or written to disk, because when the program ends, the results stored in RAM will be lost.

You can think of RAM as an ordered sequence of boxes. Each of these boxes is in one of two states: either the box is full when it represents 1 or the box is empty when it represents 0. Therefore, each box represents one binary digit, either 0 or 1. The computer sometimes thinks of these in terms of *true* and *false*: 1 is true and 0 is false. Each of these boxes is called a *bit*, which is a contraction of *binary digit*.

© German Gonzalez-Morris and Ivor Horton 2020

G. Gonzalez-Morris and I. Horton, *Beginning C*, https://doi.org/10.1007/978-1-4842-5976-4_2

■ **Note** If you can't remember or have never learned about binary numbers and you want to find out a little bit more, there is more detail in Appendix A. However, you needn't worry about these details if they don't appeal to you. The important point here is that the computer can only deal with 1s and 0s—it can't deal with decimal numbers directly. All the data that your program works with, including the program instructions themselves, will consist of binary numbers inside your PC.

For convenience, the bits in memory are grouped into sets of eight, and each set of eight bits is called a *byte*. To allow you to refer to the contents of a particular byte, each byte has been labeled with a number, starting from 0 for the first byte, 1 for the second byte, and so on, up to whatever number of bytes you have in your computer's memory. This label for a byte is called its *address*. Thus, the address of each byte is unique. Just as a street address identifies a particular house, the address of a byte uniquely references that byte in your computer's memory.

To summarize, memory consists of a large number of bits that are in groups of eight (called bytes), and each byte has a unique address. Byte addresses start from 0. A bit can only be either 1 or 0. This is illustrated in Figure 2-1.

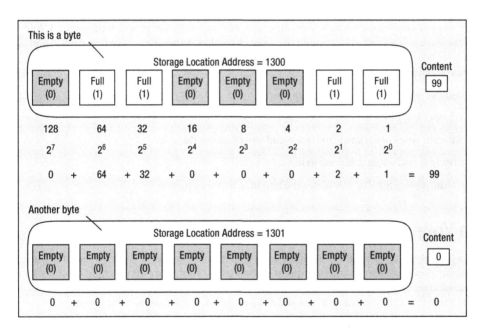

Figure 2-1. *Bytes in memory*

The amount of memory your computer has is expressed in terms of so many kilobytes, megabytes, or gigabytes and, in the case of large disk drives/SSD, terabytes. Here's what those words mean:

- 1 kilobyte (or 1 KB) is 1,024 bytes.

- 1 megabyte (or 1 MB) is 1,024 kilobytes, which is 1,048,576 bytes.

- 1 gigabyte (or 1 GB) is 1,024 megabytes, which is 1,073,741,824 bytes.

- 1 terabyte (or 1 TB) is 1,024 gigabytes, which is 1,099,511,627,776 bytes.

If you have a gigabyte of RAM in your PC, byte addresses will be from 0 to 1,073,741,823 inclusive. You might be wondering why we don't work with simpler, more rounded numbers, such as a thousand or a million or a billion. The reason is this: there are 1,024 numbers from 0 to 1,023, and 1,023 happens to be 10 bits that are all 1 in binary—11 1111 1111, which is a very convenient binary value. So while 1,000 is a very convenient decimal value, it's actually rather inconvenient in a binary machine—it's 11 1110 1000, which is not exactly neat and tidy. The kilobyte (1,024 bytes) is therefore defined in a manner that's convenient for your computer, rather than for you. Similarly, for a megabyte, you need 20 bits, and for a gigabyte, you need 30 bits.

Confusion can arise with hard disk drive (HDD) or solid-state drive (SSD) capacities. Disk drive manufacturers often refer to a HDD/SSD as having a capacity of 256 gigabytes or 1 terabyte, when they really mean 256 billion bytes and 1 trillion bytes. Of course, 256 billion bytes is only 231 gigabytes, and 1 trillion bytes is only 911 gigabytes, so a manufacturer's specification of the capacity of a HDD/SSD looks more impressive than it really is. Now that you know a bit about bytes, let's see how you use memory in your programs to store data.

It is essential to understand how the C memory is structured. This is mainly made by heap, stack, global constant, and code. However, the most important are heap and stack. They belong to RAM (memory); therefore, they're volatile and frequently change at runtime.

Local variables of a function are created in the stack; meanwhile, the heap is where pointers are manually handled by your program (i.e., malloc/free). The scope of stack is the function that is being executed.

The stack is designed to have smaller variables than heap; the philosophy is speed for volatile variables.

On the other hand, the heap is to handle larger variables (dynamically allocated space); of course, there is a speed trade-off accessing objects from each segment. They are manually handled by the developer (implicitly, it may occur a memory leak). The variables in the heap are global and can be accessed through pointers (which will be seen in later chapters).

The stack is a LIFO (last-in-first-out) structure; this is very useful for recursive function (which we'll see later in the next chapter). Every time a variable is declared, it will exist on the top of that segment (yes, it is a stack-LIFO structure, using push-pop functions).

Figure 2-1a. *Memory representation*

What Is a Variable?

A *variable* in a program is a specific piece of memory that consists of one or more contiguous bytes, typically 1, 2, 4, 8, or 16 bytes. Every variable in a program has a name, which will correspond to the memory address for the variable. You use the variable name to store a data value in memory or retrieve the data that the memory contains.

Let's start with a program that outputs your salary. It will use the printf() function we learned about in Chapter 1. Assuming your salary is $10,000 per month, you can already write that program very easily:

```
// Program 2.1 What is a Variable?
#include <stdio.h>

int main(void)
{
  printf("My salary is $10000");
  return 0;
}
```

I'm sure you don't need any more explanation about how this works; it's almost identical to the programs you saw in Chapter 1. So how can we modify this program to allow you to customize the message depending on a value stored in memory? There are several other ways of doing this. A more useful approach uses a variable.

You could allocate a piece of memory that you could name salary, say, and store the value 10000 in it. When you want to display your salary, you could use the variable name, salary, and the value that's stored in it (10000) would be output. Wherever you use a variable name in a program, the computer accesses the value that's stored there. You can access a variable however many times you need to in your program. When your salary changes, you can simply change the value stored in the variable salary, and the program will work with the new value. Of course, all the values will be stored in salary as binary numbers.

You can have as many variables as you like in a program. The value that each variable contains, at any point during the execution of that program, is determined by the instructions contained in your program. The value of a variable isn't fixed, and you can change it whenever you need to throughout a program.

■ **Note**   I said that a variable can be one or more bytes, so you may be wondering how the computer knows how many bytes it is. You'll see later in the next section that every variable has a *type* that specifies the kind of data the variable can store. The type of a variable determines how many bytes are allocated for it.

Naming Variables

The name you give to a variable, conveniently referred to as a *variable name*, can be defined with some flexibility. A variable name is a sequence of one or more uppercase or lowercase letters, digits, and underscore characters (_) that begin with a letter (incidentally, the underscore character counts as a letter). Examples of legal variable names are as follows:

```
Radius   diameter   Auntie_May   Knotted_Wool   D678
```

A variable name must not begin with a digit, so 8_Ball and 6_pack aren't legal names. A variable name must not include characters other than letters, underscores, and digits, so Hash! and Mary-Lou aren't allowed as names. This last example is a common mistake, but Mary_Lou would be quite acceptable. Because spaces aren't allowed in a name, Mary Lou would be interpreted as two variable names, Mary and Lou. Variables starting with one or two underscore characters are often used in the header files, so don't use the underscore as the first character in your variable names; otherwise, you run the risk of your name clashing with the name of a variable used in the standard library. For example, names such as _this and _that are best avoided. Another very important point to remember about variable names is that they are case sensitive. Thus, the names Democrat and democrat are distinct.

Although you can call variables whatever you want within the preceding constraints, it's worth calling them something that gives you a clue as to what they contain. Assigning the name x to a variable that stores a salary isn't very helpful. It would be far better to call it salary and leave no doubt as to what it is. In the end, the variable's name must be a clear representation of its meaning.

■ **Caution**   The maximum number of characters that you can have in a variable name will depend on your compiler. A minimum of 31 characters must be supported by a compiler that conforms to the C standard, so you can always use names up to this length without any problems. I suggest that you don't make your variable names longer than this anyway. Very long names become tedious to type and make the code hard to follow. Some compilers will truncate names that are too long.

Variables That Store Integers

There are several different types of variables, and each type of variable is used for storing a particular kind of data. There are several types that store integers, types that store nonintegral numerical values, and types that store characters. Where there are several types to store a particular kind of data, such as integers, the difference between the types is in the amount of memory they occupy and the range of values they can hold. I will introduce variables that you use to store integers first.

An integer is any whole number without a decimal point. Here are some examples:

123   10,999,000,000   20,000   88   1

You will recognize these values as integers, but what I've written here isn't quite correct so far as your program is concerned. You can't include commas in an integer, so the second value would actually be written in a program as 10999000000 and the third value would be 20000.

Here are some examples of numbers that are *not* integers:

1.234   999.9   2.0   −0.0005   3.14159265

Normally, 2.0 would be described as an integer because it's a whole number, but as far as your computer is concerned, it isn't because it is written with a decimal point. If you want an integer, you must write it as 2 with no decimal point. Integers are always written in C without a decimal point; if there's a decimal point, it isn't an integer—it's a floating-point value, which I'll get to later. Before I discuss integer variables in more detail (and believe me, there's a lot more detail!), let's look at a simple variable in action in a program, just so you can get a feel for how they're used.

TRY IT OUT: USING A VARIABLE

Let's return to a program to output your salary. You can rewrite the previous program to use a variable of type int, which is an integer type:

```
//  Program 2.2 Using a variable
#include <stdio.h>

int main(void)
{
  int salary;                           // Declare a variable called salary
  salary = 10000;                       // Store 10000 in salary
  printf("My salary is %d.\n", salary);
  return 0;
}
```

Type in this example and compile, link, and execute it. You'll get the following output:

```
My salary is 10000.
```

How It Works

The first three lines are essentially the same as in all the previous programs. Let's look at the new stuff. The statement that identifies the memory that you're using to store your salary is the following:

```
  int salary;                    // Declare a variable called salary
```

This statement is called a *variable declaration* because it declares the name of the variable. The name, in this case, is salary.

■ **Caution**   Notice that the variable declaration ends with a semicolon. If you omit the semicolon, your program will generate an error when you try to compile it.

The variable declaration also specifies the type of data that the variable will store. You've used the keyword int to specify that the variable, salary, will be used to store an integer value of type int. The keyword int precedes the name of the variable. This is just one of several different types you can use to store integers.

■ **Note**   Remember, keywords are words that are reserved in C because they have a special meaning. You must not use keywords as names for variables or other entities in your code. If you do, your compiler will produce error messages.

The declaration for the variable, salary, is also a *definition* because it causes some memory to be allocated to hold an integer value, which you can access using the name salary.

■ **Note** A *declaration* introduces a variable name, and a *definition* causes memory to be allocated for it. The reason for this distinction will become apparent later in the book.

Of course, you have not specified what the value of salary should be yet, so at this point it will contain a junk value—whatever was left behind from when this bit of memory was used last.

The next statement is `salary = 10000;`   `// Store 10000 in salary`

This is a simple arithmetic assignment statement. It takes the value to the right of the equal sign and stores it in the variable on the left of the equal sign. Here you're declaring that the variable salary will have the value 10000. You're storing the value on the right (10000) in the variable on the left (salary). The = symbol is called the assignment operator because it assigns the value on the right to the variable on the left.

You then have the familiar printf() statement, but it's a little different from how you've seen it in action before:

```
printf("My salary is %d.\n", salary);
```

There are now two *arguments* inside the parentheses, separated by a comma. An argument is a value that's passed to a function. In this program statement, the two arguments to the printf() function are as follows:

- The first argument is a *control string*, so called because it controls how the output specified by the following argument or arguments is to be presented. This is the character string between the double quotes. It is also referred to as a *format string* because it specifies the format of the data that are output.

- The second argument is the name of the variable, salary. The control string in the first argument determines how the value of salary will be displayed.

The control string is fairly similar to the previous example, in that it contains some text to be displayed. However, if you look carefully, you'll see %d embedded in it. This is called a *conversion specifier* for the value of the variable. Conversion specifiers determine how variable values are displayed on the screen. In other words, they specify the form to which an original binary value is to be converted before it is displayed. In this case, you've used a d, which is a decimal specifier that applies to integer values. It just means that the second argument, salary, will be represented and output as a decimal (base 10) number.

■ **Note** Conversion specifiers always start with a % character so that the printf() function can recognize them. Because a % in a control string always indicates the start of a conversion specifier, you must use the escape sequence %% when you want to output a % character.

TRY IT OUT: USING MORE VARIABLES

Let's try a slightly longer example:

```
// Program 2.3 Using more variables
#include <stdio.h>

int main(void)
{
  int brothers;                           // Declare a variable called brothers
  int brides;                             // and a variable called brides

  brothers = 7;                           // Store 7 in the variable brothers
  brides = 7;                             // Store 7 in the variable brides

  // Display some output
  printf("%d brides for %d brothers\n", brides, brothers);
  return 0;
}
```

If you run this program, you should get the following output:

```
7 brides for 7 brothers
```

How It Works

This program works in a similar way to the previous example. You first declare two variables, brides and brothers, with these statements:

```
  int brothers;                           // Declare a variable called brothers
  int brides;                             // and a variable called brides
```

You specify both variables as type int so they both can only store integer values. Notice that they have been declared in separate statements. Because they are both of the same type, you could have saved a line of code and declared them together like this:

```
int brothers, brides;
```

When you declare several variables of a given type in one statement, the variable names following the data type are separated by commas, and the whole line ends with a semicolon. This can be a convenient format, but the downside is that it isn't so obvious what each variable is for; because if they appear on a single line, you can't add individual comments to describe each variable so easily. Always comment on the code to have more precise details of what the code is supposed to do. However, you could write this single statement spread over two lines:

```
  int brothers,                           // Declare a variable called brothers
      brides;                             // and a variable called brides
```

By spreading the statement out over two lines, you're able to put the comments back in. Comments are ignored by the compiler so it's the exact equivalent of the original statement without the comments. You can spread C statements over as many lines as you want. The semicolon determines the end of the statement, not the end of the line.

Of course, you might as well write the preceding statement as two statements, and in general it is a better practice to define each variable in a separate statement. Variable declarations often appear at the beginning of the executable code for a function, but you are not obliged to do so. You typically put declarations for variables that you intend to use in a block of code that is between a pair of braces immediately following the opening brace, {.

The next two statements assign the same value, 7, to each variable:

```
brothers = 7;                          // Store 7 in the variable brothers
brides = 7;                            // Store 7 in the variable brides
```

Note that the statements that declared these variables precede these statements. If one or the other of the declarations were missing or appeared later in the code, the program wouldn't compile. A variable does not exist in your code before its declaration. You must always declare a variable before you use it.

The next statement calls the printf() function. The first argument is a control string that will display a line of text. This string also contains specifications for how the values of subsequent arguments will be interpreted and displayed within the text. The %d conversion specifiers within the control string will be replaced by the values currently stored in the variables that appear as the second and third arguments to the printf() function call—in this case, brides and brothers:

```
printf("%d brides for %d brothers\n", brides, brothers);
```

The conversion specifiers are replaced in order by the values of the variables that appear as the second and subsequent arguments to the printf() function, so the value of brides corresponds to the first specifier, and the value of brothers corresponds to the second. This would be more obvious if you changed the statements that set the values of the variables as follows:

```
brothers = 8;                          // Store 8 in the variable brothers
brides = 4;                            // Store 4 in the variable brides
```

In this somewhat dubious scenario, the printf() statement would show clearly which variable corresponds to which conversion specifier, because the output would be the following:

```
4 brides for 8 brothers
```

You can demonstrate that variables are case sensitive by changing the printf() statement so that one of the variable names starts with a capital letter, as follows:

```
// Program 2.3A Using more variables
#include <stdio.h>

int main(void)
{
  int brothers;                        // Declare a variable called brothers
  int brides;                          // and a variable called brides

  brothers = 7;                        // Store 7 in the variable brothers
  brides = 7;                          // Store 7 in the variable brides
```

```
  // Display some output
  printf("%d brides for %d brothers\n", Brides, brothers);
  return 0;
}
```

You'll get an error message when you try to compile this. The compiler interprets the names `brides` and `Brides` as different, so it doesn't understand what `Brides` refers to because you have not declared it. This is a common error. As I've said before, punctuation and spelling mistakes are the main causes of trivial errors. You must always declare a variable before you use it; otherwise, the compiler will not recognize it and will flag the statement as an error.

Using Variables

You now know how to name and declare your variables, but so far this hasn't been much more useful than what you learned in Chapter 1. Let's try another program in which you'll use the values in the variables before you produce some output.

TRY IT OUT: DOING A SIMPLE CALCULATION

This program does a simple calculation using the values of the variables:

```
// Program 2.4 Simple calculations
#include <stdio.h>

int main(void)
{
  int total_pets;
  int cats;
  int dogs;
  int ponies;
  int others;

  // Set the number of each kind of pet
  cats = 2;
  dogs = 1;
  ponies = 1;
  others = 46;

  // Calculate the total number of pets
  total_pets = cats + dogs + ponies + others;

  printf("We have %d pets in total\n", total_pets);   // Output the result
  return 0;
}
```

This example produces this output:

```
We have 50 pets in total
```

How It Works

As in the previous examples, all the statements between the braces are indented by the same amount. This makes it clear that all these statements belong together. You should always organize your programs the way you see here: indent a group of statements that lie between an opening and closing brace by the same amount. It makes your programs much easier to read.

You first define five variables of type `int`:

```
int total_pets;
int cats;
int dogs;
int ponies;
int others;
```

Because these variables will be used to store a count of a number of animals, they are definitely going to be whole numbers. As you can see, they're all declared as type `int`.

The variables are given specific values in these four assignment statements:

```
cats = 2;
dogs = 1;
ponies = 1;
others = 46;
```

At this point, the variable `total_pets` doesn't have an explicit value set. It will get its value as a result of the calculation using the other variables:

```
total_pets = cats + dogs + ponies + others;
```

In this arithmetic statement, you calculate the sum of all your pets on the right of the assignment operator by adding the values of each of the variables together. This total value is then stored in the variable `total_pets` that appears on the left of the assignment operator. The new value replaces any old value that was stored in the variable `total_pets`.

The `printf()` statement presents the result of the calculation by displaying the value of `total_pets`:

```
printf("We have %d pets in total\n", total_pets);
```

Try changing the numbers of some of the types of animals, or maybe add some more of your own. Remember to declare them, initialize their value, and include them in the `total_pets` statement.

Initializing Variables

In the previous example, you declared each variable with a statement such as this:

```
int cats;                          // The number of cats as pets
```

You set the value of the variable `cats` using this statement:

```
cats = 2;
```

This sets the value of cats to 2. So what was the value before this statement was executed? Well, it could be anything. The first statement creates the variable called cats, but its value will be whatever was left in memory from the last program that used this memory. The assignment statement that appeared later sets the value to 2, but it would be much better to initialize the variable when you declare it. You can do this with the following statement:

```
int cats = 2;
```

This statement declares cats as type int *and* sets its initial value to 2. Initializing variables as you declare them is very good practice. It avoids any doubt about what the initial values are, and if the program doesn't work as it should, it can help you track down the errors. Avoid leaving spurious values for variables when you create them, which reduces the chances of your computer crashing when things do go wrong. Inadvertently working with junk values can cause all kinds of problems. From now on, you'll always initialize variables in the examples, even if it's just to 0.

The previous program is the first one that really did something. It is very simple—just adding a few numbers—but it is a significant step forward. It is an elementary example of using an *arithmetic statement* to perform a calculation. Now let's look at some more sophisticated calculations that you can do.

Basic Arithmetic Operations

An arithmetic statement is of the following form:

```
variable_name = arithmetic_expression;
```

The arithmetic expression on the right of the = operator specifies a calculation using values stored in variables or explicit numbers that are combined using arithmetic operators such as addition (+), subtraction (–), multiplication (*), and division (/). There are also other operators you can use in an arithmetic expression, as you'll see.

In the previous example, the arithmetic statement was the following:

```
total_pets = cats + dogs + ponies + others;
```

The effect of this statement is to calculate the value of the arithmetic expression to the right of the = and store that value in the variable specified on the left.

The = symbol in C defines an action. It doesn't specify that the two sides are equal, as it does in mathematics. It specifies that the value that results from evaluating the expression on the right is to be stored in the variable on the left. This means that you could have the following statement:

```
total_pets = total_pets + 2;
```

This would be ridiculous as a mathematical equation, but in programming, it's fine. Let's look at it in context. Imagine you'd rewritten the last part of the program to include the preceding statement. Here's a fragment of the program as it would appear with the statement added:

```
total_pets = cats + dogs + ponies + others;
total_pets = total_pets + 2;
printf("The total number of pets is: %d", total_pets);
```

After executing the first statement here, total_pets will contain the value 50. Then, in the second line, you extract the value of total_pets, add 2 to that value, and store the results back in the variable total_ pets. The final total that will be displayed is therefore 52.

■ **Note** In an assignment operation, the expression on the right of the = sign is evaluated first, and the result is then stored in the variable on the left. The new value replaces the value that was previously contained in the variable to the left of the assignment operator. The variable on the left of the assignment is called an lvalue, because it is a location that can store a value. The value that results from executing the expression on the right of the assignment is called an rvalue because it is a value that results from evaluating the expression and is not an lvalue.

An arithmetic expression is any expression that results in a numerical value. The following are arithmetic expressions:

```
3      1 + 2      total_pets      cats + dogs - ponies      -data
```

Evaluating any of these expressions produces a single numeric value. Note that just a variable name is an expression that produces a value, which is the value that the variable contains. The last example has a value that is the negation of data, so if data contains -5, the value of the expression -data is 5. Of course, the value of data is still -5. In a moment, we'll take a closer look at how an expression is made up, and we'll look into the rules governing its evaluation. First, though, you can try some working examples using the basic arithmetic operators. Table 2-1 shows these operators.

Table 2-1. *Basic Arithmetic Operators*

Operator	Action
+	Addition
-	Subtraction
*	Multiplication
/	Division
%	Modulus

The items of data that an operator applies to are generally referred to as *operands*. All these operators produce an integer result when both operands are integers. You may not have come across the *modulus operator* before. It calculates the remainder after dividing the value of the expression on the left of the operator by the value of the expression on the right. For this reason, it's sometimes referred to as the *remainder operator*. The expression 12 % 5 produces 2, because 12 divided by 5 leaves a remainder of 2. We'll look at this in more detail in the next section. All these operators work as you'd expect, with the exception of division, which is slightly nonintuitive when applied to integers, as you'll see. Let's try some more arithmetic operations.

■ **Note** The values that an operator is applied to are called *operands*. An operator that requires two operands, such as %, is called a *binary operator*. An operator that applies to a single value is called a *unary operator*. Thus, - is a binary operator in the expression a - b and a unary operator in the expression -data.

TRY IT OUT: SUBTRACTION AND MULTIPLICATION

Let's look at a food-based program that demonstrates subtraction and multiplication:

```
// Program 2.5 Calculations with cookies
#include <stdio.h>

int main(void)
{
  int cookies = 5;
  int cookie_calories = 125;            // Calories per cookie
  int total_eaten = 0;                  // Total cookies eaten

  int eaten = 2;                        // Number to be eaten
  cookies = cookies - eaten;            // Subtract number eaten from cookies
  total_eaten = total_eaten + eaten;
  printf("\nI have eaten %d cookies.  There are %d cookies left",
                                              eaten, cookies);

  eaten = 3;                            // New value for cookies eaten
  cookies = cookies - eaten;            // Subtract number eaten from cookies
  total_eaten = total_eaten + eaten;
  printf("\nI have eaten %d more.  Now there are %d cookies left\n", eaten, cookies);
  printf("\nTotal energy consumed is %d calories.\n", total_eaten*cookie_calories);
  return 0;
}
```

This program produces the following output:

```
I have eaten 2 cookies.  There are 3 cookies left
I have eaten 3 more.  Now there are 0 cookies left

Total energy consumed is 625 calories.
```

How It Works

You first declare and initialize three variables of type `int`:

```
int cookies = 5;
int cookie_calories = 125;            // Calories per cookie
int total_eaten = 0;                  // Total cookies eaten
```

You'll use the `total_eaten` variable to accumulate the total number of cookies eaten as the program progresses, so you initialize it to 0.

Next, you declare and initialize a variable that holds the number of cookies to be eaten:

```
int eaten = 2;                        // Number to be eaten
```

You use the subtraction operator to subtract `eaten` from the value of `cookies`:

```
cookies = cookies - eaten;            // Subtract number eaten from cookies
```

The result of the subtraction is stored back in the variable cookies, so the value of cookies will now be 3.

Because you've eaten some cookies, you increment the count of the total that you've eaten by the value of eaten:

```
total_eaten = total_eaten + eaten;
```

You add the current value of eaten, which is 2, to the current value of total_eaten, which is 0. The result is stored back in the variable total_eaten.

The printf() statement displays the number of cookies that have been eaten and that are left:

```
printf("\nI have eaten %d cookies.  There are %d cookies left",
                                                    eaten, cookies);
```

I chose to put the part of the statement that follows the first comma on a new line. You can spread statements out like this to make them easier to read or fit within a given width on the screen. Note that you *cannot* split the string that is the first argument in this way. An explicit newline character isn't allowed in the middle of a string. When you need to split a string over two or more lines, each segment of the string on a line must have its own pair of double quotes delimiting it. For example, you could write the previous statement as follows:

```
printf("\nI have eaten %d cookies. "
       " There are %d cookies left",
       eaten, cookies);
```

Where there are two or more strings immediately following one another like this, the compiler will join them to form a single string.

You display the values stored in eaten and cookies using the conversion specifier, %d, for integer values. The value of eaten will replace the first %d in the output string, and the value of cookies will replace the second. The string is displayed starting on a new line because of the \n at the beginning.

The next statement sets the variable eaten to a new value:

```
eaten = 3;                              // New value for cookies to be eaten
```

The new value replaces the previous value stored in eaten, which was 2. You then go through the same sequence of operations as you did before:

```
cookies = cookies - eaten;              // Subtract number eaten from cookies
total_eaten = total_eaten + eaten;
printf("\nI have eaten %d more.  Now there are %d cookies left\n", eaten, cookies);
```

Finally, before executing the return statement that ends the program, you calculate and output the number of calories corresponding to the number of cookies eaten:

```
printf("\nTotal energy consumed is %d calories.\n", total_eaten*cookie_calories);
```

Here the second argument to the printf() function is an arithmetic expression rather than just a variable. The compiler will arrange for the result of the expression total_eaten*cookie_calories to be stored in a temporary variable, and that value will be passed as the second argument to the printf() function. You can always use an expression for an argument to a function as long as it evaluates to a result of the required type.

Easy, isn't it? Let's take a look at an example using division and the modulus operator.

TRY IT OUT: DIVISION AND THE MODULUS OPERATOR

Suppose you have a jar of 45 cookies and a group of seven children. You'll divide the cookies equally among the children and work out how many each child has. Then you'll work out how many cookies are left over:

```c
// Program 2.6 Cookies and kids
#include <stdio.h>

int main(void)
{
  int cookies = 45;                     // Number of cookies in the jar
  int children = 7;                     // Number of children
  int cookies_per_child = 0;            // Number of cookies per child
  int cookies_left_over = 0;            // Number of cookies left over

  // Calculate how many cookies each child gets when they are divided up
  cookies_per_child = cookies/children;      // Number of cookies per child
  printf("You have %d children and %d cookies\n", children, cookies);
  printf("Give each child %d cookies.\n", cookies_per_child);

  // Calculate how many cookies are left over
  cookies_left_over = cookies%children;
  printf("There are %d cookies left over.\n", cookies_left_over);
  return 0;
}
```

When you run this program, you'll get this output:

```
You have 7 children and 45 cookies
Give each child 6 cookies.
There are 3 cookies left over.
```

How It Works

I'll go through this program step by step. Four integer variables, `cookies`, `children`, `cookies_per_child`, and `cookies_left_over`, are declared and initialized with the following statements:

```c
  int cookies = 45;                     // Number of cookies in the jar
  int children = 7;                     // Number of children
  int cookies_per_child = 0;            // Number of cookies per child
  int cookies_left_over = 0;            // Number of cookies left over
```

The number of cookies is divided by the number of children by using the division operator / to produce the number of cookies given to each child:

```c
  cookies_per_child = cookies/children;      // Number of cookies per child
```

The next two statements output what is happening, including the value stored in `cookies_per_child`:

```
printf("You have %d children and %d cookies\n", children, cookies);
printf("Give each child %d cookies.\n", cookies_per_child);
```

You can see from the output that `cookies_per_child` has the value 6. This is because the division operator always produces an integer result when the operands are integers. The result of dividing 45 by 7 is 6, with a remainder of 3. You calculate the remainder in the next statement by using the modulus operator:

```
cookies_left_over = cookies%children;
```

The expression to the right of the assignment operator calculates the remainder that results when the value of `cookies` is divided by the value of `children`.

Finally, you output the remainder in the last statement:

```
printf("There are %d cookies left over.\n", cookies_left_over);
```

More on Division with Integers

Let's look at the result of using the division and modulus operators where one of the operands is negative. With division, the result will always be negative if the operands have different signs. Thus, the expression –45/7 produces the same result as the expression 45/–7, which is –6. If the operands in a division are of the same sign, either positive or negative, the result is always positive. Thus, 45/7 produces the same result as –45/–7, which is 6.

With the modulus operator, the sign of the result is always the same as the sign of the left operand whether or not the operands have different signs. Thus, 45 % –7 results in the value 3, whereas –45 % 7 results in the value –3; the expression -45 % -7 also evaluates to -3.

Unary Operators

For example, the multiplication sign is a binary operator because it has two operands, and the effect is to multiply one operand value by the other. However, there are some operators that are unary, meaning that they only need one operand. I'll present more examples later, but for now we'll just take a look at the single most common unary operator.

Unary Minus Operator

The operators that we've dealt with so far have been binary operators that require two operands. There are also unary operators in C that apply to a single operand. The unary minus operator is one example. It produces a positive result when applied to a negative operand and a negative result when the operand is positive. You might not immediately realize when you would use this, but think about keeping track of your bank account. Say you have $200 in the bank. You record what happens to this money in a book with two columns, one for money that you pay out and another for money that you receive. One column is your expenditure, and the other is your revenue.

You decide to buy a CD for $50 and a book for $25. If all goes well, when you compare the initial value in the bank and subtract the expenditure ($75), you should end up with what's left. Table 2-2 shows how these entries could typically be recorded.

Table 2-2. *Recording Revenues and Expenditures*

Entry	Revenue	Expenditure	Bank balance
Check received	$200		$200
CD		$50	$150
Book		$25	$125
Closing balance	$200	$75	$125

If these numbers were stored in variables, you could enter both the revenue and expenditure as positive values, which would allow you to calculate the sum of each as positive totals. You then only make an expenditure value negative when you want to calculate how much is left in your account. You could do this by simply placing a minus sign (–) in front of the variable name.

To output the amount you had spent as a negative value, you could write the following:

```
int expenditure = 75;
printf("Your balance has changed by %d.", -expenditure);
```

This would result in the following output:

```
Your balance has changed by -75.
```

The minus sign will remind you that you've spent this money rather than gained it. Of course, the expression -expenditure doesn't change the value stored in expenditure—it's still 75. The value of the *expression* is –75.

The unary minus operator in the expression -expenditure specifies an action, the result of which is the value of expenditure with its sign inverted: negative becomes positive and positive becomes negative. This is subtly different from when you use the minus operator when you write a negative number such as –75 or –1.25. In this case, the minus doesn't result in an action, and no instructions need to be executed when your program is running. The minus sign is part of the constant and determines that it is negative.

Variables and Memory

So far you've only looked at integer variables without considering how much space they take up in memory. Each time you declare a variable of a given type, the compiler allocates sufficient space in memory to store values of that particular type of variable. Every variable of a particular type will always occupy the same amount of memory—the same number of bytes. Variables of different types may require different amounts of memory to be allocated.

We saw at the beginning of this chapter how your computer's memory is organized into bytes. Each variable will occupy some number of bytes in memory, so how many bytes are needed to store an integer? Well, it depends on how big the integer value is. A single byte can store an integer value from –128 to +127. This would be enough for some of the values that we've seen so far, but what if you want to store a count of the average number of stitches in a pair of knee-length socks? One byte would not be anywhere near enough. On the other hand, if you want to record the number of hamburgers a person can eat in two minutes, a single byte is likely to be enough, and allocating more bytes for this purpose would be wasting memory. Not only do you have variables of different types in C that store numbers of different types, one of which happens to be integers; you also have several varieties of integer variables to provide for different ranges of integers to be stored.

Signed Integer Types

We have five basic flavors of variables that we can declare that can store signed integer values, so positive and negative values can be stored (I'll get to unsigned integer values in the next section). Each type is specified by a different keyword or combination of keywords, as shown in Table 2-3.

Table 2-3. *Type Names for Integer Variable Types*

Type name	Number of bytes
signed char	1
short	2
int	4
long	4
long long	8

Here are some declarations for variables of these types:

```
short shoe_size;
int house_number;
long long star_count;
```

The type names short, long, and long long can be written as short int, long int, and long long int, and they can optionally have the keyword signed in front. However, these types are almost always written in their abbreviated forms as shown in Table 2-3. Type int can also be written as signed int, but you won't see this often either. Table 2-3 reflects the typical number of bytes for each type. The amount of memory occupied by variables of these types, and therefore the range of values you can store, depends on the particular compiler you're using. It's easy to find out what the limits are for your compiler because they are defined in the limits.h header file, and I'll show you how to do this later in the chapter.

Unsigned Integer Types

Some kinds of data are always positive, the number of pebbles on a beach, for example. In such cases, you don't need to provide for negative values. For each type that stores signed integers, there is a corresponding type that stores unsigned integers, and the unsigned type occupies the same amount of memory as the signed type. Each unsigned type name is essentially the signed type name prefixed with the keyword unsigned. Table 2-4 shows the basic set of unsigned integer types that you can use.

Table 2-4. *Type Names for Unsigned Integer Types*

Type name	Number of bytes
unsigned char	1
unsigned short or unsigned short int	2
unsigned int	4
unsigned long or unsigned long int	4
unsigned long long or unsigned long long int	8

With a given number of bits, the number of different values that can be represented is fixed. A 32-bit integer variable can represent any of 4,294,967,296 different values. Thus, using an unsigned type doesn't provide more values than the corresponding signed type, but it does allow numbers to be represented that are twice the magnitude.

Here are examples of unsigned integer variable declarations:

```
unsigned int count;
unsigned long population;
```

■ **Note** Variables of different types that occupy the same number of bytes are still different. Type long and type int may occupy the same amount of memory, but they are still different types.

Specifying Integer Constants

Because you can have different types of integer variables, you might expect to have different kinds of integer constants, and you do. If you just write the integer value 100, for example, this will be of type int. If you want to make sure it is type long, you must append an uppercase or lowercase letter L to the numeric value. So 100 as a long value is written as 100L. Although it's perfectly legal to use it, a lowercase letter l is best avoided because it's easily confused with the digit 1.

To declare and initialize the variable Big_Number, you could write this:

```
long Big_Number = 1287600L;
```

You write negative integer constants with a minus sign, for example:

```
int decrease = -4;
long  below_sea_level = -100000L;
```

You specify integer constants to be of type long long by appending two Ls:

```
long long really_big_number = 123456789LL;
```

To specify a constant to be of an unsigned type, you append a U, as in these examples:

```
unsigned int count = 100U;
unsigned long value = 999999999UL;
```

To store integers with the largest magnitude, you could define a variable like this:

```
 unsigned long long metersPerLightYear = 9460730472580800ULL;
```

The ULL specifies that the initial value is type unsigned long long.

Hexadecimal Constants

You can write integer values in hexadecimal form—that is, to base 16. The digits in a hexadecimal number are the equivalent of decimal values 0–15, and they're represented by 0-9 and A–F (or a–f). Because there needs to be a way to distinguish between 99_{10} and 99_{16}, hexadecimal numbers are written with the prefix 0x or 0X. You would therefore write 99₁₆ in your program as 0x99 or as 0X99. Hexadecimal constants can also have a suffix. Here are some examples of hexadecimal constants:

```
0xFFFF    0xdead    0xfade    0xFade    0x123456EE    0xafL    0xFABABULL
```

The last example is of type unsigned long long, and the second to last example is of type long.

Hexadecimal constants are most often used to specify bit patterns, because each hexadecimal digit corresponds to 4 bits. Two hexadecimal digits specify a byte. The bitwise operators that you'll learn about in Chapter 3 are usually used with hexadecimal constants that define masks. If you're unfamiliar with hexadecimal numbers, you can find a detailed discussion of them in Appendix A.

Octal Constants

An octal value is a number to base 8. Each octal digit has a value from 0 to 7, which corresponds to 3 bits in binary. Octal values originate from the days long ago when computer memory was in terms of 36-bit words, so a word was a multiple of 3 bits. Thus, a 36-bit binary word could be written as 12 octal digits. Octal constants are rarely used these days, but you need to be aware of them so you don't specify an octal constant by mistake.

An integer constant that starts with a zero, such as 014, will be interpreted by your compiler as an octal number. Thus, 014 is the octal equivalent of the decimal value 12. If you meant it to be the decimal value 14, it is obviously wrong, so don't put a leading zero in your integers unless you really want to specify an octal value. There is rarely a need to use octal values.

Default Integer Constant Types

As we have learned, an integer constant without a suffix will be of type int by default, but what if the value is too large for type int? In this case, the compiler will create a constant of a type that it determines based on any suffix that is present whether or not the value is decimal. Table 2-5 shows what the compiler will decide in various situations.

Table 2-5. *Type Names for Unsigned Integer Types*

Suffix	Decimal constant	Octal or hexadecimal constant
none	1. int 2. long 3. long long	1. int 2. unsigned int 3. long 4. unsigned long 5. long long 6. unsigned long long
U	1. unsigned int 2. unsigned long□ 3. unsigned long long	1. unsigned int 2. unsigned long 3. unsigned long long
L	1. long 2. long long	1. λονγ 2. unsigned long 3. long long 4. unsigned long long

(*continued*)

Table 2-5. (*continued*)

Suffix	Decimal constant	Octal or hexadecimal constant
UL	1. `unsigned long` 2. `unsigned long long`	1. `unsigned long` 2. `unsigned long long`
LL	1. `long long`	1. `long long` 2. `unsigned long long`
ULL	1. `unsigned long long`	1. `unsigned long long`

The compiler chooses the first type that accommodates the value, as the numbers in the table entries indicate. For instance, a hexadecimal constant with u or U appended will be `unsigned int` by default; otherwise, it will be `unsigned long`, and if the range for that is too limited, it will be `unsigned long long`. Of course, if you specify an initial value for a variable that does not fit within the range of the variable type, you will get an error message from the compiler.

Working with Floating-Point Numbers

Floating-point numbers hold values that are written with a decimal point, so you can represent fractional as well as integral values. The following are examples of floating-point values:

1.6   0.00008   7655.899 100.0

The last constant is integral, but it will be stored as a floating-point value because of the presence of the decimal point. Because of the way floating-point numbers are represented, they define a fixed number of digits. Limiting accuracy to a fixed number of digits is a bit of a disadvantage, but floating-point numbers can represent a very wide range of values—much wider than integer types, which more than compensates. Floating-point numbers are often expressed as a decimal value multiplied by some power of 10, where the power of 10 is called the *exponent*. For example, each of the examples of preceding floating-point numbers could be expressed as shown in Table 2-6.

Table 2-6. *Expressing Floating-Point Numbers*

Value	With an exponent	Can also be written in C as
1.6	0.16×10^1	0.16E1
0.00008	0.8×10^{-4}	0.8E-4
7655.899	0.7655899×10^4	0.7655899E4
100.0	1.0×10^2	1.0E2

The center column shows how the numbers in the left column could be written with an exponent. This isn't how you write these numbers in C; it's just an alternative way of representing the values. The right column shows how the representation in the center column can be expressed in C. The E in each of the numbers is for exponent, and you could equally well use a lowercase e. Of course, you can write each of these numbers in your program without an exponent, just as they appear in the left column, but for very large or very small numbers, the exponent form is very useful. I'm sure you would rather write 0.5E-15 than 0.0000000000000005, wouldn't you?

Floating-Point Number Representation

Internal floating-point number representation is a little complicated. You can skip this section if you are not really interested in what goes on inside your computer. I am including this explanation here because an understanding of how your computer handles floating-point values will give you much better insight into why the range of such values is what it is. Figure 2-2 shows how a floating-point number is stored in a 4-byte word in memory on an Intel PC.

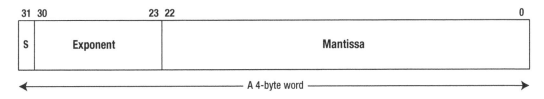

Figure 2-2. *A single-precision floating-point value in memory 32 bit*

(1 bit for sign, 11 bits for exponent, and 52 bits for mantissa)

This is a single-precision floating-point value, which occupies 4 bytes of memory. The value consists of three parts:

- A sign bit that is 0 for a positive value and 1 for a negative value

- An 8-bit exponent

- A 23-bit mantissa

The *mantissa* contains the digits in the number and occupies 23 bits. It is assumed to be a binary value of the form 1.bbb...b, with 23 bits to the right of the binary point. Thus, the value of the mantissa is always greater than or equal to 1 and less than 2. I'm sure you are wondering how you get a 24-bit value into 23 bits, but it's quite simple. The leftmost bit is always 1, so it does not need to be stored. Adopting this approach provides an extra binary digit of precision.

The *exponent* is an unsigned 8-bit value, so the exponent value can be from 0 to 255. The actual value of the floating-point number is the mantissa multiplied by 2 to the power of the exponent, or 2^{exp}, where exp is the exponent value. You need negative exponent values to allow small fractional numbers to be represented. To accommodate this, the actual exponent for a floating-point value has 127 added to it. This allows for values from –127 to 128 to be represented as an 8-bit unsigned value. Thus, an exponent of –6 will be stored as 121, and an exponent of 6 will be stored as 133. However, there are a few complications.

An actual exponent of –127, which corresponds to a stored exponent of 0, is reserved for a special case. A floating-point value of zero is represented by a word with all bits in the mantissa and exponent as 0, so the actual exponent value of –127 cannot be used for other values.

Another complication arises because it is desirable to be able to detect division by zero. Two more special values are reserved that represent +infinity and -infinity, the values that result from dividing a positive number or a negative number by zero. (This can be achieved when there is an overflow or underflow for the data type of the variable since the C99 compiler handles these boundaries—by multiplying or dividing—by replacing the result with -+INF.) Dividing a positive number by zero will generate a result with a zero sign bit, all the exponent bits 1, and all the mantissa bits 0. This value is special and represents +infinity and not the value 1 × 2 and all the mantissa bits 0. Dividing a negative number by zero results in the negation of that value, so -1×2^{128} is a special value too.

The last complication arises because it is desirable to be able to represent the result dividing zero by zero. This is referred to as "Not a Number" (NaN). The value reserved for this has all exponent bits 1 and the leading digit in the mantissa as 1 or 0 depending on whether the NaN is a *quiet* NaN, which allows execution to continue, or it is a *signaling* NaN, which causes an exception in the code that can terminate execution. When NaN has a leading 0 in the mantissa, at least one of the other mantissa bits is 1 to distinguish it from infinity.

47

Also, there are other definitions for the IEEE-754 standard, for example, double precision which contains for its representation 1 bit for sign, 11 bits for exponent, and 52 bits for mantissa. These will be described later for float, double, and long double.

▦ **Caution**   Because your computer stores a floating-point value as a binary mantissa combined with a binary exponent, some fractional decimal values cannot be represented exactly in this way. The binary places to the right of the binary point in the mantissa, .1, .01, .001, .0001, and so on, are equivalent to the decimal fractions 1/2, 1/4, 1/8, 1/16, and so on. Thus, the fractional part of the binary mantissa can only represent decimal values that are the sum of a subset of these decimal fractions. You should be able to see that values such as 1/3 or 1/5 cannot be represented exactly in a binary mantissa because there is no combination of the binary digits that will sum to these values.

Floating-Point Variables

Floating-point variable types only store floating-point numbers. You have a choice of three types of floating-point variables, and these are shown in Table 2-7.

Float

Table 2-7. *Floating-Point Variable Types*

Keyword	Number of bytes	Range of values
float	4	$\pm3.4E\pm38$ (6–7 decimal digits of precision)
double	8	$\pm1.7E\pm308$ (15 decimal digits of precision)
long double	12	$\pm1.19E\pm4932$ (18 decimal digits of precision)

These are typical values for the number of bytes occupied and for the ranges of values that are supported. Like the integer types, the memory occupied and the range of values are dependent on the machine and the compiler. The type long double (it exists since C90) is sometimes exactly the same as type double with some compilers. Note that the number of decimal digits of precision is an approximation because floating-point values will be stored internally in binary form, and a binary mantissa does not map to an exact number of decimal digits.

You declare a floating-point variable in a similar way to an integer variable. You just use the keyword for the floating-point type that you want:

```
float radius;
double biggest;
```

If you need to store numbers with up to roughly seven decimal digits of accuracy (typically with a range of 10^{-38}–10^{+38}), you should use variables of type float. Values of type float are known as *single-precision* floating-point numbers. This type will occupy 4 bytes in memory, as you can see from the table. Using variables of type double will allow you to store *double-precision* floating-point values (64 bit). Each variable of type double will occupy 8 bytes in memory and provide roughly 15-digit precision with a range of 10^{-308}–10^{+308}. Variables of type double suffice for the majority of requirements, but some specialized applications require even more accuracy and range. The long double type typically provides the exceptional range and precision shown in the table, but this depends on the compiler.

To write a constant of type float, you append an f to the number to distinguish it from type double. You could initialize the previous two variables when you declare them like this:

```
float radius = 2.5f;
double biggest = 123E30;
```

The variable radius has the initial value 2.5, and the variable biggest is initialized to the number that corresponds to 123 followed by 30 zeroes. Any number that you write containing a decimal point is of type double unless you append the F to make it type float. When you specify an exponent value with E or e, the constant need not contain a decimal point. For instance, 1E3f is of type float, and 3E8 is of type double.

To specify a long double constant, you append an uppercase or lowercase letter L, as in the following example:

```
long double huge = 1234567.89123L;
```

Division Using Floating-Point Values

You have seen that division with integer operands always produces an integer result. Unless the left operand of a division is an exact multiple of the right operand when dividing one integer by another, the result will be inherently inaccurate. Of course, the way integer division works is an advantage if you're distributing cookies to children, but it isn't particularly useful when you want to cut a 10-foot plank into four equal pieces. This is a job for floating-point values.

Division with floating-point operands will give you an exact result—at least, a result that is as exact as it can be with a fixed number of digits of precision. The next example illustrates how division operations work with variables of type float.

TRY IT OUT: DIVISION WITH VALUES OF TYPE FLOAT

Here's a simple example that divides one floating-point value by another and outputs the result:

```
// Program 2.7 Division with float values
#include <stdio.h>

int main(void)
{
  float plank_length = 10.0f;          // In feet
  float piece_count = 4.0f;            // Number of equal pieces
  float piece_length = 0.0f;           // Length of a piece in feet

  piece_length = plank_length/piece_count;
  printf("A plank %f feet long can be cut into %f pieces %f feet long.\n",
                            plank_length, piece_count, piece_length);

  return 0;
}
```

This program produces the following output:

```
A plank 10.000000 feet long can be cut into 4.000000 pieces 2.500000 feet long.
```

You should not have any trouble understanding how you chop the plank into equal pieces. You use a new format specifier for values of type float in the printf() statement:

```
printf("A plank %f feet long can be cut into %f pieces %f feet long.\n",
                            plank_length, piece_count, piece_length);
```

You use the format specifier %f to display floating-point values. In general, the format specifier that you use must correspond to the type of value you're outputting. If you output a value of type float with the specifier %d that's to be used with integer values, you'll get garbage. This is because the float value will be interpreted as an integer, which it isn't. Similarly, if you use %f with a value of an integer type, you'll also get garbage as output.

Controlling the Number of Decimal Places in the Output

In the previous example, you got a lot of decimal places in the output that you really didn't need. You may be good with a ruler and a saw, but you aren't going to be able to cut the plank with a length of 2.500000 feet rather than 2.500001 feet. You can specify the number of places that you want to see after the decimal point in the format specifier. To obtain the output to two decimal places, you would write the format specifier as %.2f. To get three decimal places, you would write %.3f.

You can change the printf() statement in the previous example so that it will produce more suitable output:

```
printf("A plank %.2f feet long can be cut into %.0f pieces %.2f feet long.\n",
                            plank_length, piece_count, piece_length);
```

The first format specification applies to the value of plank_length and will produce output with two decimal places. The second specification will produce no decimal places—this makes sense here because the piece_count value is a whole number. The last specification is the same as the first. Thus, if you run the example with this version of the last statement, the output will be the following:

```
A plank 10.00 feet long can be cut into 4 pieces 2.50 feet long.
```

This is much more appropriate and looks a lot better. Of course, you could make piece_count an integer type, which would be better still.

Controlling the Output Field Width

The *field width* for an output value is the total number of characters used for the value including spaces. In this program, it has been determined by default. The printf() function works out how many character positions will be required for a value, given the number of decimal places you specify, and uses that as the field width. However, you can specify the field width. You can also specify the number of decimal places. A fixed field width is essential if you want to output a column of values so they align vertically. If you let the printf() function work out the field width, you're likely to get a ragged column of output. The general form of the format specifier for floating-point values can be written like this:

```
%[width][.precision][modifier]f
```

The square brackets here aren't part of the specification. They enclose bits of the specification that are optional. Thus, you can omit width or .precision or modifier or any combination of these. The width value is an integer specifying the total number of characters in the output including spaces, so it is the output field width. The precision value is an integer specifying the number of decimal places that are to appear after the decimal point. The modifier part is L when the value you are outputting is type long double; otherwise, you omit it.

You could rewrite the printf() call in the previous example to specify the field width as well as the number of digits you want after the decimal point:

```
printf("A %8.2f plank foot can be cut into %5.0f pieces %6.2f feet long.\n",
                                    plank_length, piece_count, piece_length);
```

I changed the text a little here because of the page width in the book. The first output value now has a field width of eight and two decimal places after the decimal point. The second output value, which is the count of the number of pieces, has a field width of five characters and no decimal places. The third output value will be presented in a field width of six characters with two decimal places.

When you specify the field width, the output value will be right aligned by default. If you want the value to be left aligned in the field, just put a minus sign following the %. For instance, the specification %-10.4f will output a floating-point value left aligned in a field width of ten characters with four digits following the decimal point.

You can also specify a field width and the alignment in the field with a specification for outputting an integer value. For example, %-15d specifies an integer value will be presented left aligned in a field width of 15 characters. This is not all there is to format specifiers. We'll learn more about them later. Try out some variations using the previous example. In particular, see what happens when the field width is too small for the value.

More Complicated Expressions

Of course, arithmetic can get a lot more complicated than just dividing one number by another. If that were the case, you could get by with paper and pencil. With more complicated calculations, you will often need more control over the sequence of operations when an expression is evaluated. Parentheses in an arithmetic expression provide you with this capability. They can also help to make complicated expressions clearer.

Parentheses in arithmetic expressions work much as you'd expect. Subexpressions that are enclosed within parentheses are evaluated in sequence, starting with the expression in the innermost pair of parentheses and progressing through to the outermost. The normal rules you're used to for operator precedence apply, so multiplication and division happen before addition or subtraction. For example, the expression 2 * (3 + 3 * (5 + 4)) evaluates to 60. You start with the expression 5 + 4, which produces 9. The result is multiplied by 3, which gives 27. Then you add 3 to that total (giving 30) and finally multiply 30 by 2.

You can insert spaces to separate operands from operators to make your arithmetic statements more readable, or you can leave them out when you need to make the code more compact. Either way, the compiler doesn't mind, as it will ignore spaces. If you're not quite sure of how an expression will be evaluated according to the precedence rules, you can always put in some parentheses to make sure it produces the result you want.

TRY IT OUT: ARITHMETIC IN ACTION

This time you'll have a go at calculating the circumference and area of a circular table from an input value for its diameter. You may remember from elementary math the equations to calculate the area and circumference of a circle using π or pi (circumference $= 2\pi r$ and area $= \pi r^2$, where r is the radius). If you don't, don't worry. This isn't a math book, so just look at how the program works:

```c
// Program 2.8 calculations on a table
#define _CRT_SECURE_NO_WARNINGS
#include <stdio.h>

int main(void)
{
  float radius = 0.0f;                    // The radius of the table
  float diameter = 0.0f;                  // The diameter of the table
  float circumference = 0.0f;             // The circumference of the table
  float area = 0.0f;                      // The area of the table
  float Pi = 3.14159265f;

  printf("Input the diameter of the table:");
  scanf("%f", &diameter);                 // Read the diameter from the keyboard

  radius = diameter/2.0f;                 // Calculate the radius
  circumference = 2.0f*Pi*radius;         // Calculate the circumference
  area = Pi*radius*radius;                // Calculate the area

  printf("\nThe circumference is %.2f", circumference);
  printf("\nThe area is %.2f.\n", area);
  return 0;
}
```

scanf could overflow the buffer, generating problems; for the corresponding error-prone behavior, the C11 version standard defined in Annex K safer functions (they have suffix _s in their names) that handle these possible overflows. We are introducing scanf_s later in Chapter 6. This doesn't mean that scanf is deprecated (although MS declares it). GCC and other compilers still use it. Microsoft compiler implements an approximation of these safer functions. If you still want to use the original scanf, then you must define _CRT_SECURE_NO_WARNINGS to avoid an error from the Visual Studio compiler.

Here's some typical output from this example:

```
Input the diameter of the table: 6

The circumference is 18.85.
The area is 28.27.
```

How It Works

Up to the first `printf()`, the program looks much the same as those you've seen before:

```
float radius = 0.0f;                    // The radius of the table
float diameter = 0.0f;                  // The diameter of the table
float circumference = 0.0f;             // The circumference of the table
float area = 0.0f;                      // The area of the table
float Pi = 3.14159265f;
```

You declare and initialize five variables, where `Pi` has its usual value. Note how all the initial values have an f at the end because you're initializing values of type `float`. Without the f, the values would be of type `double`. They would still work here, but you would be introducing some unnecessary conversion that the compiler would have to arrange, from type `double` to type `float`. There are more digits in the value of `Pi` that type `float` can accommodate, so the compiler will chop off the least significant part so it fits.

The next statement outputs a prompt for input from the keyboard: `printf("Input the diameter of the table:");`

The next statement deals with reading the value for the diameter of the table. You use a new standard library function, the `scanf()` function, to do this:

```
scanf("%f", &diameter);                 // Read the diameter from the keyboard
```

The `scanf()` function is another function that requires the `stdio.h` header file to be included. This function handles input from the keyboard. In effect, it takes what you enter through the keyboard and interprets it as specified by the first argument, which is a control string between double quotes. In this case, the control string is `"%f"` because you're reading a value of type `float`. It stores the result in the variable specified by the second argument, `diameter` in this instance. The first argument is a control string similar to what we used with the `printf()` function, except here it controls input rather than output. We'll learn more about the `scanf()` function in Chapter 10; and, for reference, Appendix D summarizes the control strings you can use with it.

You've undoubtedly noticed something new here: the & preceding the variable name `diameter`. This is called the *address of* operator, and it's needed to allow the `scanf()` function to store the value that is read from the keyboard in your variable, `diameter`. The reason for this is bound up with the way argument values are passed to a function. For the moment, I won't go into a more detailed explanation of this; you'll see more on this in Chapter 8. Just remember to use the address of operator (the & sign) before a variable when you're using the `scanf()` function and not to use it when you use the `printf()` function.

Within the control string for the `scanf()` function, the % character identifies the start of a format specification for an item of data. The f that follows the % indicates that the input should be interpreted as a floating-point value. In general, there can be several format specifications within the control string, in which case these determine how each of a succession of input values will be interpreted. There must be as many argument variables following the control string in the `scanf()` function call as there are format specifications. We'll learn a lot more on how `scanf()` works later in the book, but for now the basic set of format specifiers you can use for reading data of various types are shown in Table 2-8.

Table 2-8. *Format Specifiers for Reading Data*

Action	Required control string
To read a value of type short	%hd
To read a value of type int	%d
To read a value of type long	%ld
To read a value of type float	%f or %e
To read a value of type double	%lf or %le

In the %ld and %lf format specifiers, l is lowercased. Don't forget you must *always* prefix the name of the variable that's receiving the input value with &. Also, if you use the wrong format specifier—if you read a value into a variable of type float with %d, for instance—the data value in your variable won't be correct, but you'll get no indication that a junk value has been stored.

Next, you have three statements that calculate the results you're interested in:

```
radius = diameter/2.0f;                // Calculate the radius
circumference = 2.0f*Pi*radius;        // Calculate the circumference
area = Pi*radius*radius;               // Calculate the area
```

The first statement calculates the radius as half of the value of the diameter that was entered. The second statement computes the circumference of the table, using the value that was calculated for the radius. The third statement calculates the area. Note that if you forget the f in 2.0f, you'll probably get a warning message from your compiler. This is because without the f, the constant is of type double, and you would be mixing different types in the same expression. You'll see more about this later.

You could have written the statements to calculate the circumference and area like this:

```
circumference = 2.0f*Pi*(diameter/2.0f);            // Calculate the circumference
area = Pi*(diameter/2.0f)*(diameter/2.0f);          // Calculate the area
```

The parentheses ensure that the value for the radius is calculated first in each statement. They also help to make it clear that it is the radius that is being calculated. A disadvantage to these statements is that the radius calculation is potentially carried out three times, when it is only necessary for it to be carried out once. A clever compiler can optimize this code and arrange for the radius calculation to be done only once.

The next two statements output the values you've calculated:

```
printf("\nThe circumference is %.2f.", circumference);
printf("\nThe area is %.2f.\n", area);
```

These printf() statements output the values of the variables circumference and area using the format specifier %.2f. The format specification outputs the values with two decimal places after the point. The default field width will be sufficient in each case to accommodate the value that is to be displayed.

Of course, you can run this program and enter whatever values you want for the diameter. You could experiment with different forms of floating-point input here, and you could try entering something like 1E1f, for example.

Defining Named Constants

Although Pi is defined as a variable in the previous example, it's really a constant value that you don't want to change. The value of π is always a fixed number with an unlimited number of decimal digits. The only question is how many digits of precision you want to use in its specification. It would be nice to make sure its value stayed fixed in a program so it couldn't be changed by mistake.

There are a couple of ways in which you can approach this. The first is to define Pi as a symbol that's to be replaced in the program by its value during compilation. In this case, Pi isn't a variable at all, but more a sort of alias for the value it represents. Let's try that out.

TRY IT OUT: DEFINING A CONSTANT

Let's look at specifying the name PI as an alias for its value:

```
// Program 2.9 More round tables
#define _CRT_SECURE_NO_WARNINGS
#include <stdio.h>
#define PI    3.14159f                        // Definition of the symbol PI

int main(void)
{
  float radius = 0.0f;
  float diameter = 0.0f;
  float circumference = 0.0f;
  float area = 0.0f;

  printf("Input the diameter of a table:");
  scanf("%f", &diameter);

  radius = diameter/2.0f;
  circumference = 2.0f*PI*radius;
  area = PI*radius*radius;

  printf("\nThe circumference is %.2f. ", circumference);
  printf("\nThe area is %.2f.\n", area);
  return 0;
}
```

This produces the same output as the previous example.

How It Works

After the comment and the #include directive for the header file, there is the following preprocessing directive:

```
#define PI    3.14159f                        // Definition of the symbol PI
```

This defines PI as a symbol that is to be replaced in the code by the string 3.14159f. I used PI rather than Pi, because it's a common convention in C to write identifiers that appear in a #define directive in capital letters. Wherever you reference PI within an expression in the program, the preprocessor will substitute the string that you have specified for it in the #define directive. All the substitutions will be made before compiling the program. When the program is ready to be compiled, it will no longer contain references to PI, because all occurrences will have been replaced by the sequence of characters you've specified in the #define directive. This all happens internally while your program is processed by the compiler. Your source file will not be changed; it will still contain the symbol PI.

■ **Caution** The preprocessor makes the substitution for a symbol in the code without regard for whether it makes sense. If you make an error in the substitution string, if you wrote 3.14.159f, for example, the preprocessor will still replace every occurrence of PI in the code with this, and the program will not compile.

Your other option is to define Pi as a variable, but to tell the compiler that its value is fixed and must not be changed. You can fix the value of any variable when you declare it by prefixing the type name with the keyword const, for example:

```
  const float Pi = 3.14159f;                    // Defines the value of Pi as fixed
```

The advantage of defining Pi in this way is that you are now defining it as a constant numerical value with a specified type. In the previous example, PI was just a sequence of characters that replaced all occurrences of PI in your code.

The keyword const in the declaration for Pi causes the compiler to check that the code doesn't attempt to change its value. Any code that does so will be flagged as an error, and the compilation will fail. Let's see a working example of this.

TRY IT OUT: DEFINING A VARIABLE WITH A FIXED VALUE

You can use a const variable in a variation of the previous example but with the code shortened a little:

```
// Program 2.10 Round tables again but shorter
#define _CRT_SECURE_NO_WARNINGS
#include <stdio.h>

int main(void)
{
  float diameter = 0.0f;                    // The diameter of a table
  float radius = 0.0f;                      // The radius of a table
  const float Pi = 3.14159f;                // Defines the value of Pi as fixed

  printf("Input the diameter of the table:");
  scanf("%f", &diameter);

  radius = diameter/2.0f;

  printf("\nThe circumference is %.2f.", 2.0f*Pi*radius);
  printf("\nThe area is %.2f.\n", Pi*radius*radius);
  return 0;
}
```

How It Works

Following the declaration for the variable `radius` is this statement:

```
const float Pi = 3.14159f;                    // Defines the value of Pi as fixed
```

This declares the variable `Pi` and defines a value for it; `Pi` is still a variable here, but the initial value cannot be changed. The `const` modifier achieves this effect. It can be applied to the definition of any variable of any type to fix its value. The compiler will check your code for attempts to change variables that you've declared as `const`, and if it discovers an attempt to change a `const` variable, it will complain. There are ways to trick the compiler to allow a `const` variable to be changed, but this defeats the whole point of using `const` in the first place.

The two statements that produce the output from the program are

```
printf("\nThe circumference is %.2f.", 2.0f*Pi*radius);
printf("\nThe area is %.2f.\n", Pi*radius*radius);
```

In this example, you no longer use variables to store the circumference and area of the circle. The expressions for these now appear as arguments in the `printf()` statements, where they're evaluated, and their values are passed directly to the function.

As we learned before, a value that you pass to a function can be the result of an expression. In this case, the compiler creates a temporary variable to hold the value of the result of the expression, and that will be passed to the function. The temporary variable is subsequently discarded. This is fine, as long as you don't want to use these values elsewhere.

Knowing Your Limitations

Of course, it may be important to be able to determine within a program exactly what the limits are on the values that can be stored by a given integer type. As I mentioned earlier, the `limits.h` header file defines symbols that represent values for the limits for each type. Table 2-9 shows the symbol names corresponding to the limits for each signed integer type.

Table 2-9. *Symbols Representing Range Limits for Integer Types*

Type	Lower limit	Upper limit
char	CHAR_MIN	CHAR_MAX
short	SHRT_MIN	SHRT_MAX
int	INT_MIN	INT_MAX
long	LONG_MIN	LONG_MAX
long long	LLONG_MIN	LLONG_MAX

The lower limits for the unsigned integer types are all 0, so there are no symbols for these. The symbols corresponding to the upper limits for the unsigned integer types are UCHAR_MAX, USHRT_MAX, UINT_MAX, ULONG_MAX, and ULLONG_MAX.

To be able to use any of these symbols in a program, you must have an #include directive for the limits.h header file in the source file:

```
#include <limits.h>
```

You could initialize a variable with the maximum possible value for type int like this:

```
int number = INT_MAX;
```

This statement sets the value of number to be the maximum possible, whatever that may be for the compiler used to compile the code.

The float.h header file defines symbols that characterize floating-point values. Some of these are quite technical, so I'll just mention those you are most likely to be interested in. The symbols defining the maximum and minimum positive values that can be represented by the three floating-point types are shown in Table 2-10. You can also access the symbols FLT_DIG, DBL_DIG, and LDBL_DIG that indicate the number of decimal digits that can be represented by the binary mantissa of the corresponding types. Let's explore in a working example how to access some of the symbols characterizing integers and floating-point values.

Table 2-10. *Symbols Representing Range Limits for Floating-Point Types*

Type	Lower limit	Upper limit
float	FLT_MIN	FLT_MAX
double	DBL_MIN	DBL_MAX
long double	LDBL_MIN	LDBL_MAX

TRY IT OUT: FINDING THE LIMITS

This program outputs the values corresponding to the symbols defined in the header files, so it will tell you the limits for your compiler:

```
// Program 2.11 Finding the limits
#include <stdio.h>                    // For command line input and output
#include <limits.h>                   // For limits on integer types
#include <float.h>                    // For limits on floating-point types

int main(void)
{
  printf("Variables of type char store values from %d to %d\n", CHAR_MIN, CHAR_MAX);
  printf("Variables of type unsigned char store values from 0 to %u\n", UCHAR_MAX);
  printf("Variables of type short store values from %d to %d\n", SHRT_MIN, SHRT_MAX);
  printf("Variables of type unsigned short store values from 0 to %u\n", USHRT_MAX);
  printf("Variables of type int store values from %d to %d\n", INT_MIN,  INT_MAX);
  printf("Variables of type unsigned int store values from 0 to %u\n", UINT_MAX);
  printf("Variables of type long store values from %ld to %ld\n", LONG_MIN, LONG_MAX);
  printf("Variables of type unsigned long store values from 0 to %lu\n", ULONG_MAX);
  printf("Variables of type long long store values from %lld to %lld\n", LLONG_MIN,
  LLONG_MAX);
  printf("Variables of type unsigned long long store values from 0 to %llu\n",
  ULLONG_MAX);
```

```
printf("\nThe size of the smallest positive non-zero value of type float is
%.3e\n", FLT_MIN);
printf("The size of the largest value of type float is %.3e\n", FLT_MAX);
printf("The size of the smallest non-zero value of type double is %.3e\n", DBL_MIN);
printf("The size of the largest value of type double is %.3e\n", DBL_MAX);
printf("The size of the smallest non-zero value of type long double is %.3Le\n",
LDBL_MIN);
printf("The size of the largest value of type long double is %.3Le\n",  LDBL_MAX);

printf("\n Variables of type float provide %u decimal digits precision. \n", FLT_DIG);
printf("Variables of type double provide %u decimal digits precision. \n", DBL_DIG);
printf("Variables of type long double provide %u decimal digits precision. \n",
                                                                  LDBL_DIG);

return 0;
}
```

You'll get output somewhat similar to the following, which corresponds to what my compiler offers:

```
Variables of type char store values from -128 to 127
Variables of type unsigned char store values from 0 to 255
Variables of type short store values from -32768 to 32767
Variables of type unsigned short store values from 0 to 65535
Variables of type int store values from -2147483648 to 2147483647
Variables of type unsigned int store values from 0 to 4294967295
Variables of type long store values from -2147483648 to 2147483647
Variables of type unsigned long store values from 0 to 4294967295
Variables of type long long store values from -9223372036854775808 to 9223372036854775807
Variables of type unsigned long long store values from 0 to 18446744073709551615

The size of the smallest positive non-zero value of type float is 1.175e-038
The size of the largest value of type float is 3.403e+038
The size of the smallest non-zero value of type double is 2.225e-308
The size of the largest value of type double is 1.798e+308
The size of the smallest non-zero value of type long double is 3.362e-4932
The size of the largest value of type long double is 1.190e+4932

Variables of type float provide 6 decimal digits precision.
Variables of type double provide 15 decimal digits precision.
Variables of type long double provide 18 decimal digits precision.
```

How It Works

You output the values of symbols that are defined in the limits.h and float.h header files in a series of printf() function calls. Numbers in your computer are always limited in the range of values that can be stored, and the values of these symbols represent the boundaries for values of each numerical type. You have used the %u specifier to output the unsigned integer values. If you use %d for the maximum value of an unsigned type, values that have the leftmost bit (the sign bit for signed types) as 1 won't be interpreted correctly.

You use the %e specifier for the floating-point limits, which presents the values in exponential form. You also specify just three digits' precision, as you don't need the full accuracy in the output. The L modifier is necessary when the value being displayed by the printf() function is type long double. Remember, this has to be a capital letter L; a lowercase letter won't do here. The %f specifier presents values without an exponent, so it's rather inconvenient for very large or very small values. If you try it in the example, you'll see what I mean.

Introducing the sizeof Operator

You can find out how many bytes are occupied by a given type by using the sizeof operator. Of course, sizeof is a keyword in C. The expression sizeof(int) will result in the number of bytes occupied by a variable of type int, and the result is an integer of type size_t. Type size_t is defined in the standard header file stddef.h, as well as several other headers, and will correspond to one of the basic integer types. Because the choice of type that corresponds to type size_t may differ between one C library and another, it's best to use variables of size_t to store the value produced by the sizeof operator, even when you know the basic type to which it corresponds. Here's how you could store a value that results from applying the sizeof operator:

```
size_t size = sizeof(long long);
```

You can also apply the sizeof operator to an expression, in which case the result is the size of the value that results from evaluating the expression. In this context, the expression would usually be just a variable of some kind. The sizeof operator has uses other than just discovering the memory occupied by a value of a basic type, but for the moment, let's just use it to find out how many bytes are occupied by each type.

TRY IT OUT: DISCOVERING THE NUMBER OF BYTES OCCUPIED BY A TYPE

This program will output the number of bytes occupied by each numeric type:

```c
// Program 2.12 Finding the size of a type
#include <stdio.h>

int main(void)
{
  printf("Variables of type char occupy %u bytes\n", sizeof(char));
  printf("Variables of type short occupy %u bytes\n", sizeof(short));
  printf("Variables of type int occupy %u bytes\n", sizeof(int));
  printf("Variables of type long occupy %u bytes\n", sizeof(long));
  printf("Variables of type long long occupy %u bytes\n", sizeof(long long));
  printf("Variables of type float occupy %u bytes\n", sizeof(float));
  printf("Variables of type double occupy %u bytes\n", sizeof(double));
  printf("Variables of type long double occupy %u bytes\n", sizeof(long double));
  return 0;
}
```

On my system I get the following output:

```
Variables of type char occupy 1 bytes
Variables of type short occupy 2 bytes
Variables of type int occupy 4 bytes
Variables of type long occupy 4 bytes
Variables of type long long occupy 8 bytes
Variables of type float occupy 4 bytes
Variables of type double occupy 8 bytes
Variables of type long double occupy 12 bytes
```

How It Works

Because the `sizeof` operator results in an unsigned integer value, you output it using the %u specifier. Note that you can also obtain the number of bytes occupied by a variable, var_name, with the expression `sizeof var_name`. Obviously, the space between the `sizeof` keyword and the variable name in the expression is essential.

Now you know the range limits and the number of bytes occupied by each numeric type with your compiler.

▮ **Note** If you want to apply the `sizeof` operator to a type, the type name must be between parentheses, like this: `sizeof(long double)`. When you apply `sizeof` to an expression, the parentheses are optional.

Choosing the Correct Type for the Job

You have to be careful to select the type of variable that you're using in your calculations so that it accommodates the range of values you expect. If you use the wrong type, you may find that errors creep into your programs that can be hard to detect. (Besides the undefined behavior that may occur, there are known exploits of buffer overflow; however, they are beyond this book's scope. Please check OWASP Buffer Overflow.) This is best shown with an example.

TRY IT OUT: THE RIGHT TYPES OF VARIABLES

Here's an example that shows how things can go horribly wrong if you choose an unsuitable type for your variables:

```c
// Program 2.13 Choosing the correct type for the job  1
#include <stdio.h>

int main(void)
{
  const float Revenue_Per_150 = 4.5f;
  short JanSold = 23500;                            // Stock sold in January
  short FebSold = 19300;                            // Stock sold in February
  short MarSold = 21600;                            // Stock sold in March
  float  RevQuarter = 0.0f;                         // Sales for the quarter

  short QuarterSold = JanSold + FebSold + MarSold;  // Calculate quarterly total

  // Output monthly sales and total for the quarter
  printf("Stock sold in\n Jan: %d\n Feb: %d\n Mar: %d\n", JanSold, FebSold, MarSold);
  printf("Total stock sold in first quarter: %d\n", QuarterSold);

  // Calculate the total revenue for the quarter and output it
   RevQuarter = QuarterSold/150*Revenue_Per_150;
  printf("Sales revenue this quarter is:$%.2f\n", RevQuarter);
  return 0;
}
```

These are fairly simple calculations, and you can see that the total stock sold in the quarter should be 64400. This is just the sum of each of the monthly totals, but if you run the program, the output you get is this:

```
Stock sold in
 Jan: 23500
 Feb: 19300
 Mar: 21600
Total stock sold in first quarter: -1136
Sales revenue this quarter is:$-31.50
```

Obviously there is something wrong here. It doesn't take a genius or an accountant to tell you that adding three big, positive numbers together should not produce a negative result.

How It Works

First, you define a constant that will be used in the calculation:

```c
  const float Revenue_Per_150 = 4.5f;
```

This defines the revenue obtained for every 150 items sold. There's nothing wrong with that.

Next, you declare four variables and assign initial values to them:

```
short JanSold = 23500;                  // Stock sold in January
short FebSold = 19300;                  // Stock sold in February
short MarSold = 21600;                  // Stock sold in March
float  RevQuarter = 0.0f;               // Sales for the quarter
```

The first three variables are of type short, which is quite adequate to store the initial value. The RevQuarter variable is of type float because you want two decimal places for the quarterly revenue.

The next statement declares the variable QuarterSold and stores the sum of the sales for each of the months:

```
short QuarterSold = JanSold + FebSold + MarSold;    // Calculate quarterly total
```

It looks like the cause of the erroneous results is in the declaration of the QuarterSold variable. You've declared it to be of type short and given it the initial value of the sum of the three monthly figures. You know that their sum is 64400 and that the program outputs a negative number. The error must therefore be in this statement.

The problem arises because you've tried to store a number that's too large for type short. If you recall, the maximum value that a short variable can hold is 32767. The computer can't interpret the value of QuarterSold correctly and happens to give a negative result. A secondary consideration is that the quantity sold is not going to be negative, so perhaps an unsigned type would be more appropriate. The solution to the problem is to use a variable of type unsigned long for QuarterSold that will allow you to store much larger numbers. You can also specify the variables holding the monthly figures as unsigned.

Solving the Problem

Try changing the program and running it again. You need to change only five lines in the body of the function main(). The new and improved program is as follows:

```
// Program 2.14 Choosing the correct type for the job  2
#include <stdio.h>

int main(void)
{
  const float Revenue_Per_150 = 4.5f;
  unsigned short JanSold =23500;              // Stock sold in January
  unsigned short FebSold =19300;              // Stock sold in February
  unsigned short MarSold =21600;              // Stock sold in March
  float  RevQuarter = 0.0f;                   // Sales for the quarter

  unsigned long QuarterSold = JanSold + FebSold + MarSold; // Calculate quarterly
                                                           total

  // Output monthly sales and total for the quarter
  printf("Stock sold in\n Jan: %d\n Feb: %d\n Mar: %d\n", JanSold, FebSold, MarSold);
  printf("Total stock sold in first quarter: %ld\n", QuarterSold);
```

```
// Calculate the total revenue for the quarter and output it
RevQuarter = QuarterSold/150*Revenue_Per_150;
printf("Sales revenue this quarter is:$%.2f\n", RevQuarter);
return 0;
}
```

When you run this program, the output is more satisfactory:

```
Stock sold in
    Jan: 23500
    Feb: 19300
    Mar: 21600
  Total stock sold in first quarter: 64400
Sales revenue this quarter is :$1930.50
```

The stock sold in the quarter is correct, and you have a reasonable result for revenue. Notice that you use %ld to output the total stock sold. This tells the compiler that it is to use a long conversion for the output of this value. Just to check the program, calculate the result of the revenue yourself with a calculator.

The result you should get is, in fact, $1,932. Somewhere you've lost a dollar and a half. Not such a great amount, but try telling that to an accountant. You need to find the lost $1.50. Consider what's happening when you calculate the value for revenue in the program:

```
RevQuarter = QuarterSold/150*Revenue_Per_150;
```

Here you're assigning a value to RevQuarter. The value is the result of the expression on the right of the = sign. The result of the expression will be calculated, step by step, according to the precedence rules you have already learned in this chapter. Here you have quite a simple expression that's calculated from left to right, since division and multiplication have the same priority. Let's work through it:

- QuarterSold/150 is calculated as 64400/150, which should produce the result 429.333.

This is where your problem arises. QuarterSold is an integer, and so the computer truncates the result of the division to an integer, ignoring the .333. This means that when the next part of the calculation is evaluated, the result will be slightly off:

- 429*Revenue_Per_150 is calculated as 429 * 4.5 which is 1930.50.

You now know where the error has occurred, but what can you do about it? You could change all of your variables to floating-point types, but that would defeat the purpose of using integers in the first place. The numbers entered really are integers, so you'd like to store them as such. Is there an easy solution to this? In this case, there are two. First, you can rewrite the statement as follows:

```
RevQuarter = Revenue_Per_150*QuarterSold/150;
```

Now the multiplication will occur first; and because of the way arithmetic works with operands of different types, the result will be of type float. The compiler will automatically arrange for the integer operand to be converted to floating point. When you then divide by 150, that operation will execute with float values too, with 150 being converted to 150f. The net effect is that the result will now be correct.

Second, you could just use 150.0 as the divisor. The dividend will then be converted to floating point before the division is executed.

However, there's more to it than that. Not only do you need to understand more about what happens with arithmetic between operands of different types but you also need to understand how you can control conversions from one type of data to another. In C, you have the ability to explicitly convert a value of one type to another type.

Explicit Type Conversion

Let's look again at the original expression to calculate the quarterly revenue in Program 2.14 and see how you can control what goes on so that you end up with the correct result:

```
RevQuarter = QuarterSold/150*Revenue_Per_150;
```

You know that if the result is to be correct, this statement has to be amended so that the expression is evaluated with floating-point operands throughout. If you could convert the value of QuarterSold to type float, the expression will be evaluated as floating point, and your problem would be solved. To convert the value of a variable to another type, you place the type you want to cast the value to in parentheses in front of the variable. Thus, the statement to calculate the result correctly will be the following:

```
RevQuarter = (float)QuarterSold/150*Revenue_Per_150;
```

This is exactly what you require. You're using the right types of variables in the right places. You're also ensuring you don't use integer arithmetic when you want to keep the fractional part of the result of a division. An explicit conversion from one type to another is called a *cast*.

Of course you can cast the result of an expression to another type. In this case, you should put the expression between parentheses, for example:

```
double result = 0.0;
int a = 5;
int b = 8;
result = (double)(a + b)/2 - (a + b)/(double)(a*a + b*b);
```

By casting the result of evaluating (a + b) to type double, you ensure that the division by 2 is done as a floating-point operation. The value 2 will be converted to type double, so it is the same type as the left operand for the division operation. Casting the integer result of the divisor, (a*a + b*b), to type double has a similar effect on the second division operation; the value of the left operand will be promoted to type double before the division is executed.

Automatic Conversions

Look at the output from the second version of the program again:

```
Sales revenue this quarter is :$1930.50
```

Even without the explicit cast in the expression, the result is in floating-point form, though it is clearly wrong. The result is floating point because binary operators require the operands to be of the same type. The compiler automatically converts one of the operands to be the same type as the other when an operation involves operands of different types. Whenever you use operands in a binary operation that are of different types, the compiler arranges for the value that is of a type with a more limited range to be converted to the type of the other operand. This is called an *implicit conversion*. So referring back to the expression to calculate revenue:

```
QuarterSold / 150 * Revenue_Per_150
```

It is evaluated as 64400 (int)/150 (int), which equals 429 (int). Then 429, after an implicit conversion from type int to type float, is multiplied by 4.5 (float), giving the result 1930.5 (float).

An implicit conversion always applies when a binary operator involves operands of different types, including different integer types. With the first operation, the numbers are both of type int, so the result is of type int. With the second operation, the first value is type int and the second value is type float. Type int is more limited in its range than type float, so the value of type int is automatically cast to type float. Whenever there is a mixture of types in an arithmetic expression, your compiler will use specific rules to decide how the expression will be evaluated. Let's have a look at these rules now.

Rules for Implicit Conversions

The mechanism that determines which operand in a binary operation is to be changed to the type of the other is relatively simple. Broadly, it works on the basis that the operand with the type that has the more restricted range of values will be converted to the type of the other operand, although in some instances both operands will be promoted.

To express accurately in words how this works is somewhat more complicated than the description in the previous paragraph, so you may want to ignore the fine detail that follows and refer back to it if you need to. If you want the full story, read on.

The compiler determines the implicit conversion to use by checking the following rules in sequence until it finds one that applies:

1. If one operand is of type long double, the other operand will be converted to type long double.

2. Otherwise, if one operand is of type double, the other operand will be converted to type double.

3. Otherwise, if one operand is of type float, the other operand will be converted to type float.

4. Otherwise, if the operands are both of signed integer types or both of unsigned integer types, the operand of the type of lower rank is converted to the type of the other operand.

   a. The unsigned integer types are ranked from low to high in the following sequence: signed char, short, int, long, long long.

   b. Each unsigned integer type has the same rank as the corresponding signed integer type, so type unsigned int has the same rank as type int, for example.

5. Otherwise, if the operand of the signed integer type has a rank that is less than or equal to the rank of the unsigned integer type, the signed integer operand is converted to the unsigned integer type.

6. Otherwise, if the range of values the signed integer type can represent includes the values that can be represented by the unsigned integer type, the unsigned operand is converted to the signed integer type.

7. Otherwise, both operands are converted to the unsigned integer type corresponding to the signed integer type.

Implicit Conversions in Assignment Statements

You can also cause an implicit conversion to be applied when the value of the expression on the right of the assignment operator is a different type from the variable on the left. In some circumstances, this can cause values to be truncated so information is lost. For instance, if an assignment operation stores a value of type float or double to a variable of type int or long, the fractional part of the float or double will be lost, and just the integer part will be stored. The following code fragment illustrates this situation:

```
int number = 0;
float value = 2.5f;
number = value;
```

The value stored in number will be 2. Because you've assigned the value of value (2.5) to the variable number, which is of type int, the fractional part, .5, will be lost and only the 2 will be stored.

An assignment statement that may lose information because an automatic conversion has to be applied will usually result in a warning from the compiler. However, the code will still compile, so there's a risk that your program may be doing things that will lead to incorrect results. Generally, it's better to put explicit casts in your code wherever conversions that may result in information being lost are necessary.

Let's look at an example to see how the conversion rules in assignment operations work in practice. Look at the following code fragment:

```
double price = 10.0;                    // Product price per unit
long count = 5L;                        // Number of items
float ship_cost = 2.5F;                 // Shipping cost per order
int discount = 15;                      // Discount as percentage
long double total_cost = (count*price + ship_cost)*((100L - discount)/100.0F);
```

This defines four variables and computes the total cost of an order from the values of these variables. I chose the types primarily to demonstrate implicit conversions; these types would not represent a sensible choice in normal circumstances. Let's see what happens in the last statement to produce the value for total_cost:

1. count*price is evaluated first, and count will be implicitly converted to type double to allow the multiplication to take place, and the result will be of type double. This results from the second rule.

2. Next, ship_cost is added to the result of the previous operation; and, to make this possible, the value of ship_cost is converted to the type of the previous result, type double. This conversion also results from the second rule.

3. Next, the expression 100L - discount is evaluated, and to allow this to occur, the value of discount will be converted to type long, the type of the other operand in the subtraction. This is a result of the fourth rule, and the result will be type long.

4. Next, the result of the previous operation (of type long) is converted to type float to allow the division by 100.0F (of type float) to take place. This is the result of applying the third rule, and the result is of type float.

5. The result of step 2 is divided by the result of step 4, and to make this possible, the float value from the previous operation is converted to type double. This is a consequence of applying the second rule, and the result is of type double.

6. Finally, the previous result is stored in the variable `total_cost` as a result of the assignment operation. An assignment operation always causes the type of the right operand to be converted to that of the left when the operand types are different, regardless of the types of the operands, so the result of the previous operation is converted to type `long double`. No compiler warning will occur because all values of type `double` can be represented as type `long double`.

■ **Caution**   If you find that you are having to use a lot of explicit casts in your code, you may have made a poor choice of types for storing the data.

More Numeric Data Types

To complete the basic set of numeric data types, I'll now cover those that I haven't yet discussed. The first is one that I mentioned previously: type `char`. A variable of type `char` can store the code for a single character. Because it stores a character code, which is an integer, it's considered to be an integer type. Because it's an integer type, you can treat a `char` value just like any other integer so you can use it in arithmetic calculations.

Character Type

Values of type `char` occupy the least amount of memory of all the data types. They typically require just 1 byte. The integer that's stored in a variable of type `char` may be a signed or unsigned value, depending on your compiler. As an unsigned type, the value stored in a variable of type `char` can range from 0 to 255. As a signed type, a variable of type `char` can store values from –128 to +127. Of course, both ranges correspond to the same set of bit patterns: from 0000 0000 to 1111 1111. With unsigned values, all 8 bits are data bits, so 0000 0000 corresponds to 0, and 1111 1111 corresponds to 255. With signed values, the leftmost bit is a sign bit, so –128 is the binary value 1000 0000, 0 is 0000 0000, and 127 is 0111 1111. The value 1111 1111 as a signed binary value is the decimal value –1.

From the point of view of representing character codes, which are bit patterns, it doesn't matter whether type `char` is regarded as signed or unsigned. Where it *does* matter is when you perform arithmetic operations with values of type `char`.

You can specify the initial value for a variable of type `char` by a *character constant*. A character constant can be just a character written between single quotes. Here are some examples:

```
char letter = 'A';
char digit = '9';
char exclamation = '!';
```

You can use an escape sequence between a pair of single quotes to specify a character constant too:

```
char newline = '\n';
char tab = '\t';
char single_quote = '\'';
```

Of course, in every case, the variable will be set to the code for the character between single quotes. In principle, the actual code value depends on your computer environment, but by far the most common is American Standard Code for Information Interchange (ASCII). You can find the ASCII character codes in Appendix B.

You can also initialize a variable of type char with an integer value, as long as the value fits into the range for type char with your compiler, as in this example:

```
char character = 74;                   // ASCII code for the letter J
```

A variable of type char has a sort of dual personality: you can interpret it as a character or as an integer. Here's an example of an arithmetic operation with a value of type char:

```
char letter = 'C';                     // letter contains the decimal code value 67
letter = letter + 3;                   // letter now contains 70, which is 'F'
```

Thus, you can perform arithmetic on a value of type char and still treat it as a character.

▪ **Note**   Regardless of whether type char is implemented as a signed or unsigned type, the types char, signed char, and unsigned char are all different and require conversions to map from one of these types to another.

Character Input and Character Output

You can read a single character from the keyboard and store it in a variable of type char using the scanf() function with the format specifier %c, for example:

```
char ch = 0;
scanf("%c", &ch);                      // Read one character
```

As we learned earlier, you must add an #include directive for the stdio.h header file to any source file in which you use the scanf() function.

To write a single character to the command line with the printf() function, you use the same format specifier, %c:

```
printf("The character is %c\n", ch);
```

Of course, you can output the numeric value of a character too:

```
printf("The character is %c and the code value is %d\n", ch, ch);
```

This statement will output the value in ch as a character and as a numeric value.

TRY IT OUT: CHARACTER BUILDING

If you're completely new to programming, you may be wondering how on earth the computer knows whether it's dealing with a character or an integer. The reality is that it doesn't. It's a bit like when Alice encounters Humpty Dumpty who says, "When I use a word, it means just what I choose it to mean—neither more nor less." An item of data in memory can mean whatever you choose it to mean. A byte containing the value 70 is a perfectly good integer. It's equally correct to regard it as the code for the letter F.

Let's look at an example that should make it clear. Here, you'll use the conversion specifier %c, which indicates that you want to output a value of type char as a character rather than an integer:

```
// Program 2.15 Characters and numbers
#include <stdio.h>

int main(void)
{
  char first = 'T';
  char second = 63;

  printf("The first example as a letter looks like this - %c\n", first);
  printf("The first example as a number looks like this - %d\n", first);
  printf("The second example as a letter looks like this - %c\n", second);
  printf("The second example as a number looks like this - %d\n", second);
  return 0;
}
```

The output from this program is the following:

```
The first example as a letter looks like this - T
The first example as a number looks like this - 84
The second example as a letter looks like this - ?
The second example as a number looks like this - 63
```

How It Works

The program starts off by declaring two variables of type char:

```
  char first = 'T';
  char second = 63;
```

You initialize the first variable with a character constant and the second variable with an integer.

The next four statements output the value of each variable in two ways:

```
  printf("The first example as a letter looks like this - %c\n", first);
  printf("The first example as a number looks like this - %d\n", first);
  printf("The second example as a letter looks like this - %c\n", second);
  printf("The second example as a number looks like this - %d\n", second);
```

The %c conversion specifier interprets the contents of the variable as a single character, and the %d specifier interprets it as an integer. The numeric values that are output are the codes for the corresponding characters. These are ASCII codes in this instance, and will be in most instances, so that's what you'll assume throughout this book.

■ **Tip**   As noted earlier, not all computers use the ASCII character set, so you may get different values than those shown previously. As long as you use the character notation for a character constant, you'll get the character you want regardless of the character coding in effect.

You can also output the integer values of the variables of type char as hexadecimal values by using the format specifier %x instead of %d. You might like to try that.

TRY IT OUT: ARITHMETIC WITH VALUES THAT ARE CHARACTERS

Let's look at another example in which you apply arithmetic operations to values of type char:

```c
// Program 2.16 Using type char
#include <stdio.h>

int main(void)
{
  char first = 'A';
  char second = 'B';
  char last = 'Z';

  char number = 40;

  char ex1 = first + 2;                  // Add 2 to 'A'
  char ex2 = second - 1;                 // Subtract 1 from 'B'
  char ex3 = last + 2;                   // Add 2 to 'Z'

  printf("Character values     %-5c%-5c%-5c\n", ex1, ex2, ex3);
  printf("Numerical equivalents %-5d%-5d%-5d\n", ex1, ex2, ex3);
  printf("The number %d is the code for the character %c\n", number, number);
  return 0;
}
```

When you run the program, you should get the following output:

```
Character values     C    A    \
Numerical equivalents 67   65   92
The number 40 is the code for the character (
```

How It Works

This program demonstrates how you can happily perform arithmetic with char variables that you've initialized with characters. The first three statements in the body of main() are as follows:

```c
  char first = 'A';
  char second = 'B';
  char last = 'Z';
```

These initialize the variables `first`, `second`, and `last` to the character values you see. The numerical values of these variables will be the ASCII codes for the respective characters. Because you can treat them as numeric values as well as characters, you can perform arithmetic operations with them.

The next statement initializes a variable of type `char` with an integer value:

```
char number = 40;
```

The initializing value must be within the range of values that a 1-byte variable can store; so with my compiler, where `char` is a signed type, it must be between -128 and 127. Of course, you can interpret the contents of the variable as a character. In this case, it will be the character that has the ASCII code value 40, which happens to be a left parenthesis.

The next three statements declare three more variables of type `char`:

```
char ex1 = first + 2;               // Add 2 to 'A'
char ex2 = second - 1;              // Subtract 1 from 'B'
char ex3 = last + 2;                // Add 2 to 'Z'
```

These statements create new values and therefore new characters from the values stored in the variables `first`, `second`, and `last`; the results of these expressions are stored in the variables `ex1`, `ex2`, and `ex3`.

The next two statements output the three variables `ex1`, `ex2`, and `ex3` in two different ways:

```
printf("Character values      %-5c%-5c%-5c\n", ex1, ex2, ex3);
printf("Numerical equivalents %-5d%-5d%-5d\n", ex1, ex2, ex3);
```

The first statement interprets the values stored as characters by using the `%-5c` conversion specifier. This specifies that the value should be output as a character that is left aligned in a field width of five. The second statement outputs the same variables again, but this time interprets the values as integers by using the `%-5d` specifier. The alignment and the field width are the same, but `d` specifies the output is an integer. You can see that the two lines of output show the three characters on the first line with their ASCII codes aligned on the line beneath.

The last line outputs the variable `number` as a character and as an integer:

```
printf("The number %d is the code for the character %c\n", number, number);
```

To output the variable value twice, you just write it twice—as the second and third arguments to the `printf()` function. It's output first as an integer value and then as a character.

This ability to perform arithmetic with characters can be very useful. For instance, to convert from uppercase to lowercase, you can simply add the result of `'a'-'A'` (which is 32 for ASCII) to the uppercase character. To achieve the reverse, just subtract the value of `'a'-'A'`. You can see how this works if you have a look at the decimal ASCII values for the alphabetic characters in Appendix B of this book. Of course, this operation depends on the character codes for a–z and A–Z being a contiguous sequence of integers. If this is not the case for the character coding used by your computer, this won't work.

▓ **Note**   The standard library `ctype.h` header provides the `toupper()` and `tolower()` functions for converting a character to uppercase or lowercase.

Enumerations

Situations arise quite frequently in programming when you want a variable that will store a value from a very limited set of possible values. One example is a variable that stores a value representing the current month in the year. You really would only want such a variable to be able to assume one of 12 possible values, corresponding to January–December. The *enumeration* in C is intended specifically for such purposes.

With an enumeration, you define a new integer type where variables of the type have a fixed range of possible values that you specify. Here's an example of a statement that defines an enumeration type with the name Weekday:

```
enum Weekday {Monday, Tuesday, Wednesday, Thursday, Friday, Saturday, Sunday};
```

This statement defines a type—not a variable. The name of the new type, Weekday in this instance, follows the enum keyword, and this type name is referred to as the *tag* of the enumeration. Variables of type Weekday can have any of the values specified by the names that appear between the braces that follow the type name. These names are called *enumerators* or *enumeration constants*, and there can be as many of these as you want. Each enumerator is identified by the unique name you assign, and the compiler will assign a value of type int to each name. An enumeration is an integer type, and the enumerators that you specify will correspond to integer values. By default, the enumerators will start from zero, with each successive enumerator having a value of one more than the previous one. Thus, in this example, the values Monday–Sunday will have values 0-6.

You could declare a variable of type Weekday and initialize it like this:

```
enum Weekday today = Wednesday;
```

This declares a variable with the name today, and it initializes it to the value Wednesday. Because the enumerators have default values, Wednesday will correspond to the value 2. The actual integer type that is used for a variable of an enumeration type is implementation defined, and the choice of type may depend on how many enumerators there are.

It is also possible to declare variables of the enumeration type when you define the type. Here's a statement that defines an enumeration type plus two variables:

```
enum Weekday {Monday, Tuesday, Wednesday, Thursday,
                    Friday, Saturday, Sunday} today, tomorrow;
```

This declares the enumeration type Weekday and two variables of that type, today and tomorrow. Naturally you could also initialize the variable in the same statement, so you could write this:

```
enum Weekday {Monday, Tuesday, Wednesday, Thursday,
                  Friday, Saturday, Sunday} today = Monday, tomorrow = Tuesday;
```

This initializes today and tomorrow to Monday and Tuesday, respectively.

Because variables of an enumeration type are of an integer type, they can be used in arithmetic expressions. You could write the previous statement like this:

```
enum Weekday {Monday, Tuesday, Wednesday, Thursday,
              Friday, Saturday, Sunday} today = Monday, tomorrow = today + 1;
```

Now the initial value for tomorrow is one more than that of today. However, when you do this kind of thing, it is up to you to ensure that the value that results from the arithmetic is a valid enumerator value.

■ **Note** Although you specify a fixed set of values for an enumeration type, there is no checking mechanism to ensure that only these values are used in your program. It is up to you to ensure that you use only valid values for a given enumeration type. You can do this by only using the names of enumeration constants to assign values to variables.

Choosing Enumerator Values

You can specify your own integer value for any or all of the enumerators explicitly. Although the names you use for enumerators must be unique, there is no requirement for the enumerator values themselves to be unique. Unless you have a specific reason for making some of the values the same, it is usually a good idea to ensure that they are unique. Here's how you could define the Weekday type so that the enumerator values start from 1:

```
enum Weekday {Monday = 1, Tuesday, Wednesday, Thursday, Friday, Saturday, Sunday};
```

Now the enumerators Monday–Sunday will correspond to values 1–7. The enumerators that follow an enumerator with an explicit value will be assigned successive integer values. This can cause enumerators to have duplicate values, as in the following example:

```
enum Weekday {Monday = 5, Tuesday = 4, Wednesday,
              Thursday = 10, Friday = 3, Saturday, Sunday};
```

Monday, Tuesday, Thursday, and Friday have explicit values specified. Wednesday will be set to Tuesday+1 so it will be 5, the same as Monday. Similarly, Saturday and Sunday will be set to 4 and 5, so they also have duplicate values. There's no reason why you can't do this, although unless you have a good reason for making some of the enumeration constants the same, it does tend to be confusing.

You can use an enumeration in any situation where you want a variable with a specific limited number of possible values. Here's another example of defining an enumeration:

```
enum Suit{clubs = 10, diamonds, hearts, spades};
enum Suit card_suit = diamonds;
```

The first statement defines the enumeration type Suit, so variables of this type can have one of the four values between the braces. The second statement defines a variable of type Suit and initializes it with the value diamonds, which will correspond to 11. You could also define an enumeration to identify card face values like this:

```
enum FaceValue { two=2, three, four, five, six, seven,
                 eight, nine, ten, jack, queen, king, ace};
```

In this enumeration, the enumerators will have integer values that match the card values with ace as high.

When you output the value of a variable of an enumeration type, you'll just get the numeric value. If you want to output the enumerator name, you have to provide the program logic to do this. You'll be able to do this with what you learn in the next chapter.

Unnamed Enumeration Types

You can create variables of an enumeration type without specifying a tag, so there's no enumeration type name, for example:

```
enum {red, orange, yellow, green, blue, indigo, violet} shirt_color;
```

There's no tag here, so this statement defines an unnamed enumeration type with the possible enumerators from red to violet. The statement also declares one variable of the unnamed type with the name shirt_color.

You can assign a value to shirt_color in the normal way:shirt_color = blue;

Obviously, the major limitation on unnamed enumeration types is that you must declare all the variables of the type in the statement that defines the type. Because you don't have a type name, there's no way to define additional variables of this type later in the code.

Variables That Store Boolean Values

The type _Bool stores Boolean values. A *Boolean value* typically arises from a comparison where the result may be true or false; you'll learn about comparisons and using the results to make decisions in your programs in Chapter 3. The value of a variable of type _Bool can be either 0 or 1, corresponding to the Boolean values false and true, respectively, and because the values 0 and 1 are integers, type _Bool is regarded as an integer type. You declare a _Bool variable just like any other, for example:

```
_Bool valid = 1;                        // Boolean variable initialized to true
```

_Bool is not an ideal type name. The name bool would be less clumsy looking and more readable. The Boolean type was introduced into the C language in C99 version, so the type name was chosen to minimize the possibility of conflicts with existing code. If bool had been chosen as the type name, any program that used the name bool for some purpose most probably would not compile with a compiler that supported bool as a built-in type.

Having said that, you *can* use bool as the type name. You just need to add an #include directive for the standard header file stdbool.h to your source file. As well as defining bool to be the equivalent of _Bool, the header file also defines the symbols true and false to correspond to 1 and 0, respectively. Thus, if you include the header in your source file, you can rewrite the previous declaration as the following:

```
bool valid = true;                      // Boolean variable initialized to true
```

This looks much clearer than the previous version, so it's best to include the stdbool.h header unless you have a good reason not to. I'll use bool for the Boolean type throughout the rest of the book, but keep in mind that you need the appropriate header to be included and that the fundamental type name is _Bool.

You can cast between Boolean values and other numeric types. A nonzero numeric value will result in 1 (true) when cast to type bool, and 0 will cast to 0 (false). If you use a bool variable in an arithmetic expression, the compiler will insert an implicit conversion where necessary. Type bool has a rank lower than any of the other types, so in an operation involving type bool and a value of another type, it is the bool value that will be converted to the other type. I won't elaborate further on working with Boolean variables at this point. You'll learn more about using them in the next chapter.

The op= Form of Assignment

C is a very concise language, and it provides you with abbreviated ways of specifying some operations. Consider the following statement:

```
number = number + 10;
```

This sort of assignment, in which you're incrementing or decrementing a variable, occurs very often, so there's a shorthand version:

```
number += 10;
```

The += operator after the variable name is one example of a family of op= operators. This statement has exactly the same effect as the previous one, and it saves a bit of typing. The op in op= can be any of these arithmetic operators:

```
+  -  *  /  %
```

If you suppose number has the value 10, you can write the following statements:

```
number *= 3;      // number will be set to number*3 which is 30
number /= 3;      // number will be set to number/3 which is 3
number %= 3;      // number will be set to number%3 which is 1
```

The op in op= can also be a few other operators that you haven't encountered yet:

```
<<  >>  &  ^  |
```

I'll defer discussion of these until Chapter 3.

The op= set of operators always works the same way. Here is the general form of statements using op=:

```
lhs op= rhs;
```

where rhs represents any expression on the right-hand side of the op= operator. The effect is the same as the following statement form:

```
lhs = lhs op (rhs);
```

Note the parentheses around the rhs expression. This means that the right operand of op is the value that results from evaluating the entire rhs expression, whatever it is. Just to reinforce your understanding of this, I'll show you a few more examples. First, consider this statement:
```
variable *= 12;
```

```
This is the same asvariable = variable * 12;
```

You now have two different ways of incrementing an integer variable by 1. Both of the following statements increment count by 1:

```
count = count + 1;
count += 1;
```

You'll learn about yet another way to do this in the next chapter. This amazing level of choices tends to make it virtually impossible for indecisive individuals to write programs in C.

Because the op in op= applies to the result of evaluating the rhs expression, the statement

```
a /= b + 1;
```

is the same as

```
a = a/(b + 1);
```

Your computational facilities have been somewhat constrained so far. You've been able to use only a basic set of arithmetic operators. You can put more power in your calculating elbow using a few more standard library facilities. Before I come to the final example in this chapter, I'll introduce some of the mathematical functions that the standard library offers.

Mathematical Functions

The math.h header file includes declarations for a wide range of mathematical functions. To give you a feel for what's available, I'll describe those that are used most frequently. All the functions return a value of type double.

You have the set of functions shown in Table 2-11 available for numerical calculations of various kinds. These all require arguments to be of type double.

Table 2-11. *Functions for Numerical Calculations*

Function	Operation
floor(x)	Returns the largest integer that isn't greater than x as type double
ceil(x)	Returns the smallest integer that isn't less than x as type double
fabs(x)	Returns the absolute value of x
log(x)	Returns the natural logarithm (base e) of x
log10(x)	Returns the logarithm to base 10 of x
exp(x)	Returns the base e exponential of x
sqrt(x)	Returns the square root of x
pow(x, y)	Returns the value x^y

There are also versions of these for types float and long double that have f or l, respectively, appended to the function name, so ceilf() applies to float values and sqrtl() applies to long double values, for example. Here are some examples demonstrating use of the functions presented in Table 2-11:

```
double x = 2.25;
double less = 0.0;
double more = 0.0;
double root = 0.0;
less = floor(x);                    // Result is 2.0
more = ceil(x);                     // Result is 3.0
root = sqrt(x);                     // Result is 1.5
```

You also have a range of trigonometric functions available, and some of them are shown in Table 2-12. Those for type `float` and type `long double` have f or l, respectively, appended to the name. Arguments and values returned are of type `float`, type `double`, or type `long double`; and angles are expressed in radians.

Table 2-12. *Functions for Trigonometry*

Function	Operation
`sin(x)`	Sine of x expressed in radians
`cos(x)`	Cosine of x
`tan(x)`	Tangent of x

If you're into trigonometry, the use of these functions will be fairly self-evident. Here are some examples:

```
double angle = 45.0;                    // Angle in degrees
double pi = 3.14159265;
double sine = 0.0;
double cosine = 0.0;
sine = sin(pi*angle/180.0);             // Angle converted to radians
cosine = cos(pi*angle/180.0);           // Angle converted to radians
```

Because 180 degrees is the same angle as π radians, dividing an angle measured in degrees by 180 and multiplying by the value of π will produce the angle in radians, as required by these functions.

You also have the inverse trigonometric functions available, `asin()`, `acos()`, and `atan()`, as well as the hyperbolic functions `sinh()`, `cosh()`, and `tanh()`. Don't forget, you must include `math.h` into your program if you wish to use any of these functions. If this stuff is not your bag, you can safely ignore this section. Remember to use the flag –lm to the frontend compiler-linker on Linux because most of them will not find the math.h library and it must be declared explicitly in the command line.

Designing a Program

Now it's time for the end-of-chapter real-life example. This will enable you to try out some of the numeric types. I'll take you through the basic elements of the process of writing a program from scratch. This involves receiving an initial specification of the problem, analyzing it, preparing a solution, writing the program, and, of course, running and testing the program to make sure it works. Each step in the process can introduce problems, beyond just the theory.

The Problem

The height of a tree is of great interest to many people. For one thing, if a tree is being cut down, knowing its height tells you how far away *safe* is. This is very important to those with a nervous disposition. Your problem is to find out the height of a tree without using a very long ladder, which itself would introduce risk to life and limb. To find the height of a tree, you're allowed the help of a friend—preferably a short friend unless you yourself are short, in which case you need a tall friend. You should assume that the tree you're measuring is taller than both you and your friend. Trees that are shorter than you present little risk, unless they're of the spiky kind.

The Analysis

Real-world problems are rarely expressed in terms that are directly suitable for programming. Before you consider writing a line of code, you need to be sure you have a complete understanding of the problem and how it's going to be solved. Only then can you estimate how much time and effort will be involved in creating the solution.

The analysis phase involves gaining a full understanding of the problem and determining the logical process for solving it. Typically this requires a significant amount of work. It involves teasing out any detail in the specification of the problem that is vague or missing. Only when you fully understand the problem can you begin to express the solution in a form that's suitable for programming.

You're going to determine the height of a tree using some simple geometry and the heights of two people: you and one other. Let's start by naming the tall person (you) Lofty and the shorter person (your friend) Shorty. If you're vertically challenged, the roles can be reversed. For more accurate results, the tall person should be significantly taller than the short person. If they are not, the tall person could consider standing on a box. The diagram in Figure 2-3 will give you an idea of what you're trying to do in this program.

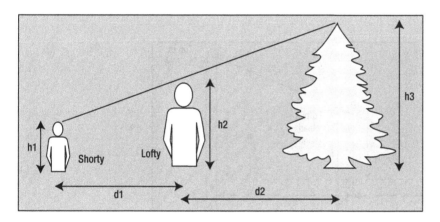

Figure 2-3. *The height of a tree*

Finding the height of the tree is actually quite simple. You can get the height of the tree, h_3, if you know the other dimensions shown in the illustration: h_1 and h_2, which are the heights of Shorty and Lofty, and d_1 and d_2, which are the distances between Shorty and Lofty and Lofty and the tree, respectively. You can use the technique of similar triangles to work out the height of the tree. You can see this in the simplified diagram in Figure 2-4.

Here, because the triangles are similar, `height1` divided by `distance1` is equal to `height2` divided by `distance2`. Using this relationship, you can get the height of the tree from the height of Shorty and Lofty and the distances to the tree, as shown in Figure 2-5.

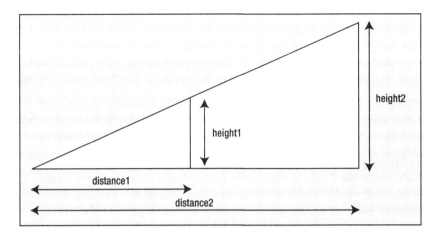

Figure 2-4. *Similar triangles*

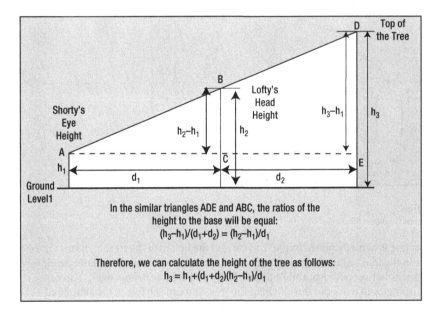

Figure 2-5. *Calculating the tree height*

The triangles ADE and ABC are the same as those shown in Figure 2-4. The triangles are *similar*, which just means that if you divide the length of any side of one triangle by the length of the corresponding side of the other, you'll always get the same result. You can use this to calculate the height of the tree, as shown in the equation at the bottom of Figure 2-5.

Thus you can calculate the height of the tree in your program from four values:

- The distance between Shorty and Lofty, d_1 in the diagram. You'll use the variable `shorty_to_lofty` to store this value.

- The distance between Lofty and the tree, d_2 in the diagram. You'll use the variable `lofty_to_tree` to store this value.

- The height of Lofty from the ground to the top of his head, h_2 in the diagram. You'll use the variable lofty to store this value.

- The height of Shorty's eyes from the ground, h_1 in the diagram. You'll use the variable shorty to store this value.

You can plug these values into the equation for the height of the tree.

Your first task in your program is to read these four values from the keyboard. You can then use your ratios to find out the height of the tree and finally output the answer. The steps are as follows:

1. Read in the values you need.

2. Calculate the height of the tree using the equation in Figure 2-5.

3. Display the answer.

The Solution

This section outlines the programming steps you'll take to solve the problem.

Step 1

Your first step is to get the values you need. This means you have to include the stdio.h header file, because you will need to use both printf() and scanf(). First, you must define the variables that will store the input values. Then you can use printf() to prompt for the input and scanf() to read the values from the keyboard.

You'll provide for the heights of the participants to be entered in feet and inches for the convenience of the user. Inside the program, it will be easier to work with all heights and distances in the same units, so you'll convert all measurements to inches. You'll need two variables to store the heights of Shorty and Lofty in inches. You'll also need variables to store the distance between Lofty and Shorty and the distance from Lofty to the tree—both distances in inches.

In the input process, you'll first read Lofty's height as a number of whole feet and then the number of inches as a second value, prompting for each value as you go along. You can use two more variables for this: one to store the feet value and the other to store the inches value. You'll then convert these into just inches and store the result in the variable you've reserved for Lofty's height. You'll do the same thing for Shorty's height (which is only up to the height of their eyes), and finally you'll read in the value for the distance between them. For the distance to the tree, you'll use only whole feet, because this will be accurate enough— and you'll convert the distance to inches for calculation purposes. You can reuse the same variables for each measurement in feet and inches that is entered. So here goes with the first part of the program:

```
// Program 2.17  Calculating the height of a tree
#define _CRT_SECURE_NO_WARNINGS
#include <stdio.h>

int main(void)
{
  long shorty = 0L;                           // Shorty's height in inches
  long lofty = 0L;                            // Lofty's height in inches
  long feet = 0L;
  long inches = 0L;
  long shorty_to_lofty = 0L;                  // Distance from Shorty to Lofty in inches
  long lofty_to_tree = 0L;                    // Distance from Lofty to the tree in inches
  const long inches_per_foot = 12L;
```

```
  // Get Lofty's height
  printf("Enter Lofty's height to the top of his/her head, in whole feet: ");
  scanf("%ld", &feet);
  printf("                    ...and then inches: ");
  scanf("%ld", &inches);
  lofty = feet*inches_per_foot + inches;

  // Get Shorty's height up to his/her eyes
  printf("Enter Shorty's height up to his/her eyes, in whole feet: ");
  scanf("%ld", &feet);
  printf("                        ... and then inches: ");
  scanf("%ld", &inches);
  shorty = feet*inches_per_foot + inches;

  // Get the distance from Shorty to Lofty
  printf("Enter the distance between Shorty and Lofty, in whole feet: ");
  scanf("%ld", &feet);
  printf("                        ... and then inches: ");
  scanf("%ld", &inches);
  shorty_to_lofty = feet*inches_per_foot + inches;

  // Get the distance from Lofty to the tree
  printf("Finally enter the distance from Lofty to the tree to the nearest foot: ");
   scanf("%ld", &feet);
  lofty_to_tree = feet*inches_per_foot;

  // The code to calculate the height of the tree will go here

  // The code to display the result will go here
  return 0;
}
```

Notice how the program code is spaced out to make it easier to read. You don't have to do this, but if you want to change the program next year, it will make it much easier to see how the program works if it's well laid out. You should always add comments to your programs to help with this. It's particularly important to at least make clear what the variables are used for and to document the basic logic of the program.

You use a variable that you've declared as const to convert from feet to inches. The variable name, inches_per_foot, makes it reasonably obvious what's happening when it's used in the code. This is much better than using the "magic number" 12. Here you're dealing with feet and inches, and people in the United States or the United Kingdom will be aware that there are 12 inches in a foot. In other countries that use the metric system and in other circumstances, the significance of numeric constants may not be so obvious. If you're using the value 0.22 in a program calculating salaries, it's not obvious what this represents. Consequently, the calculation may seem rather obscure. If you use a const variable tax_rate that is initialized to 0.22, then the mist clears. The variables are strongly recommended to be meaningful. There are real-life examples where the physics unit was assumed to be one, but, nevertheless, was implemented a totally different force unit. This happened to Mars Climate Orbiter by confusing pound-force seconds (lbf*s) instead of the SI units of newton-seconds (N*s).

Step 2

Now that you have all the required data, you can calculate the height of the tree. You just need to express the equation for the tree height in terms of your variables. You'll need to declare another variable to store the height of the tree. You can add the code that's shown here in bold type to do this:

```c
// Program 2.18  Calculating the height of a tree
#define _CRT_SECURE_NO_WARNINGS
#include <stdio.h>

int main(void)
{
  long shorty = 0L;                         // Shorty's height in inches
  long lofty = 0L;                          // Lofty's height in inches
  long feet = 0L;
  long inches = 0L;
  long shorty_to_lofty = 0L;                // Distance from Shorty to Lofty in inches
  long lofty_to_tree = 0L;                  // Distance from Lofty to the tree in inches
  long tree_height = 0L;                    // Height of the tree in inches
  const long inches_per_foot = 12L;

  // Get Lofty's height
  printf("Enter Lofty's height to the top of his/her head, in whole feet: ");
  scanf("%ld", &feet);
  printf("                                      ...and then inches: ");
  scanf("%ld", &inches);
  lofty = feet*inches_per_foot + inches;

  // Get Shorty's height up to his/her eyes
  printf("Enter Shorty's height up to his/her eyes, in whole feet: ");
  scanf("%ld", &feet);
  printf("                                ... and then inches: ");
  scanf("%ld", &inches);
  shorty = feet*inches_per_foot + inches;

  // Get the distance from Shorty to Lofty
  printf("Enter the distance between Shorty and Lofty, in whole feet: ");
  scanf("%ld", &feet);
  printf("                                ... and then inches: ");
  scanf("%ld", &inches);
  shorty_to_lofty = feet*inches_per_foot + inches;

  // Get the distance from Lofty to the tree
  printf("Finally enter the distance from Lofty to the tree to the nearest foot: ");
  scanf("%ld", &feet);
  lofty_to_tree = feet*inches_per_foot;

  // Calculate the height of the tree in inches
  tree_height = shorty + (shorty_to_lofty + lofty_to_tree)*(lofty-shorty)/
                                              shorty_to_lofty;
```

```
  // The code to display the result will go here
  return 0;
}
```

The statement to calculate the height is essentially the same as the equation in the diagram. It's a bit messy, but it translates directly to the statement in the program to calculate the height.

Step 3

Finally, you need to output the height of the tree. To present the results in the most easily understandable form, you can convert the results that you've stored in tree_height—which are in inches—back into feet and inches:

```
// Program 2.18  Calculating the height of a tree
#include <stdio.h>

int main(void)
{
  long shorty = 0L;                      // Shorty's height in inches
  long lofty = 0L;                       // Lofty's height in inches
  long feet = 0L;
  long inches = 0L;
  long shorty_to_lofty = 0L;             // Distance from Shorty to Lofty in inches
  long lofty_to_tree = 0L;               // Distance from Lofty to the tree in inches
  long tree_height = 0L;                 // Height of the tree in inches
  const long inches_per_foot = 12L;

  // Get Lofty's height
  printf("Enter Lofty's height to the top of his/her head, in whole feet: ");
  scanf("%ld", &feet);
  printf("                                    ... and then inches: ");
  scanf("%ld", &inches);
  lofty = feet*inches_per_foot + inches;

  // Get Shorty's height up to his/her eyes
  printf("Enter Shorty's height up to his/her eyes, in whole feet: ");
  scanf("%ld", &feet);
  printf("                                ... and then inches: ");
  scanf("%ld", &inches);
  shorty = feet*inches_per_foot + inches;

  // Get the distance from Shorty to Lofty
  printf("Enter the distance between Shorty and Lofty, in whole feet: ");
  scanf("%ld", &feet);
  printf("                                 ... and then inches: ");
  scanf("%ld", &inches);
  shorty_to_lofty = feet*inches_per_foot + inches;

  // Get the distance from Lofty to the tree
  printf("Finally enter the distance from Lofty to the tree to the nearest foot: ");
  scanf("%ld", &feet);
  lofty_to_tree = feet*inches_per_foot;
```

```
// Calculate the height of the tree in inches
tree_height = shorty + (shorty_to_lofty + lofty_to_tree)*(lofty-shorty)/
                                                          shorty_to_lofty;

// Display the result in feet and inches
printf("The height of the tree is %ld feet and %ld inches.\n",
                  tree_height/inches_per_foot, tree_height% inches_per_foot);
return 0;
}
```

And there you have it. The output from the program looks something like this:

```
Enter Lofty's height to the top of his/her head, in whole feet first: 6
                             ... and then inches: 2
Enter Shorty's height up to his/her eyes, in whole feet: 4
                    ... and then inches: 6
Enter the distance between Shorty and Lofty, in whole feet : 5
                         ... and then inches: 0
Finally enter the distance to the tree to the nearest foot: 20
The height of the tree is 12 feet and 10 inches.
```

Summary

This chapter covered quite a lot of ground. By now, you know how a C program is structured, and you should be fairly comfortable with any kind of arithmetic calculation. You should also be able to choose variable types to suit the job at hand. Aside from arithmetic, you've added some input and output capability to your knowledge. You should now feel at ease with inputting values into variables via scanf(). You can output text and the values of character and numeric variables to the screen. You won't remember it all the first time around, but you can always look back over this chapter if you need to. Not bad for the first two chapters, is it?

In the next chapter, you'll start looking at how you can control the program by making decisions depending on the values you enter. As you can probably imagine, this is key to creating interesting and professional programs.

Table 2-13 summarizes the variable types you've used so far. You can look back at these when you need a reminder as you continue through the book.

Table 2-13. *Variable Types and Typical Value Ranges*

Type	Typical number of bytes	Typical range of values
char	1	–128 to +127 or 0 to +255
unsigned char	1	0 to +255
short	2	–32,768 to +32,767
unsigned short	2	0 to +65,535
int	2 or 4	–32,768 to +32,767 or –2,147,438,648 to +2,147,438,647
unsigned int	4	0 to +65,535 or 0 to +4,294,967,295

(continued)

Table 2-13. (*continued*)

Type	Typical number of bytes	Typical range of values
long	4	–2,147,438,648 to +2,147,438,647
unsigned long	4	0 to +4,294,967,295
long long	8	–9,223,372,036,854,775,808 to +9,223,372,036,854,775,807
unsigned long long	8	0 to +18,446,744,073,709,551,615
float	4	±3.4E±38 (6 digits)
double	8	±1.7E±308 (15 digits)
long double	12	±1.2E±4932 (19 digits)

You have seen and used some of the data output format specifications with the printf() function in this chapter, and you'll find the complete set described in Appendix D, which also describes the input format specifiers you use to control how data are interpreted when they are read from the keyboard by the scanf() function. Whenever you are unsure about how you deal with a particular kind of data for input or output, just look in Appendix D.

EXERCISES

The following exercises enable you to try out what you've learned in this chapter. If you get stuck, look back over the chapter for help. If you're still stuck, you can download the solutions from the Source Code/Download section of the Apress website (www.apress.com), but that really should be a last resort.

Exercise 2-1. Write a program that prompts the user to enter a distance in inches and then outputs that distance in yards, feet, and inches. (For those unfamiliar with imperial units, there are 12 inches in a foot and 3 feet in a yard.)

Exercise 2-2. Write a program that prompts for input of the length and width of a room in feet and inches and then calculates and outputs the floor area in square yards with two decimal places after the decimal point.

Exercise 2-3. You're selling a product that's available in two versions: type 1 is a standard version priced at $3.50, and type 2 is a deluxe version priced at $5.50. Write a program using only what you've learned up to now that prompts for the user to enter the product type and a quantity and then calculates and outputs the price for the quantity entered.

Exercise 2-4. Write a program that prompts for the user's weekly pay in dollars and the hours worked to be entered through the keyboard as floating-point values. The program should then calculate and output the average pay per hour in the following form:

```
Your average hourly pay rate is 7 dollars and 54 cents.
```

CHAPTER 3

■ ■ ■

Making Decisions

In this chapter, you'll greatly extend the range of programs you can write and the flexibility you can build into them by adding one of the most powerful programming tools to your inventory: the ability to compare the values of expressions and, based on the outcome, choose to execute one set of statements or another. This means that you will be able to control the sequence in which statements are executed.

In this chapter, you'll learn

- How to make decisions based on arithmetic comparisons

- What logical operators are and how you can use them

- More about reading data from the keyboard

- How you can write a program that can be used as a calculator

The Decision-Making Process

Decision making in a program is focused on choosing to execute one set of program statements rather than another based on the data. Fundamentally, this is no different from decisions in everyday life. Unless you are independently wealthy, every morning you must decide whether it's a good idea to go to work. You may go through these questions:

> Do I feel well? If the answer is no, stay in bed. If the answer is yes, go to work.

You could rewrite this as

> If I feel well, I will go to work. Otherwise, I will stay in bed.

That was a straightforward decision. Later, while you're having breakfast, you may notice it's raining, so you think this:

> If it is raining as hard as it did yesterday, I will take the bus. If it is raining harder
> than yesterday, I will drive to work. Otherwise, I will risk it and walk.

This is a more complex decision process. It's a decision based on several levels in the amount of rain falling, and it can have any of three different results. All of these decisions involve comparisons. Let's start by exploring how you compare numeric values in C.

© German Gonzalez-Morris and Ivor Horton 2020
G. Gonzalez-Morris and I. Horton, *Beginning C*, https://doi.org/10.1007/978-1-4842-5976-4_3

Arithmetic Comparisons

Comparing things in C involves some new operators. You have six *relational operators* that you use to compare two values, as shown in Table 3-1.

Table 3-1. *Relational Operators*

Operator	Comparison
<	Is the left operand *less than* the right operand
<=	Is the left operand *less than or equal* to the right operand
==	Is the left operand *equal to* the right operand
!=	Is the left operand *not equal to* the right operand
>	Is the left operand *greater than* the right operand
>=	Is the left operand *greater than or equal to* the right operand

Each of these operations results in a value of type int. The result of each operation is 1 if the comparison is true and 0 if the comparison is false. You'll recall from the previous chapter that the stdbool.h header defines the symbols true and false for these values. Thus, 2 != 3 results in true, as do 5L > 3L and 6 <= 12. The expressions 2 == 3, 5 < 4, and 1.2 >= 1.3 all result in the value 0, which is false.

These expressions are called *logical expressions* or *Boolean expressions* because they result in just one of two values: either true or false. Because a relational operator produces a Boolean result, you can store the result in a variable of type bool, for example:

```
bool result = 5 < 4;                    // result will be false
```

Keep in mind that any nonzero numerical value will result in true when it is converted to type bool. This implies that you can assign the result of an arithmetic expression to a bool variable and store true if it is nonzero and false otherwise.

▓ **Note** The equal to operator has *two* successive equal signs (==). You'll almost certainly use one equal sign on occasion by mistake.

This will cause considerable confusion until you spot the problem. If you type my_weight = your_weight, it's an assignment operation that stores the value of your_weight in the variable my_weight.

If you type the expression my_weight == your_weight, you're comparing the two values: you're asking whether they're exactly the same—you're not making them the same. If you use = where you intended to use ==, the compiler will often be unable to determine that it is an error because either can be valid.

The Basic if Statement

Now that you have the relational operators for making comparisons, you need a statement allowing you to make a decision. The simplest is the if statement. If you want to compare your weight with that of someone else and print a different sentence depending on the result, you could write the body of a program as follows:

```
int my_weight = 169;                    // Weight in lbs
int your_weight = 175;                  // Weight in lbs
if(your_weight > my_weight)
  printf("You are heavier than me.\n");

if(your_weight < my_weight)
  printf("I am heavier than you.\n");

if(your_weight == my_weight)
  printf("We are exactly the same weight.\n");
```

There are three if statements here. The expression for the comparison in each case appears between the parentheses that immediately follow the keyword if. If the result of a comparison is true, the statement immediately after the if will be executed; if it is false, the statement will be skipped. Note how the statement following each if is indented. This is to show that it's dependent on the result of the if test.

Let's go through the code and see how it works. The first if tests whether the value in your_weight is greater than the value in my_weight. This will output the message

```
You are heavier than me.
```

This is because your_weight is greater than my_weight. When the expression between the parentheses evaluates to true, the statement that follows will be executed.

Execution will then continue with the next if statement. In this case, the expression between the parentheses is false. The statement immediately following the if will be skipped, so the message won't be displayed. It will be displayed only if your_weight is less than my_weight. The statement following the third if will also be skipped because our weights are not the same. The overall effect of these statements is to print one message that will depend on whether your_weight is greater than, less than, or equal to my_weight. Only one message will be displayed because only one of these can be true.

The general form or syntax of the if statement is

```
if(expression)
  Statement1;

Next_statement;
```

Notice that there is no semicolon at the end of the first line. This is because the line with the if keyword and the following line are tied together and form a single statement. The second line could be written directly following the first, like this:

```
if(expression) Statement1;
```

However, for the sake of clarity, in most instances, people usually put Statement1 on a new line.

The expression in parentheses can be any expression that results in a value of true or false. If the expression is true, Statement1 is executed, after which the program continues with Next_statement. If the expression is false, Statement1 is skipped, and execution continues immediately with Next_statement. This is illustrated in Figure 3-1.

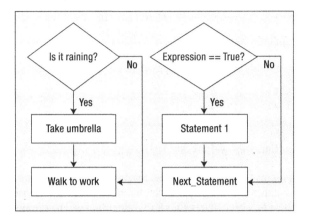

Figure 3-1. *The operation of the if statement*

Don't forget what I said earlier about what happens when a numerical value is converted to type bool. Because the control expression for an if statement is expected to produce a Boolean result, the compiler will arrange to convert the result of an if expression that produces a numerical result to type bool. You'll sometimes see this used in programs to test for a nonzero result of a calculation. Here's a statement that illustrates this:

```
if(count)
  printf("The value of count is not zero.\n");
```

This will only produce output if count is not 0, because a 0 value for count will result in false for the value of the if expression. Any nonzero value for count will result in true for the expression.

TRY IT OUT: CHECKING CONDITIONS

In this program, the user enters a number between 1 and 10, and the output tells the user how that number relates to 5 or 6:

```
// Program 3.1 A simple example of the if statement
#define _CRT_SECURE_NO_WARNINGS
#include <stdio.h>

int main(void)
{
  int number = 0;
  printf("\nEnter an integer between 1 and 10: ");
  scanf("%d",&number);

  if(number > 5)
    printf("You entered %d which is greater than 5\n", number);

  if(number < 6)
    printf("You entered %d which is less than 6\n", number);
  return 0;
}
```

Sample output from this program is as follows:

```
Enter an integer between 1 and 10: 7
You entered 7 which is greater than 5
```

or

```
Enter an integer between 1 and 10: 3
You entered 3 which is less than 6
```

How It Works

As usual, you include a comment at the beginning as a reminder of what the program does. You include the stdio.h header file to allow you to use the printf() and scanf() functions. You then have the beginning of the main() function of the program. This function returns an integer value, as indicated by the keyword int:

```
// Program 3.1 A simple example of the if statement
#include <stdio.h>

int main(void)
{
```

In the first three statements in the body of main(), you read an integer from the keyboard after prompting the user for the data:

```
    int number = 0;
    printf("\nEnter an integer between 1 and 10: ");
    scanf("%d",&number);
```

You declare an integer variable called number that you initialize to o, and then you prompt the user to enter a number between 1 and 10. This value is then read using the scanf() function and stored in number.

The next statement is an if that tests the value that was entered:

```
    if(number > 5)
      printf("You entered %d which is greater than 5\n", number);
```

You compare the value in number with the value 5. If number is greater than 5, you execute the next statement, which displays a message, and you go to the next part of the program. If number isn't greater than 5, the printf() is skipped. You've used the %d conversion specifier for integer values to output the number the user typed in.

You then have another if statement comparing number with 6:

```
    if(number < 6)
      printf("You entered %d which is less than 6\n", number);
```

If number is less than 6, you execute the next statement to display a message. Otherwise, the printf() is skipped and the program ends. Only one of the two possible messages will be displayed because the number will always be less than 6 or greater than 5.

The if statement enables you to be selective about what input you accept and what you finally do with it. For instance, if you have a variable and you want to have its value specifically limited at some point, even though higher values may arise somehow in the program, you could write this:

```
if(x > 90)
  x = 90;
```

This would ensure that if anyone entered a value of x that was larger than 90, your program would automatically change it to 90. This would be invaluable if you had a program that could only specifically deal with values within a range. You could also check whether a value was lower than a given number and, if not, set it to that number. In this way, you could ensure that the value was within the given range. Naturally, it would be a good idea to output a message when your program does this kind of thing.

Finally, you have the return statement that ends the program and returns control to the operating system:

```
return 0;
```

Extending the if statement: if-else

You can extend the if statement with a small addition that gives you a lot more flexibility. Imagine it rained a little yesterday. You could write the following:

> If the rain today is worse than the rain yesterday,
>
> I will take my umbrella.
>
> Else
>
> I will take my jacket.
>
> Then I will go to work.

This is exactly the kind of decision making the if-else statement provides. The syntax of the if-else statement is as follows:

```
if(expression)
  Statement1;
else
  Statement2;

Next_statement;
```

Here, you have an either-or situation. You'll always execute either Statement1 or Statement2 depending on whether expression results in the value true or false:

> If expression evaluates to true, Statement1 is executed, and the program continues with Next_statement.

> If expression evaluates to false, Statement2 that follows the else keyword is executed, and the program continues with Next_statement.

The sequence of operations involved here is shown in Figure 3-2.

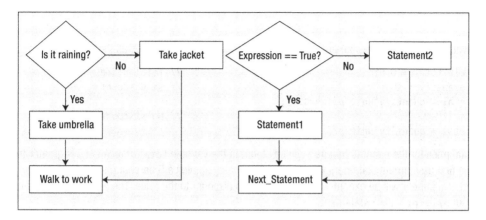

Figure 3-2. *The operation of the if-else statement*

TRY IT OUT: USING IF TO ANALYZE NUMBERS

Let's suppose that you're selling a product at a single-unit price of $3.50, and for order quantities greater than ten, you offer a 5 percent discount. You can use the if-else statement to calculate and output the price for a given quantity:

```
// Program 3.2 Using if statements to decide on a discount
#define _CRT_SECURE_NO_WARNINGS
#include <stdio.h>

int main(void)
{
  const double unit_price = 3.50;                    // Unit price in dollars
  int quantity = 0;
  printf("Enter the number that you want to buy:");  // Prompt message
  scanf(" %d", &quantity);                           // Read the input

  // Test for order quantity qualifying for a discount
  double total = 0.0;                                // Total price
  if(quantity > 10)                                  // 5% discount
    total = quantity*unit_price*0.95;
  else                                               // No discount
    total = quantity*unit_price;
  printf("The price for %d is $%.2f\n", quantity, total);
  return 0;
}
```

Typical output from this program is as follows:

```
Enter the number that you want to buy:20
The price for 20 is $66.50
```

How It Works

Once your program has read the order quantity, the if-else statement does all the work:

```
double total = 0.0;                            // Total price
if(quantity > 10)                              // 5% discount
   total = quantity*unit_price*0.95;
else                                           // No discount
   total = quantity*unit_price;
```

The total price for the quantity required will be stored in the variable total. If quantity is greater than ten, the first assignment statement will be executed, which applies a 5 percent discount. Otherwise, the second assignment will be executed, which applies no discount to the price. The result of the calculation is output by the printf() statement:

```
printf("The price for %d is $%.2f\n", quantity, total);
```

The %d specifier applies to quantity because it is an integer of type int. The %.2f specifier applies to the floating-point variable, total, and outputs the value with two digits after the decimal point.

There are a couple of points about this program worth mentioning. First, you can solve the problem with a simple if statement by replacing the if-else and printf() statements with the following code:

```
double discount = 0.0;                         // Discount allowed
if(quantity > 10)
   discount = 0.05;                            // 5% discount
printf("\nThe price for %d is $%.2f\n", quantity,
                          quantity*unit_price*(1.0-discount));
```

This simplifies the code considerably. The expression in the printf() call applies the discount that is set, either 0 or 5 percent. With a variable storing the discount value, it's also clearer what is happening in the code.

The second point is that floating-point variables aren't ideal for calculations involving money because of the potential rounding that can occur. Provided that the amounts of money are not extremely large, one alternative is to use integer values and just store cents, for example:

```
const long unit_price = 350L;                  // Unit price in cents
int quantity = 0;
printf("Enter the number that you want to buy:");  // Prompt message
scanf(" %d", &quantity);                       // Read the input

long discount = 0L;                            // Discount allowed
if(quantity > 10)
   discount = 5L;                              // 5% discount
long total_price = quantity*unit_price*(100-discount)/100;
long dollars = total_price/100;
long cents = total_price%100;
printf("\nThe price for %d is $%ld.%ld\n", quantity, dollars, cents);
```

Of course you also have the possibility of storing the dollars and cents for each monetary value in separate integer variables. It gets a little more complicated because you then have to keep track of when the cents value reaches or exceeds 100 during arithmetic operations and update the dollars and cents values.

Using Blocks of Code in if Statements

You can replace either Statement1 or Statement2, or even both, in an if statement with a block of statements enclosed between braces {}. This means that you can supply several statements that are to be executed when the value of an if expression is true, simply by placing these statements together between braces. I can illustrate the mechanics of this by considering a real-life situation:

> If the weather is sunny:
>
> I will walk to the park, eat a picnic, and walk home.
>
> Else
>
> I will stay in, watch football, and drink beer.

The general form for an if statement that involves statement blocks would look like this:

```
if(expression)
{
  StatementA1;
  StatementA2;
   ...
}
else
{
  StatementB1;
  StatementB2;
   ...
}

Next_statement;
```

All the statements that are in the block between the braces following the if condition will be executed when expression evaluates to true. If expression evaluates to false, all the statements between the braces following the else will be executed. In either case, execution continues with Next_statement. Look at the indentation. The braces aren't indented, but the statements between the braces are. This makes it clear that all the statements between an opening and a closing brace belong together.

■ **Note** Although I've been talking about using a block of statements in place of a single statement in an if statement, this is just one example of a general rule. Wherever you can have a single statement, you can equally well have a block of statements between braces. This also means that you can nest one block of statements inside another.

Nested if Statements

It's also possible to have ifs within ifs. These are called *nested ifs,* for example:

> If the weather is good,
>
> I will go out in the yard.
>
> And if it's cool enough,

I will sit in the sun.

Else

I will sit in the shade.

Else

I will stay indoors.

I will then drink some lemonade.

In programming terms, this corresponds to the following:

```
if(expression1)                        // Weather is good?
{
  StatementA;                          // Yes - Go out in the yard
  if(expression2)                      // Cool enough?
    StatementB;                        // Yes - Sit in the sun
  else
    StatementC;                        // No - Sit in the shade
}
else
  StatementD;                          // Weather not good - stay in
Statement E;                           // Drink lemonade in any event
```

Here, the second if condition, expression2, is only checked if the first if condition, expression1, is true. The braces enclosing StatementA and the second if are necessary to make both of these statements a part of what is executed when expression1 is true. Note how the else is aligned with the if to which it belongs. The logic of this is illustrated in Figure 3-3.

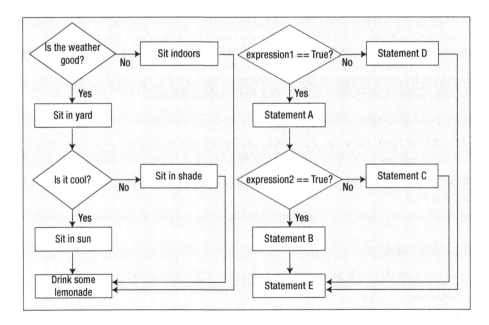

Figure 3-3. *Nested if statements*

TRY IT OUT: ANALYZING NUMBERS

You'll now exercise your if skills with a couple more examples. This program tests to see whether you enter an odd or an even number, and if the number is even, it then tests to see whether half that number is also even:

```
// Program 3.3 Using nested ifs to analyze numbers
#define _CRT_SECURE_NO_WARNINGS
#include <stdio.h>
#include <limits.h>                 // For LONG_MAX

int main(void)
{
  long test = 0L;                   // Stores the integer to be checked

  printf("Enter an integer less than %ld:", LONG_MAX);
  scanf(" %ld", &test);

  // Test for odd or even by checking the remainder after dividing by 2
  if(test % 2L == 0L)
  {
    printf("The number %ld is even", test);

    // Now check whether half the number is also even
    if((test/2L) % 2L == 0L)
    {
      printf("\nHalf of %ld is also even", test);
      printf("\nThat's interesting isn't it?\n");
    }
  }
  else
    printf("The number %ld is odd\n", test);
  return 0;
}
```

The output will look something like this:

```
Enter an integer less than 2147483647:20
  The number 20 is even
  Half of 20 is also even
That's interesting isn't it?
```

or this:

```
Enter an integer less than 2147483647:999
The number 999 is odd
```

How It Works

The prompt for input makes use of the LONG_MAX symbol that's defined by a macro in the limits.h header file. This specifies the maximum value of type long. You can see from the output that on my system the upper limit for long values is 2147483647 (in your system, you may get 9223372036854775807; this happens because they are 32 and 64 compiler values, respectively).

The first if condition tests for an even number:

```
if(test % 2L == 0L)
```

For any even number, the remainder after dividing by 2 will be 0. When the expression is true, the block that follows will be executed:

```
{
  printf("The number %ld is even", test);

  // Now check whether half the number is also even
  if((test/2L) % 2L == 0L)
  {
    printf("\nHalf of %ld is also even", test);
    printf("\nThat's interesting isn't it?\n");
  }
}
```

After outputting a message where the value is even, you have another if statement. This is called a nested if because it's inside the first if. The nested if condition divides the original value by 2 and tests whether the result is even, using the same mechanism as in the first if statement. There's an extra pair of parentheses in the nested if condition around the expression test/2L. These aren't strictly necessary, but they help to make what's going on clear. Making programs easier to follow is the essence of good programming style. If the result of the nested if condition is true, the two further printf() statements in the block following the nested if will be executed.

Try adding code to make the nested if an if-else that will output "Half of %ld is odd".

If the original input value isn't even, the statement following the else keyword will be executed:

```
else
  printf("The number %ld is odd\n", test);
```

■ **Note**   You can nest ifs anywhere inside another if, but I don't recommend this as a technique you should use extensively. If you do, your program is likely to end up being very hard to follow, and you are more likely to make mistakes.

To make the nested if statement output a message when the condition is false, you would need to insert the following after the closing brace:

```
else
  printf("\nHalf of %ld is odd", test);
```

Testing Characters

A char value may be expressed either as an integer or as a keyboard character between quotes, such as 'A'. Don't forget that values stored as type char may be signed or unsigned, depending on how your compiler implements the type. When type char is signed, values can be from –128 to +127. When char is an unsigned type, values can be from 0 to 255. Here are a few examples of comparing values of type char:

```
'Z' >= 'A'        'Q' <= 'P'       'B' <= 'b'       'B' != 66
```

The first expression is true, because 'Z' has the code value 90 and 'A' has the code value 65. The second is false, because the code for 'Q' is greater than the code for 'P'. The third expression is true. This is because the ASCII codes for lowercase letters are 32 higher than their uppercase equivalents. The last expression is false. The value 66 is indeed the decimal ASCII code for the character 'B'.

TRY IT OUT: CONVERTING UPPERCASE TO LOWERCASE

This example uses some of the new logical operators. The program will convert any uppercase letter that is entered to lowercase:

```c
// Program 3.4 Converting uppercase to lowercase
#define _CRT_SECURE_NO_WARNINGS
#include <stdio.h>

int main(void)
{
  char letter = 0;                      // Stores a character

  printf("Enter an uppercase letter:"); // Prompt for input
  scanf("%c", &letter);                 // Read a character

  // Check whether the input is uppercase
  if(letter >= 'A')                     // Is it A or greater?
    if(letter <= 'Z')                   // and is it Z or lower?
    {                                   // It is uppercase
      letter = letter - 'A' + 'a';      // Convert from upper- to lowercase
      printf("You entered an uppercase %c\n", letter);
    }
    else                                // It is not an uppercase letter
      printf("Try using the shift key! I want a capital letter.\n");
  return 0;
}
```

Sample output from this program might be the following:

```
Enter an uppercase letter:G
You entered an uppercase g
```

---

or

```
Enter an uppercase letter:s
Try using the shift key! I want a capital letter.
```

How It Works

In the first three statements, you declare a variable of type char called letter, you prompt the user to input an uppercase letter, and you store the character entered in letter:

```
char letter = 0;                         // Stores a character

printf("Enter an uppercase letter:");    // Prompt for input
scanf("%c", &letter);                    // Read a character
```

If a capital letter is entered, the character in letter must be between 'A' and 'Z', so the next if checks whether the character is greater than or equal to 'A':

```
if(letter >= 'A')                        // Is it A or greater?
```

If the expression is true, you continue with the nested if that tests whether letter is less than or equal to 'Z':

```
if(letter <= 'Z')                        // and is it Z or lower?
```

If this expression is true, you convert the character to lowercase and output a message by executing the block of statements following the if:

```
{                                        // It is uppercase
  letter = letter - 'A' + 'a';           // Convert from upper- to lowercase
  printf("You entered an uppercase %c\n", letter);
}
```

Also, another approach would be merge both if statements to only one by using && (AND) operator:

```
if((letter >= 'A') && (letter <= 'Z'))
```

To convert to lowercase, you subtract the character code for 'A' from letter and add the character code for 'a'. If letter contained 'A', subtracting 'A' would produce 0, and adding 'a' would result in 'a'. If letter contained 'B', subtracting 'A' would produce 1, and adding 'a' would result in the code for 'b'. You can see this conversion works for any uppercase letter. Note that although this works fine for ASCII, there are coding systems (such as Extended Binary Coded Decimal Interchange Code [EBCDIC]) in which this won't work because the character codes for letters are not in a contiguous sequence. Another trick to convert to lowercase is by using bitwise that will be discussed later in this chapter (anyway for the impatient, the snippet code is letter = (letter | ' ');). If you want to be sure that the conversion works for any code, you can use the standard library function tolower(). This converts the character passed as an argument to lowercase if it's an uppercase letter; otherwise, it returns the character code value unchanged. To use this function, you need to include the header file ctype.h in your source file. This header file also declares the complementary function, toupper(), which will convert lowercase letters to uppercase.

If the expression letter <= 'Z' is false, you go straight to the statement following else and display a different message:

```
else                                     // It is not an uppercase letter
  printf("Try using the shift key! I want a capital letter.\n");
```

There's something wrong, though. What if the character that was entered was less than 'A'? There's no else clause for the first if, so the program just ends without outputting anything. To deal with this, you must add another else clause at the end of the program. The complete nested if would then be

```
// Check whether the input is uppercase
if(letter >= 'A')                         // Is it A or greater?
  if(letter <= 'Z')                       // and is it Z or lower?
  {                                       // It is uppercase
    letter = letter - 'A' + 'a';          // Convert from upper- to lowercase
    printf("You entered an uppercase %c\n", letter);
  }
  else                                    // It is not an uppercase letter
    printf("Try using the shift key! I want a capital letter.\n");
else
  printf("You didn't enter a letter\n");
```

Now you always get a message. Note the indentation to show which else belongs to which if. The indentation doesn't determine what belongs to what. It just provides a visual cue. An else always belongs to the if that immediately precedes it that isn't already spoken for by another else. The original code for the if and the code here are poor in style. It would be much clearer with an extra pair of braces around the outer if condition:

```
if(letter >= 'A')                         // Is it A or greater?
{
  if(letter <= 'Z')                       // and is it Z or lower?
  {                                       // It is uppercase
    letter = letter - 'A' + 'a';          // Convert from upper- to lowercase
    printf("You entered an uppercase %c\n", letter);
  }
  else                                    // It is not an uppercase letter
    printf("Try using the shift key! I want a capital letter.\n");
}
else
  printf("You didn't enter a letter\n");
```

Now there is no doubt that the inner if-else executes when letter is not less than 'A' and that the last else belongs to the outer if.

However, there's still something wrong. Try running the example again and entering [. This time you get the message telling you to use the Shift key, which won't help at all. If you look in Appendix B, you'll see that the code for [is greater than the codes for both A and Z, but it isn't a letter at all. Within the inner else, we really need to check that the code for the character entered is not less than 'a' and also that it is not greater than 'z'. The code to do this looks like this:

```
if(letter >= 'A')                         // Is it A or greater?
{
  if(letter <= 'Z')                       // and is it Z or lower?
  {                                       // It is uppercase
    letter = letter - 'A' + 'a';          // Convert from upper- to lowercase
    printf("You entered an uppercase %c\n", letter);
  }
  else                                    // It is not an uppercase letter
  {
    if(letter >= 'a')
    {
```

```
      if(letter <= 'z')
        printf("Try using the shift key! I want a capital letter.\n");
    }
    else
      printf("You didn't enter a letter\n");
  }
}
else
  printf("You didn't enter a letter\n");
```

Now you only get the Shift key message when you enter a lowercase letter, and if you enter any character that is not a letter, you get the correct message. Who would have thought that sorting out capital letters could be so complicated? The version including the preceding code is in the code download as `Program3_04A.c`.

Logical Operators

Sometimes it just isn't enough to perform a single test for a decision. You may want to combine two or more checks on values and perform a certain action only when they're all `true`. This was the case in the previous example. You wanted to discover when a letter was not less than `'A'` and not greater than `'Z'`. Or you may want to perform a calculation if one or more of a set of conditions is `true`. Other combinations arise too. For example, you may only want to go to work if you're feeling well *and* it's a weekday. Just because you feel great doesn't mean you want to go in on a Saturday or a Sunday. Alternatively, you could say that you'll stay at home if you feel ill *or* if it's a weekend day. These are exactly the sorts of circumstances for which the logical operators are intended.

The AND Operator &&

The logical AND operator, &&, is a binary operator that combines two logical expressions—that is, two expressions that evaluate to `true` or `false`. Consider this expression:

```
test1 && test2
```

This expression evaluates to `true` if both expressions `test1` and `test2` evaluate to `true`. If either or both of the operands are `false`, the result of the operation is `false`.

The obvious place to use the && operator is in an `if` expression. Here's an example:

```
if(age > 12 && age < 20)
  printf("You are officially a teenager.");
```

The `printf()` statement will be executed only if age has a value from 13 to 19 inclusive.

Of course, the operands of the && operator can be `bool` variables. You could replace the previous statement with the following:

```
bool test1 = age > 12;
bool test2 = age < 20;
if(test1 && test2)
  printf("You are officially a teenager.");
```

The values of the two logical expressions checking the value of age are stored in the variables test1 and test2. The if expression is now much simpler using bool variables as operands.

Naturally, you can use more than one of these logical operators in an expression:

```
if(age > 12 && age < 20 && savings > 5000)
  printf("You are a rich teenager.");
```

All three conditions must be true for the printf() to be executed. That is, the printf() will be executed only if the value of age is between 13 and 19 inclusive and the value of savings is greater than 5,000.

The OR Operator ||

The logical OR operator, ||, covers the situation in which you want to check for any of two or more conditions being true. If either or both operands of the || operator are true, the result is true. The result is false only when both operands are false. Here's an example of using this operator:

```
if(a < 10 || b > c || c > 50)
  printf("At least one of the conditions is true.");
```

The printf() will be executed only if *at least* one of the three conditions, a<10, b>c, or c>50, is true. When a, b, and c all have the value 9, for instance, this will be the case. Of course, the printf() will also be executed when two or all three of the conditions are true.

You can use the && and || logical operators in combination, as in the following code fragment:

```
if((age > 12 && age < 20) || savings > 5000)
  printf ("Either you're a teenager, or you're rich, or possibly both.");
```

The printf() statement will be executed if the value of age is between 12 and 20 or the value of savings is greater than 5,000 or both. As you can see, when you use more operators in combination, things can get confusing. The parentheses around the expression that is the left operand of the || operator are not strictly necessary, but I put them in to make the condition easier to understand. Making use of Boolean variables can help. You could replace the previous statement with the following:

```
bool over_12 = age > 12;
bool undere_20 = age < 20;
bool age_check = over_12 && under_20;
bool savings_check = savings > 5000;
if(age_check || savings_check)
 printf ("Either you're a teenager, or you're rich, or possibly both.");
```

Now you have declared four Boolean variables using bool, which assumes the stdbool.h header has been included into the source file. You should be able to see that the if statement works with essentially the same test as before. Of course, you could define the value of age_check in a single step, like this:

```
bool age_check = age > 12 && age < 20;
bool savings_check = savings > 5000;
if(age_check || savings_check)
 printf ("Either you're a teenager, or you're rich, or possibly both.");
```

This reduces the number of variables you use and still leaves the code reasonably clear.

The NOT Operator !

Last but not least is the logical NOT operator, represented by !. The ! operator is a unary operator, because it applies to just one operand. The logical NOT operator reverses the value of a logical expression: true becomes false, and false becomes true. Suppose that you have two variables, a and b, with the values 5 and 2, respectively; then the expression a>b is true. If you use the logical NOT operator, the expression !(a>b) is false. I recommend that you avoid using this operator as much as possible; it tends to result in code that becomes difficult to follow. As an illustration of how not to use NOT, you can rewrite the previous example as follows:

```
if((!(age <= 12) && !(age >= 20)) || !(savings <= 5000))
{
  printf("\nYou're either not a teenager and rich ");
  printf("or not rich and a teenager,\n");
  printf("or neither not a teenager nor not rich.");
}
```

As you can see, it becomes incredibly difficult to unravel the nots!

TRY IT OUT: A BETTER WAY TO CONVERT LETTERS

Earlier in this chapter, you tried a program in which the user was prompted to enter an uppercase character. The program used a nested if to ensure that the input was of the correct type and then wrote the lowercase letter equivalent to the command line or a remark indicating that the input was of the wrong type.

You can now see that all this was completely unnecessary because you can achieve the same result like this:

```
// Program 3.5    Testing letters an easier way
#define _CRT_SECURE_NO_WARNINGS
#include <stdio.h>

int main(void)
{
  char letter = 0;                              // Stores an input character

  printf("Enter an upper case letter:");        // Prompt for input
  scanf(" %c", &letter);                        // Read the input character

  if((letter >= 'A') && (letter <= 'Z'))        // Verify uppercase letter
  {
    letter += 'a'-'A';                          // Convert to lowercase
    printf("You entered an uppercase %c.\n", letter);
  }
  else
    printf("You did not enter an uppercase letter.\n");
  return 0;
}
```

The output will either indicate that you did not enter an uppercase letter or tell you which uppercase letter you entered.

How It Works

This version is better than the version that's in the file Program3_04A.c. Compare the mechanisms to test the input in the two programs, and you'll see how much neater the second solution is. Instead of the confusing nested if statements, you now check that the character entered is greater than or equal to 'A' *and* less than or equal to 'Z' in one statement. Notice that you put extra parentheses around the two expressions to be checked. They aren't really needed in this case, but they don't hurt, and they leave you or any other programmer in no doubt as to the order of execution.

There's also a slightly simpler way of expressing the conversion to lowercase:

```
letter += 'a'-'A';                        // Convert to lowercase
```

Now you use the += operator to add the difference between 'a' and 'A' to the character code value stored in letter. Again here, we may use a beautiful bitwise trick to convert to lowercase as it is described in Program 3.4 and detailed later on this chapter. There is its similar trick to convert to uppercase as well.

If you add an #include directive for the ctype.h standard header file to the source, you could make the code even simpler. This header declares functions isalpha(), isupper(), and islower() that test the character you pass as the argument. They return true if the argument is alphabetic, uppercase, or lowercase, respectively. It also declares the toupper() and the tolower() functions to convert a character to uppercase and lowercase, respectively. The code for the program can be written like this:

```
#include <stdio.h>
#include <ctype.h>

int main(void)
{
    char letter = 0;                            // Stores a character
    printf("Enter an uppercase letter:");       // Prompt for input
    scanf("%c", &letter);                       // Read a character
  if(isalpha(letter) && isupper(letter))
    printf("You entered an uppercase %c.\n", tolower(letter));
  else
    printf("You did not enter an uppercase letter.\n");
  return 0;
}
```

The lowercase letter that the tolower() function returns is passed directly to the printf() function.

The Conditional Operator

The *conditional operator* evaluates to one of two expressions, depending on whether a logical expression evaluates true or false.

Because three operands are involved—the logical expression plus two other expressions—this operator is also referred to as the *ternary operator*. The general representation of an expression using the conditional operator looks like this:

```
condition ? expression1 : expression2
```

Notice how the operator is arranged in relation to the operands. The ? character follows the logical expression, condition. On the right of ? are two operands, expression1 and expression2, that represent choices. The value that results from the operation will be the value of expression1 if condition evaluates to true or the value of expression2 if condition evaluates to false. Note that only one, either expression1 or expression2, will be evaluated. Normally this is of little significance, but sometimes this is important. You can use the conditional operator in a statement such as this:

```
x = y > 7 ? 25 : 50;
```

This statement results in x being set to 25 if y is greater than 7 or to 50 otherwise. This is a nice shorthand way of producing the same effect as this:

```
if(y > 7)
  x = 25;
else
  x = 50;
```

The conditional operator enables you to express some things economically. An expression for the maximum or minimum of two variables can be written very simply using the conditional operator. For example, you could write an expression that compared two salaries and obtained the greater of the two like this:

```
your_salary > my_salary ? your_salary : my_salary
```

Of course you can use the conditional operator in more complex expressions. Earlier in Program 3.2, you calculated a quantity price for a product using an if-else statement. The price was $3.50 per item with a discount of 5 percent for quantities over ten. You can do this sort of calculation in a single step with the conditional operator:

```
total_price = unit_price*quantity*(quantity > 10 ? 0.95 : 1.0);
```

TRY IT OUT: USING THE CONDITIONAL OPERATOR

This discount business could translate into a short example. Suppose you have the unit price of the product still at $3.50, but you now offer three levels of discount: 15 percent for purchasing more than 50, 10 percent for more than 20, and the original 5 percent for more than 10. Here's how you can handle that:

```
// Program 3.6 Multiple discount levels
#define _CRT_SECURE_NO_WARNINGS
#include <stdio.h>

int main(void)
{
  const double unit_price = 3.50;        // Unit price in dollars
  const double discount1 = 0.05;         // Discount for more than 10
  const double discount2 = 0.1;          // Discount for more than 20
  const double discount3 = 0.15;         // Discount for more than 50
  double total_price = 0.0;
  int quantity = 0;

  printf("Enter the number that you want to buy:");
```

```
    scanf(" %d", &quantity);

    total_price = quantity*unit_price*(1.0 -
                        (quantity > 50 ? discount3 : (
                            quantity > 20 ? discount2 : (
                                quantity > 10 ? discount1 : 0.0))));

    printf("The price for %d is $%.2f\n", quantity, total_price);
    return 0;
}
```

Some typical output from the program is as follows:

```
Enter the number that you want to buy:60
The price for 60 is $178.50
```

How It Works

The interesting bit here is the statement that calculates the total price for the quantity that's entered. The statement uses three conditional operators, so it takes a little unraveling:

```
    total_price = quantity*unit_price*(1.0 -
                        (quantity > 50 ? discount3 : (
                            quantity > 20 ? discount2 : (
                                quantity > 10 ? discount1 : 0.0))));
```

You can understand how this produces the correct result by breaking it into pieces. The basic price is produced by the expression `quantity*unit_price`, which simply multiplies the unit price by the quantity ordered. The result of this has to be multiplied by a factor that depends on the quantity. If the quantity is over 50, the basic price must be multiplied by (`1.0-discount3`). This is determined by an expression such as

`(1.0 - quantity > 50 ? discount3 : something_else)`

If `quantity` is greater than 50 here, the expression will evaluate to (`1.0-discount3`), and the right side of the assignment is complete. Otherwise, it will be (`1.0 - something_else`), where `something_else` is the result of another conditional operator.

Of course if `quantity` isn't greater than 50, it may still be greater than 20, in which case you want `something_else` to be `discount2`. This is produced by the conditional operator that appears in the `something_else` position in the statement:

`(quantity > 20 ? discount2 : something_else_again)`

This will result in `something_else` being `discount2` if the value of `quantity` is more than 20, which is precisely what you want, and `something_else_again` if it isn't. You want `something_else_again` to be `discount1` if `quantity` is more than 10 and 0 if it isn't. The last conditional operator that occupies the `something_else_again` position in the statement does this:

`(quantity > 10 ? discount1 : 0.0)`

And that's it!

In spite of its odd appearance, you'll see the conditional operator come up quite frequently in C programs. A very handy application of this operator that you'll see in examples in this book and elsewhere is to vary the contents of a message or prompt depending on the value of an expression. For example, if you want to display a message indicating the number of pets that a person has and you want the message to change between singular and plural automatically, you could write this:

```
printf("You have %d pet%s.", pets, pets == 1 ? "" : "s" );
```

You use the %s specifier when you want to output a string. If pets is equal to 1, an empty string will be output in place of the %s; otherwise, "s" will be output. Thus, if pets has the value 1, the statement will output this message:

```
You have 1 pet.
```

However, if the variable pets is 5, you will get this output:

```
You have 5 pets.
```

You can use this mechanism to vary an output message depending on the value of an expression in many different ways: she instead of he, wrong instead of right, and so on.

Operator Precedence: Who Goes First?

With all the parentheses you've used in the examples in this chapter, now is a good time to revisit operator precedence. *Operator precedence* determines the sequence in which operators in an expression are executed. This order of precedence can affect the result of an expression substantially. For example, suppose you are to process job applications and you want to only accept applicants who are 25 or older and have graduated from Harvard or Yale. Here's the age condition you can represent by this conditional expression:

```
Age >= 25
```

Suppose that you represent graduation by the variables Yale and Harvard, which may be true or false. Now you can write the condition as follows:

```
Age >= 25 && Harvard || Yale
```

Unfortunately, this will result in protest because you will now accept Yale graduates who are under 25. In fact, this statement will accept Yale graduates of any age. But if you're from Harvard, you must be 25 or over to be accepted. Because of operator precedence, this expression is effectively the following:

```
(Age >= 25 && Harvard) || Yale
```

So now you take anybody at all from Yale. I'm sure those wearing a Y-front sweatshirt will claim that this is as it should be, but what you really meant was this:

```
Age >= 25 && (Harvard || Yale)
```

Because of operator precedence, you must put the parentheses in the expression to force the order of operations to be what you want.

In general, the precedence of the operators in an expression determines whether it is necessary for you to put parentheses in to get the result you want, but if you are unsure of the precedence of the operators you are using, it does no harm to put the parentheses in. Table 3-2 shows the order of precedence for all the operators in C, from highest at the top to lowest at the bottom.

There are quite a few operators listed in the table that we haven't addressed yet. You'll see the operators ~, <<, >>, &, ^, and | used later in this chapter in the "Bitwise Operators" section; and you'll learn about the rest later in the book.

All the operators that appear in the same row in the table are of equal precedence. In an expression, operators with higher precedence are executed before operators of lower precedence. The sequence of execution for operators of equal precedence is determined by their associativity, which determines whether they're selected from left to right or from right to left. Naturally, parentheses around an expression come at the very top of the list of operators because they override all other precedence rules.

Table 3-2. *Operator Order of Precedence*

Precedence	Operators	Description	Associativity
1	( ) [ ] . -> ++ --	Parenthesized expression Array subscript Member selection by object Member selection by pointer Postfix increment and prefix decrement	Left to right
2	+ - ++ -- ! ~ * & sizeof (type)	Unary + and - Prefix increment and prefix decrement Logical NOT and bitwise complement Dereference (also called indirection operator) Address of Size of expression or type Explicit cast to type such as (int) or (double)	Right to left
3	* / %	Multiplication and division and modulus (remainder)	Left to right
4	+ -	Addition and subtraction	Left to right
5	<< >>	Bitwise shift left and bitwise shift right	Left to right
6	< <= > >=	Less than and less than or equal to Greater than and greater than or equal to	Left to right
7	== !=	Equal to and not equal to	Left to right
8	&	Bitwise AND	Left to right
9	^	Bitwise exclusive OR (XOR)	Left to right
10			Bitwise OR	Left to right
11	&&	Logical AND	Left to right
12	||	Logical OR	Left to right
13	?:	Conditional operator	Right to left

(continued)

Table 3-2. *(continued)*

Precedence	Operators	Description	Associativity
14	=	Assignment	Right to left
	+= -=	Addition assignment and subtraction assignment	
	/= *=	Division assignment and multiplication assignment	
	%=	Modulus assignment	
	<<= >>=	Bitwise shift left assignment and bitwise shift right assignment	
	&= |=	Bitwise AND assignment and bitwise OR assignment	
	^=	Bitwise exclusive OR assignment	
15	,	Comma operator	Left to right

As you can see from Table 3-2, all the comparison operators are below the binary arithmetic operators in precedence, and the binary logical operators are below the comparison operators. As a result, arithmetic is done first, then comparisons, and then logical combinations. Assignments come last in this list, so they're only performed once everything else has been completed. The conditional operator squeezes in just above the assignment operators.

Note that the ! operator is highest within the set of logical operators. Consequently, parentheses around a logical expression are essential when you want to negate the value of the entire logical expression.

TRY IT OUT: USING LOGICAL OPERATORS WITHOUT CONFUSION

Suppose you want a program that will take applicant interviews for a large pharmaceutical corporation. The program should offer interviews to applicants who meet certain educational specifications. An applicant who meets any of the following criteria should be accepted for an interview:

1. Graduates over 25 who studied chemistry and who didn't graduate from Yale

2. Graduates from Yale who studied chemistry

3. Graduates from Harvard who studied economics and aren't older than 28

4. Graduates from Yale who are over 25 and who didn't study chemistry

One program to implement this policy is as follows:

```
// Program 3.7 A confused recruiting policy
#define _CRT_SECURE_NO_WARNINGS
#include <stdio.h>
#include <stdbool.h>

int main(void)
{
  int age = 0;             // Age of the applicant
  int college = 0;         // Code for college attended
  int subject = 0;         // Code for subject studied
  bool interview = false;  // true for accept, false for reject

  // Get data on the applicant
  printf("\nWhat college? 1 for Harvard, 2 for Yale, 3 for other: ");
  scanf("%d",&college);
  printf("\nWhat subject? 1 for Chemistry, 2 for Economics, 3 for other: ");
```

```
  scanf("%d", &subject);
  printf("\nHow old is the applicant? ");
  scanf("%d",&age);

  // Check out the applicant
  if((age > 25 && subject == 1) && (college == 3 || college == 1))
    interview = true;
  if(college == 2 && subject == 1)
    interview = true;
  if(college == 1 && subject == 2 && !(age > 28))
    interview = true;
  if(college == 2 && (subject == 2 || subject == 3) && age > 25)
    interview = true;

  // Output decision for interview
  if(interview)
    printf("\n\nGive 'em an interview\n");
  else
    printf("\n\nReject 'em\n");
  return 0;
}
```

The output from this program should be something like this:

```
What college? 1 for Harvard, 2 for Yale, 3 for other: 2
What subject? 1 for Chemistry, 2 for Economics, 3 for other: 1
How old is the applicant? 24

Give 'em an interview
```

How It Works

The program works in a fairly straightforward way. The only slight complication is with the number of operators and if statements needed to check out a candidate:

```
  if((age>25 && subject==1) && (college==3 || college==1))
    interview =true;
  if(college==2 && subject ==1)
    interview = true;
  if(college==1 && subject==2 && !(age>28))
    interview = true;
  if(college==2 && (subject==2 || subject==3) && age>25)
    interview = true;
```

The final if statement tells you whether to invite the applicant for an interview or not; it uses the variable interview:

```
  if(interview)
    printf("\n\nGive 'em an interview");
  else
    printf("\n\nReject 'em");
```

111

The variable `interview` is initialized to `false`, but if any of the criteria are met, you assign the value `true` to it. The `if` expression is just the variable `interview`.

This could be a lot simpler though. Let's look at the conditions that result in an interview. You can specify each criterion with an expression, as shown in Table 3-3.

Table 3-3. *Expressions for Selecting Candidates*

Criterion	Expression
Graduates over 25 who studied chemistry and who didn't graduate from Yale	`age > 25 && subject == 1 && college != 2`
Graduates from Yale who studied chemistry	`college == 2 && subject == 1`
Graduates from Harvard who studied economics and aren't older than 28	`college == 1 && subject == 2 && age <= 28`
Graduates from Yale who are over 25 and who didn't study chemistry	`college == 2 && age > 25 && subject != 1`

The variable `interview` should be set to `true` if any of these four conditions is true, so you can now combine them using the `||` operator to set the value of the variable `interview`:

```
interview = (age>25 && subject == 1 && college!=2) ||
            (college==2 && subject==1) ||
            (college==1 && subject==2 && age<=28) ||
            (college==2 && age>25 && subject!=1);
```

Now you don't need the `if` statements to check the conditions at all. You just store the logical value, `true` or `false`, which arises from combining these expressions. In fact, you could dispense with the variable `interview` altogether by just putting the combined expression for the checks into the last `if`:

```
if((age>25 && subject == 1 && college!=2) || (college == 2 && subject == 1) ||
           (college == 1 && subject == 2 && age <= 28) ||
                  (college == 2 && age > 25 && subject != 1))
  printf("\n\nGive 'em an interview\n");
else
  printf("\n\nReject 'em\n");
```

You end up with a much shorter, if somewhat less readable, program.

Multiple-Choice Questions

Multiple-choice questions come up quite often in programming. One example is selecting a different course of action depending on whether a candidate is from one or another of six different universities. Another example is when you want to choose to execute a particular set of statements depending on which day of the week it is. You have two ways to handle multiple-choice situations in C. One is a form of the `if` statement described as the else-if that provides the most general way to deal with multiple choices. The other is the switch statement, which is restricted in the way a particular choice is selected; but where it does apply, it provides a very neat and easily understood solution. Let's look at the else-if statement first.

Using else-if Statements for Multiple Choices

The use of the else-if statement for selecting one of a set of choices looks like this:

```
if(choice1)
  // Statement or block for choice 1
else if(choice2)
  // Statement or block for choice 2
else if(choice3)
  // Statement or block for choice 3

/* … and so on …   */
else
  // Default statement or block
```

Each if expression can be anything as long as the result is true or false, which I'm sure you will remember is equivalent to nonzero or zero. If the first if expression, choice1, is false, the next if is executed. If choice2 is false, the next if is executed. This continues until an expression is found to be true, in which case the statement or block of statements for that if is executed. This ends the sequence, and the statement following the sequence of else-if statements is executed next.

If all the if conditions are false, the statement or block following the final else will be executed. You can omit this final else, in which case the sequence will do nothing if all if conditions are false. Here's a simple illustration of this:

```
if(salary<5000)
  printf("Your pay is very poor.");        // pay < 5000
else if(salary<15000)
  printf("Your pay is not good.");         // 5000 <= pay < 15000
else if(salary<50000)
  printf("Your pay is not bad.");          // 15000 <= pay < 50000
else if(salary<100000)
  printf("Your pay is very good.");        // 50000 <= pay < 100000
else
  printf("Your pay is exceptional.");    // pay >= 100000
```

Note that you don't need to test for lower limits in the if conditions after the first. This is because if you reach a particular if, the previous test must have been false. However, many times when you are learning to code, it is good to have redundant source code if that redundancy helps to achieve a more human-readable code. Don't be afraid about this type of coding until you have more experience and release a more elegant one.

Because any logical expressions can be used as the if conditions, this statement is very flexible and allows you to express a selection from virtually any set of choices. The switch statement isn't as flexible, but it's simpler to use in many cases. Let's take a look at the switch statement.

The switch Statement

The switch statement enables you to choose one course of action from a set of possible actions, based on the result of an integer expression. Let's start with a simple illustration of how it works.

Imagine that you're running a raffle or a sweepstakes. Suppose ticket number 35 wins first prize, number 122 wins second prize, and number 78 wins third prize. You could use the switch statement to check for a winning ticket number as follows:

```
switch(ticket_number)
{
  case 35:
    printf("Congratulations! You win first prize!");
    break;
  case 122:
    printf("You are in luck - second prize.");
    break;
  case 78:
    printf("You are in luck - third prize.");
    break;
  default:
    printf("Too bad, you lose.");
    break;
}
```

The value of the expression in parentheses following the keyword switch, which is ticket_number in this case, determines which of the statements between the braces will be executed. If the value of ticket_number matches the value specified after one of the case keywords, the following statements will be executed. If ticket_number has the value 122, for example, this message will be displayed:

```
You are in luck - second prize.
```

The effect of the break statement following the printf() is to skip over the other statements within that block and continue with whatever statement follows the closing brace. If you were to omit the break statement for a particular case, when the statements for that case are executed, execution would continue with the statements for the next case. If ticket_number has a value that doesn't correspond to any of the case values, the statements that follow the default keyword are executed, so you simply get the default message. The break statement following default is not strictly necessary here because it is the last case, but it is a good idea to always include it because you may add more cases to the switch at a later date. The case statements can be in any sequence, and default and break are also keywords in C.

The general way of describing the switch statement is as follows:

```
switch(integer_expression)
{
  case constant_expression_1:
    statements_1;
    break;
    ....
  case constant_expression_n:
    statements_n;
    break;
```

```
  default:
    statements;
    break;
}
```

The test is the value of `integer_expression`. If that value corresponds to one of the case values defined by the associated `constant_expression_n` values, the statements following that case value are executed. If the value of `integer_expression` differs from every one of the case values, the statements following `default` are executed. Because you can't reasonably expect to select more than one case, all the case values must be different. If they aren't, you'll get an error message when you try to compile the program. The case values must all be *constant expressions*, which are expressions that can be evaluated by the compiler. This means that a case value cannot be dependent on a value that's determined when your program executes. Of course, the test expression `integer_expression` can be anything at all, as long as it evaluates to an integer.

You can omit the `default` keyword and its associated statements. If none of the case values matches the value of `integer_expression`, then nothing happens. Notice, however, that all of the case values for the associated `constant_expression` must be different. The `break` statement jumps to the statement after the closing brace.

Notice the punctuation and formatting. There's no semicolon at the end of the first `switch` expression because it forms a single statement with the following block of code. The body of the `switch` statement is always enclosed within braces. The `constant_expression` value for a case is followed by a colon, and each subsequent statement ends with a semicolon, as usual.

Because an enumeration type is an integer type, you can use a variable of an enumeration type to control a `switch`. Here's an example:

```
enum Weekday {Monday, Tuesday, Wednesday, Thursday, Friday, Saturday, Sunday};
enum Weekday today = Wednesday;
switch(today)
{
  case Sunday:
    printf("Today is Sunday.");
    break;
  case Monday:
    printf("Today is Monday.");
    break;
  case Tuesday:
    printf("Today is Tuesday.");
    break;
  case Wednesday:
    printf("Today is Wednesday.");
    break;
  case Thursday:
    printf("Today is Thursday.");
    break;
  case Friday:
    printf("Today is Friday.");
    break;
  case Saturday:
    printf("Today is Saturday.");
    break;
}
```

This `switch` selects the case that corresponds to the value of the variable `today`, so in this case the message will be that today is Wednesday. There's no default case in the `switch`, but you could put one in to guard against an invalid value for `today`.

You can associate several case values with one group of statements. You can also use an expression that results in a value of type char as the control expression for a `switch`. Suppose you read a character from the keyboard into a variable, `ch`, of type char. You can classify this character in a `switch` like this:

```
switch(tolower(ch))
{
  case 'a': case 'e': case 'i': case 'o': case 'u':
    printf("The character is a vowel.\n");
    break;
  case 'b': case 'c': case 'd': case 'f': case 'g': case 'h': case 'j': case 'k':
  case 'l': case 'm': case 'n': case 'p': case 'q': case 'r': case 's': case 't':
  case 'v': case 'w': case 'x': case 'y': case 'z':
    printf("The character is a consonant.\n");
    break;
  default:
    printf("The character is not a letter.\n");
    break;
}
```

Because you use the function `tolower()` that is declared in the `ctype.h` header file to convert the value of ch to lowercase, you only need to test for lowercase letters. When ch contains the character code for any vowel, you output a message to that effect because for the five case values corresponding to vowels, you execute the same `printf()` statement. Similarly, you output a suitable message when ch contains a consonant. If ch contains a code that's neither a consonant nor a vowel, the `default` case is executed.

You could simplify the `switch` by making use of the `isalpha()` function from the `ctype.h` header that you saw earlier. The function returns a nonzero integer (thus `true`) if the character that's passed as the argument is an alphabetic character, and it will return 0 (`false`) if the character isn't alphabetic. You could therefore produce the same result as the previous `switch` with the following code:

```
if(!isalpha(ch))
    printf("The character is not a letter.\n");
else
{
  switch(tolower(ch))
  {
    case 'a': case 'e': case 'i': case 'o': case 'u':
      printf("The character is a vowel.\n");
    break;
    default:
    printf("The character is a consonant.\n");
    break;
  }
}
```

The `if` statement tests for ch not being a letter, and if this is so, it outputs a message. If ch is a letter, the `switch` statement will sort out whether it is a vowel or a consonant. The five vowel case values produce one output, and the `default` case produces the other. Because you know that ch contains a letter when the `switch` statement executes, if ch isn't a vowel, it must be a consonant.

In addition to the tolower(), toupper(), and isalpha() functions that I've mentioned, the ctype.h header also declares several other useful functions for testing a character. The complete set is shown in Table 3-4.

Table 3-4. *Functions for Testing Characters*

Function	Tests For
islower()	Lowercase letter
isupper()	Uppercase letter
isalnum()	Uppercase or lowercase letter or a decimal digit
iscntrl()	Control character
isprint()	Any printing character including space
isgraph()	Any printing character except space
isdigit()	Decimal digit ('0'-'9')
isxdigit()	Hexadecimal digit ('0'-'9', 'A'-'F', 'a'-'f')
isblank()	Standard blank characters (space, '\t')
isspace()	Whitespace character (space, '\n', '\t', '\v', '\r', '\f')
ispunct()	Printing character for which isspace() and isalnum() return false
isalpha()	Uppercase or lowercase letter
tolower()	Convert to lowercase
toupper()	Convert to uppercase

In each case, the function returns a nonzero integer value (which is interpreted as true) if it finds what it's testing for and 0 (false) otherwise.

Let's look at the switch statement in action with an example.

TRY IT OUT: PICKING A LUCKY NUMBER

This example assumes that you're operating a lottery in which there are three winning numbers. Participants are required to guess a winning number, and the switch statement is designed to end the suspense and tell them about any valuable prizes they may have won:

```
// Program 3.8 Lucky Lotteries
#define _CRT_SECURE_NO_WARNINGS
#include <stdio.h>

int main(void)
{
  int choice = 0;              // The number chosen

  // Get the choice input
  printf("Pick a number between 1 and 10 and you may win a prize! ");
  scanf("%d", &choice);
```

```
  // Check for an invalid selection
  if((choice > 10) || (choice < 1))
    choice = 11;                  // Selects invalid choice message

  switch(choice)
  {
    case 7:
      printf("Congratulations!\n");
      printf("You win the collected works of Amos Gruntfuttock.\n");
      break;                      // Jumps to the end of the block

    case 2:
      printf("You win the folding thermometer-pen-watch-umbrella.\n");
      break;                      // Jumps to the end of the block

    case 8:
      printf("You win the lifetime supply of aspirin tablets.\n");
      break;                      // Jumps to the end of the block

    case 11:
      printf("Try between 1 and 10. You wasted your guess.\n");
                                  // No break - so continue with the next statement

    default:
      printf("Sorry, you lose.\n");
      break;                      // Defensive break - in case of new cases
  }
  return 0;
}
```

Typical output from this program will be the following:

```
Pick a number between 1 and 10 and you may win a prize! 3
Sorry, you lose.
```

   or:

```
Pick a number between 1 and 10 and you may win a prize! 7
Congratulations!
You win the collected works of Amos Gruntfuttock.
```

   or if you enter an invalid number:

```
Pick a number between 1 and 10 and you may win a prize! 92
Try between 1 and 10. You wasted your guess.
Sorry, you lose.
```

How It Works

You do the usual sort of thing to start with. You declare an integer variable `choice`. Then you ask the user to enter a number between 1 and 10 and store the value the user enters in `choice`:

```
int choice = 0;                    // The number chosen

// Get the choice input
printf("Pick a number between 1 and 10 and you may win a prize! ");
scanf("%d", &choice);
```

Before you do anything else, you check that the user has really entered a number between 1 and 10:

```
// Check for an invalid selection
if((choice > 10) || (choice < 1))
  choice = 11;                // Selects invalid choice message
```

If the value is anything else, you automatically change it to 11. You don't have to do this, but to ensure the user is advised of his or her mistake, you set the variable `choice` to 11, which produces the error message generated by the `printf()` for that case value.

Next, you have the `switch` statement, which will select from the cases between the braces that follow depending on the value of `choice`:

```
switch(choice)
{
  ...
}
```

If `choice` has the value 7, the case corresponding to that value will be executed:

```
case 7:
  printf("Congratulations!\n");
  printf("You win the collected works of Amos Gruntfuttock.\n");
  break;                     // Jumps to the end of the block
```

The two `printf()` calls are executed, and the `break` will jump to the statement following the closing brace for the block (which ends the program, in this case, because it is the `return` statement).

The same applies to the next two cases:

```
case 2:
  printf("You win the folding thermometer-pen-watch-umbrella.\n");
  break;                        // Jumps to the end of the block

case 8:
  printf("You win the lifetime supply of aspirin tablets.\n");
  break;                        // Jumps to the end of the block
```

These correspond to value 2 or 8 for the variable `choice`.

The next case is a little different:

```
case 11:        printf("Try between 1 and 10. You wasted your guess.\n");
                        // No break - so continue with the next statement
```

There's no break statement, so execution continues with the printf() for the default case after displaying the message. The upshot of this is that you get both lines of output if choice has been set to 11. This is entirely appropriate in this case, but usually you'll want to put a break statement at the end of each case. Remove the break statements from the program and try entering 7 to see why. You'll get all the output messages following any particular case.

The default case is

```
default:
    printf("Sorry, you lose.\n");
    break;                      // Defensive break - in case of new cases
```

This will be selected if the value of choice doesn't correspond to any of the other case values. You also have a break statement here. Although it isn't strictly necessary, many programmers put a break statement after the default case statement or whichever is the last case in the switch. This provides for the possibility of adding further case statements to the end of the block. If you were to forget to add the break after the last case in such circumstances, the switch won't do what you want. The case statements can be in any order in a switch, and default doesn't have to be the last.

TRY IT OUT: YES OR NO

Let's look at the switch statement in action, which is controlled by a variable of type char where the value is entered by the user. You'll prompt the user to enter the value 'y' or 'Y' for one action and 'n' or 'N' for another. On its own, this program may not seem useful, but you'll encounter many situations in which a program needs to ask just this question and then perform some action as a result (e.g., saving a file):

```
// Program 3.9 Testing cases
#define _CRT_SECURE_NO_WARNINGS
#include <stdio.h>

int main(void)
{
  char answer = 0;                 // Stores an input character

  printf("Enter Y or N: ");
  scanf(" %c", &answer);

  switch(answer)
  {
    case 'y': case 'Y':
      printf("You responded in the affirmative.\n");
      break;

    case 'n': case 'N':
      printf("You responded in the negative.\n");
      break;

    default:
      printf("You did not respond correctly...\n");
      break;
  }
  return 0;
}
```

Typical output from this is the following:

```
Enter Y or N: y
You responded in the affirmative.
```

How It Works

When you declare the variable `answer` as type `char`, you also take the opportunity to initialize it to 0. You then ask the user to type something in and store that value as usual:

```
char answer = 0;                    // Stores an input character

printf("Enter Y or N: ");
scanf(" %c", &answer);
```

The `switch` statement uses the character stored in `answer` to select a case:

```
switch(answer)
{
  ...
}
```

The first case in the `switch` provides for the possibility of the user entering an uppercase or a lowercase letter Y:

```
  case 'y': case 'Y':
    printf("You responded in the affirmative.\n");
    break;
```

Both values `'y'` and `'Y'` will result in the same `printf()` being executed. In general, you can put as many cases together like this as you want. Notice the punctuation for this. The two cases just follow each other, and each has a terminating colon after the case value.

The negative input is handled in a similar way:

```
  case 'n': case 'N':
    printf("You responded in the negative.\n");
    break;
```

If the character entered doesn't correspond with any of the case values, the default case is selected:

```
  default:
    printf("You did not respond correctly...\n");
    break;
```

Note the `break` statement after the `printf()` statements for the default case, as well as the legal case values. As before, this causes execution to break off at that point and continue after the end of the `switch` statement. Again, without it you would get the statements for succeeding cases executed and, unless there's a break statement preceding the valid cases, you would get the following statement (or statements), including the default statement, executed as well.

Of course, you could also use the `toupper()` or `tolower()` function to simplify the cases in the `switch`. By using one or the other, you can nearly halve the number of cases:

```
switch(toupper(answer))
{
  case 'Y':
    printf("You responded in the affirmative.\n");
    break;
  case 'N':
    printf("You responded in the negative.\n");
    break;
  default:
    printf("You did not respond correctly...\n");
    break;
}
```

Remember, you need an `#include` directive for `ctype.h` if you want to use the `toupper()` function.

The goto Statement

The `if` statement provides you with the ability to choose one or the other of two blocks of statements, depending on a test. This is a powerful tool that enables you to alter the natural sequence of execution. You no longer have to go from A to B to C to D. You can go to A and then decide whether to skip B and C and go straight to D.

The `goto` statement, on the other hand, is a blunt instrument. It directs the flow of statements to change *unconditionally*—do not pass Go, do not collect $200, or go directly to jail. When your program hits a `goto`, it does just that. It goes to the place you send it, without checking any values or asking the user whether this is really what they want.

I'm only going to mention the `goto` statement very briefly because it isn't as great as it might at first seem. The problem with `goto` statements is that they seem too easy. This might sound perverse, but the important word is *seem*. It feels so simple that you can be tempted into using it all over the place, where it would be better to use a different statement. This can result in heavily tangled code.

When you use the `goto` statement, the position in the code to be moved to is defined by a *statement label* at that point. A statement label is defined in exactly the same way as a variable name, which is a sequence of letters and digits, the first of which must be a letter. The statement label is followed by a colon (`:`) to separate it from the statement it labels. If you think this sounds like a case label in a `switch`, you would be right. Case labels are statement labels.

Like other statements, the `goto` statement ends with a semicolon:

```
goto there;
```

The destination statement must have the same label as appears in the `goto` statement, which is there in this case. As I said, the label is written preceding the statement it applies to, with a colon separating the label from the rest of the statement, as in this example:

```
there: x = 10;                    // A labeled statement
```

The `goto` statement can be used in conjunction with an `if` statement, as in the following example:

```
...
if(dice == 6)
  goto Waldorf;
```

```
else
  goto Jail;                        // Go to the statement labeled Jail

Waldorf:
  comfort = high;
  ...
  // Code to prevent falling through to Jail

Jail:                               // The label itself. Program control is sent here
  comfort = low;
  ...
```

You roll the dice. If you get 6, you go to `Waldorf`; otherwise, you go to `Jail`. This might seem perfectly fine; but, at the very least, it's confusing. To understand the sequence of execution, you need to hunt for the destination labels. Code that is littered with gotos is very difficult to follow and perhaps even more difficult to fix when things go wrong. So it's best to avoid the goto statement as much as possible. In theory, it's always possible to avoid using the goto statement, but there are one or two instances in which it's a useful option. It is known the computer scientist Dijkstra's crusade against goto statement; this was called spaghetti code, which gave strength for modular, object-oriented programming and other paradigms. You'll look into loops in Chapter 4, but for now, know that exiting from the innermost loop of a deeply nested set of loops can be much simpler with a goto statement than with other mechanisms.

Bitwise Operators

Before you come to the big example for this chapter, you'll examine a group of operators that look something like the logical operators you saw earlier but in fact are quite different. These are called the *bitwise operators*, because they operate on the bits in integer values. There are six bitwise operators, as shown in Table 3-5.

Table 3-5. *Bitwise Operators*

Operator	Description
&	Bitwise AND operator
|	Bitwise OR operator
^	Bitwise exclusive OR (XOR) operator
~	Bitwise NOT operator, also called the 1's complement operator
>>	Bitwise shift right operator
<<	Bitwise shift left operator

All of these only operate on integer types. The ~ operator is a unary operator—it applies to one operand—and the others are binary operators.

The bitwise AND operator, &, combines the corresponding bits of its operands in such a way that if both bits are 1, the resulting bit is 1; otherwise, the resulting bit is 0. Suppose you declare the following variables:

```
int x = 13;
int y = 6;
int z = x & y;                      // AND corresponding bits of x and y
```

After the third statement, z will have the value 4 (binary 100). This is because the corresponding bits in x and y are combined as follows:

x	0	0	0	0	1	1	0	1
y	0	0	0	0	0	1	1	0
x & y	0	0	0	0	0	1	0	0

Obviously the variables would have more bits than I have shown here, but the additional bits would all be 0. There is only one instance where corresponding bits in the variables x and y are both 1, and that is the third bit from the right; this is the only case where the result of ANDing the bits is 1.

▪ **Caution**   It's important not to confuse the bitwise operators and the logical operators. The expression x & y will produce quite a different result from x && y in general. Try it out and see.

The bitwise OR operator, |, results in 1 if either or both of the corresponding bits are 1; otherwise, the result is 0. Let's look at a specific example. If you combine the same values of x and y using the | operator in a statement such as this

```
int z = x | y;              // OR the bits of x and y
```

the result would be as follows:

x	0	0	0	0	1	1	0	1
y	0	0	0	0	0	1	1	0
x | y	0	0	0	0	1	1	1	1

The value stored in z would therefore be 15 (binary 1111).

The bitwise XOR operator, ^, produces a 1 if both bits are different and 0 if they're the same. Again, using the same initial values, look at this statement:

```
int z = x ^ y;              // Exclusive OR the bits of x and y
```

This results in z containing the value 11 (binary 1011), because the bits combine as follows:

x	0	0	0	0	1	1	0	1
y	0	0	0	0	0	1	1	0
x ^ y	0	0	0	0	1	0	1	1

The unary operator, ~, flips the bits of its operand, so 1 becomes 0 and 0 becomes 1. You could apply this operator to x with the value 13 as before:

```
int z = ~x;                 // Store 1's complement of x
```

After executing this statement, z will have the value 14. The bits are set as follows:

x	0	0	0	0	1	1	0	1
~x	1	1	1	1	0	0	1	0

The value 1111 0010 is 14 in two's complement representation of negative integers. If you're not familiar with the two's complement form and you want to find out about it, it is described in Appendix A.

The shift operators shift the bits in the left operand by the number of positions specified by the right operand. You could specify a shift left operation with the following statements:

```
int value = 12;
int shiftcount = 3;                   // Number of positions to be shifted
int result = value << shiftcount;     // Shift left shiftcount positions
```

The variable result will contain the value 96. The binary number in value is 0000 1100. The bits are shifted to the left three positions, and 0s are introduced on the right, so the value of value << shiftcount, as a binary number, will be 0110 0000.

The right shift operator moves the bits to the right, but it's a little more complicated than a left shift. For unsigned values, the bits that are introduced on the left (in the vacated positions as the bits are shifted right) are filled with zeros. Let's see how this works in practice. Suppose you declare a variable:

```
unsigned int value = 65372U;
```

As a binary value in a 2-byte variable, this is 1111 1111 0101 1100.
Suppose you now execute the following statement:

```
unsigned int result = value >> 2;     // Shift right two bits
```

The bits in value will be shifted two places to the right, introducing zeros at the left end, and the resultant value will be stored in result. In binary, this will be 0011 1111 1101 0111, which is the decimal value 16343.

For signed values that are negative, the leftmost bit will be 1, and the result of a right shift depends on your system. In most cases, the sign bit is propagated, so the bits introduced on the right are 1 bits, but on some systems zeros are introduced in this case too. Let's see how this affects the result. Suppose you define a variable with this statement:

```
int new_value = -164;
```

This happens to be the same bit pattern as the unsigned value that you used earlier, 1111 1111 0101 1100; remember that this is the two's complement representation of the value. Suppose you now execute this statement:

```
int new_result = new_value >> 2;      // Shift right two bits
```

This will shift the value in new_value two bit positions to the right, and the result will be stored in new_result. If, as is usually the case, the sign bit is propagated, 1s will be inserted on the left as the bits are shifted to the right, so new_result will end up as 1111 1111 1101 0111. This is the decimal value –41, which is what you might expect because it amounts to –164/4. If the sign bit isn't propagated, however, as can occur on some computers, the value in new_result will be 0011 1111 1101 0111. So shifting right by 2 bits in this case has changed the value –164 to +16343, perhaps a rather unexpected result.

The op= Use of Bitwise Operators

You can use all of the binary bitwise operators in the op= form of assignment. The exception is the operator ~, which is a unary operator. As you saw in Chapter 2, a statement of the form

```
lhs op= rhs;
```

is equivalent to the statement

```
lhs = lhs op (rhs);
```

This means that if you write

```
value <<= 4;
```

the effect is to shift the contents of the integer variable, value, left by four bit positions. It's exactly the same as the following:

```
value = value << 4;
```

You can do the same kind of thing with the other binary operators. For example, you could write the following statement:

```
value &= 0xFF;
```

where value is an integer variable. This is equivalent to the following:

```
value = value & 0xFF;
```

The effect of this is to keep the rightmost 8 bits unchanged and to set all the others to 0. This is called masking because it is like putting a mask (bit pattern) over the byte and its bits are hidden behind the | operator.

Using Bitwise Operators

The bitwise operators look interesting in an academic kind of way; they are a great set of tools that each programmer must know. There are some situations that an elegant solution could be implemented using them; for instance, in networking exists subnet masking to divide networks of IPv4 (32 bit) by using AND bitwise (it is such an important task that there are subnet calculators to facilitate it; nevertheless, it's essential to understand the bitwise operations underneath). Bitwise is actively used in programming competitions where the code must be as short as possible and sometimes obfuscated (www.ioccc.org). However, what use are they? They don't come up in everyday programs, but in some areas they are very useful. One major use of the bitwise AND, &, and the bitwise OR, |, is in operations to test and set individual bits in an integer variable. With this capability, you can use individual bits to store data that involve one of two choices. For example, you could use a single integer variable to store several characteristics of a person. You could store whether the person is male or female with 1 bit, and you could use other 3 bits to specify whether the person can speak French, German, or Italian. You might use another bit to record whether the person's salary is $50,000 or more. So in just 4 bits, you have a substantial set of data recorded. Let's see how this would work out.

The fact that you only get a 1 bit when both of the bits being combined are 1 means that you can use the & operator to select a part of an integer variable or even just a single bit. You first define a value, usually called a *mask*, that you use to select the bit or bits that you want. It will contain a bit value of 1 for the bit positions you want to keep and a bit value of 0 for the bit positions you want to discard. You can then AND this mask with the value that you want to select from. Let's look at an example. You can define masks with the following statements:

```
unsigned int male      = 0x1;      // Mask selecting first (rightmost) bit
unsigned int french    = 0x2;      // Mask selecting second bit
unsigned int german    = 0x4;      // Mask selecting third bit
unsigned int italian   = 0x8;      // Mask selecting fourth bit
unsigned int payBracket = 0x10;    // Mask selecting fifth bit
```

In each case, a 1 bit will indicate that the particular condition is true. These masks in binary each pick out an individual bit, so you could have an unsigned int variable, personal_data, which would store five items of information about a person. If the first bit is 1, the person is male, and if the first bit is 0, the person is female. If the second bit is 1, the person speaks French, and if it is 0, the person doesn't speak French, and so on for all 5 bits at the right end of the data value.

You could therefore test the variable, personal_data, for a German speaker with the following statement:

```
if(personal_data & german)
  /* Do something because they speak German */
```

The expression personal_data & german will be nonzero—that is, true—if the bit corresponding to the mask, german, is 1; otherwise, it will be 0.

Of course, there's nothing to prevent you from combining several expressions that involves using masks to select individual bits with the logical operators. You could test whether someone is a female who speaks French or Italian with the following statement:

```
if(!(personal_data & male) && ((personal_data & french) ||
                                        (personal_data & italian)))
  // We have a French or Italian speaking female
```

As you can see, it's easy enough to test individual bits or combinations of bits. You could also write the if statement like this:

```
if(!(personal_data & male) && (personal_data & (french | italian)))
  // We have a French or Italian speaking female
```

Here the french and italian masks are ORed together to produce a value with both of these bits as 1. ANDing this result with personal_data will result in 1 if either the french or italian bit is on in personal_data.

The only other thing you need to understand is how to set individual bits. The OR operator swings into action here. You can use the OR operator to set individual bits in a variable using the same mask as you use to test the bits. If you want to set personal_data to record a person as speaking French, you can do it with this statement:

```
personal_data |= french;           // Set second bit to 1
```

Just to remind you, the preceding statement is exactly the same as the following statement:

```
personal_data = personal_data|french;   // Set second bit to 1
```

The second bit from the right in personal_data will be set to 1, and all the other bits will remain as they were. Because of the way the | operator works, you can set multiple bits in a single statement:

```
personal_data |= french | german | male;
```

This sets the bits to record a French- and German-speaking male. If personal_data previously recorded that the person spoke Italian, that bit would still be set, because the OR operator is additive. If a bit is already set, it will stay set.

What about resetting a bit? Suppose you want to change the male bit to female. This amounts to resetting a 1 bit to 0, and it requires the use of the ~ operator with the bitwise AND:

```
personal_data &= ~male;              // Reset male to female
```

This works because ~male will have a 0 bit set for the bit that indicates male and all the other bits as 1. Thus, the bit corresponding to male will be set to 0: 0 ANDed with anything is 0, and all the other bits will be as they were. If another bit is 1, then 1&1 will still be 1. If another bit is 0, then 0&1 will still be 0.

I've used the example of using bits to record specific items of personal data. If you want to program a PC using the Windows application programming interface (API), you'll often use individual bits to record the status of various window parameters, so the bitwise operators can be very useful in this context.

Other good examples (tips and tricks or, better called, techniques) are the following:

Convert a letter to lowercase (this was mentioned earlier in this chapter):

```
letter = (letter | ' ');
```

The trick is that space ASCII value is 32 since 'a' lowercase is 65 and uppercase is 97 (97 – 65 = 32).

Swap two integers: This known trick is used to swap two integers by using only two integer variables. The beauty of it is that we don't need a temporary variable.

The most common solution would be for exchanging variables x and y:

```
tmp = x;
x = y;
y = tmp;
```

On the other hand, this algorithm does the same:

```
x ^= y;
y = x ^ y;
x ^= y;
```

This is a very known bitwise trick that saves one step for exchanging two integers; however, this is not clear at first sight. Probably it isn't recommended for beginners, and it can be factorized in a function with a meaningful function name and comments.

Always consider the suggestion that sometimes it is better to have longer/verbose code than a smart thin code (until you have empowered enough the language itself).

As mentioned earlier, there are bitwise techniques to convert characters to lowercase/uppercase or invert between those states:

```
Invert text case letter ^= ' ';
Lowercase: letter |= ' ';
Uppercase: letter &= '_';
```

Right and left shift operators were seen in the last example (3.9), n << 1; and n >> 1;, respectively, and easily we can check if the number is odd—(n & 1) == 1—and of course negate it to check if it is even.

Switching bits can be obtained by using the XOR operator (^). Bit switch if XORing with 1 (mask), and keeps its value if the mask is 0. This way, with bit 1 mask, we switch values without worrying about what the first bit's value is. Therefore, if we apply a mask to a string XORing then will become a different (hidden) string, and later we can reverse their values by using the very same mask. It is a popular (naive) cipher to encrypt text (although XOR can be used for more advanced cipher algorithms that are beyond the scope of this book):

```c
// Program 3.9d XOR switching, encryption
#include <stdio.h>
#include <string.h>

int main(void)
{

    char key = 'C';
    char sentence[] = "Fibonacci allows converting miles to kms";
    int len = strlen(sentence);    //function included in string.h, String's length

    //encoding message (switching bits con XOR)
    printf("encoded message:\n");
    for (int i = 0; i < len; i++)
    {
        sentence[i] = sentence[i] ^ key;
        printf("%c", sentence[i]);
    }
    printf("\n\n");

    //decoding message
    printf("decoded message:\n");
    for (int i = 0; i < len; i++)
    {
        sentence[i] = sentence[i] ^ key;
        printf("%c", sentence[i]);
    }

  return 0;
}
```

Don't worry about the string.h header in the example. We will review strings in the next chapters.

Even more complex calculations can be done with bitwise, for example, CRC (Cyclic Redundancy Check) for checking errors in the packets, and also average, factorial, prime calculations, counting bits, permutation, and so on.

Just remember it is not always good to optimize source code. Current compilers are smart enough (including optimization parameters) to handle these bitwise tips and tricks and more; however, they are always helpful for this kind of language that is high level with statements to manage low-level computer resources (memory, sockets, etc.).

TRY IT OUT: USING BITWISE OPERATORS

Let's exercise some of the bitwise operators in a slightly different example, but using the same principles discussed previously. This example illustrates how you can use a mask to select multiple bits from a variable. You'll write a program that sets a value in a variable and then uses the bitwise operators to reverse the sequence of hexadecimal digits. Here's the code:

```
// Program 3.10 Exercising bitwise operators
#include <stdio.h>

int main(void)
{
  unsigned int original = 0xABC;
  unsigned int result = 0;
  unsigned int mask = 0xF;      // Rightmost four bits

  printf("\n original = %X", original);

  // Insert first digit in result
  result |= original & mask;   // Put right 4 bits from original in result

  // Get second digit
  original >>= 4;                 // Shift original right four positions
  result <<= 4;                   // Make room for next digit
  result |= original & mask;     // Put right 4 bits from original in result

  /* Get third digit */
  original >>= 4;                 // Shift original right four positions
  result <<= 4;                   // Make room for next digit
  result |= original & mask;   // Put right 4 bits from original in result
  printf("\t result = %X\n", result);
  return 0;
}
```

This will produce the following output:

```
original = ABC  result = CBA
```

How It Works

This program uses the idea of masking that I discussed previously. The rightmost hexadecimal digit in `original` is obtained by ANDing the value with `mask` in the expression `original & mask`. This sets all the other hexadecimal digits to 0. The value of `mask` as a binary number is

```
0000 0000 0000 1111
```

You can see that only the first 4 bits on the right in `original` are kept. Any of these 4 bits that is 1 will stay as 1 in the result, and any that are 0 will stay as 0. All the other bits will be 0 because 0 ANDed with anything is 0.

Once you've selected the rightmost 4 bits, you then store the result with the following statement:

```
result |= original & mask;  // Put right 4 bits from original in result
```

The content of `result` is ORed with the hexadecimal digit that's produced by the expression on the right of `|=`.

To get at the second digit in `original`, you need to move it to where the first digit was. You do this by shifting the contents of `original` right by four bit positions:

```
original >>= 4;              // Shift original right four positions
```

The first digit is shifted out and is lost.

To make room for the next digit from `original`, you shift the contents of `result` left by four bit positions with this statement:

```
result <<= 4;                // Make room for next digit
```

Now you want to insert the second digit from `original`, which is now in the first digit position, into `result`. You do this with the following statement:

```
result |= original & mask;   // Put right 4 bits from original in result
```

To get the third digit, you just repeat the process. Clearly, you could repeat this for as many digits as you want.

Designing a Program

You've reached the end of Chapter 3 successfully, and now you'll apply what you have learned so far to build a useful program.

The Problem

The problem is to write a simple calculator that can add, subtract, multiply, divide, and find the remainder when one number is divided by another. The program must allow the calculation that is to be performed to be keyed in a natural way, such as 5.6 * 27 or 3 + 6.

The Analysis

All the math involved is simple, but the processing of the input adds a little complexity. You need to make checks on the input to make sure that the user hasn't asked the computer to do something impossible. You must allow the user to input a calculation in one go, for example:

```
34.87 + 5
```

or

```
9 * 6.5
```

The steps involved in writing this program are as follows:

1. Get the user's input for the calculation that the user wants the computer to perform.

2. Check that input to make sure that it's understandable.

3. Perform the calculation.

4. Display the result.

The Solution

This section outlines the steps you'll take to solve the problem.

Step 1

Getting the user input is quite easy. You'll be using printf() and scanf(), so you need to include the stdio.h header file. The only new thing I'll introduce is in the way in which you'll get the input. As I said earlier, rather than asking the user for each number individually and then asking for the operation to be performed, you'll get the user to type it in more naturally. You can do this because of the way scanf() works, but I'll discuss the details of that after you've seen the first part of the program. Let's kick off the program with the code to read the input:

```
// Program 3.11 A calculator
#define _CRT_SECURE_NO_WARNINGS
#include <stdio.h>

int main(void)
{
  double number1 = 0.0;          // First operand value a decimal number
  double number2 = 0.0;          // Second operand value a decimal number
  char operation = 0;             // Operation - must be +, -, *, /, or %

  printf("\nEnter the calculation\n");
  scanf("%lf %c %lf", &number1, &operation, &number2);

  /* Plus the rest of the code for the program */
  return 0;
}
```

The scanf() input function is fairly clever. In general, you don't need to enter each input data item on a separate line. All that's required is one or more whitespace characters between each item of input. (You create a whitespace character by pressing the spacebar, the Tab key, or the Enter key.) Here though, you don't even need a whitespace character because the numbers are separated by an operator, and scanf() will not process the operator as part of the first number.

Step 2

Next, you must check to make sure that the input is correct. The most obvious check to perform is that the operation to be performed is valid. You've already decided that the valid operations are +, -, /, *, and %, so you need to check that the operation is one of these.

You also need to check the second number to see if it's 0 if the operation is either / or %. If the right operand is 0, these operations are invalid. You could do all these checks using if statements, but a switch statement provides a far better way of doing this because it is easier to understand than a sequence of if statements:

```
// Program 3.11 A calculator
#include <stdio.h>

int main(void)
{
  double number1 = 0.0;           // First operand value a decimal number
  double number2 = 0.0;           // Second operand value a decimal number
  char operation = 0;             // Operation - must be +, -, *, /, or %

  printf("\nEnter the calculation\n");
  scanf("%lf %c %lf", &number1, &operation, &number2);

  switch(operation)
  {
    case '+':                     // No checks necessary for add
      /* Code for addition */
      break;

    case '-':                     // No checks necessary for subtract
      /* Code for subtraction */
      break;

    case '*':                     // No checks necessary for multiply
      /* Code for multiplication */
      break;

    case '/':
      if(number2 == 0)            // Check second operand for zero
        printf("\n\n\aDivision by zero error!\n");
      else
       /* Code for division */
     break;

    case '%':                     // Check second operand for zero
      if((long)number2 == 0)
        printf("\n\n\aDivision by zero error!\n");
      else
      /* Code for remainder operation */
      break;
```

```
    default:                        // Operation is invalid if we get to here
      printf("\n\n\aIllegal operation!\n");
      break;
  }

  /* Plus the rest of the code for the program */
  return 0;
}
```

The remainder operator doesn't make sense on float or double types because they can represent the exact result. It makes sense to only apply the % operator to integer operands. You therefore convert the operands to integers before applying the operator. You are casting the second operand to an integer type when the operator is %. This is because it isn't sufficient to just check the second operand against 0—you must check that number2 doesn't have a value that will result in 0 when it's cast to type long. The value 0.5, for example, is not zero, but will be zero when cast to an integer.

Steps 3 and 4

So now that you've checked the input, you can calculate the result. You have a choice here. You could calculate each result in the switch and store it to be output after the switch, or you could simply output the result for each case. Let's go for the latter approach. The code you need to add is as follows:

```
// Program 3.11 A calculator
#include <stdio.h>

int main(void)
{
  double number1 = 0.0;        //* First operand value a decimal number  */
  double number2 = 0.0;        //* Second operand value a decimal number */
  char operation = 0;            //* Operation - must be +, -, *, /, or %  */

  printf("\nEnter the calculation\n");
  scanf("%lf %c %lf", &number1, &operation, &number2);

  switch(operation)
  {
    case '+':                      // No checks necessary for add
      printf("= %lf\n", number1 + number2);
      break;

    case '-':                      // No checks necessary for subtract
      printf("= %lf\n", number1 - number2);
      break;

    case '*':                      // No checks necessary for multiply
      printf("= %lf\n", number1 * number2);
      break;

    case '/':
      if(number2 == 0)             // Check second operand for zero
        printf("\n\n\aDivision by zero error!\n");
```

```
      else
        printf("= %lf\n", number1 / number2);
      break;

    case '%':                       // Check second operand for zero
      if((long)number2 == 0)
        printf("\n\n\aDivision by zero error!\n");
      else
        printf("= %ld\n", (long)number1 % (long)number2);
      break;

    default:                        // Operation is invalid if we get to here
      printf("\n\n\aIllegal operation!\n");
      break;
  }

  return 0;
}
```

Notice how you cast the two numbers from double to long when you calculate the modulus. This is because the % operator only works with integers in C.

All that's left is to try it out! Here's some typical output:

```
Enter the calculation
25*13
= 325.000000
```

Here's another example:

```
Enter the calculation
999/3.3
= 302.727273
```

And just one more:

```
Enter the calculation
7%0

Division by zero error!
```

Summary

This chapter ends with quite a complicated example. In the first two chapters, you could do some reasonably useful things, but you couldn't control the sequence of operations in the program once it had started. In this chapter, you learned how you can use data entered by the user or results calculated during execution to determine what happens next.

You have learned how to compare values and use `if`, `if-else`, `else-if`, and `switch` statements to determine the sequence of execution depending on the outcome. You also now know how to use logical operators to combine the results of comparisons into more complex logical expressions. You should now have a good grasp of making decisions and selecting different paths through your program code.

In the next chapter, you'll learn how to write even more powerful programs: programs that can repeat a set of statements until some condition is met. By the end of Chapter 4, the calculator will be small fry.

EXERCISES

The following exercises enable you to try out what you've learned in this chapter. If you get stuck, look back over the chapter for help. If you're still stuck, you can download the solutions from the Source Code/Download area of the Apress website (www.apress.com), but that really should be a last resort.

Exercise 3-1. Write a program that will first allow a user to choose one of two options:

1. Convert a temperature from degrees Celsius to degrees Fahrenheit.

2. Convert a temperature from degrees Fahrenheit to degrees Celsius.

The program should then prompt for the temperature value to be entered and output the new value that results from the conversion. To convert from Celsius to Fahrenheit, you can multiply the value by 1.8 and then add 32. To convert from Fahrenheit to Celsius, you can subtract 32 from the value, then multiply by 5, and divide the result by 9.

Exercise 3-2. Write a program that prompts the user to enter the date as three integer values for the month, the day in the month, and the year. The program should then output the date in the form 31st December 2003 when the user enters 12 31 2003, for example.

You will need to work out when *th*, *nd*, *st*, and *rd* need to be appended to the day value. Don't forget 1st, 2nd, 3rd, and 4th, but 11th, 12th, 13th, and 14th and 21st, 22nd, 23rd, and 24th.

Exercise 3-3. Write a program that will calculate the price for a quantity entered from the keyboard, given that the unit price is $5 and there is a discount of 10 percent for quantities over 30 and a 15 percent discount for quantities over 50.

Exercise 3-4. Modify the last example in the chapter that implemented a calculator so that the user is given the option to enter y or Y to carry out another calculation and n or N to end the program. (Note: You'll have to use a `goto` statement for this here, but you'll learn a better way of doing this in the next chapter.)

CHAPTER 4

Loops

In this chapter, you'll learn how you can repeat a block of statements until some condition is met. The programming mechanism for this is called a *loop*. The number of times that a loop is repeated can be controlled simply by a count—repeating the statement block a given number of times—or it can be more complex, repeating a block until some condition is met, such as the user entering "quit", for instance. The latter would enable you to program the calculator example in the previous chapter to repeat as many times as required without having to use a goto statement.

In this chapter, you'll learn

- How you can repeat a statement, or a block of statements, as many times as you want

- How you can repeat a statement or a block of statements until a particular condition is fulfilled

- How you use the for, while, and do-while loops

- What the increment and decrement operators do and how you can use them

- How you can write a program that plays a Simple Simon game

How Loops Work

The loop is a fundamental programming tool with the ability to compare items. A comparison of some kind is always implicit in a loop because it provides the way for the loop to end. A typical loop would repeat a block of statements a given number of times. This kind of loop maintains a count of the number of times the loop block has been executed. The count is compared with the required number of loop block iterations, and the result decides when the loop should end.

In the lottery example in Chapter 3 in Program 3.8, you could change the code to give the user exactly three guesses—in other words, you could let them continue to guess until a variable called number_of_ guesses, for instance, equals 3. This would involve a loop to repeat the code that reads a guess from the keyboard and checks the accuracy of the value entered. Figure 4-1 illustrates the way a typical loop would work in this case.

© German Gonzalez-Morris and Ivor Horton 2020
G. Gonzalez-Morris and I. Horton, *Beginning C*, https://doi.org/10.1007/978-1-4842-5976-4_4

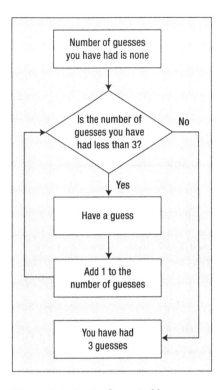

Figure 4-1. *Logic of a typical loop*

More often than not, you'll find that you want to apply the same calculation to different sets of data values; a payroll program is an obvious example. Without loops, you would need to write out the instructions to be performed as many times as there were sets of data values to be processed, which is not very practical. A loop allows you to use the same program code for any number of sets of data to be entered.

Before I discuss the first type of loop, I'll introduce two more arithmetic operators that you'll encounter frequently: the *increment operator* and the *decrement operator*. These operators are often used with loops, which is why I'll discuss them now. I'll start with a brief introduction and then go straight into an example of how you can use them in a loop. Once I have explained the basics of how the loop works, I'll return to the increment and decrement operators to explain some of their idiosyncrasies.

Introducing the Increment and Decrement Operators

The increment operator (++) and the decrement operator (--) will increment or decrement the value stored in the integer variable that they apply to by one. Suppose you have defined an integer variable, number, that currently has the value 6. You can increment it by 1 with the following statement:

```
++number;                          // Increase the value by 1
```

After executing this statement, number will contain the value 7. Similarly, you could decrease the value of number by 1 with the following statement:

```
--number;                          // Decrease the value by 1
```

These operators are different from the other arithmetic operators you have encountered. When you use any of the other arithmetic operators, you create an expression that will result in a value that you can store in a variable or use as part of a more complex expression. They do not directly modify the value stored in a variable. The increment and decrement operators do modify the value of their operand. The expression --number modified the value in number by subtracting 1 from it. The expression ++number adds 1 to the value stored.

The for Loop

You typically use the for loop to execute a block of statements a given number of times. Let's suppose you want to display the numbers from 1 to 10. Instead of writing ten statements that call printf(), you could write this:

```
for(int count = 1 ; count <= 10 ; ++count)
{
  printf("  %d", count);
}
```

The for loop operation is controlled by what appears between the parentheses that follow the keyword for. This is illustrated in Figure 4-2. The action that you want to repeat each time the loop repeats is the block containing the statement that calls printf(). Because you have just a single statement here, you could omit the braces. Figure 4-2 shows the three control expressions that are separated by semicolons. These expressions control the operation of the loop.

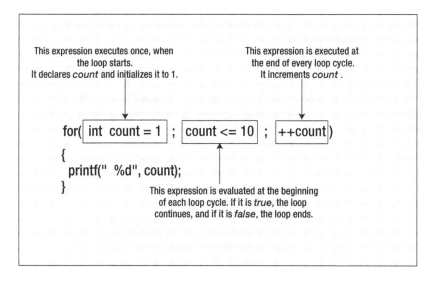

Figure 4-2. *Control expressions in a for loop*

The effect of each control expression is explained in Figure 4-2, but let's take a closer look at exactly what's going on:

- The first control expression, int count = 1, is executed only once, when the loop starts. In the example, this creates a variable, count, with the initial value 1. This variable is local to the loop and does not exist outside the loop. If you attempt to reference count after the loop, your code will not compile.

- The second control expression must be a logical expression that ultimately can result in true or false. In this case, it's the expression count <= 10, which will evaluate to true as long as count is not greater than ten. The second expression is evaluated at the beginning of each loop iteration. If the expression evaluates to true, the loop continues, and if it's false, the loop ends and execution of the program continues with the first statement following the loop block or loop statement. Remember that false is a zero value and any nonzero value is true. Thus, the loop will execute the printf() statement as long as count is less than or equal to ten. The loop will end when count reaches 11.

- The third control expression, ++count in this case, is executed at the end of each loop iteration. Here you use the increment operator to add 1 to the value of count. On the first iteration, count will be 1, so the printf() will output 1. On the second iteration, count will have been incremented to 2, so the printf() will output the value 2. This will continue until the value 10 has been displayed. At the start of the next iteration, count will have been incremented to 11, and because the second control expression will then be false, the loop will end.

Notice the punctuation in the loop statement. The for loop control expressions between the parentheses are separated by semicolons. The two semicolons must always be present. You can omit any or all of the control expressions, but when you do, you must still include the semicolons. For example, you could declare and initialize count to 1 outside the loop:

```
int count = 1;
```

Of course this statement must precede the loop because a variable only exists and is accessible in statements that follow its declaration. Now you don't need to specify the first control expression at all, and the for loop could look like this:

```
for( ; count <= 10 ; ++count)
{
  printf("  %d", count);
}
```

Because you define count before the loop, it will still exist after the loop, so you could output its value. As a trivial example, you could make this into a working program simply by adding a few lines of code:

```
// Program 4.1 List ten integers
#include <stdio.h>

int main(void)
{
  int count = 1;
  for( ; count <= 10 ; ++count)
```

```
   {
      printf("  %d", count);
   }
   printf("\nAfter the loop count has the value %d.\n", count);
   return 0;
}
```

This program will list the numbers from 1 to 10 on the first line followed by the value of count after the loop on the second line:

```
 1  2  3  4  5  6  7  8  9  10
After the loop count has the value 11.
```

The flow chart in Figure 4-3 illustrates the logic of this program.

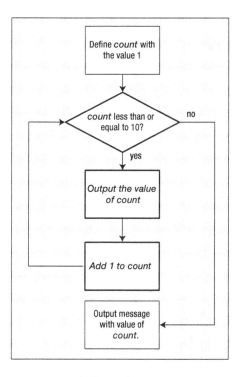

Figure 4-3. *The logic of Program 4.1*

The steps with a bold outline are within the for loop. Let's try a slightly different example.

TRY IT OUT: DRAWING A BOX

Suppose that you want to draw a box on the screen using asterisks. You could just use the `printf()` statement many times, but the typing would be exhausting. You can use a `for` loop to draw a box much more easily. Let's try it:

```
// Program 4.2 Drawing a box
#include <stdio.h>

int main(void)
{
  printf("\n**************");          // Draw the top of the box

  for(int count = 1 ; count <= 8 ; ++count)
    printf("\n*              *");      // Draw the sides of the box

  printf("\n**************\n");        // Draw the bottom of the box
  return 0;
}
```

No prizes for guessing, but the output for this program looks like this:

```
**************
*              *
*              *
*              *
*              *
*              *
*              *
*              *
*              *
**************
```

How It Works

The program itself is really very simple. The first `printf()` statement outputs the top of the box:

```
  printf("\n**************");          // Draw the top of the box
```

The next statement is the `for` loop:

```
  for(int count = 1 ; count <= 8 ; ++count)
    printf("\n*              *");   // Draw the sides of the box
```

This repeats the `printf()` statement eight times to output the sides of the box. You probably understand this, but let's look again at how it works and pick up a bit more jargon. The loop control is the following:

```
  for(int count = 1 ; count <= 8 ; ++count)
```

The operation of the loop is controlled by the three expressions that appear between the parentheses following the keyword `for`. The first expression is the following:

```
int count = 1
```

This creates and initializes the *loop control variable*, or *loop counter*, which in this case is an integer variable, `count`. You could have used other types of variables for this, but integers are the most suitable here. The next loop control expression is

```
count <= 8
```

This is the *continuation condition* for the loop. This is checked *before* each loop iteration to see whether the loop should continue. If the expression is `true`, the loop continues. When it's `false`, the loop ends, and execution continues with the statement following the loop. In this example, the loop continues as long as `count` is less than or equal to 8. The last expression is

```
++count
```

This increments the loop counter and is executed at the end of each loop iteration. The loop statement that outputs the sides of the box will therefore be executed eight times. After the eighth iteration, `count` will be incremented to 9 and the continuation condition will be `false`, so the loop will end.

Program execution will then continue by executing the statement that follows the loop:

```
printf("\n*************\n");   // Draw the bottom of the box
```

This outputs the bottom of the box on the screen.

General Form of the for Loop

The general pattern for the `for` loop is

```
for(starting_condition; continuation_condition ; action_per_iteration)
  loop_statement;

next_statement;
```

The statement to be repeated is represented by `loop_statement`. In general, this could equally well be a block of several statements enclosed between braces.

The `starting_condition` usually (but not always) sets an initial value to a loop control variable. The *loop control variable* is typically, but not necessarily, a counter of some kind that tracks how often the loop has been repeated. You can also declare and initialize several variables of the same type here with the declarations separated by commas; in this case, all the variables will be local to the loop and will not exist once the loop ends.

The `continuation_condition` is a logical expression evaluating to `true` or `false`. This determines whether the loop should continue to be executed. As long as this condition has the value `true`, the loop continues. It typically checks the value of the loop control variable, but you can put any logical or arithmetic expression here as long as you know what you're doing.

As you've already seen, the `continuation_condition` is tested at the beginning of the loop rather than at the end. This obviously means that the `loop_statement` will not be executed at all if the `continuation_condition` starts out as `false`.

The `action_per_iteration` is executed at the end of each loop iteration. It is usually (but again, not necessarily) an increment or decrement of one or more loop control variables. Where several variables are modified, you separate the expressions that modify the variables by commas. At each loop iteration, `loop_statement` is executed. The loop is terminated, and execution continues with `next_statement` as soon as the `continuation_condition` is `false`.

Here's an example of a loop with two variables declared in the first loop control condition:

```
for(int i = 1, j = 2 ; i <= 5 ; ++i, j = j + 2)
  printf("  %5d", i*j);
```

The output produced by this fragment will be the values 2, 8, 18, 32, and 50 on a single line.

More on the Increment and Decrement Operators

Now that you've seen an increment operator in action, let's delve a little deeper and find out what else these increment and decrement operators can do. They're both *unary operators*, which means that they're used with only one operand. You know they're used to increment (increase) or decrement (decrease) a value stored in a variable of one of the integer types by 1.

The Increment Operator

Let's start with the increment operator ++. Assuming the variables are of type `int`, the following three statements all have exactly the same effect:

```
count = count + 1;
count += 1;
++count;
```

Each statement increments `count` by 1. The last form is clearly the most concise.

You can also use the increment operator in an expression. The action of this operator in an expression is to increment the value of the variable, and the incremented value is used in the evaluation of the expression. For example, suppose `count` has the value 5 and you execute this statement:

```
total = ++count + 6;
```

The variable `count` will be incremented to 6, and this value will be used in the evaluation of the expression on the right of the assignment. Consequently, `total` will be assigned the value 12, so the one statement modifies two variables, `count` and `total`.

The Prefix and Postfix Forms of the Increment Operator

Up to now you've written the operator ++ in front of the variable to which it applies. This is called the *prefix* form of the operator. You can also write the operator after the variable to which it applies, and this is referred to as the *postfix* form. The effect of the postfix form of the increment operator is significantly different from the prefix form when it's used in an expression. If you write `count++` in an expression, the incrementing of `count` occurs *after* its value has been used. This sounds more complicated than it really is. Let's look at a variation on the earlier example:

```
total = 6 + count++;
```

With the same initial value of 5 for count, total is assigned the value 11. This is because the initial value of count is used to evaluate the expression on the right of the assignment (6 + 5). The variable count is incremented by 1 after its value has been used in the expression. The preceding statement is therefore equivalent to these two statements:

```
total = 6 + count;
++count;
```

Note, however, that when you use the increment operator in a statement by itself (as in the preceding second statement, which increments count), it doesn't matter whether you write the prefix or the postfix version of the operator. They both have the same effect.

Where you have an expression such as a++ + b—or, worse, a+++b—it's less than obvious what is meant to happen or what the compiler will achieve. The expressions are actually the same, but in the second case you might really have meant a + ++b, which is different because it evaluates to one more than the other two expressions.

For example, suppose a is 10 and b is 5 in the following statement:

```
x = a++ + b;
```

x will be assigned the value 15 (from 10 + 5) because a is incremented after the expression is evaluated. The next time you use the variable a, however, it will have the value 11.

On the other hand, suppose you execute the following statement, with the same initial values for a and b:

```
y = a + (++b);
```

y will be assigned the value 16 (from 10 + 6) because b is incremented before the statement is evaluated.

It's a good idea to use parentheses in all these cases to make sure there's no confusion. So you should write these statements as follows:

```
x = (a++) + b;
y = a + (++b);
```

The Decrement Operator

The decrement operator works in much the same way as the increment operator. It takes the form -- and subtracts 1 from the variable it acts on. It's used in exactly the same way as ++. For example, assuming the variables are of type int, the following three statements all have exactly the same effect:

```
count = count - 1;
count -= 1;
--count;
```

They each decrement the variable count by 1.

It works similarly to the increment operator in an expression. For example, suppose count has the value 10 in the following statement:

```
total = --count + 6;
```

The variable total will be assigned the value 15 (from 9 + 6). The variable count, with the initial value of 10, has 1 subtracted from it before it is used in the expression so that its value will be 9.

Exactly the same rules that I discussed in relation to the prefix and postfix forms of the increment operator apply to the decrement operator. For example, suppose count has the value 5 in this statement:

```
total = --count + 6;
```

total will be assigned the value 10 (from 4 + 6). In this statement

```
total = 6 + count-- ;
```

total will be assigned the value 11 (from 6 + 5).

Both the increment and decrement operators can only be applied to integer types, but this does include integer types that store character codes.

The for Loop Revisited

Now that you understand a bit more about the ++ and -- operators, let's look at another example that uses a loop.

TRY IT OUT: SUMMING NUMBERS

This is a more useful and interesting program than drawing a box with asterisks (unless what you really need is a box drawn with asterisks). I'm sure that you have always wanted to know what all the house numbers on your street totaled. It's such a wonderful ice-breaker at parties. Here you're going to find out by creating a program that reads in the highest house number and then uses a for loop to sum all the numbers from 1 to the value that was entered:

```c
// Program 4.3 Sum the integers from 1 to a user-specified number
#define _CRT_SECURE_NO_WARNINGS
#include <stdio.h>

int main(void)
{
  unsigned  long long sum = 0LL;          // Stores the sum of the integers
  unsigned int count = 0;                 // The number of integers to be summed

  // Read the number of integers to be summed
  printf("\nEnter the number of integers you want to sum: ");
  scanf(" %u", &count);

  // Sum integers from 1 to count
  for(unsigned int i = 1 ; i <= count ; ++i)
    sum += i;

  printf("\nTotal of the first %u numbers is %llu\n", count, sum);
  return 0;
}
```

The typical output you should get from this program is the following:

```
Enter the number of integers you want to sum: 10

Total of the first 10 integers is 55
```

How It Works

You start by declaring and initializing two variables that you'll need during the calculation:

```
unsigned  long long sum = 0LL;           // Stores the sum of the integers
unsigned int count = 0;                  // The number of integers to be summed
```

You use `sum` to hold the final result of your calculations. You declare it as type `unsigned long long` to allow the maximum total you can deal with to be as large an integer as possible. The variable `count` stores the integer that's entered as the number of integers to be summed, and you'll use this value to control the number of iterations in the `for` loop.

You deal with the input by means of the following statements:

```
printf("\nEnter the number of integers you want to sum: ");
scanf(" %u", &count);
```

After the prompt, you read in the integer that will define the sum required. If the user enters 4, for instance, the program will compute the sum of 1, 2, 3, and 4.

The sum is calculated in the following loop:

```
for(unsigned int i = 1 ; i <= count ; ++i)
  sum += i;
```

The loop variable `i` is declared and initialized to 1 by the starting condition in the `for` loop. On each iteration, the value of `i` is added to `sum`. Because `i` is incremented on each iteration, the values 1, 2, 3, and so on, up to the value stored in `count`, will be added to `sum`. The loop ends when the value of `i` exceeds the value of `count`.

As I've hinted by saying "not necessarily" in my descriptions of how the `for` loop is controlled, there is a lot of flexibility about what you can use as control expressions. The next program demonstrates how this flexibility might be applied to shortening the previous example slightly.

TRY IT OUT: THE FLEXIBLE FOR LOOP

This example demonstrates how you can carry out a calculation within the third control expression in a `for` loop:

```
// Program 4.4 Summing integers - compact version
#define _CRT_SECURE_NO_WARNINGS
#include <stdio.h>

int main(void)
{
  unsigned  long long sum = 0LL;         // Stores the sum of the integers
  unsigned int count = 0;                // The number of integers to be summed

  // Read the number of integers to be summed
  printf("\nEnter the number of integers you want to sum: ");
  scanf(" %u", &count);
```

```
    // Sum integers from 1 to count
    for(unsigned int i = 1 ; i <= count ; sum += i++);

    printf("\nTotal of the first %u numbers is %llu\n", count, sum);
    return 0;
}
```

Typical output would be the following:

```
Enter the number of integers you want to sum: 6789

Total of the first 6789 numbers is 23048655
```

How It Works

This program will execute exactly the same as the previous program. The only difference is that you've placed the operation that accumulates the sum in the third control expression for the loop:

```
    for(unsigned int i = 1 ; i<= count ; sum += i++);
```

The loop statement is empty: it's just the semicolon after the closing parenthesis. This expression adds the value of i to sum and then increments i for the next iteration. It works this way because you've used the postfix form of the increment operator. If you use the prefix form here, you'll get the wrong answer because count+1 will be added to sum on the last iteration of the loop, instead of just count.

Modifying the for Loop Control Variable

Of course, you are not limited to incrementing the loop control variable by 1. You can change it by any amount, positive or negative. You could sum the first *n* integers backward if you wish, as in the following example:

```
// Program 4.5 Summing integers backward
#define _CRT_SECURE_NO_WARNINGS
#include <stdio.h>

int main(void)
{
  unsigned  long long sum = 0LL;            // Stores the sum of the integers
  unsigned int count = 0;                   // The number of integers to be summed

  // Read the number of integers to be summed
  printf("\nEnter the number of integers you want to sum: ");
  scanf(" %u", &count);

  // Sum integers from count to 1
  for(unsigned int i = count ; i >= 1 ; sum += i--);

  printf("\nTotal of the first %u numbers is %llu\n", count, sum);
  return 0;
}
```

This produces the same output as the previous example. The only change is in the loop control expressions. The loop counter is initialized to count, rather than to 1, and it's *decremented* on each iteration. The effect is to add the values count, count-1, count-2, and so on to sum, down to 1. Again, if you used the prefix form, the answer would be wrong, because you would start by adding count-1 instead of count.

Just to keep any mathematically inclined readers happy, I should mention that it's quite unnecessary to use a loop to sum the first *n* integers. The tidy little formula $\frac{1}{2}n(n+1)$ for the sum of the integers from 1 to *n* will do the trick much more efficiently (just as Gauss did being a kid). However, it wouldn't teach you much about loops, would it?

A for Loop with No Parameters

As I've already mentioned, you have no obligation to put any parameters in the for loop statement. The minimal for loop looks like this:

```
for( ;; )
{
  /* statements */
}
```

The loop body could be a single statement, but when there are no loop parameters, it is usually a block of statements. Because the condition for continuing the loop is absent, the loop will continue indefinitely. Unless you want your computer to be indefinitely doing nothing, the loop body must contain the means of exiting from the loop. To stop the loop, the loop body must contain two things: a test of some kind to determine when the condition for ending the loop has been reached and a statement that will end the current loop iteration and continue execution with the statement that follows the loop.

The break Statement in a Loop

You encountered the break statement in the context of the switch statement in Chapter 3. Its effect was to stop executing the code within the switch block and continue with the first statement following the switch. The break statement works essentially the same way within the body of a loop—any kind of loop—for instance:

```
char answer = 0;
for( ;; )
{
  /* Code to read and process some data */

  printf("Do you want  to enter some more(y/n): ");
  scanf("%c", &answer);
  if(tolower(answer) == 'n')
    break;                          // Go to statement after the loop
}
/* Statement after the loop */
```

Here you have a loop that will potentially execute indefinitely. The scanf() function reads a character into answer, and if the character entered is n or N, the break statement will be executed. The effect is to stop executing the loop and to continue with the first statement following the loop. Let's see this in action in another example.

TRY IT OUT: A MINIMAL FOR LOOP

This example computes the average of an arbitrary number of values:

```c
// Program 4.6 The almost indefinite loop - computing an average
#define _CRT_SECURE_NO_WARNINGS
#include <stdio.h>
#include <ctype.h>                    // For tolower() function

int main(void)
{
  char answer = 'N';                  // Decision to continue the loop
  double total = 0.0;                 // Total of values entered
  double value = 0.0;                 // Value entered
  unsigned int count = 0;             // Number of values entered

  printf("\nThis program calculates the average of"
                          " any number of values.");

  for( ;; )                           // Indefinite loop
  {
    printf("\nEnter a value: ");      // Prompt for the next value
    scanf(" %lf", &value);            // Read the next value
    total += value;                   // Add value to total
    ++count;                          // Increment count of values

    // check for more input
    printf("Do you want to enter another value? (Y or N): ");
    scanf(" %c", &answer);            // Read response Y or N

    if(tolower(answer) == 'n')        // look for any sign of no
      break;                          // Exit from the loop
  }
  // Output the average to 2 decimal places
  printf("\nThe average is %.2lf\n", total/count);
  return 0;
}
```

Typical output from this program is the following:

```
This program calculates the average of any number of values.
Enter a value: 2.5
Do you want to enter another value? (Y or N): y

Enter a value: 3.5
Do you want to enter another value? (Y or N): y

Enter a value: 6
Do you want to enter another value? (Y or N): n

The average is 4.00
```

How It Works

The general logic of the program is illustrated in Figure 4-4.

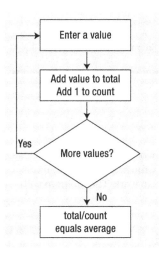

Figure 4-4. *Basic logic of the program*

You've set up the loop to continue indefinitely because the for loop has no end condition specified—or indeed any loop control expressions:

```
for( ;; )                          // Indefinite loop
```

Therefore, so far as the loop control is concerned, the block of statements enclosed between the braces will be repeated indefinitely.

You display a prompt and read an input value in the loop with these statements:

```
printf("\nEnter a value: ");       // Prompt for the next value
scanf(" %lf", &value);             // Read the next value
```

Next, you add the value entered to your variable total and increment count:

```
total += value;                    // Add value to total
++count;                           // Increment count of values
```

Having read a value and added it to the total, you check with the user to see if more input is to be entered:

```
// check for more input
printf("Do you want to enter another value? (Y or N): ");
scanf(" %c", &answer);             // Read response Y or N
```

This prompts for either Y or N to be entered. The character entered is checked in the if statement:

```
if(tolower(answer) == 'n')         // look for any sign of no
    break;                         // Exit from the loop
```

The character stored in answer is converted to lowercase by the tolower() function that's declared in the ctype.h header file, so you only need to test for n. If you enter N, or n, to indicate that you've finished entering data, the break statement will be executed. Executing break within a loop has the effect of immediately ending the loop, so execution continues with the statement following the closing brace for the loop block. This is the statement:

```
printf("\nThe average is %.2lf\n", total/count);
```

This statement calculates the average of the values entered by dividing the value in total by the count of the number of values. The result is then displayed.

Limiting Input Using a for Loop

You can use a for loop to limit the amount of input from the user. Each iteration of the loop will permit some input to be entered. When the loop has completed a given number of iterations, the loop ends so no more data can be entered. You can write a simple program to demonstrate how this can work. The program will implement a guessing game.

TRY IT OUT: A GUESSING GAME

With this program, the user has to guess a number that the program has picked as the lucky number. It uses one for loop and plenty of if statements. I've also thrown in a conditional operator, just to make sure you haven't forgotten how to use it!

```
// Program 4.7 A Guessing Game
#define _CRT_SECURE_NO_WARNINGS
#include <stdio.h>

int main(void)
{
  int chosen = 15;                  // The lucky number
  int guess = 0;                    // Stores a guess
  int count = 3;                    // The maximum number of tries

  printf("\nThis is a guessing game.");
  printf("\nI have chosen a number between 1 and 20"
                          " which you must guess.\n");

  for( ; count > 0 ; --count)
  {
    printf("\nYou have %d tr%s left.", count, count == 1 ? "y" : "ies");
    printf("\nEnter a guess: ");     // Prompt for a guess
    scanf("%d", &guess);             // Read in a guess

    // Check for a correct guess
    if(guess == chosen)
    {
      printf("\nCongratulations. You guessed it!\n");
      return 0;                      // End the program
    }
```

```
    else if(guess < 1 || guess > 20)        // Check for an invalid guess
      printf("I said the number is between 1 and 20.\n ");
    else
      printf("Sorry, %d is wrong. My number is %s than that.\n",
                          guess, chosen > guess ? "greater" : "less");
  }
  printf("\nYou have had three tries and failed. The number was %d\n",
                                                          chosen);

  return 0;
}
```

Some sample output would be the following:

```
This is a guessing game.
I have chosen a number between 1 and 20 which you must guess.

You have 3 tries left.
Enter a guess: 11
Sorry, 11 is wrong. My number is greater than that.

You have 2 tries left.
Enter a guess: 15

Congratulations. You guessed it!
```

How It Works

You first declare and initialize three variables of type int—chosen, guess, and count:

```
  int chosen = 15;                   // The lucky number
  int guess = 0;                     // Stores a guess
  int count = 3;                     // The maximum number of tries
```

These store the number that's to be guessed, the user's guess, and the number of guesses the user is permitted, respectively.

You provide the user with an initial explanation of the program:

```
  printf("\nThis is a guessing game.");
  printf("\nI have chosen a number between 1 and 20"
                              " which you must guess.\n");
```

The number of guesses that can be entered is controlled by this loop:

```
for( ; count > 0 ; --count)
  {
    ...
  }
```

All the operational details of the game are within this loop, which will continue as long as count is positive, so the loop will repeat count times.

There's a prompt for a guess to be entered, and the guess itself is read by these statements:

```
printf("\nYou have %d tr%s left.", count, count == 1 ? "y" : "ies");
printf("\nEnter a guess: ");        // Prompt for a guess
scanf("%d", &guess);               // Read in a guess
```

The first printf() looks a little complicated, but all it does is insert "y" after "tr" in the output when count is 1 and "ies" in all other cases. It's important to get your plurals right.

After reading a guess value using scanf(), you check whether it's correct with these statements:

```
if(guess == chosen)
{
  printf("\nCongratulations. You guessed it!\n");
  return 0;                        // End the program
}
```

If the guess is correct, you display a suitable message and execute the return statement. This ends the function main(), so the program ends. You'll learn more about the return statement when I discuss functions in greater detail in Chapter 8.

The program will reach the subsequent checks in the loop if the guess is incorrect:

```
else if(guess < 1 || guess > 20)      // Check for an invalid guess
  printf("I said the number is between 1 and 20.\n ");
else
  printf("Sorry, %d is wrong. My number is %s than that.\n",
                    guess, chosen > guess ? "greater" : "less");
```

This group of statements first tests whether the value entered is within the prescribed limits. If it isn't, a message is displayed reiterating the limits. If it's a valid guess, a message is displayed to the effect that it's incorrect, and that gives a clue as to where the correct answer is.

The loop ends after three iterations and thus three guesses. The statement after the loop is the following:

```
printf("\nYou have had three tries and failed. The number was %d\n",
                                                        chosen);
```

This will be executed only if all three guesses were wrong. It displays an appropriate message, revealing the number to be guessed, and then the program ends.

The program is designed so that you can easily change the value of the variable chosen and have endless fun. Well, endless fun for a short while, anyway.

Generating Pseudo-random Integers

The previous example would have been much more entertaining if the number to be guessed could have been generated within the program so that it was different each time the program executed. Well, you can do that using the rand() function that's declared in the stdlib.h header file:

```
int chosen = 0;
chosen = rand();   // Set to a random integer
```

Each time you call the rand() function, it will return a random integer. The value will be from zero to a maximum of RAND_MAX, the value of which is defined in stdlib.h. The integers generated by the rand() function are described as *pseudo-random* numbers because truly random numbers can arise only in natural processes and can't be generated algorithmically.

The sequence of numbers that's generated by the rand() function uses a starting seed number, and for a given seed, the sequence will always be the same. If you use the function with the default seed value, as in the previous snippet, you'll always get exactly the same sequence, which won't make the game very challenging but is useful when you are testing a program. However, stdlib.h provides another standard function, srand(), which you can call to initialize the sequence with a particular seed that you pass as an argument to the function.

At first sight, this doesn't seem to get you much further with the guessing game, as you now need to generate a different seed each time the program executes. Yet another library function can help with this: the time() function that's declared in the time.h header file. The time() function returns the number of seconds that have elapsed since January 1, 1970, as an integer. (This is called an epoch that is commonly a representation of time in a 32-bit integer that starts counting from the mentioned date above. It is a de facto standard because it is not defined in the standard and follows POSIX specification.) Be aware these are seconds since 1970; so if you are trying to execute the same program at the same time, it will be necessary to handle micro- or nanoseconds in the seed. Otherwise, the sequence of pseudo-random numbers will be repeated (or use a different seed like PID), and because time always marches on, you get a different value returned by the time() function each time the program executes. The time() function requires an argument to be specified, which you'll specify here as NULL. NULL is a symbol that's defined in stdlib.h that represents a memory address that doesn't refer to anything. I'll discuss the use and significance of NULL further in Chapter 7.

Thus, to get a different sequence of pseudo-random numbers each time a program is run, you can use the following statements:

```
srand(time(NULL));              // Use clock value as starting seed
int chosen = 0;
chosen = rand();                // Set to a random integer 0 to RAND_MAX
```

You only need to call srand() once in a program to initialize the sequence. Each time you call rand() subsequently, you'll get another pseudo-random number. The value of the upper limit, RAND_MAX, is likely to be quite large—often the maximum value that can be stored as type int. When you need a more limited range of values, you can scale the value returned by rand() to provide values within the range you want. Suppose you want to obtain values in a range from zero up to, but not including, limit. The simplest approach to obtaining values in this range is like this:

```
srand(time(NULL));              // Use clock value as starting seed - time can be casted
                                // to (unsigned int) to avoid possible overflow
int limit = 20;                 // Upper limit for pseudo-random values
int chosen = 0;
chosen = rand() % limit;        // 0 to limit-1 inclusive
```

Of course, if you want numbers from 1 to limit, you can write this:

```
chosen = 1 + rand() % limit;    // 1 to limit  inclusive
```

This works reasonably well with the implementation of rand() in my compiler and library. However, this isn't a good way in general of limiting the range of numbers produced by a pseudo-random number generator. This is because you're essentially chopping off the high-order bits in the value that's returned and implicitly assuming that the bits that are left will also represent random values. This isn't necessarily the case.

You could try using rand() in a variation of the previous example:

```
// Program 4.7a A More Interesting Guessing Game
#define _CRT_SECURE_NO_WARNINGS
#include <stdio.h>
#include <stdlib.h>              // For rand() and srand()
#include <time.h>               // For time() function

int main(void)
{
  int chosen = 0;              // The lucky number
  int guess = 0;                 // Stores a guess
  int count = 3;                 // The maximum number of tries
  int limit = 20;              // Upper limit for pseudo-random values

  srand((unsigned int)time(NULL));       // Use clock value as starting seed
  chosen = 1 + rand() % limit;   // Random int 1 to limit

  printf("\nThis is a guessing game.");
  printf("\nI have chosen a number between 1 and 20"
                              " which you must guess.\n");

  for( ; count > 0 ; --count)
  {
    printf("\nYou have %d tr%s left.", count, count == 1 ? "y" : "ies");
    printf("\nEnter a guess: ");     // Prompt for a guess
    scanf("%d", &guess);             // Read in a guess

    // Check for a correct guess
    if(guess == chosen)
    {
      printf("\nCongratulations. You guessed it!\n");
      return 0;                      // End the program
    }
    else if(guess < 1 || guess > 20)       // Check for an invalid guess
      printf("I said the number is between 1 and 20.\n ");
    else
      printf("Sorry, %d is wrong. My number is %s than that.\n",
                      guess, chosen > guess ? "greater" : "less");
  }
  printf("\nYou have had three tries and failed. The number was %d\n",
                                              chosen);
  return 0;
}
```

This version of the program should give you a different number to guess most of the time.

More for Loop Control Options

You've seen how you can increment or decrement the loop counter by 1 using the ++ and -- operators. You can increment or decrement the loop counter by any amount that you wish. Here's an example of how you can do this:

```
long sum = 0L;
for(int n = 1 ; n < 20 ; n += 2)
  sum += n;
printf("Sum is %ld", sum);
```

The loop in the preceding code fragment sums all the odd integers from 1 to 20. The third control expression increments the loop variable n by 2 on each iteration. You can write any expression here, including any assignment. For instance, to sum every seventh integer from 1 to 1,000, you could write the following loop:

```
for(int n = 1 ; n < 1000 ; n = n + 7)
  sum += n;
```

Now the third loop control expression increments n by 7 at the end of each iteration, so you'll get the sum 1 + 8 + 15 + 22 +...up to 1,000.

You aren't limited to a single loop control expression. You could rewrite the loop in the first code fragment, summing the odd numbers from 1 to 20, like this:

```
for(int n = 1 ; n<20 ; sum += n, n += 2)
  ;
```

Now the third control expression consists of two expressions separated by a comma. These will execute in sequence at the end of each loop iteration. So first the expression sum += n will add the current value of n to sum. Next, the second expression n += 2 will increment n by 2. Because these expressions execute in sequence from left to right, you must write them in the sequence shown. If you reverse the sequence, the result will be incorrect.

You aren't limited to just two expressions either. You can have as many expressions here as you like, as long as they're separated by commas. Of course, you should make use of this only when there is a distinct advantage in doing so. Too much of this can make your code hard to understand. The first and second control expressions can also consist of several expressions separated by commas, but the need for this is quite rare.

Floating-Point Loop Control Variables

The loop control variable can also be a floating-point variable. Here's a loop to sum the fractions from 1/1 to 1/10:

```
double sum = 0.0;
for(double x = 1.0 ; x < 11 ; x += 1.0)
  sum += 1.0/x;
```

You'll find this sort of thing isn't required very often. It's important to remember that fractional values often don't have an exact representation in floating-point form, so it's unwise to rely on equality as the condition for ending a loop, for example:

```
for(double x = 0.0 ; x != 2.0 ; x+= 0.2)       // Indefinite loop!!!
  printf("\nx = %.2lf",x);
```

This loop is supposed to output the values of x from 0.0 to 2.0 in steps of 0.2, so there should be 11 lines of output. Because 0.2 doesn't have an exact representation as a binary floating-point value, x may never have the value 2.0. The loop will take over your computer and run indefinitely when this is the case (until you stop it; press Ctrl+C under Microsoft Windows).

Chars loop Control Variables

Float is not the only new data type that can be handled in a for loop; although there is a trick, we can use char to iterate in a for loop too. For C, char's are integers underneath. Thus, its use is straightforward.

For instance, this is an example to show the English alphabet:

```
//  Program 4.7b loop with char's
#include <stdio.h>
int main(void)
{
  char c;
  printf("\nPrinting out alphabet.\n");
  for (c = 'A'; c <= 'Z'; c++)
    printf("%c ", c);
  printf("\n");
  return 0;
}
```

■ **Note**   Your compiler converts decimal floating-point values to binary. Even though 0.2 has no exact representation in binary, it is still possible that the previous loop may end normally. This is because the precise binary value for 0.2 depends on the algorithm used to generate it.

The while Loop

Now that you've seen several examples of for loops, let's look at a different kind of loop: the while loop. With a while loop, the mechanism for repeating a set of statements allows execution to continue for as long as a specified logical expression evaluates to true. I could describe this in words as follows:

```
While this condition is true
   Keep on doing this
```

Alternatively, here's a particular example:

```
While you are hungry
   Eat sandwiches
```

This means that you ask yourself "Am I hungry?" before eating the next sandwich. If the answer is yes, then you eat a sandwich and then ask yourself "Am I still hungry?" You keep eating sandwiches until the answer is no, at which point you go on to do something else—drink some coffee maybe. One word of caution: Enacting a loop in this way yourself is probably best done in private.

The general syntax for the while loop is as follows:

```
while( expression )
  statement1;

statement2;
```

As always, statement1 and statement2 could each be a block of statements.

The logic of the while loop is shown in Figure 4-5.

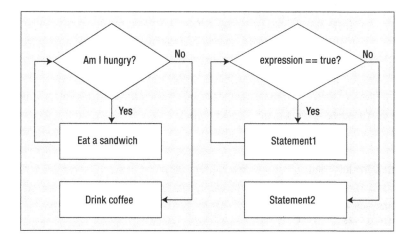

Figure 4-5. *The logic of the while loop*

Just like the for loop, the condition for continuation of the while loop is tested at the start, so if expression starts out false, none of the loop statements will be executed. If you answer the first question with "No, I'm not hungry," then you don't get to eat any sandwiches at all, and you move straight to the coffee. Clearly, if the loop condition starts out as true, the loop body must contain a mechanism for changing this if the loop is to end.

Be careful. A typical beginner error is that the expression of the while loop could be an assignment such as while (value = 1) instead of a correct comparison while (value == 1).

Using an assignment, the value always will be the number that is being set (this means true, unless we assign zero), and the while loop will become indefinite.

TRY IT OUT: USING THE WHILE LOOP

The while loop looks fairly straightforward, so let's go right into applying it in that old favorite, humming, and summing house numbers:

```
// Program 4.8 While programming and summing integers
#define _CRT_SECURE_NO_WARNINGS
#include <stdio.h>

int main(void)
{
  unsigned long sum = 0UL;          // The sum of the integers
  unsigned int i = 1;               // Indexes through the integers
  unsigned int count = 0;           // The count of integers to be summed

  // Get the count of the number of integers to sum
  printf("\nEnter the number of integers you want to sum: ");
  scanf(" %u", &count);

  // Sum the integers from 1 to count
  while(i <= count)
    sum += i++;

  printf("Total of the first %u numbers is %lu\n", count, sum);
  return 0;
}
```

Typical output from this program is the following:

```
Enter the number of integers you want to sum: 7
Total of the first 7 numbers is 28
```

How It Works

Well, really this works pretty much the same as when you used the for loop. The only aspect of this example worth discussing is the while loop:

```
while(i <= count)
  sum += i++;
```

The loop body contains a single statement that accumulates the total in sum. This continues to be executed with i values up to and including the value stored in count. Because you have the postfix increment operator here (the ++ comes after the variable), i is incremented *after* its value is used to compute sum on each iteration. What the statement really means is this:

```
sum += i;
i++;
```

So the value of sum isn't affected by the incremented value of i until the next loop iteration.

This example uses the increment operator as postfix. How could you change the preceding program to use the prefix form of the ++ operator? Have a try and see whether you can work it out before looking at the answer in the next section.

The obvious bit of code that will change will be the `while` loop:

```
sum += ++i;
```

Try just changing this statement in Program 4.8. If you run the program now, you get the wrong answer:

```
Enter the number of integers you want to sum: 3
Total of the first 3 numbers is 9
```

This is because the `++` operator is adding 1 to the value of `i` before it stores the value in `sum`. The variable `i` starts at 1 and is increased to 2 on the first iteration, whereupon that value is added to `sum`.

To make the first loop iteration work correctly, you need to start with `i` as 0. This means that the first increment would set the value of `i` to 1, which is what you want. So you must change the definition of `i` to the following:

```
unsigned int i = 0;
```

However, the program still doesn't work properly because it continues the calculation until the value in `i` is greater than `count`, so you get one more iteration than you need. To fix this, you must change the control expression so that the loop continues while `i` is less than but not equal to `count`:

```
while(i < count)
```

Now the program will produce the correct answer. This example should help you understand better the effects of postfixing and prefixing these operators.

Nested Loops

Sometimes you may want to place one loop inside another. You might want to count the number of occupants in each house on a street. You step from house to house, and for each house you count the number of occupants. Going through all the houses could be an outer loop, and for each iteration of the outer loop, you would have an inner loop that counts the occupants.

The simplest way to understand how a nested loop works is to look at a simple example. Program 4.2 outputs a box with a fixed height and width. Suppose you wanted to generalize this example so it would output a box of any given width and height. The first step would be to define variables that specify the number of characters for the width and the height:

```
unsigned int width = 0;
unsigned int height = 0;
```

A width or height less than 3 is not acceptable because the box would have no interior. You can define a variable representing a minimum dimension value for the box:

```
const unsigned int MIN_SIZE = 3;        // Minimum width and height values
```

You could read in the width and height next:

```
printf("Enter values for the width and height (minimum of %u):", MIN_SIZE);
scanf("%u%u", &width, &height);
```

In spite of the message, you would probably want to verify that the values entered are at least the minimum:

```
if(width < MIN_SIZE)
{
  printf("\nWidth value of %u is too small. Setting it to %u.", width, MIN_SIZE);
  width = MIN_SIZE;
}
if(height < MIN_SIZE)
{
  printf("\nHeight value of %d is too small. Setting it to %u.", height, MIN_SIZE);
  height = MIN_SIZE;
}
```

Finally, you could draw the box with the given height and width:

```
// Output the top of the box with width asterisks
for(unsigned int i = 0 ; i < width ; ++i)
  printf("*");

// Output height-2 rows of width characters with * at each end and spaces inside
for(unsigned int j = 0 ; j < height - 2 ; ++j)
{
  printf("\n*");                             // First asterisk

  // Next draw the spaces
  for(unsigned int i = 0 ; i < width - 2 ; ++i)
    printf(" ");

  printf("*");                               // Last asterisk
}

// Output the bottom of the box
printf("\n");                                // Start on newline
for(unsigned int i = 0 ; i < width ; ++i)
  printf("*");

printf("\n");                                // Newline at end of last line
```

You can assemble this into a complete example.

TRY IT OUT: USING NESTED LOOPS

Here's the complete program:

```c
// Program 4.9 Output a box with given width and height
#define _CRT_SECURE_NO_WARNINGS
#include <stdio.h>

int main(void)
{
  const unsigned int MIN_SIZE = 3;          // Minimum width and height values
  unsigned int width = 0;
  unsigned int height = 0;

  // Read in required width and height
  printf("Enter values for the width and height (minimum of %u):", MIN_SIZE);
  scanf("%u%u", &width, &height);

  // Validate width and height values
  if(width < MIN_SIZE)
  {
    printf("\nWidth value of %u is too small. Setting it to %u.", width, MIN_SIZE);
    width = MIN_SIZE;
  }
  if(height < MIN_SIZE)
  {
    printf("\nHeight value of %u is too small. Setting it to %u.", height, MIN_SIZE);
    height = MIN_SIZE;
  }
  printf("\n");
  // Output the top of the box with width asterisks
  for(unsigned int i = 0 ; i < width ; ++i)
    printf("*");

  // Output height-2 rows of width characters with * at each end and spaces inside
  for(unsigned int j = 0 ; j < height - 2 ; ++j)
  {
    printf("\n*");                           // First asterisk

    // Next draw the spaces
    for(unsigned int i = 0 ; i < width - 2 ; ++i)
      printf(" ");

    printf("*");                             // Last asterisk

  }
  // Output the bottom of the box
  printf("\n");                              // Start on newline
  for(unsigned int i = 0 ; i < width ; ++i)
    printf("*");

  printf("\n");                              // Newline at end of last line
  return 0;
}
```

Here is some sample output:

```
Enter values for the width and height (minimum of 3): 24 7
************************
*                      *
*                      *
*                      *
*                      *
*                      *
************************
```

How It Works

The top and bottom of the box are created by simple identical loops. The number of iterations is the number of asterisks in each line. You generate the interior rows of output in a nested loop. The outer loop with the control variable j repeats height - 2 times. There are height rows in the box, so you subtract 2 for the top and bottom rows, which are created outside this loop. The inner loop with the control variable i outputs width - 2 spaces after a newline followed by an asterisk, which is written to the output. When the inner loop ends, another asterisk is written to the output to complete the line. Thus, a newline, followed by a complete execution of the inner loop, followed by another newline, occurs for every iteration of the outer loop. We can try a nested loop performing some calculations next.

TRY IT OUT: ARITHMETIC IN A NESTED LOOP

This example is based on the summing integers program. Originally, you produced the sum of all the integers from 1 up to the value entered. Now for every house, you'll produce the sum of all the numbers from the first house, 1, up to the current house. If you look at the program output, it will become clearer:

```c
// Program 4.10 Sums of successive integer sequences
#define _CRT_SECURE_NO_WARNINGS
#include <stdio.h>

int main(void)
{
  unsigned long sum = 0UL;              // Stores the sum of integers
  unsigned int count = 0;               // Number of sums to be calculated

  // Prompt for, and read the input count
  printf("\nEnter the number of integers you want to sum: ");
  scanf(" %u", &count);

  for(unsigned int i = 1 ; i <= count ; ++i)
  {
    sum = 0UL;                          // Initialize sum for the inner loop

    // Calculate sum of integers from 1 to i
    for(unsigned int j = 1 ; j <= i ; ++j)
      sum += j;
```

```
    printf("\n%u\t%5lu", i, sum);        // Output sum of 1 to i
  }
  printf("\n");
  return 0;
}
```

You should see some output like this:

```
Enter the number of integers you want to sum: 5

1    1
2    3
3    6
4    10
5    15
```

As you can see, if you enter **5**, the program calculates the sums of the integers from 1 to 1, from 1 to 2, from 1 to 3, from 1 to 4, and from 1 to 5.

How It Works

The program calculates the sum of the integers from 1 up to each value, for all values from 1 up to the value of count that you enter. The inner loop completes all its iterations for each iteration of the outer loop. Thus, the outer loop sets up the value of i that determines how many times the inner loop will repeat:

```
  for(unsigned int i = 1 ; i <= count ; ++i)
  {
    sum = 0UL;                          // Initialize sum for the inner loop

    // Calculate sum of integers from 1 to i
    for(unsigned int j = 1 ; j <= i ; ++j)
      sum += j;

    printf("\n%u\t%5lu", i, sum);       // Output sum of 1 to i
  }
```

The outer loop starts off by initializing i to 1, and the loop is repeated for successive values of i up to count. For each iteration of the outer loop, and therefore for each value of i, sum is initialized to 0, the inner loop is executed, and the result is displayed by the printf() statement. The inner loop accumulates the sum of all the integers from 1 to the current value of i.

Each time the inner loop finishes, the printf() to output the value of sum is executed. Control then goes back to the beginning of the outer loop for the next iteration.

You use variables of unsigned integer types throughout because none of the values can be negative. It would still work with signed integer types, but using unsigned type ensures that a negative value cannot be stored and also provides for values of greater magnitude.

Look at the output again to see the action of the nested loop. The first loop simply sets sum to 0 each time around, and the inner loop accumulates all the integers from 1 to the current value of i. You could modify the nested loop to use a while loop for the inner loop and to produce output that would show what the program is doing a little more explicitly.

TRY IT OUT: NESTING A WHILE LOOP WITHIN A FOR LOOP

In the previous two examples, you nested a for loop inside a for loop. In this example, you'll nest a while loop inside a for loop:

```c
// Program 4.11 Sums of integers with a while loop nested in a for loop
#define _CRT_SECURE_NO_WARNINGS
#include <stdio.h>

int main(void)
{
  unsigned long sum = 1UL;        // Stores the sum of integers
  unsigned int j = 1U;            // Inner loop control variable
  unsigned int count = 0;         // Number of sums to be calculated

  // Prompt for, and read the input count
  printf("\nEnter the number of integers you want to sum: ");
  scanf(" %u", &count);

  for(unsigned int i = 1 ; i <= count ; ++i)
  {
    sum = 1UL;                    // Initialize sum for the inner loop
    j=1;                          // Initialize integer to be added
    printf("\n1");

    // Calculate sum of integers from 1 to i
    while(j < i)
    {
      sum += ++j;
      printf(" + %u", j);         // Output +j - on the same line
    }
    printf(" = %lu", sum);        // Output  = sum
  }
  printf("\n");
  return 0;
}
```

This program produces the following output:

```
Enter the number of integers you want to sum: 5

1 = 1
1 + 2 = 3
1 + 2 + 3 = 6
1 + 2 + 3 + 4 = 10
1 + 2 + 3 + 4 + 5 = 15
```

How It Works

The differences are inside the outer loop. The outer loop control is exactly the same as before. What occurs during each iteration has been changed. The variable sum is initialized to 1 within the outer loop, because the while loop will add integers to sum starting with 2. The value to be added is stored in j, which is also initialized to 1. The first printf() in the outer loop just outputs a newline character followed by 1, the first integer in the set to be summed. The inner loop adds the integers from 2 up to the value of i. For each integer value in j that's added to sum, the printf() in the inner loop outputs + j on the same line as the initial value, 1. Thus, the inner loop will output + 2, then + 3, and so on for as long as j is less than i. Of course, for the first iteration of the outer loop, i is 1, so the inner loop will not execute at all, because j < i (1 < 1) is false from the beginning.

When the inner loop ends, the last printf() statement is executed. This outputs an equal sign followed by the value of sum. Control then returns to the beginning of the outer loop for the next iteration.

Nested Loops and the goto Statement

You've learned how you can nest one loop inside another, but it doesn't end there. You can nest as many loops one inside another as you want, for instance:

```
for(int i = 0 ; i < 10 ; ++i)
{
  for(int j = 0 ; j < 20 ; ++j)          // Loop executed 10 times
  {
    for(int k = 0 ; k < 30 ; ++k)        // Loop executed 10x20 times
    {                                    // Loop body executed 10x20x30 times
      /* Do something useful */
    }
  }
}
```

The inner loop controlled by j will execute once for each iteration of the outer loop that is controlled by i. The innermost loop controlled by k will execute once for each iteration of the loop controlled by j. Thus, the body of the innermost loop will be executed 6,000 times.

Occasionally with deeply nested loops like this, you'll want to break out of all the nested loops from the innermost loop and then continue with the statement following the outermost loop. A break statement in the innermost loop will only break out of that loop, and execution will continue with the loop controlled by j. To escape the nested loops completely using break statements therefore requires quite complicated logic to break out of each level until you escape the outermost loop. This is one situation in which the goto statement can be very useful because it provides a way to avoid all the complicated logic, for example:

```
for(int i = 0 ; i < 10 ; ++i)
{
  for(int j = 0 ; j < 20 ; ++j)          // Loop executed 10 times
  {
    for(int k = 0 ; k < 30 ; ++k)        // Loop executed 10x20 times
    {                                    // Loop body executed 10x20x30 times
      /* Do something useful */
```

```
        if(must_escape)
          goto out;
     }
   }
}
out: /*Statement following the nested loops */
```

This fragment presumes that must_escape can be altered within the innermost loop to signal that the whole nested loop should end. If the variable must_escape is true, you execute the goto statement to branch directly to the statement with the label out. So you have a direct exit from the complete nest of loops without any complicated decision making in the outer loop levels.

As we declared in the last chapter, the goto statement is a very "dangerous" statement that will create a spaghetti code that highly probably will finish in problems; please use goto with moderation.

The do-while Loop

The third type of loop is the do-while loop. You may be wondering why you need this when you already have the for loop and the while loop. There's a subtle difference between the do-while loop and the other two. The test for whether the loop should continue is at the *end* of the loop, so the loop statement or statement block always executes at least once. The while loop and the for loop test at the beginning of the loop, so the body of the loop won't execute at all when the condition is false at the outset. Look at this fragment of code:

```
int number = 4;

while(number < 4)
{
  printf("\nNumber = %d", number);
  number++;
}
```

Here, you would never output anything. The control expression number < 4 is false from the start, so the loop block is never executed.

You can see how the do-while loop differs if you replace the preceding while loop with a do-while loop and leave the body of the loop the same:

```
int number = 4;

do
{
  printf("\nNumber = %d", number);
  number++;
}
while(number < 4);
```

Now when you execute this loop, you get Number = 4 displayed. This is because the expression number < 4 is checked after the loop body executes.

The general representation of the do-while loop is

```
do
{
  /* Statements for the loop body */
}
while(expression);
```

If the loop body is just one statement, you can omit the braces. Notice the semicolon after the parentheses in a do-while loop. There isn't one in the while loop. In a do-while loop, if the value of expression is true (nonzero), the loop continues. The loop will exit only when the value of expression becomes false (zero). You can see how this works more clearly in Figure 4-6.

Here, you can see that you eat a sandwich *before* you check whether you're hungry. You'll always eat at least one sandwich, so this loop is not to be used as part of a calorie-controlled diet!

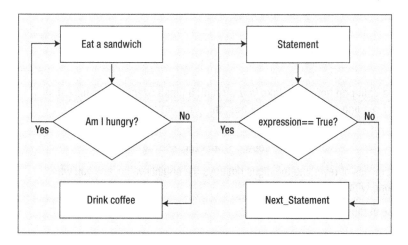

Figure 4-6. *Operation of the do-while loop*

TRY IT OUT: USING A DO-WHILE LOOP

You can try out the do-while loop with a little program that reverses the digits of a positive number:

```
// Program 4.12 Reversing the digits
#define _CRT_SECURE_NO_WARNINGS
#include <stdio.h>

int main(void)
{
  unsigned int number = 0;            // The number to be reversed
  unsigned int rebmun = 0;            // The reversed number
  unsigned int temp = 0;              // Working storage

  // Read in the value to be reversed
  printf("\nEnter a positive integer: ");
  scanf(" %u", &number);

  temp = number;                      // Copy to working storage
```

```
  // Reverse the number stored in temp
  do
  {
    rebmun = 10*rebmun + temp % 10;      // Add rightmost digit of temp to rebmun
    temp = temp/10;                       // and remove it from temp
  } while(temp);                          // Continue as long as temp is not 0
  printf("\nThe number %u reversed is  %u rebmun ehT\n", number, rebmun );
  return 0;
}
```

The following is a sample of output from this program:

```
Enter a positive integer: 234567

The number 234567 reversed is 765432 rebmun ehT
```

How It Works

The best way to explain what's going on here is to take you through a small example. Assume that 43 is entered by the user. After reading this value into number, the program copies the value in number to temp:

```
  temp = number;                          // Copy to working storage
```

This is necessary because the process of reversing the digits destroys the original value, and you want to output the original integer along with the reversed version.

The reversal of the digits is done in the do-while loop:

```
  do
  {
    rebmun = 10*rebmun + temp % 10;      // Add rightmost digit of temp to rebmun
    temp = temp/10;                       // and remove it from temp
  } while(temp);                          // Continue as long as temp is not 0
```

The do-while loop is most appropriate here because any positive number will have at least one digit. You get the rightmost decimal digit from the value stored in temp using the modulus operator, %, to obtain the remainder after dividing by 10. Because temp originally contains 43, temp%10 will be 3. You assign the value of the expression 10*rebmun + temp%10 to rebmun. Initially, the value of rebmun is 0, so on the first iteration, 3 is stored in rebmun.

You've now stored the rightmost digit of the input in rebmun so you remove this digit from temp by dividing temp by 10. Because temp contains 43, temp/10 will be 4.

At the end of the loop, the condition is checked, which is just the value of temp. Because temp contains the value 4, the condition is true and another iteration begins.

■ **Note** Remember, any nonzero integer will convert to true. The Boolean value false corresponds to zero.

This time, the value stored in `rebmun` will be 10 times `rebmun`, which is 30, plus the remainder when `temp` is divided by 10, which is 4, so the result is that `rebmun` becomes 34. You again divide `temp` by 10, so it will contain 0. Now `temp` is 0 at the end of the loop iteration, which is `false`, so the loop finishes and you have reversed the digits from `number`. You should be able to see that this works just as well with values with more decimal digits.

This form of loop is used relatively rarely, compared with the other two forms. Keep it in the back of your mind, though; when you need a loop that always executes at least once, the `do-while` loop delivers the goods.

The continue Statement

Sometimes a situation arises where you don't want to end a loop, but you want to skip the current iteration and continue with the next. The `continue` statement in the body of a loop does this and is written as

```
continue;
```

Of course, `continue` is a keyword, so you must not use it for other purposes. Here's an example of how the `continue` statement works:

```
enum Day { Monday, Tuesday, Wednesday, Thursday, Friday, Saturday, Sunday};
for(enum Day day = Monday; day <= Sunday ; ++day)
{
  if(day == Wednesday)
    continue;

  printf("It's not Wednesday!\n");
  /* Do something useful with day */
}
```

I used an enumeration here to remind you that it is an integer type and you can use a variable of an `enum` type to control for a loop. This loop will execute with values of day from Monday to Sunday (which will correspond to 0–6 by default). When day has the value `Wednesday`, however, the `continue` statement will execute and the rest of the current iteration is skipped. The loop continues with the next iteration when day will be `Thursday`.

You'll see more examples that use the `continue` statement later in the book.

Designing a Program

It's time to try your skills on a bigger programming problem and to apply some of what you've learned so far. I'll introduce a few more standard library functions that you're sure to find useful.

The Problem

The problem that you're going to solve is to write a program to play a game of Simple Simon. Simple Simon is a memory test game. In this game, the computer displays a sequence of digits on the screen for a short period of time. You then have to memorize them, and when the digits disappear from the screen, you must enter exactly the same sequence of digits. Each time you succeed, the process repeats with a longer sequence of digits for you to try. The objective is to continue the process for as long as possible.

The Analysis

The logic of the program is quite straightforward. The program must generate a sequence of integers between 0 and 9 and display the sequence on the screen for one second before erasing it. The program should then read the player's pathetic attempt to enter the identical sequence of digits. If the player is lucky enough to get the sequence correct, the computer should repeat with another sequence of the same length. If the player's luck holds out for three successive sequences of a given length, the program should continue by displaying a longer sequence for the player to try. This continues until the player's luck runs out and they get a sequence wrong. The program will then calculate a score based on the number of successful tries and the time taken and invite the player to play again.

You could express the program logic in general terms in the flow chart shown in Figure 4-7.

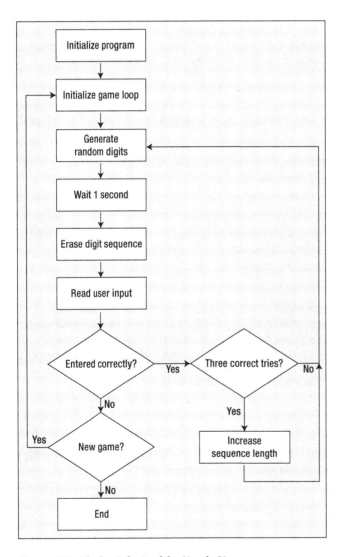

Figure 4-7. *The basic logic of the Simple Simon program*

Each box describes an action in the program, and the diamond shapes represent decisions. It's reasonable to assume that at least one game will be played so the check for a new game is at the end of the game loop. Three successful sequence entries trigger an increase in the length of the next sequence. Entering an incorrect sequence ends the game. Let's use the flow chart as the basis for coding the program.

The Solution

This section outlines the steps you'll take to solve the problem. In the context of this program, I'll introduce some additional aspects to managing input from the keyboard. I'll also explain how you can time operations within a program.

Step 1

You can start identifying the basic functional blocks of code, including the main loop for the game. The loop check should go at the end of the loop so the do-while loop fits the bill very nicely. The initial program code will be this:

```
// Program 4.13 Simple Simon
#define _CRT_SECURE_NO_WARNINGS
#include <stdio.h>                    // For input and output
#include <ctype.h>                    // For toupper() function

int main(void)
{

  char another_game = 'Y';           // Records if another game is to be played
  const unsigned int DELAY = 1;      // Display period in seconds

  /* More variable declarations for the program */

  // Describe how the game is played
  printf("\nTo play Simple Simon, ");
  printf("watch the screen for a sequence of digits.");
  printf("\nWatch carefully, as the digits are only displayed"
                          " for %u second%s ", DELAY, DELAY > 1 ? "s!" :"!");
  printf("\nThe computer will remove them, and then prompt you ");
  printf("to enter the same sequence.");
  printf("\nWhen you do, you must put spaces between the digits.\n");
  printf("\nGood Luck!\nPress Enter to play\n");
  scanf("%c", &another_game);

  // Game loop - one outer loop iteration is a complete game
  do
  {
    /* Initialize a game                          */

    /* Inner loop to play the game                */

    /* Output the score when a game is finished */
```

```
  // Check if a new game is required
  printf("\nDo you want to play again (y/n)? ");
  scanf("%c", &another_game);
} while(toupper(another_game) == 'Y');

return 0;
}
```

The another_game variable that you define at the beginning of main() controls whether or not another game is started when the current game finishes. A character is read from the keyboard at the end of the main game loop into this variable, and its value is checked in the loop condition. If y or Y is entered, the loop continues for another game. Otherwise, the program ends. By converting another_game to uppercase, you avoid having to check for either y or Y.

The DELAY variable is a fixed integer value that specifies the number of seconds the digit sequence will be displayed before it is erased. You'll use this to control how long the program waits before erasing a sequence of digits. It is 1 here, but you can increase this to make the game easier.

The first block of code consists of printf() function calls that output an explanation of how the game is played. Note how you automatically concatenate two strings in this printf() statement:

```
printf("\nWatch carefully, as the digits are only displayed"
                     " for %u second%s ", DELAY, DELAY > 1 ? "s!" :"!");
```

This is a convenient way of splitting a long string over two or more lines. You just put each piece of the string between its own pair of double quote characters, and the compiler takes care of assembling them into a single string. This statement also uses the conditional operator to append "s!" to the output instead of "!" when DELAY is more than 1 second.

Step 2

Next, you can add a declaration for another variable with the name correct that you'll use to record whether or not the entry from the player is correct. You'll use this variable to control the inner loop that plays a single game:

```
// Program 4.13 Simple Simon
#define _CRT_SECURE_NO_WARNINGS
#include <stdio.h>                  // For input and output
#include <ctype.h>                  // For toupper() function
#include <stdbool.h>                // For bool, true, false

int main(void)
{
  char another_game = 'Y';          // Records if another game is to be played
  const unsigned int DELAY = 1;     // Display period in seconds
  bool correct = true;              // true for correct sequence, false otherwise

  /* Rest of the declarations for the program */

  // statements describing how the game is played as before ...
```

```
// Game loop - one outer loop iteration is a complete game
do
{
  correct = true;                    // Indicates correct sequence entered

  /* Other code to initialize the game */

  // Inner loop continues as long as sequences are entered correctly
  while(correct)
  {
    /* Statements to play the game    */
  }

  /* Output the score when the game is finished */

  // Check if new game required
  printf("\nDo you want to play again (y/n)? ");
  scanf("%c", &another_game);
} while(toupper(another_game) == 'Y');
  return 0;
}
```

You are using the _Bool variable correct here. Because you have added an #include directive for the stdbool.h header, you can use bool as the type name. The stdbool.h header also defines the symbols true and false to correspond to 1 and 0, respectively. The while loop continues as long as correct has the value true. You will set it to false when the player enters a sequence incorrectly.

■ **Caution**   The code will compile as it is, and you should compile it to check it out, but you should not run it yet. If you run this as it is, program execution will never end because it contains an indefinite loop—the inner while loop. The condition for this loop is always true because the loop doesn't change the value of correct. However, you'll be adding that bit of the program shortly.

As you develop a program, it's a good approach to make sure that the code will at least compile at each step. If you write all the code in one attempt, you are likely to end up with larger numbers of errors to correct, and as you correct one problem, more may appear. This can be very frustrating. If you develop and check out the code incrementally, the errors will be easier to identify and development will be faster. This brings me back to our current program.

Step 3

You have a slightly trickier task next: generating the sequence of random digits. There are two problems to be solved. The first is how you generate the sequence of random digits. The second is how you check the player's input against the computer-generated sequence.

The digits in the sequence that you generate have to be random. You'll use the functions rand(), srand(), and time(), which you used earlier in this chapter, to do this. These require the standard library headers stdlib.h and time.h to be included in the source file. You can get a random digit by using the % operator to obtain the remainder after dividing the integer that rand() returns by 10.

You call the srand() function with a seed value produced by the time() function as the argument to initialize the sequence of values produce by rand(). By passing the value returned by time() to srand(), you ensure that the sequence produced by rand() will be different each time.

The time() function accepts the address of a variable as an argument in which the time value is to be stored, and it also returns the same value. If you store the return value, you may not want to supply the address of a variable as the argument. In this case, you specify the argument as NULL, which is an address that doesn't refer to anything. In the game program, you will pass the address of a variable to time() in which the time value will be stored as well as make use of the value returned.

Now let's consider how creating and checking the sequence is going to work. You'll need a given sequence of random digits twice: first to output it for a limited time and second to check the player's input against it. You could consider saving the sequence of digits as an integer value. The problem with this is that the sequence could get very long if the player is good, and it could exceed the upper limit for the digits in integer values of type unsigned long long. Ideally the program should allow sequences to be of unlimited length. There is a simple approach you can adopt that will allow this.

The sequence of integers that the rand() function produces is determined by the seed value. Each time you pass a given seed value to srand(), rand() will return the same sequence of integers. If you store the seed value you use when you call srand() to initialize the sequence that you output, you can use this a second time to reinitialize the sequence when you are checking the user's input. Calls to rand() will then generate the same sequence again.

You can add code to the program to generate the sequence of random digits and check them against what the player enters:

```
// Program 4.13 Simple Simon
#define _CRT_SECURE_NO_WARNINGS
#include <stdio.h>                    // For input and output
#include <ctype.h>                    // For toupper() function
#include <stdbool.h>                  // For bool, true, false
#include <stdlib.h>                   // For rand() and srand()
#include <time.h>                     // For time() function

int main(void)
{
  char another_game = 'Y';          // Records if another game is to be played
  const unsigned int DELAY = 1;     // Display period in seconds
  bool correct = true;              // true for correct sequence, false otherwise
  unsigned int tries = 0;           // Number of successful entries for sequence length
  unsigned int digits = 0;          // Number of digits in a sequence
  time_t seed = 0;                  // Seed value for random number sequence
  unsigned int number = 0;          // Stores an input digit

  /* Rest of the declarations for the program */

  // statements describing how the game is played as before ...

  // Game loop - one outer loop iteration is a complete game
  do
  {
    // Initialize game
    correct = true;                 // Indicates correct sequence entered
    tries = 0;                      // Initialize count of successful tries
    digits = 2;                     // Initial length of digit sequence
```

```
/* Other code to initialize the game        */

// Inner loop continues as long as sequences are entered correctly
while(correct)
{
  ++tries;                            // A new attempt

  // Generate a sequence of digits and display them
  srand((unsigned int)time(&seed));              // Initialize the random sequence
  for(unsigned int i = 1 ; i <= digits ; ++i)
    printf("%d ", rand() % 10);      // Output a random digit

  /* Code to wait one second               */

  /* Code to overwrite the digit sequence */

  /* Code to prompt for the input sequence */

  srand((unsigned int)seed);                      // Reinitialize the random sequence
  for(unsigned int i = 1; i <= digits; ++i)
  // Read the input sequence & check against the original
  {
    scanf("%u", &number);           // Read a digit
    if(number != rand() % 10)       // Compare with generated digit
    {
      correct = false;              // Incorrect entry
      break;                        // No need to check further...
    }
  }

  // On every third successful try, increase the sequence length
  if(correct && ((tries % 3) == 0))
    ++digits;

  printf("%s\n", correct ? "Correct!" : "Wrong!");
}

/* Output the score when the game is finished */

// Check if new game required
printf("\nDo you want to play again (y/n)? ");
scanf("%c", &another_game);
} while(toupper(another_game) == 'Y');
return 0;
}
```

You've declared four new variables that you need to implement the inner while loop that continues to execute as long as the player is successful. Each loop iteration displays a sequence of digits that the player must memorize and enter when it is no longer shown: tries records the number of times that the player is successful, and digits records the current length of the sequence of digits. Although you initialize these variables when you declare them, you must also initialize them in the do-while loop before the nested while loop to ensure that the correct initial conditions are set for each game. You declare a variable, seed, of type time_t, that you use to record the value produced by the time() function. You'll use this to initialize the random number sequence returned by the function rand(). The value for seed is set in the while loop by passing its address to the standard library function time(). The same seed value is returned by the time() function, and you use this as the argument to the first call of srand() to initialize the random sequence from which you obtain the digits for display.

At the beginning of the while loop, you increase the value stored in tries because a new attempt occurs on each loop iteration. At the end of the loop, you increment digits each time three correct attempts have been entered.

You obtain a digit between 0 and 9 by taking the remainder after dividing the random integer returned by rand() by 10. This isn't the best method for obtaining random digits, but it's a very easy way and is adequate for our purposes. Although the numbers that rand() generates are randomly distributed, the low-order decimal digit for numbers in the sequence is not necessarily random. To get properly random digits, you should be dividing the entire range of values produced by rand() into ten segments and associating a different decimal digit with each segment. The digit corresponding to a given pseudo-random number is then selected based on the segment in which the number lies.

The sequence of digits is displayed by the for loop. The loop just outputs the low-order decimal digit of the value returned by rand(). You then have some comments indicating the other code that you still have to add that will delay the program for 1 second and then erase the sequence from the screen. This is followed by the code to check the sequence that was entered by the player. This reinitializes the random number–generating process by calling srand() with the seed value that you stored in seed. Each digit that is entered is compared with the low-order digit of the value returned by rand(). If there's a discrepancy, the player got it wrong so you set correct to false and execute a break statement, which will cause the for loop to end. When the value of correct is false, the outer while loop will also end.

Of course, if you try to run this code as it is, the sequence won't be erased, so it isn't usable yet. The next step is to add the code to the while loop that will erase the sequence.

Step 4

You must erase the sequence after waiting DELAY seconds. How can you get the program to wait? One way is to use another standard library function. The clock() function in the time.h header returns the time since the program started, in units of *clock ticks*, where the duration of a clock tick depends on your processor. The time.h header file defines a symbol CLOCKS_PER_SEC that corresponds to the number of clock ticks in one second, so you can use this to convert from clock ticks to seconds. If you cause the program to wait until the value returned by clock() has increased by DELAY*CLOCKS_PER_SEC, then DELAY seconds will have passed. You can cause the program to wait by storing the value returned by the function clock() and then checking in a loop for when the value returned by clock() is DELAY*CLOCKS_PER_SEC more than the value that you saved. With a variable wait_start to store the current time, the code for the loop would be as follows:

```
for( ;clock() - wait_start < DELAY*CLOCKS_PER_SEC; );      // Wait DELAY seconds
```

This loop executes repeatedly until the condition is false, whereupon the program will continue.

You need to erase the sequence of computer-generated digits next. This is actually quite easy. You can move the command-line cursor to the beginning of the current output line by outputting the escape character '\r', which is a carriage return. You can then output a sufficient number of spaces to overwrite the sequence of digits. Let's fill out the code you need in the while loop:

```
// Program 4.13 Simple Simon
// include directives as before...
```

```
int main(void)
{
  // Variable definitions as before...

  time_t wait_start = 0;                    // Stores current time

  /* Rest of the declarations for the program */

  // statements describing how the game is played as before ...

  // Game loop - one outer loop iteration is a complete game
  do
  {
    correct = true;              // Indicates correct sequence entered
    tries = 0;                   // Initialize count of successful tries
    digits = 2;                  // Initial length of digit sequence

    /* Other code to initialize the game      */

    // Inner loop continues as long as sequences are entered correctly
    while(correct)
    {
      ++tries;                   // A new attempt
      wait_start = clock();      // record start time for sequence

      // Code to generate a sequence of digits and display them as before...

      for( ; clock() - wait_start < DELAY*CLOCKS_PER_SEC ; );  // Wait DELAY seconds

      // Now overwrite the digit sequence
      printf("\r");                    // Go to beginning of the line
      for(unsigned int i = 1 ; i <= digits ; ++i)
        printf("  ");                  // Output two spaces

      if(tries == 1)                   // Only output message for 1st try
        printf("\nNow you enter the sequence  - don't forget"
                                       " the spaces\n");
      else
        printf("\r");                  // Back to the beginning of the line

      // Code to check the digits entered as before...

      // Code to update digits and display a message as before...
    }

    /* Output the score when the game is finished */
```

```
    // Check if new game required
    printf("\nDo you want to play again (y/n)? ");
    scanf("%c", &another_game);
  } while(toupper(another_game) == 'Y');
  return 0;
}
```

You record the time that `clock()` returns before you output the sequence. The `for` loop that's executed after the sequence has been displayed and continues until the value returned by `clock()` exceeds the time recorded in `wait_start` by `DELAY*CLOCKS_PER_SEC`.

Because you did not output a newline character when you displayed the sequence, the same output line is still current. You can move the cursor back to the start of the current line by executing a carriage return without a linefeed; outputting `"\r"` does just that. You then output two spaces for each digit that was displayed, thus overwriting each of them. You then output a prompt for the player to enter the sequence that was displayed. You output this message only once; otherwise, it gets rather tedious. On subsequent tries, you just back up to the beginning of the now blank line, ready for the user's input.

Step 5

You need to generate a score at the end of a game, which will be given when the player gets a sequence wrong. Ideally the score should be a number of points that reflects the length of the longest sequence entered successfully as well as how fast the game was played. You'll need four more variables in `main()` for this:

```
clock_t start_time = 0;          // Game start time in clock ticks
unsigned int score = 0;          // Game score
unsigned int total_digits = 0;   // Total of digits entered in a game
unsigned int game_time = 0;      // Game time in seconds
```

As a starting point for the score, you could arbitrarily award ten points for each digit in the longest sequence that was entered correctly:

```
score = 10*(digits - (tries % 3 == 1));
```

The `digits` value is the length of the current sequence. If the player failed on the first attempt at a sequence of `digits` length, the value in `digits` is 1 too many for scoring purposes. On the first try for a sequence of a given length, `tries` will have a value of the form `3*n+1` because three tries are necessary at each sequence length. Thus, the expression (`tries % 3 == 1`) will be 1 (true) when the player fails at the first try for a sequence of a given length, so the effect in the statement is to reduce the `digits` value by 1 when this is the case.

To work out the points scored for a faster time, you need to define a standard time for entry of a digit and find out how long the game took. You can allow 1 second as the standard time to enter a digit. You can award a further ten points for each second less than the standard that the player needed to enter all the digits in a complete game. To calculate this, you must figure out how many digits were entered. You can start by calculating the number of digits entered for the sequence length when the player failed.

If the player fails on the last attempt of the set of three for a given length, `tries` will be a multiple of 3. In this case, `3*digits` is the number of digits entered. If `tries` is not a multiple of 3, then the digit count is the value of `digits` multiplied by the remainder after dividing `tries` by 3. Thus, the number of digits entered for all attempts at the current length is produced by this statement: total_digits = digits*((tries % 3 == 0) ? 3 : tries % 3);

You now need to work out the number of digits entered for all sequence lengths less than the current length. These sequences have lengths from 2 to digits-1, and there must have been three successful tries at each length.

The sum of the integers from 1 to n is given by the formula $\frac{1}{2}n(n+1)$. You can obtain the count of all digits entered for sequences prior to the current length as three times the sum of the integers from 2 to digits-1. You can get this value by using the formula to sum the digits from 1 to digits-1 and then subtracting 1 from the result. Finally, you need to multiply by 3 because there are three tries at each length. Thus, you can increment total_digits to include this with the following if statement:

```
if(digits > 2)
  total_digits += 3*((digits - 1)*(digits)/2 - 1);
```

The value in total_digits is also the number of seconds required as standard for all the input because each digit is allowed 1 second. You must get the actual time for digit entry and compare it to this. You recorded the time when the game started in start_time as a number of clock ticks. The overall elapsed time for the game in seconds will therefore be (clock() - start_time)/CLOCKS_PER_SEC. Each sequence is displayed for DELAY seconds, so to be fair to the player, you must subtract the total delay time for all sequences. This will be tries*DELAY.

The final value of score can be calculated like this:

```
game_time = (clock() - start_time)/CLOCKS_PER_SEC - tries*DELAY;
if(total_digits > game_time)
  score += 10*( total_digits - game_time);
```

Unfortunately, the program is still not quite correct. The program starts to read and check digits after the player presses Enter at the end of a sequence. If an incorrect digit is entered and it isn't the last in the sequence, the reading of digits stops and the remaining digits will be left in the keyboard buffer. This will result in the next digit being read as the answer to the prompt for another game. You need to remove any information that's still in the keyboard buffer before prompting for the next game for the program to work correctly. This implies that you need a way to clear the keyboard buffer.

■ **Note**   The *keyboard buffer* is memory that's used by the operating system to store input characters from the keyboard. The scanf() function reads input from the keyboard buffer rather than getting it directly from the keyboard itself.

With standard input and output—that is, input from the keyboard and output to the command line on the screen—there are two buffers: one that holds input characters and one for holding output. The operating system manages the transfer of data between these buffers and the physical devices. The standard input and output streams are identified by the names stdin and stdout, respectively.

There's a standard library function, fflush(), for clearing out the contents of an input or an output buffer. This function is typically used for file buffers, which you'll learn about in Chapter 12, but it works for any buffer. To clear a buffer for a given stream, you call fflush() with the name of the stream as the argument. For an input buffer, the data will be cleared. For an output buffer, the data will be written to the destination, thus emptying the buffer. To remove the contents of the keyboard buffer, you call fflush() with the name of the keyboard input stream as the argument:

```
fflush(stdin);                        // Flush the stdin buffer
```

Here's the complete program, which includes calculating a score and flushing the input buffer:

```
// Program 4.13 Simple Simon
#define _CRT_SECURE_NO_WARNINGS
#include <stdio.h>                    // For input and output
#include <ctype.h>                    // For toupper() function
#include <stdbool.h>                  // For bool, true, false
#include <stdlib.h>                   // For rand() and srand()
#include <time.h>                     // For time() function

int main(void)
{
  char another_game = 'Y';           // Records if another game is to be played
  const unsigned int DELAY = 1;      // Display period in seconds
  bool correct = true;               // true for correct sequence, false otherwise
  unsigned int tries = 0;            // Number of successful entries for sequence length
  unsigned int digits = 0;           // Number of digits in a sequence
  time_t seed = 0;                   // Seed value for random number sequence
  unsigned int number = 0;           // Stores an input digit
  time_t wait_start = 0;             // Stores current time
  clock_t start_time = 0;            // Game start time in clock ticks
  unsigned int score = 0;            // Game score
  unsigned int total_digits = 0;     // Total of digits entered in a game
  unsigned int game_time = 0;        // Game time in seconds

  // Describe how the game is played
  printf("\nTo play Simple Simon, ");
  printf("watch the screen for a sequence of digits.");
  printf("\nWatch carefully, as the digits are only displayed"
                        " for %u second%s ", DELAY, DELAY > 1 ? "s!" :"!");
  printf("\nThe computer will remove them, and then prompt you ");
  printf("to enter the same sequence.");
  printf("\nWhen you do, you must put spaces between the digits.\n");
  printf("\nGood Luck!\nPress Enter to play\n");
  scanf("%c", &another_game);

  // Game loop - one outer loop iteration is a complete game
  do
  {
    // Initialize game
    correct = true;                  // Indicates correct sequence entered
    tries = 0;                       // Initialize count of successful tries
    digits = 2;                      // Initial length of digit sequence
    start_time = clock();            // Record time at start of game

    // Inner loop continues as long as sequences are entered correctly
    while(correct)
    {
      ++tries;                       // A new attempt
      wait_start = clock();          // record start time for sequence
```

```
  // Generate a sequence of digits and display them
  srand((unsigned int)time(&seed));              // Initialize the random sequence
  for(unsigned int i = 1 ; i <= digits ; ++i)
    printf("%u ", rand() % 10);      // Output a random digit

  for( ; clock() - wait_start < DELAY*CLOCKS_PER_SEC; );  // Wait DELAY seconds

  // Now overwrite the digit sequence
  printf("\r");                      // Go to beginning of the line
  for(unsigned int i = 1 ; i <= digits ; ++i)
    printf("  ");                    // Output two spaces

  if(tries == 1)                     // Only output message for 1st try
    printf("\nNow you enter the sequence  - don't forget"
                                    " the spaces\n");
  else
    printf("\r");                    // Back to the beginning of the line

  srand((unsigned int)seed);                       // Reinitialize the random sequence
  for(unsigned int i = 1 ; i <= digits ; ++i)
  // Read the input sequence & check against the original
  {
    scanf("%u", &number);            // Read a digit
    if(number != rand() % 10)        // Compare with generated digit
    {
      correct = false;               // Incorrect entry
      break;                         // No need to check further...
    }
  }

  // On every third successful try, increase the sequence length
  if(correct && ((tries % 3) == 0))
    ++digits;

  printf("%s\n", correct ? "Correct!" : "Wrong!");
}

// Calculate and output the game score
score = 10*(digits - ((tries % 3) == 1));          // Points for sequence length
total_digits = digits*(((tries % 3) == 0) ? 3 : tries % 3);
if(digits > 2)
  total_digits += 3*((digits - 1)*(digits)/2 - 1);

game_time = (clock() - start_time)/CLOCKS_PER_SEC - tries*DELAY;

if(total_digits > game_time)
  score += 10*(total_digits - game_time);          // Add points for speed
printf("\n\nGame time was %u seconds. Your score is %u", game_time, score);

fflush(stdin);                                      // Clear the input buffer
```

```
    // Check if new game required
    printf("\nDo you want to play again (y/n)? ");
    scanf("%c", &another_game);

  }while(toupper(another_game) == 'Y');
  return 0;
}
```

The declaration required for the function fflush() is in the stdio.h header file, for which you already have an #include directive. Now you just need to see what happens when you actually play:

```
To play Simple Simon, watch the screen for a sequence of digits.
Watch carefully, as the digits are only displayed for 1 second!
The computer will remove them, and then prompt you to enter the same sequence.
When you do, you must put spaces between the digits.

Good Luck!
Press Enter to play

Now you enter the sequence  - don't forget the spaces
2 1
Correct!
8 7
Correct!
4 1
Correct!
7 9 6
Correct!
7 5 4
Wrong!

 Game time was 11 seconds. Your score is 30
Do you want to play again (y/n)? n
```

Summary

In this chapter, I covered all you need to know about repeating actions using loops. With the powerful set of programming tools you've learned up to now, you should be able to create quite complex programs on your own. You have three different loops you can use to repeatedly execute a block of statements:

- The for loop, which you typically use for counting loops where the value of a control variable is incremented or decremented by a given amount on each iteration until some final value is reached.

- The while loop, which you use when the loop continues as long as a given condition is true. If the loop condition is false at the outset, the loop block will not be executed at all.

- The do-while loop, which works like the while loop except that the loop condition is checked at the end of the loop block. Consequently, the loop block is always executed at least once.

In keeping with this chapter topic, I'll now reiterate some of the rules and recommendations I've presented in the book so far:

- *Before you start programming, work out the logic of the process and computations you want to perform, and write it down—preferably in the form of a flow chart.* Try to think of lateral approaches to a problem; there may be a better way than the obvious approach.

- *Understand operator precedence in order to get complex expressions right.* Whenever you are not sure about operator precedence, use parentheses to ensure expressions do what you want. Use parentheses to make complex expressions more readily understood.

- *Comment your programs to explain all aspects of their operation and use.* Assume the comments are for the benefit of someone else reading your program with a view to extend or modify it. Explain the purpose of each variable as you declare it.

- *Program with readability foremost in your mind.*

- *In complicated logical expressions, avoid using the operator ! as much as you can.*

- *Use indentation to visually indicate the structure of your program.*

Prepared with this advice, you can now move on to the next chapter—after you've completed all the exercises, of course!

EXERCISES

The following exercises enable you to try out what you've learned in this chapter. If you get stuck, look back over the chapter for help. If you're still stuck, you can download the solutions from the Source Code/Download section of the Apress website (www.apress.com), but that really should be a last resort.

Exercise 4-1. Write a program that will generate a multiplication table of a size entered by the user. A table of size 4, for instance, would have four rows and four columns. The rows and columns would be labeled from 1 to 4. Each cell in the table will contain the product of the corresponding row and column numbers, so the value in the position corresponding to the third row and the fourth column would contain 12.

Exercise 4-2. Write a program that will output the printable characters for character code values from 0 to 127. Output each character code along with its symbol with two characters to a line. Make sure the columns are aligned. (Hint: You can use the isgraph() function that's declared in ctype.h to determine when a character is printable.)

Exercise 4-3. Extend the previous program to output the appropriate name, such as "newline," "space," "tab," and so on, for each whitespace character.

Exercise 4-4. Modify Program 4.13 to determine the random digits by selecting a digit based on where the number returned by rand() lies within the entire range of possible values.

Exercise 4-5. Modify the Simple Simon game implemented in Program 4.7A so that the program will continue with an option to play another game when the player fails to guess the number correctly and will allow as many games as the player requires.

Exercise 4-6. Calculate number Pi by using the Leibniz Formula:

$$1 - \frac{1}{3} + \frac{1}{5} - \frac{1}{7} + \frac{1}{9} - \cdots = \frac{\pi}{4}$$

This formula has low convergence rate; then please use at least 500,000 iterations to have an accurate Pi approximation.

CHAPTER 5

Arrays

You'll often need to store many data values of a particular kind in your programs. In a program to track the performance of a basketball team, you might want to store the scores for a season of games and the scores for individual players. You could then output the scores for a particular player over the season or work out an ongoing average as the season progresses. Armed with what you've learned so far, you could write a program that does this using a different variable for each score. However, if there are a lot of games in the season, this will be rather tedious because you'll need as many variables for each player as there are games. All your basketball scores are really the same kind of thing. The values are different, but they're all basketball scores. Ideally, you want to be able to group these values together under a single name—perhaps the name of the player—so that you wouldn't need separate variables for each item of data.

This chapter will show you how to do just that using arrays. I'll then show you how powerful referencing a set of values through a single name can be when you process arrays.

In this chapter, you'll learn

- What arrays are
- How to use arrays in your programs
- How memory is used by an array
- What a multidimensional array is
- How to write a program to work out your hat size
- How to write a game of tic-tac-toe

An Introduction to Arrays

The best way to show you what an array is and how powerful it can be is to go through an example. This will demonstrate how much easier a program becomes when you use an array. For this example, you'll look at ways in which you can find the average grade score for the students in a class.

Programming Without Arrays

To find the average grade of a class of students, I'll assume that there are only ten students in the class (mainly to avoid having to type in a lot of numbers). To work out the average of a set of numbers, you add them all together and then divide by how many there are (in this case, ten):

```
// Program 5.1 Averaging ten grades without storing them
#define _CRT_SECURE_NO_WARNINGS
#include <stdio.h>
```

© German Gonzalez-Morris and Ivor Horton 2020
G. Gonzalez-Morris and I. Horton, *Beginning C*, https://doi.org/10.1007/978-1-4842-5976-4_5

```
int main(void)
{
  int grade = 0;                      // Stores a grade
  unsigned int count = 10;            // Number of values to be read
  long sum = 0L;                      // Sum of the grades
  float average = 0.0f;               // Average of the grades

  // Read the ten grades to be averaged
  for(unsigned int i = 0 ; i < count ; ++i)
  {
    printf("Enter a grade: ");
    scanf("%d", & grade);             // Read a grade
    sum += grade;                     // Add it to sum
  }

  average = (float)sum/count;         // Calculate the average

  printf("\nAverage of the ten grades entered is: %f\n", average);
  return 0;
}
```

If you're interested only in the average, then you don't have to remember what the previous grades were. You accumulate the sum of all the values, which you then divide by count, which has the value 10. This program uses a single variable, grade, to store each grade as it is entered within the loop. The loop repeats for values of i from 0 to 9, so there are ten iterations.

Let's assume you want to develop this into a more sophisticated program in which you need to store the values entered. Perhaps you want to output each person's grade, with the average grade next to it. In the previous program, you had only one variable. Each time you add a grade, the old value is overwritten, and you can't get it back.

So how can you store all the grades? You could declare ten integer variables to store the grades, but then you can't use a loop to enter the values. You must include code that will read the values individually. This works, but it's quite tiresome:

```
// Program 5.2 Averaging ten grades - storing values the hard way
#define _CRT_SECURE_NO_WARNINGS
#include <stdio.h>

int main(void)
{
  int grade0 = 0, grade1 = 0, grade2 = 0, grade3 = 0, grade4 = 0;
  int grade5 = 0, grade6 = 0, grade7 = 0, grade8 = 0, grade9 = 0;

  long sum = 0L;          // Sum of the grades
  float average = 0.0f;   // Average of the grades

  // Read the ten grades to be averaged
  printf("Enter the first five grades,\n");
  printf("use a space or press Enter between each number.\n");
  scanf("%d%d%d%d%d", & grade0, & grade1, & grade2, & grade3, & grade4);
  printf("Enter the last five numbers in the same manner.\n");
  scanf("%d%d%d%d%d", & grade5, & grade6, & grade7, & grade8, & grade9);
```

```
// Now we have the ten grades, we can calculate the average
sum = grade0 + grade1 + grade2 + grade3 + grade4 +
      grade5 + grade6 + grade7 + grade8 + grade9;
average = (float)sum/10.0f;

printf("\nAverage of the ten grades entered is: %f\n", average);
return 0;
}
```

This is more or less okay for ten students, but what if your class has 30 students or 100 or 1,000? How can you do it then? This approach would become wholly impractical, and an alternative mechanism is essential.

What Is an Array?

An *array* is a fixed number of data items that are all of the same type. The data items in an array are referred to as *elements*. The elements in an array are all of type int or of type long or all of any type you choose. The following array declaration is similar to a declaration for a normal variable that contains a single value, except that you've placed a number between square brackets [ ] following the name:

```
long numbers[10];
```

The number between square brackets defines how many elements the array contains and is called the array *dimension*. An array has a type, which is a combination of the element type and the number of elements in the array. Thus, two arrays are of the same type if they have the same number of elements of the same type.

Each of the data items stored in an array is accessed by the same name; in the previous statement, the array name is numbers. You select a particular element by using an *index value* between square brackets following the array name. Index values are sequential integers that start from zero, and 0 is the index value for the first array element. The index values for the elements in the numbers array run from 0 to 9, so the index value 0 refers to the first element and the index value 9 refers to the last element. Therefore, you access the elements in the numbers array as numbers[0], numbers[1], numbers[2], and so on, up to numbers[9]. You can see this in Figure 5-1.

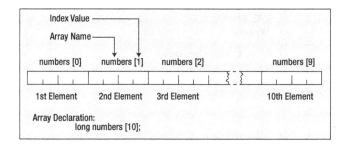

Figure 5-1. *Accessing the elements of an array*

Don't forget, index values start from zero, not one. It's a common mistake to assume that they start from one when you're working with arrays for the first time, and this is sometimes referred to as the *off-by-one error*. In a ten-element array, the index value for the last element is 9. To access the fourth value in your array, you use the expression numbers[3]. You can think of the index value for an array element as the offset from the first element. The first element is the first element, so its offset is 0. The second element is offset by 1 from the first element, the third element is offset by 2 from the first element, and so on.

189

You can specify an index for an array element by an expression in the square brackets following the array name. The expression must result in an integer value that corresponds to one of the possible index values. For example, you could write numbers[i-2]. If i is 3, this accesses numbers[1], the second element in the array. Thus, you can use a simple integer to explicitly reference the element that you want to access, or you can use an integer expression that's evaluated during the execution of the program. When you use an expression, the only constraints are that it must produce an integer result and the result must be a legal index value for the array.

Note that if you use an expression for an index value that's outside the legal range for the array, the program won't work properly. The compiler can't check for this, so your program will still compile, but execution is likely to be less than satisfactory. You'll pick up a junk value from somewhere so that the results are incorrect and may vary from one run to the next. It's possible that the program may overwrite something important and lock up your computer, so a reboot becomes necessary. It is also possible that the effect will be much more subtle with the program sometimes working and sometimes not, or the program may appear to work, but the results are wrong but not obviously so. It is therefore most important to ensure that your array indexes are always within bounds.

Using an Array

Let's put what you've just learned about arrays into practice in calculating average grades.

TRY IT OUT: AVERAGES WITH ARRAYS

You can use an array to store all the scores you want to average. This means that all the values will be saved and you'll be able to reuse them. You can now rewrite the program to average ten scores:

```
// Program 5.3 Averaging ten grades - storing the values the easy way
#define _CRT_SECURE_NO_WARNINGS
#include <stdio.h>

int main(void)
{
  int grades[10];                     // Array storing 10 values
  unsigned int count = 10;            // Number of values to be read
  long sum = 0L;                      // Sum of the numbers
  float average = 0.0f;               // Average of the numbers

  printf("\nEnter the 10 grades:\n"); // Prompt for the input

  // Read the ten numbers to be averaged
  for(unsigned int i = 0 ; i < count ; ++i)
  {
    printf("%2u> ",i + 1);
    scanf("%d", &grades[i]);          // Read a grade
    sum += grades[i];                 // Add it to sum
  }

  average = (float)sum/count;         // Calculate the average
  printf("\nAverage of the ten grades entered is: %.2f\n", average);
  return 0;
}
```

The output from the program looks something like this:

```
Enter the ten grades:
 1> 450
 2> 765
 3> 562
 4> 700
 5> 598
 6> 635
 7> 501
 8> 720
 9> 689
10> 527

Average of the ten grades entered is: 614.70
```

How It Works

You start off the program with the ubiquitous #include directive for stdio.h because you want to use printf() and scanf(). At the beginning of main(), you declare an array of ten integers and then the other variables that you'll need for calculation:

```
int grades[10];                 // Array storing 10 values
unsigned int count = 10;        // Number of values to be read
long sum = 0L;                  // Sum of the numbers
float average = 0.0f;           // Average of the numbers
```

The count variable is type unsigned int because it must be nonnegative.

You prompt for the input to be entered with this statement:

```
printf("\nEnter the 10 grades:\n");    // Prompt for the input
```

Next, you have a loop to read the values and accumulate the sum:

```
for(unsigned int i = 0 ; i < count ; ++i)
{
  printf("%2u> ",i + 1);
  scanf("%d", &grades[i]);             // Read a grade
  sum += grades[i];                    // Add it to sum
}
```

The for loop is in the standard form with the loop continuing as long as i is less than the limit, count. Because the loop counts from 0 to 9, rather than from 1 to 10, you can use the loop variable i directly to reference each of the members of the array. The printf() call outputs the current value of i + 1 followed by >, so it has the effect you see in the output. By using %2u as the format specifier, you ensure that each value is output in a two-character field, so the numbers are aligned. If you used %u instead, the output for the tenth value would be out of alignment.

You read each grade into element i of the array using the scanf() function; the first value will be stored in grades[0], the second number entered will be stored in grades[1], and so on up to the tenth value entered, which will be stored in grades[9]. You add each grade value to sum on each loop iteration.

191

When the loop ends, you calculate the average and display it with these statements:

```
average = (float)sum/count;                    // Calculate the average
printf("\nAverage of the ten grades entered is: %.2f\n", average);
```

You've calculated the average by dividing sum by count, the number of grades. Notice how you convert sum (which is type long) to type float in the call to printf(). This conversion ensures that the division is done using floating-point values, so you don't discard any fractional part of the result. The format specification, %.2f, limits the output value for the average to two decimal places.

TRY IT OUT: USING THE ELEMENT VALUES

I can expand the previous example to demonstrate one of the advantages of using an array. I've made only a minor change to the original program (highlighted in the following code in **bold**), so the program displays all the values that were typed in. Having the values stored in an array means that you can access those values whenever you want and process them in many different ways:

```
// Program 5.4 Reusing the numbers stored
#define _CRT_SECURE_NO_WARNINGS
#include <stdio.h>

int main(void)
{
  int grades[10];                        // Array storing 10 values
  unsigned int count = 10;               // Number of values to be read
  long sum = 0L;                         // Sum of the numbers
  float average = 0.0f;                  // Average of the numbers

  printf("\nEnter the 10 grades:\n");    // Prompt for the input

  // Read the ten numbers to be averaged
  for(unsigned int i = 0 ; i < count ; ++i)
  {
    printf("%2u> ",i + 1);
    scanf("%d", &grades[i]);             // Read a grade
    sum += grades[i];                    // Add it to sum
  }
  average = (float)sum/count;            // Calculate the average

  // List the grades
  for(unsigned int i = 0 ; i < count ; ++i)
    printf("\nGrade Number %2u is %3d", i + 1, grades[i]);

  printf("\nAverage of the ten grades entered is: %.2f\n", average);
  return 0;
}
```

Typical output from this program would be as follows:

```
Enter the 10 grades:
 1> 77
 2> 87
 3> 65
```

```
 4> 98
 5> 52
 6> 74
 7> 82
 8> 88
 9> 91
10> 71

Grade Number  1 is  77
Grade Number  2 is  87
Grade Number  3 is  65
Grade Number  4 is  98
Grade Number  5 is  52
Grade Number  6 is  74
Grade Number  7 is  82
Grade Number  8 is  88
Grade Number  9 is  91
Grade Number 10 is  71
Average of the ten grades entered is: 78.50
```

How It Works

I'll just explain the new bit where you reuse the array elements in a loop:

```
for(unsigned int i = 0 ; i < count ; ++i)
  printf("\nGrade Number %2u is %3d", i + 1, grades[i]);
```

This for loop steps through the elements in the array and outputs each value. You use the loop control variable to produce the sequence number for the value of the number of the element and to access the corresponding array element. These values obviously correspond to the numbers you typed in. To get the grades starting from 1, you use the expression i + 1 in the output statement so grades are numbered from 1 to 10 because i runs from 0 to 9.

Before I go any further with arrays, I'll explain a bit more about the address of operator and how arrays are stored in memory.

The Address of Operator

The *address of* operator, &, produces the address in memory of its operand. You have been using the address of operator extensively with the scanf() function. You've been using it as a prefix to the name of the variable where the input is to be stored. This makes the address that the variable occupies available to scanf(), which allows the function to store the data that are entered from the keyboard in the variable. When you use the variable name by itself as an argument to a function, only the value stored in the variable is available to the function. Prefixing the variable name with the address of operator makes the address of the variable available to the function. This enables the function to modify the value that's stored in the variable. You will learn why this is so in Chapter 8. Let's see what some addresses look like.

TRY IT OUT: USING THE ADDRESS OF OPERATOR

The following program outputs the addresses of some variables:

```
// Program 5.5 Using the & operator
#include<stdio.h>

int main(void)
{
  // Define some integer variables
  long a = 1L;
  long b = 2L;
  long c = 3L;

  // Define some floating-point variables
  double d = 4.0;
  double e = 5.0;
  double f = 6.0;

  printf("A variable of type long occupies %u bytes.", sizeof(long));
  printf("\nHere are the addresses of some variables of type long:");
  printf("\nThe address of a is: %p  The address of b is: %p", &a, &b);
  printf("\nThe address of c is: %p", &c);
  printf("\n\nA variable of type double occupies %u bytes.", sizeof(double));
  printf("\nHere are the addresses of some variables of type double:");
  printf("\nThe address of d is: %p  The address of e is: %p", &d, &e);
  printf("\nThe address of f is: %p\n", &f);
  return 0;
}
```

Output from this program will be something like this:

```
A variable of type long occupies 4 bytes.
Here are the addresses of some variables of type long:
The address of a is: 000000000012ff14  The address of b is: 000000000012ff10
The address of c is: 000000000012ff0c

A variable of type double occupies 8 bytes.
Here are the addresses of some variables of type double:
The address of d is: 000000000012ff00  The address of e is: 000000000012fef8
The address of f is: 000000000012fef0
```

The addresses that you get will almost certainly be different from these. The addresses depend on the operating system you're using and how your compiler allocates memory.

How It Works

You declare three variables of type `long` and three of type `double`:

```
// Define some integer variables
long a = 1L;
long b = 2L;
long c = 3L;

// Define some floating-point variables
double d = 4.0;
double e = 5.0;
double f = 6.0;
```

Next, you output the number of bytes occupied by variables of type `long`, followed by the addresses of the three variables of that type that you created:

```
printf("A variable of type long occupies %u bytes.", sizeof(long));
printf("\nHere are the addresses of some variables of type long:");
printf("\nThe address of a is: %p   The address of b is: %p", &a, &b);
printf("\nThe address of c is: %p", &c);
```

You use `%u` for the value produced by `sizeof` because it will be an unsigned integer value. You use a new format specifier, `%p`, to output the addresses of the variables. This format specifier is for outputting a memory address, and the value is presented in hexadecimal format. A memory address is typically 32 or 64 bits, and the size of the address will determine the maximum amount of memory that can be referenced. A memory address on my computer is 64 bits and is presented as 16 hexadecimal digits; on your machine, it may be different.

You then output the size of variables of type `double`, followed by the addresses of the three variables of that type that you also created:

```
printf("\n\nA variable of type double occupies %u bytes.", sizeof(double));
printf("\nHere are the addresses of some variables of type double:");
printf("\nThe address of d is: %p   The address of e is: %p", &d, &e);
printf("\nThe address of f is: %p\n", &f);
```

The interesting part isn't the program itself so much as the output. Look at the addresses that are displayed. You can see that the value of the address gets steadily lower in a regular pattern, as shown in Figure 5-2. On my computer, the address of b is 4 lower than that of a, and c is also lower than b by 4. This is because each variable of type `long` occupies 4 bytes. There's a similar situation with the variables d, e, and f, except that the difference is 8. This is because 8 bytes are used to store a value of type `double`.

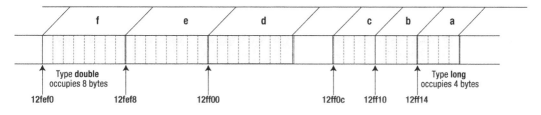

Figure 5-2. *Addresses of variables in memory*

There's a gap between the locations of the variables d and c in Figure 5-2. Why is this? Many compilers allocate space for variables at addresses that are a multiple of their size, so 4-byte variables are at addresses that are a multiple of 4, and 8-byte variables are at addresses that are a multiple of 8. This ensures that accessing the memory is done most efficiently. My compiler left the 4-byte gap between d and c to make the address of d a multiple of 8. If the program defined another variable of type long following c, it would occupy the 4-byte gap, and no gap would be apparent.

■ **Caution**   If the output shows that the addresses for the variables of the same type are separated by greater amounts than the size for the type, it is most likely because you compiled the program as a debug version. In debug mode, your compiler allocates extra space to store additional information about the variable that will be used when you're executing the program in debug mode.

Arrays and Addresses

Here's a declaration for an array with four elements:

```
long number[4];
```

The array name, number, identifies the address in memory where the array elements are stored. The specific location of an element is found by combining the address corresponding to the array name with the index value, because the index value represents the offset of a number of elements from the beginning of the array.

When you declare an array, you give the compiler all the information it needs to allocate the memory for it. The type of value determines the number of bytes that each element will require, and the array dimension specifies the number of elements. The number of bytes that an array will occupy is the number of elements multiplied by the size of each element. The address of an array element is going to be the address where the array starts, plus the product of the index value for the element and the number of bytes required to store each element. Figure 5-3 represents the way that array variables are held in memory.

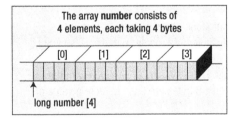

Figure 5-3. *The organization of an array in memory*

You can obtain the address of an array element in the same way as for an ordinary variable. For a variable with the name value, you would use the following statement to print its address:

```
printf("\n%p", &value);
```

To output the address of the third element of an array with the name number, you could write the following:

```
printf("\n%p", &number[2]);
```

The following fragment sets a value for each element in an array and outputs the address and contents of each element:

```
int data[5];
for(unsigned int i = 0 ; i < 5 ; ++i)
{
  data[i] = 12*(i + 1);
  printf("data[%d] Address: %p  Contents: %d\n", i, &data[i], data[i]);
}
```

The for loop variable i iterates over all the legal index values for the data array. Within the loop, the value of the element at index position i is set to 12*(i + 1). The output statement displays the current element with its index value, the address of the current array element determined by the current value of i, and the value stored within the element. If you make this fragment into a program, the output will be similar to the following:

```
data[0] Address: 000000000012fee4  Contents: 12
data[1] Address: 000000000012fee8  Contents: 24
data[2] Address: 000000000012feec  Contents: 36
data[3] Address: 000000000012fef0  Contents: 48
data[4] Address: 000000000012fef4  Contents: 60
```

The value of i is displayed between the square brackets following the array name. You can see that the address of each element is 4 greater than the previous element, so each element occupies 4 bytes.

Initializing an Array

Of course you will want to assign initial values for the elements of your array most of the time, even if it's only for safety's sake. Defining initial values for array elements makes it easier to detect when things go wrong. To initialize the elements of an array, you just specify the list of initial values between braces and separate them by commas in the declaration, for example:

```
double values[5] = { 1.5, 2.5, 3.5, 4.5, 5.5 };
```

This declares the values array with five elements. The elements are initialized with values[0] having the value 1.5, value[1] having the initial value 2.5, and so on.

To initialize the whole array, there must be one value for each element. If there are fewer initializing values than elements, the elements without initializing values will be set to 0. Thus, if you write

```
double values[5] = { 1.5, 2.5, 3.5 };
```

the first three elements will be initialized with the values between braces, and the last two elements will be initialized with 0.

Knowing that the compiler will supply zeroes for elements for which you don't provide, an initial value offers an easy way to initialize an entire array to zero. You just need to supply one element with the value of 0:

```
double values[5] = {0.0};
```

The entire array will then be initialized with 0.0.

If you put more initializing values than there are array elements, you'll get an error message from the compiler. However, you can omit the size of the array when you specify a list of initial values. In this case, the compiler will assume that the number of elements is the number of values in the list:

```
int primes[] = { 2, 3, 5, 7, 11, 13, 17, 19, 23, 29};
```

The size of the array is determined by the number of initial values in the list, so the primes array will have ten elements.

Finding the Size of an Array

You've already seen that the sizeof operator computes the number of bytes that a variable of a given type occupies. You can apply the sizeof operator to a type name like this:

```
printf("The size of a variable of type long is %zu bytes.\n", sizeof(long));
```

The parentheses around the type name following the sizeof operator are required. If you leave them out, the code won't compile. As you know, you can also apply the sizeof operator to a variable, and it will compute the number of bytes occupied by the variable.

■ **Note** The sizeof operator produces a value of type size_t, which is an implementation-defined unsigned integer type. If you use the %u specifier for output and your compiler happens to define size_t as unsigned long or unsigned long long, you may get warning messages from the compiler that the specifier %u does not match the value being output by the printf() function. Using %zu will eliminate the warning messages.

The sizeof operator works with arrays too. Suppose that you declare an array with the following statement:

```
double values[5] = { 1.5, 2.5, 3.5, 4.5, 5.5 };
```

You can output the number of bytes that the array occupies with the following statement:

```
printf("The size of the array, values, is %zu bytes.\n", sizeof values);
```

This will produce the following output:

```
The size of the array, values, is 40 bytes.
```

You can also obtain the number of bytes occupied by a single element of the array with the expression sizeof values[0]. This expression will have the value 8. Of course, any legal index value for an element could be used to produce the same result. The memory occupied by an array is the size of a single element multiplied by the number of elements. Thus, you can use the sizeof operator to calculate the number of elements in an array:

```
size_t element_count = sizeof values/sizeof values[0];
```

After executing this statement, element_count will contain the number of elements in the values array. I declared element_count to be type size_t because that is the type that the sizeof operator produces.

Because you can apply the sizeof operator to a data type, you could have written the previous statement to calculate the number of array elements as follows:

```
size_t element_count = sizeof values/sizeof(double);
```

The result is the same as before because the array is of type double, so sizeof(double) produces the number of bytes occupied by an element. There's the risk that you might accidentally use the wrong type, so it's better to use the former statement in practice.

Although the sizeof operator doesn't require the use of parentheses when applied to a variable, it's common practice to use them anyway, so the earlier example could be written as follows:

```
double values[5] = { 1.5, 2.5, 3.5, 4.5, 5.5 };
size_t element_count = sizeof(values)/sizeof(values[0]);
printf("The size of the array is %zu bytes ", sizeof(values));
printf("and there are %u elements of %zu bytes each\n", element_count, sizeof(values[0]));
```

The output from these statements will be the following:

```
The size of the array is 40 bytes and there are 5 elements of 8 bytes each
```

You can use the sizeof operator when you use a loop to process all the elements in an array, for example:

```
double values[5] = { 1.5, 2.5, 3.5, 4.5, 5.5 };
double sum = 0.0;
for(unsigned int i = 0 ; i < sizeof(values)/sizeof(values[0]) ; ++i)
  sum += values[i];
printf("The sum of the values is %.2f", sum);
```

This loop totals the values of all the array elements. Using sizeof to compute the number of elements in the array ensures that the upper limit for the loop variable, i, is always correct, whatever the size of the array.

Multidimensional Arrays

Let's start with two dimensions and work our way up. A two-dimensional array can be declared as follows:

```
float carrots[25][50];
```

This declares the carrots array with 25 sets of 50 floating-point elements. Note how each dimension is between its own pair of square brackets.

Similarly, you could declare another two-dimensional array of floating-point numbers with this statement:

```
float numbers[3][5];
```

You can visualize a two-dimensional array as a rectangular arrangement like rows of vegetables in a field. You can visualize the numbers array as having three rows and five columns. They're actually stored in memory sequentially by row, as shown in Figure 5-4. You can see that the rightmost index varies most rapidly. The left index conceptually selects a row, and the right index selects an element within the row.

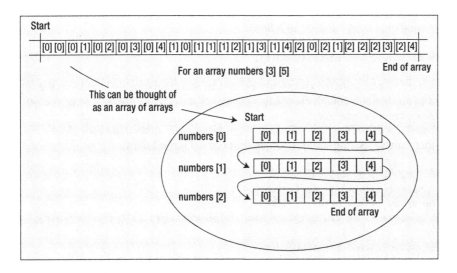

Figure 5-4. *Organization of a 3 × 5 element array in memory*

There's another way of looking at a two-dimensional array. Figure 5-4 also illustrates how you can envision a two-dimensional array as a one-dimensional array of elements, where each element is itself a one-dimensional array. You can view the numbers array as a one-dimensional array of three elements, where each element is an array containing five elements of type float. The first row of five is located at the address labeled numbers[0], the next row at numbers[1], and the last row of five elements at numbers[2].

The amount of memory allocated to each element is, of course, dependent on the type of variables that the array contains. An array of type double will need more memory to store each element than an array of type float or type int. Figure 5-5 illustrates how an array with four rows of ten elements of type float is stored.

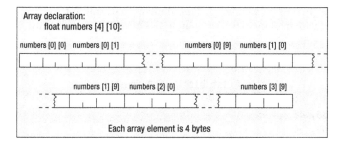

Figure 5-5. *Memory occupied by a 4 × 10 array*

Because the array elements are of type float, which on my machine occupies 4 bytes, the total memory occupied by this array on my computer will be 4 × 10 × 4 bytes, which amounts to a total of 160 bytes.

A three-dimensional array is a straightforward extension of a two-dimensional array:

```
double beans[4] [10][20];        // 4 fields, each with 10 rows of 20 beans
```

This declares an array with 800 elements. You can visualize it as storing yields from bean plants where there are three fields, each containing 10 rows of 20 plants. I'm sure you can see that the idea can be extended to define arrays with as many dimensions as you require.

Initializing Multidimensional Arrays

Initializing a two-dimensional array is similar to what you have seen for a one-dimensional array. The difference is that you put the initial values for each row between braces, {}, and then enclose all the rows between braces:

```
int numbers[3][4] = {
                { 10, 20, 30, 40 },        // Values for first row
                { 15, 25, 35, 45 },        // Values for second row
                { 47, 48, 49, 50 }         // Values for third row
            };
```

Each set of values that initializes the elements in a row is between braces, and the whole lot goes between another pair of braces. The values for a row are separated by commas, and each set of row values is separated from the next set by a comma.

If you specify fewer initializing values than there are elements in a row, the values will be assigned to row elements in sequence, starting with the first. The remaining elements in a row that are left when the initial values have all been assigned will be initialized to 0. You can initialize the whole array to 0 by supplying just one value:

```
int numbers[3][4] = {0};
```

For arrays of three or more dimensions, the process is extended. A three-dimensional array, for example, will have three levels of nested braces, with the inner level containing sets of initializing values for a row:

```
int numbers[2][3][4] = {
                        {                           // First block of 3 rows
                          { 10, 20, 30, 40 },
                          { 15, 25, 35, 45 },
                          { 47, 48, 49, 50 }
                        },
                        {                           // Second block of 3 rows
                          { 10, 20, 30, 40 },
                          { 15, 25, 35, 45 },
                          { 47, 48, 49, 50 }
                        }
                       };
```

As you can see, the initializing values are between an outer pair of braces that enclose two blocks of three rows, each between braces. Each row is also between braces, so you have three levels of nested braces for a three-dimensional array. This is true generally; for instance, a six-dimensional array will have six levels of nested braces enclosing the initial values for the elements. You can omit the braces around the list for each row, and the initialization will still work; but including the braces for the row values is much safer because you are much less likely to make a mistake. Of course, if you want to supply fewer initial values than there are elements in a row, you must include the braces around the row values.

You need a nested loop to process all the elements in a multidimensional array. The level of nesting will be the number of array dimensions. Here's how you could sum the elements in the previous numbers array:

```
int sum = 0;
for(int i = 0 ; i < 2 ; ++i)
{
  for(int j = 0 ; j < 3 ; ++j)
  {
    for(int k = 0 ; k < 4 ; ++k)
    {
      sum += numbers[i][j][k];
    }
  }
}
printf("The sum of the values in the numbers array is %d.", sum);
```

Each loop iterates over one array dimension. For each value of i, the loop controlled by j will execute completely, and for each value of j, the loop controlled by k will execute completely.

You can use the sizeof operator to work out the number of elements in each dimension of a multidimensional array. You just need to be clear on what the sizeof operator is producing. Here's the previous loop using the sizeof operator to compute the loop control limits:

```
for(int i = 0 ; i < sizeof(numbers)/sizeof(numbers[0]) ; ++i)
{
  for(int j = 0 ; j < sizeof(numbers[0])/sizeof(numbers[0][0]) ; ++j)
  {
    for(int k = 0 ; k < sizeof(numbers[0][0])/sizeof(numbers[0][0][0]) ; ++k)
```

```
    {
      sum += numbers[i][j][k];
    }
  }
}
```

You can visualize the numbers array as an array of two-dimensional arrays. The expression sizeof(numbers) results in the number of bytes that the entire numbers array occupies, and sizeof(numbers[0]) results in the number of bytes occupied by one of the two-dimensional subarrays. Thus, the expression sizeof(numbers)/sizeof(numbers[0]) is going to result in the number of elements in the first array dimension. Similarly, you can visualize each two-dimensional subarray as a one-dimensional array of one-dimensional arrays. Dividing the size of a two-dimensional array by the size of one of its subarrays results in the number of subarrays, which is the second numbers dimension. Finally, dividing the size of the one-dimensional sub-subarray by the size of one element results in the third dimension value.

TRY IT OUT: USING MULTIDIMENSIONAL ARRAYS

Let's move away from vegetables and turn to a more practical application. You can use arrays in a program to avoid a significant health and safety issue. As you may know, wearing a hat that is too large is dangerous. It can fall over your eyes, so you may bump into things, causing injury or even death. Equally, wearing a hat that is too small can result in persistent headaches and make you look foolish. This invaluable program will use arrays to work out your correct hat size in the units commonly used in the United States and the United Kingdom, where hat sizes typically vary from 6 1/2 to 7 7/8. Other countries have more transparent hat sizes that cause fewer problems at home, but if you are a foreign visitor to the United States or the United Kingdom, buying a hat while you are away can be even more hazardous. You just enter the circumference of your head, in inches of course, and your hat size will be displayed instantly:

```
// Program 5.6 Know your hat size - if you dare...
#define _CRT_SECURE_NO_WARNINGS
#include <stdio.h>
#include <stdbool.h>

int main(void)
{
    /*****************************************************
     * The size array stores hat sizes from 6 1/2 to 7 7/8 *
     * Each row defines one character of a size value so   *
     * a size is selected by using the same index for each *
     * the three rows. e.g. Index 2 selects 6 3/4.         *
     *****************************************************/
    char size[3][12] = {            // Hat sizes as characters
       {'6', '6', '6', '6', '7', '7', '7', '7', '7', '7', '7', '7'},
       {'1', '5', '3', '7', ' ', '1', '1', '3', '1', '5', '3', '7'},
       {'2', '8', '4', '8', ' ', '8', '4', '8', '2', '8', '4', '8'}
                    };
    int headsize[12] =              // Values in 1/8 inches
        {164,166,169,172,175,178,181,184,188,191,194,197};
```

```c
  float cranium = 0.0f;                    // Head circumference in decimal inches
  int your_head = 0;                       // Headsize in whole eighths
  bool hat_found = false;                  // Indicates when a hat is found to fit

  // Get the circumference of the head
  printf("\nEnter the circumference of your head above your eyebrows "
      "in inches as a decimal value: ");
  scanf(" %f", &cranium);

  your_head = (int)(8.0f*cranium);         // Convert to whole eighths of an inch

  /******************************************************************
   * Search for a hat size:                                        *
   * Either your head corresponds to the 1st headsize element or   *
   * a fit is when your_head is greater that one headsize element  *
   * and less than or equal to the next.                           *
   * In this case the size is the second headsize value.           *
   ******************************************************************/
  size_t i = 0;                     // Loop counter
  if(your_head == headsize[i])  // Check for min size fit
    hat_found = true;
  else
  {
    for (i = 1 ; i < sizeof(headsize) ; ++i)
    {
      // Find head size in the headsize array
      if(your_head > headsize[i - 1] && your_head <= headsize[i])
      {
        hat_found = true;
        break;
      }
    }
  }

  if(hat_found)
  {
    printf("\nYour hat size is %c %c%c%c\n",
           size[0][i], size[1][i],
           (size[1][i]==' ') ? ' ' : '/', size[2][i]);
  }
  else  // If no hat was found, the head is too small, or too large
  {
    if(your_head < headsize[0])        // check for too small
      printf("\nYou are the proverbial pinhead. No hat for"
                                        " you I'm afraid.\n");
    else                              // It must be too large
      printf("\nYou, in technical parlance, are a fathead."
                              " No hat for you, I'm afraid.\n");
  }
  return 0;
}
```

Typical output from this program would be this:

```
Enter the circumference of your head above your eyebrows in inches as a decimal
  value: 22.5
Your hat size is 7 1/4
```

or possibly this:

```
Enter the circumference of your head above your eyebrows in inches as a decimal
  value: 29
You, in technical parlance, are a fathead. No hat for you I'm afraid.
```

How It Works

Before I start discussing this example, I should give you a word of caution. Do not allow large football players to use it to determine their hat size unless they're known for their sense of humor.

The example looks a bit complicated because of the nature of the problem, but it does illustrate using arrays. Let's go through what's happening.

The first declaration in the body of main() is a two-dimensional array:

```
char size[3][12] = {              // Hat sizes as characters
    {'6', '6', '6', '6', '7', '7', '7', '7', '7', '7', '7', '7'},
    {'1', '5', '3', '7', ' ', '1', '1', '3', '1', '5', '3', '7'},
    {'2', '8', '4', '8', ' ', '8', '4', '8', '2', '8', '4', '8'}
                 };
```

Apart from hats that are designated as "one size fits all" or as small, medium, and large, hats are typically available in sizes from 6 1/2 to 7 7/8 in increments of 1/8 inch. The size array shows one way in which you could store such sizes in the program. This array corresponds to 12 possible hat sizes, each of which comprises three values. For each hat size, you store three characters, making it more convenient to output the fractional sizes. The smallest hat size is 6 1/2, so the first three characters corresponding to the first size are in size[0][0], size[1][0], and size[2][0]. They contain the characters '6', '1', and '2', representing the size 6 1/2. The biggest hat size is 7 7/8, and it's stored in the elements size[0][11], size[1][11], size[2][11].

You then declare the headsize array that provides the reference head dimensions in this declaration:

```
int headsize[12] =        // Values in 1/8 inches
                  {164,166,169,172,175,178,181,184,188,191,194,197};
```

The values in the array are all whole eighths of an inch. They correspond to the values in the size array containing the hat sizes. This means that a head size of 164 eighths of an inch (20.5 inches) will give a hat size of 6 1/2, and at the other end of the scale, 197 eighths corresponds to a hat size of 7 7/8.

Notice that the head sizes don't run consecutively. You could get a head size of 171, for example, which doesn't fall into a definite hat size. You need to be aware of this later in the program so that you can decide which is the closest hat size for the head size.

After declaring your arrays, you then declare the variables you're going to need:

```
float cranium = 0.0f;          // Head circumference in decimal inches
int your_head = 0;             // Headsize in whole eighths
bool hat_found = false;        // Indicates when a hat is found to fit
```

Notice that cranium is declared as type float, but your_head is type int. This becomes important later. You declare the variable hat_found as type bool so you use the symbol false to initialize this. The hat_found variable will record when you have found a size that fits.

Next, you prompt for your head size to be entered in inches, and the value is stored in the variable cranium (remember it's type float, so you can store values that aren't whole numbers):

```
printf("\nEnter the circumference of your head above your eyebrows "
       "in inches as a decimal value: ");
scanf(" %f", &cranium);
```

The value stored in cranium is then converted into eighths of an inch with this statement:

```
your_head = (int)(8.0f*cranium);
```

Because cranium contains the circumference of a head in inches, multiplying by 8.0f results in the number of eighths of an inch that that represents. Thus, the value stored in your_head will then be in the same units as the values stored in the array headsize. Note that you need to cast the result of the multiplication to type int here to avoid a warning message from the compiler. The code will still work if you omit the cast, but the compiler must then insert the cast to type int. The warning is because this cast potentially loses information. The parentheses around the expression (8.0f*cranium) are also necessary; without them, you would only cast the value 8.0f to type int, not the whole expression.

You use the value stored in your_head to find the closest value in the headsize array:

```
size_t i = 0;                      // Loop counter
if(your_head == headsize[i])       // Check for min size fit
  hat_found = true;
else
{
  for (i = 1 ; i < sizeof(headsize) ; ++i)
  {
    // Find head size in the headsize array
    if(your_head > headsize[i - 1] && your_head <= headsize[i])
    {
      hat_found = true;
        break;
    }
  }
}
```

You declare the loop index, i, before the loop because you want to use the value outside the loop. The if-else statement first checks for the head size matching the first headsize array element, in which case you have found it. When this is not the case, the for loop is executed. The loop index runs from the second element in the array to the last element. This is necessary because you use i - 1 to index the headsize array in the if expression. On each loop iteration, you compare your head size with a pair of successive values stored in the headsize array to find the element value that is greater than or equal to your input size with the preceding value less than your input size. The index found will correspond to the hat size that fits.

Next, you output the hat size if the value of hat_found is true:

```
if(hat_found)
{
  printf("\nYour hat size is %c %c%c%c\n",
          size[0][i], size[1][i],
          (size[1][i]==' ') ? ' ' : '/', size[2][i]);
}
```

As I said earlier, the hat sizes are stored in the array size as characters to simplify the outputting of fractions. The printf() uses the conditional operator to decide when to output a space and when to output a slash (/) for the fractional output value. For example, the fifth element of the headsize array corresponds to a hat size of exactly 7. You want to output 7 rather than 7/. Therefore, you customize the printf() output depending on whether or not the size[1][i] element contains a space character. In this way, you omit the slash for any size where the numerator of the fractional part is a space, so this will still work even if you add new sizes to the array.

Of course, it may be that no hat was found because either the head was too small or too large for the hat sizes available, and the else clause for the if statement deals with that situation because the else executes if hat_found is false:

```
// If no hat was found, the head is too small, or too large
else
{
  if(your_head < headsize[0])        // check for too small
    printf("\nYou are the proverbial pinhead. No hat for"
                                    " you I'm afraid.\n");
  else                               // It must be too large
    printf("\nYou, in technical parlance, are a fathead."
                        " No hat for you, I'm afraid.\n");
}
```

If the value in your_head is less than the first headsize element, the head is too small for the available hats; otherwise, it must be too large.

Remember that if you lie about the size of your head when you use this program, your hat won't fit. The more mathematically astute, and any hatters reading this book, will appreciate that the hat size is simply the diameter of a notionally circular head. Therefore, if you have the circumference of your head in inches, you can produce your hat size by dividing this value by π.

Constant Arrays

We have seen constants in integers so far. In present times, the immutable concept can be a beneficial and safe way to code (trendy in functional programming), but this is not the case; however, we would like to achieve the same behavior.

Sometimes we need to manage constant values of past events, such as the best 10 ELO scores of all time; this can implement like

```
const int elo[10] = {2882, 2851, 2844, 2830, 2822, 2820, 2819, 2817, 2816, 2810};
```

The keyword "const" can also be used for generating string literal or constant string (to learn more details of strings, please check the next chapter).

This means that if, after definition, we try to modify the value, a compilation error will be thrown (see Program 5.6a).

Another practical example is to give relative values to chess pieces and add them up, retrieving a final score to choose which is the best move (a technique for pruning in a search tree algorithm).

The value can vary depending on the state of the game (opening, middle game, ending). We will use the most traditional values:

Values of the pieces: pawn = 1 knight = 3 bishop = 3 rook = 5 queen = 9

```c
// Program 5.1b  Modifying constant array
#include <stdio.h>

//these constants are redundant for educational purpose
// King's value is undefined
#define king 0
#define pawn 1
#define knight 2
#define bishop 3
#define rook 4
#define queen 5

//white pieces respectively:
// 6 7 8 9 10

int main(void)
{
  const int values[6] = {0, 1, 3, 3, 5, 9};

  int board[8][8] = { // chessboard
          { 0, 0, 4, 0, 0, 0, 0, 0,},
          { 4, 0, 0, 2, 5, 0, 1, 0,},
          { 1, 0, 0, 0, 1, 0, 0, 1,},
          { 0, 0, 1, 0, 0, 0, 0, 0,},
          { 0, 0, 0, 1, 6, 6, 0, 0,},
          { 0, 0, 0, 0, 0, 0, 0,10,},
          { 6, 6, 0, 0, 8, 0, 6, 6,},
          { 0, 0, 9, 0, 0, 9, 0, 0,}
  };

  int score = 0;

  for(int i=0; i<8; i++) {
    for(int j=0; j<8; j++) {
      //we separate colors:
          if(board[i][j]<6)
            score += values[board[i][j]];
          else
            score -= values[board[i][j]%6];
      }
  }
```

```
  printf("\nScore : %d\n", score);

  if(score>0) printf("\nSpassky is winning to Fischer");
  else printf("\nFischer is winning to Spassky");

  printf("... for now !\n");

  return 0;
}
```

Then we can iterate the chessboard and check the final score.

Variable-Length Arrays

So far, all the arrays have had fixed dimensions that you specify in the code. You can also define arrays where the dimensions are determined at runtime, when you execute the program. Here's an example:

```
size_t size = 0;
printf("Enter the number of elements you want to store: ");
scanf("%zd", &size);
float values[size];
```

In this fragment, you read a value from the keyboard into size. The value of size is then used to specify the dimension for the values array. Because size_t is an implementation-defined integer type, you may get compiler errors if you try to read such a value using %d. The z in %zd tells the compiler that it applies to size_t, so the compiler will make the specifier suitable for reading whatever integer type size_t is.

You can also define arrays with two or more dimensions with any or all of the dimensions determined at execution time, for example:

```
size_t rows = 0;
size_t columns = 0;
printf("Enter the number of rows you want to store: ");
scanf("%zd", &rows);
printf("Enter the number of columns in a row: ");
scanf("%zd", &columns);
float beans[rows][columns];
```

Here you read both dimensions for a two-dimensional array from the keyboard. Both array dimensions are determined at execution time.

A C11-conforming compiler does not have to implement support for variable-length arrays (VLAs) because it is an optional feature. If it does not, the symbol __STDC_NO_VLA__ must be defined as 1. You can check for support for variable-length arrays using this code:

```
#ifdef    __STDC_NO_VLA__
  printf("Variable length arrays are not supported.\n");
  exit(1);
#endif
```

This uses preprocessor directives that you'll learn about in Chapter 13. The printf() statement and the following exit() statement will be included in the program if the symbol __STDC_NO_VLA__ is defined. If you place this fragment at the beginning of main(), if variable-length arrays are not supported, you'll see a message from the printf() function call, and the program will end immediately. Despite the fact that constant __STDC_NO_VLA__ is 1 in Visual Studio 2019, this compiler does not support VLA.

You can see a variable-length, one-dimensional array working in a revised version of Program 5.3 as shown in Program 5.7.

TRY IT OUT: USING A VARIABLE-LENGTH ARRAY

This program calculates an average grade, but this time allocates an array that accommodates the exact number of grades to be entered:

```c
// Program 5.7 Averaging a variable number of grades
#define _CRT_SECURE_NO_WARNINGS
#include <stdio.h>

int main(void)
{
  size_t nGrades = 0;                          // Number of grades
  printf("Enter the number of grades: ");
  scanf("%zd", &nGrades);
  int grades[nGrades];                         // Array storing nGrades values
  long sum = 0L;                               // Sum of the numbers
  float average = 0.0f;                        // Average of the numbers

  printf("\nEnter the %zd grades:\n", nGrades); // Prompt for the input

  // Read the ten numbers to be averaged
  for(size_t i = 0 ; i < nGrades ; ++i)
  {
    printf("%2zd> ",i + 1);
    scanf("%d", &grades[i]);                   // Read a grade
    sum += grades[i];                          // Add it to sum
  }

  printf("The grades you entered are:\n");
  for(size_t i = 0 ; i < nGrades ; ++i)
  {
    printf("Grade[%2zd] = %3d  ", i + 1, grades[i]);

    if((i+1) % 5 == 0)                         // After 5 values
      printf("\n");                            // Go to a new line
  }
  average = (float)sum/nGrades;                // Calculate the average

  printf("\nAverage of the %zd grades entered is: %.2f\n", nGrades, average);
}
```

Here is some typical output:

```
Enter the number of grades: 12

Enter the 12 grades:
 1> 56
 2> 67
 3> 78
 4> 67
 5> 68
 6> 56
 7> 88
 8> 98
 9> 76
10> 75
11> 87
12> 72
The grades you entered are:
Grade[ 1] =  56  Grade[ 2] =  67  Grade[ 3] =  78  Grade[ 4] =  67  Grade[ 5] =  68
Grade[ 6] =  56  Grade[ 7] =  88  Grade[ 8] =  98  Grade[ 9] =  76  Grade[10] =  75
Grade[11] =  87  Grade[12] =  72
Average of the 12 grades entered is: 74.00
```

How It Works

You define a variable, nGrades, that will store the number of grades to be entered and read the value from the keyboard:

```
size_t nGrades = 0;                              // Number of grades
printf("Enter the number of grades: ");
scanf("%zd", &nGrades);
```

You use the value read into nGrades to define the grades array with the exact number of elements required:

```
int grades[nGrades];                             // Array storing nGrades values
```

Obviously, the value for the array dimension must be defined prior to this statement.

The rest of the code is what you have seen before, except that input and output of the size_t values use the %zd specifier. Note how the remainder operator is used in the loop that outputs the grades to start a new line after every fifth output value.

▒ **Note** The Microsoft Windows command line may be too narrow to display five grades. If so, you can output fewer per line by changing the code, or you can change the default size of the window by clicking the icon at the left of the title bar and selecting Properties from the menu.

Designing a Program

Now that you've learned about arrays, let's see how you can apply them in a bigger problem. Let's try writing another game—tic-tac-toe—also known as noughts and crosses.

The Problem

Implementing the game with the computer as the adversary is beyond what I have covered up to now, so you are just going to write a program that allows two people to play tic-tac-toe.

The Analysis

Tic-tac-toe is played on a 3 × 3 grid of squares. Two players take turns entering either an **X** or an **O** in the grid. The first player to get three of his or her symbols in a line horizontally, vertically, or diagonally is the winner. You know how the game works, but how does that translate into designing your program? You'll need the following:

- *A 3 × 3 grid in which to store the turns of the two players*: That's easy. You can use a two-dimensional array with three rows of three elements.

- *A simple way for a player to select a square on his or her turn*: You can label the nine squares with digits from 1 to 9. A player will just need to enter the number of the square to select it.

- *A way to get the two players to take alternate turns*: You can identify the two players as 1 and 2, with player 1 going first. You can then determine the player number by the number of the turn. On odd-numbered turns, it's player 1. On even-numbered turns, it's player 2.

- *Some way of specifying where to place the player symbol on the grid and checking to see if it's a valid selection*: A valid selection is a digit from 1 to 9. If you label the first row of squares with 1, 2, and 3, the second row with 4, 5, and 6, and the third row with 7, 8, and 9, you can calculate a row index and a column index from the square number. Let's assume the player's choice is stored in a variable, choice.

  - If you subtract 1 from the player's chosen square number in choice, the square numbers are effectively 0 through 8, as shown in the following image:

Original

Subtract 1

1	2	3
4	5	6
7	8	9

0	1	2
3	4	5
6	7	8

- Then the expression choice/3 gives the row number, as you can see here:

Original less 1

0	1	2
3	4	5
6	7	8

Divide by 3

0	0	0
1	1	1
2	2	2

- The expression choice%3 will give the column number:

Original less 1

0	1	2
3	4	5
6	7	8

Remainder after divide by 3

0	1	2
0	1	2
0	1	2

- *A method of finding out if one of the players has won*: After each turn, you must check to see if any row, column, or diagonal in the board grid contains identical symbols. If it does, the last player has won.

- *A way to detect the end of the game*: Because the board has nine squares, a game consists of up to nine turns. The game ends when a winner is discovered or after nine turns.

The Solution

This section outlines the steps you'll take to solve the problem.

Step 1

You can first add the code for the main game loop and the code to display the board:

```c
// Program 5.8 Tic-Tac-Toe
#include <stdio.h>

int main(void)
{
  int player = 0;                    // Current player number - 1 or 2
  int winner = 0;                    // The winning player number

  char board[3][3] = {               // The board
              {'1','2','3'},         // Initial values are characters '1' to '9'
              {'4','5','6'},         // used to select a vacant square
              {'7','8','9'}          // for a player's turn.
                  };
```

```
  // The main game loop. The game continues for up to 9 turns
  // as long as there is no winner
  for(unsigned int i = 0; i < 9 && winner == 0; ++i)
  {
    // Display the board
    printf("\n");
    printf(" %c | %c | %c\n", board[0][0], board[0][1], board[0][2]);
    printf("---+---+---\n");
    printf(" %c | %c | %c\n", board[1][0], board[1][1], board[1][2]);
    printf("---+---+---\n");
    printf(" %c | %c | %c\n", board[2][0], board[2][1], board[2][2]);

    player = i%2 + 1;                    // Select player

    /* Code to play the game */
  }

  /* Code to output the result */

  return 0;
}
```

Here, you've declared the following variables: i, for the loop variable; player, which stores the identifier for the current player, 1 or 2; winner, which contains the identifier for the winning player; and the array board, which is of type char, because you want to place the symbol 'X' or 'O' in the squares. You initialize the array with the characters for the digits that identify the squares. The main game loop continues for as long as the loop condition is true. It will be false if winner contains a value other than 0 (which indicates that a winner has been found) or the loop counter is equal to or greater than 9 (which will be the case when all nine squares on the board have been filled).

When you display the grid in the loop, you use vertical bars and dash characters to delineate the squares. When a player selects a square, the symbol for that player will replace the digit character.

Step 2

Next, you can implement the code for the player to select a square and to ensure that the square is valid:

```
// Program 5.8 Tic-Tac-Toe
#include <stdio.h>

int main(void)
{
  int player = 0;                      // Current player number - 1 or 2
  int winner = 0;                      // The winning player number
  int choice = 0;                      // Chosen square
  unsigned int row = 0;                // Row index for a square
  unsigned int column = 0;             // Column index for a square

  char board[3][3] = {                 // The board
              {'1','2','3'},           // Initial values are characters '1' to '9'
              {'4','5','6'},           // used to select a vacant square
              {'7','8','9'}            // for a player's turn.
                    };
```

```
// The main game loop. The game continues for up to 9 turns
// as long as there is no winner
for(unsigned int i = 0; i < 9 && winner == 0; ++i)
{
  // Code to display the board as before...

  player = i%2 + 1;                    // Select player

  // Get valid player square selection
  do
  {
    printf("Player %d, please enter a valid square number "
           "for where you want to place your %c: ",
              player,(player == 1) ? 'X' : 'O');
    scanf("%d", &choice);

    row = --choice/3;                  // Get row index of square
    column = choice % 3;               // Get column index of square
  }while(choice < 0 || choice > 8 || board[row][column] > '9');

  // Insert player symbol
  board[row][column] = (player == 1) ? 'X' : 'O';

  /* Code to check for a winner */
}
  /* Code to output the result      */
  return 0;
}
```

You prompt the current player for input in the do-while loop and read the square number into choice. You use this value to compute the row and column index values in the array using the expressions you saw earlier. You store the row and column index values in row and column. The do-while loop condition verifies that the square selected is valid. There are three ways an invalid choice could be made:

- The square number is less than the minimum, 0.

- The square number is greater than the maximum, 8.

- The square number selects a square that already contains 'X' or 'O'.

In the latter case, the contents of the square will have a value greater than the character '9', because the character codes for 'X' and 'O' are greater than the character code for '9'. If the choice falls on any of these conditions, you just repeat the request to select a valid square.

Step 3

You can add the code to check for a winning line next. This needs to be executed after every turn:

```
// Program 5.8 Tic-Tac-Toe
#define _CRT_SECURE_NO_WARNINGS
#include <stdio.h>
```

```
int main(void)
{
  // Variable declarations as before...

  // Definition of the board array as before...

  // The main game loop. The game continues for up to 9 turns
  // as long as there is no winner
  for(size_t i = 0; i < 9 && winner == 0; ++i)
  {
    // Code to display the board as before...

    player = i%2 + 1;                      // Select player

    // Loop to get valid player square selection as before...

    // Insert player symbol
    board[row][column] = (player == 1) ? 'X' : 'O';

    // Check for a winning line - diagonals first
    if((board[0][0]==board[1][1] && board[0][0]==board[2][2]) ||
       (board[0][2]==board[1][1] && board[0][2]==board[2][0]))
      winner = player;
    else
    {
      // Check rows and columns for a winning line
      for(unsigned int line = 0; line <= 2; ++line)
      {
        if((board[line][0] == board[line][1] && board[line][0] == board[line][2]) ||
           (board[0][line] == board[1][line] && board[0][line] == board[2][line]))
          winner = player;
      }
    }
  }
  /* Code to output the result */
  return 0;
}
```

To check for a winning line, you compare one element in a line with the other two to test for equality. If all three are identical, then you have a winning line. You check both diagonals in the board array with the if expression, and if either diagonal has identical symbols in all three elements, you set winner to the current player. The current player must be the winner because he or she was the last to place a symbol on a square. If neither diagonal has identical symbols, you check the rows and the columns in the else clause using a for loop. The for loop body consists of one if statement that checks both a row and a column for identical elements on each iteration. If either is found, winner is set to the current player. Of course, if winner is set to a value here, the main loop condition will be false, so the loop ends and execution continues with the code following the main loop.

Step 4

The final task is to display the grid with the final position and to display a message for the result. If winner is 0, the game is a draw; otherwise, winner contains the winning player number. Here's the complete code for the program:

```
// Program 5.8 Tic-Tac-Toe
#define _CRT_SECURE_NO_WARNINGS
#include <stdio.h>

int main(void)
{
  int player = 0;                      // Current player number - 1 or 2
  int winner = 0;                      // The winning player number
  int choice = 0;                      // Chosen square
  unsigned int row = 0;                // Row index for a square
  unsigned int column = 0;             // Column index for a square
  char board[3][3] = {                 // The board
              {'1','2','3'},           // Initial values are characters '1' to '9'
              {'4','5','6'},           // used to select a vacant square
              {'7','8','9'}            // for a player's turn.
                    };

  // The main game loop. The game continues for up to 9 turns
  // as long as there is no winner
  for(unsigned int i = 0; i < 9 && winner == 0; ++i)
  {
    // Display the board
    printf("\n");
    printf(" %c | %c | %c\n", board[0][0], board[0][1], board[0][2]);
    printf("---+---+---\n");
    printf(" %c | %c | %c\n", board[1][0], board[1][1], board[1][2]);
    printf("---+---+---\n");
    printf(" %c | %c | %c\n", board[2][0], board[2][1], board[2][2]);

    player = i%2 + 1;                  // Select player

    // Get valid player square selection
    do
    {
      printf("Player %d, please enter a valid square number "
              "for where you want to place your %c: ",
                player,(player == 1) ? 'X' : 'O');
      scanf("%d", &choice);

      row = --choice/3;                // Get row index of square
      column = choice % 3;             // Get column index of square
    }while(choice < 0 || choice > 8|| board[row][column] > '9');
```

```
  // Insert player symbol
  board[row][column] = (player == 1) ? 'X' : 'O';

  // Check for a winning line - diagonals first
  if((board[0][0]==board[1][1] && board[0][0]==board[2][2]) ||
     (board[0][2]==board[1][1] && board[0][2]==board[2][0]))
    winner = player;
  else
  {
    // Check rows and columns for a winning line
    for(unsigned int line = 0; line <= 2; ++line)
    {
      if((board[line][0] == board[line][1] && board[line][0] == board[line][2]) ||
         (board[0][line] == board[1][line] && board[0][line] == board[2][line]))
        winner = player;
    }
  }
}
// Game is over so display the final board
printf("\n");
printf(" %c | %c | %c\n", board[0][0], board[0][1], board[0][2]);
printf("---+---+---\n");
printf(" %c | %c | %c\n", board[1][0], board[1][1], board[1][2]);
printf("---+---+---\n");
printf(" %c | %c | %c\n", board[2][0], board[2][1], board[2][2]);

// Display result message
if(winner)
  printf("\nCongratulations, player %d, YOU ARE THE WINNER!\n", winner);
else
  printf("\nHow boring, it is a draw\n");
  return 0;
}
```

Typical output from this program and a very bad player number 2 would be as follows:

```
1 | 2 | 3
---+---+---
4 | 5 | 6
---+---+---
7 | 8 | 9
```

Player 1, please enter a valid square number for where you want to place your X: 1

```
X | 2 | 3
---+---+---
4 | 5 | 6
---+---+---
7 | 8 | 9
```

```
Player 2, please enter a valid square number for where you want to place your O: 3

 X | 2 | O
---+---+---
 4 | 5 | 6
---+---+---
 7 | 8 | 9

Player 1, please enter a valid square number for where you want to place your X: 5

 X | 2 | O
---+---+---
 4 | X | 6
---+---+---
 7 | 8 | 9

Player 2, please enter a valid square number for where you want to place your O: 6

 X | 2 | O
---+---+---
 4 | X | O
---+---+---
 7 | 8 | 9

Player 1, please enter a valid square number for where you want to place your X: 9

 X | 2 | O
---+---+---
 4 | X | O
---+---+---
 7 | 8 | X

Congratulations, player 1, YOU ARE THE WINNER!
```

Summary

This chapter explored the ideas behind arrays. An array is a fixed number of elements of the same type, and you access any element within the array using the array name and one or more index values. Index values for an array are unsigned integer values starting from zero, and there is one index for each array dimension.

Processing an array with a loop provides a powerful programming capability. The amount of program code you need for the operation on array elements within a loop is essentially the same, regardless of how many elements there are. You have also seen how you can organize your data using multidimensional arrays. You can structure an array such that each array dimension selects a set of elements with a particular characteristic, such as the data pertaining to a particular time or location. By applying nested loops to multidimensional arrays, you can process all the array elements with a very small amount of code.

Up until now, you've mainly concentrated on processing numbers. The examples haven't really dealt with text to any great extent. In the next chapter, you'll learn how you can process and analyze strings of characters, but first some exercises to establish what you have learned in this chapter.

```
┌─────────────────────────────────────────────────────────────────────────┐
│                              EXERCISES                                    │
└─────────────────────────────────────────────────────────────────────────┘
```

The following exercises enable you to try out what you've learned about arrays. If you get stuck, look back over the chapter for help. If you're still stuck, you can download the solutions from the Source Code/Download area of the Apress website (www.apress.com), but that really should be a last resort.

Exercise 5-1. Write a program that will read five values of type double from the keyboard and store them in an array. Calculate the reciprocal of each value (the reciprocal of value x is 1.0/x) and store it in a separate array. Output the values of the reciprocals and calculate and output the sum of the reciprocals.

Exercise 5-2. Define an array, data, with 100 elements of type double. Write a loop that will store the following sequence of values in corresponding elements of the array:

1/(2*3*4)   1/(4*5*6)   1/(6*7*8) … up to 1/(200*201*202)

Write another loop that will calculate the following:

data[0] - data[1] + data[2] - data[3] + … -data[99]

Multiply the result of this by 4.0, add 3.0, and output the final result. Do you recognize the value you get?

Exercise 5-3. Write a program that will read five values from the keyboard and store them in an array of type float with the name amounts. Create two arrays of five elements of type long with the names dollars and cents. Store the whole number part of each value in the amounts array in the corresponding element of dollars and the fractional part of the amount as a two-digit integer in cents (e.g., 2.75 in amounts[1] would result in 2 being stored in dollars[1] and 75 being stored in cents[1]). Output the values from the two arrays of type long as monetary amounts (e.g., $2.75).

Exercise 5-4. Define a two-dimensional array, data[11][5], of type double. Initialize the elements in the first column with values from 2.0 to 3.0 inclusive in steps of 0.1. If the first element in a row has value x, populate the remaining elements in each row with the values 1/x, x^2, x^3, and x^4. Output the values in the array with each row on a separate line and with a heading for each column.

Exercise 5-5. Write a program that will calculate the average grade for the students in each of an arbitrary number of classes. The program should read in all the grades for students in all classes before calculating the averages. Output the student grades for each class followed by the average for that class.

CHAPTER 6

■ ■ ■

Applications with Strings and Text

In this chapter, you'll extend your knowledge of arrays by exploring how you use an array of characters to represent a string. You'll frequently need to work with a text string as a single entity. C doesn't provide a string data type. Instead, C uses an array of elements of type char to store a string. This chapter will show you how to create and work with variables that store strings and how the standard library functions greatly simplify string processing (including the C Library Extension 1).

In this chapter, you'll learn

- How to create string variables

- How to join two or more strings together to form a single string

- How to compare strings

- How to use arrays of strings

- What library functions are available to handle strings and how you can apply them

What Is a String?

You've already seen many examples of string constants. A *string constant* (**string literal is another synonym for this data structure**) is a sequence of characters or symbols between a pair of double quote characters. Anything between a pair of double quotes is interpreted by the compiler as a string, including any special characters and embedded spaces. Every time you've displayed a message using the printf() function, you have defined the message as a string constant. The following statements illustrate this:

```
printf("This is a string.");
printf("This is on\ntwo lines!");
printf("For \" you write \\\".");
```

The three strings used in the preceding code are shown in Figure 6-1. The decimal values of the character codes that will be stored in memory are shown below the characters.

© German Gonzalez-Morris and Ivor Horton 2020
G. Gonzalez-Morris and I. Horton, *Beginning C*, https://doi.org/10.1007/978-1-4842-5976-4_6

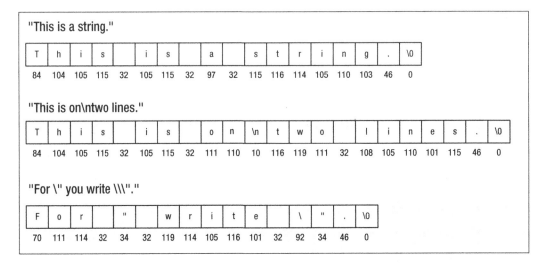

Figure 6-1. *Examples of strings in memory*

The first string is a straightforward sequence of letters followed by a period. The printf() function will output this string as

```
This is a string.
```

The second string has a newline character embedded in it, so the string will be displayed over two lines:

```
This is on
two lines!
```

The third string may look a little confusing, but the output should make it clearer:

```
For " you write \".
```

You must specify a double quote within a string as the escape sequence \" because the compiler will interpret an explicit double quote without a preceding backslash as a string delimiter. You must also use the escape sequence \\ when you want to include a backslash in a string because a backslash in a string always signals the start of an escape sequence to the compiler.

As Figure 6-1 shows, a special character with the code value 0 is added to the end of each string to mark where it ends. This character is known as the *null character*, and you write it as \0. A string is always terminated by a null character, so the length of a string is always one greater than the number of characters in the string.

■ **Caution**   Don't confuse the null character with NULL. The null character is a string terminator, whereas NULL is a symbol that represents a memory address that doesn't reference anything.

There's nothing to prevent you from adding a \0 character to the end of a string explicitly, but if you do, you'll end up with two of them. You can see how the null character works with a simple example. Have a look at the following program:

```
// Program 6.1 Displaying a string
#include <stdio.h>

int main(void)
{
  printf("The character \0 is used to terminate a string.");
  return 0;
}
```

If you compile and run this program, you'll get this output:

```
The character
```

It's probably not quite what you expected: only the first part of the string has been displayed. The output ends after the first two words because the function stops outputting the string when it reaches the first null character. There's another \0 at the end of the string, but it will never be reached. The first \0 that's found in a character sequence always marks the end of the string.

Variables That Store Strings

C has no specific provision within its syntax for variables that store strings, and because there are no string variable types, there are no special operators in the language for processing strings. This is not a problem though, because the standard library provides an extensive range of functions to handle strings. First, let's see how you create variables that represent strings.

As I said at the beginning of this chapter, you use an array of type char to hold strings. This is the simplest form of string variable. You can declare an array variable like this:

```
 char saying[20];
```

This variable can accommodate a string that contains up to 19 characters, because you must allow one element for the termination character. Of course, you could also use this array to store 20 characters that are not a string.

■ **Caution**   Remember that when you specify the dimension of an array that you intend to use to store a string, it must be at least one greater than the number of characters in the string that you want to store. The compiler automatically adds \0 to the end of every string constant.

You can initialize a string variable when you declare it:

```
char saying[] = "This is a string.";
```

Here you haven't explicitly defined the array dimension. The compiler will assign a value to the dimension that is sufficient to accommodate the initializing string constant. In this case, it will be 18, which is 17 elements for the characters in the string plus an extra element for the terminating \0. You can specify the dimension explicitly, but if you leave it for the compiler to figure out, you can be sure it will be correct.

You can initialize just part of an array of elements of type char with a string, for example:

```
char str[40] = "To be";
```

The compiler will initialize the first five elements, str[0]-str[4], with the characters of the string constant, and str[5] will contain the null character, '\0'. Of course, space is allocated for all 40 elements of the array, and they're all available to use in any way you want.

Initializing a char array and declaring it as constant is a good way of handling standard messages:

```
const char message[] = "The end of the world is nigh.";
```

Because you declare message as const, it's protected from being modified explicitly within the program. Any attempt to do so will result in an error message from the compiler. This technique for defining standard messages is particularly useful if they're used in many places within a program. It prevents accidental modification of such constants in other parts of the program. Of course, if you do need to be able to change the message, then you shouldn't specify the array as const.

When you want to refer to the string stored in an array, you just use the array name by itself. For instance, to output the string stored in message using the printf() function, you could write this:

```
printf("\nThe message is: %s", message);
```

The %s specification is for outputting a null-terminated string. At the position where the %s appears in the string that is the first argument, the printf() function will insert successive characters from the message array up to the '\0' character, which will not be inserted. Of course, an array with elements of type char behaves in exactly the same way as an array of elements of any other type, so you can use it in exactly the same way. Only the special string handling functions are sensitive to the '\0' character, so outside of that, there really is nothing special about an array that holds a string.

If you use a single char array to hold a variety of different strings, you have to declare it with a dimension that will accommodate the maximum string length you're likely to want to process. In most circumstances, the typical string length will be somewhat less than the maximum, so determining the length of a string is important, especially if you want to add to it. Let's look at how you do this using an example.

TRY IT OUT: FINDING OUT THE LENGTH OF A STRING

In this example, you're going to initialize two strings and then find out how many characters there are in each, excluding the null character:

```
// Program 6.2 Lengths of strings
#include <stdio.h>
int main(void)
{
  char str1[] = "To be or not to be";
  char str2[] = ",that is the question";
  unsigned int count = 0;                  // Stores the string length

  while (str1[count] != '\0')              // Increment count till we reach the
    ++count;                               //   terminating character.

  printf("The length of the string \"%s\" is %d characters.\n", str1, count);

  count = 0;                               // Reset count for next string
  while (str2[count] != '\0')              // Count characters in second string
    ++count;

  printf("The length of the string \"%s\" is %d characters.\n", str2, count);
  return 0;
}
```

The output you will get from this program is

```
The length of the string "To be or not to be" is 18 characters.
The length of the string ",that is the question" is 21 characters.
```

How It Works

First, you have the declarations for the variables that you'll be using:

```
char str1[] = "To be or not to be";
char str2[] = ",that is the question";
unsigned int count = 0;                    // Stores the string length
```

You declare two arrays of type char that are each initialized with a string. The compiler will set the size of each array to accommodate the string, including its terminating null. You declare and initialize a counter, count, which you'll use to record the length of a string.

Next, you have a while loop that determines the length of the first string:

```
while (str1[count] != '\0')          // Increment count till we reach the
  ++count;                           //   terminating character.
```

You use count to step through the elements in the str1 array. To find the length of str1, you increment count in the while loop as long as you haven't reached the null character that marks the end of the string. When the loop ends, count will contain the number of characters in the string, excluding the terminating null.

The while loop condition compares the value of the str1[count] element with '\0'. However, this loop would often be written like this:

```
while(str1[count])
  ++count;
```

The ASCII code value for the '\0' character is zero, which corresponds to the Boolean value false. All other ASCII code values are nonzero and therefore correspond to the Boolean value true. Thus, this version of the loop continues as long as str1[count] is not '\0', which is the same as the previous version.

▄ **Caution**   You might be tempted to write the loop like this:

```
while (str1[count++] != '\0');       // Wrong!
```

You increment the value of count using the postfix operator, so it is incremented after its value is used in the expression. However, this produces the wrong result. Thus, count will be incremented in this case even when the loop condition is false, so the value will be one greater that it should be.

Once you've determined the length, you display the string with the following statement:

```
printf("The length of the string \"%s\" is %d characters.\n", str1, count);
```

This displays the count of the number of characters that the string contains, excluding the terminating null. You use the new format specifier, %s, that you saw earlier to output the string. This outputs characters from the string until it reaches the terminating null. If there was no terminating null character, the function would continue to output characters until it found a null character somewhere in memory. This could mean *a lot* of output or the program might even crash. You use the \" escape sequence to include a double quote in the string. If you don't precede the double quote character with the backslash, the compiler will assume that it marks the end of the string that is the first argument to the printf() function, and the statement will not compile. You find the length of the second string and display the result in exactly the same way as the first string.

Arrays of Strings

It may have occurred to you by now that you can use a two-dimensional array of elements of type char to store strings, where each row holds a separate string. In this way, you can store a whole bunch of strings and refer to any of them through a single variable name, as in this example:

```
char sayings[3][32] = {
                        "Manners maketh man.",
                        "Many hands make light work.",
                        "Too many cooks spoil the broth."
                      };
```

This definition creates an array of three rows of 32 characters. The strings between the braces will be assigned in sequence to the three rows of the array, sayings[0], sayings[1], and sayings[2]. Note that you don't need to put braces around each string. The compiler deduces that each string is intended to initialize one row of the array. The first dimension specifies the number of strings that the array can store. The second dimension is specified as 32, which is just sufficient to accommodate the longest string, including its terminating \0 character.

You'll recall from the previous chapter that when you're referring to an element of an array, sayings[i][j], for instance, the first index, i, identifies a row in the array, and the second index, j, identifies a character within a row. When you want to refer to a complete row containing one of the strings, you just use a single index value between square brackets. For instance, sayings[1] refers to the second string in the array "Many hands make light work."

Although you must specify the second dimension in an array of strings, you can leave it to the compiler to figure out how many strings there are. You could write the previous definition as

```
char sayings[][32] = {
                        "Manners maketh man.",
                        "Many hands make light work.",
                        "Too many cooks spoil the broth."
                      };
```

Because there are three initializing strings, the compiler will make the first array dimension 3. Of course, you must still make sure that the second dimension is large enough to accommodate the longest string, including its terminating null character.

You could output the three sayings with the following code:

```
for(unsigned int i = 0 ; i < sizeof(sayings)/ sizeof(sayings[0]) ; ++i)
    printf("%s\n", sayings[i]);
```

You determine the number of strings in the array using the sizeof operator. You learned why this works in the previous chapter. A char array is no different from other types of arrays. In the example, sayings is an array of one-dimensional arrays. You reference a row of the array using a single index in the expression sayings[i]. This accesses the one-dimensional array that is at index position i in the sayings array.

TRY IT OUT: ARRAYS OF STRINGS

Let's change the previous example so that it finds the number of strings in a two-dimensional array and the length of each string:

```c
// Program 6.3 Arrays of strings
#include <stdio.h>

int main(void)
{
  char str[][70] =  {
              "Computers do what you tell them to do, not what you want them to do.",
              "When you put something in memory, remember where you put it.",
              "Never test for a condition you don't know what to do with.",
                  };
  unsigned int count = 0;                                  // Length of a string
  unsigned int strCount = sizeof(str)/sizeof(str[0]);   // Number of strings
  printf("There are %u strings.\n", strCount);

  // find the lengths of the strings
  for(unsigned int i = 0 ; i < strCount ; ++i)
  {
    count = 0;
    while (str[i][count])
      ++count;

    printf("The string:\n    \"%s\"\n contains %u characters.\n", str[i], count);
  }

  return 0;
}
```

The output from this program is

```
There are 3 strings.
The string:
    "Computers do what you tell them to do, not what you want them to do."
 contains 68 characters.
The string:
    "When you put something in memory, remember where you put it."
 contains 60 characters.
The string:
    "Never test for a condition you don't know what to do with."
 contains 58 characters.
```

How It Works

You declare a single two-dimensional char array where the first dimension is determined from the initializing strings:

```
char str[][70] =  {
            "Computers do what you tell them to do, not what you want them to do.",
            "When you put something in memory, remember where you put it.",
            "Never test for a condition you don't know what to do with.",
                };
```

The second index value has to be sufficient to accommodate the number of characters in the longest string, plus 1 for \0 at the end. The first initializing string is stored with the first index value as 0, the second is stored with the first index value as 1, and the third is stored with the first index value as 2. Of course you can add as many initializing strings as you want between the braces, and the compiler will adjust the first array dimension to accommodate them.

The first dimension is the number of strings in the str array, and you calculate this value using the sizeof operator and store it in strCount. The string lengths are calculated in a nested loop:

```
for(unsigned int i = 0 ; i < strCount ; ++i)
{
  count = 0;
  while (str[i][count])
    ++count;

  printf("The string:\n    \"%s\"\n contains %u characters.\n", str[i], count);
}
```

The outer for loop iterates over the strings, and the inner while loop iterates over the characters in the current string selected by the first index value, i. After the while loop ends, the string and the number of characters it contains are output. This approach obviously works for any number of strings in the array. A disadvantage of this approach is that if your strings contain significantly fewer characters than provided for by the second array dimension, you waste quite a bit of memory in the array. In the next chapter, you'll learn how you can avoid this and store each string in the most efficient manner.

Operations with Strings

The previous example shows the code for finding the length of a string, but you never really need to write such code in practice. The standard library provides a function to do this along with many other functions for processing strings. To use these, you must include the string.h header file into your source file.

The task-oriented sections that follow focus on new string functions introduced in the C11 standard. These new functions are safer and more robust than the traditional functions you may be used to using. They offer greater protection against errors such as buffer overflow. However, that protection is dependent on careful and correct coding.

Checking for C11/C17 Support

The default set of string processing functions that the standard library provides are not secure. They provide considerable potential for errors in your code that sometimes can be difficult to find. A bigger problem is that they allow programs to be subverted by malicious code when they are used in a network environment.

These problems can occur primarily because there is no verification that arrays are large enough for the operations. For these reasons, the C17 (since C11) standard includes optional versions of the string processing functions that are more secure and less prone to errors because the dimensions of arrays are checked to ensure they are large enough. Writing secure and less error-prone code is of such importance that I will concentrate on the optional string processing functions that do bounds checking for arrays. In my view, any C17-conforming compiler worth its salt should implement the optional string functions. All the optional functions have names that end with _s.

It is easy to determine whether the standard library that comes with your C compiler supports these optional functions. Just compile and execute the following code:

```
// Program 6.1a Check C11/C17 versions
#include <stdio.h>

int main(void)
{
        //this line shouldn't compile in MS Visual Studio, comment it if necessary
        printf("__STDC_VERSION__ = %d\n", __STDC_VERSION__);

#if defined __STDC_LIB_EXT1__
  printf("Optional functions are defined.\n");
#else
  printf("Optional functions are not defined.\n");
#endif
  return 0;
}
```

The __STDC_VERSION__ macro should yield value 201710L or 201112L for C17 and C11 versions, respectively.

A compiler that implements the optional functions according to the C11/C17 standard will define the symbol __STDC_LIB_EXT1__ (C Library Extension 1). This code uses preprocessor directives to insert one of two printf() statements, depending on whether the symbol __STDC_LIB_EXT1__ is defined. If this symbol is defined, the code will output the message

```
Optional functions are defined.
```

If the symbol __STDC_LIB_EXT1__ is not defined, you will see the following output:

```
Optional functions are not defined.
```

The preprocessor directives I have used here (these are the lines that begin with #) work much like the if statement you know and love. I'll explain preprocessor directives in more detail in Chapter 13.

To use the optional functions in string.h, you must define the __STDC_WANT_LIB_EXT1__ symbol in your source file to represent the value 1, prior to the include directive for string.h, like this:

```
#define __STDC_WANT_LIB_EXT1__ 1    // Make optional versions of functions available
#include <string.h>                 // Header for string functions
```

If you don't define this symbol as 1, only the standard set of string processing functions will be available. You may wonder why such an elaborate mechanism is necessary to make use of the optional string functions. The reason is so it does not break old code that was written before the C11 standard was around. It is obviously possible that old code may use one or more of the new function names. In particular, many programmers implemented their own safer string handling functions in the past, so this could easily cause name conflicts with the C11/C17 library. When conflicts occur, the old code can be compiled with a C11/C17 compiler by defining __STDC_WANT_LIB_EXT1__ as 0, which inhibits the availability of the optional functions.

GCC doesn't have this new C11/C17 feature implemented; meanwhile, Microsoft Windows compiler and Pelles C do. Therefore, check if it is implemented by default or it is necessary to use an external library.

Finding the Length of a String

The strnlen_s() function that returns the length of a string requires two arguments: the address of the string, which is the array name for a one-dimensional char array, and the size of the array. Knowing the size of the array enables the function to avoid accessing memory beyond the last element when there is no terminating \0 character present.

The function returns the length of the string as an integer value of type size_t. If the first argument is NULL, 0 will be returned. If the array specified by the first argument does not contain a \0 character within the number of elements specified by the second argument, the second argument value will be returned for the length of the string.

We can rewrite the loop in Program 6.3 to use the strnlen_s() function to obtain the lengths of the strings:

```
for(unsigned int i = 0 ; i < strCount ; ++i)
  {
    printf("The string:\n    \"%s\"\n contains %zu characters.\n",
                             str[i], strnlen_s(str[i], sizeof(str[i])));
  }
```

As before, the for loop iterates over the first dimension of the two-dimensional str array so it selects each string in turn. The original inner while loop is no longer required, and the loop body is now just one statement. The third argument to printf() calls the strnlen_s() function to obtain the length of the string in str[i]. Applying the sizeof operator to str[i] provides the second argument value for strnlen_s().

■ **Note**   The standard function to obtain the length of a string is strlen(). It requires just the address of the string as the argument. This function will overrun the end of the string when no \0 is present.

Unfortunately you can't use the assignment operator to copy a string from one variable to another in the way you do with int and double variables. To achieve the equivalent of an arithmetic assignment with strings, the string in one variable has to be copied element by element to the other. In fact, performing any operation on string variables is very different from the arithmetic operations with numeric variables you've seen so far. Let's explore some common operations that you might want to perform with strings and how you can use library functions to carry them out.

Copying Strings

The strcpy_s() function provides the effect of assigning the contents of one string variable to another. The first argument identifies the destination for the copy, the second argument is an integer specifying the size of the first argument, and the third argument is the source string. Knowing the length of the destination enables the function to avoid overwriting memory beyond the end of the last character in the destination. This could occur if the source string is longer than the size of the destination. The function returns an integer that is zero when everything goes well and nonzero when it doesn't. Here's an example:

```
char source[] = "Only the mediocre are always at their best.";
char destination[50];
if(strcpy_s(destination, sizeof(destination), source))
  printf("An error occurred copying the string.\n");
```

The condition for the if statement is an expression that calls strcpy_s() to copy the contents of the source array to the destination array. The value of the expression is the value returned by strcpy_s(). This will be 0 if the copy works and nonzero if it doesn't. A nonzero integer value corresponds to true, so in this case the printf() call will be executed to output an error message.

■ **Note**   The standard copy function is strcpy(). This copies the string specified by the second argument to the location specified by the first argument. There is no check on the capacity of the destination.

The strncpy_s() function provides the possibility of copying part of the source string to the destination. The additional n in the name compared to strcpy_s() indicates that up to some given n, characters may be copied. The first three arguments are the same as for strcpy_s(), and the fourth argument specifies the maximum number of characters to be copied from the source string identified by the third argument. If a \0 is found in the source string before the maximum specified characters have been copied, copying ceases, and the \0 is appended to the destination.

Here's how you might use strncpy_s():

```
char source[] = "Only the mediocre are always at their best.";
char destination[50];
if(strncpy_s(destination, sizeof(destination), source, 17))
  printf("An error occurred copying the string.\n");
```

Up to 17 characters from source will be copied to destination. No \0 appears in the first 17 characters in source, so all 17 characters will be copied, and the function will append \0 as the character in destination[18], and destination will then contain "Only the mediocre".

Concatenating Strings

Concatenation is the fancy term for joining one string to the end of another. This is a common requirement. For instance, you might want to assemble a single message from two or more strings. You might define the error messages in a program as a few basic text strings to which you append one of a variety of strings to make the message specific to a particular error.

When you are copying one string to the end of another, you need to be sure of two things if the operation is to be secure: first, that the space available in the destination string is not exceeded—otherwise, other data or even code could be overwritten—and, second, that the resultant combined string will have a \0 character at the end. The optional strcat_s() function in string.h meets this requirement.

The strcat_s() requires three arguments: the address of the string that is to be appended to, the maximum length of the string that can be stored by the first argument, and the address of the string that is to be appended to the first argument. The function returns an integer error code as a value of type errno_t, which is an integer type that is compiler dependent.

Here's an example of using strcat_s():

```
char str1[50] = "To be, or not to be, ";
char str2[] = "that is the question.";
int retval = strcat_s(str1, sizeof(str1), str2);
if(retval)
  printf("There was an error joining the strings. Error code = %d",retval);
else
  printf("The combined strings:\n%s\n", str1);
```

The strings str1 and str1 belong together, so this fragment uses strcat_s() to append str2 to str1. The operation copies str2 to the end of str1, overwriting the \0 in str1 and then appending a final \0. When everything works as it should, strcat_s() returns 0. If str1 is not large enough to allow str2 to be appended or there is some other constraint preventing the operation from being carried out, the return value will be nonzero.

In a similar way to strncpy_s(), you have an optional function, strncat_s(), that concatenates part of one string to another. This also has an extra argument specifying the maximum number of characters to be concatenated. Here's how that works:

```
char str1[50] = "To be, or not to be, ";
char str2[] = "that is the question.";
int retval = strncat_s(str1, sizeof(str1), str2, 4);
if(retval)
  printf("There was an error joining the strings. Error code = %d",retval);
else
  printf("The combined strings:\n%s\n", str1);
```

Because the fourth argument to strncat_s() is 4, this fragment will append "that" from str2 to str1 and add \0. A \0 appearing in str2 before the maximum number of characters had been copied would end the process.

Let's see how copying and concatenating strings work in an example.

TRY IT OUT: JOINING STRINGS

This example assembles four strings into a single string:

```
// Program 6.4 Joining strings
#define __STDC_WANT_LIB_EXT1__ 1        // Make optional versions of functions
available
#include <string.h>                     // Header for string functions
#include <stdio.h>

int main(void)
{
  char preamble[] = "The joke is:\n\n";
  char str[][60] = {
                    "My dog hasn\'t got any nose.\n",
```

```
                   "How does your dog smell then?\n",
                   "My dog smells horrible.\n",
                                  //jokes from C11 standard footnote, which are
                                  removed in C17:
                                  "Atomic objects are neither active nor
                                  radioactive\n",
                                  "Among other implications, atomic variables
                                  shall not decay\n"
             };

  unsigned int strCount = sizeof(str)/sizeof(str[0]);

  // Find the total length of all the strings in str
  unsigned int length = 0;
  for(unsigned int i = 0 ; i < strCount ; ++i)
    length += strnlen_s(str[i], sizeof(str[i]));

  // Create array to hold all strings combined
  char joke[length + strnlen_s(preamble, sizeof(preamble)) + 1];

  if(strncpy_s(joke, sizeof(joke), preamble, sizeof(preamble)))
  {
    printf("Error copying preamble to joke.\n");
    return 1;
  }

  // Concatenate strings in joke
  for(unsigned int i = 0 ; i < strCount ; ++i)
  {
    if(strncat_s(joke, sizeof(joke), str[i], sizeof(str[i])))
    {
      printf("Error copying string str[%u].", i);
      return 2;
    }
  }

  printf("%s", joke);
  return 0;
}
```

The output from this program will be the following:

```
The joke is:

My dog hasn't got any nose.
How does your dog smell then?
My dog smells horrible.
```

How It Works

Note the definition for the __STDC_WANT_LIB_EXT1__ symbol at the beginning of the source file. Without this, the optional string functions would not be accessible.

The preamble array contains the first of the four strings to be assembled into a single string, and the two-dimensional str array contains the other three. The total length of the strings in the str array is determined by the for loop:

```
for(unsigned int i = 0 ; i < strCount ; ++i)
  length += strnlen_s(str[i], sizeof(str[i]));
```

This uses strnlen_s() to obtain the number of characters in each string. The second argument is the length of the array containing a string, and it prevents the function from accessing memory beyond the last element.

The size of the joke array that will hold the result of concatenating all four strings is determined at runtime from the length of the string in the preamble array and the total length of all three strings from the str array:

```
char joke[length + strnlen_s(preamble, sizeof(preamble)) + 1];
```

Note the +1 in the dimension specification to provide for the \0 at the end. You must always remember to allow space for the terminating \0.

The string in preamble is copied to joke using strncpy_s() like this:

```
if(strncpy_s(joke, sizeof(joke), preamble, sizeof(preamble)))
{
  printf("Error copying preamble to joke.\n");
  return 1;
}
```

The fourth argument to strncpy_s() ensures that no more characters are copied than the capacity of the source string, preamble. If the value returned by strncpy_s() is nonzero, an error of some kind prevented the copy from being completed. This would be the case if joke was too small to accommodate the string, for example. In this case, the if condition would be true, and the printf() call would output an error message, and the program would end with the return code 1.

■ **Caution** You cannot concatenate a string to an array that does not contain a string. If you wanted to use strcat_s() or strncat_s() to copy preamble to joke, you would need to initialize joke to an empty string. The compiler will not allow you to initialize an array in the declaration statement when the dimension is determined at runtime. To initialize joke to an empty array, you could store '\0' in joke[0] using an assignment.

The next step is to concatenate the strings from the str array to joke in a for loop:

```
for(unsigned int i = 0 ; i < strCount ; ++i)
{
  if(strncat_s(joke, sizeof(joke), str[i], sizeof(str[i])))
  {
```

```
        printf("Error copying string str[%u].", i);
        return 2;
    }
}
```

The `strncat_s()` function is called in the condition to the `if` statement to check the return value, just like with `strncpy_s()`. If something goes wrong, an error message is displayed, and the program ends with return code 2.

Finally, the program outputs the combined string in `joke`, and the output shows that everything went well after all.

■ **Note** Any nonzero return value to end a program is an abnormal end. By using different nonzero values for abnormal returns, you can identify where in the code the abnormal end occurred.

Comparing Strings

The standard library provides functions for comparing strings and deciding whether one string is greater than or less than another. It may sound a bit odd applying such terms as greater than and less than to strings, but the result is produced quite simply. Successive corresponding characters of the two strings are compared based on the numerical value of their character codes. This mechanism is illustrated graphically in Figure 6-2, in which the character codes in the strings `str1` and `str2` are shown as hexadecimal values.

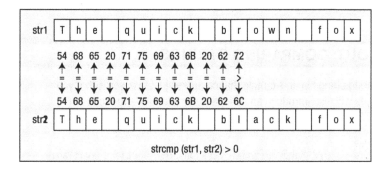

Figure 6-2. *Comparing two strings*

If two strings are identical, then of course they're equal. The first pair of corresponding characters that are different in two strings determines whether the first string is less than or greater than the second. So, for example, if the character code for the character in the first string is less than the character code for the character in the second string, the first string is less than the second. This mechanism for comparing two strings generally corresponds to what you expect when you're arranging strings in alphabetical order.

■ **Note** There are no optional functions for comparing strings.

The standard function strcmp(str1, str2) compares two strings, str1 and str2. It returns a value of type int that is less than, equal to, or greater than 0, depending on whether str1 is less than, equal to, or greater than str2. You can express the comparison illustrated in Figure 6-2 in the following code fragment:

```
char str1[] = "The quick brown fox";
char str2[] = "The quick black fox";
if(strcmp(str1, str2) > 0)
  printf("str1 is greater than str2.\n");
```

The printf() statement will execute only if the strcmp() function returns a positive integer. This will happen when the strcmp() function finds a pair of corresponding characters in the two strings that do not match and the character code in str1 is greater than the character code in str2.

The strncmp() function compares up to a given number, n, of characters of the two strings. The first two arguments are the same as for the strcmp() function, and the number of characters to be compared is specified by a third argument, which is an integer of type size_t. This function would be useful if you were processing strings with a prefix of ten characters, say, that represented a part number or a sequence number. You could use the strncmp() function to compare just the first ten characters of two strings to determine which should come first:

```
if(strncmp(str1, str2, 10) <= 0)
  printf("\n%s\n%s", str1, str2);
else
  printf("\n%s\n%s", str2, str1);
```

These statements output strings str1 and str2 that are arranged in ascending sequence according to the first ten characters in the strings.

Let's try comparing strings in a working example.

TRY IT OUT: COMPARING STRINGS

I can demonstrate the use of comparing strings in an example that compares just two words that you enter from the keyboard. This example will also introduce an optional safer alternative to the scanf() function for keyboard input, scanf_s(), which is declared in stdio.h:

```
// Program 6.5 Comparing strings
#define __STDC_WANT_LIB_EXT1__ 1      // Make optional versions of functions available
#include <stdio.h>
#include <string.h>

#define MAX_LENGTH 21                 // Maximum char array length
int main(void)
{
  char word1[MAX_LENGTH];                            // Stores the first word
  char word2[MAX_LENGTH];                            // Stores the second word

  printf("Type in the first word (maximum %d characters): ", MAX_LENGTH - 1);
  int retval = scanf_s("%s", word1, sizeof(word1));       // Read the first word
  if(EOF == retval)
  {
    printf("Error reading the word.\n");
    return 1;
  }
```

```
  printf("Type in the second word (maximum %d characters): ", MAX_LENGTH - 1);
  retval = scanf_s("%s", word2, sizeof(word2));          // Read the second word
  if(EOF == retval)
  {
    printf("Error reading the word.\n");
    return 2;
  }

  // Compare the words
  if(strcmp(word1,word2) == 0)
    printf("You have entered identical words");
  else
    printf("%s precedes %s\n",
                    (strcmp(word1, word2) < 0) ? word1 : word2,
                    (strcmp(word1, word2) < 0) ? word2 : word1);

  return 0;
}
```

The program will read in two words and then tell you which word comes before the other alphabetically. The output looks something like this:

```
Type in the first word (maximum 20 characters): Eve
Type in the second word (maximum 20 characters): Adam
Adam precedes Eve
```

How It Works

The comparison functions are standard in `string.h`, so you don't need to define `__STDC_WANT_LIB_EXT1__` for those, but you do need to define it as 1 to access the safer replacement for `scanf()` in `stdio.h`. You have the `#include` directives for the header files for the standard input and output library and the string handling library following the `#define` directive:

```
#define __STDC_WANT_LIB_EXT1__ 1   // Make optional versions of functions available
#include <stdio.h>
#include <string.h>
```

You also define a symbol for use in the program code:

```
#define MAX_LENGTH 21                 // Maximum char array length
```

This symbol specifies the maximum array size to store the input, so the maximum word length that can be entered will be `MAX_LENGTH-1`. Using this symbol in the code will allow the length of the input to the program to be changed just by changing the value for this symbol.

In the body of `main()`, you declare two character arrays to store the words that you'll read from the keyboard:

```
  char word1[MAX_LENGTH];             // Stores the first word
  char word2[MAX_LENGTH];             // Stores the second word
```

You set the size of the arrays to MAX_LENGTH. It's *your* responsibility to check that the user input does not exceed the array capacity. The function scanf_s() will help with this. Here's how you prompt for, and read, the first input word:

```
printf("Type in the first word (maximum %d characters): ", MAX_LENGTH - 1);
int retval = scanf_s("%s", word1, sizeof(word1));    // Read the first word
if(EOF == retval)
{
  printf("Error reading the word.\n");
  return 1;
}
```

The prompt produced by the printf() call displays MAX_LENGTH-1 as the maximum-length word that can be entered. This allows for the terminating \0. The scanf_s() function requires two arguments for each value to be read using the %s input specification. The first is the address of where the input is to be stored, and the second is the maximum number of characters. You supply word1 and sizeof(word1) as the arguments corresponding to the %s format specification. Note how you use just the array name, word1, with no & as the starting address for where input is to be stored. You saw in Chapter 5 that the array name by itself is the address where the array starts. In fact, word1 is the equivalent of &word[0], so you could use either. I'll explain more about this in the next chapter.

The scanf_s() function returns an integer value that will be the value of the symbol EOF if the character limit is exceeded. The stdio.h header defines EOF. The if statement outputs a message and terminates the program when the maximum input limit is exceeded. You read the input for word2 essentially the same way, reusing the retval variable to store the value returned by scanf_s().

When you use the scanf_s() function to read characters using the %c conversion specification, it also requires two arguments for each %c in the format string. To read a single character, you would code it like this:

```
char ch;
scanf_s("%c", &ch, sizeof(ch));
```

Up to now, you have only used %c to read a single character, but you can also use it to read multiple characters into a char array. This is where the maximum input character count becomes important, for example:

```
char ch[5];
if(EOF == scanf_s("%c", ch, sizeof(ch)))
  printf("Error reading characters.\n");
```

The scanf_s() function will store up to five characters in the ch array. No \0 is added. If you enter abcde, each character will be stored in a successive element of ch. If you enter more than five characters, the operation will fail, and the function will return EOF. The standard scanf() function would happily overwrite memory beyond the end of the ch array when more characters than the maximum are entered.

Note that the scanf_s() function requires two arguments for each %[conversion specifier in the format string. This specification reads characters that must be from a given set, and this is explained in Appendix D.

Finally, in the example, you used the strcmp() function to compare the two words that were entered:

```
    if(strcmp(word1,word2) == 0)
      printf("You have entered identical words");
    else
      printf("%s precedes %s\n",
                      (strcmp(word1, word2) < 0) ? word1 : word2,
                      (strcmp(word1, word2) < 0) ? word2 : word1);
```

If the value returned by the strcmp() function is 0, the two strings are equal, and you display a message to this effect. If not, you output a message specifying which word precedes the other. You do this using the conditional operator to specify which word you want to output first and which you want to output second.

Searching a String

The string.h header file declares several string searching functions. Before I get into these, we'll take a peek at the subject of the next chapter, namely, pointers. You need an appreciation of the basics of this in order to understand how to use the functions that search strings.

The Idea of a Pointer

As you'll learn in detail in the next chapter, C provides a remarkably useful type of variable called a pointer. A *pointer* is a variable that stores an address—that is, its value is the address of another location in memory that can contain a value. You already used an address when you used the scanf() and scanf_s() functions. A pointer variable with the name pNumber is defined by the second of the following two statements:

```
int Number = 25;
int *pNumber = &Number;
```

You declare a variable, Number, with the value 25, and a pointer, pNumber, which contains the address of Number. You can now use the variable pNumber in the expression *pNumber to obtain the value contained in Number. The * is the dereference operator, and its effect is to access the data stored at the address specified by a pointer.

Figure 6-3 illustrates what happens when these two statements are executed.

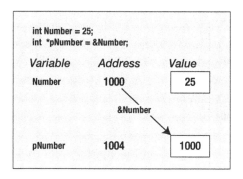

Figure 6-3. An example of a pointer

The memory addresses for Number and pNumber in Figure 6-3 are arbitrary. The value of &Number is the address where Number is located, and this value is used to initialize pNumber in the second statement.

The main reason for introducing the idea of pointers here is that the functions that I'll discuss in the following sections return pointers, so you could be a bit confused by them if there were no explanation here at all. If you end up confused anyway, don't worry—all will be illuminated in the next chapter.

Searching a String for a Character

The strchr() function searches a given string for a specified character. The first argument to the function is the string to be searched (which will be the address of a char array), and the second argument is the character that you're looking for. The function will search the string starting at the beginning and return a pointer to the first position in the string where the character is found. This is the address of this position in memory and is of type char* described as the "pointer to char." So to store the value that's returned, you must create a variable that can store the address of a character. If the character isn't found, the function returns a special value NULL, which, as you know, is the equivalent of 0 for a pointer and represents a pointer that doesn't point to anything.

You can use the strchr() function like this:

```
char str[] = "The quick brown fox";    // The string to be searched
char ch = 'q';                          // The character we are looking for
char *pGot_char = NULL;                 // Pointer initialized to NULL
pGot_char = strchr(str, ch);            // Stores address where ch is found
```

The first argument to strchr() is the address of the first location to be searched. Here, it is the first element of str. The second argument is the character that is sought, so in this case it is ch, which is of type char. The strchr() function expects its second argument to be of type int, so the compiler will convert the value of ch to this type before passing it to the function.

You could just as well define ch as type int like this:

```
int ch = 'q';                           // Initialize with character code for q
```

Functions are often implemented so that a character is passed as an argument of type int because it's simpler to work with type int than type char. This is because the EOF character that indicates end of file is a negative integer, and if type char is an unsigned type, it cannot represent a negative integer.

Figure 6-4 illustrates the result of this search using the strchr() function.

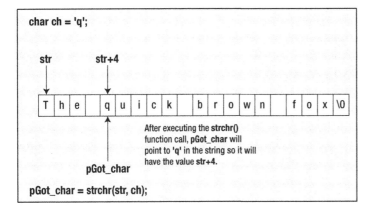

Figure 6-4. Searching for a character

The address of the first character in the string is given by the array name, str. Because 'q' appears as the fifth character in the string, its address will be str + 4, an offset of 4 bytes from the first character. Thus, the variable pGot_char will contain the address str + 4.

Using the variable name pGot_char in an expression will access the address it contains. If you want to access the character that's stored at that address, then you must *dereference* the pointer. To dereference a pointer, you precede the pointer variable name with the dereference operator *, for example:

```
printf("Character found was %c.", *pGot_char);
```

I'll go into more detail on using the dereference operator in the next chapter.

Of course, it's always possible that the character you're searching for might not be found in the string, so you should ensure that you don't attempt to dereference a NULL pointer. If you do try to dereference a NULL pointer, your program will crash. This is very easy to avoid with an if statement, like this:

```
if(pGot_char)
  printf("Character found was '%c'.", *pGot_char);
```

A NULL pointer value converts to the bool value false, and a non-NULL pointer value converts to true. If pGot_char is NULL, the if expression will be false, so the printf() function will not be called. Now you only execute the printf() statement to output the character when pGot_char isn't NULL. The output from this fragment will be

```
Character found was 'q'.
```

Of course, pGot_char contains the address of the substring that starts with ch, so you could output this with the statement

```
printf("The substring beginning with '%c' is: \"%s\"\n", ch, pGot_char);
```

This statement will produce the output

```
The substring beginning with 'q' is: "quick brown fox"
```

You can search for multiple occurrences of a character quite easily using

```
char str[] = "Peter piper picked a peck of pickled pepper.";     // The string to be searched
char ch = 'p';                              // The character we are looking for
char *pGot_char = str;                      // Pointer initialized to string start
int count = 0;                              // Number of times found
while(pGot_char = strchr(pGot_char, ch))    // As long as NULL is not returned...
{                                           // ...continue the loop.
  ++count;                                  // Increment the count
  ++pGot_char;                              // Move to next character address
  }
printf("The character '%c' was found %d times in the following string:\n\"%s\"\n",
                                           ch, count, str);
```

You may get a warning from your compiler that the = operator is used in the loop condition. Many compilers issue this warning because it is usually a mistake, indicating it should be ==, but not in this case. This code fragment produced the output

```
The character 'p' was found 8 times in the following string:
"Peter piper picked a peck of pickled pepper."
```

The pGot_char pointer is initialized with the address of the string, str. The search occurs in the while loop condition. The strchr() function is called to start searching for ch at the address in pGot_char, which will be the start of str initially. The return value is stored back in pGot_char, so this value determines whether the loop continues. If ch is found, pGot_char will be assigned the address of where it is found in the string, and the loop will continue. In the loop body, you increment the count of the number of times that the character has been found. You also increment pGot_char so the address it contains will refer to the character following the position where ch was found. Thus, the next loop iteration will search from this new address. The loop ends when strchr() returns NULL.

The strrchr() function is basically similar in operation to the strchr() function and expects the same two arguments, the first being the address of the string to be searched and the second the character to be found. However, the difference is that strrchr() searches for the character in reverse sequence starting from the end of the string. Thus, it will return the address of the *last* occurrence of the character in the string or NULL if the character isn't found. The terminating \0 is considered to be part of the string.

Searching a String for a Substring

The strstr() function is probably the most useful of all the searching functions. It searches one string for the first occurrence of a substring and returns a pointer to the position in the first string where the substring is found. If it doesn't find a match, it returns NULL. So if the value returned here isn't NULL, you can be sure that the searching function you're using has found an occurrence of what it was searching for. The first argument to the function is the string that is to be searched, and the second argument is the substring you're looking for.

Here is an example of how you might use the strstr() function:

```
char text[] = "Every dog has his day";
char word[] = "dog";
char *pFound = NULL;
pFound = strstr(text, word);
```

This searches text for the first occurrence of the string stored in word. Because the string "dog" appears starting at the seventh character in text, pFound will be set to the address text + 6. The search is case sensitive, so if you search the text string for "Dog", it won't be found.

TRY IT OUT: SEARCHING A STRING

Here's some of what I've been talking about in action:

```
// Program 6.6 A demonstration of seeking and finding
#include <stdio.h>
#include <string.h>
```

```
int main(void)
{
  char str1[] = "This string contains the holy grail.";
  char str2[] = "the holy grail";
  char str3[] = "the holy grill";

  // Search str1 for the occurrence of str2
  if(strstr(str1, str2))
    printf("\"%s\" was found in \"%s\"\n",str2, str1);
  else
    printf("\n\"%s\" was not found.", str2);

  // Search str1 for the occurrence of str3
  if(!strstr(str1, str3))
    printf("\"%s\" was not found.\n", str3);
  else
    printf("\nWe shouldn't get to here!");
  return 0;
}
```

This program produces the following output:

```
"the holy grail" was found in "This string contains the holy grail."
"the holy grill" was not found.
```

How It Works

The #include directive for string.h is necessary when you want to use any of the string processing functions. You have three strings defined: str1, str2, and str3:

```
char str1[] = "This string contains the holy grail.";
char str2[] = "the holy grail";
char str3[] = "the holy grill";
```

In the first if statement, you use the library function strstr() to search for the occurrence of the second string in the first string:

```
  if(strstr(str1, str2))
    printf("\"%s\" was found in \"%s\"\n",str2, str1);
  else
    printf("\n\"%s\" was not found.", str2);
```

You display a message corresponding to the result by testing the returned value of strstr(). If the value returned is not NULL, this indicates that str2 was found in str1. The if expression converts to true in this case, so the first printf() executes. If str2 is not found in str1, the if expression is NULL, which converts to false so the else is executed. In this case, a message is displayed indicating that the string was not found.

You then repeat the process in the second `if` statement and check for the occurrence of the third string in the first:

```
if(!strstr(str1, str3))
  printf("\"%s\" was not found.\n", str3);
else
  printf("\nWe shouldn't get to here!");
```

In this case, `str3` does not appear in `str1`, so `strstr()` will return `NULL`. The expression `!NULL` converts to `true`, so the first `printf()` statement will be executed. If you get output from the last `printf()` in the program, something is seriously wrong.

Tokenizing a String

A *token* is a sequence of characters within a string that is bounded by some predefined delimiter characters. For example, considering this sentence as a string, the words are delimited by spaces, commas, and a period.

Breaking a sentence into words is called *tokenizing*. The standard library provides the `strtok()` function for tokenizing a string. It requires two arguments: the string to be tokenized and a string containing all the possible delimiter characters. There is also an optional tokenizing function, `strtok_s()`, that is safer to use than the standard function, so I will describe how that works. Because it's an optional standard function, you need to define the `__STDC_WANT_LIB_EXT1__` symbol as 1 to use it.

The way `strtok_s()` works is a little complicated because it provides for the possibility of multiple calls of the function to find successive tokens in a single string. I'll first explain the arguments you must supply and then explain the operation of the function.

The `strtok_s()` function requires four arguments:

(C17 and Microsoft Visual Studio strtok_s have a different signature. C17 has one more parameter.)

> `str`: The address of the string to be tokenized, or `NULL` for second and subsequent tokenizing operations after the first on the same string.

> `str_size`: The address of an integer variable containing the size of the array in which the first argument is stored. This will be updated by the function, so it stores the number of characters left to be searched in the string to be tokenized after the current search. (This parameter does not exist in Microsoft implementation and must not be written.)

> `delimiters`: The address of a string that contains all possible token delimiters.

> `pptr`: A pointer to a variable of type char* in which the function will store information to allow it to continue searching for tokens after the first has been found.

■ **Note** A pointer to a variable of type char* will be of type char**. You'll learn more about this in the next chapter. Of course, for a variable, `ptr`, of type char*, a pointer to it is &ptr.

The function returns a pointer of type char* that points to the first character of a token or `NULL` if no token is found, which implies the string is empty or consists entirely of delimiters. The operation of `strtok_s()` when searching for multiple tokens proceeds like this:

1. On the first function call with str, not NULL, str is searched to find the first character that is not a delimiter. If no such character is found, there are no tokens in the string, and the function returns NULL. If a nondelimiter character is found, the function searches subsequent characters for a delimiter character. When such a delimiter is found, it is replaced by \0 to terminate the token, and you can call the function again with NULL as the first argument to find another token.

2. On the second and subsequent calls to search a given string, the first argument must be NULL, and the second and fourth arguments must be the same arguments that you used in the first function call. You can supply a different delimiters string argument if you know what you are doing. The function searches for a nondelimiter character starting at the position in str following the previous \0 that was inserted. If no such character is found, NULL is returned. If such a character is found, subsequent characters in str are searched to find a delimiter from delimiters. If a delimiter is found, it is replaced by \0 to terminate the token, and you can call the function again with NULL as the first argument to find another token.

If the operation of strtok_s() still seems a little confusing, a working example will shed some light. But to use it with text entered from the keyboard, you need a way to read a sequence of characters. The gets_s() function in stdio.h is one way to do this. This is an optional function because it replaces gets(), which is now a deprecated function, so you should not use it. (Of course, it could be found in older code.)

The gets_s() function expects two arguments. The first is the address of an array, str, say, in which the characters read are to be stored; and the second is the size of the array. The function reads up to a maximum of one less character than the size of the array from the keyboard, including spaces. If there are more characters entered after the maximum has been stored in str, they are discarded. Pressing Enter terminates the input. The function appends \0 following the last character read. If you just press Enter without entering characters, then str[0] will be set to \0. If everything works as it should, gets_s() returns str; otherwise, NULL is returned. You'll see it working in the next example, which tokenizes some text that you enter.

TRY IT OUT: TOKENIZING A STRING

This program will extract all the words from text that you enter:

```
// Program 6.7 Find all the words
#define __STDC_WANT_LIB_EXT1__ 1    // Make optional versions of functions available
#include <stdio.h>
#include <string.h>
#include <stdbool.h>

int main(void)
{
  char delimiters[] = " \".,;:!?)(";      // Prose delimiters
  char buf[100];                          // Buffer for a line of keyboard input
  char str[1000];                         // Stores the prose to be tokenized
  char* ptr = NULL;                       // Pointer used by strtok_s()
  str[0] = '\0';                          // Set 1st character to null

  size_t str_len = sizeof(str);
  size_t buf_len = sizeof(buf);
  printf("Enter some prose that is less than %zd characters.\n"
         "Terminate input by entering an empty line:\n", str_len);
```

```
  // Read multiple lines of prose from the keyboard
  while(true)
  {
    if(!gets_s(buf, buf_len))                // Read a line of input
    {
      printf("Error reading string.\n");
      return 1;
    }
    if(!strnlen_s(buf, buf_len))             // An empty line ends input
      break;

    if(strcat_s(str, str_len, buf))          // Concatenate the line with str
    {
      printf("Maximum permitted input length exceeded.\n");
      return 1;
    }
  }
  printf("The words in the prose that you entered are:\n");

  // Find and list all the words in the prose
  unsigned int word_count = 0;
  char * pWord = strtok_s(str, &str_len, delimiters, &ptr);  // Find 1st word
  // use this line instead, for Microsoft compiler:
  // char * pWord = strtok_s(str, delimiters, &ptr);  // Find 1st word  if(pWord)
  {
    do
    {
      printf("%-18s", pWord);
      if(++word_count % 5 == 0)
        printf("\n");
      pWord = strtok_s(NULL, &str_len, delimiters, &ptr);  // Find subsequent words
      // use this line instead, for Microsoft compiler:
      //pWord = strtok_s(NULL, delimiters, &ptr);    // Find subsequent words
        }while(pWord);                        // NULL ends tokenizing
    printf("\n%u words found.\n", word_count);
  }
  else
    printf("No words found.\n");

  return 0;
}
```

Here is an example of some output from the program:

```
Enter some prose that is less than 1000 characters.
Terminate input by entering an empty line:
My father's family name being Pirrip, and my Christian name Philip,
 my infant tongue could make of both names nothing longer
  or more explicit than Pip.
So, I called myself Pip, and came to be called Pip.
```

```
The words in the prose that you entered are:
My              father's        family          name            being
Pirrip          and             my              Christian       name
Philip          my              infant          tongue          could
make            of              both            names           nothing
longer          or              more            explicit        than
Pip             So              I               called          myself
Pip             and             came            to              be
called          Pip
37 words found.
```

How It Works

The set of delimiters is somewhat arbitrary, but it includes most characters you would normally find delimiting words in prose:

```
char delimiters[] = " \".,;:!?)(";        // Prose delimiters
```

There are two arrays declared: buf to store a line of input and str, which will hold the complete prose to be tokenized. The next variable is for use in the tokenizing process:

```
char* ptr = NULL;                         // Pointer used by strtok_s()
```

The ptr variable holds a string address, and this will be used by the strtok_s() function to record a position in a string being tokenized, which it will use the next time it is called. In order for the function to update ptr, it needs access to its memory address. The address of ptr is &ptr, and this will be passed to the function as the fourth argument.

You initialize the first element of str to \0, so it contains an empty string. This is necessary to allow the first input string to be concatenated to str.

After prompting for input, one or more lines of input are read in a loop:

```
while(true)
{
  if(!gets_s(buf, buf_len))               // Read a line of input
  {
    printf("Error reading string.\n");
    return 1;
  }
  if(!strnlen_s(buf, buf_len))            // An empty line ends input
    break;

  if(strcat_s(str, str_len, buf))         // Concatenate the line with str
  {
    printf("Maximum permitted input length exceeded.\n");
    return 1;
  }
}
```

The while loop continues until a break statement in the body of the loop is executed. We use gets_s() to read the input because it can read a string, including spaces, whereas scanf_s() cannot. The gets_s() function will read up to buf_len-1 characters into buf and append a \0. As with any input or output operation, things can go wrong. If an error of some kind prevents the gets_s() function from reading the input successfully, it will return NULL (normally, it returns the address passed as the argument, buffer, in this case). You therefore check that the read operation was successful using the if statement. This will output a message and end the program if the read operation fails for any reason. Errors on keyboard input are relatively rare, so I won't always include this testing when reading from the keyboard in subsequent examples, but if you are reading from a file, verifying that the read was successful is essential.

When an empty line is entered, the length of the string in buf will be 0, and this terminates the input operation by causing the break statement to be executed, thus ending the loop. Each line of input is concatenated to the current contents of str by the strcat_s() function. The function returns a nonzero value when the operation potentially exceeds the capacity of str, and this will cause a message to be output, and the program will be terminated by returning 1.

The first token is found and extracted by this statement:

```
char * pWord = strtok_s(str, &str_len, delimiters, &ptr);   // Find 1st word
   // use this line instead, for Microsoft compiler:
   // char * pWord = strtok_s(str, delimiters, &ptr);   // Find 1st word
```

The call of strok_s() to find the first token has str as the first argument. Subsequent calls to find further tokens must have the first argument as NULL to indicate to the function that this is a continuing operation. The address that is returned is tested in the if statement to make sure there is at least one token before trying to find more tokens. The strtok_s() returns NULL when no token is found.

The tokenizing of the input after the first token has been found is done in a do-while loop:

```
do
{
  printf("%-18s", pWord);
  if(++word_count % 5 == 0)
    printf("\n");
  pWord = strtok_s(NULL, &str_len, delimiters, &ptr);   // Find subsequent words
  // use this line instead, for Microsoft compiler:
  //pWord = strtok_s(NULL, delimiters, &ptr);     // Find subsequent words
}while(pWord);                                          // NULL ends tokenizing
```

The token found by the previous call to strtok_s() is output in the loop body, and the function is called again to find the next token. If this is NULL, the loop will end. The count recorded in word_count is used to control the output, so there are up to five tokens per line. Whenever the value is a multiple of five, a newline character is output. The %-18s conversion specification for a token outputs the token left justified (because of the -) in a field width of 18 characters. I chose the field width to allow five columns to fit within the width of a page in the book, rather than as a suitable width to accommodate most words.

Besides, strtok and strchr could be replaced with strbrk (string pointer break), as definition stands: Upon successful completion, strpbrk() shall return a pointer to the byte or a null pointer if no byte from s2 occurs in s1.

In other words, it will return a pointer to the first occurrence of any of the delimiter characters provided.

Reading Newline Characters into a String

Program 6.7 has a problem. Each line of input is terminated by pressing Enter, which enters a newline character, but this is not stored in the input array by gets_s(). This means that if you don't add a space at either the end of one line or the beginning of the next, the last word in one line will be concatenated with the first word in the next, as though they were a single word. This makes the input process rather unnatural. You could implement the input process better by using the fgets() function, which stores the newline character in a string that is entered to end the input operation. This is a more general input function that you can use to read files as well as reading keyboard input. You'll learn about file input and output in Chapter 12.

The fgets() function requires three arguments: the address of the input array, str, say; the maximum number of characters to be read, which is usually the size of str; and the source of the input, which for the keyboard will be stdin. The function reads at most one less than the number of characters specified by the second argument and appends \0. Pressing Enter causes \n to be stored in str. This ends the input operation, so a \0 will also be stored to terminate the string. An alternative version of Program 6.7 will demonstrate this in operation.

TRY IT OUT: READING NEWLINE CHARACTERS

Only three lines need to be changed from the previous version of Program 6.7. The delimiters array now includes an \n character, the input operation calls fgets() instead of gets_s(), and the condition for ending the input loop now detects \n as the first character in buf:

```
// Program 6.7A Reading newline characters
#define __STDC_WANT_LIB_EXT1__ 1   // Make optional versions of functions available
#include <stdio.h>
#include <string.h>
#include <stdbool.h>

int main(void)
{
  char delimiters[] = " \n\".,;:!?)(";      // Prose delimiters

  // Other declarations as Program 6.7...

  printf("Enter some prose that is less than %zd characters.\n"
         "Terminate input by entering an empty line:\n", str_len);

  // Read multiple lines of prose from the keyboard
  while(true)
  {
    if(!fgets(buf, buf_len, stdin))         // Read a line of input
    {
      printf("Error reading string.\n");
      return 1;
    }
    if(buf[0] == '\n')                      // An empty line ends input
      break;
```

```
    if(strcat_s(str, str_len, buf))          // Concatenate the line with str
    {
      printf("Maximum permitted input length exceeded.");
      return 1;
    }
  }
  // Rest of the code as for Program 6.7...
  return 0;
}
```

How It Works

The program works essentially as before except that it is more user-friendly. Newlines are stored in the input and act as delimiters, thus removing the problem that occurred with the previous version of the program. When you enter an empty line, the newline is stored in the first element of buf. This is used to decide when to end the input loop. You could also end the loop when the string in buf is of length 1.

Analyzing and Transforming Strings

You can examine the characters in a string using the library functions that are declared in the ctype.h header, which was introduced in Chapter 3. These provide a very flexible range of analytical functions that enable you to test what kind of character you have. They also have the advantage that they're independent of the character code on the computer you're using. Just to remind you, Table 6-1 shows the functions that will test for various categories of characters.

Table 6-1. *Character Classification Functions*

Function	Tests for
islower()	Lowercase letter
isupper()	Uppercase letter
isalpha()	Uppercase or lowercase letter
isalnum()	Uppercase or lowercase letter or a digit
iscntrl()	Control character
isprint()	Any printing character including space
isgraph()	Any printing character except space
isdigit()	Decimal digit ('0'-'9')
isxdigit()	Hexadecimal digit ('0'-'9', 'A'-'F', 'a'-'f')
isblank()	Standard blank characters (space, '\t')
isspace()	Whitespace character (space, '\n', '\t', '\v', '\r', '\f')
ispunct()	Printing character for which isspace() and isalnum() return false

The argument to a function is the character to be tested. All these functions return a nonzero value of type int if the character is within the set that's being tested for; otherwise, they return 0. Of course, these return values convert to true and false, respectively, so you can use them as Boolean values. Let's see how you can use these functions for testing the characters in a string.

TRY IT OUT: CLASSIFYING CHARACTERS

The following example determines how many digits, letters, and punctuation characters there are in a string that's entered from the keyboard:

```
// Program 6.8 Testing characters in a string
#define __STDC_WANT_LIB_EXT1__ 1    // Make optional versions of functions available
#include <stdio.h>
#include <ctype.h>
#define BUF_SIZE 100

int main(void)
{
  char buf[BUF_SIZE];              // Input buffer
  int nLetters = 0;                // Number of letters in input
  int nDigits = 0;                 // Number of digits in input
  int nPunct = 0;                  // Number of punctuation characters

  printf("Enter an interesting string of less than %d characters:\n", BUF_SIZE);
  if(!gets_s(buf, sizeof(buf)))  // Read a string into buffer
  {
    printf("Error reading string.\n");
    return 1;
  }
  size_t i = 0;                    // Buffer index
  while(buf[i])
  {
    if(isalpha(buf[i]))
      ++nLetters;                  // Increment letter count
    else if(isdigit(buf[i]))
      ++nDigits;                   // Increment digit count
    else if(ispunct(buf[i]))
      ++nPunct;
    ++i;
  }
  printf("\nYour string contained %d letters, %d digits and %d punctuation
characters.\n",
                                      nLetters, nDigits, nPunct);
  return 0;
}
```

The following is typical output from this program:

```
Enter an interesting string of less than 100 characters:
I was born on the 3rd of October 1895, which is long ago.

Your string contained 38 letters, 5 digits and 2 punctuation characters.
```

How It Works

This example is quite straightforward. You read the string into the array, buf, within the following if statement:

```
if(!gets_s(buf, sizeof(buf)))   // Read a string into buffer
{
  printf("Error reading string.\n");
  return 1;
}
```

The string you enter is read into the buf array using the optional standard library function, gets_s(). This is accessible because you defined __STDC_WANT_LIB_EXT1__ as 1. The gets_s() function has the advantage that it will read all the characters entered from the keyboard, including blanks, up to when you press the Enter key as long as there are sufficient elements in the buf array. A '\0' will be appended to the string automatically.

The statements that analyze the string are as follows:

```
while(buf[i])
{
  if(isalpha(buf[i]))
    ++nLetters;                 // Increment letter count
  else if(isdigit(buf[i]))
    ++nDigits;                  // Increment digit count
  else if(ispunct(buf[i]))
    ++nPunct;
  ++i;
}
```

The input string is tested character by character in the while loop. The loop continues as long as buf[i] does not contain \0. Checks are made for alphabetic characters, digits, and punctuation characters in the if statements. When one is found, the appropriate counter is incremented. The index, i, is incremented after checking buf[i], so the next character will be checked on the next iteration.

Converting Character Case

You've already seen that the standard library also includes two conversion functions that you get access to through ctype.h. The toupper() function converts from lowercase to uppercase, and the tolower() function does the reverse. Both functions return either the converted character or the same character for characters that are already in the correct case or are not convertible such as punctuation characters. You can therefore convert a string to uppercase using this statement:

```
for(int i = 0 ; (buf[i] = (char)toupper(buf[i])) != '\0' ; ++i);
```

This loop will convert the entire string in the buf array to uppercase by stepping through the string one character at a time, converting lowercase to uppercase, and leaving uppercase and nonconvertible characters unchanged. The loop stops when it reaches the string termination character '\0'. This sort of pattern in which everything is done inside the loop control expressions is quite common in C. The cast to type char is there because toupper() returns type int. Without the cast, you'll get a warning from the compiler.

Let's try a working example that applies these functions to a string.

TRY IT OUT: CONVERTING CHARACTERS

You can use the function toupper() in combination with the strstr() function to find out whether one string occurs in another, ignoring case. Look at the following example:

```c
// Program 6.9 Finding occurrences of one string in another
#define __STDC_WANT_LIB_EXT1__ 1        // Make optional versions of functions available
#include <stdio.h>
#include <string.h>
#include <ctype.h>
#define TEXT_LEN 100                     // Maximum input text length
#define SUBSTR_LEN 40                    // Maximum substring length

int main(void)
{
  char text[TEXT_LEN];                   // Input buffer for string to be searched
  char substring[SUBSTR_LEN];            // Input buffer for string sought

  printf("Enter the string to be searched (less than %d characters):\n", TEXT_LEN);
  gets_s(text, TEXT_LEN);

  printf("\nEnter the string sought (less than %d characters):\n", SUBSTR_LEN);
  gets_s(substring, SUBSTR_LEN);

  printf("\nFirst string entered:\n%s\n", text);
  printf("Second string entered:\n%s\n", substring);

  // Convert both strings to uppercase.
  for(int i = 0 ; (text[i] = (char)toupper(text[i])) != '\0' ; ++i);
  for(int i = 0 ; (substring[i] = (char)toupper(substring[i])) != '\0' ; ++i);

  printf("The second string %s found in the first.\n",
            ((strstr(text, substring) == NULL) ? "was not" : "was"));
  return 0;
}
```

Typical operation of this example will produce the following output:

```
Enter the string to be searched (less than 100 characters):
Cry havoc, and let slip the dogs of war.

Enter the string sought (less than 40 characters):
The Dogs of War

First string entered:
Cry havoc, and let slip the dogs of war.
Second string entered:
The Dogs of War
The second string was found in the first.
```

<u>How It Works</u>

This program has three distinct phases: reading in the input strings, converting both strings to uppercase, and searching the first string for an occurrence of the second.

First, you use `printf()` to prompt the user for the input, and you use the `fgets()` function to read the input into `text`:

```
printf("Enter the string to be searched (less than %d characters):\n", TEXT_LEN);
gets_s(text, TEXT_LEN);
```

You read the substring to be searched for into the `substring` array in the same way. The `gets_s()` function here will read in any string from the keyboard, including spaces, the input being terminated when the Enter key is pressed. The input process will only allow TEXT_LEN-1 characters to be entered for the first string, `text`, and SUBSTR_LEN-1 characters for the second string, `substring`. If more characters are entered, they will be ignored, so the operation of the program is safe.

Of course if you exceed the limits for input, the strings will be truncated, and the results are unlikely to be correct. This will be evident from the listing of the two strings that is produced by the following statements:

```
printf("\nFirst string entered:\n%s\n", text);
printf("Second string entered:\n%s\n", substring);
```

The conversion of both strings to uppercase is accomplished using the following statements:

```
// Convert both strings to uppercase.
for(int i = 0 ; (text[i] = (char)toupper(text[i])) != '\0' ; ++i);
for(int i = 0 ; (substring[i] = (char)toupper(substring[i])) != '\0' ; ++i);
```

You use `for` loops to do the conversion, and the work is done entirely within the control expressions for the loops. The first `for` loop initializes `i` to 0 and then converts the `i` character of `text` to uppercase in the loop condition and stores that result back in the same position in `text`. The loop continues as long as the character code stored in `text[i]` in the second loop control expression is nonzero, which will be for any character except NULL. The index `i` is incremented in the third loop control expression. The second loop works exactly the same way to convert a substring to uppercase.

With both strings in uppercase, you can test for the occurrence of `substring` in `text`, regardless of the case of the characters in the original strings. The test is done inside the output statement that reports the result:

```
printf("The second string %s found in the first.\n",
            ((strstr(text, substring) == NULL) ? "was not" : "was"));
```

The conditional operator chooses either "was not" or "was" to be part of the output string, depending on whether the `strstr()` function returns NULL. You saw earlier that the `strstr()` function returns NULL when the string specified by the second argument isn't found in the first. Otherwise, it returns the address where the substring was found.

Converting Strings to Numerical Values

The `stdlib.h` header file declares functions that you can use to convert a string to a numerical value. Each of the functions in Table 6-2 requires an argument that's a pointer to a string or an array of type char containing a string representing a numerical value.

Table 6-2. *Functions That Convert Strings to Numerical Values*

Function	Returns
atof()	A value of type double that is produced from the string argument. Infinity as a double value is recognized from the string "INF" or "INFINITY" where any character can be in uppercase or lowercase and "Not a Number" is recognized from the string "NAN" in uppercase or lowercase
atoi()	A value of type int that is produced from the string argument
atol()	A value of type long that is produced from the string argument
atoll()	A value of type long long that is produced from the string argument

For all four functions, leading whitespace (characters for which isspace() returns true) is ignored. Any characters following the character representation of the value that cannot form part of the value are also ignored.

Although these functions are defined since C99, in C17 the definition is fixed (redefined for clarification) such that the nan, nanf, and nanl functions convert a pointed string according to the following rules. The call nan("n-char-sequence") is equivalent to strtod("NAN(n-char-sequence)", (char**) NULL); the call nan("") is equivalent to strtod("NAN()", (char**) NULL). Where n-char-sequence is a sequence of alphanumeric characters.

These functions are very easy to use. Here's a sample snippet code from Program 6.9a:

```
char value_str[] = "98.4";
double value = atof(value_str);         // Convert string to floating-point
```

The value_str array contains a string representation of a value of type double. You pass the array name as the argument to the atof() function to convert it to type double. You use the other three functions in a similar way.

These functions are particularly useful when you need to read numerical input in the format of a string. This can happen when the sequence of the data input is uncertain, so you need to analyze the string in order to determine what it contains. Once you've figured out what kind of numerical value the string represents, you can use the appropriate library function to convert it.

You also have some more sophisticated functions available that can convert several substrings in a string to floating-point values. These are shown in Table 6-3.

Table 6-3. *Functions for Converting a Substring to a Floating-Point Value*

Function	Returns
strtod()	A value of type double is produced from the initial part of the string specified by the first argument. The second argument is a pointer to a variable, ptr, say, of type char* in which the function will store the address of the first character following the substring that was converted to the double value. If no string was found that could be converted to type double, the variable ptr will contain the address passed as the first argument
strtof()	A value of type float. In all other respects, it works as strtod()
strtold()	A value of type long double. In all other respects, it works as strtod()

These functions recognize "INF", "INFINITY", and "NAN", as discussed for the previous functions in this section. They will recognize floating-point values with or without an exponent in decimal or hexadecimal form. A hexadecimal value must be preceded by 0x or 0X; a hexadecimal floating-point constant is a very rare beast in my experience. Here's how you might convert several substrings from a single string to double values, snippet code from Program 6.9b:

```
double value = 0;
char str[] = "3.5 2.5 1.26";      // The string to be converted
char *pstr = str;                 // Pointer to the string to be converted
char *ptr = NULL;                 // Pointer to character position after conversion
while(true)
{
  value = strtod(pstr, &ptr);     // Convert starting at pstr
  if(pstr == ptr)                 // pstr stored if no conversion...
    break;                        // ...so we are done
  else
  {
    printf(" %f", value);         // Output the resultant value
    pstr = ptr;                   // Store start for next conversion
  }
}
```

Executing this fragment will output the three floating-point values from the string. When strtod() stores the address you passed as the first argument in ptr, no character sequence was found that could be converted. So pstr starts out with the address of the beginning of str. When a substring is converted, the function stores the address of the character following the substring in ptr. This becomes the starting address for the next substring to be converted because you store it in pstr.

You have functions for converting integer values too. The strtol() function returns a long value produced from a substring. It expects three arguments:

- The first argument is the address of the substring to be converted.

- The second argument is a pointer to a variable, ptr, say, of type char* in which the function will store the address of the first character following the substring that was converted to the long value. If no string was found that could be converted to type long, ptr will contain the address passed as the first argument.

- The third argument is a value of type int that specifies the number base for the integer. This can be 0 to specify a decimal, octal, or hexadecimal integer constant with or without a sign. It can also be a value from 2 to 36 specifying a base of the value specified. For base 16, the substring can optionally begin with 0x or 0X. For number bases of ten or greater, digits in excess of nine are represented by letters in sequence beginning with uppercase or lowercase a.

You also have the functions strtoll(), strtoul(), and strtoull() available, which convert a substring to a value of type long long, unsigned long, and unsigned long long, respectively. These work essentially the same way as strtol().

All the names of the preceding functions have suffix based on the data type that each function can convert: u unsigned, l long, d double, and f float. Thus, for instance, we can deduce strtold is conversion to long double.

Here's how you might convert several values in a string, snippet code from Program 6.9c:

```
char str[] = "123   234   0xAB      111011";
char *pstr = str;
char *ptr = NULL;
long a = strtol(pstr, &ptr, 0);          // Convert base 10 value        a = 123
pstr = ptr;                              // Start is next character
unsigned long b = strtoul(pstr, &ptr, 0); // Convert base 10 value        b = 234L
pstr = ptr;                              // Start is next character
long c = strtol(pstr, &ptr, 16);         // Convert a hexadecimal value c = 171
pstr = ptr;                              // Start is next character
long d = strtol(pstr, &ptr, 2);          // Convert binary value         d = 59
```

The values stored are shown in the comments. The hexadecimal substring would still be converted correctly without the initial 0x. Because it has an initial 0x, you could specify the base as 0.

Designing a Program

You've almost come to the end of this chapter. All that remains is to go through a larger example to use some of what you've learned so far.

The Problem

You are going to develop a program that will read a paragraph of text of an arbitrary length that is entered from the keyboard and determine the frequency of which each word in the text occurs, ignoring case. The paragraph length won't be completely arbitrary, as you'll have to specify some limit for the array size within the program, but you can make the array that holds the text as large as you want.

The Analysis

To read the paragraph from the keyboard, you need to be able to read input lines of arbitrary length and assemble them into a single string that will ultimately contain the entire paragraph. You don't want lines truncated either, so fgets() looks like a good candidate for the input operation. If you define a symbol at the beginning of the code that specifies the array size to store the paragraph, you will be able to change the capacity of the program by changing the definition of the symbol.

The text will contain punctuation, so you will have to deal with that somehow if you are to be able to separate one word from another. It would be easy to extract the words from the text if each word is separated from the next by one or more spaces. You can arrange for this by replacing all characters that are not characters that appear in a word with spaces. You'll remove all the punctuation and any other odd characters that are lying around in the text. We don't need to retain the original text, but if you did, you could just make a copy before eliminating the punctuation.

Separating out the words will be simple. All you need to do is extract each successive sequence of characters that are not spaces as a word. You can store the words in another array. Since you want to count word occurrences, ignoring case, you can store each word as lowercase. As you find a new word, you'll have to compare it with all the existing words you have found to see if it occurs previously. You'll only store it in the array if it is not already there. To record the number of occurrences of each word, you'll need another array to store the word counts. This array will need to accommodate as many counts as the number of words you have provided for in the program.

The Solution

This section outlines the steps you'll take to solve the problem. The program boils down to a simple sequence of steps that are more or less independent of one another. At the moment, the approach to implementing the program will be constrained by what you have learned up to now, and by the time you get to Chapter 9, you'll be able to implement this much more efficiently.

Step 1

The first step is to read the paragraph from the keyboard. As this is an arbitrary number of input lines, it will be necessary to involve an indefinite loop. Here's the initial code to do that:

```c
// Program 6.10 Analyzing text
#define __STDC_WANT_LIB_EXT1__ 1            // Make optional versions of functions available
#include <stdio.h>
#include <string.h>
#include <stdbool.h>

#define TEXT_LEN   10000                    // Maximum length of text
#define BUF_SIZE 100                        // Input buffer size
#define MAX_WORDS   500                     // Maximum number of different words
#define WORD_LEN      12                    // Maximum word length

int main(void)
{
  char delimiters[] = " \n\".,;:!?)(";      // Word delimiters
  char text[TEXT_LEN] = "";                 // Stores the complete text
  char buf[BUF_SIZE];                       // Stores one input line
  char words[MAX_WORDS][WORD_LEN];          // Stores words from the text
  int nword[MAX_WORDS] = {0};               // Number of word occurrences
  int word_count = 0;                       // Number of words stored

  printf("Enter text on an arbitrary number of lines.");
  printf("\nEnter an empty line to end input:\n");

  // Read an arbitrary number of lines of text
  while(true)
  {
    // An empty string containing just a newline
    // signals end of input
    fgets(buf, BUF_SIZE, stdin);
    if(buf[0] == '\n')
      break;

    // Concatenate new string & check if we have space for latest input    if(strcat_s(text,
      TEXT_LEN, buf))
    {
      printf("Maximum capacity for text exceeded. Terminating program.\n");
      return 1;
    }
}
```

```
// The code to find the words in the text array...

// The code to output the words...

  return 0;
}
```

You can compile and run this code as it stands if you like. The delimiters array is a string identifying all possible delimiters for words. The symbols TEXT_LEN and BUF_SIZE specify the capacity of the text and buf arrays, respectively. The text array will store the entire paragraph, and the buf array stores a line of input. The text array is initialized with an empty string because you will want to append input lines to this.

The MAX_WORDS and WORD_LEN symbols define the maximum number of words that will be accommodated and the maximum length of a word, respectively. I chose the WORD_LEN value for page width considerations rather than for what length words might occur. Words will be stored in the two-dimensional array, words. Each element of the nword array stores the count of the number of occurrences of the word in the corresponding row of the words array. All elements of nword are initialized to 0. The word_count variable will store the number of unique words that have been found and will also act as an index to the words and nword arrays.

To indicate the end of the input operation, the user enters an empty line. The fgets() function stores a newline character in the input array, so just pressing Enter results in the string "\n", so the first character in buf will be \n. The fgets() function reads a maximum of BUF_SIZE - 1 characters from stdin. If the user enters a line longer than this, it won't really matter. The characters that are in excess of BUF_SIZE - 1 will be left in the input stream and will be read on the next loop iteration. You can check that this works by setting BUF_SIZE to 10 and then entering lines longer than ten characters.

The strcat_s() function returns a nonzero integer if the concatenation could not be completed. In this case, this can result because there is insufficient unused space in the text array to accommodate the latest input, so you use the value returned by strcat_s() to detect when this occurs. In this case, the program ends abnormally after outputting a message.

Here's an example of output that results from executing this input operation:

```
Enter text on an arbitrary number of lines.
Enter an empty line to end input:
Mary had a little lamb,
Its feet were black as soot,
And into Mary's bread and jam,
His sooty foot he put.
```

Step 2

The next step is to extract the words from the text array and store them in the words array. As each word is found, the code must check whether the word has been found previously. If it has been, the count for that word in nword must be incremented. If a new word has been found, the word will be copied to the next available row in the words array and the corresponding count in nword set to 1. Because of the way strtok_s() works, you'll find the first word before finding the remaining words. Here's the code to do that:

```
size_t len = TEXT_LEN;
char *ptr = NULL;
char* pWord = strtok_s(text, &len, delimiters, &ptr);    // Find 1st word
// use this line instead, for Microsoft compiler:
//char* pWord = strtok_s(text, delimiters, &ptr);    // Find 1st word
```

```
if(!pWord)
{
  printf("No words found. Ending program.\n");
  return 1;
}
strcpy_s(words[word_count], WORD_LEN, pWord);
++nword[word_count++];
```

The len and ptr variables are used by the strtok_s() function to record data that it will use when finding the words in text that are separated by characters from the delimiters array. Because the function needs to modify the values stored in these variables, you must pass the address of the variables as arguments, not the variables themselves. The strtok_s() function returns the address of the word that was found, and this must certainly be non-NULL because this is the first word. After confirming that pWord is not NULL, you copy the word into the words array, increment the value in the corresponding nword element from 0 to 1, and increment word_count to 1. Because you use the postfix version of the increment operator, word_count will be incremented after its current value has been used to index the nword array. Thus, words[0] will contain the first word, and nword[0] will be 1.

Now you need to find the remaining words in text:

```
bool new_word = true;                                   // False for an existing word
while(true)
{
  pWord = strtok_s(NULL, &len, delimiters, &ptr);       // Find subsequent word
  // use this line instead, for Microsoft compiler:
  //pWord = strtok_s(NULL, delimiters, &ptr);            // Find subsequent word
  if(!pWord)
    break;                                              // NULL ends tokenizing

  // Check for existing word
  for(int i = 0 ; i < word_count ; ++i)
  {
    if(strcmp(words[i], pWord) == 0)
    {
      ++nword[i];
      new_word = false;
    }
  }

  if(new_word)                                          // True if new word
  {
    strcpy_s(words[word_count], WORD_LEN, pWord);       // Copy to array
    ++nword[word_count++];                              // Increment count and index
  }
  else
    new_word = true;                                    // Reset new word flag

  if(word_count > MAX_WORDS - 1)
  {
    printf("Capacity to store words exceeded.\n");
    return 1;
  }
}
```

The new_word variable will be set to false when the word found is a duplicate. Searching for words is carried out in the indefinite while loop. The NULL first argument to strtok_s() indicates that the call is to find words in the string previously passed to the function. If a NULL is returned, there are no more words, so you exit the loop. When a word is found, the for loop compares the word with the words previously stored in the words array. If the word already exists in the words array, the corresponding value in the nword array is incremented, and new_word is set to false to signal that the word is a duplicate and does not need to be stored. Following the for loop, you check new_word in the if statement. If it has the value true, pWord points to a new word, so you copy it to the next free element in words and increment the corresponding element in nword. The latter operation also increments word_count. If new_word was false, indicating that a duplicate word was found, you just reset it to true, and it is ready for the next iteration of the while loop. At the end of each loop iteration, we check for exceeding the bounds of the words and nword arrays.

Step 3

The last code you need to add will output the words and their frequencies of occurrence. Here's a complete listing of the program with the additional code from step 2, and this step is highlighted in bold font:

```
// Program 6.10 Analyzing text
#define __STDC_WANT_LIB_EXT1__ 1      // Make optional versions of functions available
#include <stdio.h>
#include <string.h>
#include <stdbool.h>

#define TEXT_LEN  10000               // Maximum length of text
#define BUF_SIZE 100                  // Input buffer size
#define MAX_WORDS   500               // Maximum number of different words
#define WORD_LEN      12              // Maximum word length

int main(void)
{
  char delimiters[] = " \n\".,;:!?)(";    // Word delimiters
  char text[TEXT_LEN] = "";                // Stores the complete text
  char buf[BUF_SIZE];                      // Stores one input line
  char words[MAX_WORDS][WORD_LEN];         // Stores words from the text
  int nword[MAX_WORDS] = {0};              // Number of word occurrences
  int word_count = 0;                      // Number of words stored

  printf("Enter text on an arbitrary number of lines.");
  printf("\nEnter an empty line to end input:\n");

  // Read an arbitrary number of lines of text
  while(true)
  {
    // An empty string containing just a newline
    // signals end of input
    fgets(buf, BUF_SIZE, stdin);
    if(buf[0] == '\n')
      break;

    // Concatenate new string & check if we have space for latest input
    if(strcat_s(text, TEXT_LEN, buf))
```

```
    {
      printf("Maximum capacity for text exceeded. Terminating program.\n");
      return 1;
    }
}

// Find  the first word
size_t len = TEXT_LEN;
char *ptr = NULL;
char* pWord = strtok_s(text, &len, delimiters, &ptr);    // Find 1st word
// use this line instead, for Microsoft compiler:
//char* pWord = strtok_s(text, delimiters, &ptr);    // Find 1st word
if(!pWord)
{
  printf("No words found. Ending program.\n");
  return 1;
}
strcpy_s(words[word_count], WORD_LEN, pWord);
++nword[word_count++];

// Find  the rest of the words
bool new_word = true;                                  // False for an existing word
while(true)
{
  pWord = strtok_s(NULL, &len, delimiters, &ptr);      // Find subsequent word
  // use this line instead, for Microsoft compiler:
  //pWord = strtok_s(NULL, delimiters, &ptr);          // Find subsequent word
  if(!pWord)
    break;                                             // NULL ends tokenizing

  // Check for existing word
  for(int i = 0 ; i < word_count ; ++i)
  {
    if(strcmp(words[i], pWord) == 0)
    {
      ++nword[i];
      new_word = false;
    }
  }

  if(new_word)                                         // True if new word
  {
    strcpy_s(words[word_count], WORD_LEN, pWord);      // Copy to array
    ++nword[word_count++];                             // Increment count and index
  }
  else
    new_word = true;                                   // Reset new word flag

  if(word_count > MAX_WORDS - 1)
  {
    printf("Capacity to store words exceeded.\n");
```

```
      return 1;
    }
  }

  // List the words
  for(int i = 0; i < word_count ; ++i)
  {
    printf(" %-13s  %3d", words[i], nword[i]);
    if((i + 1) % 4 == 0)
      printf("\n");
  }
  printf("\n");

  return 0;
}
```

The words and corresponding frequencies are output in a for loop that iterates over the number of words. The loop code arranges for four words plus frequencies to be output per line by writing a newline character to stdout if the value of i+1 is a multiple of four.

When you have learned the complete C language, you would organize this program very differently with the code segmented into several much shorter functions. By Chapter 9, you'll be in a position to do this, and I would encourage you to revisit this example when you reach the end of Chapter 9. Here's a sample of output from the complete program:

```
Enter text on an arbitrary number of lines.
Enter an empty line to end input:
When I makes tea I makes tea, as old mother Grogan said.
And when I makes water I makes water.
Begob, ma'am, says Mrs Cahill, God send you don't make them in the same pot.

    When          1  I        4  makes     4  tea      2
    as            1  old      1  mother    1  Grogan   1
    said          1  And      1  when      1  water    2
    Begob         1  ma'am    1  says      1  Mrs      1
    Cahill        1  God      1  send      1  you      1
    don't         1  make     1  them      1  in       1
    the           1  same     1  pot       1
```

Summary

In this chapter, you applied the techniques you acquired in earlier chapters to the general problem of dealing with character strings. Strings present a different, and perhaps more difficult, problem than numeric data types.

Most of the chapter dealt with handling strings using arrays, but I also introduced pointers. These will provide you with even more flexibility in dealing with strings and many other things besides, as you'll discover in the next chapter, but first some exercises to reinforce what you have learned.

EXERCISES

The following exercises enable you to try out what you've learned in this chapter. If you get stuck, look back over the chapter for help. If you're still stuck, you can download the solutions from the Source Code/Download section of the Apress website (www.apress.com), but that really should be a last resort.

Exercise 6-1. Write a program that will prompt for and read a positive integer less than 1,000 from the keyboard and then create and output a string that is the value of the integer in words. For example, if **941** is entered, the program will create the string "Nine hundred and forty one".

Exercise 6-2. Write a program that will allow a list of words to be entered separated by commas and then extract the words and output them one to a line, removing any leading or trailing spaces. For example, if the input is

```
John  ,  Jack ,   Jill
```

then the output will be

```
John
Jack
Jill
```

Exercise 6-3. Write a program that will output a randomly chosen thought for the day from a set of at least five thoughts of your own choosing.

Exercise 6-4. A palindrome is a phrase that reads the same backward as forward, ignoring whitespace and punctuation. For example, "Madam, I'm Adam" and "Are we not drawn onward, we few? Drawn onward to new era?" are palindromes. Write a program that will determine whether a string entered from the keyboard is a palindrome.

CHAPTER 7

Pointers

You had a glimpse of pointers in the last chapter and just a small hint at what you can use them for. Here, you'll delve a lot deeper into the subject of pointers and see what else you can do with them. I'll cover a lot of new concepts here, so you may need to repeat some sections a few times. This is a long chapter, so spend some time on it and experiment with the examples. Remember that the basic ideas are very simple, but you can apply them to solving complicated problems. By the end of this chapter, you'll be equipped with an essential element for effective C programming.

In this chapter, you'll learn

- What a pointer is and how it's used

- What the relationship between pointers and arrays is

- How to use pointers with strings

- How you can declare and use arrays of pointers

- How to write an improved calculator program

A First Look at Pointers

You have now come to one of the most extraordinarily powerful tools in the C language. It's also potentially the most confusing, so it's important you get the ideas straight in your mind at the outset and maintain a clear idea of what's happening as you dig deeper.

I discussed memory back in Chapters 2 and 5. I talked about how your computer allocates an area of memory when you declare a variable. You refer to this area in memory using the variable name in your program, but once your program is compiled and running, your computer references it by the address of the memory location. This is the number that the computer uses to refer to the "box" in which the value of the variable is stored.

Look at the following statement:

```
int number = 5;
```

Here an area of memory is allocated to store an integer, and you can access it using the name number. The value 5 is stored in this area. The computer references the area using an address. The specific address where these data will be stored depends on your computer and what operating system and compiler you're using. Although the variable name is fixed in the source program, the address is likely to be different on different systems.

© German Gonzalez-Morris and Ivor Horton 2020
G. Gonzalez-Morris and I. Horton, *Beginning C*, https://doi.org/10.1007/978-1-4842-5976-4_7

Variables that can store addresses are called *pointers*, and the address that's stored in a pointer is usually that of another variable, as illustrated in Figure 7-1. You have a pointer pnumber that contains the address of another variable, called number, which is an integer variable containing the value 99. The value that's stored in pnumber is the address of the first byte of number. The word *pointer* is also used to refer to just an address, as in the phrase "the strcat_s() function returns a pointer."

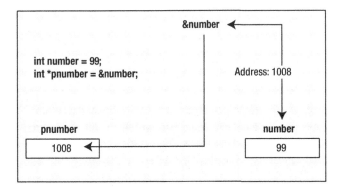

Figure 7-1. *How a pointer works*

The first thing to appreciate is that it's not enough to know that a particular variable, such as pnumber, is a pointer. You and, more importantly, the compiler must know the *type* of data stored in the variable to which it points. Without this information, it's virtually impossible to know how much memory is occupied or how to handle the contents of the memory to which it points. A pointer to a value of type char is pointing to a value occupying 1 byte, whereas a pointer to a value of type long is usually pointing to the first byte of a value occupying 4 bytes. This means that every pointer will be associated with a specific variable type, and it can be used only to point to variables of that type. So pointers of type "pointer to int" can point only to variables of type int, pointers of type "pointer to float" can point only to variables of type float, and so on. In general, a pointer of a given type is written type* for any given type name type.

The type name void means absence of any type, so a pointer of type void* can contain the address of a data item of any type. Type void* is often used as a parameter type or return value type with functions that deal with data in a type-independent way. Any kind of pointer can be passed around as a value of type void* and then cast to the appropriate type when you come to use it. The address of a variable of type int can be stored in a pointer variable of type void*, for example. When you want to access the integer value at the address stored in the void* pointer, you must first cast the pointer to type int*. Although this is the safer and better practice to work with void pointers, it is not always necessary to do an explicit cast; this can be handled with pointer arithmetic as well. Of course, it is mandatory to know the length of the data type. A related and fundamental feature declared in the C standard is as follows: A pointer to void must have the same representation and address memory alignment as a pointer to a char.

qsort is a popular function to order elements that uses void pointers in its signature (parameters) to accept different types; however, it needs next to cast to a specific type to be utilized later.

You'll learn about the malloc() library function later in this chapter, which allocates memory for use in your program and returns a pointer to the memory of type void*.

Declaring Pointers

You can declare a pointer to a variable of type int with the following statement:

```
int *pnumber;
```

The type of the variable with the name pnumber is int*. It can store the address of any variable of type int. Note that you can also write the statement like this:

```
int* pnumber;
```

This is exactly the same as the previous statement in its effect. You can use either notation, but it is best to stick to one or the other.

The statement just creates the pnumber variable but doesn't initialize it. Uninitialized pointers are particularly hazardous, much more dangerous than an ordinary variable that is uninitialized, so you should always initialize a pointer when you declare it. You can initialize pnumber so that it doesn't point to anything by rewriting the declaration like this:

```
int *pnumber = NULL;
```

NULL is a constant that's defined in the standard library and is the equivalent of zero for a pointer. NULL is a value that's guaranteed not to point to any location in memory. This means that it implicitly prevents the accidental overwriting of memory by using a pointer that doesn't point to anything specific. NULL is defined in several standard library header files, including stddef.h, stdlib.h, stdio.h, string.h, time.h, wchar.h, and locale.h. Anytime that it's not recognized by the compiler, just add an #include directive for stddef.h to your source file.

If you want to initialize your variable pnumber with the address of a variable you've already declared, you use the *address of* operator, &:

```
int number = 99;
int *pnumber = &number;
```

Now the initial value of pnumber is the address of the variable number. Note that the declaration of number must precede the declaration of the pointer that stores its address. If this isn't the case, the code won't compile. The compiler must have already allocated space and thus an address for number to use it to initialize pnumber.

There's nothing special about the declaration of a pointer. You can declare regular variables and pointers in the same statement, for example:

```
double value, *pVal, fnum;
```

This statement declares two double-precision floating-point variables, value and fnum, and a variable pVal of type "pointer to double." With this statement, it is obvious that only the second variable, pVal, is a pointer, but consider this statement:

```
int *p, q;
```

This declares a pointer, p, of type int* and a variable, q, that is of type int. It is a common mistake to think that both p and q are pointers.

Accessing a Value Through a Pointer

You use the *indirection operator*, *, to access the value of the variable pointed to by a pointer. This operator is also referred to as the *dereference operator* because you use it to "dereference" a pointer. Suppose you declare the following variables:

```
int number = 15;
```

```
int *pointer = &number;
int result = 0;
```

The pointer variable contains the address of the variable number, so you can use this in an expression to calculate a new value for result, like this:

```
result = *pointer + 5;
```

The expression *pointer will evaluate to the value stored at the address contained in the pointer. This is the value stored in number, 15, so result will be set to 15 + 5, which is 20.

So much for the theory. Let's look at a small program that will highlight some of the characteristics of this special kind of variable.

TRY IT OUT: DECLARING POINTERS

In this example, you're simply going to declare a variable and a pointer. You'll then output their addresses and the values they contain:

```c
// Program 7.1 A simple program using pointers
#include <stdio.h>

int main(void)
{
  int number = 0;                // A variable of type int initialized to 0
  int *pnumber = NULL;           // A pointer that can point to type int

  number = 10;
  printf("number's address: %p\n", &number);              // Output the address
  printf("number's value: %d\n\n", number);               // Output the value

  pnumber = &number;             // Store the address of number in pnumber

  printf("pnumber's address: %p\n", (void*)&pnumber);     // Output the address
  printf("pnumber's size: %zd bytes\n", sizeof(pnumber)); // Output the size
  printf("pnumber's value: %p\n", pnumber);  // Output the value (an address)
  printf("value pointed to: %d\n", *pnumber);             // Value at the address
  return 0;
}
```

The output from the program will look something like the following. Remember the actual address is likely to be different on your machine:

```
number's address: 000000000012ff0c
number's value: 10

pnumber's address: 000000000012ff00
pnumber's size: 8 bytes
pnumber's value: 000000000012ff0c
value pointed to: 10
```

You can see that the pointers occupy 8 bytes and the addresses have 16 hexadecimal digits. This is because my machine has a 64-bit operating system and my compiler supports 64-bit addresses. Some compilers only support 32-bit addressing, in which case addresses will be 32-bit addresses.

How It Works

You first declare a variable of type int and a pointer:

```
int number = 0;                        // A variable of type int initialized to 0
int *pnumber = NULL;                   // A pointer that can point to type int
```

The pointer is of type "pointer to int."

After the declarations, you store the value 10 in the variable called number and then output its address and its value with these statements:

```
number = 10;
printf("number's address: %p\n", &number);              // Output the address
printf("number's value: %d\n\n", number);               // Output the value
```

To output the address of the variable called number, you use the output format specifier %p. This outputs a pointer value as a memory address in hexadecimal form.

The next statement obtains the address of the variable number and stores that address in pnumber, using the address of operator, &:

```
pnumber = &number;              // Store the address of number in pnumber
```

Remember, the only kind of value that you should store in pnumber is an address.

Next, you have four printf() statements that output, respectively, the address of pnumber (which is the first byte of the memory location that pnumber occupies), the number of bytes that the pointer occupies, the value stored in pnumber (which is the address of number), and the value stored at the address that pnumber contains (which is the value stored in number).

Just to make sure you're clear about this, let's go through these line by line. The first output statement is as follows:

```
printf("pnumber's address: %p\n", (void*)&pnumber);       // Output the address
```

Here, you output the address of pnumber. Remember a pointer itself has an address, just like any other variable. You use %p as the conversion specifier to display an address, and you use the & (address of) operator to reference the address that the pnumber variable occupies. The cast to void* is to prevent a possible warning from the compiler. The %p specification expects the value to be some kind of pointer type, but the type of &pnumber is "pointer to pointer to int."

Next, you output the size of pnumber:

```
printf("pnumber's size: %d bytes\n", sizeof(pnumber));    // Output the size
```

You use the sizeof operator to obtain the number of bytes a pointer occupies, just like any other variable, and the output on my machine shows that a pointer occupies 8 bytes, so a memory address on my machine is 64 bits. You may get a compiler warning for this statement. Because size_t is an implementation-defined integer type, it can potentially be any basic integer type, although types char and short are unlikely to be chosen. To prevent the warning, you could cast the argument to type int like this:

```
printf("pnumber's size: %d bytes\n", (int)sizeof(pnumber)); // Output the size
```

The next statement outputs the value stored in pnumber:

```
printf("pnumber's value: %p\n", pnumber);  // Output the value (an address)
```

The value stored in pnumber is the address of number. Because this is an address, you use %p to display it, and you use the variable name, pnumber, to access the address value.
The last output statement is

```
printf("value pointed to: %d\n", *pnumber);                // Value at the address
```

Here, you use the pointer to access the value stored in number. The effect of the * operator is to access the data contained in the address stored at pnumber. You use %d because you know it's an integer value. The variable pnumber stores the address of number, so you can use that address to access the value stored in number. As I said earlier, the * operator is called the *indirection operator* or sometimes the *dereference operator*.

The addresses shown will be different on different computers. They will sometimes be different at different times on the same computer. This is because your program won't necessarily be loaded at the same place in memory. One possible dependency is what other code has been loaded previously into the same address space, and there are other factors that affect this.

You'll certainly have noticed that the indirection operator, *, is also the symbol for multiplication, and it is used to specify pointer types. Fortunately, there's no risk of confusion for the compiler. Depending on where the asterisk appears, the compiler will understand whether it should interpret it as an indirection operator, as a multiplication sign, or as part of a type specification. The context determines what it means in any instance.

Figure 7-2 illustrates using a pointer. In this case, the pointer is type char*, which is a pointer to char. The pChar variable can only store addresses of variables of type char. The value stored in ch is changed through the pointer.

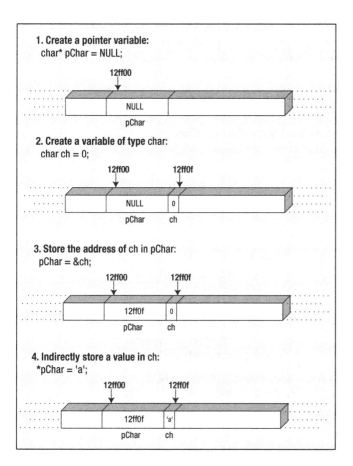

1. **Create a pointer variable:**
   char* pChar = NULL;

2. **Create a variable of type** char:
   char ch = 0;

3. **Store the address of** ch in pChar:
   pChar = &ch;

4. **Indirectly store a value in** ch:
   *pChar = 'a';

Figure 7-2. *Using a pointer*

Using Pointers

Because you can access the contents of number through the pointer pnumber, you can use a dereferenced pointer to a numerical *type* in arithmetic statements, for example:

```
*pnumber += 25;
```

This statement increments the value of whatever variable pnumber currently addresses by 25. The * indicates you're accessing the contents to which the variable called pnumber is pointing. In this case, it's the contents of the variable called number.

The variable pnumber can store the address of any variable of type int. This means you can change the variable that pnumber points to like this:

```
int value = 999;
pnumber = &value;
```

Suppose you repeat the same statement that you used previously:

```
*pnumber +=  25;
```

271

The statement will operate with the new variable, value, so the new contents of value will be 1024. A pointer can contain the address of any variable of the appropriate type, so you can use one pointer variable to change the values of many different variables, as long as they're of a type compatible with the pointer type.

TRY IT OUT: USING POINTERS

This example uses pointers to modify values stored in some other variables:

```
// Program 7.2  What's the pointer of it all
#include <stdio.h>

int main(void)
{
  long num1 = 0L;
  long num2 = 0L;
  long *pnum = NULL;

  pnum = &num1;                              // Get address of num1
  *pnum = 2L;                                // Set num1 to 2
  ++num2;                                    // Increment num2
  num2 += *pnum;                             // Add num1 to num2

  pnum = &num2;                              // Get address of num2
  ++*pnum;                                   // Increment num2 indirectly

  printf("num1 = %ld   num2 = %ld  *pnum = %ld  *pnum + num2 = %ld\n",
                          num1, num2, *pnum, *pnum + num2);

  return 0;
}
```

When you run this program, you should get the following output:

```
num1 = 2   num2 = 4   *pnum = 4   *pnum + num2 = 8
```

How It Works

The comments should make the program easy to follow up to the printf(). First, in the body of main(), you have these declarations:

```
long num1 = 0L;
long num2 = 0L;
long *pnum = NULL;
```

This ensures that you set out with initial values for the two variables, num1 and num2, at 0. The third statement declares an integer pointer, pnum, which is initialized with NULL.

■ **Caution** You should always initialize pointers when you declare them. Using a pointer that isn't initialized to store an item of data is dangerous. Who knows what you might overwrite when you use the pointer to store a value.

The next statement is an assignment:

```
pnum = &num1;                              // Get address of num1
```

The pointer pnum is set to point to num1 here, because you take the address of num1 using the & operator.

The next two statements are

```
*pnum = 2L;                                // Set num1 to 2
++num2;                                    // Increment num2
```

The first statement exploits your newfound power of the pointer to set the value of num1 to 2 indirectly by dereferencing pnum. Then, num2 gets incremented by 1 in the normal way, using the increment operator.

The next statement is

```
num2 += *pnum;                             // Add num1 to num2
```

This adds the contents of the variable pointed to by pnum to num2. Because pnum still points to num1, num2 is being increased by the value of num1.

The next two statements are

```
pnum = &num2;                              // Get address of num2
++*pnum;                                   // Increment num2 indirectly
```

First, pnum is reassigned to point to num2. The variable num2 is then incremented indirectly through pnum. You can see that the expression ++*pnum increments the value pointed to by pnum without any problem. However, if you wanted to use the postfix increment operator, you would have to write the expression as (*pnum)++. The parentheses are essential, assuming that you want to increment the value rather than the address. If you omit them, the address contained in pnum would be incremented, and the result is dereferenced. This is because the operators ++ and unary * (and unary & for that matter) share the same precedence level and are evaluated from right to left. This is a common source of error when incrementing values through pointers, so it's a good idea to use parentheses in any event.

Finally, before the return statement that ends the program, you have the following printf() statement:

```
printf("num1 = %ld   num2 = %ld   *pnum = %ld   *pnum + num2 = %ld\n",
                       num1, num2, *pnum, *pnum + num2);
```

This displays the values of num1, num2, and num2 through pnum and, lastly, num2 in the guise of pnum, with the value of num2 added.

Pointers can be confusing when you encounter them for the first time. The multiple levels of meaning are the source of the confusion. You can work with addresses or values, pointers or variables, and sometimes it's hard to work out what exactly is going on. The best thing to do is to keep writing short programs that use the things I've described: getting values using pointers, changing values, printing addresses, and so on. This is the only way to really get confident about using pointers.

I've mentioned the importance of operator precedence again in this discussion. Don't forget that Table 3-2 in Chapter 3 shows the precedence of all the operators in C, so you can always refer to it when you are uncertain about the precedence of an operator.

Let's look at an example that will show how pointers work with input from the keyboard.

TRY IT OUT: USING A POINTER WHEN RECEIVING INPUT

Until now, when you've used `scanf()` to input values, you've used the & operator to obtain the address of the variable that is to receive the input and used that as the argument to the function. When you have a pointer that already contains an address, you can use the pointer name as an argument. You can see this in the following example:

```c
// Program 7.3  Using pointer arguments to scanf_s
#define __STDC_WANT_LIB_EXT1__ 1
#include <stdio.h>

int main(void)
{
  int value = 0;
  int *pvalue = &value;                  // Set pointer to refer to value

  printf ("Input an integer: ");
  scanf_s(" %d", pvalue);                // Read into value via the pointer

  printf("You entered %d.\n", value);    // Output the value entered
  return 0;
}
```

This program will just echo what you enter. How unimaginative can you get? Typical output is something like this:

```
Input an integer: 10
You entered 10.
```

How It Works

Everything should be pretty clear up to the `scanf_s()` statement:

```c
  scanf_s(" %d", pvalue);
```

You normally store the value entered by the user at the address of the variable. You could have used &value, but the pvalue pointer is used to pass the address of value to `scanf()`. You already stored the address of value in pvalue when you created it:

```c
  int *pvalue = &value;                  // Set pointer to refer to value
```

Here, pvalue and &value are the same, so you can use either.

You then just display value:

```c
  printf("You entered %d\n", value);
```

Although this is a somewhat pointless example, it isn't pointerless and not entirely pointless because it illustrates how pointers and variables can work together.

Testing for a NULL Pointer

Suppose that you create a pointer like this:

```
int *pvalue = NULL;
```

As you know, NULL is a special symbol in C that represents the pointer equivalent to 0 with ordinary numbers. The symbol is often defined as ((void*)0). When you assign 0 to a pointer, it's the equivalent of setting it to NULL, so you could write the following:

```
int *pvalue = 0;
```

Because NULL is the equivalent of zero, if you want to test whether pvalue is NULL, you can write this:

```
if(!pvalue)
{
  // Tell everyone! - the pointer is NULL! ...
}
```

When pvalue is NULL, !pvalue will be true, so the block of statements will be executed only if pvalue is NULL. Alternatively, you can write the test as follows:

```
if(pvalue == NULL)
{
  // Tell everyone! - the pointer is NULL! ...
}
```

Pointers to Constants

You can use the const keyword when you declare a pointer to indicate that the value pointed to must not be changed. Here's an example of a declaration of a pointer to a const value:

```
long value = 9999L;
const long *pvalue = &value;        // Defines a pointer to a constant
```

Because you have declared the value pointed to by pvalue to be const, the compiler will check for any statements that attempt to modify the value pointed to by pvalue and flag such statements as an error. For example, the following statement will now result in an error message from the compiler:

```
*pvalue = 8888L;                     // Error - attempt to change const location
```

You have only asserted that what pvalue points to must not be changed. You are quite free to do what you want with value:

```
value = 7777L;
```

The value pointed to has changed, but you did not use the pointer to make the change. Of course, the pointer itself is not constant, so you can still change what it points to:

```
long number = 8888L;
pvalue = &number;                    // OK - changing the address in pvalue
```

This will change the address stored in pvalue to point to number. You still cannot use the pointer to change the value that is stored though. You can change the address stored in the pointer as much as you like, but using the pointer to change the value pointed to is not allowed, even after you have changed the address stored in the pointer.

Constant Pointers

Of course you might also want to ensure that the address stored in a pointer cannot be changed. You can arrange for this to be the case by using the const keyword slightly differently in the declaration of the pointer. Here's how you could ensure that a pointer always points to the same thing:

```
int count = 43;
int *const pcount = &count;          // Defines a constant pointer
```

The second statement declares and initializes pcount and indicates that the address stored must not be changed. The compiler will therefore check that you do not inadvertently attempt to change what the pointer points to elsewhere in your code, so the following statements will result in an error message when you compile:

```
int item = 34;
pcount = &item;                      // Error - attempt to change a constant pointer
```

You can still change the value that pcount points to using pcount though:

```
*pcount = 345;                       // OK - changes the value of count
```

This references the value stored in count through the pointer and changes its value to 345. Of course, you could also use count directly to change the value.

You can create a constant pointer that points to a value that is also constant:

```
int item = 25;
const int *const pitem = &item;
```

The pitem is a constant pointer to a constant, so everything is fixed. You cannot change the address stored in pitem, and you cannot use pitem to modify what it points to. You can still change the value of item directly though. If you wanted to make everything fixed and inviolable, you could specify item as const.

Naming Pointers

You've already started to write some quite large programs. As you can imagine, when your programs get even bigger, it may be difficult to remember which variables are normal variables and which are pointers. Therefore, it's a good idea to use names beginning with p as pointer names. If you follow this method religiously, you stand a reasonable chance of knowing which variables are pointers and which are not.

Arrays and Pointers

You'll need a clear head for this section. Let's recap for a moment and recall what an array is and what a pointer is:

> An *array* is a collection of objects of the same type that you can refer to using a single name. For example, an array called scores[50] could contain all the basketball scores for a 50-game season. You use a different index value to refer to each element in the array. The array scores[0] is the first score, and scores[49] is the last score. If you had ten games each month, you could use a multidimensional array, scores[12][10]. If you start to play in January, the third game in June would be referenced by scores[5][2].

> A *pointer* is a variable that has as its value a memory address that can reference another variable or constant of a given type. You can use a pointer to hold the address of different variables at different times, as long as they're all of the same type.

Arrays and pointers seem quite different, and indeed they are, but they are really very closely related and can sometimes be used interchangeably. Let's consider strings. A string is just an array of elements of type char. If you want to input a single character with scanf_s(), you could use this:

```
char single = 0;
scanf_s("%c", &single, sizeof(single));
```

Here you need the address of operator (&) applied to single for scanf_s() to work because scanf_s() needs the address of the location where the input data are to be stored; otherwise, it could not modify the location.
However, if you're reading in a string, you can write this:

```
char multiple[10];
scanf_s("%s", multiple, sizeof(multiple));
```

Here you don't use the & operator. You're using the array name just like a pointer. If you use the array name in this way without an index value, it refers to the address of the first element in the array. Always keep in mind, though, that arrays are *not* pointers and there's an important difference between them. You can change the address contained in a pointer, but you can't change the address referenced by an array name.
Let's go through some examples to see how arrays and pointers work together. These examples link together as a progression. With practical examples of how arrays and pointers can work together, you should find it fairly easy to grasp the main ideas behind pointers and their relationship to arrays.

TRY IT OUT: ARRAYS AND POINTERS

Just to further illustrate that an array name by itself refers to an address, try running the following program:

```
// Program 7.4  Arrays and pointers
#include <stdio.h>

int main(void)
{
  char multiple[] = "My string";
```

```
    char *p = &multiple[0];
    printf("The address of the first array element  : %p\n", p);

    p = multiple;
    printf("The address obtained from the array name: %p\n", multiple);
    return 0;
}
```

On my computer, the output is

```
The address of the first array element  : 000000000012ff06
The address obtained from the array name: 000000000012ff06
```

How It Works

You can conclude from the output that the expression &multiple[0] produces the same value as the expression multiple. This is what you might expect because multiple evaluates to the address of the first byte of the array and &multiple[0] evaluates to the first byte of the first element of the array, and it would be surprising if these were not the same. So let's take this a bit further. If you set p to multiple, which has the same value as &multiple[0], what does p + 1 correspond to? Let's try that in an example.

TRY IT OUT: ARRAYS AND POINTERS TAKEN FURTHER

This program demonstrates the effect of adding an integer value to a pointer:

```
// Program 7.5 Incrementing a pointer to an array
#define __STDC_WANT_LIB_EXT1__ 1
#include <stdio.h>
#include <string.h>

int main(void)
{
  char multiple[] = "a string";
  char *p = multiple;

  for(size_t i = 0 ; i < strnlen_s(multiple, sizeof(multiple)) ; ++i)
    printf("multiple[%zu] = %c   *(p+% zu) = %c   &multiple[%zu] = %p   p+% zu = %p\n",
                    i, multiple[i], i, *(p+i), i, &multiple[i], i, p+i);

  return 0;
}
```

The output is the following:

```
multiple[0] = a  *(p+0) = a  &multiple[0] = 000000000012feff  p+0 = 000000000012feff
multiple[1] =    *(p+1) =    &multiple[1] = 000000000012ff00  p+1 = 000000000012ff00
multiple[2] = s  *(p+2) = s  &multiple[2] = 000000000012ff01  p+2 = 000000000012ff01
multiple[3] = t  *(p+3) = t  &multiple[3] = 000000000012ff02  p+3 = 000000000012ff02
```

```
multiple[4] = r   *(p+4) = r   &multiple[4] = 000000000012ff03   p+4 = 000000000012ff03
multiple[5] = i   *(p+5) = i   &multiple[5] = 000000000012ff04   p+5 = 000000000012ff04
multiple[6] = n   *(p+6) = n   &multiple[6] = 000000000012ff05   p+6 = 000000000012ff05
multiple[7] = g   *(p+7) = g   &multiple[7] = 000000000012ff06   p+7 = 000000000012ff06
```

How It Works

Look at the list of addresses to the right in the output. Because p is set to the address of multiple, p + n is essentially the same as multiple + n, so you can see that multiple[n] is the same as *(multiple + n). The addresses differ by 1, which is what you would expect for an array of elements that each occupy 1 byte. You can see from the two columns of output to the left that *(p + n), which is dereferencing the address that you get by adding an integer n to the address in p, evaluates to the same thing as multiple[n].

TRY IT OUT: DIFFERENT TYPES OF ARRAYS

The previous program is interesting, but you already knew that the computer could add numbers together without much difficulty, so let's change to a different type of array and see what happens:

```
// Program 7.6 Incrementing a pointer to an array of integers
#include <stdio.h>

int main(void)
{
  long multiple[] = {15L, 25L, 35L, 45L};
  long *p = multiple;

  for(int i = 0 ; i < sizeof(multiple)/sizeof(multiple[0]) ; ++i)
    printf("address p+%d (&multiple[%d]): %llu        *(p+%d)   value: %d\n",
                           i, i, (unsigned long long)(p+i), i,  *(p+i));

  printf("\n   Type long occupies: %d bytes\n", (int)sizeof(long));
  return 0;
}
```

If you compile and run this program, you get an entirely different result:

```
address p+0 (&multiple[0]): 1244928        *(p+0)   value: 15
address p+1 (&multiple[1]): 1244932        *(p+1)   value: 25
address p+2 (&multiple[2]): 1244936        *(p+2)   value: 35
address p+3 (&multiple[3]): 1244940        *(p+3)   value: 45
     Type long occupies: 4 bytes
```

How It Works

This time the pointer, p, is set to the address that results from `multiple`, where `multiple` is an array of elements of type `long`. The pointer will initially contain the address of the first byte in the array, which is also the first byte of the element `multiple[0]`. This time the addresses are displayed using the `%llu` conversion specification after casting them to type `unsigned long long` so they will be decimal values. This will make it easier to see the difference between successive addresses.

Look at the output. With this example, p is 1244928 and p+1 is equal to 1244932. You can see that 1244932 is 4 greater than 1244928, although you only added 1 to p. This isn't a mistake. The compiler presumes that when you add 1 to an address value, what you actually want to do is access the next variable of that type. This is why you have to specify the *type* of variable that's to be pointed to when you declare a pointer. Remember that `char` data are stored in 1 byte and that variables declared as `long` typically occupy 4 bytes. As you can see, on my computer variables declared as `long` are 4 bytes. Incrementing a pointer to type `long` by 1 on my computer increments the address by 4, because a value of type `long` occupies 4 bytes. On a computer that stores type `long` in 8 bytes, incrementing a pointer to `long` by 1 will increase the address value by 8.

Note that you could use the array name directly in this example. You could write the `for` loop as

```
for(int i = 0 ; i < sizeof(multiple)/sizeof(multiple[0]) ; ++i)
  printf("address p+%d (&multiple[%d]): %llu        *(p+%d)   value: %d\n",
              i, i, (unsigned long long)(multiple+i), i, *(multiple+i));
```

This works because the expressions `multiple` and `multiple+i` both evaluate to an address. We output the values of these addresses and output the value at these addresses by using the * operator. The arithmetic with addresses works the same here as it did with the pointer p. Incrementing `multiple` by 1 results in the address of the next element in the array, which is 4 bytes further along in memory. However, don't be misled; an array name refers to a fixed address and is not a pointer. You can use an array name and thus the address it references in an expression, but you cannot modify it.

Multidimensional Arrays

So far, you have looked at one-dimensional arrays in relation to pointers; but is it the same story with arrays that have two or more dimensions? Well, to some extent it is. However, the differences between pointers and array names start to become more apparent. Let's consider the array that you used for the tic-tac-toe program at the end of Chapter 5. You declared the array as follows:

```
char board[3][3] = {
                      {'1','2','3'},
                      {'4','5','6'},
                      {'7','8','9'}
                    };
```

I'll use this array for the examples in this section to explore multidimensional arrays in relation to pointers.

TRY IT OUT: TWO-DIMENSIONAL ARRAYS AND POINTERS

Let's look at some of the addresses related to the board array with this example:

```
// Program 7.7 Two-dimensional arrays and pointers
#include <stdio.h>

int main(void)
{
  char board[3][3] = {
                       {'1','2','3'},
                       {'4','5','6'},
                       {'7','8','9'}
                     };
  printf("address of board      : %p\n", board);
  printf("address of board[0][0] : %p\n", &board[0][0]);
  printf("value of board[0]      : %p\n", board[0]);
  return 0;
}
```

The output might come as a bit of a surprise to you:

```
address of board       : 000000000012ff07
address of board[0][0] : 000000000012ff07
value of board[0]      : 000000000012ff07
```

How It Works

As you can see, all three output values are the same, so what can you deduce from this? When you declare a one-dimensional array as x[n1], the [n1] after the array name tells the compiler that it's an array with n1 elements. When you declare a two-dimensional array as y[n1][n2], the compiler conceptually creates a one-dimensional array of size n1, in which each element is an array of size n2.

As you learned in Chapter 5, when you declare a two-dimensional array, you're notionally creating an array of one-dimensional subarrays. So when you access the two-dimensional array using the array name with a single index value, board[0], for example, you're referencing the address of one of the subarrays. Using the two-dimensional array name by itself references the address of the beginning of the array of subarrays, which is also the address of the beginning of the first subarray.

To summarize the expressions:

```
board
board[0]
&board[0][0]
```

These all have the same value, but they aren't the same thing: board is the address of a two-dimensional array of char elements, board[0] is the address of a one-dimensional array of char elements that is a subarray of board, and &board[0][0] is the address of an array element of type char. Just because the nearest gas station is 6 1/2 miles away doesn't make it the same thing as your hat size. The expression board[1] results in the same address as the expression &board[1][0]. It should be reasonably easy to understand that this is so because the latter expression is the first element of the second subarray, board[1].

When you use pointer notation to get to the values within a two-dimensional array, you still use the indirection operator, but you must be careful. If you change the preceding example to display the value of the first element, you'll see why:

```
// Program 7.7A Two-dimensional arrays and pointers
#include <stdio.h>

int main(void)
{
  char board[3][3] = {
                        {'1','2','3'},
                        {'4','5','6'},
                        {'7','8','9'}
                     };
  printf("value of board[0][0] : %c\n", board[0][0]);
  printf("value of *board[0]   : %c\n", *board[0]);
  printf("value of **board     : %c\n", **board);
  return 0;
}
```

The output from this program is as follows:

```
value of board[0][0] : 1
value of *board[0]   : 1
value of **board     : 1
```

As you can see, if you use board as a means of obtaining the value of the first element, you need to apply two indirection operators to get it: **board. If you use only one *, you will get the address of the first element of the array of arrays, which is the address referenced by board[0]. The relationship between the multidimensional array and its subarrays is shown in Figure 7-3.

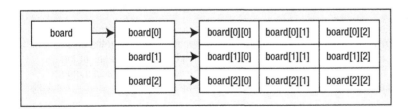

Figure 7-3. *Referencing an array, its subarrays, and its elements*

As Figure 7-3 shows, board refers to the address of the first element in the array of subarrays, and board[0], board[1], and board[2] refer to the addresses of the first element in each of the corresponding subarrays. Using two index values accesses the value stored in an element of the array. So, with this clearer picture of what's going on in your multidimensional array, let's see how you can use board to get to all the values in that array. You'll do this in the next example.

■ **Note** Although you can visualize a two-dimensional array as an array of one-dimensional arrays, this is not how it is laid out in memory. The array elements will be stored as a large one-dimensional array, and the compiler ensures that you can access it as an array of one-dimensional arrays.

TRY IT OUT: GETTING VALUES IN A TWO-DIMENSIONAL ARRAY

This example takes the previous example a bit further using a for loop:

```
// Program 7.8  Getting values in a two-dimensional array
#include <stdio.h>

int main(void)
{
  char board[3][3] = {
                      {'1','2','3'},
                      {'4','5','6'},
                      {'7','8','9'}
                      };
  // List all elements of the array
  for(int i = 0 ; i < 9 ; ++i)
    printf(" board: %c\n", *(*board + i));
  return 0;
}
```

The output from the program is as follows:

```
board: 1
board: 2
board: 3
board: 4
board: 5
board: 6
board: 7
board: 8
board: 9
```

How It Works

Notice how you dereference board in the loop:

```
printf(" board: %c\n", *(*board + i));
```

You use the expression *(*board + i) to get the value of an array element. The expression between the parentheses, *board + i, produces the address of the element in the board array that is at offset i.

Using board by itself is effectively using an address value of type char**. Dereferencing board produces the same address value, but of type char*. Adding i to this results in an address of type char* that is i elements further on in memory, which is a character in the array. Dereferencing that results in the contents of the memory at that address.

It's important that the brackets are included. Leaving them out would give you the value pointed to by board (i.e., the value stored in the location referenced by the address stored in board) with the value of i added to this value. So if i had the value 2, you would simply output the value of the first element of the array plus 2. What you actually want to do, and what your expression does, is to add the value of i to the *address* contained in board and then dereference this new address to obtain a value.

To make this clearer, let's see what happens if you omit the parentheses in the example. To see what is happening, you need to change the initial values for the array so that the characters go from '9' to '1' with the brackets in the expression in the printf() call omitted so it reads like this:

```
printf(" board: %c\n", **board + i);
```

The output looks like this:

```
board: 9
board: :
board: ;
board: <
board: =
board: >
board: ?
board: @
board: A
```

This output results because you're adding the value of i to the contents of the first element of the array, board, which is accessed by the expression **board. The characters you get as a result come from the ASCII table, starting at '9' and continuing to 'A'.

Using the expression **(board + i) will give erroneous results. In this case, **(board + 0) points to board[0][0], whereas **(board + 1) points to board[1][0], and **(board + 2) points to board[2][0]. If you use higher increments, you access memory locations outside the array because there isn't a fourth element in the array of arrays.

Multidimensional Arrays and Pointers

So now that you've used an array name using pointer notation for referencing a two-dimensional array, let's use a variable that you've declared as a pointer. As I've already stated, this is where there's a significant difference. If you declare a pointer and assign the address of the array to it, then you can use that pointer to access the members of the array by modifying the address it contains.

TRY IT OUT: MULTIDIMENSIONAL ARRAYS AND POINTERS

You can see multidimensional arrays and pointers in action here:

```
// Program 7.9  Multidimensional arrays and pointers
#include <stdio.h>

int main(void)
{
  char board[3][3] = {
                       {'1','2','3'},
                       {'4','5','6'},
                       {'7','8','9'}
                     };

  char *pboard = *board;              // A pointer to char
  for(int i = 0 ; i < 9 ; ++i)
    printf(" board: %c\n", *(pboard + i));

  return 0;
}
```

Here, you get the same output as for Program 7.8.

How It Works

You initialize pboard with the address of the first element of the array, and then you use normal pointer arithmetic to move through the array:

```
  char *pboard = *board;              // A pointer to char
  for(int i = 0 ; i < 9 ; ++i)
    printf(" board: %c\n", *(pboard + i));
```

Note how you dereference board to obtain the address you want (with *board). This is necessary because board by itself is of type char**, a pointer to a pointer, and is the address of the subarray board[0]. It is not the address of an element, which must be of type char*. You could have initialized pboard by using the following:

```
  char *pboard = &board[0][0];
```

This amounts to the same thing. You might think you could initialize pboard using this statement:

```
  pboard = board;                     // Wrong level of indirection!
```

This is wrong. You should at least get a compiler warning if you do this, and ideally it should not compile at all. Strictly speaking, this isn't legal because pboard and board have *different levels of indirection*. That's a great jargon phrase that just means that pboard refers to an address that contains a value of type char, whereas board refers to an address that *refers to an address* containing a value of type char. There's an extra level with board compared to pboard. Consequently, pboard needs one * to get to the value, and board needs two **. Some compilers will allow you to get away with this and just give you a warning about what you've done. However, it is an error, so you shouldn't do it!

Accessing Array Elements

Now you know that, for a two-dimensional array, you have several ways of accessing the elements in that array. Table 7-1 lists these ways of accessing your board array. The left column contains row index values to the board array, and the top row contains column index values. The entry in the table corresponding to a given row index and column index shows the various possible expressions for referring to that element.

Table 7-1. *Pointer Expressions for Accessing Array Elements*

board	0	1	2
0	board[0][0] *board[0] **board	board[0][1] *(board[0]+1) *(*board+1)	board[0][2] *(board[0]+2) *(*board+2)
1	board[1][0] *(board[0]+3) *board[1] *(*board+3)	board[1][1] *(board[0]+4) *(board[1]+1) *(*board+4)	board[1][2] *(board[0]+5) *(board[1]+2) *(*board+5)
2	board[2][0] *(board[0]+6) *(board[1]+3) *board[2] *(*board+6)	board[2][1] *(board[0]+7) *(board[1]+4) *(board[2]+1) *(*board+7)	board[2][2] *(board[0]+8) *(board[1]+5) *(board[2]+2) *(*board+8)

Let's see how you can apply what you've learned so far about pointers in a program that you previously wrote without using pointers. Then you'll be able to see how the pointer-based implementation differs. You'll recall that in Chapter 5 you wrote an example, Program 5.6, that worked out your hat size. Let's see how you could have done things a little differently.

TRY IT OUT: KNOW YOUR HAT SIZE REVISITED

Here's a rewrite of the hat sizes example using pointer notation:

```
// Program 7.10  Understand pointers to your hat size - if you dare
#define __STDC_WANT_LIB_EXT1__ 1
#include <stdio.h>
#include <stdbool.h>

int main(void)
{
  char size[3][12] = {              // Hat sizes as characters
      {'6', '6', '6', '6', '7', '7', '7', '7', '7', '7', '7', '7'},
      {'1', '5', '3', '7', ' ', '1', '1', '3', '1', '5', '3', '7'},
      {'2', '8', '4', '8', ' ', '8', '4', '8', '2', '8', '4', '8'}
                  };

  int headsize[12] =                // Values in 1/8 inches
      {164,166,169,172,175,178,181,184,188,191,194,197};

  char *psize = *size;
  int *pheadsize = headsize;
```

```
  float cranium = 0.0f;                  // Head circumference in decimal inches
  int your_head = 0;                     // Headsize in whole eighths
  bool hat_found = false;                // Indicates when a hat is found to fit

  // Get the circumference of the head
  printf("\nEnter the circumference of your head above your eyebrows"
                                   " in inches as a decimal value: ");
  scanf_s(" %f", &cranium);

  your_head = (int)(8.0f*cranium);       // Convert to whole eighths of an inch

  /****************************************************************
   * Search for a hat size:                                      *
   * Either your head corresponds to the 1st headsize element or *
   * a fit is when your_head is greater that one headsize element*
   * and less than or equal to the next.                         *
   * In this case the size is the second headsize value.         *
   ****************************************************************/
  unsigned int i = 0;                    // Loop counter
  if(your_head == *pheadsize)            // Check for min size fit
    hat_found = true;
  else
  {
    // Find head size in the headsize array
    for (i = 1 ; i < sizeof(headsize)/sizeof(*headsize) ; ++i)
    {
      if(your_head > *(pheadsize + i - 1) && your_head <= *(pheadsize + i))
      {
        hat_found = true;
        break;
      }
    }
  }

  if(hat_found)
  {
    printf("\nYour hat size is %c %c%c%c\n",
           *(psize + i),                                          // 1st row of size
           *(psize + 1*sizeof(*size)/sizeof(**size) + i),   // 2nd row of size
           (*(psize + 1*sizeof(*size)/sizeof(**size) + i) == ' ') ?' ' : '/',
           *(psize + 2* sizeof(*size)/sizeof(**size) + i));  // 3rd row of size
  }

  // If no hat was found, the head is too small, or too large
  else
  {
    if(your_head < *pheadsize)         // check for too small
      printf("\nYou are the proverbial pinhead. No hat for"
                                      " you I'm afraid.\n");
    else                             // It must be too large
      printf("\nYou, in technical parlance, are a fathead."
                                 " No hat for you, I'm afraid.\n");
  }
  return 0;
}
```

287

The output from this program is the same as that given in Chapter 5, so I won't repeat it here. It's the code that's of interest, so let's look at the new elements in this program.

How It Works

The program works in essentially the same way as the example from Chapter 5. The differences arise because the implementation is now in terms of the pointers `pheadsize` and `psize` that contain the addresses of the start of the `headsize` and `size` arrays, respectively. The `for` loop iterates over the head sizes starting at the second array element. Note that `sizeof(*headsize)` is equivalent to `sizeof(headsize[0])`. In the `for` loop, the value in `your_head` is compared with the values in the `headsize` array in the following statement:

```
if(your_head > *(pheadsize + i - 1) && your_head <= *(pheadsize + i))
{
  hat_found = true;
    break;
}
```

The expression on the far right side of the comparison, `*(pheadsize + i)`, is equivalent to `headsize[i]` in array notation. The bit between the parentheses adds `i` to the address of the beginning of the array. Remember that adding an integer `i` to an address will add `i` times the length of each element. Therefore, the subexpression between parentheses produces the byte address of the element corresponding to the index value `i`. The dereference operator `*` then obtains the contents of this element for the comparison operation with the value in the variable `your_head`. The expression `*(pheadsize + i - 1)` is equivalent to `headsize[i - 1]`.

The `printf()` that outputs a hat size shows the effect of two array dimensions on the pointer expression that access an element in a particular row:

```
printf("\nYour hat size is %c %c%c%c\n",
          *(psize + i),                                      // 1st row of size
          *(psize + 1*sizeof(*size)/sizeof(**size) + i),     // 2nd row of size
          (*(psize + 1*sizeof(*size)/sizeof(**size) + i) == ' ') ?' ' : '/',
          *(psize + 2* sizeof(*size)/sizeof(**size) + i));   // 3rd row of size
```

The first expression for an output value is `*(psize + i)` that accesses the `i`th element in the first row of size, so this is equivalent to `size[0][i]`. Remember, `psize` is of type `char*`, not `char**`, so applying a single indirection gets you to an array element. The second expression is `*(psize + 1*sizeof(*size)/sizeof(**size) + i)`, which accesses the `i`th element in the second row of size, so it is equivalent to `size[1][i]`. Here `sizeof(*size)` is the size of a row, and you must divide that by `sizeof(**size)`, the size of a single element, to get the number of elements in a row. I have written the expression to show that the address of the start of the second row is obtained by adding the number of elements in a row to `psize`. You then add `i` to that to get the element within the second row. To get the element in the third row of the size array, you use the expression `*(psize + 2* sizeof(*size)/sizeof(**size) + i)`, which is equivalent to `size[2][i]`.

Using Memory As You Go

Pointers are an extremely flexible and powerful tool for programming over a wide range of applications. The majority of programs in C use pointers to some extent. C also has a further facility called *dynamic memory allocation* that depends on the concept of a pointer and provides a strong incentive to use pointers in your code. Dynamic memory allocation allows memory for storing data to be allocated dynamically when your program executes. Allocating memory dynamically is possible only because you have pointers available.

The majority of production programs will use dynamic memory allocation. Your email client does, for example. When you retrieve your email, the program has no prior knowledge of how many emails there will be or how much memory each requires. The email client will obtain sufficient memory at runtime to manage the number and size of your emails.

Think back to the program in Chapter 5 that calculated the average scores for a group of students. At the moment, it works for only ten students. Ideally, the program should work for any number of students without knowing the number of students in the class in advance and without using any more memory than necessary for the number of student scores specified. Dynamic memory allocation allows you to do just that. You can create arrays at runtime that are just large enough to hold the amount of data you require for the task.

When you explicitly allocate memory at runtime in a program, space is reserved for you in a memory area called the *heap*. There's another memory area called the *stack* associated with a program in which space to store function arguments and local variables in a function is allocated. (As we already discussed, there are more areas of components for memory. The heap and stack are the essential segments for our chapter scope, but you can check the figure in Chapter 2 for more details.) When the execution of a function ends, the space allocated to store arguments and local variables is freed. The memory in the heap is different in that it is controlled by you. As you'll see in this chapter, when you allocate memory on the heap, it is up to you to keep track of when the memory you have allocated is no longer required and free the space you have allocated to allow it to be reused.

Dynamic Memory Allocation: The malloc() Function

You saw in Chapter 5 how arrays can be created at runtime by specifying the dimensions by variables. You can also allocate memory at runtime explicitly. The simplest standard library function that allocates memory at runtime is called malloc(). You need to include the stdlib.h header file in your program when you use this function. When you use the malloc() function, you specify the number of bytes of memory that you want allocated as the argument. The function returns the address of the first byte of memory that it allocated in response to your request. Because you get an address returned, a pointer is the only place to put it.

A typical example of dynamic memory allocation might be this:

```
int *pNumber = (int*)malloc(100);
```

Here, you've requested 100 bytes of memory and assigned the address of this memory block to pNumber. As long as you haven't modified it, any time that you use the variable pNumber, it will point to the first int location at the beginning of the 100 bytes that were allocated. This whole block can hold 25 int values on my computer, because they require 4 bytes each. The statement kind of assumes that type int requires 4 bytes. It would be better to remove this assumption. Writing the statement like this will do that:

```
int *pNumber = (int*)malloc(25*sizeof(int));
```

Now the argument to malloc() is clearly indicating that sufficient bytes for accommodating 25 values of type int should be made available.

Notice the cast (int*), which converts the address returned by the function to the type pointer to int. The function malloc() is a general-purpose function that is used to allocate memory for any type of data. The function has no knowledge of what you want to use the memory for, so it returns a pointer of type pointer to void, which, as you know, is written as void*. Pointers of type void* can point to any kind of data. However, you can't dereference a pointer of type pointer to void because what it points to is unspecified. Your compiler will always arrange for the address returned by malloc() to be automatically converted to the pointer type on the left of the assignment, but it doesn't hurt to put an explicit cast.

■ **Note**   Where possible, the compiler will *always* convert the value of an expression that is the right operand of an assignment to the type required to store it in the left operand.

You can request any number of bytes, subject only to the amount of free memory on the computer and the lismit on malloc() imposed by a particular implementation. If the memory that you request can't be allocated for any reason, malloc() returns a pointer with the value NULL. This is the equivalent of 0 for pointers. It's always a good idea to check any dynamic memory request immediately using an if statement to make sure the memory is actually there before you try to use it. As with money, attempting to use memory you don't have is generally catastrophic. For that reason, you might write this:

```
int *pNumber = (int*)malloc(25*sizeof(int));
if(!pNumber)
{
  // Code to deal with memory allocation failure ...
}
```

Now you can at least display a message and terminate the program. This would be much better than allowing the program to continue and crash when it uses a NULL address to store something. In some instances, you may be able to free up a bit of memory that you've been using elsewhere, which might give you enough memory to continue.

Releasing Dynamically Allocated Memory

When you allocate memory dynamically, you should always release the memory when it is no longer required. Memory that you allocate on the heap will be automatically released when your program ends, but it is better to explicitly release the memory when you are done with it, even if it's just before you exit from the program. In more complicated situations, you can easily have a memory leak. A *memory leak* occurs when you allocate some memory dynamically and you do not retain the reference to it, so you are unable to release the memory. This often occurs within a loop, and because you do not release the memory when it is no longer required, your program consumes more and more of the available memory on each loop iteration and eventually may occupy it all (or not enough left space for the rest of the program).

Of course, to free memory that you have allocated dynamically, you must still have access to the address that references the block of memory. To release the memory for a block of dynamically allocated memory whose address you have stored in the pointer pNumber, you just write this statement:

```
free(pNumber);
pNumber = NULL;
```

The free() function has a formal parameter of type void*, and because any pointer type can be automatically converted to this type, you can pass a pointer of any type as the argument. As long as pNumber contains the address that was returned when the memory was allocated, the entire block of memory will be freed for further use. You should always set the pointer to NULL after the memory that it points to has been freed.

▓ **Caution**   You must ensure that a pointer to heap memory does not get overwritten by another address before you have freed the memory to which it points.

If you pass a NULL pointer to the free() function, the function does nothing. You should avoid attempting to free the same memory area twice, because the behavior of the free() function is undefined in this instance and therefore unpredictable. You are most at risk of trying to free the same memory twice when you have more than one pointer variable that references the memory you have allocated, so take particular care when you are doing this.

TRY IT OUT: DYNAMIC MEMORY ALLOCATION

You can put the concept of dynamic memory allocation into practice by using pointers to help calculate prime numbers. In case you've forgotten, a prime number is an integer that's exactly divisible only by 1 or by the number itself.

The process for finding a prime is quite simple. First, you know by inspection that 2, 3, and 5 are the first three prime numbers, because they aren't divisible by anything other than 1 and themselves. Because all the other prime numbers must be odd (otherwise, they would be divisible by 2), you can work out the next number to check by starting at the last prime you have and adding 2. When you've checked out that number, you add another 2 to get the next to be checked, and so on.

To check whether a number is actually prime rather than just odd, you could divide by all the odd numbers less than the number that you're checking, but you don't need to do as much work as that. If a number is *not* prime, it must be divisible by one of the primes lower than the number you're checking. Because you'll obtain the primes in sequence, it will be sufficient to check a candidate by testing whether any of the primes you've already found is an exact divisor.

You'll implement this program using pointers and dynamic memory allocation:

```c
// Program 7.11  A dynamic prime example
#define __STDC_WANT_LIB_EXT1__ 1
#include <stdio.h>
#include <stdlib.h>
#include <stdbool.h>

int main(void)
{
  unsigned long long *pPrimes = NULL;  // Pointer to primes storage area
  unsigned long long trial = 0;        // Integer to be tested
  bool found = false;                  // Indicates when we find a prime
  int total = 0;                       // Number of primes required
  int count = 0;                       // Number of primes found
```

```
    printf("How many primes would you like - you'll get at least 4?   ");
    scanf_s("%d", &total);                // Total is how many we need to find
    total = total < 4 ? 4 : total;        // Make sure it is at least 4

    // Allocate sufficient memory to store the number of primes required
    pPrimes = (unsigned long long*)malloc(total*sizeof(unsigned long long));
    if(!pPrimes)
    {
        printf("Not enough memory. It's the end I'm afraid.\n");
        return 1;
    }

    // We know the first three primes so let's give the program a start
    *pPrimes = 2ULL;                      // First prime
    *(pPrimes + 1) = 3ULL;                // Second prime
    *(pPrimes + 2) = 5ULL;                // Third prime
    count = 3;                            // Number of primes stored
    trial = 5ULL;                         // Set to the last prime we have

    // Find all the primes required
    while(count < total)
    {
      trial += 2ULL;                      // Next value for checking

      // Divide by the primes we have. If any divide exactly - it's not prime
      for(int i = 1 ; i < count ; ++i)
      {
        if(!(found = (trial % *(pPrimes + i))))
          break;                          // Exit if zero remainder
      }

      if(found)                           // We got one - if found is true
        *(pPrimes + count++) = trial;     // Store it and increment count
    }
    // Display primes 5-up
    for(int i = 0 ; i < total ; ++i)
    {
      printf ("%12llu", *(pPrimes + i));
      if(!((i+1) % 5))
        printf("\n");                     // Newline after every 5
    }
    printf("\n");                         // Newline for any stragglers

    free(pPrimes);                        // Release the heap memory ...
    pPrimes = NULL;                       // ... and reset the pointer
    return 0;
}
```

The output from the program looks something like this:

```
How many primes would you like - you'll get at least 4? 25
         2           3           5           7          11
        13          17          19          23          29
        31          37          41          43          47
        53          59          61          67          71
        73          79          83          89          97
```

How It Works

You enter the number of prime numbers you want the program to generate. The pPrimes pointer variable refers to a memory area that will be used to store the prime numbers as they're calculated. No memory is defined initially in the program. The space is allocated after you've entered how many you want:

```
printf("How many primes would you like - you'll get at least 4?  ");
scanf_s("%d", &total);            // Total is how many we need to find
total = total < 4 ? 4 : total;    // Make sure it is at least 4
```

After the prompt, the number you enter is stored in total. The next statement then ensures that total is at least 4. This is because you'll define and store the three primes you know (2, 3, and 5) by default.

You use the value in total to allocate the memory to store the primes:

```
pPrimes = (unsigned long long*)malloc(total*sizeof(unsigned long long));
if(!pPrimes)
{
   printf("Not enough memory. It's the end I'm afraid.\n");
   return 1;
}
```

Primes grow in size quite rapidly, so you store them as type unsigned long long. Because you're going to store each prime as type unsigned long long, the number of bytes you require is total*sizeof(unsigned long long). If malloc() returns NULL, no memory was allocated, so you display a message and end the program.

The maximum number of primes you can specify depends on two things: the memory available on your computer and the maximum memory the implementation of malloc() can allocate at one time. The former is probably the major constraint. The argument to malloc() is of type size_t, so the integer type that corresponds to size_t with your compiler will limit the number of bytes you can specify. If size_t corresponds to a 4-byte unsigned integer, you will be able to allocate up to 4,294,967,295 bytes at one time.

You define the first three primes and store them in the first three positions in the memory area pointed to by pPrimes:

```
*pPrimes = 2ULL;          // First prime
*(pPrimes+1) = 3ULL;      // Second prime
*(pPrimes+2) = 5ULL;      // Third prime
```

As you can see, referencing successive locations in memory that is acquired dynamically is simple. Because pPrimes is of type pointer to unsigned long long, pPrimes+1 refers to the address of the second location—the address that results from the expression being pPrimes plus the number of bytes required to store one data item of type unsigned long long. To store each value, you use the indirection operator. If you fail to dereference a pointer variable such as pPrimes, you would be modifying the address itself, and if you fail to dereference an expression that evaluates to an address such as pPrimes+1, you will get a compiler error.

You have three primes, so you set count to 3 and initialize the variable trial with the last prime you stored:

```
count = 3;                          // Number of primes stored
trial = 5ULL;                       // Set to the last prime we have
```

The value in trial will be incremented by 2 to get the next value to be tested when you start searching for the next prime.

All the primes are found in the while loop:

```
while(count < total)
{
  ...
}
```

The variable count is incremented within the loop as each prime is found, and when it reaches the value of total, the loop ends.

Within the while loop, you first increase the value in trial by 2 and then test whether the value is prime in a for loop:

```
for(int i = 1 ; i < count ; ++i)
{
  if(!(found = (trial % *(pPrimes + i))))
      break;                        // Exit if zero remainder
}
```

The loop body does the testing. You don't bother to divide by the first prime, 2, because total is always odd. The remainder after dividing trial by each of the other primes that you have so far is stored in the bool variable, found. The remainder will be converted automatically to type bool, with a nonzero value converting to true and 0 resulting in false. If the division is exact, the remainder will be 0, and therefore found will be set to false. If you find the remainder is 0, it means that the value in trial isn't a prime, and you can continue with the next candidate.

When found is false, the break statement will be executed, and the for loop will end.

If none of the primes divides into trial exactly, the for loop will end when all the primes have been tried, and found will contain the bool value resulting from converting the last remainder value, which will be true. When the for loop ends, you can use the value stored in found to determine whether you've found a new prime:

```
if(found)                           // We got one - if found is true
    *(pPrimes + count++) = trial;   // Store it and increment count
```

If found is true, you store the value of trial in the next available slot in the memory area. The address of the next available slot is pPrimes + count. Remember that the first slot is pPrimes, so when you have count number of primes, the last prime occupies the location pPrimes+count-1. The statement storing the new prime also increments the value of count after the new prime has been stored.

The while loop repeats the process until you have the number of primes requested. You then output the primes five on a line:

```
for(int i = 0 ; i < total ; ++i)
{
  printf ("%12llu", *(pPrimes + i));
  if(!((i+1) % 5))
    printf("\n");                        // Newline after every 5
}
printf("\n");                            // Newline for any stragglers
```

The for loop outputs total number of primes. The printf() that displays each prime value appends the output to the current line, but the if statement outputs a newline character after every fifth iteration, so there will be five primes on each line. Because the number of primes may not be an exact multiple of five, you output a newline after the loop ends to ensure that there's always at least one newline character at the end of the output.

Finally, you release the memory you allocated to store the primes:

```
free(pPrimes);                 // Release the heap memory ...
pPrimes = NULL;                // ... and reset the pointer
```

You should always set a pointer to heap memory to NULL when the memory has been freed. This eliminates the possibility of attempting to use memory that is no longer available, which is always disastrous.

▓ **Tip**   The previous example demonstrates the use of malloc() to allocate memory and free() to release it. However, you could implement the example much more easily by using a dynamic array. With a dynamic array, you have no need for malloc() or free(), and there is no need to mess about with pointers.

Memory Allocation with the calloc() Function

The calloc() function that is declared in the stdlib.h header offers a couple of advantages over malloc(). First, it offers the small advantage that it allocates memory as a number of elements of a given size. Second and more importantly, it initializes the memory that is allocated so that all bytes are zero. The calloc() function requires two argument values: the number of data items for which space is required and the size of each data item. Both arguments are expected to be of type size_t. The function still doesn't know the type of the data you wish to store, so the address of the area that is allocated is returned as type void*.

Here's how you could use calloc() to allocate memory for an array of 75 elements of type int:

```
int *pNumber = (int*) calloc(75, sizeof(int));
```

The return value will be NULL if it was not possible to allocate the memory requested, so you should still check for this. This is very similar to using malloc(), but the big plus is that you know the memory area will be initialized to 0. Of course, you can let the compiler take care of supplying the cast:

```
int *pNumber = calloc(75, sizeof(int));
```

I'll omit the cast in subsequent code.

To make Program 7.11 use `calloc()` instead of `malloc()` to allocate the memory required, you only need to change one statement. The rest of the code is identical:

```
pPrimes = calloc((size_t)total, sizeof(unsigned long long));
if (primes == NULL)
{
  printf("Not enough memory. It's the end I'm afraid.\n");
  return 1;
}
```

Extending Dynamically Allocated Memory

The `realloc()` function enables you to reuse or extend memory that you previously allocated using `malloc()` or `calloc()` (or `realloc()`). The `realloc()` function expects two argument values: a pointer containing an address that was previously returned by a call to `malloc()`, `calloc()`, or `realloc()` and the size in bytes of the new memory that you want allocated.

The `realloc()` function allocates the amount of memory you specify by the second argument and transfers the contents of the previously allocated memory referenced by the pointer that you supply as the first argument to the newly allocated memory up to the lesser of the old and new memory extents. The function returns a `void*` pointer to the new memory or `NULL` if the operation fails for some reason. The new memory extent can be larger or smaller than the original. If the first argument to `realloc()` is `NULL`, the new memory specified by the second argument is allocated, so it behaves just like `malloc()` in this case. If the first argument is not `NULL` but does not point to previously allocated memory or points to memory that has been freed, the result is undefined.

The most important feature of this operation is that `realloc()` *preserves the contents of the original memory area* up to the lesser of the old and new memory extents. If the new memory extent is greater than the old, then the additional memory is not initialized and will contain junk values.

You can see how `realloc()` can be used with a revised version of Program 7.11 that calculates primes in the example here.

TRY IT OUT: EXTENDING DYNAMICALLY ALLOCATED MEMORY

In this program, the user enters the upper limit for the magnitude of the primes that are to be calculated. This means that there is no advance knowledge of how many there will be:

```
// Program 7.12  Extending dynamically allocated memory
#define __STDC_WANT_LIB_EXT1__  1
#include <stdio.h>
#include <stdlib.h>
#include <stdbool.h>
#define CAP_INCR   10                   // New memory increment

int main(void)
{
  unsigned long long *pPrimes = NULL;  // Pointer to primes storage area
  bool found = false;                  // Indicates when we find a prime
  unsigned long long limit = 0LL;      // Upper limit for primes
  int count = 0;                       // Number of primes found
```

```
printf("Enter the upper limit for primes you want to find: ");
scanf_s("%llu", &limit);

// Allocate some initial memory to store primes
size_t capacity = 10;
pPrimes = calloc(capacity, sizeof(unsigned long long));
if(!pPrimes)
{
   printf("Not enough memory. It's the end I'm afraid.\n");
   return 1;
}

// We know the first three primes so let's give the program a start
*pPrimes = 2ULL;                       // First prime
*(pPrimes + 1) = 3ULL;                 // Second prime
*(pPrimes + 2) = 5ULL;                 // Third prime
count = 3;                             // Number of primes stored

// Find all the primes required starting with the next candidate
unsigned long long trial = *(pPrimes + 2) + 2ULL;
unsigned long long *pTemp = NULL;      // Temporary pointer store
while(trial <= limit)
{
  // Divide by the primes we have. If any divide exactly - it's not prime
  for(int i = 1 ; i < count ; ++i)
  {
    if(!(found = (trial % *(pPrimes + i))))
      break;                           // Exit if zero remainder
  }

  if(found)                            // We got one - if found is true
  {
    if(count == capacity)
    { // We need more memory
      capacity += CAP_INCR;
      pTemp = realloc(pPrimes, capacity*sizeof(unsigned long long));
      if(!pTemp)
      {
        printf("Unfortunately memory reallocation failed.\n");
        free(pPrimes);
        pPrimes = NULL;
        return 2;
      }
      pPrimes = pTemp;
    }
    *(pPrimes + count++) = trial;  // Store the new prime & increment count
  }
  trial += 2ULL;
}
// Display primes 5-up
printf("%d primes found up to %llu:\n", count, limit);
for(int i = 0 ; i < count ; ++i)
```

```
  {
    printf("%12llu", *(pPrimes + i));
    if(!((i+1) % 5))
      printf("\n");                      // Newline after every 5
  }
  printf("\n");                          // Newline for any stragglers

  free(pPrimes);                         // Release the heap memory ...
  pPrimes = NULL;                        // ... and reset the pointer
  return 0;
}
```

Here's some sample output:

```
Enter the upper limit for primes you want to find: 100000
9592 primes found up to 100000:
           2           3           5           7          11
          13          17          19          23          29
          31          37          41          43          47
and lots more primes until...
       99817       99823       99829       99833       99839
       99859       99871       99877       99881       99901
       99907       99923       99929       99961       99971
       99989       99991
```

I omitted 1,912 lines of output because they were boring.

■ **Tip**   To see all the output for large numbers of primes under Microsoft Windows, you will need to increase the buffer size for the output window.

How It Works

With this example, you can enter the upper limit for the prime numbers you want the program to generate. The pPrimes pointer variable refers to a memory area that will be used to store the prime numbers as they're calculated. Memory for capacity primes is allocated initially in the program:

```
size_t capacity = 10;
pPrimes = calloc(capacity, sizeof(unsigned long long));
```

The second statement allocates space for ten values of type unsigned long long. The amount of memory will be extended as necessary. There's the standard check for a NULL return value from calloc() following these two statements.

The process for finding primes is essentially the same as in Program 7.11, the only difference being the while loop control that continues the loop as long as the trial value is less than or equal to the limit value that was entered.

When a prime is found, it's necessary to check whether there is sufficient memory to accommodate it:

```
if(count == capacity)
{ // We need more memory
    capacity += CAP_INCR;
    pTemp = realloc(pPrimes, capacity*sizeof(unsigned long long));
    if(!pTemp)
    {
        printf("Unfortunately memory reallocation failed.\n");
        free(pPrimes);
        return 2;
    }
    pPrimes = pTemp;
}
```

When `count`, the number of primes found, reaches `capacity`, the number of primes for which there is memory allocated, more memory must be acquired. The `capacity` is increased by the amount specified by the value of the symbol `CAP_INCR`, so each time all the currently allocated memory is occupied, there is provision for an additional ten primes. I chose the increment value as a low number to ensure that extending the memory would occur relatively frequently to illustrate the mechanism, but it is generally inefficient to allocate memory in such small amounts. The `realloc()` function makes the new memory available and preserves the original contents of the old memory in the new memory. The pointer that is returned by `realloc()` is stored in `pTemp`. This avoids overwriting the address in `pPrimes` when the allocation fails. In general, you are likely to want to access the original memory that was allocated when `realloc()` fails, possibly to make use of the data it contains and also to release the memory. The rest of the program proceeds as the previous example, so I won't discuss it further.

Here are some basic guidelines for working with memory that you allocate dynamically:

- *Avoid allocating lots of small amounts of memory.* Allocating memory on the heap carries some overhead with it, so allocating many small blocks of memory will carry much more overhead than allocating fewer larger blocks.

- *Only hang on to the memory as long as you need it.* As soon as you are finished with a block of memory on the heap, release the memory.

- *Always ensure that you provide for releasing memory that you have allocated.* Decide where in your code you will release the memory when you write the code that allocates it.

- *Make sure you do not inadvertently overwrite the address of memory you have allocated on the heap before you have released it;* otherwise, your program will have *a memory leak.* You need to be especially careful when allocating memory within a loop.

■ **Note**   Calling `free()` after failing to allocate memory using `realloc()` may result in a warning from your compiler. Calling `free()` here is valid because memory was allocated previously, but the compiler does not know this.

Handling Strings Using Pointers

You have up to now primarily used arrays of elements of type char to store strings, but using a variable of type pointer to char to reference a string will give you a lot of flexibility in handling strings, as you'll see in the section that follows. You can declare a variable of type pointer to char with a statement such as this:

```
char *pString = NULL;
```

At this point, it's worth noting yet again that a pointer is just a variable that can store the address of another memory location. So far, you've created a pointer, but you have not created the space you need to store a string. To store a string, you need to allocate some memory and store its address in the pointer variable. The dynamic memory allocation capabilities are going to be very useful in this context, for example:

```
const size_t BUF_SIZE = 100;            // Input buffer size
char buffer[BUF_SIZE];                  // A 100 byte input buffer
scanf_s("%s", buffer, BUF_SIZE);        // Read a string

// Allocate space for the string
size_t length = strnlen_s(buffer, BUF_SIZE) + 1;
char *pString = malloc(length);
if(!pString)
{
  printf("Memory allocation failed.\n");
  return 1;
}
strcpy_s(pString, length, buffer);      // Copy string to new memory
printf("%s", pString);
free(pString);
pString = NULL;
```

This fragment reads a string into an array of char elements, allocates space on the heap for the string that is read, and copies the string to the new memory. Copying the string to the memory referenced by pString allows buffer to be reused to read more data. The obvious next step would be to read another string, so how can you handle multiple strings of arbitrary length?

Using Arrays of Pointers

Of course, when you are dealing with several strings, you can use an array of pointers to store references to the strings on the heap. Suppose you wanted to read ten strings from the keyboard and store them. You could create an array of pointers to store the locations of the strings:

```
char *pS[10] = { NULL };
```

This declares an array, pS, that has ten elements of type char*. Each element in pS can store the address of a string. You learned in Chapter 5 that if you supply fewer initial values than elements in an array initializer list, the remaining elements will be initialized with 0. Thus, just specifying the list with one value, NULL, will initialize all the elements of an array of pointers of any size to NULL.

Here's how you might use this array of pointers:

```
#define STR_COUNT  10                          // Number of string pointers
const size_t BUF_SIZE = 100;                   // Input buffer size
char buffer[BUF_SIZE];                         // A 100 byte input buffer
char *pS[STR_COUNT] = {NULL};                  // Array of pointers
size_t str_size = 0;

for(size_t i = 0 ; i < STR_COUNT ; ++i)
{
  scanf_s("%s", buffer, BUF_SIZE);             // Read a string
  str_size = strnlen_s(buffer, BUF_SIZE) + 1;  // Bytes required
  pS[i] = malloc(str_size);                    // Allocate space for the string
  if(!pS[i]) return 1;                         // Allocation failed so end
  strcpy_s(pS[i], str_size, buffer);           // Copy string to new memory
}
// Do things with the strings...

// Release the heap memory
for(size_t i = 0 ; i < STR_COUNT ; ++i)
{
  free(pS[i]);
  pS[i] = NULL;
}
```

Each element of the pS array holds the address of a different string that is read from the keyboard. The array has STR_COUNT elements . Note that you cannot use a variable to specify the dimension when you want to initialize an array, even if you declare the variable as const. An array with its dimension specified by a variable is a variable-length array for which initialization is not allowed, although you can always set the element values in a loop once the array has been created. A symbol is replaced by what it represents before the code is compiled, so at compilation time, the dimension for pS will be 10.

Strings are input in the for loop. When a string has been read into buffer, sufficient space is allocated on the heap to hold the string using malloc(), and the pointer that malloc() returns is stored in an element of the pS array. The string in buffer is then copied to the memory that was allocated for it, making buffer available for use in reading the next string. You end up with an array of strings, where each string occupies exactly the number of bytes it requires and no more, so this is very efficient. But what if you don't know how many strings there are going to be? You can see how you can handle that situation through a working example.

TRY IT OUT: ALLOCATING MEMORY FOR STRINGS

This is a revised version of Program 6.10 that finds the number of occurrences of each unique word in some arbitrary prose. This version allocates memory on the heap to store the prose, the words, and the word counts. Because it's quite a lot of code, I have omitted the checks for NULL pointers from the memory allocation functions to keep the number of lines of code down, but you should always include them. Here's the code:

```
// Program 7.13 Extending dynamically allocated memory for strings
#define __STDC_WANT_LIB_EXT1__  1
#include <stdio.h>
```

```
#include <string.h>
#include <stdbool.h>
#include <stdlib.h>

#define BUF_LEN        100                    // Input buffer size
#define INIT_STR_EXT   50                     // Initial space for prose
#define WORDS_INCR     5                      // Words capacity increment

int main(void)
{
  char delimiters[] = " \n\".,;:!?)(";        // Prose delimiters
  char buf[BUF_LEN];                          // Buffer for a line of keyboard input
  size_t str_size = INIT_STR_EXT;             // Current memory to store prose
  char* pStr = malloc(str_size);              // Pointer to prose to be tokenized
  *pStr = '\0';                               // Set 1st character to null

  printf("Enter some prose with up to %d characters per line.\n"
         "Terminate input by entering an empty line:\n", BUF_LEN);

  // Read multiple lines of prose from the keyboard
  while(true)
  {
    fgets(buf, BUF_LEN, stdin);               // Read a line of input
    if(buf[0] == '\n')                        // An empty line ends input
      break;

    if(strnlen_s(pStr, str_size) + strnlen_s(buf, BUF_LEN) + 1 > str_size)
    {
      str_size = strnlen_s(pStr, str_size) + strnlen_s(buf, BUF_LEN) + 1;
      pStr = realloc(pStr, str_size); }
    }

    if(strcat_s(pStr, str_size, buf))          // Concatenate the line with pStr
    {
      printf("Something's wrong. String concatenation failed.\n");
      return 1;
    }
  }

  // Find and list all the words in the prose}

  size_t maxWords = 10;                               // Current maximum word count
  int word_count = 0;                                 // Current word count
  size_t word_length = 0;                             // Current word length
  char** pWords = calloc(maxWords, sizeof(char*));  // Stores pointers to the words
  int* pnWord = calloc(maxWords, sizeof(int));      // Stores count for each word

  size_t str_len = strnlen_s(pStr, str_size);   // Length used by strtok_s()
  char* ptr = NULL;                             // Pointer used by strtok_s()
  char* pWord = strtok_s(pStr, &str_len, delimiters, &ptr); // Find 1st word
  // use this line instead, for Microsoft compiler:
  //char* pWord = strtok_s(pStr, delimiters, &ptr);  // Find 1st word
```

```c
  if(!pWord)
  {
    printf("No words found. Ending program.\n");
    return 1;
  }

  bool new_word = true;                        // False for an existing word
  while(pWord)
  {
    // Check for existing word
    for(int i = 0 ; i < word_count ; ++i)
    {
      if(strcmp(*(pWords + i), pWord) == 0)
      {
        ++*(pnWord + i);
        new_word = false;
        break;
      }
    }
}
    if(new_word)                               // Check for new word
    {
      //Check for sufficient memory
      if(word_count == maxWords)
      { // Get more space for pointers to words}

        maxWords += WORDS_INCR;
        pWords = realloc(pWords, maxWords*sizeof(char*));

        // Get more space for word counts
        pnWord = realloc(pnWord, maxWords*sizeof(int));
      }

      // Found a new word so get memory for it and copy it there
      word_length = ptr - pWord;                       // Length of new word
      *(pWords + word_count) = malloc(word_length);    // Allocate memory for word
      strcpy_s(*(pWords + word_count), word_length, pWord); // Copy to array
      *(pnWord + word_count++) = 1;                    // Set new word count
    }
    else
      new_word = true;                         // Reset new word flag

    pWord = strtok_s(NULL, &str_len, delimiters, &ptr); // Find subsequent word
    // use this line instead, for Microsoft compiler:
    //pWord = strtok_s(NULL, delimiters, &ptr);       // Find subsequent word
  }

  // Output the words and counts
  for(int i = 0; i < word_count ; ++i)
  {
    printf("  %-13s  %3d", *(pWords + i), *(pnWord + i));
    if((i + 1) % 4 == 0)
      printf("\n");
  }
```

```
    printf("\n");
    // Free the memory for words
    for(int i = 0; i < word_count ; ++i)
    {
      free(*(pWords + i));                      // Free memory for word
      *(pWords + i) = NULL;                      // Reset the pointer
    }
  }
    free(pWords);                                // Free memory for pointers to words
    pWords = NULL;
    free(pnWord);                                // Free memory for word counts
    pnWord = NULL;
    free(pStr);                                  // Free memory for prose
    pStr = NULL;
    return 0;
}
```

Here's an example of output from this program:

```
Enter some prose with up to 100 characters per line.
Terminate input by entering an empty line:
Peter Piper picked a peck of pickled pepper.
A peck of pickled pepper Peter Piper picked.
If Peter Piper picked a peck of pickled pepper,
Where's the peck of pickled pepper Peter Piper picked?
```

Peter	4	Piper	4	picked	4	a	2
peck	4	of	4	pickled	4	pepper	4
A	1	If	1	Where's	1	the	1

How It Works

This version now handles prose input of unlimited length containing an unlimited number of words. Some initial memory is allocated to accommodate the input:

```
size_t str_size = INIT_STR_EXT;              // Current memory to store prose
char* pStr = malloc(str_size);                // Pointer to prose to be tokenized
*pStr = '\0';                                 // Set 1st character to null
```

The symbol INIT_STR_EXT specifies the initial extent of the memory to which pStr points. The current number of bytes available is recorded in the variable str_size, and this will be incremented when more memory is needed. As before, the first character pointed to by pStr is set to '\0', so you can concatenate input with the contents of this memory right from the start.

The input process is similar to what was used originally, the difference being that heap memory is extended to accommodate each new input line:

```
    if(strnlen_s(pStr, str_size) + strnlen_s(buf, BUF_LEN) + 1 > str_size)
    {
      str_size = strnlen_s(pStr, str_size) + strnlen_s(buf, BUF_LEN) + 1;
      pStr = realloc(pStr, str_size);
    }
```

If the memory pointed to by pStr is less than what is required to add the new line of input, the memory is extended by calling realloc(). The input is then appended to pStr using strcat_s():

```
if(strcat_s(pStr, str_size, buf))              // Concatenate the line with pStr
{
  printf("Something's wrong. String concatenation failed.\n");
  return 1;
}
```

Memory for maxWords pointers to words and memory for the count for each word are also allocated on the heap using calloc():

```
char** pWords = calloc(maxWords, sizeof(char*));   // Stores pointers to the words
int* pnWord = calloc(maxWords, sizeof(int));       // Stores count for each word
```

The term pWords points to memory that stores pointers of type char*, so pWords has to be of type char**, type pointer to pointer to char. The term pnWord points to memory that accommodates maxWords count values of type int. Of course, no memory has yet been allocated to store the words themselves.

As before, you define a variable, str_len, that contains the initial length of pStr and a pointer, ptr, both of which will be used by the strtok_s() function. When strtok_s() finds a word, it updates the value of str_len to reflect the number of bytes in pStr following the word. It also stores the address of the character following the word in ptr. Both of these are for use in a subsequent call of the function.

After calling strtok_s() to obtain the address of the first word, that word and all subsequent words are processed in the while loop, which continues as long as pWord is not NULL.

As each word is found, you check whether the word is a duplicate of a previously found word:

```
for(int i = 0 ; i < word_count ; ++i)
{
  if(strcmp(*(pWords + i), pWord) == 0)
  {
    ++*(pnWord + i);
    new_word = false;
    break;
  }
}
```

If the word that pWord points to already exists, the corresponding count is incremented, and new_word is set to false. The term pnWord + i is the address of the ith count, so you dereference the result of this expression before applying the increment operator. The if statement that follows tests new_word, and if it's false, it is reset to true.

When new_word is true, you check if there is sufficient memory for the pWords and pnWord arrays, and if there isn't, they are extended using realloc(). Next, heap memory is allocated to store the new word:

```
word_length = ptr - pWord;                        // Length of new word
*(pWords + word_count) = malloc(word_length);     // Allocate memory for word
strcpy_s(*(pWords + word_count), word_length, pWord);// Copy to array
*(pnWord + word_count++) = 1;                     // Set new word count
```

You record the number of characters occupied by the word that pWord points to in word_length. Remember ptr holds the address in pStr of the character that follows the terminating \o in the word, and pWord holds the address of the first character in the word. Subtracting the address in pWord from the address in ptr will give the length of the word. It's easy to see that this is the case through a simple example. Suppose the word is "and", which is length 4 including the null character; pWord will point to 'a' and pWord+3 will point to the null character. The next character is at pWord+4, which will be the address contained in ptr. Subtracting pWord from this results in 4, the length of the string including the null character.

You use word_length in the malloc() call to allocate heap memory for the word and store the address of the new memory in the next available position in the memory pointed to by pWords. You set the corresponding count to 1. Note that it is important to set the value here because the additional heap memory that is allocated by realloc() will contain junk values.

Finally, in the while loop, you call strtok_s() to find the next word:

```
pWord = strtok_s(NULL, &str_len, delimiters, &ptr);      // Find subsequent word
```

When a new word is found, its address is recorded in pWord, and it is processed on the next loop iteration. When there are no more words, pWord will be NULL so the while loop will end.

When the while loop ends, you list all the words and associated counts:

```
for(int i = 0; i < word_count ; ++i)
{
  printf(" %-13s  %3d", *(pWords + i), *(pnWord + i));
  if((i + 1) % 4 == 0)
    printf("\n");
}
printf("\n");
```

The for loop index runs from 0 to word_count-1. The first printf() call in the loop outputs a word left justified in a field width of 13 followed by the count for the word. After every fifth output, a newline is written by the second printf() call in the loop.
Finally, you release all the heap memory:

```
for(int i = 0; i < word_count ; ++i)
{
  free(*(pWords + i));                     // Free memory for word
  *(pWords + i) = NULL;                     // Reset the pointer
}

free(pWords);                              // Free memory for pointers to words
pWords = NULL;
free(pnWord);                              // Free memory for word counts
pnWord = NULL;
free(pStr);                                // Free memory for prose
pStr = NULL;
```

The memory allocated for words is freed in the for loop. Obviously, you must free the memory for words before you free the memory for the pointers to the words. It's easy to forget to free the memory for the words in this situation. Note that each pointer is set to NULL when the memory it points to is released. It's not essential here because the program ends immediately, but it's a good habit.

Note that it is not really necessary to copy the words in this example. You could avoid the need to copy the words by just storing the pointers that strtok_s() returns in pWords. I implemented it this way to give you the extra experience in heap memory allocation.

Pointers and Array Notation

The previous example used pointer notation throughout, but you don't have to do this. You can use array notation with a variable that is a pointer to a block of heap memory that provides for storing several items of data of the same type. For example, suppose you allocate some memory of the heap like this:

```
int count = 100;
double* data = calloc(count, sizeof(double));
```

This allocates sufficient memory to store 100 values of type double and initializes them to 0.0. The address of this memory is stored in data. You can access this memory as though data was an array of 100 elements of type double. For example, you can set different values in the memory with a loop:

```
for(int i = 0 ; i < count ; ++i)
  data[i] = (double)(i + 1)*(i + 1);
```

This sets the values to 1.0, 4.0, 9.0, and so on. You just use the pointer name with the index value between square brackets, just as you would with an array. It's important not to forget that data is a pointer and not an array. The expression sizeof(data) results in the number of bytes required to store an address, which is 8 on my system. If data were an array, the expression would result in the number of bytes occupied by the array, which would be 800.

You could rewrite the for loop in Program 7.13 that checks whether the latest word is a duplicate using array notation:

```
for(int i = 0 ; i < word_count ; ++i)
{
  if(strcmp(pWords[i], pWord) == 0)
  {
    ++pnWord[i];
    new_word = false;
    break;
  }
}
```

The expression pWords[i] accesses the ith element with pWords considered to be the starting address of an array of elements of type char*. Thus, this expression accesses the ith word and is exactly the same as the original expression *(pWords + i). Similarly, pnWord[i] is the equivalent of *(pnWord + i). Array notation is a lot easier to understand than pointer notation, so it's a good idea to use it when it applies. Let's try an example that uses array notation with heap memory.

```
┌─────────────────────────────────────────────────────────────────────┐
│              TRY IT OUT: SORTING STRINGS USING POINTERS               │
└─────────────────────────────────────────────────────────────────────┘
```

I can demonstrate the use of array notation with pointers through an example using a simple method for sorting data:

```c
// Program 7.14 Using array notation with pointers to sort strings
#define __STDC_WANT_LIB_EXT1__ 1
#include <stdio.h>
#include <stdlib.h>
#include <stdbool.h>
#include <string.h>

#define BUF_LEN 100                  // Length of input buffer
#define COUNT       5                // Initial number of strings

int main(void)
{
  char buf[BUF_LEN];                 // Input buffer
  size_t str_count = 0;              // Current string count
  size_t capacity = COUNT;           // Current maximum number of strings
  char **pS = calloc(capacity, sizeof(char*));    // Pointers to strings
  char** psTemp = NULL;              // Temporary pointer to pointer to char
  char* pTemp = NULL;                // Temporary pointer to char
  size_t str_len = 0;                // Length of a string
  bool sorted = false;               // Indicated when strings are sorted

  printf("Enter strings to be sorted, one per line. Press Enter to end:\n");

  // Read in all the strings
  char *ptr = NULL;
  while(true)
  {
    ptr = fgets(buf, BUF_LEN, stdin);
    if(!ptr)                         // Check for read error
    {
      printf("Error reading string.\n");
      free(pS);
      pS = NULL;
      return 1;
    }

    if(*ptr == '\n') break;          // Empty line check

    if(str_count == capacity)
    {
      capacity += capacity/4;        // Increase capacity by 25%

      if(!(psTemp = realloc(pS, capacity))) return 1;

      pS = psTemp;
    }
    str_len = strnlen_s(buf, BUF_LEN) + 1;
    if(!(pS[str_count] = malloc(str_len))) return 2;
    strcpy_s(pS[str_count++], str_len, buf);
  }
```

```
  // Sort the strings in ascending order
  while(!sorted)
  {
    sorted = true;
    for(size_t i = 0 ; i < str_count - 1 ; ++i)
    {
      if(strcmp(pS[i], pS[i + 1]) > 0)
      {
        sorted = false;              // We were out of order so...
        pTemp= pS[i];                // swap pointers pS[i]...
        pS[i] = pS[i + 1];           //        and...
        pS[i + 1]  = pTemp;          //      pS[i + 1]
      }
    }
  }

  // Output the sorted strings
  printf("Your input sorted in ascending sequence is:\n\n");
  for(size_t i = 0 ; i < str_count ; ++i)
  {
    printf("%s", pS[i]);
    free(pS[i]);                     // Release memory for the word
    pS[i] = NULL;                    // Reset the pointer
  }
  free(pS);                          // Release the memory for pointers
  pS = NULL;                         // Reset the pointer
  return 0;
}
```

Typical output from this program is

```
Enter strings to be sorted, one per line. Press Enter to end:
Many a mickle makes a muckle.
A fool and your money are soon partners.
Every dog has his day.
Do unto others before they do it to you.
A nod is as good as a wink to a blind horse.
The bigger they are, the harder they hit.
Least said, soonest mended.

Your input sorted in ascending sequence is:

A fool and your money are soon partners.
A nod is as good as a wink to a blind horse.
Do unto others before they do it to you.
Every dog has his day.
Least said, soonest mended.
Many a mickle makes a muckle.
The bigger they are, the harder they hit.
```

How It Works

This example will really sort the wheat from the chaff. You use the input function `fgets()` for the input process, which reads a complete string up to the point when you press Enter and then adds \0 to the end, following the \n character. The function `fgets()` ensures that the capacity of buf will not be exceeded. The first argument is a pointer to the memory area where the string is to be stored, the second is the maximum number of characters that can be stored, and the third is the input source, the standard input stream in this case. Its return value is either the address where the input string is stored—buf, in this case—or NULL if an error occurs. When an empty line is entered, buf will contain '\n' as the first character, and this will terminate the loop.

Before you can deal with a string read into buf, you must check whether space is available in pS to store the pointer to the string:

```
if(str_count == capacity)
{
  capacity += capacity/4;          // Increase capacity by 25%
  if(!(psTemp = realloc(pS, capacity))) return 1;
  pS = psTemp;
}
```

When `str_count` is equal to `capacity`, all the space for pointers is occupied, so you increase the value of capacity by 25 percent and use `realloc()` to extend the memory that is pointed to by pS. There's a check for a NULL return from `realloc()`, which would indicate the memory could not be allocated for some reason.

With sufficient space in pS for the string pointer ensured, you allocate the exact amount of memory required for the string:

```
str_len = strnlen_s(buf, BUF_LEN) + 1;
if(!(pS[str_count] = malloc(str_len))) return 2;
```

The pointer equivalent of `pS[str_count]` is `*(pS + str_count)`, but this is less clear than the array notation.

With the memory allocated, you copy the string from buf to the new memory that is pointed to by `pS[str_count]`:

```
strcpy_s(pS[str_count++], str_len, buf);
```

`str_count` is incremented after the value is used to index pS, ready for the next iteration.

Once all the strings are safely stowed away, you sort them using the simplest and probably the most inefficient sort going, but it's easy to follow:

```
while(!sorted)
{
  sorted = true;
  for(size_t i = 0 ; i < str_count - 1 ; ++i)
  {
    if(strcmp(pS[i], pS[i + 1]) > 0)
```

```
    {
      sorted = false;           // We were out of order so...
      pTemp= pS[i];             // swap pointers pS[i]...
      pS[i] = pS[i + 1];        //       and...
      pS[i + 1]  = pTemp;       //       pS[i + 1]
    }
  }
}
```

Sorting the strings takes place inside the while loop, which continues as long as sorted is false. The sort proceeds by comparing successive pairs of strings using the strcmp() function inside the for loop. If the first string is greater than the second string, you swap pointer values. Using pointers is a very economical way of changing the order of the strings. The strings themselves remain undisturbed exactly where they were in memory. It's just the sequence of their addresses that changes in the pointer array, pS. The time needed to swap pointers is a fraction of that required to move all the strings around.

The swapping continues through all the string pointers. If it's necessary to interchange any pair of strings, sorted is set to false to repeat the whole thing. If the whole thing is repeated without interchanging any strings, then they're in order, and the sort is finished. You track the status of this with the bool variable sorted. This is set to true at the beginning of each cycle, but if any interchange occurs, it gets set back to false. If you exit a cycle with sorted still true, it means that no interchanges occurred, so everything must be in order; therefore, you exit from the while loop.

The reason this sort is not so good is that each pass through all the items only moves a value by one position in the list. In the worst case, when you have the first entry in the last position, the number of times you have to repeat the process is one less than the number of entries in the list. This inefficient but nevertheless famous method of sorting is known as a *bubble sort*.

Handling strings and other kinds of data using pointers in this way is an extremely powerful mechanism in C. You can throw the basic data (the strings, in this case) into a bucket of memory in any order, and then you can process them in any sequence you like without moving the data at all. You just change the pointers. You could use ideas from this example as a base for programs for sorting any text. You had better find a better sort of sort, though.

■ **Note** The stdlib.h header provides the qsort() function that can sort an array of any kind of data. You need to know a bit more about functions in order to use this to sort strings. You'll learn all about functions in the next two chapters.

Designing a Program

Congratulations! You made it through a really tough part of the C language, and now I can show you an application using some of what you've learned—pointer notation in particular. I'll follow the usual process, taking you through the analysis and design and writing the code step by step. Let's look at the final program for this chapter.

The Problem

The problem is to rewrite the calculator program from Chapter 3 with some new features, but this time using pointers. The main improvements are as follows:

- Allow the use of signed decimal numbers, including a decimal point with an optional leading sign, – or +, as well as signed integers.

- Permit expressions to combine multiple operations such as 2.5 + 3.7 – 6/6.

- Add the ^ operator, which will be exponentiation, so 2 ^ 3 is 2 cubed, which will produce 8.

- Allow a line to operate on the previous result. If the previous result is 2.5, then writing =*2 + 7 will produce the result 12. Any input line that starts with an assignment operator will automatically assume the left operand for the next arithmetic operation is the previous result.

You're also going to cheat a little by not taking into consideration the precedence of the operators. You'll simply evaluate an expression from left to right, applying each operator to the previous result and the right operand. This means that the expression

```
1 + 2*3 - 4*-5
```

will be evaluated as

```
((1 + 2)*3 - 4)*(-5)
```

The Analysis

You don't know in advance how long an expression is going to be or how many operands are going to be involved. You'll read in a complete string and then analyze this to see what the operand values and operators are. You'll evaluate each intermediate result as soon as you have an operator with a left and a right operand.

There are eight basic operations to be performed by the program:

1. Read an input string entered by the user and exit if it is quit.

2. Remove spaces from the input string.

3. Check for an = at the start of the input, and when it is found, make the left operand of the next arithmetic operation the result of the previous input string.

4. Extract the input characters corresponding to the left operand for the next arithmetic operation and convert the substring to type double.

5. Extract the arithmetic operator and remember it.

6. Extract the input characters corresponding to the right operand and convert the substring to a value of type double.

7. Execute the operation and store the result as the next left operand.

8. If it's not the end of the string, go back to step 6, and if it is the end of the string, go back to step 1.

The Solution

This section outlines the steps you'll take to solve the problem. The steps correspond to the operations outlined in the previous section. Before I start describing how the steps can be implemented, I'll set out the basics required for the program.

Several standard header files will be needed for this program:

```
// Program 7.15 An improved calculator
#define __STDC_WANT_LIB_EXT1__ 1
#include <stdio.h>              // Standard input/output
#include <string.h>             // For string functions
#include <ctype.h>              // For classifying characters
#include <stdlib.h>             // For converting strings to numeric values
#include <stdbool.h>            // For bool values
#include <math.h>               // For power() function
#define BUF_LEN 256             // Length of input buffer
```

You'll be using the optional string functions, so you define the symbol that makes them available. Of course this also makes the optional functions in stdio.h available. You define BUF_LEN as 256. Defining the length of the input buffer by the BUF_LEN symbol makes it easy to change, because changing the symbol definition changes all references to it throughout the code.

You will need several variables for working storage that you can define at the beginning of main():

```
int main(void)
{
  char buf[BUF_LEN];        // Input expression
  char op = 0;              // Stores an operator
  size_t index = 0;         // Index of the current character in buf
  size_t to = 0;            // To index for copying buf to itself
  size_t buf_length = 0;    // Length of the string in buf
  double result = 0.0;      // The result of an operation
  double number = 0.0;      // Stores the value of number_string
  char* endptr = NULL;      // Stores address of character following a number
  // Rest of the code for the calculator...

  return 0;
}
```

The comments should make the use of these clear enough. The next thing required in main() is a comprehensive prompt for the user to explain how the calculator works:

```
  printf("To use this calculator, enter any expression with"
                          " or without spaces.");
  printf("\nAn expression may include the operators");
  printf(" +, -, *, /, %%, or ^(raise to a power).");
  printf("\nUse = at the beginning of a line to operate on ");
  printf("\nthe result of the previous calculation.") ;
  printf("\nEnter quit to stop the calculator.\n\n");
```

Step 1

This step reads the input string. You'll read the input expression using the fgets() function that is declared in the stdio.h header file. This will read an entire line of input, including spaces and the newline character. You can combine the input and the overall program loop together like this:

```
int main(void)
{
  // Variable declarations...
  // Input prompt...

  char *ptr = NULL;
  while(true)
  {
    ptr = fgets(buf, BUF_LEN, stdin);
    if(!ptr)                             // Check for read error
    {
      printf("Error reading input.\n");
      return 1;
    }

    if(strcmp(buf, "quit\n") == 0) break;    // Quit check

    buf_length = strnlen_s(buf, BUF_LEN);    // Get the input string length
    buf[--buf_length] = '\0';                // Remove newline at the end

    /* Code to implement the calculator */
  }
  return 0;
}
```

You store the address returned by fgets() for checking purposes. After verifying that NULL was not returned, which indicates an error, you call strcmp() in the if statement to see whether quit was entered. The function will return 0 if the argument strings are equal, and executing break will end the loop.

The function fgets() stores the newline character that is generated when you press the Enter key. This is not needed in the string, so you remove it by overwriting it with the null character. You decrement buf_length so it will now be the string length including the null character.

Step 2

This step removes spaces from the input. You could start analyzing the input right away, but it would be better if you removed all spaces from the string. Because the input string is well defined, you don't need spaces to separate the operators from their operands. You can add the next block of code inside the while loop to remove any spaces:

```
for(to = 0, index = 0 ; index <= buf_length ; ++index)
{
  if(*(buf + index) != ' ')              // If it is not a space...
    *(buf + to++) = *(buf + index);      // ...copy the character
}

buf_length = strnlen_s(buf, BUF_LEN);    // Get the new string length
```

You remove spaces by copying the string stored in buf to itself. You need to keep track of two indexes in the copy loop: the to index records the position in buf where the next nonspace character is to be copied to, and index records the position of the next character that is a candidate to be copied. In the loop, you don't copy spaces. When you find a space, you just increment index to move to the next character. The to index gets incremented only when a character is copied. After the loop ends, you store the new string length in buf_length.

You could equally well write the loop using array notation:

```
for(to = 0, index = 0 ; index <= buf_length ; ++index)
{
  if(buf[index] != ' ')                    // If it's not a space...
    buf[to++] = buf[index];                // ...copy the character
}
```

For my taste, the code is much clearer using array notation, but I'll continue with pointer notation because you need the practice.

Step 3

This step looks for '=' as the first character. The input expression has two possible forms. It can start with an assignment operator, indicating that the last result is to be taken as the left operand, or it can start with a number with or without a sign that is the left operand. You can differentiate these two situations by looking for the '=' character first. If you find one, the left operand is the previous result.

The code you need to add next in the while loop will look for an '=':

```
index = 0;                               // Start at the first character
if(buf[index]== '=')                     // If there's = ...
  index++;                               // ...skip over it
else
{ // No =, so look for left operand
  // Code to extract the left operand for the 1st operator...
}
// Code to find the operator for the left operand...
```

The if statement checks for '=' as the first character in the input, and if it's found, index is incremented to skip over it. The program will then go straight to looking for the operator. If '=' isn't found, you execute the else block, which will contain code to look for a numeric left operand.

Step 4

This step finds the left operand when the first input character is not '='. You want to convert all the characters that make up the number to a value of type double that you will store in result. The strtod() function declared in stdlib.h can help. The function requires two arguments. The first is the address of where the number string starts. The second is the address of a pointer in which the function will store the address of the first character that did not form part of the number. It returns the converted value of the string as type double. If no conversion was possible, strtod() returns 0. Here's how we can get the value of the first operand and store it in result:

```
result = strtod(buf + index, &endptr);      // Store the number
index = endptr - buf;                        // Get index for next character
```

After executing strtod(), endptr contains the address of the character in buf that follows the characters specifying the operand. You increment index by the difference between buf and ptr, which corresponds to the number of characters for the first operand.

Step 5

This step defines a loop that starts by discovering what the operator is. At this point, what follows in the input string must be an operator followed by a number that is the right operand for the operation. Of course, the number you found previously or the previous result is the left operand, and either will have been stored in result. This op-number combination may also be followed by another, so you may have a succession of op-number combinations through to the end of the string. You can look for these combinations in a while loop, which will work like this:

```
// Now look for 'op number' combinations
while(index < buf_length)
{
  op = *(buf + index++);                          // Get the operator
  // Extract the right operand...
  // Execute the operation, storing the result in result...
}
```

The first statement in this while loop extracts the operator from the input and stores it in op for use when the right operand value has been obtained.

Step 6

This step adds the code to the while loop from the previous step to extract and store the right operand:

```
number = strtod(buf + index, &endptr);      // Convert & store the number
index = endptr - buf;                        // Get index for next character
```

This uses strtod() again in the same way as for the left operand, but instead stores the value that is returned in number.

Step 7

This step executes the operation with the left operand in result and right operand in number. This code follows the code of the previous step inside the while loop from step 5:

```
switch(op)
{
  case '+':                        // Addition
    result += number;
    break;
  case '-':                        // Subtraction
    result -= number;
    break;
```

```
      case '*':                            // Multiplication
        result *= number;
        break;
      case '/':                            // Division
        // Check second operand for zero
        if(number == 0) printf("\n\n\aDivision by zero error!\n");
        else
          result /= number;
        break;
      case '%':                            // Modulus operator - remainder
        // Check second operand for zero
        if((long long)number == 0LL) printf("\n\n\aDivision by zero error!\n");
        else
          result = (double)((long long)result % (long long)number);
        break;
      case '^':                            // Raise to a power
        result = pow(result, number);
        break;
      default:                             // Invalid operation or bad input
        printf("\n\n\aIllegal operation!\n");
        break;
    }
```

The switch statement selects the operation to be performed based on the value stored in op. There are checks for a zero right operand when the operation is division or the modulus operator. The % operator only applies to integer operands, so both operands must be converted to integers. It is necessary to convert the right operand to an integer before checking for zero because it could be less than one. The result of an expression on the right of an assignment will always be converted to the type of the left operand, but including an explicit cast in such cases shows that you wanted this to happen.

You have added the final block of code to the loop that started in step 5. This loop continues by executing another iteration that starts with the code to retrieve the next operator/operand combination until the end of the string is reached. On reaching the end of the string, the while loop from step 5 ends.

Step 8

When the end of the string is reached, you output result with a statement that follows the closing brace for the while loop that started in step 5:

```
printf("= %f\n", result);                 // Output the result
```

After executing this statement, control returns to step 1 to start a new iteration of the outer while loop that reads a line of input. When "quit" is entered, the outer while loop from step 1 ends, and the following statement will end the program:

```
return 0;
```

This is the last statement in main().

The Complete Program

The complete program code is as follows:

```c
// Program 7.15 An improved calculator
#define __STDC_WANT_LIB_EXT1__ 1
#include <stdio.h>                    // Standard input/output
#include <string.h>                   // For string functions
#include <ctype.h>                    // For classifying characters
#include <stdlib.h>                   // For converting strings to numeric values
#include <stdbool.h>                  // For bool values
#include <math.h>                     // For power() function
#define BUF_LEN 256                   // Length of input buffer

int main(void)
{
  char buf[BUF_LEN];                  // Input expression
  char op = 0;                        // Stores an operator
  size_t index = 0;                   // Index of the current character in buf
  size_t to = 0;                      // To index for copying buf to itself
  size_t buf_length = 0;              // Length of the string in buf
  double result = 0.0;                // The result of an operation
  double number = 0.0;                // Stores the value of right operand
  char* endptr = NULL;                // Stores address of character following a number

  printf("To use this calculator, enter any expression with"
                            " or without spaces.");
  printf("\nAn expression may include the operators");
  printf(" +, -, *, /, %%, or ^(raise to a power).");
  printf("\nUse = at the beginning of a line to operate on ");
  printf("\nthe result of the previous calculation.");
  printf("\nEnter quit to stop the calculator.\n\n");

  // The main calculator loop
  char *ptr = NULL;
  while(true)
  {
    ptr = fgets(buf, BUF_LEN, stdin);
    if(!ptr)                                      // Check for read error
    {
      printf("Error reading input.\n");
      return 1;
    }

    if(strcmp(buf, "quit\n") == 0) break;         // Quit check

    buf_length = strnlen_s(buf, BUF_LEN);         // Get the input string length
    buf[--buf_length] = '\0';                     // Remove newline at the end
```

```
  // Remove spaces from the input by copying the string to itself
  for(to = 0, index = 0 ; index <= buf_length ; ++index)
  {
    if(*(buf + index) != ' ')                      // If it's not a space...
      *(buf + to++) = *(buf + index);              // ...copy the character
  }

  buf_length = strnlen_s(buf, BUF_LEN);            // Get the new string length

  index = 0;                                       // Start at the first character
if(buf[index]== '=')                               // If there's = ...
  index++;                                         // ...skip over it
else
{ // No =, so look for left operand
    result = strtod(buf + index, &endptr);         // Convert & store the number
    index = endptr - buf;                          // Get index for next character
}

  // Now look for 'op number' combinations
  while(index < buf_length)
  {
    op = *(buf + index++);                          // Get the operator
    number = strtod(buf + index, &endptr);         // Convert & store the number
    index = endptr - buf;                          // Get index for next character

    // Execute operation, as 'result op= number'
    switch(op)
    {
      case '+':                                     // Addition
        result += number;
        break;
      case '-':                                     // Subtraction
        result -= number;
        break;
      case '*':                                     // Multiplication
        result *= number;
        break;
      case '/':                                     // Division
        // Check second operand for zero
        if(number == 0) printf("\n\n\aDivision by zero error!\n");
        else
          result /= number;
        break;
      case '%':                                     // Modulus operator - remainder
        // Check second operand for zero
        if((long long)number == 0LL) printf("\n\n\aDivision by zero error!\n");
        else
          result = (double)((long long)result % (long long)number);
        break;
      case '^':                                     // Raise to a power
        result = pow(result, number);
        break;
```

```
            default:                                    // Invalid operation or bad input
                printf("\n\n\aIllegal operation!\n");
                break;
        }
    }
    printf("= %f\n", result);                           // Output the result
    }
    return 0;
}
```

Typical output from the calculator program is as follows:

```
To use this calculator, enter any expression with or without spaces.
An expression may include the operators +, -, *, /, %, or ^(raise to a power).
Use = at the beginning of a line to operate on
the result of the previous calculation.
Enter quit to stop the calculator.

2.5 + 3.3/2
= 2.900000
= *3
= 8.700000
= ^ 4
= 5728.976100
1.3 + 2.4 - 3.5 + -7.8
= -7.600000
= *-2
= 15.200000
quit
```

And there you have it!

Summary

This chapter covered a lot of ground. You explored pointers in detail. You should now understand the relationship between pointers and arrays (both one-dimensional and multidimensional arrays) and have a good grasp of their uses. I introduced the malloc(), calloc(), and realloc() functions for dynamically allocating memory, which provide the potential for your programs to use just enough memory for the data being processed in each run. You also learned about the complementary function free() that you use to release memory previously allocated by malloc(), calloc(), or realloc(). You should have a clear idea of how you can use pointers with strings and how you can use arrays of pointers, and you should be very comfortable with using pointer notation by now.

The topics I've discussed in this chapter are fundamental to a lot of what follows in the rest of the book, and of course to writing C programs effectively, so make sure you're comfortable with the material in this chapter before moving on to the next.

You may have noticed that the code in many of the examples in this chapter is quite unwieldy. The number of statements in main() is becoming so large it's quite difficult to work with the code. This is especially true of Program 7.15, where main() is more than 100 lines of code. This is not good C programming. C programs are ideally composed of many short functions that perform well-defined operations. You may have noticed that the logic of Program 7.15 fell naturally into several different well-defined operations that were relatively independent of one another. There was also code duplication—the code for retrieving a left operand was virtually identical to the code for obtaining a right operand, for example. The next chapter is all about structuring your programs using functions. When you've learned more about functions, you'll be able to do a much better job of implementing Program 7.15.

EXERCISES

The following exercises enable you to try out what you've learned in this chapter. If you get stuck, look back over the chapter for help. If you're still stuck, you can download the solutions from the Source Code area of the Apress website (www.apress.com), but that really should be a last resort.

Exercise 7-1. Write a program to calculate the average for an arbitrary number of floating-point values that are entered from the keyboard. Store all values in memory that's allocated dynamically before calculating and displaying the average. The user shouldn't be required to specify in advance how many values there will be.

Exercise 7-2. Write a program that will read an arbitrary number of proverbs from the keyboard and store them in memory that's allocated at runtime. The program should then output the proverbs ordered by their length, starting with the shortest and ending with the longest.

Exercise 7-3. Write a program that will read a string from the keyboard and display it after removing all spaces and punctuation characters. All operations should use pointers.

Exercise 7-4. Write a program that will read a series of temperature recordings as floating-point values for an arbitrary number of days, in which six recordings are made per day. The temperature readings should be stored in memory that's allocated dynamically and that's the exact amount of memory required to store for the number of temperature values that are entered. Calculate the average temperature per day for all days entered. Output the recordings for each day together with the average on a single line with one decimal place after the point.

■ ■ ■

CHAPTER 8

Structuring Your Programs

I mentioned in Chapter 1 that breaking up a program into reasonably self-contained units is basic to the development of any program of a practical nature. When confronted with a big task, the most sensible thing to do is break it up into manageable chunks. You can then deal with each small chunk fairly easily, and you can be reasonably sure that you've done it properly. If you design the chunks of code carefully, you may be able to reuse some of them in other programs.

One of the key ideas in the C language is that every program should be segmented into functions that are relatively short. Even with the examples that you have seen so far that were written as a single main() function, other functions are inevitably involved because you have used a variety of standard library functions for input and output, for mathematical operations, and for handling strings.

In this chapter, you'll look at how you can make your programs more effective and easier to develop by implementing them in terms of several short functions, each with a well-defined purpose.

In this chapter, you'll learn

- How data are passed to a function

- How to return results from a function

- How to define your own functions

- What function prototypes are and when you need to use them

- The advantages of pointers as arguments to functions

Program Structure

As I said at the outset, a C program consists of one or more functions, the most important of which is the function main() where execution starts. When you use library functions such as printf() or scanf_s(), you see how one function is able to call up another function in order to carry out some particular task and then continues execution back in the calling function when the task is complete. Except for side effects on data stored at global scope (I'll discuss global variables in the next chapter) or data that can be accessed through a pointer that is passed as an argument, each function in a program is a self-contained unit that carries out a particular operation. When a function is called, the code within the body of that function is executed, and when the function has finished executing, control returns to the point at which that function was called. This is illustrated in Figure 8-1, where you can see an idealized representation of a C program structured as five functions. It doesn't show any details of the statements involved—just the sequence of execution.

© German Gonzalez-Morris and Ivor Horton 2020

G. Gonzalez-Morris and I. Horton, *Beginning C*, https://doi.org/10.1007/978-1-4842-5976-4_8

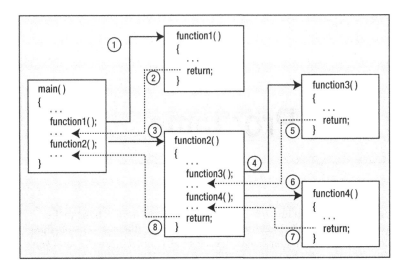

Figure 8-1. *Execution of a program made up of several functions*

The program steps through the statements in sequence in the normal way until it comes across a call to a particular function. At that point, any argument values are transferred to the function, and execution moves to the start of that function—that is, the first statement in the body of the function. Execution of the program continues through the function statements until it hits a return statement or reaches the closing brace marking the end of the function body. This signals that execution should go back to the point immediately after the point the function was originally called.

The set of functions that make up a program link together through the function calls and their return statements to perform the various tasks necessary for the program to achieve its purpose. Figure 8-1 shows each function in the program executed just once. In practice, each function can be executed many times and can be called from several points within a program. You've already seen this in the examples that called the printf() and scanf_s() functions several times.

Before you look in more detail at how to define your own functions, I need to explain a particular aspect of the way variables behave that I've glossed over so far.

Variable Scope and Lifetime

In all the examples up to this point, you've declared the variables for the program at the beginning of the block that define the body of the function main(). But you can actually define variables anywhere in the body of a function. Does this make a difference? "It most certainly does, Stanley," as Ollie would have said. Variables exist only within the block in which they're defined. They're created when they are declared, and they cease to exist at the next closing brace.

This is also true of variables that you declare within blocks that are inside other blocks. The variables declared at the beginning of an outer block also exist in the inner block. These variables are freely accessible, as long as there are no other variables with the same name in the inner block, as you'll see.

Variables that are created when they're declared and destroyed at the end of a block are called *automatic variables*, because they're automatically created and destroyed. The extent within the program code where a given variable is visible and can be referenced is called the *variable's scope*. When you use a variable within its scope, everything is okay. But if you try to reference a variable outside its scope, you'll get an error message when you compile the program because the variable doesn't exist outside its scope. The general idea is illustrated in the following code fragment:

```
{
  int a = 0;                                      // Create a
  // Reference to a is OK here
  // Reference to b is an error here - it hasn't been created yet
  {
    int b = 10;                                   // Create b
    // Reference to a and b is OK here
  }                                               // b dies here
  // Reference to b is an error here - it has been destroyed
  // Reference to a is OK here
}                                                 // a dies here
```

All the variables that are declared within a block are destroyed and no longer exist after the closing brace of the block. The variable a is visible within both the inner and outer blocks because it's declared in the outer block. The variable b is visible only within the inner block because it's declared within that block.

During program execution, a variable is created, and memory is allocated for it when the statement that defines it is executed. For automatic variables, the memory that the variable occupies is returned back to the system at the end of the block in which the variable is declared. Of course, while functions called within the block are executing, the variable continues to exist; it is only destroyed when execution reaches the end of the block in which it was created. The time period during which a variable is in existence is referred to as the *lifetime* of the variable.

Let's explore the implications of a variable's scope through an example.

TRY IT OUT: UNDERSTANDING SCOPE

This example involves a nested block that happens to be the body of a loop:

```
// Program 8.1 Scoping out scope
#include <stdio.h>

int main(void)
{
  int count1 = 1;                                 // Declared in outer block

  do
  {
    int count2 = 0;                               // Declared in inner block
    ++count2;
    printf("count1 = %d    count2 = %d\n", count1, count2);
  } while( ++count1 <= 5);

  // count2 no longer exists

  printf("count1 = %d\n", count1);
  return 0;
}
```

You will get the following output from this program:

```
count1 = 1     count2 = 1
count1 = 2     count2 = 1
count1 = 3     count2 = 1
```

```
count1 = 4      count2 = 1
count1 = 5      count2 = 1
count1 = 6
```

<u>How It Works</u>

The block that encloses the body of main() contains an inner block that is the do-while loop. You declare and define count2 inside the loop block:

```
do
{
  int count2 = 0;                          // Declared in inner block
  ++count2;
  printf("count1 = %d     count2 = %d\n", count1, count2);
} while( ++count1 <= 5);
```

So count2 is recreated on every loop iteration with the initial value 0, and its value is never more than 1. During each loop iteration, count2 is created, initialized, incremented, and destroyed. It only exists from the statement that declares it down to the closing brace for the loop. The variable count1, on the other hand, exists at the main() block level. It continues to exist while it is incremented, so the last printf() produces the value 6.

If you modify the program to make the last printf() output the value of count2, it won't compile. The error is caused because count2 no longer exists at the point where the last printf() is executed.

TRY IT OUT: MORE ABOUT SCOPE

Let's try a slight modification of the previous example:

```
// Program 8.2 More scope in this example
#include <stdio.h>

int main(void)
{
  int count = 0;                         // Declared in outer block
  do
  {
    int count = 0;                       // This is another variable called count
    ++count;                             // this applies to inner count
    printf("count = %d\n", count);
  }
  while( ++count <= 5);                  // This works with outer count

  printf("count = %d\n", count);    // Inner count is dead, this is outer count
  return 0;
}
```

It's not a good idea to do so, but you have used the same variable name, count, at the main() block level and in the loop block. Observe what happens when you compile and run this:

```
count = 1
count = 1
count = 1
count = 1
count = 1
count = 1
count = 6
```

How It Works

The output is boring, but interesting at the same time. You have two variables called count, but inside the loop block the local variable will "hide" the version of count that exists at the main() block level. The compiler will assume that when you use the name count, you mean the one that was declared in the current block. Inside the do-while loop, only the local version of count can be reached, so that is the variable being incremented. The printf() inside the loop block displays the local count value, which is always 1, for the reasons given previously. As soon as you exit the loop, the outer count variable becomes visible, and the last printf() displays its final value from the loop as 6.

Clearly, the variable that is controlling the loop is the one declared at the beginning of main(). This little example demonstrates why it isn't a good idea to use the same variable name for two different variables in a function, even though it's legal. At best, it's most confusing. At worst, you'll be thinking "that's another fine mess I've gotten myself into."

Variable Scope and Functions

The last point to note, before I get into the detail of creating functions, is that the body of every function is a block (which may contain other blocks, of course). As a result, the automatic variables you declare within a function are local to the function and don't exist elsewhere. Therefore, the variables declared within one function are quite independent of those declared in another function or in a nested block. There's nothing to prevent you from using the same name for variables in different functions; they will remain quite separate. Indeed, this is an advantage. It would be very hard to keep coming up with distinct names for all of the variables in a large program. It's handy to be able to use the same name such as count in different functions. It's still a good idea to avoid any unnecessary or misleading overlapping of variable names in your various functions, and, of course, you should try to use names that are meaningful to make your programs easy to follow.

Functions

You've already used built-in functions such as printf() and strcpy_s() quite extensively in your programs. You've seen how these built-in functions are executed when you reference them by name and how you are able to transfer information to a function by means of arguments between parentheses following the function name. With the printf() function, for instance, the first argument is usually a string literal, and the succeeding arguments (of which there may be none) are a series of variables or expressions whose values are to be displayed.

You've also seen how you can receive information back from a function in two ways. The first way is through one of the function arguments. When you provide an address of a variable through an argument to a function, the function can modify the value of that variable. When you use scanf_s() to read data from the keyboard, for instance, the input is stored in an address that you supply as an argument. The second way you can receive information back from a function is as a return value. With the `strnlen_s()` function, for instance, the length of the string that you supply as the first argument appears in the program code in the position where the function call is made. Thus, if `str` is an array containing the string `"example"`, in the expression `2*strnlen_s(str, sizeof(str))`, the function returns the value 7 and this replaces the function call in the expression. The expression will amount to `2*7`. Where a function returns a value of a given type, the function call can appear as part of any expression where a variable of the same type could be used. Of necessity, you've written the function `main()` in all your programs, so you already have the basic knowledge of how a function is constructed. So let's look at what makes up a function in more detail.

Defining a Function

When you create a function, you specify the function header as the first line of the function definition, followed by the executable code for the function enclosed between braces. The block of code between braces following the function header is called the *function body*:

- The *function header* defines the name of the function, the function parameters (which specify the number and types of values that are passed to the function when it's called), and the type for the value that the function returns.

- The *function body* contains the statements that are executed when the function is called, and these have access to any values that are passed as arguments to the function.

The general form of a function looks like this:

```
Return_type  Function_name( Parameters - separated by commas )
{
   // Statements...
}
```

The statements in the function body can be absent, but the braces must be present. If there are no statements in the body of a function, the return type must be `void`, and the function will have no effect. You'll recall that I said that the type `void` means "absence of any type," and here it means that the function doesn't return a value. A function that has statements in the function body but does not return a value must also have the return type specified as `void`. Conversely, for a function that does not have a `void` return type, every return statement in the function body must return a value of the specified return type.

Defining a function with an almost content-free body is often useful during the testing phase of a complicated program, for example, a function defined so that it just contains a return statement, perhaps returning a default value. This allows you to run the program with only selected functions actually doing something; you can then add the detail for the function bodies step by step, testing at each stage, until the whole thing is implemented and fully tested.

The term *parameter* refers to a placeholder in a function definition that specifies the type of value that should be passed to the function when it is called. The value passed to a function corresponding to a parameter is referred to as an *argument*. A function parameter consists of the type followed by the parameter name that is used within the body of the function to refer to the corresponding argument value that is transferred when the function is called. I'll explain parameters in more detail in the "Function Parameters" section later in this chapter.

▧ **Note** The statements in the body of a function can contain nested blocks of statements. However, you can't define a function inside the body of another function.

The general form for calling a function is the following expression:

```
Function_name(List of Arguments - separated by commas)
```

You simply use the function's name followed by a list of arguments separated by commas in parentheses, just as you've been doing with functions such as `printf()` and `scanf_s()`. A function call can appear as a statement on a line by itself, like this:

```
printf("I used to be indecisive but now I'm not so sure.");
```

A function that's called like this can be a function that returns a value. In this case, the value that's returned is simply discarded. A function that has been defined with a return type of `void` can *only* be called like this. A function that returns a value can, and usually does, participate in an expression, for example:

```
result = 2.0*sqrt(2.0);
```

Here, the value that's returned by the `sqrt()` function (declared in the `math.h` header file) is multiplied by 2.0, and the result is stored in the variable `result`. Obviously, because a function with a `void` return type doesn't return anything, it cannot be part of an expression.

Naming a Function

The name of a function can be any legal name in C that isn't a reserved word (such as `int`, `double`, `sizeof`, etc.) and isn't the same as the name of another function in your program. You should ensure that you do not use the same names as any of the standard library functions because this not only would prevent you from using the library function but would also be very confusing. Of course, if you do use a library function name and include the header file for the function into your source file, your program will not compile.

One way of differentiating your function names from those in the standard library is to start them with a capital letter, although some programmers find this rather restricting. Names starting with a capital letter are also often reserved for use as `struct` type names, which you'll learn about in Chapter 11. A legal name has the same form as that of a variable: a sequence of letters and digits, the first of which must be a letter. As with variable names, the underline character counts as a letter. Other than that, the name of a function can be anything you like, but ideally the name that you choose should give some clue as to what the function does and should not be too long. Examples of valid function names that you might create are as follows:

```
cube_root    FindLast findNext    Explosion    Back2Front
```

You'll often want to define function names (and variable names too) that consist of more than one word. There are three common approaches you can adopt that happen to be illustrated in the first three examples:

- Separate each of the words in a function name with an underline character
- Capitalize the first letter of each word
- Capitalize words after the first

All three approaches work well, but the third form of name is more often used for variables. Which one you choose is up to you, but it's a good idea to pick an approach and stick to it. You can, of course, use one approach for functions and another for variables. Within this book, I have sprinkled these approaches around to give you a feel for how they look. By the time you reach the end of the book, you'll probably have formed your own opinion as to which approach is best for you.

Function Parameters

Function parameters are defined within the function header and are placeholders for the arguments that need to be specified when the function is called. The parameters for a function are a list of parameter names with their types, and successive parameters are separated by commas. The entire list of parameters is enclosed between the parentheses that follow the function name. A function can have no parameters, in which case you should put void between the parentheses.

Parameters provide the means by which you specify the information that is passed from the calling function to the function that is called. The names of the parameters are local to the function, and they will assume the values of the arguments that are passed when the function is called. The computation in the body of the function is written using these parameter names and is executed with their current values when the function is called. Of course, a function body may have locally defined automatic variables that are destroyed when execution of the function ends. When the execution of a function ends, the function returns an appropriate value back to the original calling statement if the return type is not void, and execution continues at that point.

When you want to pass an array as an argument to a function, you must also pass an additional argument specifying the size of the array. Without this, the function has no means of knowing how many elements there are in the array.

Some examples of function headers are shown in Table 8-1.

Table 8-1. *Examples of Function Headers*

Function header	Description
bool SendMessage(char *text)	This function has one parameter, text, which is of type "pointer to char," and it returns a value of type bool
void PrintData(double *data, int count)	This function has two parameters, one of type "pointer to double" and the other of type int. The function does not return a value
int SumIt(int x[], size_t n)	The first parameter to this function is an array of type int[], and the second parameter specifies the number of elements in an array as a value of type size_t. The function returns a value of type int
char* GetMessage(void)	This function has no parameters and returns a pointer of type char*

As you know, you call a function by using the function name followed by the arguments to the function between parentheses. When you call the function, the values of the arguments that you specify in the call will be assigned to the parameters in the function. When the function executes, the computation proceeds using the values you supplied as arguments. The arguments you specify when you call a function should agree in type, number, and sequence with the parameters in the function header. The relationship and information passing between the calling and called functions are illustrated in Figure 8-2.

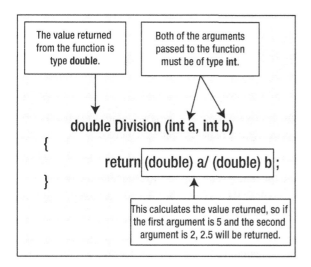

Figure 8-2. *Passing arguments to a function*

If the type of an argument to a function does not match the type of the corresponding parameter, the compiler will insert a conversion of the argument value to the parameter type where this is possible. This may result in truncation of the argument value, when you pass a value of type double for a parameter of type int, for example, so this is a dangerous practice. If the compiler cannot convert an argument to the required type, you will get an error message.

Specifying the Return Value Type

Let's take another look at the general form of a function:

```
Return_type  Function_name(List of Parameters - separated by commas)
{
    // Statements...
}
```

The Return_type specifies the type of the value returned by the function. If the function is used in an expression or as the right side of an assignment statement, the return value supplied by the function will effectively be substituted for the function in its position. You can specify the type of value to be returned by a function as any of the legal types in C, including enumeration types and pointers.

The return type can also be type void*, which is a pointer to void. The value returned in this case is an address but with no specified type. This type is used when you want the flexibility to be able to return an address that may point to a variety of types, as in the case of the malloc() function for allocating memory, for example. As you saw earlier, the return type can be specified as void, meaning that no value is returned.

▪ **Note**   In Chapter 11, you will learn about struct types that provide a way to work with aggregates of several data items as a single unit. A function can have parameters that are struct types, or pointers to a struct type, and can also return a struct or a pointer to a struct.

The return Statement

The return statement provides the means of exiting from a function and resuming execution of the calling function at the point from which the call occurred. In its simplest form, the return statement is just this:

```
return;
```

This form of the return statement is used exclusively in a function where the return type has been declared as void. It doesn't return a value. The more general form of the return statement is

```
return expression;
```

This form of return statement must be used when the return value type for the function has been declared as some type other than void. The value that's returned to the calling program is the value that results when expression is evaluated, and this should be of the return type specified for the function.

■ **Caution** You'll get an error message if you compile a program that contains a function with a void return type that tries to return a value. You'll get an error message from the compiler if you use a bare return in a function where the return type is other than void.

If expression results in a value that's a different type from the return type in the function header, the compiler will insert a conversion from the type of expression to the one required where this is possible. The compiler will produce an error message if the conversion isn't possible. There can be more than one return statement in a function, but each return statement must supply a value that is convertible to the type specified in the function header for the return value.

We should let clear that a function can have more than one return in a function, but it is not good practice, although it is feasible. This can be done inside of a conditional statement, but it is always strongly recommended to use only one return statement at the end of each function. (Otherwise, the code will be more similar to a hidden goto statement.)

```
double Average(int n)
{
    if (n==314)
    {
        return (double)n;
    }
    else
    {
        return (double)n+1;
    }

}
```

■ **Note** The calling function doesn't have to recognize or process the value returned from a called function. It's up to you how you use any values returned from function calls.

TRY IT OUT: USING FUNCTIONS

It's always easier to understand new concepts with an example. This program consists of four functions, including main():

```c
// Program 8.3 Calculating an average using functions
#define __STDC_WANT_LIB_EXT1__ 1
#include <stdio.h>
#define MAX_COUNT 50

// Function to calculate the sum of array elements
// n is the number of elements in array x
double Sum(double x[], size_t n)
{
  double sum = 0.0;
  for(size_t i = 0 ; i < n ; ++i)
    sum += x[i];

  return sum;
}

// Function to calculate the average of array elements
double Average(double x[], size_t n)
{
   return Sum(x, n)/n;
}

// Function to read in data items and store in data array
// The function returns the number of items stored
size_t GetData(double *data, size_t max_coun t)
{
  size_t nValues = 0;
  printf("How many values do you want to enter (Maximum %zd)? ", max_count);
  scanf_s("%zd", &nValues);
  if(nValues > max_count)
  {
    printf("Maximum count exceeded. %zd items will be read.", max_count);
    nValues = max_count;
  }
  for( size_t i = 0 ; i < nValues ; ++i)
    scanf_s("%lf", &data[i]);

  return nValues;
}

// main program - execution always starts here
int main(void)
{
  double samples[MAX_COUNT] = {0.0};
  size_t sampleCount = GetData(samples, MAX_COUNT);
  double average = Average(samples, sampleCount);
  printf("The average of the values you entered is: %.2lf\n", average);

  return 0;
}
```

Typical output of this program is

```
How many values do you want to enter (Maximum 50)? 5
1.0 2.0 3.0 4.0 5.0
The average of the values you entered is: 3.00
```

How It Works

This example illustrates several aspects of using functions. I'll go through this example step by step. After the usual #define and #include directives, you have a definition for the Sum() function:

```
double Sum(double x[], size_t n)
{
  double sum = 0.0;
  for(size_t i = 0 ; i < n ; ++i)
    sum += x[i];

  return sum;
}
```

The first parameter is of an array type, so the corresponding argument can be an array name or a pointer of type double*. The second parameter is of an integer type, and the corresponding argument should specify the number of array elements. The body of the function computes the sum of the elements in the array that is passed to it and returns the sum as a value of type double. The for loop could be written more concisely as

```
  for(size_t i = 0 ; i < n ; sum += x[i++]);
```

It's more concise, but not necessarily clearer.

The next function definition is

```
double Average(double x[], size_t n)
{
    return Sum(x, n)/n;
}
```

The parameters are the same as for Sum(). This function computes and returns the average of the elements in the array passed as the first argument. It calls the Sum() function in the return expression to obtain the sum of the elements and then divides the result by the number of elements in the array. The Average() function passes the arguments it receives when it is called to the Sum() function. Note that for both functions, the type of the first parameter could be specified as double*.

The third function reads in the data to be processed:

```
size_t GetData(double *data, size_t max_count)
{
  size_t nValues = 0;
  printf("How many values do you want to enter (Maximum %zd)? ", max_count);
  scanf_s("%zd", &nValues);
  if(nValues > max_count)
  {
    printf("Maximum count exceeded. %zd items will be read.", max_count);
```

```
    nValues = max_count;
  }
  for( size_t i = 0 ; i < nValues ; ++i)
    scanf_s("%lf", &data[i]);

  return nValues;
}
```

This reads values from the keyboard and stores them in the memory referenced by the argument. The max_count parameter specifies the number of array elements. In general, the first argument can be an array, or it can be a block of memory created on the heap. I won't explain the input process in detail because you have seen it before. Note the use of the z qualifier with %d to read a value of size_t. This qualifier is specifically used for reading size_t values, which, because the type is implementation defined, may be any integer type. As Appendix D explains, you can use the z qualifier with the d, i, o, u, x, X, or n conversion specifier. Obviously the calling program will need to know how many elements have been placed in the array so the GetData() function returns the number of values read as size_t, which is a convenient type for use with array index values.

■ **Tip**   I have not done it in the book for reasons of space, but it's generally a good idea to add comments before each of your own function definitions that explain what the function does and how the arguments are to be used.

The main() function welds everything together, and Figure 8-3 illustrates the order of execution and how data pass between the functions in the example.

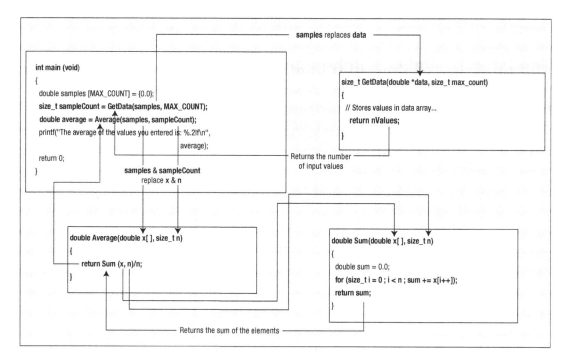

Figure 8-3. *Order of execution*

Execution begins at the first executable statement of the function main(). After defining the samples array, main() calls the GetData() function:

```
size_t sampleCount = GetData(samples. MAX_COUNT);
```

This passes the samples array and the number of elements it contains to GetData(), and the function stores data in the array and returns the number of data items. Each occurrence of data in the body of the GetData() function will refer to samples. The count of values that is returned by the GetData() function is stored in sampleCount.

The main() function calls Average() next:

```
double average = Average(samples, sampleCount);
```

The arguments are the array name, samples, and the count of the number of values in the array, sampleCount, which contains the value returned by GetData().

The Average() function calls Sum(), but what goes on in Average() behind the scenes is of no consequence to main().

Note how all four functions, including main(), are short and easy to understand, much easier than if all the code was in main(). The main() function could be a bit shorter because you don't need to store the value returned by Average(). You could pass it directly to the printf() function in the output statement, like this:

```
printf("The average of the values you entered is: %.2lf\n",
                                              Average(samples, sampleCount));
```

Now the body of main() is only four statements, including the return.

The Pass-by-Value Mechanism

When you pass an argument to a function, the argument value, whatever it is, is not passed directly to the function. A copy of the argument value is made first and stored on the stack (remember, from Chapters 2 and 7, stack is a part of the memory that each function has to persist local variables and arguments from the signature), and it is this copy that is made available to the function, not the original value. This is illustrated in Figure 8-4.

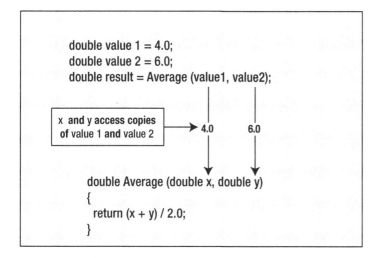

Figure 8-4. *Passing arguments to a function*

The Average() function in Figure 8-4 just computes the average of its two arguments that map to parameters x and y. The Average() function has no access to the variables, value1 and value2, that are passed as arguments when the function is called. It only has access to the copies of the values of these arguments. This means that the function can't change the values stored in value1 and value2. This mechanism is how *all* argument values are passed to functions in C, and it's termed the *pass-by-value mechanism*.

The only way that a called function can change the value of a variable belonging to the calling function is by receiving an argument value that's the address of the variable. When you pass an address to a function, it's still only a copy of the address that's passed, not the original. However, the copy is still the same address and still references the original variable. This is the reason why you must pass the addresses of variables to scanf_s(). Without the addresses, the function cannot store the values in the original variables.

There's an interesting consequence of the pass-by-value mechanism when you pass an array as an argument. As I said when I discussed arrays in Chapter 5, an array name by itself references the address of the start of the array, but it is not a pointer and you cannot modify this address. However, when you use an array name as an argument, a copy of the address is made, and this copy is passed to the function. The copy is now just an address so the called function *can* modify this address in any way it wishes. Of course the original array address is unaffected. This is not a recommended approach, but it means that you could implement the Sum() function from Program 8.3 like this:

```
double Sum(double x[], size_t n)
{
  double sum = 0.0;
  for(size_t i = 0 ; i < n ; ++i)
    sum += *(x++);
  return sum;
}
```

This treats the array name, x, just like a pointer. This is legal because whatever you pass as the argument for the parameter x will end up as a value of type double*.

The value that is returned from a function is also a copy. This is necessary because automatic variables defined within the body of a function and any other local storage cease to exist when the function returns. The GetData() function in Program 8.3 returns the value of nValues, which no longer exists when the function ends, but a copy of its value is made and that is passed back to main().

Function Prototypes

In a variation of Program 8.3, you could define the function main() first and then the function Average() followed by Sum() and GetData():

```
// #include & #define directives...

int main(void)
{
  // Code in main() ...
}

double Average(double x[], size_t n)
{
   return Sum(x, n)/n;
}

double Sum(double x[], size_t n)
{
  // Statements...
}

size_t GetData(double *data, size_t max_count)
{
  // Statements...
}
```

As it stands, this won't compile, but why not? When the compiler comes across the call to the Average() function in main(), it will have no idea what to do with it because at that point the Average() function has not been defined. This is similar to the GetData() function call in main(). Further, when the compiler begins compiling Average(), Sum() has not yet been defined, so it cannot deal with a call to that function either. For this program to compile, you must add something before the definition of main() that tells the compiler about the Average(), Sum(), and GetData() functions.

A *function declaration*, also called a *function prototype*, is a statement that defines the essential characteristics of a function. It defines its name, its return value type, and the type of each of its parameters. You can write a prototype for a function exactly the same as the function header and just add a semicolon at the end. A function declaration is referred to as a function prototype because it provides all the external specifications for the function. A function prototype enables the compiler to generate the appropriate instructions at each point where you call the function and to check that you use it correctly in each case. When you include a standard header file in a program, the header file adds the function prototypes for library functions to the program. For example, the header file stdio.h contains function prototypes for printf() and scanf_s(), among others.

To get the variation of Program 8.3 to compile, you just need to add the function prototypes for the three functions other than main() before the definition of main():

```
// #include & #define directives...

// Function prototypes
double Average(double data_values[], size_t count);
double Sum(double *x, size_t n);
size_t GetData(double*, size_t);
```

338

```
int main(void)
{
  // Code in main() ...
}

// Definitions for Average(), Sum() and GetData()...
```

Now the compiler can compile the call to Average() in main() because it knows all its characteristics, its name, its parameter types, and its return type. Technically, you could put the declaration for the function Average() within the body of main() prior to the function call, but this is never done. Function prototypes generally appear at the beginning of a source file prior to the definitions of any of the functions or in a header file. The function prototypes are then external to all of the functions in the source file, and their scope extends to the end of the source file, thereby allowing any of the functions in the file to call any function regardless of where you've placed the definitions of the functions.

Note that the parameter names do not have to be the same as those used in the function definition. It is not even required to include the names of parameters in a function prototype. I have deliberately made them significantly different and omitted the parameter names in the GetData() prototype. This is to illustrate the range of possibilities and not a recommended approach. Note that the parameter type double* is equivalent to the parameter type double[] in the function definition. One use for using different names in a function prototype is to make the names longer and more self-explanatory in the prototype and in the function definition to keep the parameter names short and the code concise.

There may be situations where a function, fun1(), say, calls a function fun2(), which in turn calls fun1(). In such circumstances, you must define prototypes for the functions to allow them to be compiled. It's good practice to always include declarations for all of the functions in a program source file, regardless of where they're called. This approach will help keep your programs more consistent in design, and it will prevent any errors from occurring if, at any stage, you choose to call a function from another part of your program. Of course, you never need a function prototype for main() because this function is called by the host environment when execution of a program starts.

Pointers As Parameters and Return Types

You've already seen how it's possible to specify a function parameter as a pointer type and pass an address as the corresponding argument to the function. More than that, you've seen that this is essential if a function is to modify the value of a variable that's defined in the calling function. In fact, this is the only way it can be done.

You have also seen that when you pass an array as an argument to a function with a pointer parameter, you are only passing a copy of the address of the array, not the array itself. The values of the elements in an array that are defined in a function can be modified in a function to which the array is passed as an argument. The called function will need to know the number of elements in an array that is passed to it. You have seen two ways to do this. The first way is to just define an additional parameter that is the number of elements in the array. For a function with a pointer parameter, p, and an element count, n, the array elements can be accessed through their addresses, which run from p to p+n-1. This arrangement is equivalent to passing two pointers, one, p, that points to the first array element and another, p+n, that points to one past the last element. This mechanism is used frequently in other programming languages such as C++. A second way is to store a special unique value in the last array element that the function can look for. This mechanism is used for strings, where an array of char elements that represents a string will have '\0' stored in the last element. This mechanism can sometimes be applied to arrays of other types of data. For example, an array of temperature values could store -1000 in the last element to mark the end of the array because this is never a valid temperature.

const Parameters

You can qualify a function parameter using the const keyword, which indicates that the function will treat the argument that is passed for this parameter as a constant. Because arguments are passed by value, using const is only useful when the parameter is a pointer. Typically you apply the const keyword to a parameter that is a pointer to specify that a function will not change the value to which the argument points. Here's an example of a function with a const parameter:

```
bool SendMessage(const char* pmessage)
{
  // Code to send the message
  return true;
}
```

The type of the parameter, pmessage, is a pointer to a const char. In other words, it's the char value that's const, not its address. Putting the const keyword right at the start specifies the data pointed to are const. The compiler will verify that the code in the body of the function does not use the pmessage pointer to modify the message text. You could specify the pointer itself as const too, but this makes little sense because the address is passed by value, so you cannot change the original pointer in the calling function.

Using const with a pointer parameter has another useful purpose. The const modifier implies that the function will not change the data that are pointed to, so the compiler knows that an argument that is a pointer to constant data will be safe. On the other hand, if you do not use the const modifier with the parameter, so far as the compiler is concerned, the function may modify the data pointed to by the argument. Your compiler will at least give you an error message when you pass a pointer to constant data as the argument for a parameter that you did not declare as const.

This is valid, whether it is an array too. The array is treated as a pointer (as stated earlier at "Pass-by-Value Mechanism"):

```
// Program 8.4a const in a array function prototype
#include <stdio.h>
void int_out (const int array[], size_t); // Outputs the integers
void int_out (const int array[], size_t n)
{
        printf ( "The integers are:\n");

        for(size_t i = 0 ; i < n ; ++i)
        {
                printf("%d\n", array[i]); // Display an integer

                //try modifying a constant value should throw an error at compilation
                //array[i] = 3;
        }
}

int main(void)
{
        int array[] = { 2, 7, 1, 8, 2, 8 };
        int_out(array, 6);

        return 0;
}
```

Tip If your function does not modify the data pointed to by a pointer parameter, declare the function parameter as const. That way the compiler will verify that your function indeed does not change the data. It will also allow a pointer to a constant to be passed to the function without issuing an error message.

With parameters that are pointers to pointers, working with them gets a little trickier. The argument corresponding to a parameter that is a pointer to a pointer is passed by value just like any other argument, so there is no point in making the pointer const. However, you might conceivably make the pointer that the pointer points to const, which would prevent modification of the pointer that is pointed to. It is more likely, though, that you will just want to make the data that are ultimately pointed to const. Here is one possible use of const with parameters that are pointers to pointers:

```
void sort(const char** str, size_t n);
```

This is a prototype for a sort() function where the first parameter is of type pointer to pointer to const char. Considering the first parameter to be an array of strings, it is the strings themselves that are const, not their addresses and not the address of the array. This is appropriate in this case because the function will rearrange the addresses stored in the array and will not modify the strings to which they point.

A second possibility is this:

```
void replace(char *const *str, size_t n);
```

The first parameter here is of type pointer to const pointer to char. The argument will be an array of strings where the function can modify the strings but cannot change the addresses in the array. The function could replace punctuation characters with spaces, for instance, but could not rearrange the sequence of strings in the array.

The last possibility for using const with a parameter that is a pointer to a pointer is this:

```
size_t max_length(const char* const* str, size_t n);
```

In this function prototype, the first parameter is of type pointer to const pointer to const char. The pointers in the array are const, and so are the strings to which they point. The function can access the array but cannot modify it in any way. This function notionally returns the maximum length of the strings, which can be obtained without changing anything.

TRY IT OUT: PASSING DATA USING POINTERS

You can exercise passing data to a function using pointers in a variety of ways with a revised version of the example from the previous chapter, Program 7.14, for sorting strings. The source code defines five functions in addition to main(). I'll show the main() function implementation and the function prototypes first. Then I'll explain the implementation of each of the other functions:

```
// Program 8.4 The functional approach to string sorting
#define __STDC_WANT_LIB_EXT1__  1
#include <stdio.h>
#include <stdlib.h>
#include <stdbool.h>
#include <string.h>
#define BUF_LEN   256                      // Input buffer length
#define INIT_NSTR  2                       // Initial number of strings
#define NSTR_INCR  2                       // Increment to number of strings
```

```c
char* str_in();                             // Reads a string
void str_sort(const char**, size_t);        // Sorts an array of strings
void swap(const char**, const char**);      // Swaps two pointers
void str_out(const char* const*, size_t);   // Outputs the strings
void free_memory(char**, size_t);           // Free all heap memory

// Function main - execution starts here
int main(void)
{
  size_t pS_size = INIT_NSTR;                     // count of pS elements
  char **pS = calloc(pS_size, sizeof(char*));     // Array of string pointers
  if(!pS)
  {
    printf("Failed to allocate memory for string pointers.\n");
    exit(1);
  }

  char **pTemp = NULL;                      // Temporary pointer

  size_t str_count = 0;                     // Number of strings read
  char *pStr = NULL;                        // String pointer
  printf("Enter one string per line. Press Enter to end:\n");
  while((pStr = str_in()) != NULL)
  {
    if(str_count == pS_size)
    {
      pS_size += NSTR_INCR;
      if(!(pTemp = realloc(pS, pS_size*sizeof(char*))))
      {
        printf("Memory allocation for array of strings failed.\n");
        return 2;
      }
      pS = pTemp;
    }
    pS[str_count++] = pStr;
  }
  str_sort((const char**)pS, str_count);    // Sort strings
    str_out((const char**)pS, str_count);    // Output strings
      free_memory(pS, str_count);             // Free all heap memory
    return 0;
}
```

I chose the values for symbols used by the code to ensure that memory reallocation would occur frequently. You can add printf() calls if you want to trace this activity. In a real-world program, values would be chosen to minimize the likelihood of repeated heap memory allocation to avoid the overhead in that.

With the function prototypes at the beginning of the source file, the definitions of the functions can appear in any order. Strings will be stored in heap memory, and a pointer to each string will be stored in an element of the pS array, which is also in heap memory. The array pS has an initial capacity to store the number of pointers defined by the INIT_NSTR symbol. The operation of main() is very simple. It reads strings from the keyboard using str_in(), it calls str_sort() to sort the strings, the strings are output in their sorted sequence by calling str_out(), and then the heap memory that has been allocated is freed by calling the free_memory() function.

A string is read from the keyboard by str_in(), which is implemented like this:

```
char* str_in(void)
{
  char buf[BUF_LEN];                        // Space to store input string
  if(!gets_s(buf, BUF_LEN))                 // If NULL returned...
  {                                         // ...end the operation
    printf("\nError reading string.\n");
    return NULL;
  }

  if(buf[0] == '\0')                        // If empty string read...
    return NULL;                            // ...end the operation

  size_t str_len = strnlen_s(buf, BUF_LEN) + 1;
  char *pString = malloc(str_len);

  if(!pString)                              // If no memory allocated...
  {
    printf("Memory allocation failure.\n");
    return NULL;                            // ...end the operation
  }

  strcpy_s(pString, str_len, buf);          // Copy string read to new memory
  return pString;
}
```

The return type is char*, a pointer to a string. A string is read into the local array, buf. Sufficient heap memory is allocated to accommodate the string that was read, and its address is stored in the local variable, pString. The string in buf is copied to the heap memory, and the address stored in pString is returned. If an empty string is read, the function returns NULL. In main(), strings are read in a loop that ends when str_in() returns NULL. A non-NULL string address is stored in the next available element in the pS array. When the array is full, its size is increased by NSTR_INCR elements by calling the realloc() function. As you know, existing data are maintained in the new memory allocated by realloc(), even if it cannot be located at the same address.

When all strings have been read, they are sorted in ascending sequence by calling the str_sort() function, which is implemented like this:

```
void str_sort(const char **p, size_t n)
{
  bool sorted = false;               // Strings sorted indicator
  while(!sorted)                     // Loop until there are no swaps
  {
    sorted = true;                   // Initialize to indicate no swaps
    for(size_t i = 0 ; i < n - 1 ; ++i)
    {
      if(strcmp(p[i], p[i + 1]) > 0)
      {
        sorted = false;              // indicate we are out of order
        swap(&p[i], &p[i + 1]);      // Swap the string addresses
```

```
        }
      }
    }
  }
}
```

This uses the bubble sort to sort the strings, like the example in Chapter 7. The process it applies to some arbitrary array of pointers to strings, pS, is illustrated in Figure 8-5.

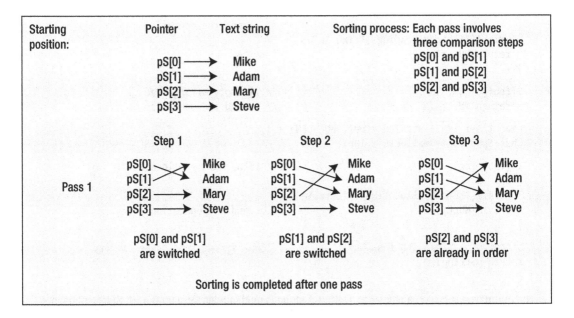

Figure 8-5. *Sorting the strings*

The process compares successive pairs of adjacent array elements, and if they are not in sequence, they are swapped. In the example shown in Figure 8-5, the elements are in sequences after a single pass through all the elements, but in general the process repeats as many times as is necessary.

The first parameter to str_sort() is of type const char**, which is a pointer to a pointer to a const char. This is an array of pointers to strings, where the strings are constant, not their addresses. The sorting process will rearrange the addresses stored in the array elements so the strings appear in ascending sequence. The strings themselves are not changed, nor are their addresses in heap memory. The second argument is the number of strings pointed to by the array elements, which is essential because without this the function has no way to know how many strings there are. Note that there is no return statement in the definition of the str_sort() function. Coming to the end of the function body during execution is equivalent to executing a return statement without a return expression. Obviously this only applies with functions that have a void return type.

The str_sort() function calls swap() to interchange two pointers. It's important to be clear on what this function is doing in order to understand why the parameter types are what they are. Remember arguments are passed by value, so you must pass the address of a variable to a function to allow the function to change the value in the calling function. The arguments to the swap() function are &p[i] and &p[i+1]. These are the addresses of p[i] and p[i+1]—in other words, pointers to these elements.

And what type are these elements? They are pointers to const char, which is type const char*. Put these together, and you have the type of the parameters for the swap() function: const char**, which is pointer to a pointer to const char. You must specify the parameters in this way because the swap() function will modify the contents of elements in the p array. If you use only one * in the parameter type definition and just use p[i] and p[i+1] as the arguments, the function receives whatever is contained in these elements, which isn't what you want at all. Of course, type const char** is the same as type const char*[ ], which is an array of elements of type const char*. You could use either type specification here, but you'll have to write const char* p1[ ],not const char*[ ] p1.

The swap() function is implemented like this:

```
void swap(const char** p1, const char** p2)
{
  const char *pT = *p1;
  *p1 = *p2;
  *p2 = pT;
}
```

If you understand the reasons why the parameter types are what they are, the interchange code should be easy to understand. The function is interchanging the contents of p1 and p2. The contents of these are of type const char*, so the local temporary variable used in swapping the values has to be of this type.

The sorted array of strings is written out by calling str_out(), which is implemented like this:

```
void str_out(const char* const* pStr, size_t n)
{
  printf("The sorted strings are:\n");
  for(size_t i = 0 ; i < n ; ++i)
    printf("%s\n", pStr[i]);              // Display a string
}
```

The first parameter is of type const char* const*, which is a pointer to a const pointer to a const char. The function simply accesses the array argument; it does not change the pointers in the array or what they point to, so specifying the array elements and what they point to as const is appropriate. The second argument is the number of strings to be displayed. The code in the body of the function is what you have seen before, so I won't explain it further.

The last step in main() is to call free_memory() to release all the heap memory that has been allocated. The implementation of free_memory() is

```
void free_memory(char **pS, size_t n)
{
  for(size_t i = 0 ; i < n ; ++i)
  {
    free(pS[i]);
    pS[i] = NULL;
  }
  free(pS);
  pS = NULL;
}
```

Heap memory has to be freed in two stages. The memory allocated for storing the strings is released by stepping through the array elements in the `for` loop. Each pointer is reset to `NULL` once the memory it points to has been freed. When all the memory for strings has been freed, a single call to `free()` releases the memory that was allocated for storing the string addresses.

I've added quite a few comment lines in fancy boxes in the download file for this example. This is a good practice for longer programs that serve several functions, so you can always be sure you know what each function does.

Typical output from this program is

```
Enter one string per line. Press Enter to end:
Many a mickle makes a muckle.
Least said, soonest mended.
Pride comes before a fall.
A stitch in time saves nine.

A wise man hides the hole in his carpet.
The sorted strings are:
A stitch in time saves nine.
A wise man hides the hole in his carpet.
Least said, soonest mended.
Many a mickle makes a muckle.
Pride comes before a fall.
```

Perils of Returning Pointers

You've seen how you can return a numeric value from a function, and you know that a copy of the value is returned. Returning a pointer from a function is a particularly powerful capability, because it provides a way for you to return not just a single value but a whole set of values. In the previous example, the `str_in()` function returns a pointer to a string, and of course, a copy of the pointer value is returned in this case too. It's a mistake to conclude from this that nothing can go wrong with returning values from a function. In particular, there are specific hazards related to returning a pointer. Let's look first at a very simple example that will demonstrate where one peril lies.

TRY IT OUT: RETURNING VALUES FROM A FUNCTION

You'll use increasing your salary as the basis for the example because it's such a popular topic:

```
// Program 8.5 A function to increase your pay
#include <stdio.h>

long *IncomePlus(long* pPay);          // Prototype for increase pay function

int main(void)
{
  long your_pay = 30000L;              // Starting salary
  long *pold_pay = &your_pay;          // Pointer to pay value
  long *pnew_pay = NULL;               // Pointer to hold return value
  pnew_pay = IncomePlus(pold_pay);
  printf("Old pay = $%ld\n", *pold_pay);
```

```
    printf("   New pay = $%ld\n", *pnew_pay);
    return 0;
}

// Definition of function to increment pay
long* IncomePlus(long *pPay)
{
    *pPay += 10000L;                       // Increment the value for pay
    return pPay;                           // Return the address
}
```

When you run the program, you'll get this output:

```
Old pay = $40000
  New pay = $40000
```

How It Works

In main(), you set up an initial value in the variable your_pay and define two pointers for use with the function IncomePlus(), which is going to increase your_pay. One pointer is initialized with the address of your_pay, and the other is initialized to NULL because it's going to receive the address returned by the function IncomePlus().

The output looks satisfactory except that there's something not quite right. If you overlook what you started with ($30,000), it looks as though you didn't get any increase at all. Because the function IncomePlus() modifies the value of your_pay through the pointer pold_pay, the original value has been changed. Clearly, both pointers, pold_pay and pnew_pay, refer to the same location: your_pay. This is a result of the statement in the function IncomePlus():

```
return pPay;
```

This returns the pointer value that the function received when it was called, which is the address contained in pold_pay. The result is that you inadvertently increase the original amount you were paid so you can claim you are owed back pay for the past year—such is the power of pointers.

However, that's not the only potential problem with returning a pointer. Let's try a variation on this.

TRY IT OUT: USING LOCAL STORAGE

To avoid interfering with the variable that the argument points to, you could consider using local storage in the function IncomePlus() to hold the value that is returned. After a small modification, the example looks like this:

```
// Program 8.6 A function to increase your pay that doesn't
#include <stdio.h>

long *IncomePlus(long* pPay);          // Prototype for increase pay function

int main(void)
{
    // Code as Program 8.5 ...
}
```

```
// Definition of function to increment pay
long *IncomePlus(long *pPay)
{
  long pay = 0;                       // Local variable for the result

  pay = *pPay + 10000;                // Increment the value for pay
  return &pay;                        // Return the address of the new pay
}
```

How It Works

You will probably get a warning message when you compile this example, which will give the game away. When I run this, I now get the following result (it's likely to be different on your machine, and you may even get the correct result):

```
Old pay = $30000
  New pay = $27467656
```

Numbers like $27,467,656 with the word "pay" in the same sentence tend to be a bit startling. But you would probably hesitate before complaining about this kind of error! As I said, you may get different results on your computer, possibly the correct result this time. You should get a warning from your compiler with this version of the program. With my compiler, I get the message *"Pointer to local 'pay' is an invalid return value."* This is because I'm returning the address of the variable pay, which goes out of scope on exiting the function IncomePlus(). This is the cause of the remarkable value for the new value of pay—it's junk, just a spurious value left around by something. This is an easy mistake to make, but it can be a hard one to find if the compiler doesn't warn you about the problem.

Try combining the two printf() statements in main() into one:

```
printf("\nOld pay = $%ld   New pay = $%ld\n", *pold_pay, *pnew_pay);
```

On my computer, it now produces the following output:

```
Old pay = $30000   New pay = $40000
```

This actually looks right, in spite of the fact that you know there's a serious error in the program. In this case, although the variable pay is out of scope and therefore no longer exists, the memory it occupied hasn't been reused yet. In the example, evidently something uses the memory previously used by the variable pay and produces the enormous output value. Here's an absolutely 100 percent cast-iron rule for avoiding this kind of problem.

▒ **Cast-Iron Rule**   Never ever return the address of a local variable in a function.

So how should you implement the IncomePlus() function? Well, the first implementation is fine if you recognize that it does modify the value at the address that is passed to it. If you don't want this to happen, you could just return the new value for the pay rather than a pointer. The calling program would then need to store the value that's returned, not an address.

If you want the new pay value to be stored in another location, the IncomePlus() function could conceivably allocate space for it using malloc() and then return the address of this memory. However, you must take care when doing this because responsibility for freeing the memory would be left to the calling function. It would be better to pass two arguments to the function: one being the value of the initial pay and the other being the address of the location in which the new pay is to be stored. This way the calling function has control of the memory. If you had to pass a pointer to the initial pay for some reason, you could protect it by making the parameter type const long*.

Separating the allocation of memory at runtime from the freeing of the memory is sometimes a recipe for something called a *memory leak*. This arises when a function that allocates memory dynamically but doesn't release it gets called repeatedly in a loop. This results in more and more of the available memory being occupied, until in some instances there is none left, so the program crashes. As far as possible, you should make the function that allocates memory responsible for releasing it. When this is not possible, put in place the code to release the memory when you code the dynamic memory allocation.

Summary

You're not finished with functions yet, so I'll postpone diving into another chunky example until the end of the next chapter, which covers further aspects of using functions. So let's pause for a moment and summarize the key points you need to keep in mind when creating and using functions:

- C programs consist of one or more functions, one of which is called main(). The function main() is where execution always starts, and it's called by the operating system through a user command.

- A function is a self-contained named block of code in a program. The name of a function is in the same form as identifiers, which is a unique sequence of letters and digits, the first of which must be a letter (an underline counts as a letter).

- A function definition consists of a header and a body. The header defines the name of the function, the type of the value returned from the function, and the types and names of all the parameters to the function. The body contains the executable statements for the function, which define what the function actually does.

- All the variables that are declared in a function are local to that function.

- A function prototype is a declaration statement terminated by a semicolon that defines the name, the return type, and the parameter types for a function. A function prototype is required to provide information about a function to the compiler when the definition of a function doesn't precede its use in executable code.

- Before you use a function in your source file, you'd either define the function or declare the function with a function prototype.

- Specifying a pointer parameter as const indicates to the compiler that the function does not modify the data pointed to by the function.

- Arguments to a function should be of a type that's compatible with the corresponding parameters specified in its header. If you pass a value of type double to a function that expects an integer argument, the value will be truncated, removing the fractional part.

- A function that returns a value can be used in an expression just as if it were a value of the same type as the return value.

- Copies of the argument values are transferred to a function, not the original values in the calling function. This is referred to as the pass-by-value mechanism for transferring data to a function.

- If you want a function to modify a variable that's declared in its calling function, the address of the variable needs to be transferred as an argument.

That covers the essentials of creating your own functions. In the next chapter, you'll add a few more techniques for using functions. You'll also work through a more substantial example of applying functions in a practical context.

EXERCISES

The following exercises enable you to try what you've learned in this chapter. If you get stuck, look back over the chapter for help. If you're still stuck, you can download the solutions from the Source Code area of the Apress website (www.apress.com), but that really should be a last resort.

Exercise 8-1. Define a function that will calculate the average of an arbitrary number of floating-point values that are passed to the function in an array. Demonstrate the operation of this function by implementing a program that will accept an arbitrary number of values entered from the keyboard and output the average.

Exercise 8-2. Define a function that will return a string representation of an integer that is passed as the argument. For example, if the argument is 25, the function will return "25". If the argument is –98, the function will return "-98". Demonstrate the operation of your function with a suitable version of main().

Exercise 8-3. Extend the function that you defined for the previous exercise to accept an additional argument that specifies the field width for the result and return the string representation of the value right justified within the field. For example, if the value to be converted is –98 and the field width argument is 5, the string that is returned should be " -98". Demonstrate the operation of this function with a suitable version of main().

Exercise 8-4. Define a function that will return the number of words in a string that is passed as an argument. (Words are separated by spaces or punctuation characters. Assume the string doesn't contain embedded single or double quotes—that is, no words such as "isn't.") Define a second function that will segment a string that's passed as the first argument to the function into words and return the words stored in the array that's passed as the second argument. Define a third function that will return the number of letters in a string that's passed as the argument. Use these functions to implement a program that will read a string containing text from the keyboard and then output all the words from the text ordered from the shortest to the longest.

CHAPTER 9

■ ■ ■

More on Functions

Now that you've completed Chapter 8, you have a good grounding in the essentials of creating and using functions. In this chapter, you'll build on that foundation by exploring how functions can be used and manipulated; in particular, you'll investigate how you can access a function through a pointer. You'll also be working with some more flexible methods of communicating between functions.

In this chapter, you'll learn

- What pointers to functions are and how you use them

- How to use static variables in functions

- How to share variables between functions

- How functions can call themselves without resulting in an indefinite loop

- How to write an Othello-type game (also known as Reversi)

Pointers to Functions

Up to now, you've considered pointers as an exceptionally useful device for manipulating data and variables that contain data. It's a bit like handling things with a pair of tongs; you can manipulate a whole range of hot items with just one pair. However, you can also use pointers to handle *functions* at a distance. Because a function has an address in memory where it starts execution (i.e., its starting address), the basic information to be stored in a pointer to a function is going to be that address.

If you think about it, though, this isn't going to be enough. If a function is going to be called through a pointer, information also has to be available about the number and type of the arguments to be supplied and the type of return value to be expected. The compiler can't deduce these just from the address of the function. This means that declaring a pointer to a function is going to be a little more complicated than declaring a pointer to a data type. Just as a pointer holds an address and must also define a type, a function pointer holds an address and must also define a prototype.

Declaring a Pointer to a Function

The declaration for a pointer to a function looks a little strange and can be confusing, so let's start with a simple example:

```
int (*pfunction) (int);
```

This declares a variable that is a pointer to a function. It doesn't point to anything yet; this statement just defines the pointer variable. The name of the pointer is pfunction, and it's intended to point to functions that have one parameter of type int and that return a value of type int to the calling function. Furthermore, you can only use this particular pointer to point to functions with these characteristics. If you want a pointer to functions that accept a float argument and return float values, you need to declare another pointer with the required characteristics. The components of the declaration are illustrated in Figure 9-1.

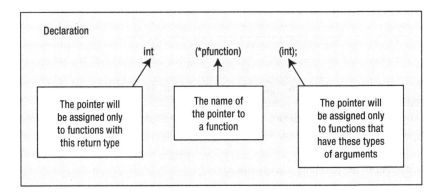

Figure 9-1. *Declaring a pointer to a function*

There are a lot of parentheses in a "pointer to function" declaration. In this example, the *pfunction part of the declaration must be between parentheses. If you omit the parentheses, you'll have a declaration for a function called pfunction() that returns a value that's a pointer to int, which isn't what you want here. The second pair of parentheses just encloses the parameter list in the same way it does with a standard function declaration. A pointer to a function can point only to functions with a given return type and a given number of parameters of given types. You can assign whatever name you like, just as with any other pointer variable.

Calling a Function Through a Function Pointer

Suppose you define a function that has the following prototype:

```
int sum(int a, int b);                  // Calculates a+b
```

This function has two parameters of type int and returns a value of type int, so you could store its address in a function pointer that you declare like this:

```
int (*pfun)(int, int) = sum;
```

This declares a function pointer with the name pfun that will store addresses of functions with two parameters of type int and a return value of type int. The statement also initializes pfun with the address of the function sum(). To supply an initial value, you just use the name of a function that has the required prototype.

You can now call sum() through the function pointer like this:

```
int result = pfun(45, 55);
```

This statement calls the sum() function through the pfun pointer with argument values of 45 and 55. You use the value returned by sum() as the initial value for the variable result, so the result will be 100. Note that you use the function pointer name just like a function name to call the function that it points to; no dereference operator is required.

Suppose you define another function that has the following prototype:

```
int product(int a, int b);           // Calculates a*b
```

You can store the address of product() in pfun with the following statement:

```
pfun = product;
```

With pfun containing the address of product(), you can call product() through the pointer:

```
result = pfun(5, 12);
```

After executing this statement, result will contain the value 60.

Let's try a simple example and see how it works.

TRY IT OUT: USING POINTERS TO FUNCTIONS

In this example, you'll define three functions that have the same parameter and return types and use a pointer to a function to call each of them in turn:

```
// Program 9.1 Pointing to functions
#include <stdio.h>

// Function prototypes
int sum(int, int);
int product(int, int);
int difference(int, int);

int main(void)
{
  int a = 10;                    // Initial value for a
  int b = 5;                     // Initial value for b
  int result = 0;                // Storage for results
  int (*pfun)(int, int);         // Function pointer declaration

  pfun = sum;                    // Points to function sum()
  result = pfun(a, b);           // Call sum() through pointer
  printf("pfun = sum        result = %2d\n", result);

  pfun = product;                // Points to function product()
  result = pfun(a, b);           // Call product() through pointer
  printf("pfun = product    result = %2d\n", result);
  pfun = difference;             // Points to function difference()
  result = pfun(a, b);           // Call difference() through pointer
  printf("pfun = difference result = %2d\n", result);
  return 0;
}
```

```
int sum(int x, int y)
{
  return x + y;
}

int product(int x, int y)
{
  return x * y;
}

int difference(int x, int y)
{
  return x - y;
}
```

The output from this program looks like this:

```
pfun = sum               result = 15
pfun = product           result = 50
pfun = difference        result = 5
```

How It Works

You declare and define three different functions to return the sum, the product, and the difference between two integer arguments. Within main(), you declare a pointer to a function with this statement:

```
int (*pfun)(int, int);             // Function pointer declaration
```

This pointer can be assigned to point to any function that accepts two int arguments and also returns a value of type int. Notice the way you assign a value to the pointer:

```
pfun = sum;                        // Points to function sum()
```

You just use a regular assignment statement that has the name of the function, completely unadorned, on the right side! You don't need to put in the parameter list or anything. If you did, it would be wrong, because it would then be a function call, not an address, and the compiler would complain. A function is very much like an array in its usage here. If you want the address of an array, you just use the name by itself, and if you want the address of a function, you also use the name by itself.

In main(), you assign the address of each function, in turn, to the function pointer pfun. You then call each function using the pointer pfun and display the results. You can see how to call a function using the pointer in this statement:

```
result = pfun(a, b);               // Call sum() through pointer
```

You use the name of the pointer as though it were a function name, followed by the argument list between parentheses. Here, you're using the pointer to function variable name as though it were the original function name, so the argument list must correspond with the parameters in the function header for the function you're calling. This is illustrated in Figure 9-2.

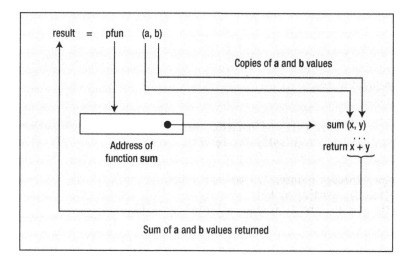

Figure 9-2. *Calling a function through a pointer*

Arrays of Pointers to Functions

Of course, a function pointer is a variable like any other. You can therefore create an array of pointers to functions.

To declare an array of function pointers, you just put the array dimension after the function pointer array name, for instance:

```
int (*pfunctions[10]) (int);
```

This declares an array, pfunctions, with ten elements. Each element in this array can store the address of a function with a return type of int and a parameter of type int. Let's see how this would work in practice.

TRY IT OUT: ARRAYS OF POINTERS TO FUNCTIONS

You can demonstrate how you can use an array of pointers to functions with a variation on the previous example:

```
// Program 9.2 Arrays of Pointers to functions
#include <stdio.h>

// Function prototypes
int sum(int, int);
int product(int, int);
int difference(int, int);

int main(void)
{
  int a = 10;                       // Initial value for a
  int b = 5;                        // Initial value for b
  int result = 0;                   // Storage for results
  int (*pfun[3])(int, int);         // Function pointer array declaration
```

355

```
  // Initialize pointers
  pfun[0] = sum;
  pfun[1] = product;
  pfun[2] = difference;

  // Execute each function pointed to
  for(int i = 0 ; i < 3 ; ++i)
  {
    result = pfun[i](a, b);          // Call the function through a pointer
    printf("result = %2d\n", result); // Display the result
  }

  // Call all three functions through pointers in an expression
  result = pfun[1](pfun[0](a, b), pfun[2](a, b));
  printf("The product of the sum and the difference = %2d\n", result);
  return 0;
}
// Definitions of sum(), product() and difference() as before...
```

The output from this program is as follows:

```
result = 15
result = 50
result =  5
The product of the sum and the difference = 75
```

How It Works

The major difference between this and the previous example is the pointer array, which you declare as follows:

```
int (*pfun[3])(int, int);     // Function pointer array declaration
```

This is similar to the previous declaration for a single pointer variable, but with the addition of the array dimension in square brackets following the pointer name. If you want a two-dimensional array, two sets of square brackets would have to appear here, just like declarations for ordinary array types. You still enclose the parameter list between parentheses, as you did in the declaration of a single pointer. Again, in parallel with what happens for ordinary arrays, all the elements of the array of pointers to functions are of the same type and will accept only the argument list specified. So, in this example, they can all only point to functions that take two arguments of type int and return an int value.

When you want to assign a value to a pointer within the array, you write it in the same way as an element of any other array:

```
pfun[0] = sum;
```

Apart from the function name on the right of the equal sign, this could be a normal data array. It's used in exactly the same way. You could have chosen to initialize all the elements of the array of pointers within the declaration itself: int (*pfun[3])(int, int) = { sum, product, difference };

This would have initialized all three elements and would have eliminated the need for the assignment statements that perform the initialization. In fact, you could have left out the array dimension too and gotten it by default:

```
int (*pfun[])(int, int) = { sum, product, difference };
```

The number of initializing values between the braces would determine the number of elements in the array. Thus, an initialization list for an array of function pointers works in exactly the same way as an initialization list for any other type of array.

When it comes to calling a function that an array element points to, you write it as follows: result = pfun[i](a, b);   // Call the function through a pointer

This, again, is much like the previous example, with just the addition of the index value in square brackets that follows the pointer name. You index this array with the loop variable i as you've done many times before with ordinary data arrays.

Look at the output. The first three lines are generated in the for loop, where the functions sum(), product(), and difference() are called in turn through the corresponding element of the pointer array. The last line of output is produced using the value result from the following statement:

```
result = pfun[1](pfun[0](a, b), pfun[2](a, b));
```

This statement shows that you can incorporate function calls through pointers into expressions, in the same way you might use a normal function call. Here, you call two of the functions through pointers, and their results are used as arguments to a third function that's called through a pointer. Because the elements of the array correspond to the functions sum(), product(), and difference() in sequence, this statement is equivalent to the following:

```
result = product(sum(a, b), difference(a, b));
```

The sequence of events in this statement is as follows:

1. Execute sum(a, b) and difference(a, b) and save the return values.

2. Execute the function product() with the returned values from step 1 as arguments, and save the value returned.

3. Store the value obtained from step 2 in the variable result.

Pointers to Functions As Arguments

You can also use a pointer to a function as an argument to a function. This allows a different function to be called, depending on which function is addressed by the pointer that's passed as the argument.

TRY IT OUT: POINTERS TO FUNCTIONS AS ARGUMENTS

You could produce a variant of the previous example that will pass a pointer to a function as an argument to a function:

```
// Program 9.3 Passing a Pointer to a function
#include <stdio.h>
```

```c
// Function prototypes
int sum(int,int);
int product(int,int);
int difference(int,int);
int any_function(int(*pfun)(int, int), int x, int y);

int main(void)
{
  int a = 10;                         // Initial value for a
  int b = 5;                          // Initial value for b
  int result = 0;                     // Storage for results
  int (*pf)(int, int) = sum;          // Pointer to function

  // Passing a pointer to a function
  result = any_function(pf, a, b);

  printf("result = %2d\n", result );

  // Passing the address of a function
  result = any_function(product,a, b);

  printf("result = %2d\n", result );

  printf("result = %2d\n", any_function(difference, a, b));
  return 0;
}

// Definition of a function to call a function
int any_function(int(*pfun)(int, int), int x, int y)
{
  return pfun(x, y);
}

// Definition of the function sum
int sum(int x, int y)
{
  return x + y;
}

// Definition of the function product
int product(int x, int y)
{
  return x * y;
}

// Definition of the function difference
int difference(int x, int y)
{
  return x - y;
}
```

The output looks like this:

```
result = 15
result = 50
result =  5
```

How It Works

The function that will accept a pointer to a function as an argument is `any_function()`. The prototype for this function is the following:

```
int any_function(int(*pfun)(int, int), int x, int y);
```

The `any_function()` function has three parameters. The first parameter type is a pointer to a function that accepts two integer arguments and returns an integer. The last two parameters are integers that will be used in the call of the function specified by the first parameter. The function `any_function()` itself returns an integer value that will be the value obtained by calling the function indicated by the first argument.

Within the definition of `any_function()`, the function specified by the pointer argument is called in the `return` statement:

```
int any_function(int(*pfun)(int, int), int x, int y)
{
  return pfun(x, y);
}
```

The name of the pointer `pfun` is used, followed by the other two parameters as arguments to the function to be called. The value of `pfun` and the values of the other two parameters `x` and `y` all originate in `main()`.

Notice how you initialize the function pointer `pf` that you declared in `main()`:

```
  int (*pf)(int, int) = sum;   // Pointer to function
```

You place the name of the function `sum()` as the initializer after the equal sign. As you saw earlier, you can initialize function pointers to the addresses of specific functions just by putting the function name as an initializing value.

The first call to `any_function()` involves passing the value of the pointer `pf` and the values of the variables `a` and `b` to `any_function()`:

```
  result = any_function(pf, a, b);
```

The pointer is used as an argument in the usual way, and the value returned by `any_function()` is stored in `result`. Because of the initial value of `pf`, `sum()` will be called in `any_function()`, so the returned value will be the sum of `a` and `b`.

The next call to `any_function()` is in this statement:

```
  result = any_function(product,a, b);
```

Here you explicitly enter the name of a function, `product`, as the first argument, so within `any_function()`, the `product()` function will be called with the values of `a` and `b` as arguments. In this case, you're effectively persuading the compiler to create an internal pointer to the function `product()` and passing that to `any_function()`.

The final call of `any_function()` takes place in the argument to the `printf()` function call:

```
  printf("result = %2d\n", any_function(difference, a, b));
```

In this case, you're also explicitly specifying the name of a function, `difference`, as an argument to `any_function()`. The compiler knows from the prototype of `any_function()` that the first argument should be a pointer to a function. Because you specify the function name, `difference`, explicitly as an argument, the compiler will pass the address of the function to `any_function()`. Lastly, the value returned by `any_function()` is passed as an argument to the function `printf()`. When all this unwinds, you eventually get the difference between the values of a and b displayed.

Take care not to confuse the idea of passing an address of a function as an argument to a function, such as in this expression

```
any_function(product, a, b)
```

with the idea of passing a value that is returned from a function, as in this statement:

```
printf("%2d\n", product(a, b));
```

In the former case, you're passing the address of `product()` as an argument, and if and when it gets called depends on what goes on inside the body of `any_function()`. In the latter case, you're calling the `product()` function before you call `printf()` and passing the result as an argument to `printf()`.

Variables in Functions

Structuring a program into functions not only simplifies the process of developing the program but also extends the power of the language to solve problems. Carefully designed functions can often be reused, making the development of new applications faster and easier. The standard library illustrates the power of reusable functions. The power of the language is further enhanced by the properties of variables within a function and some extra capabilities that C provides in declaring variables. Let's take a look at some of these.

Static Variables: Keeping Track Within a Function

So far, all the variables you've used have gone out of scope at the end of the block in which they were defined, and their memory on the stack then becomes free for use by another function. These are called *automatic variables* because they're automatically created at the point where they're declared and they're automatically destroyed when program execution leaves the block in which they were declared. This is a very efficient process because the memory-containing data in a function are only retained for as long as you're executing statements within the function in which the variable is declared.

However, there are some circumstances in which you might want to retain information from one function call to the next. You may wish to maintain a count of something within a function, such as the number of times the function has been called or the number of lines of output that have been written. With automatic variables, you have no way of doing this.

However, C provides you with a way to do this with *static variables*. You could declare a `static` variable count, for example, with this declaration:

```
static int count = 0;
```

The word `static` is a keyword. The variable declared in this statement differs from an automatic variable in two ways. First, despite the fact that it may be defined within the scope of a function, a `static` variable doesn't get destroyed when execution leaves the function. Second, whereas an automatic variable is initialized each time its scope is entered, the initialization of a variable declared as `static` occurs only once, right at the beginning of the program. Although a static variable is visible only within the function that contains its declaration, it is essentially a global variable and therefore treated in the same way. Consider that global variables always exist; therefore, they consume memory (all the time), be aware of using them only if necessary, and avoid running out of memory.

▓ **Note**   You can make any type of variable within a function a `static` variable.

TRY IT OUT: USING STATIC VARIABLES

You can see static variables in action in the following very simple example:

```c
// Program 9.4 Static versus automatic variables
#include <stdio.h>

// Function prototypes
void test1(void);
void test2(void);

int main(void)
{
  for(int i = 0 ; i < 5 ; ++i)
  {
    test1();
    test2();
  }
  return 0;
}

// Function test1 with an automatic variable
void test1(void)
{
  int count = 0;
  printf("test1   count = %d\n", ++count );
}

// Function test2 with a static variable
void test2(void)
{
  static int count = 0;
  printf("test2   count = %d\n", ++count );
}
```

This produces the following output:

```
test1    count = 1
test2    count = 1
test1    count = 1
test2    count = 2
test1    count = 1
test2    count = 3
test1    count = 1
```

```
test2   count = 4
test1   count = 1
test2   count = 5
```

How It Works

As you can see, the two variables called `count` are quite separate. The changes in the values of each show clearly that they're independent of each other. The `static` variable `count` is declared in the function `test2()`:

```
static int count = 0;
```

Although you specify an initial value, here the variable would have been initialized to 0 anyway because you declared it as static.

■ **Note**   All static variables are initialized to 0 by default if you don't specify an initial value.

The `static` variable `count` is used to count the number of times the function is called. This is initialized when program execution starts, and its current value when the function is exited is maintained. It isn't reinitialized on subsequent calls to the function. Because the variable has been declared as `static`, the compiler arranges things so that the variable will be initialized only once. Because initialization occurs before program startup, you can always be sure a static variable has been initialized when you use it.

The automatic variable `count` in the function `test1()` is declared as follows:

```
int count = 0;
```

Because this is an automatic variable, it isn't initialized by default, and if you don't specify an initial value, it will contain a junk value. This variable gets reinitialized to 0 at each entry to the function, and it's discarded on exit from `test1()`; therefore, it never reaches a value higher than 1.

Although a `static` variable will persist for as long as the program is running, it will be visible only within the scope in which it is declared, and it can't be referenced outside that original scope.

Sharing Variables Between Functions

You also have a way of sharing variables among all your functions. In the same way you can declare constants at the beginning of a program file so they're outside the scope of the functions that make up the program, you can also declare variables like this. These are called *global variables* because they're accessible anywhere. Global variables are declared in the normal way; it's the position of the declaration that's significant and determines whether they're global.

TRY IT OUT: USING GLOBAL VARIABLES

By way of a demonstration, you can modify the previous example to share the count variable between the functions:

```
// Program 9.5 Global variables
#include <stdio.h>

int count = 0;                          // Declare a global variable

// Function prototypes
void test1(void);
void test2(void);

int main(void)
{
  int count = 0;                        // This hides the global count

  for( ; count < 5 ; ++count)
  {
    test1();
    test2();
  }
  return 0;
}

// Function test1 using the global variable
void test1(void)
{
  printf("test1   count = %d\n", ++count);
}

// Function test2 using a static variable
void test2(void)
{
  static int count;                     // This hides the global count
  printf("test2   count = %d\n", ++count);
}
```

The output will be this:

```
test1   count = 1
test2   count = 1
test1   count = 2
test2   count = 2
test1   count = 3
test2   count = 3
test1   count = 4
test2   count = 4
test1   count = 5
test2   count = 5
```

How It Works

In this example, you have three separate variables called count. The first of these is the global variable count that's declared at the beginning of the file:

```
#include <stdio.h>

int count = 0;
```

This isn't a static variable (although you could make it static if you wanted to), but because it is global, it will be initialized by default to 0 if you don't initialize it otherwise. It's potentially accessible in any function from the point where it's declared to the end of the file, so it's accessible in any of the functions here.

The second variable is an automatic variable count that's declared in main():

```
  int count = 0;                     // This hides the global count
```

Because it has the same name as the global variable, the global variable count can't be accessed from main(). Any use of the name count in main() will refer to the variable declared within the body of main(). The local variable count hides the global variable.

The third variable is a static variable count that's declared in the function test2():

```
  static int count;                  // This hides the global count
```

Because this is a static variable, it will be initialized to 0 by default. This variable also hides the global variable of the same name, so only the static variable count is accessible in test2().

The function test1() works using the global count. The functions main() and test2() use their local versions of count, because the local declaration hides the global variable of the same name.

Clearly the count variable in main() is incremented from 0 to 5, because you have five calls to each of the functions test1() and test2(). This has to be different from the count variables in either of the called functions; otherwise, they couldn't have the values 1–5 that are displayed in the output.

You can further demonstrate that this is indeed the case by simply removing the declaration for count in test2() as a static variable. You'll then have made test1() and test2() share the global count, and the values displayed will run from 1 to 10. If you then put a declaration back in test2() for count as an initialized automatic variable with the statement

```
  int count = 0;
```

the output from test1() will run from 1 to 5, and the output from test2() will remain at 1, because the variable is now automatic and will be reinitialized on each entry to the function.

Global variables can replace the need for function arguments and return values. They look very tempting as the complete alternative to automatic variables. However, you should use global variables sparingly. They can be a major asset in simplifying and shortening some programs, but using them excessively will make your programs difficult to understand and prone to errors. It's very easy to modify a global variable and forget what consequences it might have throughout your program. The bigger the program, the more difficult it becomes to avoid erroneous references to global variables. The use of local variables provides very effective insulation for each function against the possibility of interference from the activities of other functions. You could try removing the local variable count from main() in Program 9.5 to see the effect of such an oversight on the output.

> ■ **Caution** As a rule, it's unwise to use the same names in C for local and global variables. There's no particular advantage to be gained, other than to demonstrate the effect, as I've done in the example.

Functions That Call Themselves: Recursion

It's possible for a function to call itself. This is termed *recursion*. You're unlikely to come across a need for recursion very often, so I won't dwell on it, but it can be a very effective technique in some contexts, providing considerable simplification of the code needed to solve particular problems. There are a few bad jokes based on the notion of recursion, but we won't dwell on those either.

Obviously, when a function calls itself, there's the immediate problem of how the process stops. Here's a trivial example of a function that obviously results in an indefinite loop:

```
void Looper(void)
{
  printf("Looper function called.\n");
  Looper();                          // Recursive call to Looper()
}
```

Calling this function would result in an indefinite number of lines of output because after executing the printf() call, the function calls itself. There is no mechanism in the code that will stop the process. This is similar to the problem you have with an indefinite loop, and the solution is similar too: a function that calls itself must also contain the means of stopping the process. Let's see how it works in practice.

TRY IT OUT: RECURSION

The primary uses of recursion tend to arise in complicated problems, so it's hard to come up with original but simple examples to show how it works. Therefore, I'll follow the crowd and use the standard illustration: the calculation of the factorial of an integer. A *factorial* of any integer is the product of all the integers from one up to the integer itself. So here you go:

```
// Program 9.6 Calculating factorials using recursion
#define __STDC_WANT_LIB_EXT1__ 1
#include <stdio.h>

unsigned long long factorial(unsigned long long);

int main(void)
{
  unsigned long long number = 0LL;
  printf("Enter an integer value: ");
  scanf_s("%llu", &number);
  printf("The factorial of %llu is %llu\n", number, factorial(number));
  return 0;
}

// A recursive factorial function
unsigned long long factorial(unsigned long long n)
{
  if(n < 2LL)
```

```
      return n;

   return n*factorial(n - 1LL);
}
```

Typical output from the program looks like this:

```
Enter an integer value: 15
The factorial of 15 is 1307674368000
```

How It Works

This is very simple once you get your mind around what's happening. Let's go through a concrete example of how it works. Assume you enter the value 4. Figure 9-3 shows the sequence of events.

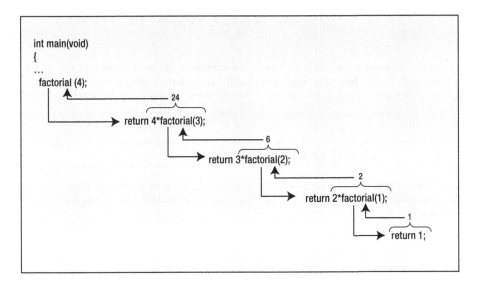

Figure 9-3. *Recursive function calls*

Within the statement

`printf("The factorial of %llu is %llu\n", number, factorial(number));`

the factorial() function gets called from main() with number having the value 4 as the argument.

Within the factorial() function itself, because the argument is greater than 1, this statement is executed:

`      return n*factorial(n - 1LL);`

This is the second return statement in the function, and it calls factorial() again with the argument value 3 from within the arithmetic expression. This expression can't be evaluated, and the return can't be completed until the value is returned from the call to the function factorial() with the argument 3.

This continues, as shown in Figure 9-3, until the argument in the last call of the `factorial()` function is 1. In this case, the first `return` statement is executed:

```
return n;
```

This returns the value 1 to the previous call point. This call point is inside the second `return` in the `factorial()` function, which can now calculate `2 * 1` and return the result to the previous call.

In this way, the whole process unwinds, ending up with the value required being returned to `main()` where it's displayed. So for any given number n, you'll have n calls to the function `factorial()`. For each call, a copy of the argument is created, and the location to be returned to is stored. This can get expensive as far as memory is concerned if there are many levels of recursion. A loop to do the same thing would be less expensive and faster. If you do need or want to use recursion, the most important thing to remember is that there has to be a way to end the process. In other words, there must be a mechanism for not repeating the recursive call. In this example, the check for whether the argument is less than 2 provides the way for the sequence of recursive calls of the `factorial()` function to end.

Note that factorial values grow very quickly. With quite modest input values, you'll exceed the capacity of an `unsigned long long` integer and start getting the wrong results.

Other algorithms and data structures can be implemented with this technique, such as binary tree traversal with Depth-First or Breadth-First Search (DFS/BFS). For a binary search, quicksort is another algorithm that shows the beauty of simplicity that recursion provides; in C its implementation is the function called qsort() and is defined in header <stdlib.h>.

Recursion makes it simpler to implement binary search like traversing a binary tree by choosing right or left branches (quicksort does the same). This is a known method called **divide-and-conquer** that breaks down the problem into smaller pieces (usually one or two) that can be called recursively; thus, the complete picture shows the beauty of the simplicity.

Let's try a simple problem of a chessboard with black and white cells, and we need to find out a path that goes from a Start to a Final cell by traversing each step for a different color (black or white). I cannot cross twice the same color.

One example board is as follows:

```
0 1 0 1 S
1 1 0 0 1
0 1 1 1 0
1 0 0 0 0
F 1 1 0 1
```

This solution can be generated only with arrays and recursion to traverse each path (there are more than one solution) of this pseudo-tree (actually a graph).

Snippet code of the solution would be

```
void search(int level)
{
    // branches/edges
    for (int b = 1; b <= graph[0][level]; b++)
    {
        if (!used[graph[b][level]])
        {
```

```
            used[graph[b][level]] = true;
            //each solution has a lineal position steps (similar to a stack)
            solution[++depth] = graph[b][level];

            //depth of the solution
            if ((graph[b][level] == Finish) && (depth >= SIZE * SIZE -1))
            {
                solfound();
            }

            search(graph[b][level]);

            solution[depth--] = 0;
            used[graph[b][level]] = false;
        }
    }
}
```

Here, we can see that "graph" is the real board already processed for available nodes to travel, and "used" is a helper array to mark if the node was visited.

Complete source code can be found in the book's online repository.

Functions with a Variable Number of Arguments

It can't have escaped your notice that some functions in the standard libraries accept a variable number of arguments. The functions printf() and scanf_s() are obvious examples. You may come up with a need to do this yourself from time to time, so the standard library stdarg.h provides you with routines to write some of your own.

The immediately obvious problem with writing a function with a variable number of parameters is how to specify its prototype. Suppose you're going to produce a function to calculate the average of two or more values of type double. Clearly, calculating the average of fewer than two values wouldn't make much sense. The prototype would be written as follows:

```
double average(double v1, double v2, ...);
```

The *ellipsis* (that's the fancy name for the three periods after the second parameter type) indicates that a variable number of arguments may follow the first two fixed arguments. You must have at least one fixed argument. The remaining specifications are as you would usually find with a function prototype. The first two arguments are of type double, and the function returns a double result.

The next problem with variable argument lists that hits you between the eyes is how you reference the arguments when writing the function. Because you don't know how many there are, you can't possibly give them names. The only conceivable way to do this is indirectly, through pointers. The stdarg.h library header provides you with routines that are usually implemented as macros to help with this, but they look and operate like functions, so I'll discuss them as though they were. You need to use three of these when implementing your own function with a variable number of arguments. They are called va_start(), va_arg(), and va_end(). The first of these has the following form:

```
void va_start(va_list parg, last_fixed_arg);
```

The name, va_start, is obtained from *variable argument start*. This function accepts two arguments: a pointer parg of type va_list and the name of the last fixed parameter you specified for the function you're writing. The va_list type is a type that is also defined in stdarg.h and is designed to store information required by the routines that support variable argument lists.

So using the function average() as an illustration, you can start to write the function as follows:

```
double average(double v1, double v2,...)
{
  va_list parg;                    // Pointer for variable argument list
  // More code to go here...
  va_start( parg, v2);
  // More code to go here...
}
```

You first declare the variable parg of type va_list. You then call va_start() with this as the first argument and specify the last fixed parameter v2 as the second argument. The effect of the call to va_start() is to set the variable parg to point to the first variable argument that is passed to the function when it is called. You still don't know what type of value this represents, and the standard library is no further help in this context. You must determine the type of each variable argument, either implicitly—all variable arguments assumed to be of a given type, for instance—or by deducing the type of each argument from information contained within one of the fixed arguments.

The average() function deals with arguments of type double, so the type isn't a problem. You now need to know how to access the value of each of the variable arguments, so let's see how this is done by completing the function average():

```
// Function to calculate the average of two or more arguments
double average( double v1, double v2,...)
{
  va_list parg;                    // Pointer for variable argument list
  double sum = v1 + v2;            // Accumulate sum of the arguments
  double value = 0.0;              // Argument value
  int count = 2;                   // Count of number of arguments

  va_start(parg,v2);               // Initialize argument pointer
  while((value = va_arg(parg, double)) != 0.0)
  {
    sum += value;
    ++count;
  }
  va_end(parg);                    // End variable argument process
  return sum/count;
}
```

You can work your way through this step by step. After declaring parg, you declare the variable sum as double and as being initialized with the sum of the first two fixed arguments, v1 and v2. You'll accumulate the sum of all the argument values in sum. The next variable, value, declared as double will be used to store the values of the variable arguments as you obtain them one by one. You then declare a counter, count, for the total number of arguments and initialize this with the value 2 because you know you have at least that many values from the fixed arguments. After you call va_start() to initialize parg, most of the action takes place within the while loop. Look at the loop condition:

```
while((value = va_arg(parg, double)) != 0.0)
```

The loop condition calls another function from stdarg.h, va_arg(). The first argument to va_arg() is the variable parg you initialized through the call to va_start(). The second argument is a specification of the type of the argument you expect to find. The function va_arg() returns the value of the current argument specified by parg, and this is stored in value. It also updates the pointer parg to point to the next argument in the list, based on the type you specified in the call. It's essential to have some means of determining the types of the variable arguments. If you don't specify the correct type, you won't be able to obtain the next argument correctly. In this case, the function is written assuming the arguments are all double. Another assumption you're making is that all the arguments will be nonzero except for the last. This is reflected in the condition for continuing the loop, being that value isn't equal to 0. Within the loop, you have familiar statements for accumulating the sum in sum and for incrementing count.

When an argument value obtained is 0.0, the loop ends, and you execute the statement

```
va_end(parg);                    // End variable argument process
```

The call to va_end() is essential to tidy up loose ends left by the process. It resets the parg pointer to NULL. If you omit this call, your program may not work properly. Once the tidying up is complete, you can return the required result with the statement

```
return sum/count;
```

TRY IT OUT: USING VARIABLE ARGUMENT LISTS

After you've written the function average(), it would be a good idea to exercise it in a little program to make sure it works:

```c
// Program 9.7 Calculating an average using variable argument lists
#include <stdio.h>
#include <stdarg.h>

double average(double v1 , double v2,...);        // Function prototype

int main(void)
{
  double v1 = 10.5, v2 = 2.5;
  int num1 = 6, num2 = 5;
  long num3 = 12L, num4 = 20L;

  printf("Average = %.2lf\n", average(v1, 3.5, v2, 4.5, 0.0));
  printf("Average = %.2lf\n", average(1.0, 2.0, 0.0));
  printf("Average = %.2lf\n", average( (double)num2, v2,(double)num1,
                                  (double)num4,(double)num3, 0.0));
  return 0;
}

// Function to calculate the average of two or more arguments
double average( double v1, double v2,...)
{
  va_list parg;                    // Pointer for variable argument list
  double sum = v1 + v2;            // Accumulate sum of the arguments
  double value = 0.0;              // Argument value
  int count = 2;                   // Count of number of arguments
```

```
  va_start(parg,v2);              // Initialize argument pointer
  while((value = va_arg(parg, double)) != 0.0)
  {
    sum += value;
    ++count;
  }
  va_end(parg);                   // End variable argument process
  return sum/count;
}
```

If you compile and run this, you should get the following output:

```
Average = 5.25
Average = 1.50
Average = 9.10
```

How It Works

This output results from three calls to average with different numbers of arguments. Remember, you must cast the variable arguments to the type double, because this is the argument type assumed by the function average(). You can call average() with as many arguments as you like as long as the last is 0.0.

You might be wondering how printf() manages to handle a mix of types. Well, remember the first argument is a control string with format specifiers. The control string supplies the information necessary to determine the types of the arguments that follow, as well as how many there are. The number of arguments following the first must match the number of format specifiers in the control string. The type of each argument after the first must match the type implied by the corresponding format specifier. You've seen how things don't work out right if you specify the wrong format for the type of variable you want to output.

Copying a va_list

It is possible that you may need to process a variable argument list more than once. The stdarg.h header defines a routine for copying an existing va_list for this purpose. Suppose you have created and initialized a va_list object, parg, within a function by using va_start(). You can now make a copy of parg like this:

```
va_list parg_copy;
va_copy(parg_copy, parg);
```

The first statement creates a new va_list variable, parg_copy. The next statement copies the contents of parg to parg_copy. You can then process parg and parg_copy independently to extract argument values using va_arg() and va_end().

Note that the va_copy() routine copies the va_list object in whatever state it's in, so if you have executed va_arg() with parg to extract argument values from the list prior to using the va_copy() routine, parg_copy will be in an identical state to parg with some argument values already extracted. Note also that you must not use the va_list object parg_copy as the destination for another copy operation before you have executed va_end() for parg_copy.

Basic Rules for Variable-Length Argument Lists

Here's a summary of the basic rules and requirements for writing functions to be called with a variable number of arguments:

- There must be at least one fixed parameter.

- You must call va_start() to initialize the value of the variable argument list pointer in your function. This pointer must be declared as type va_list.

- There needs to be a mechanism to determine the type of each argument. Either there can be a default type assumed or there can be a parameter that allows the argument type to be determined. For example, you could have an extra fixed argument in the average() function that would have the value 0 if the variable arguments were double and 1 if they were long. If the argument type specified in the call to va_arg() isn't correct for the argument value specified when your function is called, your function won't work properly.

- You must have a way to determine when the list of arguments is exhausted. For example, the last argument in the variable argument list could have a fixed value called a *sentinel* value that can be detected because it's different from all the others, or the first argument could specify the count of the number of arguments in total or in the variable part of the argument list.

- The second argument to va_arg() that specifies the type of the argument value to be retrieved must be such that the pointer to the type can be specified by appending * to the type name. Check the documentation for your compiler for other restrictions that may apply.

- You must call va_end() before you exit a function with a variable number of arguments. If you fail to do so, the function won't work properly.

You could try a few variations in Program 9.7 to understand this process better. Put some output in the function average() and see what happens if you change a few things. For example, you could display value and count in the loop in the function average(). You could then modify main() to use an argument that isn't double, or you could introduce a function call in which the last argument isn't 0.0.

The main() Function

You already know that the main() function is where execution starts. What I haven't discussed up to now is that main() can have a parameter list so that you can pass arguments to main() when you execute a program from the command line. You can write the main() function either with no parameters or with two parameters.

When you write main() with parameters, the first parameter is of type int and represents a count of the number of arguments that appear in the command that is used to execute main(), including the name of the program itself. Thus, if you add two arguments following the name of the program on the command line, the value of the first argument to main() will be 3. The second parameter to main() is an array of pointers to strings. The argument that will be passed when you write two arguments following the name of the program at the command line will be an array of three pointers. The first will point to the name of the program, and the second and third will point to the two arguments you enter at the command line, as shown in the code:

```
// Program 9.8 A program to list the command line arguments
#include <stdio.h>
int main(int argc, char *argv[])
```

```
{
  printf("Program name: %s\n", argv[0]);
  for(int i = 1 ; i<argc ; ++i)
    printf("Argument %d: %s\n", i, argv[i]);
  return 0;
}
```

The value of argc must be at least 1 because you can't execute a program without entering the program name. You therefore output argv[0] as the program name. Subsequent elements in the argv array will be the arguments that were entered at the command line, so you output these in sequence within the for loop.

My source file for this program had the name Program9_08.c, so I entered the following command to execute it:

```
Program9_08   first   second_arg   "Third is this"
```

Note the use of double quotes to enclose an argument that includes spaces. This is because spaces are normally treated as delimiters. You can always enclose an argument between double quotes to ensure it will be treated as a single argument.

The program then produces the following output as a result of the preceding command:

```
Program name: Program9_08
Argument 1: first
Argument 2: second_arg
Argument 3: Third is this
```

As you can see, putting double quotes around the last argument ensures that it is read as a single argument and not as three arguments.

All command-line arguments will be read as strings, so when numerical values are entered at the command line, you'll need to convert the string containing the value to the appropriate numerical type. You can use one of the functions shown in Table 9-1 that are declared in stdlib.h to do this.

Table 9-1. *Functions That Convert Strings to Numerical Values*

Function	Description
atof()	Converts the string passed as an argument to type double
atoi()	Converts the string passed as an argument to type int
atol()	Converts the string passed as an argument to type long
atoll()	Converts the string passed as an argument to type long long

For example, if you're expecting a command-line argument to be an integer, you might process it like this:

```
int arg_value = 0;          // Stores value of command line argument
if(argc > 1)                // Verify we have at least one argument
  arg_value = atoi(argv[1]);
else
{
  printf("Command line argument missing.");
  return 1;
}
```

Note the check on the number of arguments. It's particularly important to include this before processing command-line arguments, as it's very easy to forget to enter them.

Terminating a Program

In Program 8.4 from the previous chapter, there was more than one instance where you might want to terminate execution of the program from within a function that is called by main(). From main() you can return to end the program, but in other functions, that technique doesn't apply. Terminating the program from within a function can be a *normal* or *abnormal* program end. You might have a function that determines that computation is at an end because there are no more data to process or the user entered data that indicated the program should end. These situations would result in normal program termination. In general, the need to terminate program execution abnormally in a function usually arises when some disastrous state has been detected within the function, such as some serious error within the data that makes it nonsense to continue or some external failure that should not happen for the most part, such as failing to find a disk file or detecting errors on reading from a file.

The stdlib.h header offers several functions that you can call to terminate execution. The stdlib.h header also provides functions that enable you to identify one or more of your own functions that you want to be called when your program terminates normally. Such functions may not have parameters and have the return type specified as void. Of course, you identify a function to be called at termination by a function pointer.

The abort() Function

Calling the abort() function causes an *abnormal* termination of the program. It requires no arguments, and of course it does not return. You call it like this when you want to end a program:

```
abort();                        // Abnormal program end
```

abort() can be used when checking boundary cases and must abort the program if these constraints are hit, for instance, when trying to read a file, but it is not found in the filesystem.

The function may flush output buffers and close open streams, but whether or not it does this is implementation defined.

The exit() and atexit() Functions

Calling the exit() function causes *normal* termination of the program. The function requires an argument of type int that indicates program status at the time of termination. The argument can be 0 or EXIT_SUCCESS to indicate a successful termination, and this is returned to the host environment, for example:

```
exit(EXIT_SUCCESS);             // Normal program end
```

If the argument is EXIT_FAILURE, an indication of unsuccessful termination is returned to the host environment. In any event, the exit() function flushes all output buffers to cause the data they contain to be written to the destination and closes all open streams before returning control to the host environment. The values that may be returned to the host environment are implementation defined. Note that calling exit() causes a normal program termination, regardless of the value of the argument. You can register your own functions to be called by exit() by calling atexit().

You call the atexit() function to identify a function that is to be executed when the application terminates. Here's how you might do that:

```
void CleanUp(void);          // Prototype of function to be called on normal exit
...
if(atexit(CleanUp))
  printf("Registration of function failed!\n");
```

You pass the name of the function to be called as the argument to atexit(), which returns 0 if the registration was successful and nonzero otherwise. You can register several functions by calling atexit() several times, and a conforming C implementation must provide for registering a maximum of at least 32 functions. When several functions have been registered to be called when exit() is called, they are called in the reverse of their registration sequence on program termination. Thus, the last one to be registered by calling atexit() is called first.

The _Exit() Function

The _Exit() function does essentially the same job as exit(), in that it causes normal termination and returns the argument value to the host environment. The difference is that you cannot affect what happens at program termination that results from calling _Exit() because it will not call any registered functions. You call _Exit() like this:

```
_Exit(1);    // Exit with status code 1
```

The quick_exit() and at_quick_exit() Functions

Calling quick_exit() causes a normal termination and returns control to the host environment by calling _Exit(). The argument to quick_exit() is a status code of type int that the function passes on in the call to _Exit(). Before calling _Exit(), quick_exit() calls functions registered through calls to the at_quick_exit() function. Here's how you might register functions to be called by quick_exit():

```
// Termination function prototypes
void CloseFiles(void);
void CloseCommunicationsLinks(void);
...
at_quick_exit(CloseCommunicationsLinks);
at_quick_exit(CloseFiles);
```

With the functions registered to be called by quick_exit() by the last two statements, CloseFiles() will be called first and then CloseCommunicationLinks().

The quick_exit() function provides a parallel program termination mechanism to exit(). Functions registered to be called by exit() and quick_exit() are completely independent of one another; functions registered through atexit() calls are not called by quick_exit(), and functions registered using at_quick_exit() are not called by exit().

Enhancing Performance

You have three facilities that are intended to provide cues to your compiler to generate code with better performance. The first relates to how short function calls are compiled, and the second is concerned with the use of pointers. The effects are not guaranteed for either of these though, and they depend on your compiler's implementation. The third facility is for functions that never return. I'll discuss short functions first.

Declaring Functions Inline

The functional structure of the C language encourages the segmentation of a program into many functions, and the functions can sometimes be very short. With very short functions, it is possible to improve execution performance by replacing each function call of a short function with inline code that implements the effects of the function. This means there is no need to provide for passing values to a function or returning a value. You can indicate that you would like this technique to be applied by the compiler by specifying a short function as inline. Here's an example:

```
inline double bmi(double kg_wt, double m_height)
{
  return kg_wt/(m_height*m_height);
}
```

This function calculates an adult's body mass index from their weight in kilograms and their height in meters. This operation is sensibly defined as a function, but it is also a good candidate for inline implementation of calls because the code is so simple. This is specified by the inline keyword in the function header. There's no guarantee in general that the compiler will take note of a function being declared as inline because it's just a hint to the compiler.

Using the restrict Keyword

Sophisticated C compilers have the capability to optimize the performance of the object code, and this can involve changing the sequence in which calculations occur compared with the sequence in which you specify operations in the code. For such code optimization to be possible, the compiler must be sure that such resequencing of operations will not affect the result of the calculations, and pointers represent something of a problem in this respect. To allow optimization of code involving pointers, the compiler has to be certain that the pointers are not aliased—in other words, the data item that each pointer references is not referenced by some other means in a given scope. The restrict keyword provides a way for you to tell the compiler when this is the case and thus allows code optimization to be applied. Here's an example of a function that is declared in string.h:

```
errno_t strcpy_s(char * restrict s1, rsize_t s1max, const char * restrict s2)
{
  // Implementation of the function to copy s2 to s1
}
```

This function copies s2 to s1. The restrict keyword is applied to both pointer parameters, thus indicating that the strings referenced by s1 and s2 are only referenced through those pointers in the body of the function, so the compiler can optimize the code generated for the function. The restrict keyword only imparts information to the compiler and does not guarantee that any optimization will be applied. Of course if you use the restrict keyword where the condition does not apply, your code may produce incorrect results.

Most of the time you won't need to use the restrict keyword. Only if your code is very computationally intensive will it have any appreciable effect, and even then it depends on your compiler.

The _Noreturn Function Specifier

Sometimes you will implement a function that will never return. For example, you might define a function that you will call when the program terminates normally. Such a function would not return in the sense that control goes back to the caller as would typically be the case. In such cases, you can indicate to the compiler that the function does not return:

```
_Noreturn void EndAll(void)
{
  // Tidy up open files...
  exit(EXIT_SUCCESS);
}
```

The _Noreturn qualifier tells the compiler that this function does not return to its calling function. Because the function will not return, the only possible return type specification is void. Knowing that a function will never return allows the compiler to omit code and storage that is normally required to accommodate the process of returning control to the calling point. The stdnoreturn.h header defines the macro noreturn, which expands to _Noreturn, so you can use noreturn as long as you include the header in your source file.

Designing a Program

At this point, you have finished with functions, and because you're more than halfway through the capabilities of C, an example of reasonable complexity wouldn't come amiss. In this program, you're going to put to practical use the various elements of C that you've covered so far in the book.

The Problem

The problem that you're going to solve is to write a game. There are several reasons for choosing to write a game. First, games tend to be just as complex, if not more so, as other types of programs, even when the game is simple. And second, games are more fun.

The game is in the same vein as Othello or, if you are ancient enough to remember Microsoft Windows 3.0, Reversi. The game is played by two players who take turns placing a counter on a square board. One player has black counters, and the other has white counters. The board has an even number of squares along each side. The starting position, followed by five successive moves, is shown in Figure 9-4.

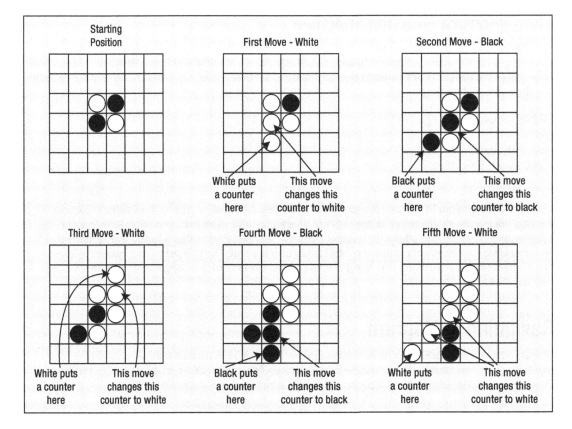

Figure 9-4. *Starting position and initial moves in Reversi*

You can only place a counter adjacent to an opponent's counter, such that one or more of your opponent's counters—in a line diagonally, horizontally, or vertically—are enclosed between two of your own counters. The opponent's counters are then changed to counters of your own color. The person with the most counters on the board at the end of the game wins. The game ends when all the squares are occupied by counters. The game can also end if neither player can place a counter legally, which can occur if you or your opponent manages to convert all the counters to the same color. The game can be played with any size of board, but you'll implement it on a 6 × 6 board. You'll also implement it as a game that you play against the computer.

The Analysis

This problem's analysis is a little different from those you've seen up to now. The whole point of this chapter is to introduce the concept of *structured programming*—in other words, breaking a problem into small pieces—which is why you've spent so much time looking at functions.

A good way to start is with a diagram. You'll start with a single box, which represents the whole program, or the main() function, if you like. Developing from this, on the next level down, you'll show the functions that will need to be directly called by the main() function, and you'll indicate what these functions have to do. Below that, you'll show the functions that those functions in turn have to use. You don't have to show the actual functions; you can show just the tasks that need to be accomplished. However, these tasks *do* tend to be functions, so this is a great way to design your program. Figure 9-5 shows the tasks your program will need to perform.

You can now go a step further than this and begin to think about the actual sequence of actions, or functions, that the program is going to perform. Figure 9-6 is a flowchart that describes the same set of functions but in a manner that shows the sequence in which they're executed and the logic involved in deciding that. You're moving closer now to a more precise specification of how the program will work.

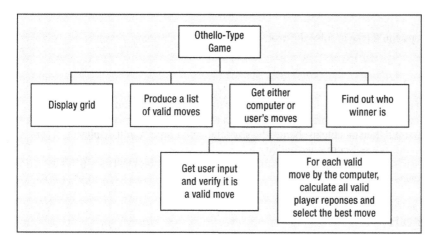

Figure 9-5. *Tasks in the Reversi program*

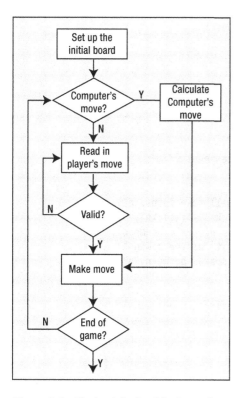

Figure 9-6. *The basic logic of the Reversi program*

This isn't absolutely complete, of course. There's a lot of detail you'll need to fill in. This sort of diagram can help you get the logic of the program clear in your mind, and from there you can progress to a more detailed definition of how the program will work.

The Solution

This section outlines the steps you'll take to solve the problem.

Step 1

The first thing to do is to set up and display the initial board. You'll use a smaller-than-normal board (6 × 6), as this makes the games shorter, but you'll implement the program with the board size as a symbol defined by a preprocessor directive. You'll then be able to change the size later if you want. You'll display the board using a separate function, as this is a self-contained activity.

Let's start with the code to declare, initialize, and display the grid. The computer will use '@' as its counter, and the player will have 'O' for their counter:

```c
// Program 9.9 REVERSI An Othello type game
#define __STDC_WANT_LIB_EXT1__ 1
#include <stdio.h>

#define SIZE 6                       // Board size - must be even
const char comp_c = '@';             // Computer's counter
const char player_c = 'O';           // Player's counter

// Function prototypes
void display(char board[][SIZE]);
void reset_board(char board[][SIZE]);

int main(void)
{
  char board [SIZE][SIZE] = {0};     // The board
  char again = 0;                    // Replay choice input
  // Prompt for how to play
  printf("\nREVERSI\n\n");
  printf("You can go first on the first game, then we will take turns.\n");
  printf("   You will be white - (%c)\n   I will be black   - (%c).\n",
                                                player_c, comp_c);
  printf("Select a square for your move by typing a digit for the row\n "
                "and a letter for the column with no spaces between.\n");
  printf("\nGood luck!  Press Enter to start.\n");
  scanf_s("%c", &again, sizeof(again));
  fflush(stdin);                     // Clear the buffer

  // The main game loop...

  return 0;
}
```

```
// Reset the board to starting state
void reset_board(char board[][SIZE])
{
  // Blank all the board squares
  for(size_t row = 0 ; row < SIZE ; ++row)
    for(size_t col = 0; col < SIZE; ++col)
      board[row][col] = ' ';

  // Place the initial four counters in the center
  size_t mid = SIZE/2;
  board[mid - 1][mid - 1] = board[mid][mid] = player_c;
  board[mid - 1][mid] = board[mid][mid - 1] = comp_c;
}

// Function to display the board in its current state
void display(char board[][SIZE])
{
  // Display the column labels
  char col_label = 'a';                              // Column label
  printf("\n ");                                     // Start top line
  for(size_t col = 0 ; col < SIZE ; ++col)
    printf("   %c", (char)(col_label + col));        // Display the top line
  printf("\n");                                      // End the top line

  // Display the rows...
  for(size_t row = 0 ; row < SIZE ; ++row)
  {
    // Display the top line for the current row
    printf("  +");
    for(size_t col = 0 ; col < SIZE ; ++col)
      printf("---+");
    printf("\n%2zd|",row + 1);

    // Display the counters in current row
    for(size_t col = 0 ; col < SIZE; ++col)
      printf(" %c |", board[row][col]);              // Display counters in row
    printf("\n");
  }

  // Finally display the bottom line of the board
  printf("  +");                                     // Start the bottom line
  for(size_t col = 0 ; col < SIZE ; ++col)
    printf("---+");                                  // Display the bottom line
  printf("\n");                                      // End the bottom  line
}
```

The initial code in main() explains how the game is played. The scanf_s() function reads a character from the keyboard that in this case will be just '\n'. It's a good idea to call fflush() as a matter of course after reading single characters to make sure there are no extra characters such as newlines left behind in the buffer. Anything left behind will be read next time you read a character, and this usually causes a problem.

The reset_board() function sets all elements in the board array to ' ' and places two counters for each player in the center of the board. The parameter is a two-dimensional array address, and the second dimension must be specified in the parameter type. The first dimension must also be SIZE because the board is square.

The display() function outputs the board with row numbers to identify the rows and the letters from 'a' onward to identify each column. This will be the reference system by which the user will select a square to place their counter. The code looks complicated, but it's quite straightforward. The first loop outputs the top line with the column label, from 'a' to 'f' with the board size. The next loop outputs the squares that can contain counters, a row at a time, with a row number at the start of each row. The last loop outputs the bottom of the last row. The board array is an argument to the display() function rather than a global variable. This is to prevent other functions from modifying the contents of board accidentally. The function will display a board of any size, but after 26 columns, the column headings will be strange characters.

Step 2

You need a function to generate all the possible moves that can be made for the current player. This function will have two uses: first, it will allow you to check that the move the player enters is valid, and, second, it will help you determine what moves the computer can make. But first you must decide how you're going to represent and store this list of moves.

So what information do you need to store, and what options do you have? Well, you've defined the grid in such a way that any cell can be referenced by a row number and a column letter. You could therefore store a move as a string consisting of a number and a letter. You would then need to accommodate a list of moves of varying length to allow for the possibility that the dimensions of the board might change to 10 × 10 or greater.

There's an easier option. You can create a second array with elements of type bool with the same dimensions as the board and store true for positions where there is a valid move and false otherwise. The function will need access to three arguments: the board array, so it can check for vacant squares; the moves array, in which the valid moves are to be recorded; and the identity of the current player, which will be the character used as a counter for the player.

The strategy will be this: For each blank square, search the squares around that square for an opponent's counter. If you find an opponent's counter, follow a line of opponent counters (horizontal, vertical, or diagonal) until you find a player counter. If you do in fact find a player counter along that line, then you know that the original blank square is a valid move for the current player.

You can add the function definition to the file following the definition of the display() function and implement it like this:

```
int valid_moves(char board[][SIZE], bool moves[][SIZE], char player)
{
  int rowdelta = 0;              // Row increment around a square
  int coldelta = 0;              // Column increment around a square
  int x = 0;                     // Row index when searching
  int y = 0;                     // Column index when searching
  int no_of_moves = 0;           // Number of valid moves

  // Set the opponent
  char opponent = (player == player_c) ? comp_c : player_c;

  // Initialize moves array to false
  for(size_t row = 0 ; row < SIZE ; ++row)
    for(size_t col = 0 ; col < SIZE ; ++col)
      moves[row][col] = false;
```

```
// Find squares for valid moves.
// A valid move must be on a blank square and must enclose
// at least one opponent square between two player squares
for(size_t row = 0 ; row < SIZE ; ++row)
{
  for(size_t col = 0 ; col < SIZE ; ++col)
  {
    if(board[row][col] != ' ')        // If it's not a blank square...
      continue;                       // ...go to the next

    // Check all the squares around the blank square for opponents counter
    for(rowdelta = -1 ; rowdelta <= 1 ; ++rowdelta)
    {
      for(coldelta = -1 ; coldelta <= 1 ; ++coldelta)
      {
        // Don't check outside the array, or the current square
        if((row == 0 && rowdelta == -1) || row + rowdelta >= SIZE ||
          (col == 0 && coldelta == -1) || col + coldelta >= SIZE ||
                                  (rowdelta == 0 && coldelta == 0))
          continue;

        // Now check the square
        if(board[row + rowdelta][col + coldelta] == opponent)
        {
          // If we find the opponent, move in the delta direction
          // over opponent counters searching for a player counter
          x = row + rowdelta;        // Move to
          y = col + coldelta;        // opponent square

          // Look for a player square in the delta direction
          for(;;)
          {
            x += rowdelta;           // Go to next square
            y += coldelta;           // in delta direction

            // If we move outside the array or it's a blank square, give up
            if(x < 0 || x >= SIZE || y < 0 || y >= SIZE || board[x][y] == ' ')
              break;

            //  If square has a player counter then we have a valid move
            if(board[x][y] == player)
            {
              moves[row][col] = true; // Mark as valid
              no_of_moves++;          // Increase valid moves count
              break;                  // Go check another square
            }
          }
        }
      }
    }
  }
}
```

```
  }
  return no_of_moves;
}
```

You can add a prototype for the valid_moves() function following the other prototypes. There are three parameters:

- The board array, which is the game board

- The moves array with the same dimensions as board where each bool element will specify whether that board position is a valid move for player

- The player, which identifies the player for whom valid moves are being determined

Because the counters are either player_c or comp_c, you can set the opponent counter in the valid_moves() function as the one that isn't the player counter that's passed as an argument. You do this with the conditional operator. You set the moves array to false in the first nested loop, so you only have to set valid positions to true. The second nested loop iterates through all the squares on the board, looking for those that are blank. When you find a blank square, you search for an opponent counter in the inner loop:

```
// Check all the squares around the blank square for opponents counter
for(rowdelta = -1 ; rowdelta <= 1 ; ++rowdelta)
{
  for(coldelta = -1 ; coldelta <= 1 ; ++coldelta)
  {
    ...
```

This will iterate over all the squares that surround the blank square and will include the blank square itself, so you skip the blank square or any squares that are off the board with this if statement:

```
// Don't check outside the array, or the current square
if((row == 0 && rowdelta == -1) || row + rowdelta >= SIZE ||
   (col == 0 && coldelta == -1) || col + coldelta >= SIZE ||
                    (rowdelta == 0 && coldelta == 0))
    continue;
```

If you get past this point, you've found a nonblank square that's on the board. If it contains the opponent's counter, then you move in the same direction, looking for either more opponent counters or a player counter. If you find a player counter, the original blank square is a valid move, so you record it. If you find a blank or run of the board, it isn't a valid move, so you look for another blank square. The function returns a count of the number of valid moves, so you can use this value to indicate whether the function returns any valid moves. Remember, any nonzero integer is true and 0 is false.

Step 3

Now that you can produce an array that contains all the valid moves, you can fill in more of the game loop in main(). You'll base this on the flowchart you saw earlier. You can start by adding two nested do-while loops: the outer one will initialize each game, and the inner one will iterate over player and computer turns:

```
int main(void)
{
  char board[SIZE][SIZE] = {0};          // The board
  bool moves[SIZE][SIZE] = { false };    // Valid moves
```

```
  int no_of_moves = 0;                           // Count of moves
  int invalid_moves = 0;                         // Invalid move count
  char again = 0;                                // Replay choice input

  // Player indicator: true for player and false for computer
  bool next_player = true;

  // Prompt for how to play - as before...

  // The main game loop
  do
  {
    reset_board(board);                          // Board in initial state

    // On even games the player starts, on odd games the computer starts
    next_player = !next_player;
    no_of_moves = 4;                             // Starts with four counters

    // The game play loop
    do
    {
      display(board);                            // Display the board
      if(true == (next_player = !next_player))   // Flip next player
      { //    It is the player's turn

        // Code to get the player's move and execute it...

      }
      else
      { // It is the computer's turn

        // Code to make the computer's move...
      }
    }while(no_of_moves < SIZE*SIZE && invalid_moves < 2);

    // Game is over
    display(board);                              // Show final board

    printf("The final score is:\n");
    printf("Computer %d\n     User %d\n\n",
             player_counters(board, comp_c), player_counters(board, player_c));
    printf("Do you want to play again (y/n): ");
    scanf_s(" %c", &again, sizeof(again));       // Get y or n
    fflush(stdin);                               // Clear the buffer
  }while(tolower(again) == 'y');                 // Go again on y or Y

  printf("\nGoodbye\n");
  return 0;
}
```

```
// Code for definition of display()...
// Code for definition of reset_board()...
// Code for definition of valid_moves()...
```

The additional code requires the stdbool.h and ctype.h headers to be included. I recommend that you don't run this program yet because you haven't written the code to handle input from the user or moves from the computer. At the moment, it will just loop indefinitely, printing a board with no new moves being made. You'll sort out those parts of the program next.

The variable player determines whose turn it is. When player is false, it's the computer's turn, and when player is true, it's the player's turn. This is set initially to true, and setting player to !player in the do-while loop will alternate who goes next. To determine who takes the next turn, you invert the value of the variable player and test the result in the if statement, which will alternate between the computer and the player automatically.

The game ends when the number of counters in no_of_moves reaches SIZE*SIZE, the number of squares on the board. It will also end if invalid_moves reaches 2. You set invalid_moves to 0 when a valid move is made and increment it each time no valid move is possible. Thus, it will reach 2 if there's no valid option for two successive moves, which means that neither player can go. At the end of a game, you output the final board and the results and offer the option of another game.

The final score is obtained by calling the player_counters() function for each player. You can add a prototype for the function and implement it like this:

```
int player_counters(char board[][SIZE], char player)
{
  int count = 0;
  for(size_t row = 0 ; row < SIZE ; ++row)
    for(size_t col = 0 ; col < SIZE ; ++col)
      if(board[row][col] == player) ++count;
  return count;
}
```

This just totals the number of counters on the board for the player specified by the second argument. You can now add the code to main(), which will make the player and computer moves:

```
// Program 9.9 REVERSI An Othello type game
#define __STDC_WANT_LIB_EXT1__ 1
#include <stdio.h>
#include <stdbool.h>
#include <ctype.h>
#include <string.h>

#define SIZE 6                    // Board size - must be even
const char comp_c = '@';          // Computer's counter
const char player_c = 'O';        // Player's counter

// Function prototypes
void display(char board[][SIZE]);
void reset_board(char board[][SIZE]);
int valid_moves(char board[][SIZE], bool moves[][SIZE], char player);
int player_counters(char board[][SIZE], char player);
void make_move(char board[][SIZE], size_t row, size_t col, char player);
void computer_move(char board[][SIZE], bool moves[][SIZE], char player);
```

```
int main(void)
{
  char board[SIZE][SIZE] = {0};          // The board
  bool moves[SIZE][SIZE] = {false};      // Valid moves
  int no_of_moves = 0;                   // Count of moves
  int invalid_moves = 0;                 // Invalid move count
  char again = 0;                        // Replay choice input
  char y = 0;                            // Column letter
  size_t x = 0;                          // Row number

  // Player indicator: true for player and false for computer
  bool next_player = true;
  // Prompt for how to play - as before...

  // The main game loop
  do
  {
    reset_board(board);                  // Board in initial state

    // On even games the player starts, on odd games the computer starts
    next_player = !next_player;
    no_of_moves = 4;                     // Starts with four counters

    // The game play loop
    do
    {
      display(board);                              // Display the board
      if(true == (next_player = !next_player))     // Flip next player
      { //    It is the player's turn
        if(valid_moves(board, moves, player_c))
        { // Read player moves until a valid move is entered
          for(;;)
          {
            printf("Please enter your move (row column - no space): ");
            scanf_s(" %zd%c", &x, &y, sizeof(y));  // Read input
            fflush(stdin);                         // Clear the buffer

            y = tolower(y) - 'a';       // Convert to column index
            --x;                        // Convert to row index
            if(y < 0 || y >= SIZE || x >= SIZE || !moves[x][y])
            {
              printf("Not a valid move, try again.\n");
              continue;
            }

            make_move(board, x, y, player_c);
            ++no_of_moves;                // Increment move count
            break;
          }
        }
      }
```

```
      else                             // No valid moves
      {
        if(++invalid_moves < 2)
        {
          printf("\nYou have to pass, press return");
          scanf_s("%c", &again, sizeof(again));
          fflush(stdin);               // Clear the buffer
        }
        else
          printf("\nNeither of us can go, so the game is over.\n");
      }
    }
    else
    { // It is the computer's turn
      if(valid_moves(board, moves, comp_c)) // Check for valid moves
      {
        invalid_moves = 0;                   // Reset invalid count
        computer_move(board, moves, comp_c);
        ++no_of_moves;                       // Increment move count
      }
      else
      {
        if(++invalid_moves < 2)
          printf("\nI have to pass, your go\n"); // No valid move
        else
          printf("\nNeither of us can go, so the game is over.\n");
      }
    }
  }while(no_of_moves < SIZE*SIZE && invalid_moves < 2);

  // Game is over
  display(board);                            // Show final board

  printf("The final score is:\n");
  printf("Computer %d\n    User %d\n\n",
         player_counters(board, comp_c), player_counters(board, player_c));
  printf("Do you want to play again (y/n): ");
  scanf_s(" %c", &again, sizeof(again));      // Get y or n
  fflush(stdin);                             // Clear the buffer
  }while(tolower(again) == 'y');             // Go again on y

  printf("\nGoodbye\n");
  return 0;
}

// Code for definition of display() as before...
// Code for definition of reset_board() as before...
// Code for definition of valid_moves() as before...
// Code for definition of player_counters() as before...
```

The code to deal with game moves uses two new functions for which you should add prototypes. The make_move() function executes a move, and the computer_move() function calculates the computer's move. For the player, you calculate the moves array for the valid moves in the if statement:

```
if(valid_moves(board, moves, player_c))
    ...
```

When the return value is positive, there are valid moves, so you read the row number and column letter for the square selected:

```
printf("Please enter your move (row column - no space): ");
scanf_s(" %zd%c", &x, &y, sizeof(y));  // Read input
```

You convert the row number to an index by subtracting 1 and the letter to an index by subtracting 'a'. You call tolower() just to be sure the value in y is lowercase. Of course, you must include the ctype.h header for this function. For a valid move, the index values must be within the bounds of the array and moves[x][y] must be true, so you check for when this is not the case and continue with the next loop iteration:

```
if(y < 0 || y >= SIZE || x >= SIZE || !moves[x][y])
{
    printf("Not a valid move, try again.\n");
    continue;
}
```

If you have a valid move, you execute it by calling the make_move() function you'll write in a moment (notice that the code won't link yet, because you make a call to this function without having defined it in the program).

If there are no valid moves for the player, you increment invalid_moves. If this is still less than 2, you output a message that the player can't go and continue with the next iteration for the computer's move. If invalid_moves isn't less than 2, however, you output a message that the game is over, and the do-while loop condition controlling game moves will be false.

For the computer's move, if there are valid moves, you call the computer_move() function to make the move and increment the move count. The circumstances in which there are no valid moves are handled in the same way as for the player.

Let's add the definition of the make_move() function next. To make a move, you must place the appropriate counter on the selected square and flip any adjacent rows, columns, or diagonals of opponent counters that are bounded at the opposite end by a player counter. You can add the code for this function at the end of the source file:

```
void make_move(char board[][SIZE], size_t row, size_t col, char player)
{
  int rowdelta = 0;                     // Row increment
  int coldelta = 0;                     // Column increment
  size_t x = 0;                         // Row index for searching
  size_t y = 0;                         // Column index for searching

  // Identify opponent
  char opponent = (player == player_c) ? comp_c : player_c;

  board[row][col] = player;             // Place the player counter
```

```
// Check all squares around this square for opponents counter
for(rowdelta = -1 ; rowdelta <= 1 ; ++rowdelta)
{
  for(coldelta = -1; coldelta <= 1; ++coldelta)
  {
    // Don't check off the board, or the current square
    if((row == 0 && rowdelta == -1) || row + rowdelta >= SIZE ||
       (col == 0 && coldelta == -1) || col + coldelta >= SIZE ||
                              (rowdelta == 0 && coldelta == 0))
      continue;

    // Now check the square
    if(board[row + rowdelta][col + coldelta] == opponent)
    { // Found opponent so search in same direction for player counter
      x = row + rowdelta;           // Move to opponent
      y = col + coldelta;           // square

      for(;;)
      {
        x += rowdelta;              // Move to the
        y += coldelta;              // next square

        if(x >= SIZE || y >= SIZE || board[x][y] == ' ')// If blank square or off board...
          break;                                        // ...give up

        // If we find the player counter, go backward from here
        // changing all the opponents counters to player
        if(board[x][y] == player)
        {
          while(board[x -= rowdelta][y -= coldelta] == opponent) // Opponent?
            board[x][y] = player;                                // Yes, change it

          break;                    // We are done
        }
      }
    }
  }
}
```

The logic here is similar to that in the valid_moves() function for checking that a square is a valid move. The first step is to search the squares around the square indexed by the parameters row and col for an opponent counter. This is done in the nested loops:

```
for(rowdelta = -1; rowdelta <= 1; rowdelta++)
{
  for(coldelta = -1; coldelta <= 1; coldelta++)
  {
    ...
  }
}
```

When you find an opponent counter, the indefinite for loop heads off in the same direction looking for a player counter. If it falls off the edge of the board or finds a blank square, the break statement ends the for loop, and the outer loop continues to move to the next square around the selected square. If you do find a player counter, you back up, changing all the opponent counters to player counters:

```
// If we find the player counter, go backward from here
// changing all the opponents counters to player
 if(board[x][y] == player)
 {
   while(board[x -= rowdelta][y -= coldelta] == opponent) // Opponent?
     board[x][y] = player;                                // Yes, change it

   break;                          // We are done
 }
```

The break statement breaks out of the indefinite for loop.

Now that you have implemented this function, you can move on to the trickiest part of the program, which is implementing the function to make the computer's move. You'll adopt a relatively simple strategy for determining the computer's move. You'll evaluate each of the possible valid moves for the computer. For each valid computer move, you'll determine what the best move is that the player could make and determine a score for that. You'll then choose the computer move for which the player's best move produces the lowest score.

Before you get to write computer_move(), you'll implement a couple of helper functions. Helper functions are just functions that help in the implementation of an operation, in this case implementing the move for the computer. The first will be the function get_score(), which will calculate the score for a given board position. You can add the following code to the end of the source file for this:

```
int get_score(char board[][SIZE], char player)
{
  return player_counters(board, player) -
                   player_counters(board, (player == player_c) ? comp_c : player_c);
}
```

This is quite simple. The score is calculated as the difference between the number of counters on the board for the player and the number of counters for the opponent.

The next helper function is best_move(), which will calculate and return the score for the best move of the current set of valid moves for a player. The code for this is as follows:

```
int best_move(char board[][SIZE], bool moves[][SIZE], char player)
{
  char new_board[SIZE][SIZE] = {0};    // Local copy of board
  int score = 0;                       // Best score
  int new_score = 0;                   // Score for current move

  // Check all valid moves to find the best
  for(size_t row = 0 ; row < SIZE ; ++row)
  {
    for(size_t col = 0 ; col < SIZE ; ++col)
    {
      if(!moves[row][col])             // if not a valid move...
        continue;                      // ...go to the next
```

```
      // Copy the board
      memcpy_s(new_board, board, sizeof(new_board));

      // Make move on the board copy
      make_move(new_board, row, col, player);

      // Get score for move
      new_score = get_score(new_board, player);

      if(score < new_score)              // If it's better...
        score = new_score;               // ...save it as best score.
    }
  }
  return score;                          // Return best score
}
```

Remember that you must add function prototypes for both of these helper functions. The complete set of function prototypes is

```
void display(char board[][SIZE]);
void reset_board(char board[][SIZE]);
int valid_moves(char board[][SIZE], bool moves[][SIZE], char player);
int player_counters(char board[][SIZE], char player);
void make_move(char board[][SIZE], size_t row, size_t col, char player);
void computer_move(char board[][SIZE], bool moves[][SIZE], char player);
int best_move(char board[][SIZE], bool moves[][SIZE], char player);
int get_score(char board[][SIZE], char player);
```

Step 4

The last piece to complete the program is the implementation of the computer_move() function. The code for this is as follows:

```
void computer_move(char board[][SIZE], bool moves[][SIZE], char player)
{
  size_t best_row = 0;                 // Best row index
  size_t best_col = 0;                 // Best column index
  int new_score = 0;                   // Score for current move
  int score = SIZE*SIZE;               // Minimum opponent score
  char temp_board[SIZE][SIZE];         // Local copy of board
  bool temp_moves[SIZE][SIZE];         // Local valid moves array

  // Identify opponent
  char opponent = (player == player_c) ? comp_c : player_c;

  // Go through all valid moves
  for(size_t row = 0 ; row < SIZE ; ++row)
  {
```

```
  for(size_t col = 0 ; col < SIZE ; ++col)
  {
    if(!moves[row][col])
      continue;

    // First make a copy of the board array
    memcpy_s(temp_board, SIZE*SIZE, board, SIZE*SIZE);

    // Now make this move on the temporary board
    make_move(temp_board, row, col, player);

    // find valid moves for the opponent after this move
    valid_moves(temp_board, temp_moves, opponent);

    // Now find the score for the opponent's best move
    new_score = best_move(temp_board, temp_moves, opponent);

    if(new_score < score)          // If it's worse...
    {                              // ...save this move
      score = new_score;           // Record new lowest opponent score
      best_row = row;              // Record best move row
      best_col = col;              // and column
    }
  }
  }
  make_move(board, best_row, best_col, player);   // Make the best move
}
```

This isn't difficult with the two helper functions. Remember you're going to choose the move for which the opponent's subsequent best move is a minimum. In the main loop that is controlled by the counters row and col, you try each valid move in turn on the copy of the current board that's stored in the local array temp_board. After each move, you call the valid_moves() function to calculate the valid moves for the opponent in that position and store the results in the temp_moves array. You then call the best_move() function to get the score for the best opponent move from the valid set stored in the array temp_moves. If that score is less than any previous score, you save the score, the row, and the column index for that computer move as a possible best move.

The variable score is initialized with a value that's higher than any possible score, and you go about trying to minimize this (because it's the strength of the opponent's next move) to find the best possible move for the computer. After all of the valid computer moves have been tried, best_row and best_col contain the row and column index, respectively, for the move that minimizes the opponent's next move. You then call make_move() to make the best move for the computer.

You can now compile and execute the game. The game starts something like this:

```
    a   b   c   d   e   f
  +---+---+---+---+---+---+
1 |   |   |   |   |   |   |
  +---+---+---+---+---+---+
2 |   |   |   |   |   |   |
  +---+---+---+---+---+---+
3 |   |   | O | @ |   |   |
  +---+---+---+---+---+---+
4 |   |   | @ | O |   |   |
  +---+---+---+---+---+---+
5 |   |   |   |   |   |   |
  +---+---+---+---+---+---+
6 |   |   |   |   |   |   |
  +---+---+---+---+---+---+
Please enter your move: 3e
    a   b   c   d   e   f
  +---+---+---+---+---+---+
1 |   |   |   |   |   |   |
  +---+---+---+---+---+---+
2 |   |   |   |   |   |   |
  +---+---+---+---+---+---+
3 |   |   | O | O | O |   |
  +---+---+---+---+---+---+
4 |   |   | @ | O |   |   |
  +---+---+---+---+---+---+
5 |   |   |   |   |   |   |
  +---+---+---+---+---+---+
6 |   |   |   |   |   |   |
  +---+---+---+---+---+---+
```

The computer doesn't play too well because it looks only one move ahead, and it doesn't have any favoritism for edge and corner cells. Also, the board is only 6 × 6. If you want to change the board size, just change the value of SIZE to another even number. The program will work just as well.

Summary

If you've arrived at this point without too much trouble, you're well on your way to becoming a competent C programmer. This chapter and the previous one have covered all you really need to write well-structured C programs. A functional structure is inherent to the C language, and you should keep your functions short with a well-defined purpose. This is the essence of good C code. You should now be able to approach your own programming problems with a functional structure in mind right from the outset.

Don't forget the flexible power that pointers give you as a C programmer. They can greatly simplify many programming problems, and you should frequently find yourself using them as function arguments and return values. After a while, it will be a natural inclination. The real teacher is experience, so going over the programs in this chapter again will be extremely useful if you don't feel completely confident. And once you feel confident with what's in this book, you should be raring to have a go at some problems of your own.

There's still one major new piece of language territory in C that you have yet to deal with, and it's all about data and how to structure them. You'll look at data in Chapter 11. But before you do that, you need to cover input/output in more detail than you have so far. Handling input and output is an important and fascinating aspect of programming, so that's where you're headed next.

EXERCISES

The following exercises enable you to try out what you've learned in this chapter. If you get stuck, look back over the chapter for help. If you're still stuck, you can download the solutions from the Source Code/Download area of the Apress website (www.apress.com), but that really should be a last resort.

Exercise 9-1. A function with the prototype

```
double power(double x, int n);
```

should calculate and return the value of x^n. That is, the expression power(5.0, 4) will evaluate 5.0 * 5.0 * 5.0 * 5.0, which will result in the value 625.0.

Implement the power() function as a recursive function (so it should call itself) and demonstrate its operation with a suitable version of main().

Exercise 9-2. Implement functions with the following prototypes:

```
double add(double a, double b);        // Returns a+b
double subtract(double a, double b);   // Returns a-b
double multiply(double a, double b);   // Returns a*b
double array_op(double array[], size_t size, double (*pfun)(double,double));
```

The parameters for the array_op() function are the array to be operated on, the number of elements in the array, and a pointer to a function defining the operation to be applied between successive elements. The array_op() function should be implemented so that when the subtract() function is passed as the third argument, the function combines the elements with alternating signs. So for an array with four elements, x_1, x_2, x_3, and x_4, it computes the value of $x_1 - x_2 + x_3 - x_4$. To multiply, it will just be the product of the elements, $x_1 \times x_2 \times x_3 \times x_4$, for example.

Demonstrate the operation of these functions with a suitable version of main().

Exercise 9-3. Define a function that will accept an array of pointers to strings as an argument and return a pointer to a string that contains all the strings joined into a single string, each terminated by a newline character. If an original string in the input array has newline as its last character, the function shouldn't add another to the string. Write a program to demonstrate this function in operation by reading a number of strings from the keyboard and outputting the resultant combined string.

Exercise 9-4. Implement a function that has the following prototype:

```
char *to_string(int count, double first, ...);
```

This function should return a string that contains string representations of the second and subsequent arguments, each to two decimal places and separated by commas. The first argument is a count of the number of arguments that follow. Write a suitable version of main() to demonstrate the operation of your function.

CHAPTER 10

Essential Input and Output

In this chapter, you're going to look in more detail at input from the keyboard and output to the screen. The bad news is that there's quite a lot of it, and it's not exactly exciting stuff. The good news is that everything in this chapter is fairly easy, although there may be moments when you feel it's all becoming a bit of a memory test, but once you have learned it, it all applies to file input and output too. Treat this as a breather from the previous two chapters. After all, you don't have to memorize everything you see here; you can always come back to it when you need it.

Like most modern programming languages, C has no input or output capability within the language. All operations of this kind are provided by functions from standard libraries. You've been using many of these functions to provide input from the keyboard and output to the screen in the preceding chapters.

This chapter will put all the pieces together into some semblance of order and round it out with the aspects I haven't explained so far. You don't have a program demonstrating a problem solution with this chapter for the simple reason that I don't really cover anything that requires any practice on a substantial example (it's that easy).

In this chapter, you'll learn

- How to read data from the keyboard

- How to format data for output on the screen

- How to deal with character output

Input and Output Streams

Up to now, you've primarily used scanf_s() for keyboard input and printf() for output to the screen. There has been nothing in particular about the way you've used these functions to specify where the input came from or where the output went. The information that scanf_s()received could have come from anywhere, as long as it was a suitable stream of characters. There was nothing that characterized the data source as the keyboard. Similarly, the output from printf()could have been going anywhere with no specific indication that it was the command line on your display. This is no accident: the standard serial input/output functions in C have been designed to be device independent, so that the details of how the transfer of data to or from a specific device is managed aren't a concern of the programmer. The C library functions and the operating system make sure that operations with a specific device are executed correctly.

Each serial input source and output destination in C is called a *stream*. An *input stream* is a serial source of data that can be read into your program, and an *output stream* is a destination for serial data that originates in your program. A stream is independent of the physical piece of equipment involved, such as the display or the keyboard. Each device that a program uses can have one or more streams associated with it, depending on whether it's simply a one-way device, such as a keyboard, or a device that can represent multiple data sources or destinations, such as a disk drive.

© German Gonzalez-Morris and Ivor Horton 2020
G. Gonzalez-Morris and I. Horton, *Beginning C*, https://doi.org/10.1007/978-1-4842-5976-4_10

A disk drive typically contains multiple files. The correspondence is between a stream and the source or destination of the data, not between a stream and the device, so you associate a file that is to be read or written with a stream. The stream that you associate with a particular file could be an input stream, so you could only read from the file. It could also be an output stream, in which case you could only write to the file. A further possibility is that the stream could allow input and output, so reading and writing to the file would both be possible. Obviously, if the stream that is associated with a file is an input stream, the file must have been written at some time so it contained some data. You could also associate a stream with a file on a CD-ROM or DVD drive. When this device is read-only, the stream would, of necessity, be an input stream.

There are two further subdivisions of input and output streams. A stream can be a *character stream*, which is also referred to as a *text stream*, or it can be a *binary stream*. The main difference between these is that data transferred to or from a character stream are treated as a sequence of characters that may be modified by the library routine performing the input/output according to a format specification. Data that are transferred to or from a binary stream are just a sequence of bytes that are not modified in any way. I'll discuss binary streams in Chapter 12 when I cover reading and writing disk files.

■ **Note**   Writing graphical output to your display or writing to a printer requires specialized functions that are provided by the host operating system.

Standard Streams

A stream will have a name that identifies it. C has three predefined *standard streams* that are automatically available in any program, provided, of course, you've included the stdio.h header file into your program. These standard streams are stdin, stdout, and stderr, which correspond to the keyboard, normal output to the command line, and error output to the command line, respectively. No initialization or preparation is necessary to use these streams because they are each preassigned to a specific physical device. You just have to apply the appropriate library function that sends data to them.

The stderr stream is the stream to which error messages from the C library are sent, and you can direct your own error messages to stderr if you wish. By default, the destination for data written to both streams is the command line. The main difference between stdout and stderr is that output to stdout is buffered in memory so the data you write to it won't necessarily be transferred immediately to the device, whereas stderr is unbuffered so data you write to it is always transferred immediately to the device. With a buffered stream, your program transfers data to or from a buffer area in memory, and the data transfer to or from the physical device occurs asynchronously. This makes the input and output operations much more efficient. The advantage of using an unbuffered stream for error messages is that you can be sure that the messages will actually be displayed, but the output operations will be inefficient; a buffered stream is efficient but may not get flushed when a program fails for some reason, so the output may never be seen. I won't discuss this further, other than to say stderr points to the display screen.

Both stdin and stdout can be reassigned to files, instead of the default of keyboard and screen, by using host operating system commands. This offers you a lot of flexibility. If you want to run your program several times with the same data, during testing, for example, you could prepare the data as a text file and redirect stdin to the file. This enables you to rerun the program with the same data without having to reenter it each time. By redirecting the output from your program to a file, you can easily retain it for future reference, and you could use a text editor to access it or search it.

Input from the Keyboard

There are two forms of input from the keyboard on stdin that you've already seen in previous chapters: *formatted input*, which is provided primarily by the scanf_s() function that is the safe version of scanf(), and *unformatted input*, in which you receive the raw character data from a function such as getchar(). There's rather more to both of these possibilities, so let's look at them in detail.

Formatted Keyboard Input

As you know, the scanf_s() function reads characters from stdin and converts them to one or more values according to the format specifiers in a format control string. The prototype of the scanf_s() function is as follows:

```
int scanf_s(const char * restrict format, ... );
```

The old scanf() function has a similar prototype. The difference between scanf() and scanf_s() is that the latter requires two arguments for each input data controlled by c, s, and [specifiers (I'll discuss these conversion specifiers later in this chapter), whereas the former just requires one argument for these. The first of the pair of arguments is the address of where the input is to be stored, and the second is the number of bytes pointed to by the first argument. The second of the pair of arguments is used to specify how many bytes are available to store the data that is read. The function will return EOF to indicate an error if the number of bytes specified is insufficient to store the data that is read. The scanf() provides no such protection because you only supply the address of where the data are to go. All other conversion specifications just require a single argument that is an address.

The format control string parameter is of type const char*, a pointer to a constant character string as shown here. However, this usually appears as an explicit argument in the function call, such as this:

```
scanf_s("%lf", &variable);
```

But there's nothing to prevent you from writing this:

```
char str[] = "%lf";
scanf_s(str, &variable);
```

The scanf_s() function makes use of the facility of handling a variable number of arguments, which you learned about in Chapter 9. The format control string is basically a coded description of how scanf_s() should convert the incoming character stream to the values required and embed them in the string. Following the format control string, you can have one or more optional arguments. For each input read with c, s, and [specifiers, the first corresponding argument is a pointer to the memory where the input is to be stored, and the second corresponding argument is the number of bytes pointed to by the previous argument. For all other conversions, the corresponding argument is an address in which the converted input value is to be stored.

The scanf_s() reads from stdin until it comes to the end of the format control string or until an error condition stops the input process. This sort of error is the result of input that doesn't correspond to what is expected with the current format specifier. Something I haven't previously noted is that scanf_s() returns a value of type int, which is the count of the number of input values read. This provides a way for you to detect when an error occurs by comparing the value returned with the number of input values you are expecting.

Input Format Control Strings

The format control string you use with scanf_s() isn't precisely the same as that used with printf(). For one thing, putting one or more whitespace characters—space ' ', tab '\t', or newline '\n'—in the format control string causes scanf_s() to read and ignore whitespace characters up to the next nonwhitespace character in the input. A single whitespace character in the format control string causes any number of consecutive whitespace characters to be ignored. You can therefore include as many whitespace characters as you wish in the format string to make it more readable. Note that whitespace characters are ignored by scanf_s() by default except when you are reading data using %c, %[ ], or %n specification (see Table 10-1).

Any nonwhitespace character other than % will cause scanf_s() to read but not store successive occurrences of the character. If you want scanf_s() to ignore commas separating values in the input, for instance, just precede each format specifier by a comma. There are other differences too, as you'll see when I discuss formatted output in the section "Output to the Screen" a bit later in this chapter.

The most general form of a format specifier is shown in Figure 10-1.

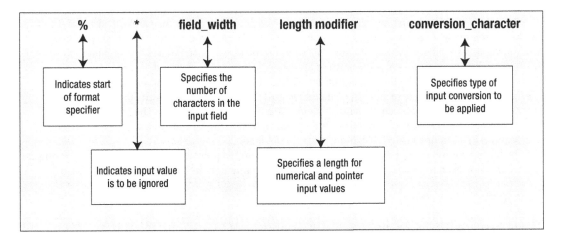

Figure 10-1. *The general form of an input specifier*

Let's take a look at what the various parts of this general form mean:

- The % simply indicates the start of the format specifier. It must always be present.

- The next * is optional. If you include it, it indicates that the next input value is to be ignored. This isn't normally used with input from the keyboard. It does become useful, however, when stdin has been reassigned to a file and you don't want to process all the values that appear within the file in your program.

- The field width is optional. It's an integer specifying the number of characters that scanf_s() should assume for the current value being input. This allows you to input a sequence of values without spaces between them. This is also often quite useful when reading files.

- The length specification is also optional, and it can be any of the following:

  - h can only be included with an integer conversion specifier that is d, i, o, u, x, X, or n and indicates that the input is to be converted as signed short or unsigned short.

  - hh applies to the same conversion specifiers as h and indicates that the input is to be converted as signed char or unsigned char.

  - l (lowercase L) indicates long or unsigned long when preceding an integer conversion specifier and double when preceding a, A, e, E, f, F, g, or G conversion specifier. Prefixing the c specification indicates that a wide character conversion is to be applied, so the input is read as type wchar_t, which I'll explain in Chapter 14.

  - L applies to the a, A, e, E, f, F, g, or G conversion specifier and indicates that the value is to be converted as type long double.

  - ll (two lowercase Ls) applies to integer conversions and specifies that the input is to be stored as type long long or unsigned long long.

  - j applies to integer conversion specifiers and indicates that the input is to be converted to type intmax_t or uintmax_t. These types are defined in the stdint.h header, and I'll explain them in Chapter 14.

  - z applies to integer conversion specifiers and indicates the input is to be converted to type size_t. Because size_t is implementation defined, you may get compiler warnings if you are reading into a variable of type size_t without using this prefix.

  - t applies to an integer conversion specifier and indicates the input is to be stored as type ptrdiff_t, which is an implementation-defined integer type for values that are the difference between two pointers. Type ptrdiff_t is defined in stdint.h.

- The conversion character specifies the type of conversion to be carried out on the input stream and therefore must be included. The possible characters and their meanings are shown in Table 10-1.

Table 10-1. *Conversion Characters and Their Meanings*

Conversion character	Meaning
d	Reads the input as a signed decimal integer
i	Reads the input as a signed integer. If the input begins with 0, then the input is assumed to be octal. If the input starts with 0x or 0X, then hexadecimal input is assumed; otherwise, decimal input is assumed
o	Reads the input assuming it is a signed octal integer
u	Reads the input as an unsigned integer
x	Reads the input as a signed hexadecimal integer
c	Reads the number of characters specified by the field width as type char, including whitespace. If the field width specification is absent, one character will be read. If you want to ignore preceding whitespace when reading characters, just precede the format specification by a whitespace character. Two arguments are required corresponding to this specification: a pointer to char and the number of bytes pointed to. If the l length modifier is present, the characters are converted to wchar_t
s	Reads a string of successive nonwhitespace characters as type char, starting with the next nonwhitespace character. This specifier required two arguments: a pointer to type char and the number of bytes pointed to. If the l length modifier is present, the characters are converted to wchar_t
[]	Reads characters from the specified set between the square brackets. The first character not found in the set ends the input. For example, the specification %[ab] will only read successive characters that are a or b. To include a ']' character in the set, it must be the first character following the initial left square bracket. Thus, %[]ab] reads characters as long as they are a, b, or]. If the first character after [is ^, then characters are read if they were not in the set that follows. The specification %[^]ab] reads characters as long as they are not a, b, or]. Two arguments are required, as for the c and s specifiers. If the l length modifier is present, the characters are converted to wchar_t
a, A, e, E, f, F, G, or g	Converts the input to type float. A sign, a decimal point, and an exponent in the input are optional
%	Reads a % character that is not stored. Thus, the specification to skip a % character is %%
p	Reads input as a pointer. The argument should be of type void**. The input form is implementation defined, so consult your compiler and library documentation
n	No input is read, but the number of characters that have been read from the keyboard up to this point is stored in the memory pointed to by the corresponding argument, which should be of type int*. Reading with this specification does not increment the value of the assignment count that is returned

The %[ ] specification provides a lot of flexibility. For example, the specification %[0123456789.-] will read a numerical value as a string, so if the input is –1.25, it will be read as "-1.25". To read a string consisting of just the lowercase letters a–z, you could use the specification %[abcdefghijklmnopqrstuvwxyz]. Although it isn't required by the standard, many C library implementations support the form %[a-z] to read a string consisting of any lowercase letters. The specification %[^,] will read everything in the string except a comma, so this form will enable you to read a series of strings separated by commas.

Table 10-2 shows a few examples of applying the various options.

Table 10-2. *Examples of Options in Conversion Specifications*

Specification	Description
%lf	Reads the next value as type double
%*d	Reads the next integer value but doesn't store it
%15c	Reads the next 15 characters as type char
\n%c	Reads the next character as type char ignoring whitespace characters
%10lld	Reads the next ten characters as an integer value of type long long
%Lf	Reads the next value as a floating-point value of type long double
%hu	Reads the next value as type unsigned short

Let's exercise some of these format control strings with practical examples.

TRY IT OUT: EXERCISING FORMATTED INPUT

This example reads various types of data three times with various format strings:

```
// Program 10.1          Exercising formatted input
#define __STDC_WANT_LIB_EXT1__ 1
#include <stdio.h>

#define SIZE  20                          // Max characters in a word
void try_input(char *prompt, char *format);   // Input test function

int main(void)
{
  try_input("Enter as input: -2.35 15 25 ready2go\n",
            "%f %d %d %[abcdefghijklmnopqrstuvwxyz] %*1d %s%n" );

  try_input("\nEnter the same input again: ",
            "%4f %4d %d %*d %[abcdefghijklmnopqrstuvwxyz] %*1d %[^o]%n");

  try_input("\nEnter as input: -2.3A 15 25 ready2go\n",
            "%4f %4d %d %*d %[abcdefghijklmnopqrstuvwxyz] %*1d %[^o]%n");
  return 0;
}
```

```
void try_input(char* prompt, char *format)
{
  int value_count = 0;                  // Count of input values read
  float fp1 = 0.0f;                     // Floating-point value read
  int i = 0;                            // First integer read
  int j = 0;                            // Second integer read
  char word1[SIZE] = " ";               // First string read
  char word2[SIZE] = " ";               // Second string read
  int byte_count = 0;                   // Count of input bytes read
  printf(prompt);
  value_count = scanf_s(format, &fp1, &i , &j,
                 word1, sizeof(word1), word2, sizeof(word2), &byte_count);
  fflush(stdin);                        // Clear the input buffer
  printf("The input format string for scanf_s() is:\n    \"%s\"\n", format);
  printf("Count of bytes read = %d\n", byte_count);
  printf("Count of values read = %d\n", value_count);
  printf("fp1 = %f   i = %d   j = %d\n", fp1, i, j);
  printf("word1 = %s   word2 = %s\n", word1, word2);
}
```

There are three sets of output from this program, and I'll discuss each set individually after I explain the code.

How It Works

The `try_input()` function has two parameters: a string that specifies what the keyboard input should be and a format string to be used by `scanf_s()` to read the input. Implementing the input as a function allows you to see what happens to the input with varying format strings with just one statement for each test.

The `try_input()` function defines the variables that will receive the input and then issues a prompt using the string passed as the first argument. The input is then read by calling `scanf_s()` with the format string specified by the second argument to `try_input()`. The function then outputs the format string that was used for input so you can see from the output what is going on. The first block of output is

```
Enter as input: -2.35 15 25 ready2go
-2.35 15 25 ready2go
The input format string for scanf_s() is:
    "%f %d %d %[abcdefghijklmnopqrstuvwxyz] %*1d %s%n"
Count of bytes read = 20
Count of values read = 5
fp1 = -2.350000   i = 15   j = 25
word1 = ready   word2 = go
```

The first three input values are read in a straightforward way using simple conversion specifiers. The fourth input value is read using the specifier %[abcdefghijklmnopqrstuvwxyz], which will read a sequence of lowercase letters as a string. This reads the string "ready" and stores it in word1. Input stops for word1 after "ready" because the character that follows is '2', and this isn't in the set between the square brackets. The '2' is still in the input buffer, so this is read using the next conversion specifier %*1d. The * in the specification causes the input to be read but not stored, and because the field width is 1, this only applies to one character. The word "go" is read next and stored in word2 using the %s specifier. The %n specifier does not extract data from the input stream; it just stores the number of bytes that the scanf_s()function has read from the input stream up to that point, and that value is stored in byte_count.

The value of value_count holds the count of the number of values processed that is returned by the scanf_s() function. As you can see, the value reflects the number of values stored and doesn't include the value read by the %*1d specification.

It isn't essential that you enter all the data on a single line. If you key in the first two values and press Enter, scanf_s() will wait for you to enter the next value on the next line.

■ **Note** The arguments following word1 and word2 are required by scanf_s()so it can make sure it does not overwrite memory that it shouldn't. If you don't have scanf_s() available, you can use scanf() and omit the length arguments for word1 and word2.

The next block of output is

```
Enter the same input again: -2.35 15 25 ready2go
The input format string for scanf_s() is:
    "%4f %4d %d %*d %[abcdefghijklmnopqrstuvwxyz] %*1d %[^o]%n"
Count of bytes read = 19
Count of values read = 5
fp1 = -2.300000   i = 5   j = 15
word1 = ready   word2 = g
```

Because you specified a field width of 4 for the floating-point value, the first four characters are taken as defining the value of the first input variable. The next integer value is read as 5, the last digit following the value read as −2.3. This shows that in spite of the fact that you specified a field width of 4 for the second integer, it appears to have been overridden. This is a consequence of the space following digit 5, which terminates the input scanning for the value being read. So whatever value you put as a field width, the scanning of the input line for a given value stops as soon as it meets the first whitespace character. You could change the specifiers for the integer values to %12d, and the result would still be the same for the given input. The integer that's stored in j is 15, and the value 25 is read and ignored by the %*d specification; word1 is read as before, and the %*1d specification reads and discards the '2' that follows. The last string is read into word2 as just "g" because the specification %[^o] accepts any character in the string except the letter 'o'. Because the letter 'o' is not read as part of the input, the byte count is now 19.

The third block of output is

```
Enter as input: -2.3A 15 25 ready2go
-2.3A 15 25 ready2go
The input format string for scanf_s() is:
    "%4f %4d %d %*d %[abcdefghijklmnopqrstuvwxyz] %*1d %[^o]%n"
Count of bytes read = 0
Count of values read = 1
fp1 = -2.300000   i = 0   j = 0
word1 =    word2 =
```

The count of the number of input values is 1, corresponding to a value for the variable fp1 being read. The count of the number of bytes read is 0, which is clearly incorrect, the reason being that you never got to the point of storing a value in byte_count. The A in the input stream is invalid in numerical input, so the whole process stops dead. No values for variables i and j, and word1 and word2 are processed, and no value is stored for the byte count. This demonstrates how unforgiving scanf_s() and scanf() really are. A single invalid character in the input stream will stop your program in its tracks. If you want to be able to recover from the situation in which invalid input is entered, you can use the return value from scanf_s() as a measure of whether all the necessary input has been processed correctly and include some code to recover from the situation when necessary.

The simplest approach would perhaps be to print an irritable message and then demand the whole input be repeated. But beware of errors in your code getting you into a permanent loop in this circumstance. You'll need to think through all of the possible ways that things might go wrong if you're going to produce a robust program.

Characters in the Input Format String

You can include a sequence of one or more characters that isn't a format conversion specifier within the input format string. If you do this, you're indicating that you expect the same characters to appear in the input and that scanf_s() should read them but not store them. These have to be matched exactly, character for character, by the data in the input stream. Any variation will terminate the input scanning process in scanf_s().

TRY IT OUT: CHARACTERS IN THE INPUT FORMAT STRING

You can illustrate the effect of including characters in the input format string with the following example:

```c
// Program 10.2 Characters in the format control string
#define __STDC_WANT_LIB_EXT1__ 1
#include <stdio.h>

int main(void)
{
  int i = 0;
  int j = 0;
  int value_count = 0;
  float fp1 = 0.0f;
```

```
    printf("Enter: fp1 = 3.14159 i = 7 8\n");

    printf("\nInput:");
    value_count = scanf_s("fp1 = %f i = %d %d", &fp1, &i , &j);

    printf("\nOutput:\n");
    printf("Count of values read = %d\n", value_count);
    printf("fp1 = %f\ti = %d\tj = %d\n", fp1, i, j);
    return 0;
}
```

Here's an example of the output:

```
Enter: fp1 = 3.14159 i = 7 8
Input:fp1 = 3.14159 i = 7 8

Output:
Count of values read = 3
fp1 = 3.141590  i = 7   j = 8
```

How It Works

It doesn't matter whether the blanks before and after the = are included in the input; they're whitespace characters and are therefore ignored. The important thing is to include the same nonwhitespace characters that appear in the format control string in the correct sequence and at the correct place in the input. Try an input line in which this isn't the case:

```
Enter: fp1 = 3.14159 i = 7 8

Input:fp1 = 3.14159

i=7 j=8

Output:
Count of values read = 2
fp1 = 3.141590  i = 7   j = 0
```

Now only two values are read. This is because the j in the input stops processing immediately, and no value is received by the variable j. The input processing of characters by scanf_s() is also case sensitive. If you input Fp1= instead of fp1=, no values will be processed at all, because the mismatch with the capital F will stop the scanning before any values are entered.

■ **Note**   The fact that scanf_s()can stop processing input in this way is a strong argument for always initializing your variables. If scanf_s() fails, at least your variables for which input was not read will have sensible values and not arbitrary junk values.

Variations on Floating-Point Input

When you're reading floating-point values formatted using scanf_s(),not only do you have a choice of specification that you use but also you can enter the values in a variety of forms. You can see this with another simple example.

TRY IT OUT: FLOATING-POINT INPUT

With this example, you can try various forms of specifier and various ways in which you can enter the input values:

```
// Program 10.3 Floating-Point Input
#define __STDC_WANT_LIB_EXT1__ 1
#include <stdio.h>

int main(void)
{
  float fp1 = 0.0f;
  float fp2 = 0.0f;
  float fp3 = 0.0f;
  int value_count = 0;
  printf("Enter: 3.14.314E1.0314e+02\n");

  printf("Input:\n");
  value_count = scanf_s("%f %f %f", &fp1, &fp2, &fp3);

  printf("\nOutput:\n");
  printf("Number of values read = %d\n", value_count);
  printf("fp1 = %f   fp2 = %f   fp3 = %f\n", fp1, fp2, fp3);
  return 0;
}
```

Here's an example of output from this program:

```
Enter: 3.14.314E1.0314e+02
Input:
3.14.314E1.0314e+02

Output:
Number of values read = 3
fp1 = 3.140000   fp2 = 3.140000   fp3 = 3.140000
```

How It Works

This example demonstrates three different ways of entering the same value. The first is a straightforward decimal value, the second has an exponent value defined by the E1 that indicates the value is to be multiplied by 10, and the third has an exponent value of e+02 and therefore the mantissa is to be multiplied by 100. As you can see, when you're reading a floating-point value with the %f specification, you have the option of whether to include an exponent. If you do include an exponent, you can define it beginning with either e or E. You also have the option to include a sign for the exponent value, + or -, and, of course, the value can be signed too. There are countless variations possible here.

You could try changing the scanf_s() statement to the following:

```
value_count = scanf_s("%e %g %a", &fp1, &fp2, &fp3);
```

The output with this statement in the program is the same as before.

Clearly all four format specifications work equally well with the various input forms. The variation between them is only when you use them for output with the printf() function. I recommend that you experiment with the various possibilities here.

Reading Hexadecimal and Octal Values

As you saw earlier, you can read hexadecimal values from the input stream using the format specifier %x. For octal values, you use %o. These are very straightforward, but let's see them working in an example.

```
┌────────────────────────────────────────────────────────────────────┐
│        TRY IT OUT: READING HEXADECIMAL AND OCTAL VALUES              │
└────────────────────────────────────────────────────────────────────┘
```

Try the following example:

```c
// Program 10.4 Reading hexadecimal and octal values
#define __STDC_WANT_LIB_EXT1__  1
#include <stdio.h>

int main(void)
{
  int i = 0;
  int j = 0;
  int k = 0;
  int n = 0;

  printf("Enter three integer values:");
  n = scanf_s(" %d %x %o", &i , &j, &k );

  printf("\nOutput:\n");
  printf("%d values read.\n", n);
  printf("i = %d   j = %d   k = %d\n", i, j, k );
  return 0;
}
```

Here's some sample output:

```
Enter three integer values:12 12 12

Output:
3 values read.
i = 12   j = 18   k = 10
```

How It Works

You read three values entered as 12 in different ways. The first is read with a decimal format specifier %d, the second with a hexadecimal format specifier %x, and the third with an octal format specifier %o. The output shows that 12 in hexadecimal is 18 in decimal notation and 12 in octal is 10 in decimal notation.

Hexadecimal data entry can be useful when you want to enter bit patterns (sequences of ones and zeros), as they're easier to specify in hexadecimal than in decimal. Each hexadecimal digit corresponds to 4 bits, so you can specify a 16-bit word as four hexadecimal digits. Octal is hardly ever used, and it appears here mainly for historical reasons.

Note the following example of output:

```
Enter three integer values:18 18 18

Output:
3 values read.
i = 18    j = 24    k = 1
```

Here the first two values are read correctly as 18, as a hexadecimal value is indeed 24 in decimal notation. However, the third value is read as 1. This is because 8 isn't a legal octal digit and therefore stops scanning. Octal digits are 0–7.

You can enter hexadecimal values using A–F or a–f or even a mixture if you're so inclined. Here's another example of output:

```
Enter three integer values:12 aA 17

Output:
3 values read.
i = 12    j = 170    k = 15
```

The hexadecimal value aA is 10 × 16 + 10, which is 170 as a decimal value. The octal value 17 is 1 × 8 + 7, which is 15 as a decimal value.

There's no difference between using "%x" and "%X" with scanf_s(), but they'll have a different effect when you use them with printf() for output. You can demonstrate this by changing the last printf() statement to the following:

```
    printf("i = %x    j = %X    k = %d\n", i, j, k );
```

This now outputs the first two values in hexadecimal notation. You can get the following output with the input shown:

```
Enter three integer values:26 ae 77

Output:
3 values read.
i = 1a    j = AE    k = 63
```

%x produces hexadecimal output using hexadecimal digits a–f, and %X produces output using A–F.

Reading Characters Using scanf_s()

You read strings in the first example, but there are more possibilities. You can read a single character and store it as type char using the format specifier %c. For a string of characters, you use either the specifier %s or the specifier %[ ]. In this case, the string is stored as a null-terminated string with ' \0 ' as the last character. With the %[ ] format specification, the string to be read must include only the characters that appear between the square brackets, or if the first character between the square brackets is ^, the string must contain only characters that are *not* among those following the ^ character. Thus, %[aeiou] will read a string that consists only of vowels. The first character that isn't a vowel will signal the end of the string. The specification %[^aeiou] reads a string that contains any character that isn't a vowel. The first vowel or whitespace character will signal the end of the string.

Note that one interesting aspect of the %[ ] specification is that it enables you to read a string containing spaces, something that the %s specification can't do. You just need to include a space as one of the characters between the square brackets.

TRY IT OUT: READING CHARACTERS AND STRINGS

You can see these character reading capabilities in operation with the following example:

```
// Program 10.5 Reading characters with scanf_s()
#define __STDC_WANT_LIB_EXT1__ 1
#include <stdio.h>
#define MAX_TOWN 10
int main(void)
{
  char initial = ' ';
  char name[80] = { ' ' };
  char age[4] = { '0' };
  printf("Enter your first initial: ");
  scanf_s("%c", &initial, sizeof(initial));
  printf("Enter your first name: " );
  scanf_s("%s", name, sizeof(name));
  fflush(stdin);

  if(initial  != name[0])
    printf("%s,you got your initial wrong.\n", name);
  else
    printf("Hi, %s. Your initial is correct. Well done!\n", name );
  printf("Enter your full name and your age separated by a comma:\n" );
  scanf_s("%[^,] , %[0123456789]", name, sizeof(name), age, sizeof(age));
  printf("\nYour name is %s and you are %s years old.\n", name, age );
  return 0;
}
```

Here's some output from this program:

```
Enter your first initial: I
Enter your first name: Ivor
Hi, Ivor. Your initial is correct. Well done!
Enter your full name and your age separated by a comma:
Ivor Horton  ,  98
Your name is Ivor Horton   and you are 98 years old.
```

How It Works

This program expects you to enter your first initial and then your first name. It checks that the first letter of your name is the same as the initial you entered. This works in a straightforward way, as you can see from the output.

Next, you're asked to enter your full name followed by your age, separated by a comma. The read operation is carried out by the following statement:

```
scanf_s("%[^,] , %[0123456789]", name, sizeof(name), age, sizeof(age));
```

I deliberately spaced out the input data so you could see that the first input specification, `%[^,]`, reads any character as part of the string that isn't a comma, including spaces, hence the extra spaces following the name in the last line of output. You then have a comma in the control string that will cause `scanf_s()` to read the comma in the input and not store it. The input for `age` is read as a string with the specifier `%[0123456789]`. This will read any sequence of consecutive digits as a string. Of course, spaces following the comma are ignored.

Note that the comma in the input string is essential for the input to be read properly. If you leave it out, `scanf_s()` will read characters and store them as the name up to the limit specified by the third argument. It will continue looking for a comma and will not scan the input for the `age` value until it finds one. The space after the comma in the format string is also necessary.

If you try entering a space and then your initial as the first input, the program will treat the space as the value for `initial` and the single character you entered as your `name`. With the way the control string is defined, the first character you enter when using the `%c` specifier is taken to be the character, whatever it is. If you don't want a space to be accepted as the initial, you can fix this by writing the input statement as follows:

```
scanf_s(" %c", &initial, sizeof(initial));
```

Now the first character in the control string is a space, so `scanf_s()` will read and ignore any number of spaces and read the first character that isn't a space into `initial`.

■ **Caution**   Don't forget that the arguments to `scanf_s()` that specify where data are to be stored *must* be pointers. Perhaps the most common error is to forget the ampersand (&) when specifying single variables as arguments, particularly because you don't need it with `printf()`. Of course, the & isn't necessary if the argument is an array name or a pointer variable or a size specification.

String Input from the Keyboard

As you've seen, the `gets_s()` function in `stdio.h` will read a complete line of text as a string. The prototype of the function is as follows:

```
char *gets_s(char *str, rsize_t n);
```

This function reads up to n-1 successive characters into the memory pointed to by str until you press the Enter key. It appends the terminating null, '\0', in place of the newline character that is read when you press the Enter key. The return value is identical to the first argument, which is the address where the string has been stored. If an error occurs during input, str[0] will be set to the '\0' character. The following example provides a reminder of how it works.

TRY IT OUT: READING A STRING

Here's a simple program using gets_s():

```
// Program 10.6 Reading a string with gets_s()
#define __STDC_WANT_LIB_EXT1__ 1
#include <stdio.h>

int main(void)
{
  char initial[3] = {' '};
  char name[80] = {' '};

  printf("Enter your first initial:  ");
  gets_s(initial, sizeof(initial));
  printf("Enter your name:  " );
  gets_s(name, sizeof(name));
  if(initial[0] != name[0])
    printf("%s, you got your initial wrong.\n", name);
  else
    printf("Hi, %s. Your initial is correct. Well done!\n", name);
  return 0;
}
```

Here's some output from this program:

```
Enter your first initial:  M
Enter your name:  Mephistopheles
Hi, Mephistopheles. Your initial is correct. Well done!
```

How It Works

You read the initial and the name as strings using gets_s(). The function is very easy to use because there's no format specification involved; gets_s() will read characters until n-1 characters have been read or when you press the Enter key. The newline character is not stored.

When you want to retain the newline character, you can use the fgets() function that works like gets_s() except that it stores the newline from when the Enter key was pressed, and you must supply a third argument specifying the input stream. You could replace the statements that manage the input with the following:

```
printf("Enter your first initial:  ");
fgets(initial, sizeof(initial), stdin);
printf("Enter your name:  " );
fgets(name, sizeof(name), stdin);
```

The fgets() function reads up to one less than the number of characters specified by the second argument and appends the terminating '\0'. The fgets() function stores a newline character in the input string corresponding to the Enter key being pressed, whereas the gets_s() function does not. To avoid a newline being output by the printf() call that outputs the name, you would need to overwrite it like this:

```
size_t length = strnlen_s(name, sizeof(name));
name[length-1] = name[length];              // Overwrite the newline
```

For string input, using gets_s() or fgets() is the preferred approach unless you want to control the content of the string, in which case you can use %[]. The %[] specification is more convenient to use when the nonstandard %[a-z] form is supported, but remember that because this is nonstandard, your code is no longer as portable as it would be if you had used the standard form.

Single-Character Keyboard Input

The getc() function in stdio.h reads a single character from a stream and returns the character code as type int. The argument to getc() is the stream identifier. When the end of a stream is read, getc() returns the value EOF (end of file), which is a symbol that is always defined in stdio.h as a negative integer. Because type char can be signed or unsigned at the whim of the compiler writer, getc() does not return type char. If it did, EOF could not be returned if char was defined as an unsigned type. In general, when a function returns a value of type int where you might expect it to return type char, it is almost certainly because it needs to allow EOF to be returned.

The getchar() function reads one character at a time from stdin and is equivalent to calling getc() with stdin as the argument. The getchar() function is defined in stdio.h, and its prototype is

```
int getchar(void);
```

The getchar() function requires no arguments, and it returns the code for the character read from the input stream as type int.

The standard header stdio.h also declares the ungetc() function that enables you to put a character you have just read back into an input stream. The function requires two arguments: the first is the character to be pushed back into the stream, and the second is the identifier for the stream, which would be stdin for the standard input stream. The ungetc() function returns a value of type int that corresponds to the character pushed back into the stream, or a special character, EOF, if the operation fails.

In principle, you can push a succession of characters back into an input stream, but only one character is guaranteed. As I noted, a failure to push a character back into a stream will be indicated by EOF being returned by the function, so you should check for this if you are attempting to return several characters to a stream.

The ungetc() function is useful when you are reading input character by character and don't know how many characters make up a data unit. You might be reading an integer value, for example, but don't know how many digits there are. In this situation, the ungetc() function makes it possible for you to read a succession of characters using getchar(), and when you find you have read a character that is not a digit, you can return it to the stream. Here's a function that ignores spaces and tabs from the standard input stream using the getchar() and ungetc() functions:

```
void eatspaces(void)
{
  char ch = 0;
  while(isspace(ch = (char)getchar()));  // Read as long as there are spaces
  ungetc(ch, stdin);                     // Put back the nonspace character
}
```

The isspace() function that is declared in the ctype.h header file returns true when the argument is a whitespace character, which could be space, \f, \n, \r, \t, or \v. The while loop continues to read characters as long as they are whitespace characters, storing each character in ch. The first nonwhitespace character that is read will end the loop, and the character will be left in ch. The call to ungetc() returns the nonwhitespace character back to the stream for future processing.

Some implementations of C include the nonstandard header file conio.h. This header dates back to the days of DOS and Windows 3.0, but it can still be useful because it provides additional functions for character input and output. One of the most useful is _getch(), which reads a character from the keyboard without displaying it on the command line. Its prototype is

```
int _getch(void);
```

Strangely, there isn't a formal method for not-buffered-keystroke input function in C standard library (any ISO C version) nor in POSIX (all functions like getchar() and getc() are buffered); therefore, there is this old nonstandard header conio.h that some compilers from Microsoft, IBM, and ncurses have functions for this purpose (_getch(), getche()).

This function is particularly useful when you need to prevent others from being able to see what's being keyed in—for example, when a password is being entered. The conio.h header also declares the _ungetch() function:

```
int _ungetch(int ch);
```

The function pushes the character passed as the argument back into the stream so it can be read by the next _getch() call. It returns ch if the operation is successful or EOF if it is not. The operation will usually fail if you call it a second time before the previously pushed back character has been read.

Let's try out the getchar() and ungetc() functions in a working example.

TRY IT OUT: READING AND UNREADING CHARACTERS

This example assumes that the input consists of an arbitrary sequence of integers and names:

```
// Program 10.7 Reading and unreading characters
#define __STDC_WANT_LIB_EXT1__  1
#include <stdio.h>
#include <ctype.h>
#include <stdbool.h>
#include <string.h>

#define LENGTH 50                     // Name buffer size

// Function prototypes
void eatspaces(void);
bool getinteger(int *n);
char *getname(char *name, size_t length);
bool isnewline(void);

int main(void)
{
  int number;
  char name[LENGTH] = {'\0'};
  printf("Enter a sequence of integers and alphabetic names in a single line:\n");
  while(!isnewline())
```

```c
  {
    if(getinteger(&number))
      printf("Integer value:%8d\n", number);
    else if(strnlen_s(getname(name, LENGTH), LENGTH) > 0)
      printf("Name: %s\n", name);
    else
    {
      printf("Invalid input.\n");
      return 1;
    }
  }
  return 0;
}

// Function to ignore spaces from standard input
void eatspaces(void)
{
  char ch = 0;
  while(isspace(ch = (char)getchar()));
  ungetc(ch, stdin);
}

// Function to read an integer from standard input
bool getinteger(int *n)
{
  eatspaces();
  int value = 0;
  int sign = 1;
  char ch = 0;

  // Check first character
  if((ch = (char)getchar()) == '-')      // should be minus
    sign = -1;
  else if(isdigit(ch))                    // ...or a digit
   value = ch - '0';
  else  if(ch != '+')                     // ...or plus
  {
    ungetc(ch, stdin);
    return false;                         // Not an integer
  }

  // Find more digits
  while(isdigit(ch = (char)getchar()))
    value = 10*value + (ch - '0');

  ungetc(ch,stdin);                       // Push back non-digit character
  *n = value*sign;                        // Set the sign
  return true;
}
```

```
// Function to read an alphabetic name from input
char* getname(char *name, size_t length)
{
  eatspaces();                          // Remove leading spaces
  size_t count = 0;
  char ch = 0;
  while(isalpha(ch = (char)getchar())) // As long as there are letters...
  {
    name[count++] = ch;                 // ...store them in name.
    if(count == length - 1)             // Check for name full
      break;
  }

  name[count] = '\0';                   // Append string terminator
  if(count < length - 1)                // If we didn't end for name full...
    ungetc(ch, stdin);                  // ...return non-letter to stream
  return name;
}

// Function to check for newline
bool isnewline(void)
{
  char ch = 0;
  if((ch = (char)getchar()) == '\n')
    return true;

  ungetc(ch, stdin);                    // Not newline so put it back
  return false;
}
```

Here's an example of output from the program:

```
Enter a sequence of integers and alphabetic names in a single line:
Fred 22 34 Mary Jack 89 Jane
Name: Fred
Integer value:     22
Integer value:     34
Name: Mary
Name: Jack
Integer value:     89
Name: Jane
```

How It Works

There are four functions using getchar() and ungetc(). You saw the eatspaces() function in the previous section. The isnewline() function reads a character from the keyboard and returns true if it is a newline character and false if it is not. If the character is not newline, it is returned to the stream. This function is used to control when input ends in main().

The getinteger() function reads an optionally signed integer of arbitrary length from the keyboard. The first step removes leading spaces by calling the eatspaces() function. After checking for a sign or the first digit, the function continues to read digits from the keyboard in a loop:

```
while(isdigit(ch = (char)getchar()))
  value = 10*value + (ch - '0');
```

The digits are read from left to right, so the latest digit is the low-order digit in the number. The digit value is obtained by subtracting the code value for the 0 digit from the code value for the current digit. This works because code values for digits are in ascending sequence. To insert the digit, you multiply the current accumulated value by ten and add the new digit value. Of course, storing the result as type int is a constraint. You could implement the function to store the value as type long long to accommodate a wider range of values. You could also include code to check for how large the number is getting and to output an error message if it cannot be stored as type int. The first character read that is not a digit ends the loop, and this character is returned to the stream so that it can be read again.

The getname() function reads an alphabetic name from the keyboard. The parameters are an array in which the name is to be stored and the length of the array so the function can ensure the capacity is not exceeded. The function returns the address of the first byte of the string as a convenience to the calling program. In principle, the process is the same as in the getinteger() function. The function continues to read characters in a loop as long as they are alphabetic:

```
while(isalpha(ch = (char)getchar())) // As long as there are letters...
{
  name[count++] = ch;                 // ...store them in name.
  if(count == length - 1)             // Check for name full
    break;
}
```

The count variable tracks the number of characters stored in the name array, and when only one element is still free, the loop ends. After the loop, the code appends '\0' to terminate the string. Of course the last character read will have been alphabetic and stored in the array if the value of count reaches length-1. You therefore only restore the last character back to the stream by calling ungetc() when this is not the case.

The main() function reads an arbitrary sequence of names and integers in a loop:

```
while(!isnewline())
{
  if(getinteger(&number))
    printf("Integer value:%8d\n", number);
  else if(strnlen_s(getname(name, LENGTH), LENGTH) > 0)
    printf("Name: %s\n", name);
  else
  {
    printf("Invalid input.\n");
    return 1;
  }
}
```

The loop continues as long as the current character is not a newline. The program expects to read either an integer or a name on each loop iteration. The loop first tries to read an integer by calling the getinteger() function. This function returns false if an integer is not found, in which case the getname() function is called to read a name. If no name is found, the input is neither a name nor an integer, so the program ends after outputting a message.

Output to the Screen

Writing data to the command line on the screen is much easier than reading input from the keyboard. You know what data you're writing; with input, you have all the vagaries of possible incorrect entry of the data. The primary function for formatted output to the stdout stream is printf(), and you have already used this extensively. The stdio.h header may also declare the optional printf_s() function, which is a safe version of printf(). The primary difference between printf() and printf_s() is that printf_s() does not permit the %n output specification to be included in the format string. This is because the %n output specification writes data to memory, and this makes it unsafe. By not accepting %n as a valid format specification, printf_s() ensures that if the format string is subverted for malicious purposes, it will not be processed. I will therefore use printf_s() in code from this point, but if it is not available with your system, you can just use printf(). As always, you must define the symbol __STDC_WANT_LIB_EXT1__ as 1 prior to the #include directives for the library headers to make the optional safe library functions available.

Fortunately—or unfortunately, depending on how you view the chore of getting familiar with this stuff—printf_s() provides myriad possible variations for the output you can obtain, much more than the scope of the format specifiers associated with scanf_s().

Formatted Output Using printf_s()

The prototype of the printf_s() function is

```
int printf_s(char *format, ...);
```

The first parameter is the format control string. The argument for this parameter is usually passed to the function as an explicit string constant, as you've seen in all the examples using printf(), but it can be a pointer to a string that you specify elsewhere. The optional arguments to the function are the values to be output in sequence, and they must correspond in number and type with the format conversion specifiers that appear in the format string. Pointer arguments to printf_s() must not be NULL. Of course, as you've also seen in earlier examples, if the output is simply the text that appears in the format string, there are no additional arguments after the first. But where there are argument values to be output, there must be at least as many arguments as there are format specifiers. If not, the results are unpredictable. If there are more arguments than specifiers, the excess is ignored. This is because the function uses the format string as the determinant of how many arguments follow and what type they have.

■ **Note** The fact that the format string alone determines how the data are interpreted is the reason why you get the wrong result with a %d specifier combined with a long long argument.

The format conversion specifiers for printf() and printf_s() are a little more complicated than those you use for input with scanf_s(). The general form of an output format specifier is shown in Figure 10-2.

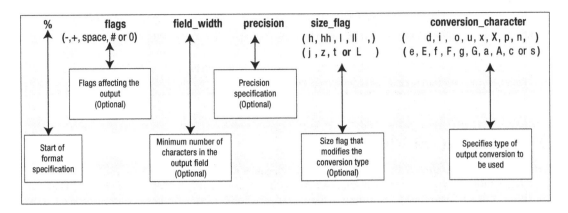

Figure 10-2. *Output format specifications for the* `printf_s()` *function*

You've seen quite a lot of the details before, but I'll go through all the elements of this general format specifier so you have them in one place.

Table 10-3 shows how the optional output flag characters affect the output.

Table 10-3. *Effects of the Optional Flag Characters in an Output Specification*

Character	Use
+	Ensures there's always a plus or minus sign preceding a signed output value. Only negative values have a sign by default
-	Specifies that the output value is left justified in the output field and padded with blanks on the right. The default positioning of the output is right justified
0	Specifies that integer or floating-point values should be padded with zeros instead of spaces to fill out the field width to the left
#	Ensures that 0 is to precede an octal output value 0x or 0X is to precede a hexadecimal output value A floating-point output value will contain a decimal point For g or G floating-point conversion characters, trailing zeros will not be omitted
Space	Specifies that positive or zero values are preceded by a space rather than a plus sign

The optional `field_width` specifies the minimum field width for the output value. If the value requires more characters, the field is simply expanded. If it requires less than the minimum specified, it is padded with blanks, unless the field width is preceded by the 0 flag, as in 09, for example, where it would be filled on the left with zeros.

The optional precision specifier is generally used with floating-point output values and consists of a period followed by an integer. A specifier of `.n` indicates that n decimal places are to be output for a floating-point value. If the value to be output has more than n significant digits, it's rounded. If you use it for integer conversions, it specifies the minimum number of digits to appear in the output.

The optional size flags are shown in Table 10-4.

Table 10-4. *Size Flag Characters in an Output Specification*

Flag	Effect
h	A following integer conversion specifier applies to a short or unsigned short argument
hh	A following integer conversion specifier applies to a signed char or unsigned char argument
l (lowercase L)	A following integer conversion specifier applies to a long or unsigned long argument. (This also specifies that a c specifier applies to a wint_t argument and an s specifier applies to a wchar_t argument)
ll (lowercase LL)	A following integer conversion specifier applies to a long long or unsigned long long argument
j	A following integer conversion specifier applies to an intmax_t or uintmax_t argument
z	A following integer conversion specifier applies to a size_t argument. This flag avoids potential compiler warnings that can arise because size_t is an implementation-defined integer type
t	A following integer conversion specifier applies to a ptrdiff_t argument
L	A following floating-point conversion specifier applies to a long double argument

The conversion character that you use defines how the output is to be converted for a particular type of value. Conversion characters are defined in Table 10-5.

Table 10-5. *Conversion Characters in an Output Specification*

Conversion character	Output produced
Applicable to integers:	Signed decimal integer
d or i	Unsigned octal integer
o	Unsigned decimal integer
u	Unsigned hexadecimal integer with lowercase hexadecimal digits
x	a, b, c, d, e, f
X	As x but with uppercase hexadecimal digits A, B, C, D, E, F
Applicable to floating point:	Signed decimal value
f or F	Signed decimal value with exponent
e	As e but with E for exponent instead of e
E	As e or f depending on size of value and precision
g	As g but with E for exponent values
G	Presents a double value in hexadecimal form with the hexadecimal
a or A	mantissa value preceded by 0x or 0X and any exponent prefixed with p or P, thus 0xh.hhhhp±d where h is a hexadecimal digit
Applicable to pointers:	Outputs the value of the argument as a pointer and the value is
p	presented in an implementation-defined way. The argument should be of type void*
Applicable to characters:	Single character or precision characters
c	All characters until '\0' is reached or precision characters
s	have been output

The %n specifier only works with printf(). The corresponding argument must be of type int*, and the effect of %n is to store the number of characters written to stdout so far.

Escape Sequences

You can include whitespace characters in the format control string for printf_s(). Whitespace characters are the newline, carriage return, form-feed, space, and tab. Some of these are represented by escape sequences, and these are shown in Table 10-6.

Table 10-6. *Escape Sequences for Whitespace Characters*

Escape sequence	Description
\b	Backspace
\f	Form-feed or page eject
\n	Newline
\r	Carriage return (for printers) or move to the beginning of the current line for output to the screen
\t	Horizontal tab

You use the escape sequence \\ in a format control string to output the backslash character, \. If this weren't the case, it would be impossible to output a backslash, because it would always be assumed that a backslash was the start of an escape sequence. To write a % character to stdout, you use %%. You can't use % by itself because this would be interpreted as the start of a format specification.

■ **Note**   Of course you can use escape sequences within any string, not just in the context of the format string for the printf_s() function.

Integer Output

Let's take a look at some of the variations that you haven't made much use of so far. Those with field width and precision specifiers are probably the most interesting.

TRY IT OUT: OUTPUTTING INTEGERS

Let's try a sample of integer output formats first:

```
// Program 10.8 Integer output variations
#define __STDC_WANT_LIB_EXT1__ 1
#include <stdio.h>

int main(void)
{
  int       i = 15,     j = 345,              k = 4567;
  long long li = 56789LL, lj = 67891234567LL, lk = 23456789LL;
```

```
    printf_s("i = %d    j = %d      k = %d     i = %6.3d    j = %6.3d    k = %6.3d\n",
                                                i ,j, k, i, j, k);
    printf_s("i = %-d    j = %+d     k = %-d    i = %-6.3d    j = %-6.3d    k ="
                                        " %-6.3d\n", i ,j, k, i, j, k);
    printf_s("li = %d    lj = %d     lk = %d\n", li, lj, lk);
    printf_s("li = %lld    lj = %lld    lk = %lld\n", li, lj, lk);
    return 0;
}
```

You may get warnings from your compiler relating to the third output statement. When you execute this example, you should see something like this:

```
i = 15    j = 345     k = 4567    i =      015    j =      345    k =    4567
i = 15    j = +345    k = 4567    i = 015         j = 345         k = 4567
li = 56789    lj = -828242169     lk = 23456789
li = 56789    lj = 67891234567    lk = 23456789
```

How It Works

This example illustrates a miscellany of options for integer output. You can see the effects of the - flag by comparing the first two lines that are produced by these statements:

```
    printf_s("i = %d    j = %d      k = %d     i = %6.3d    j = %6.3d    k = %6.3d\n",
                                                i ,j, k, i, j, k);
    printf_s("i = %-d    j = %+d     k = %-d    i = %-6.3d    j = %-6.3d    k ="
                                        " %-6.3d\n",i ,j, k, i, j, k);
```

The - flag causes the output to be left justified. The effect of the field width specifier is also apparent from the spacing of the last three outputs in each group of six. Note that the default width provides just enough output positions to accommodate the number of digits to be output, so the - flag has no effect.

You get a leading plus sign in the output of j on the second line because of the flag modifier. You can use more than one flag modifier if you want. With the second output of the value of i, you have a leading zero inserted due to the minimum precision being specified as three. You could also have obtained leading zeroes by preceding the minimum width value with a zero in the format specification and omitting the precision specification. When the precision specification is present, any leading zero is ignored.

The third output line is produced by the following statement:

```
    printf_s("li = %d    lj = %d     lk = %d\n", li, lj, lk);
```

Here you can see that failure to insert the ll (lowercase LL) modifier when outputting integers of type long long results in apparent garbage, because the output value is assumed to be a value of type int. Of course the problem arises only if long long and int are of different sizes.

You get the correct values from this statement:

```
    printf_s("li = %lld    lj = %lld    lk = %lld\n", li, lj, lk);
```

It's unwise to specify inadequate values for the width and the precision of the values to be displayed. Weird and wonderful results may be produced if you do. Try experimenting with this example to see just how much variation you can get.

TRY IT OUT: VARIATIONS ON A SINGLE INTEGER

You can try one more integer example to run the gamut of possibilities with a single integer value:

```
// Program 10.9 Variations on a single integer
#define __STDC_WANT_LIB_EXT1__ 1
#include <stdio.h>

int main(void)
{
  int k = 678;

  // Display formats as heading then display the values
  printf_s("%%d    %%o    %%x    %%X\n");
  printf_s("%d  %o  %x  %X\n", k, k, k, k );
  printf_s("\n|%%8d        |%%-8d       |%%+8d       |%%08d       |%%-+8d      |\n");
  printf_s("|%8d  |%-8d  |%+8d  |%08d  |%-+8d  |\n", k, k, k, k, k );
  return 0;
}
```

How It Works

This program may look a little confusing at first because the first of each pair of printf_s() statements displays the format used to output the number appearing immediately below. The %% specifier outputs the % character.

When you execute this example, you should get something like this:

```
%d    %o    %x    %X
678   1246  2a6   2A6

|%8d        |%-8d       |%+8d       |%08d       |%-+8d      |
|     678   |678        |    +678   |00000678   |+678       |
```

The first printf_s() statement outputs the format specifications for the values that appear on the next line of output:

```
  printf_s("%%d    %%o    %%x    %%X\n");
```

The first row of output values is produced by this statement:

```
  printf_s("%d  %o  %x  %X\n", k, k, k, k );
```

The outputs are decimal, octal, and two varieties of hexadecimal for the value 678, with the default width specification. The corresponding format appears above each value in the output.

The format specifications used next are displayed by this statement:

```
  printf_s("\n|%%8d        |%%-8d       |%%+8d       |%%08d       |%%-+8d      |\n");
```

I included the vertical bars here and in the statement that outputs the values to make it easier to see the effects of the specifiers.

The next row of output values is produced by this:

```
printf_s("|%8d  |%-8d  |%+8d  |%08d  |%-+8d  |\n", k, k, k, k, k );
```

The statement includes a variety of flag settings with a width specification of 8. The first is the default right justification in the field. The second is left justified because of the - flag. The third has a sign because of the + flag. The fourth has leading zeroes because the width is specified as 08 instead of 8. The last output value uses a specifier with both + and -, %-+8d, so the output is left justified in the field and also has a leading sign.

Tip   When you're outputting multiple rows of values on the screen, using a width specification—possibly with tabs—will enable you to line them up in columns.

Outputting Floating-Point Values

If plowing through the integer options hasn't started you nodding off, then see if the floating-point output options will do it.

TRY IT OUT: OUTPUTTING FLOATING-POINT VALUES

Look at the following example:

```
// Program 10.10 Outputting floating-point values
#define __STDC_WANT_LIB_EXT1__ 1
#include <stdio.h>

int main(void)
{
  float  fp1 = 345.675f,    fp2 = 1.234E6f;
  double fp3 = 234567898.0, fp4 = 11.22334455e-6;

  printf_s("%f  %+f  %-10.4f  %6.4f\n", fp1, fp2, fp1, fp2);
  printf_s("%e  %+E\n", fp1, fp2);
  printf_s("%f  %g  %#+f  %8.4f  %10.4g\n", fp3,fp3, fp3, fp3, fp4);
  return 0;
}
```

With my compiler, I get this output:

```
345.675000  +1234000.000000  345.6750      1234000.0000
3.456750e+02  +1.234000E+06
234567898.000000  2.34568e+08  +234567898.000000  234567898.0000   1.122e-05
```

It's possible that you may not get exactly the same output, but it should be close.

How It Works

Most of the output is a straightforward demonstration of the effects of the format conversion specifiers that I've discussed, but a few points are noteworthy. In the output generated by the statement

```
printf_s("%f  %+f  %-10.4f  %6.4f\n", fp1, fp2, fp1, fp2);
```

the second output value for fp1 shows how the number of decimal places after the point can be constrained. The output in this case is left justified in the field. The second output of fp2 has a field width specified that is too small for the number of decimal places required and is therefore overridden.

The second printf_s() statement is as follows: printf_s("%e %+E\n", fp1, fp2);

This outputs the same values in floating-point format with an exponent. Whether you get an uppercase E or a lowercase e for the exponent indicator depends on how you write the format specifier.

In the last line, you can see how the g-specified output of fp3 has been rounded up compared to the f-specified output.

■ **Note**   There are a number of possible variations for the output obtainable with printf_s(). It would be enlightening to play around with the options, trying various ways of outputting the same information.

Character Output

Now that you've looked at the various possibilities for outputting numbers, let's have a look at outputting characters. There are two flavors of output specifications you can use with printf_s() for character data: %c for single characters and %s for strings. You have used %s extensively, so I'll just demonstrate %c.

■ **Note**   %lc and %ls are used to output wide characters as you'll see in Chapter 14.

TRY IT OUT: OUTPUTTING CHARACTER DATA

This example outputs all the printable characters:

```
// Program 10.11 Outputting character data
#define __STDC_WANT_LIB_EXT1__ 1
#include <stdio.h>
#include <limits.h>              // For CHAR_MAX
#include <ctype.h>               // For isprint()

int main(void)
{
  int count = 0;

  printf_s("The printable characters are the following:\n");

  // Iterate over all values of type char
```

```
  for(int code = 0 ; code <= CHAR_MAX ; ++code)
  {
    char ch = (char)code;
    if(isprint(ch))
    {
      if(count++ % 32 == 0)
        printf_s("\n");
      printf_s(" %c", ch);
    }
  }
  printf_s("\n");
  return 0;
}
```

The output from this program is

```
The printable characters are the following:
  ! " # $ % & ' ( ) * + , - . / 0 1 2 3 4 5 6 7 8 9 : ; < = > ?
@ A B C D E F G H I J K L M N O P Q R S T U V W X Y Z [ \ ] ^ _
` a b c d e f g h i j k l m n o p q r s t u v w x y z { | } ~
```

How It Works

The block of output for the printable characters is generated in the for loop:

```
  for(int code = 0 ; code <= CHAR_MAX ; code++)
  {
    char ch = (char)code;
    if(isprint(ch))
    {
      if(count++ % 32 == 0)
        printf_s("\n");
      printf_s(" %c", ch);
    }
  }
```

First, note the type of the loop control variable, code. You might be tempted to use type char here, but this would be a serious mistake, as the loop would run indefinitely. The reason for this is that the condition for ending the loop is checked after the value of code has been incremented. On the last good iteration, code has the value CHAR_MAX, which is the maximum value that can be stored as type char. If code is type char, when 1 is added to CHAR_MAX, the result would be 0, so the loop would continue instead of ending as it should.

Within the loop, you cast the value of code to type char and store the result in ch. The explicit cast is not required for the code to compile because the compiler will insert the conversion, but it does indicate that it is intentional. You then use the isprint() function that is declared in the ctype.h header to test for a printable character. When isprint() returns true, you output the character using the %c format specification. You also arrange to output a newline character each time 32 characters have been output so you don't have output just spilling arbitrarily from one line to the next.

Other Output Functions

The stdio.h header declares the puts() function that complements the gets_s() function. The name of the function derives from its purpose: *put* string. The prototype for puts() is

```
int puts(const char *string);
```

The puts() function accepts a pointer to a string as an argument and writes the string followed by a newline character to the standard output stream, stdout. The string must be terminated by '\0'. The parameter to puts() is const, so the function does not modify the string you pass to it. The function returns a negative integer value if any errors occur on output and a nonnegative value otherwise. The puts() function is useful for outputting single-line messages, for example:

```
puts("Is there no end to input and output?");
```

This will output the string that is passed as the argument and then move the cursor to the next line. The printf_s() function requires an explicit '\n' to be included at the end of the string to do the same thing.

■ **Note** The puts() function will process embedded '\n' characters in the string to generate output on multiple lines.

Unformatted Output to the Screen

The putchar() function that complements getchar() is also declared in stdio.h. This has the prototype

```
int putchar(int c);
```

The function outputs a single character, c, to stdout and returns the character that was displayed. This allows you to output a message one character at a time, which can make your programs a bit bigger, but gives you control over whether or not you output particular characters. For example, you could simply write the following to output a string:

```
char string[] = "Beware the Jabberwock, \nmy son!";
puts(string);
```

Alternatively, you could write the string like this:

```
int i = 0;
while( string[i] != '\0')
{
  if(string[i] != '\n')
    putchar(string[i]);
  ++i;
}
```

The first fragment outputs the string over two lines, like this:

```
Beware the Jabberwock,
my son!
```

The second fragment skips newline characters in the string so the output will be

```
Beware the Jabberwock, my son!
```

Your use of putchar() need not be as simple as this. With putchar() you could choose to output a selected sequence of characters from the middle of a string bounded by a given delimiter, or you could selectively transform the occurrences of certain characters within a string before output, converting tabs to spaces, for example.

Formatted Output to an Array

You can write formatted data to an array of elements of type char in memory using the optional sprintf_s() and snprintf_s() functions that are declared in the stdio.h header file. These are safe alternatives to the standard sprintf() function in that they prevent writing beyond the end of the array. The difference between sprintf_s() and snprintf_s() is that sprintf_s() treats exceeding the extent of the array as a runtime error, whereas snprintf_s() just truncates the output to fit within the array. Apart from the name, the functions have the same prototype. I'll discuss snprintf_s(), which has the prototype

```
int snprintf_s(char * restrict str, rsize_t n, const char * restrict format, . . .);
```

The first argument is the address of an array that is the destination for the output. The second argument is the array length, which the function uses to ensure that it does not write beyond the last array element. The function writes the data specified by the fourth and subsequent arguments formatted according to the format string passed as the third argument. This works identically to printf_s() except that the data are written to str instead of stdout. The integer returned is a count of the number of characters written to str, excluding the terminating null character.

Here's a fragment illustrating how this works:

```
char result[20];               // Output destination
int count = 4;
int nchars = snprintf_s(result, sizeof(result), "A dog has %d legs.", count);
```

The effect of this is to write the value of count to result using the format string that is the third argument. The result is that result will contain the string "A dog has 4 legs". The nchars variable will contain the value 17, which is the same as the return value you would get from strnlen_s(result, sizeof(result)) after the snprintf_s() call has executed. The snprintf_s() function will return a negative integer if an encoding error occurs during the operation. One significant use for the snprintf_s() function is to create format strings programmatically.

Formatted Input from an Array

The optional sscanf_s() function complements the snprintf_s() function because it enables you to read data under the control of a format string from an array of elements of type char. It's a safe alternative to sscanf(). The principal difference is that sscanf_s() requires an address and a length argument for each c, s, or [specification, whereas sscanf() only requires the address. The prototype looks like this:

```
int sscanf_s(const char * restrict str, const char * restrict format, . . .);
```

Data will be read from str into variables that are specified by the third and subsequent arguments according to the format string, format. The function returns a count of the number of items actually read or EOF if a failure occurs before any data values are read and stored. The end of the string is recognized as the end-of-file condition, so reaching the end of the str string before any values are converted will cause EOF to be returned.

Here's a simple illustration of how the sscanf_s() function works:

```
char *source = "Fred 94";
char name[10] = {0};
int age = 0;
int items = sscanf_s(source, " %s %d", name, sizeof(name), &age);
```

The result of executing this fragment is that name will contain the string "Fred" and age will contain the value 94. The variable items will contain the value 2 because two items are read from source. The length argument for name ensures that data will not be written beyond the end of the array.

One use for the sscanf_s() function is to try various ways of reading the same data. You can always read an input line from an external stream into an array as a string. You can then use sscanf_s() to reread the same input line from the array with different format strings as many times as you like.

Summary

In this chapter, you learned about standard streams and formatted input and output for them. You also learned how to write formatted data to an array in memory and read it back. You will see in Chapter 12 that the mechanism for formatted file input and output is essentially the same as the operations you have seen in this chapter because files are also streams.

Although I chose the various specifications for formatting that you've seen in this chapter with the idea of them being as meaningful as possible, there are a lot of them. The only way you're going to become comfortable with them is through practice, and ideally this practice needs to take place in a real-world context. Understanding the various codes is one thing, but they'll only become really familiar to you once you've used them a few times in real programs. In the meantime, when you need a quick reminder, you can always look them up in Appendix D.

EXERCISES

The following exercises enable you to try out what you've learned in this chapter. If you get stuck, look back over the chapter for help. If you're still stuck, you can download the solutions from the Source Code/Download area of the Apress website (www.apress.com), but that really should be a last resort.

Exercise 10-1. Write a program that will read, store, and output the following five types of strings on separate lines. One of each type of string should be entered on successive lines:

- *Type 1:* A sequence of lowercase letters followed by a digit (e.g., number1)

- *Type 2:* Two words that both begin with a capital letter and have a hyphen between them (e.g., Seven-Up)

- *Type 3:* A decimal value (e.g., 7.35)

- *Type 4:* A sequence of uppercase and lowercase letters and spaces (e.g., Oliver Hardy)

- *Type 5:* A sequence of any characters except spaces and digits (e.g., floating-point)

The following is a sample of input that should be read as five separate strings:

babylon5John-Boy3.14159Stan Laurel'Winner!'

Exercise 10-2. Write a program that will read the numerical values in the following line of input and output the total:

    $3.50 , $4.75 , $9.95 , $2.50

Exercise 10-3. Define a function that will output an array of values of type double that is passed as an argument along with the number of elements in the array. The prototype of the function will be the following:

void show(double array[], int array_size, int field_width);

The values should be output five to a line, each with two places after the decimal point. Use the function in a program that will output the values from 1.5 to 4.5 in steps of 0.3 (i.e., 1.5, 1.8, 2.1, etc., up to 4.5) with each value in a field width of 12.

Exercise 10-4. Define a function using the getchar() function that will read a string from stdin terminated by a character that is passed as the third argument to the function. Thus, the prototype will be the following:

char *getString(char *buffer, size_t buffer, char end_char);

The return value is the pointer that is passed as the first argument. Write a program to demonstrate the use of the function to read and output five strings that are from the keyboard, each terminated by a colon. The function should output an error message if buffer is full and end_char has not been found.

CHAPTER 11

Structuring Data

So far, you've learned how to declare and define variables that can hold various types of data, including integers, floating-point values, and characters. You also have the means to create arrays of any of these types and arrays of pointers to memory locations containing data of the types available to you. Although these have proved very useful, there are many applications in which you need even more flexibility.

For instance, suppose you want to write a program that processes data about breeding horses. You need information about each horse such as its name, its date of birth, its coloring, its height, its parentage, and so on. Some items are strings and some are numeric. Clearly, you could set up arrays for each type of data and store them quite easily. However, this has limitations—for example, it doesn't allow you to refer to Dobbin's date of birth or Trigger's height particularly easily. You would need to synchronize your arrays by relating data items through a common index. Amazingly, C provides you with a much better way of doing this sort of thing, and that's what I'll discuss in this chapter.

In this chapter, you'll learn

- What structures are

- How to declare and define data structures

- How to use structures and pointers to structures

- How to use pointers as structure members

- What a linked list is and how to use it to manage data

- What a binary tree is and how to create and use it

- How to share memory between variables

- How to write a program that produces bar charts from your data

Data Structures: Using struct

The struct keyword enables you to define a collection of variables of various types called a *structure* that you can treat as a single unit. This will be clearer if you see a simple example of a structure declaration:

```
struct Horse
{
  int age;
  int height;
} silver;
```

© German Gonzalez-Morris and Ivor Horton 2020

G. Gonzalez-Morris and I. Horton, *Beginning C*, https://doi.org/10.1007/978-1-4842-5976-4_11

This example declares a *structure* type called Horse. This isn't a variable name; it's a new type. This type name is referred to as a *structure tag* or a *tag name*. The naming of the structure tag follows the same rules as for a variable name, which you should be familiar with by now.

▪ **Note** It's legal to use the same name for a structure tag name and another variable. However, I don't recommend you do this because it will make your code confusing and difficult to understand.

The variable names within the Horse structure, age and height, are called *members* or *fields*. In this case, both members are of type int. The members of the structure appear between the braces that follow the struct tag name Horse.

In the example, an instance of the structure, called silver, is declared at the same time that the structure is defined; so silver is a variable of type Horse. Now, whenever you use the variable name silver, it includes both members of the structure: the member age and the member height.

Let's look at the declaration of a slightly more complicated version of the structure type Horse:

```
struct Horse
{
  int age;
  int height;
  char name[20];
  char father[20];
  char mother[20];
} dobbin = {
            24, 17, "Dobbin", "Trigger", "Flossie"
           };
```

A variable of any type can be a member of a structure, including arrays. There are five members to this version of the Horse structure type: the integer members, age and height; and the arrays of char elements, name, father, and mother. Each struct member declaration is essentially the same as a normal variable declaration, with the type followed by the name and terminated by a semicolon. Initialization values can't be placed here because you aren't declaring variables; you're defining members of a type called Horse. A structure type is a kind of specification or blueprint that can then be used to define variables of that type—in this example, type Horse.

You define an instance of the Horse structure after the closing brace of the structure definition. This is the variable dobbin. Initial values are also assigned to the member variables of dobbin in a manner similar to those used to initialize arrays, so initial values *can* be assigned when you define instances of the type Horse.

In the declaration of the variable dobbin, the values that appear between the final pair of braces apply, in sequence, to the member variables age (24), height (17), name ("Dobbin"), father ("Trigger"), and mother ("Flossie"). The statement is finally terminated with a semicolon. The variable dobbin now refers to the complete collection of members included in the structure. The memory occupied by the structure dobbin is shown in Figure 11-1, assuming that variables of type int occupy 4 bytes. You can always obtain the amount of memory that's occupied by a structure object using the sizeof operator.

Structure Variable **dobbin**

age	height	name	father	mother
4 bytes	4 bytes	20 bytes	20 bytes	20 bytes

Figure 11-1. *Memory occupied by dobbin*

Defining Structure Types and Structure Variables

Of course you can define a structure type and a variable of a structure type in separate statements. Instead of the statements you saw previously, you could have entered the following:

```
struct Horse
{
  int age;
  int height;
  char name[20];
  char father[20];
  char mother[20];
};

struct Horse dobbin = {
                  24, 17,"Dobbin", "Trigger", "Flossie"
                  };
```

The first statement defines the structure tag Horse, and the second is a declaration of one variable of that type, dobbin. Both the structure definition and the structure variable declaration statements end with a semicolon. The initial values for the members of the dobbin structure tell you that the father of dobbin has the name "Trigger" and his mother's name is "Flossie".

You could also add a third statement to the previous two examples that would define another variable of type Horse:

```
struct Horse trigger = {
                  30, 15, "Trigger", "Smith", "Wesson"
                  };
```

Now you have a variable trigger that holds the details of the father of dobbin, where it's clear that the ancestors of trigger are called "Smith" and "Wesson".

Of course, you can also declare multiple structure variables in a single statement. This is almost as easy as declaring variables of one of the standard C types, for example:

```
struct Horse piebald, bandy;
```

This statement declares two variables of type Horse. The only additional item in the declaration, compared with standard types, is the struct keyword. The variables are not initialized here—to keep the statement simple—but in general it's wise to do so. Each variable of type Horse has its own set of fields.

The struct keyword is required when you define a new variable that stores a structure, but the code would look simpler and easier to read without it. There's a way you can remove the need to include struct every time you declare a variable by using a typedef definition, for example:

```
typedef struct Horse Horse;
```

This defines Horse to be the equivalent of struct Horse. If you put this definition at the beginning of a source file, you can define a variable of type Horse like this:

```
Horse trigger = {
                    30, 15, "Trigger", "Smith", "Wesson"
               };
```

The struct keyword is no longer necessary. This makes the code less cluttered and makes your structure type look like a first-class type. I will use this technique in the examples throughout the rest of the book.

Accessing Structure Members

Now that you know how to define a structure and declare structure variables, you need to be able to refer to the members of a structure. A structure variable name is *not* a pointer. You need a special syntax to access the members. You refer to a member of a structure by writing the variable name followed by a period, followed by the member variable name. For example, if you found that dobbin had lied about his age and was actually much younger than the initializing value would suggest, you could amend the value by writing this:

```
dobbin.age = 12;
```

The period between the structure variable name and the member name is called the *member selection operator*. This statement sets the age member of the structure referenced by dobbin to 12. Structure members are the same as variables of the same type. You can set their values and use them in expressions in the same way as ordinary variables.

The initialization for trigger in the previous section depends on getting the initial values for the fields in the correct order. This is not a problem with a Horse struct, but it could be with a structure with many more members. You have the option of specifying the member names in the initialization list, like this:

```
Horse trigger = {
                    .height = 15, .age = 30,
                    .name = "Trigger", .mother = "Wesson", .father = "Smith"
               };
```

Now there is no doubt about which member is being initialized by what value. The order of the initializers is now unimportant.

TRY IT OUT: USING STRUCTURES

You can try out what you've learned so far about structures in a simple example that's designed to appeal to horse enthusiasts:

```
// Program 11.1 Exercising the horse
#define __STDC_WANT_LIB_EXT1__ 1
#include <stdio.h>

typedef struct Horse Horse;            // Define Horse as a type name

struct Horse                           // Structure type definition
{
  int age;
  int height;
  char name[20];
  char father[20];
  char mother[20];
};

int main(void)
{
  Horse my_horse;                      // Structure variable declaration

  // Initialize  the structure variable from input data
  printf_s("Enter the name of the horse: " );
  scanf_s("%s", my_horse.name, sizeof(my_horse.name));     // Read the name

  printf_s("How old is %s? ", my_horse.name );
  scanf_s("%d", &my_horse.age );                           // Read the age

  printf_s("How high is %s ( in hands )? ", my_horse.name );
  scanf_s("%d", &my_horse.height );                        // Read the height

  printf_s("Who is %s's father? ", my_horse.name );
  scanf_s("%s", my_horse.father, sizeof(my_horse.father)); // Get pa's name

  printf_s("Who is %s's mother? ", my_horse.name );
  scanf_s("%s", my_horse.mother, sizeof(my_horse.mother)); // Get ma's name

  // Now tell them what we know
  printf_s("%s is %d years old, %d hands high,",my_horse.name, my_horse.age, my_
  horse.height);
  printf_s(" and has %s and %s as parents.\n", my_horse.father, my_horse.mother);
  return 0;
}
```

Depending on what data you key in, you should get output approximating the following:

```
Enter the name of the horse: Neddy
How old is Neddy? 12
How high is Neddy ( in hands )? 14
Who is Neddy's father? Bertie
Who is Neddy's mother? Nellie
Neddy is 12 years old, 14 hands high, and has Bertie and Nellie as parents.
```

How It Works

The way you reference members of a structure makes it very easy to follow what is going on in this example. You define the structure Horse with this statement:

```
struct Horse                          // Structure type definition
{
  int age;
  int height;
  char name[20];
  char father[20];
  char mother[20];
};
```

The structure has two integer members, age and height, and three char array members, name, father, and mother. Because there's just a semicolon following the closing brace, no variables of type Horse are declared here. This definition is preceded by a typedef statement:

```
typedef struct Horse Horse;
```

This allows you to define variables of type Horse without having to include the struct keyword.

The typedef and the definition of the struct are outside main() at global scope. This means that the Horse type can be used in any function in the source file. You could put the definition within the body of main(), in which case the type would be local to main(). Structure type definitions usually appear at global scope.

You have the following statement in main():

```
  Horse my_horse;                     // Structure variable declaration
```

This declares one variable of type Horse with the name my_horse. This variable has no initial values assigned to the members of the struct in the declaration.

You read in the data for the name member of the structure my_horse with this statement:

```
  scanf_s("%s", my_horse.name, sizeof(my_horse.name));     // Read the name
```

No address of operator (&) is necessary here, because the name member of the structure is an array, so you implicitly transfer the address of the first array element to the function scanf_s(). You reference the member by writing the structure name, my_horse, followed by a period, followed by the name of the member, name. Other than the notation used to access it, using a structure member is the same as using any other variable. The name member is a string that you are reading using %s, so you must supply the length argument as well as the address of name.

The next value you read in is for the age of the horse:

```
  scanf_s("%d", &my_horse.age );                           // Read the age
```

The age member is a variable of type int, so here you must use the & to pass the address of the structure member.

■ **Note** When you use the address of operator (&) for a member of a struct object, you place the & in front of the whole reference to the member, not in front of the member name.

The following statements read the data for each of the other members of the structure in exactly the same manner, prompting for the input in each case. Once input is complete, the values read are output to the display as a single line using the following statements:

```
printf_s("%s is %d years old, %d hands high,",
                             my_horse.name, my_horse.age, my_horse.height);
printf_s(" and has %s and %s as parents.\n", my_horse.father, my_horse.mother);
```

You have the names of the member variables as the arguments to the function following the first argument, which is the standard sort of format control string you've seen many times before.

Unnamed Structures

You don't have to give a structure a tag name. When you declare a structure and any instances of that structure in a single statement, you can omit the tag name. In the previous example, instead of the structure declaration for type Horse, followed by the instance declaration for my_horse, you could have written this statement:

```
struct
{                              // Structure declaration and...
  int age;
  int height;
  char name[20];
  char father[20];
  char mother[20];
} my_horse;                    // ...structure variable declaration combined
```

A serious disadvantage with this is that you can no longer define further instances of the structure in another statement. All the variables of this structure type that you want in your program must be defined in the one statement.

Arrays of Structures

The basic approach to keeping horse data is fine as far as it goes. But it will probably begin to be a bit cumbersome by the time you've accumulated 50 or 100 horses. You need a more stable method for handling a lot of horses. It's exactly the same problem you had with variables, which you solved by using an array. And you can do the same here: you can declare a Horse array.

TRY IT OUT: USING ARRAYS OF STRUCTURES

Let's saddle up and extend the previous example to handle several horses:

```c
// Program 11.2    Exercising the horses
#define __STDC_WANT_LIB_EXT1__ 1
#include <stdio.h>
#include <ctype.h>

typedef struct Horse Horse;           // Define Horse as a type name

struct Horse                          // Structure type definition
{
  int age;
  int height;
  char name[20];
  char father[20];
  char mother[20];
};

int main(void)
{
  Horse my_horses[50];                // Array of Horse elements
  int hcount = 0;                     // Count of the number of horses
  char test = '\0';                   // Test value for ending

  for(hcount = 0 ; hcount < sizeof(my_horses)/ sizeof(Horse) ; ++hcount)
  {
    printf_s("Do you want to enter details of a%s horse (Y or N)? ",
                                      hcount ? "nother" : "" );
    scanf_s(" %c", &test, sizeof(test));
    if(tolower(test) == 'n')
      break;

    printf_s("Enter the name of the horse: " );
    scanf_s("%s", my_horses[hcount].name, sizeof(my_horses[hcount].name));

    printf_s("How old is %s? ", my_horses[hcount].name );
    scanf_s("%d", &my_horses[hcount].age);

    printf_s("How high is %s ( in hands )? ", my_horses[hcount].name);
    scanf_s("%d", &my_horses[hcount].height);

    printf_s("Who is %s's father? ", my_horses[hcount].name);
    scanf_s("%s", my_horses[hcount].father, sizeof(my_horses[hcount].father));

    printf_s("Who is %s's mother? ", my_horses[hcount].name);
    scanf_s("%s", my_horses[hcount].mother, sizeof(my_horses[hcount].mother));
  }

  // Now tell them what we know.
  printf_s("\n");
  for (int i = 0 ; i < hcount ; ++i)
  {
    printf_s("%s is %d years old, %d hands high,",
             my_horses[i].name, my_horses[i].age, my_horses[i].height);
```

```
    printf_s(" and has %s and %s as parents.\n", my_horses[i].father,
                                            my_horses[i].mother);
  }
  return 0;
}
```

The output from this program is a little different from the previous example you saw that dealt with a single horse. The main addition is the prompt for input data for each horse. Once all the data for a few horses have been entered, or, if you have the stamina, the data on 50 horses have been entered, the program outputs a summary of all the data that have been read in, one line per horse. The whole mechanism is stable and works very well in the mane (almost an unbridled success, you might say).

How It Works

In this version of equine data processing, you first declare the Horse structure at global scope, and the following declaration in main() makes use of it:

```
  Horse my_horses[50];                    // Array of Horse elements
```

This declares the variable my_horses to be an array of 50 Horse structures. Because of the typedef, it's just like any other array declaration.

You then have a for loop controlled by the variable hcount:

```
  for(hcount = 0 ; hcount < sizeof(my_horses)/sizeof(Horse) ; ++hcount)
  {
    ...
  }
```

This creates the potential for the program to read in data for up to 50 horses. The loop control variable hcount is used to accumulate the total number of Horse structures entered. The first action in the loop is in these statements:

```
    printf_s("Do you want to enter details of a%s horse (Y or N)? ",
                                            hcount ? "nother" : "" );
  scanf_s(" %c", &test, sizeof(test));
  if(tolower(test) == 'n')
      break;
```

On each iteration, the user is prompted to indicate if they want to enter data for another horse by entering **Y** or **N**. The printf_s() statement for this uses the conditional operator to insert "nother" into the output on every iteration after the first. After reading the character that the user enters, using scanf_s(), the if statement executes a break, which immediately exits from the loop if the response is negative.

The succeeding sequence of printf_s() and scanf_s() statements is much the same as before, but there are two points to note in these. Look at this statement:

```
  scanf_s("%s", my_horses[hcount].name, sizeof(my_horses[hcount].name));
```

You can see that the method for referencing the member of one element of an array of structures is easier to write than to say! The structure array name has an index in square brackets, to which a period and the member name are appended. If you want to reference the third element of the name array for the fourth structure element, you would write my_horses[3].name[2].

░ **Note**   Of course, index values for arrays of structures start from zero as with arrays of other types, so the fourth element of the structure array has the index value 3, and the third element of the member array is accessed by the index value 2.

Now look at this statement from the example:

```
scanf_s("%d", &my_horses[hcount].age);
```

The arguments to scanf_s() don't need the & for the string array variables, such as my_horses[hcount].name, but they *do* require it for the integer arguments my_horses[hcount].age and my_horses[hcount].height. It's very easy to forget the address of operator when reading values for variables like these.

Don't be misled at this point and think that these techniques are limited to equine applications. They can perfectly well be applied to porcine problems and also to asinine exercises.

Structure Members in Expressions

You can use a structure member that is of one of the built-in types like any other variable in an expression. Using the structure from Program 11.2, you could write this rather meaningless computation:

```
my_horses[1].height = (my_horses[2].height + my_horses[3].height)/2;
```

I can think of no good reason why the height of one horse should be the average of two other horses' heights (unless there's some Frankenstein-like assembly going on), but it's a legal statement.

You can also use a complete structure element in an assignment statement:

```
my_horses[1] = my_horses[2];
```

This statement causes *all* the members of the structure my_horses[2] to be copied to the structure my_horses[1], which means that the two structures become identical. The only other operation that's possible with a whole structure is to take its address using the & operator. You can't add, compare, or perform any other operations with a complete structure. To do those kinds of things, you must write your own functions. With the preceding statement, the elements of the char array members are copied, so the name member for each structure, for example, is independent of the name member of the other.

Pointers to Structures

The ability to obtain the address of a structure raises the question of whether you can have pointers to a structure. Because you can take the address of a structure, the possibility of declaring a pointer to a structure does, indeed, naturally follow. You use the notation you've already seen with other types of variables:

```
Horse *phorse = NULL;
```

This declares a pointer, phorse, that can store the address of a structure of type Horse. Don't forget that the typedef for Horse is necessary to omit the struct keyword. Without the typedef, you must write the statement as

```
struct Horse *phorse = NULL;
```

You can now set phorse to have the value of the address of a particular structure, using exactly the same kind of statement that you've been using for other pointer types, for example:

```
Horse ahorse = { 3, 11, "Jimbo", "Trigger", "Nellie"};
phorse = &ahorse;
```

Here phorse points to the ahorse structure.

Of course, the pointer could also store the address of an element in the array of horses from the previous example:

```
phorse = &my_horses[1];
```

Now phorse points to the structure my_horses[1], which is the second element in the my_horses array. You can immediately reference elements of this structure through your pointer. So if you want to display the name member of this structure, you could write this:

```
printf_s("The name is %s.\n", (*phorse).name);
```

The parentheses around the dereferenced pointer are essential, because the precedence of the member selection operator (the period) is higher than that of the pointer-dereference operator *. However, there's another way of expressing this, and it's much more readable and intuitive. You could write the previous statement like this:

```
printf_s("The name is %s.\n", phorse->name );
```

You don't need parentheses or an asterisk. You construct the -> operator from a minus sign immediately followed by the greater than symbol. The operator is sometimes called the *pointer to member* operator for obvious reasons. This notation is almost invariably used in preference to the usual pointer-dereferencing notation you used at first, because it makes your programs so much easier to read.

Dynamic Memory Allocation for Structures

You have virtually all the tools you need to rewrite Program 11.2 with a much more economical use of memory. In the original version, you allocated the memory for an array of 50 Horse structures, even when in practice you probably didn't need anything like that amount.

To create dynamically allocated memory for structures, the only tool that's missing is an array of pointers to structures, which is declared very easily, as you can see in this statement:

```
Horse *phorses[50];
```

This statement declares an array of 50 pointers to structures of type Horse. Only memory for the pointers has been allocated by this statement. You must still allocate the memory necessary to store the actual members of each structure that you need.

TRY IT OUT: USING POINTERS WITH STRUCTURES

You can see the dynamic allocation of memory for structures at work in the following example:

```
// Program 11.3 Pointing out the horses
#define __STDC_WANT_LIB_EXT1__ 1
#include <stdio.h>
#include <ctype.h>
#include <stdlib.h>                      // For malloc()

typedef struct Horse Horse;             // Define Horse as a type name

struct Horse                            // Structure type definition
{
  int age;
  int height;
  char name[20];
  char father[20];
  char mother[20];
};

int main(void)
{
  Horse *phorses[50];                   // Array of pointers to structure
  int hcount = 0;                       // Count of the number of horses
  char test = '\0';                     // Test value for ending input

  for(hcount = 0 ; hcount < sizeof(phorses)/sizeof(Horse*) ; ++hcount)
  {
    printf_s("Do you want to enter details of a%s horse (Y or N)? ",
                                        hcount ? "nother" : "" );
    scanf_s(" %c", &test, sizeof(test));
    if(tolower(test) == 'n')
      break;

    // allocate memory to hold a horse structure
    phorses[hcount] = (Horse*) malloc(sizeof(Horse));

    printf_s("Enter the name of the horse: " );
    scanf_s("%s", phorses[hcount]->name, sizeof(phorses[hcount]->name));

    printf_s("How old is %s? ", phorses[hcount]->name );
    scanf_s("%d", &phorses[hcount]->age);

    printf_s("How high is %s ( in hands )? ", phorses[hcount]->name);
    scanf_s("%d", &phorses[hcount]->height);

    printf_s("Who is %s's father? ", phorses[hcount]->name);
    scanf_s("%s", phorses[hcount]->father, sizeof(phorses[hcount]->father));

    printf_s("Who is %s's mother? ", phorses[hcount]->name);
    scanf_s("%s", phorses[hcount]->mother, sizeof(phorses[hcount]->mother));
  }
```

```
  // Now tell them what we know.
  printf_s("\n");
  for (int i = 0 ; i < hcount ; ++i)
  {
    printf_s("%s is %d years old, %d hands high,",
               phorses[i]->name, phorses[i]->age, phorses[i]->height);
    printf_s(" and has %s and %s as parents.\n", phorses[i]->father,
                                                  phorses[i]->mother);
    free(phorses[i]);
  }
  return 0;
}
```

The output should be exactly the same as that from Program 11.2, given the same input.

How It Works

This looks very similar to the previous version, but it operates rather differently. Initially, you don't have any memory allocated for any structures. The declaration

```
Horse *phorses[50];                      // Array of pointers to structure
```

defines only 50 pointers to structures of type Horse. You still have to find somewhere to put a structure to which each of these pointers is going to point, and this statement in the for loop does that:

```
phorses[hcount] = (Horse*) malloc(sizeof(Horse));
```

This allocates the number of bytes needed to store each structure as it's required. Let's do a quick review of how the malloc() function works. The malloc() function allocates the number of bytes specified by its argument and returns the address of the block of memory allocated as type void*. In this case, you apply the sizeof operator to the Horse type to provide the argument value.

It's very important to use sizeof when you need the number of bytes occupied by a structure. It doesn't necessarily correspond to the sum of the bytes occupied by each of its individual members, so you may get it wrong if you try to work it out yourself. Variables other than type char are often stored beginning at an address that's a multiple of two for 2-byte variables, a multiple of four for 4-byte variables, and so on. This is called *boundary alignment*, and it has nothing to do with C in particular, but it can be a hardware requirement. Arranging variables to be stored in memory like this makes the transfer of data between the processor and memory faster. This arrangement can result in unused bytes occurring between member variables of different types, though, depending on their sequence. These have to be accounted for in the number of bytes allocated for a structure. Figure 11-2 presents an illustration of how this can occur.

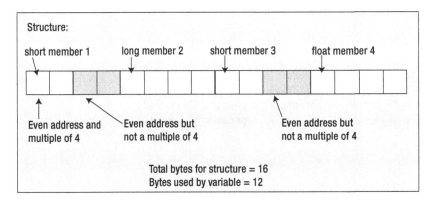

Figure 11-2. *The effect of boundary alignment on memory allocation*

■ **Note**   C has the _Alignof operator that you can use to discover the boundary alignment of a variable. You can also apply _Alignas(type) in a variable declaration to force the alignment to be at the specified type alignment.

The value returned by malloc() is a pointer to void, so you cast this to the type you require with the expression (Horse*):

```
scanf_s("%s", phorses[hcount]->name, sizeof(phorses[hcount]->name));
```

In this statement, you use the new notation for selecting members of a structure through a pointer. It's much clearer than (*phorses[hcount]).name. All subsequent references to members of a specific Horse structure use this new notation.

Lastly, in this program, you display a summary of all the data entered for each horse, freeing the memory as you go along.

More on Structure Members

So far you have seen that any of the basic data types, including arrays, can be members of a structure. But there's more. You can make a structure a member of a structure. Furthermore, pointers can be members of a structure, including pointers to structure types. This opens up a whole new range of possibilities in organizing data with structures and at the same time increases the potential for confusion. Let's look at each of these possibilities in sequence and see what they have to offer. Maybe it won't be a can of worms after all.

Structures As Members of a Structure

At the start of this chapter, you examined the needs of horse breeders and, in particular, the necessity to manage a variety of details about each horse, including its name, height, date of birth, and so on. You tried this out in Program 11.1, which carefully avoided date of birth and substituted age instead. This was partly because dates are messy things to deal with, because they're represented by three numbers and hold all the complications of leap years. However, you're now ready to tackle dates using a structure that's a member of another structure.

You can define a structure type designed to hold dates. You can specify a suitable structure with the tag name Date with this statement:

```
struct Date
{
  int day;
  int month;
  int year;
};
```

You can also include a typedef for Date as well as for Horse:

```
typedef struct Horse Horse;      // Define Horse as a type name
typedef struct Date Date;        // Define Date as a type name
```

Now you can define the Horse structure, including a date-of-birth variable, like this:

```
struct Horse
{
  Date dob;
  int height;
  char name[20];
  char father[20];
  char mother[20];
};
```

Now you have a single variable member within the structure that represents the date of birth of a horse, and this member is itself a structure. You don't need the struct keyword because you have defined Date as the equivalent of struct Date. Next, you can define an instance of the Horse structure with the usual statement:

```
Horse dobbin;
```

You can set the value of the member height with the same sort of statement that you've already seen:

```
dobbin.height = 14;
```

If you want to set the date of birth in a series of assignment statements, you can use the logical extension of this notation:

```
dobbin.dob.day = 5;
dobbin.dob.month = 12;
dobbin.dob.year = 1962;
```

You have a very old horse! The expression dobbin.dob.day is referencing a variable of type int, so you can happily use it in arithmetic or comparative expressions. But if you use the expression dobbin.dob, you would be referring to a struct variable of type Date. Because this is clearly not a basic type but a structure, you can use it only in an assignment such as this:

```
trigger.dob = dobbin.dob;
```

This *could* mean that they're twins, but it doesn't guarantee it.

If you can find a good reason to do it, you can extend the notion of structures that are members of a structure to a structure that's a member of a structure that's a member of a structure. In fact, if you can make sense of it, you can continue with further levels of structure. Your C compiler is likely to provide for at least 15 levels of such convolution. But beware: if you reach this depth of structure nesting, you're likely to be in for a bout of repetitive strain injury just typing the references to members.

Declaring a Structure Within a Structure

You could define the Date structure within the Horse structure definition, as in the following code:

```
struct Horse
{
  struct Date
  {
    int day;
    int month;
    int year;
  } dob;

  int height;
  char name[20];
  char father[20];
  char mother[20];
};
```

This has an interesting effect. Because the declaration is enclosed within the scope of the Horse structure definition, it doesn't exist outside it, so it becomes impossible to declare a Date variable external to the Horse structure. Of course, each instance of a Horse type variable would contain the Date type member, dob. But a statement such as

```
struct Date my_date;
```

may cause a compiler error. The message generated will say that the structure type Date is undefined. If you need to use Date outside the Horse structure, its definition should be placed outside the Horse structure.

As stated before, we can declare unnamed (anonymous) structures, and this can be within another structure (or union), precisely like the preceding Horse structure. They can be bundled recursively if the containing structure or union is also anonymous. The structure members can be accessed directly, as seen in the example:

```
// Program 11.3a Anonymous struct
#define _CRT_SECURE_NO_WARNINGS
#include <stdio.h>
#include <string.h>

struct Horse                  // Structure type definition
{
    char owner[9];
    struct      // Anonymous struct
    {
        int age;
```

```
        char height;
    };
};

int main(void)
{
    struct Horse rocinante;

        rocinante.age = 55;
        rocinante.height = 13;
    strcpy(rocinante.owner, "Quixote");

    printf("age: %d, height: %d, owner: %s",
            rocinante.age, rocinante.height, rocinante.owner);

    return 0;
}
```

Pointers to Structures As Structure Members

Any pointer can be a member of a structure. This includes a pointer that points to a structure. A pointer structure member that points to the same type of structure is also permitted. For example, the Horse type structure could contain a pointer to a Horse structure type. Interesting, but is it of any use? Well, as it happens, yes. It enables you to chain horses together—in a team, so wagons ho!

TRY IT OUT: POINTERS TO STRUCTURES IN STRUCTURES

You can demonstrate a structure containing a pointer to a structure of the same type with a modification of the previous example:

```
// Program 11.4    Daisy chaining the horses
#define __STDC_WANT_LIB_EXT1__ 1
#include <stdio.h>
#include <ctype.h>
#include <stdlib.h>

typedef struct Horse Horse;         // Define Horse as a type name

struct Horse                        // Structure type definition
{
  int age;
  int height;
  char name[20];
  char father[20];
  char mother[20];
  Horse *next;                      // Pointer to next Horse structure
};
```

```c
int main(void)
{
  Horse *first = NULL;                // Pointer to first horse
  Horse *current = NULL;              // Pointer to current horse
  Horse *previous = NULL;            // Pointer to previous horse

  char test = '\0';                  // Test value for ending input

  for( ; ; )
  {
    printf_s("Do you want to enter details of a%s horse (Y or N)? ",
                               first != NULL ? "nother" : "" );
    scanf_s(" %c", &test, sizeof(test));
    if(tolower(test) == 'n')
      break;

    // Allocate memory for a Horse structure
    current = (Horse*) malloc(sizeof(Horse));
    if(first == NULL)                // If there's no 1st Horse...
      first = current;               // ...set this as 1st Horse

    if(previous != NULL)             // If there was a previous...
      previous->next = current;      // ...set its next to this one

    printf_s("Enter the name of the horse: ");
    scanf_s("%s", current->name, sizeof(current->name));

    printf_s("How old is %s? ", current->name);
    scanf_s("%d", &current->age);

    printf_s("How high is %s ( in hands )? ", current -> name );
    scanf_s("%d", &current->height);

    printf_s("Who is %s's father? ", current->name);
    scanf_s("%s", current->father,sizeof(current->father));

    printf_s("Who is %s's mother? ", current->name);
    scanf_s("%s", current->mother, sizeof(current->mother));

    current->next = NULL;            // In case it's the last...
    previous = current;              // ...save its address
  }

  // Now tell them what we know...
  printf_s("\n");
  current = first;                   // Start at the beginning
  while (current != NULL)            // As long as we have a valid pointer
  { // Output the data
    printf_s("%s is %d years old, %d hands high,",
                    current->name, current->age, current->height);
    printf_s(" and has %s and %s as parents.\n", current->father,
                                     current->mother);
    previous = current;    // Save the pointer so we can free memory
    current = current->next;        // Get the pointer to the next
    free(previous);                 // Free memory for the old one
    previous = NULL;
  }
```

```
   first = NULL;
   return 0;
}
```

This example should produce the same output as Program 11.3 (given the same input), but here you have yet another mode of operation.

How It Works

You've added a member to the Horse structure with the name next that is a pointer to a Horse structure. This will be used to link all the horses you have, where each Horse structure will have a pointer containing the address of the next. The last Horse structure will be an exception, of course. Because there is no subsequent Horse structure, its next member will be NULL. The structure is otherwise exactly as you had previously. It's shown in Figure 11-3.

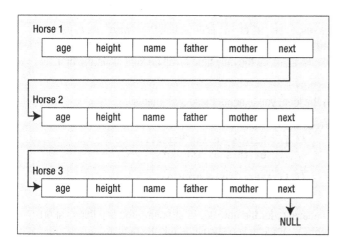

Figure 11-3. *A sequence of linked horses*

Note that with the typedef for Horse, you can use just Horse to specify the type of the next member of the Horse structure. You must always use the struct keyword when you define a structure though.

This time, not only do you have no space for structures allocated but you also have only three pointers defined initially. These pointers are declared and initialized in these statements:

```
Horse *first = NULL;          // Pointer to first horse
Horse *current = NULL;        // Pointer to current horse
Horse *previous = NULL;       // Pointer to previous horse
```

Each pointer is defined as a pointer to a Horse structure. The pointer first is used solely to store the address of the first structure. The second and third pointers are working storage: current holds the address of the current Horse structure you're dealing with, and previous keeps track of the address of the previous structure that was processed.

The input loop is the following:

```
for( ; ; )
{
  ...
}
```

The input loop is now an indefinite loop because you don't have an array to worry about. You don't need to mess around with indexes. It's also unnecessary to keep count of how many sets of data are read in, so you don't need the variable hcount or the loop variable i. Because you allocate memory for each horse, you can just take them as they come.

The initial statements in the loop are the following:

```
printf_s("Do you want to enter details of a%s horse (Y or N)? ",
                          first != NULL ? "nother" : "" );
scanf_s(" %c", &test, sizeof(test));
if(tolower(test) == 'n')
  break;
```

After the prompt, you exit from the loop if the response 'N' or 'n' is detected. Otherwise, you expect another set of structure members to be entered. You use the pointer first to get a slightly different prompt on the second and subsequent iterations, because the only time it will be NULL is on the first loop iteration.

Assuming you get past the initial question in the loop, you execute these statements:

```
current = (Horse*) malloc(sizeof(Horse));
if(first == NULL)                 // If there's no 1st Horse...
    first = current;              // ...set this as 1st Horse

if(previous != NULL)              // If there was a previous...
    previous->next = current;     // ...set its next to this one
```

On each iteration, you allocate the memory necessary for the new Horse structure. To keep things short, there's no check for a NULL return from malloc(), although you should do this in practice.

If first is NULL, you must be on the first loop iteration, and this must be the first structure about to be entered. Consequently, you set first to the address that you've just obtained from malloc() and stored in current. The address in first is the key to accessing the first horse in the chain. You can get to any of the others by starting with the address in first and then use its next member pointer to access the address of the next structure. You can step from there to the next structure and so on to any horse in the sequence.

The next pointer for each Horse object always needs to point to the next Horse structure in the chain if there is one, but the address of the next structure can be determined only once you have the next structure. Therefore, on the second and subsequent iterations, you store the address of the current structure in the next member of the previous structure, whose address you'll have saved in previous. On the first iteration, the pointer previous will be NULL, so of course you do nothing.

At the end of the loop, following all the input statements, you have these statements:

```
current->next = NULL;             // In case it's the last...
previous = current;               // ...save its address
```

The next pointer in the structure pointed to by current, which you're presently working with, is set to NULL in case this is the last structure and there's no next structure. If there is a next structure, this next pointer will be filled in on the next iteration. The previous pointer is set to current and is ready for the next iteration, when the current structure will indeed be the previous structure. Have you got that?

The strategy of the program for storing information on an unlimited number of horses is to generate a daisy chain of Horse structures in which the next member of each structure points to the next structure in the chain. The last is an exception because there's no next Horse, so its next pointer contains NULL. This arrangement is called a *linked list*.

Once you have the horse data in a linked list, you process it by starting with the first structure and then getting the next structure through the pointer member next. When the pointer next is NULL, you know that you've reached the end of the list. This is how you generate the output list of all the input.

Linked lists are invaluable in applications in which you need to process an unknown number of structures, such as you have here. The main advantages of a linked list relate to memory usage and ease of handling. You occupy only the minimum memory necessary to store and process the list. Although the memory used may be fragmented, you have no problem progressing from one structure to the next. As a consequence, in a practical situation in which you may need to deal with several different types of objects simultaneously, each can be handled using its own linked list, with the result that memory use is optimized. There is one small cloud associated with this—as there is with any silver lining—and it's that you pay a penalty in slower access to the data, particularly if you want to access it randomly.

The output process shows how you access a linked list because it steps through the linked list of Horse objects you have created with these statements:

```
current = first;                    // Start at the beginning
while (current != NULL)             // As long as we have a valid pointer
{ // Output the data
  printf_s("%s is %d years old, %d hands high,",
                    current->name, current->age, current->height);
  printf_s(" and has %s and %s as parents.\n", current->father,
                                        current->mother);
  previous = current;     // Save the pointer so we can free memory
  current = current->next;         // Get the pointer to the next
  free(previous);                  // Free memory for the old one
  previous = NULL;
}
```

The current pointer controls the output loop, and it's set to first at the outset. Remember that the first pointer contains the address of the first structure in the list. The loop steps through the list, and as the members of each structure are displayed, the address stored in the member next, which points to the next structure, is assigned to current.

The memory for the structure displayed is then freed. It's obviously fairly essential that you only free the memory for a structure once you have no further need to reference it. It's easy to fall into the trap of putting the call of the function free() immediately after you've output all of the member values for the current structure. This would create some problems, because then you couldn't legally reference the current structure's next member to get the pointer to the next Horse structure. For the last structure in the linked list, the next pointer will contain NULL, and the loop will terminate. It is not strictly necessary to set the pointers to NULL because the program ends, but it's a good policy to always set a pointer to NULL when the address it contains is no longer valid.

Doubly Linked Lists

A disadvantage of the linked list you created in the previous example is that you can only go forward. You can start with the first horse and work your way through to the last, but you can't go backward. However, a small modification of the idea enables you to create a *doubly linked list*, which will allow you to go through a list in either direction. The trick is to include an extra pointer in each structure to store the address of the previous structure in addition to the pointer to the next.

TRY IT OUT: DOUBLY LINKED LISTS

You can see a doubly linked list in action in a modified version of Program 11.4:

```c
// Program 11.5 Daisy chaining the horses both ways
#define __STDC_WANT_LIB_EXT1__ 1
#include <stdio.h>
#include <ctype.h>
#include <stdlib.h>

typedef struct Horse Horse;     // Define Horse as a type name

struct Horse                    // Structure type definition
{
  int age;
  int height;
  char name[20];
  char father[20];
  char mother[20];
  Horse *next;                  // Pointer to next structure
  Horse *previous;              // Pointer to previous structure
};

int main(void)
{
  Horse *first = NULL;          // Pointer to first horse
  Horse *current = NULL;        // Pointer to current horse
  Horse *last = NULL;           // Pointer to previous horse

  char test = '\0';             // Test value for ending input

  for( ; ; )
  {
    printf_s("Do you want to enter details of a%s horse (Y or N)? ",
                                  first != NULL ? "nother" : "");
    scanf_s(" %c", &test, sizeof(test));
    if(tolower(test) == 'n')
      break;

    // Allocate memory for each new horse structure
    current = (Horse*) malloc(sizeof(Horse));
    if(first == NULL)
    {
      first = current;          // Set pointer to first horse
     current->previous = NULL;
    }
```

```
    else
    {
      last->next = current;       // Set next address for previous horse
      current->previous = last;   // Previous address for current horse
    }

    printf_s("Enter the name of the horse: ");
    scanf_s("%s", current->name, sizeof(current->name));

    printf_s("How old is %s? ", current->name);
    scanf_s("%d", &current->age);

    printf_s("How high is %s ( in hands )? ", current -> name );
    scanf_s("%d", &current->height);

    printf_s("Who is %s's father? ", current->name);
    scanf_s("%s", current->father,sizeof(current->father));

    printf_s("Who is %s's mother? ", current->name);
    scanf_s("%s", current->mother, sizeof(current->mother));

    current->next = NULL;       // In case it's the last...
    last = current;             // ...save its address
  }
  // Now tell them what we know.
  printf_s("\n");
  while(current != NULL)        // Output horse data in reverse order
  {
    printf_s("%s is %d years old, %d hands high,",
                current->name, current->age, current->height);
    printf_s(" and has %s and %s as parents.\n", current->father,
                                        current->mother);
    last = current;                     // Save pointer to enable memory to be freed
    current = current->previous;  // current points to previous in list
    free(last);                         // Free memory for the horse we output
    last = NULL;
  }
  first = NULL;
  return 0;
}
```

For the same input, this program should produce the same output as before, except that the data on the horses you enter are displayed in reverse order to that of entry—just to show that you can do it.

How It Works

The Horse structure is defined as

```
struct Horse                        // Structure type definition
{
  int age;
  int height;
```

```
    char name[20];
    char father[20];
    char mother[20];
    Horse *next;                    // Pointer to next structure
    Horse *previous;                // Pointer to previous structure
};
```

The Horse structure now contains two pointers: one to point forward in the list, called next, and the other to point backward to the preceding structure, called previous. This allows the list to be traversed in either direction, as you demonstrate by the fact that you output the data at the end of the program in reverse order.

The initial pointer declarations are now

```
    Horse *first = NULL;            // Pointer to first horse
    Horse *current = NULL;          // Pointer to current horse
    Horse *last = NULL;             // Pointer to previous horse
```

I changed the name of the pointer recording the Horse structure entered on the previous iteration of the loop to last. This name change isn't strictly necessary, but it does help to avoid confusion with the structure member previous.

Aside from the output, the only changes to the program are to add the statements that take care of the entries for the pointer structure member previous. In the beginning of the input loop, you have the following:

```
    if(first == NULL)
    {
      first = current;              // Set pointer to first horse
      current->previous = NULL;
    }
    else
    {
      last->next = current;         // Set next address for previous horse
      current->previous = last;     // Previous address for current horse
    }
```

When first is NULL, it's the first loop iteration, so you store the address of the current Horse object in first, and because there is no previous horse, you set the previous member of first to NULL. For all subsequent structures, the previous member is set to the pointer last, whose value was saved on the preceding iteration. For all structures after the first, last will not be NULL, so you set its next member to the address of the current Horse structure.

At the end of the input loop, you do this:

```
    current->next = NULL;           // In case it's the last...
    last = current;                 // ...save its address
```

There is no next structure yet, so you set the next member of current to NULL. At this point current contains the address of the last structure so far, so you store this in last.

The output process is virtually the same as in the previous example, except that you start from the last structure in the list and work back to the first. You could also output the horses forward with a similar loop, with `current` starting out as `first` and using `current->next` in the loop body instead of `current->previous`.

As we can see, using (doubly) linked list (pointers at the end) makes our data structure more comfortable to create other methods for inserting, removing items of the list (which cannot be done in a fixed array). It is straightforward if the item is at the beginning or end of the list, but if it is a distinct item, then we need to iterate until finding it (we must iterate almost the complete list in the worst scenario). Another disadvantage is to have more significant memory footprint for handling the items, and again, it is slower by not having random (direct) access to the items.

Bit Fields in a Structure

Bit fields provide a mechanism that allows you to define variables within a structure that comprise one or more adjacent binary bits within a single integer word. You can refer to a bit field using its member name. A bit field is one or more adjacent bits in an integer word that is usually of type `unsigned int`. A bit field can also be type `_Bool` or bits in a word of type `int`.

■ **Note**   Bit fields are used most frequently when memory is at a premium and you're in a situation in which you must use it as sparingly as possible. This is rarely the case these days, so you won't see them used very often. Bit fields will slow your program down appreciably compared with using standard variable types. You must therefore assess each situation on its merits to decide whether the memory savings offered by bit fields are worth this price in execution speed for your programs. In most instances, bit fields won't be necessary or even desirable, but you still need to know about them. Bit fields are frequently used in embedded programming by the requirement of handling hardware at a low level (registers). Conclusively, bit field structures are beneficial for microcontroller memory (where the impact can be high) and the advantage of a versatile and easy interface for bit manipulation.

Bit fields are often defined within an anonymous structure. Here's an example of an anonymous structure containing only bit fields as members:

```
struct
{
  unsigned int flag1 : 1;
  unsigned int flag2 : 1;
  unsigned int flag3 : 2;
  unsigned int flag4 : 3;
} indicators;
```

This defines a variable with the name `indicators` that's an instance of an anonymous structure containing four bit fields with the names `flag1`–`flag4`. These will all be stored in a single word, as illustrated in Figure 11-4.

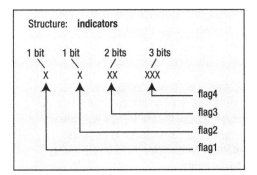

Figure 11-4. *Bit fields in a structure*

The first two bit fields, being a single bit specified by the 1 in their definition, can only assume the values 0 or 1. The third bit field, flag3, has 2 bits, so it can have a value from 0 to 3. The last bit field, flag4, can have values from 0 to 7, because it has 3 bits. These bit fields are referenced in the same manner as other structure members, for example:

```
indicators.flag4 = 5;
indicators.flag3 = indicators.flag1 = 1;
```

Where you do not occupy all the bits in a word with named bit fields, you can specify an anonymous bit field to fill up the word, for example:

```
struct
{
  unsigned int flag1 : 1;
  unsigned int flag2 : 1;
  unsigned int flag3 : 2;
  unsigned int flag4 : 3;
  unsigned int       : 25;
} indicators;
```

This ensures that the memory occupied ends on a 4-byte boundary.

A regular named struct type can contain bit fields alongside members of other types, for example:

```
struct Person
{
  char name[20];
  unsigned int sex : 1;          // Male = 1 Female = 0
  unsigned int height : 7 ;      // Height in inches
  unsigned int age : 8;          // Up to 255 years old
  unsigned int married : 1;      // Married = 1
  unsigned int       : 15;       // Unused
  char address[100];
};
```

The members of the Person structure that records the sex, age, height, and whether or not a person is married are defined as bit fields. You'll rarely, if ever, have any need for this facility. I've included bit fields here for the sake of completeness and for that strange off chance that one day bit fields will be just what you need in a particularly tight memory situation.

Structures and Functions

Structures represent a very powerful feature of the C language, and their use with functions is very important. You'll now look at how you can pass structures as arguments to a function and how you can return a structure from a function.

Structures As Arguments to Functions

There's nothing unusual in the method for passing a structure as an argument to a function. It's exactly the same as passing any other variable. Analogous to the Horse structure, you could create this structure:

```
struct Family
{
  char name[20];
  int age;
  char father[20];
  char mother[20];
};
```

Assuming that you have a typedef that defines Family as equivalent to struct Family, you could construct a function to test whether two Family objects are siblings like this:

```
bool siblings(Family member1, Family member2)
{
  if(strcmp(member1.mother, member2.mother) == 0)
    return true;
  else
    return false;
}
```

This function has two parameters, each of which is a structure. It simply compares the strings corresponding to the member mother for each structure. If they're the same, they are siblings, and true is returned. Otherwise, they can't be siblings, so false is returned. You're ignoring the effects of divorce, in vitro fertilization, cloning, artificial insemination, and any other possibilities that may make this test inadequate.

Pointers to Structures As Function Arguments

Remember that a copy of the value of an argument is transferred to a function when it's called. If the argument is a large structure, it can take quite a bit of time, as well as requiring whatever amount of memory to store the copy of the structure. Under these circumstances, you should use a pointer to a structure as an argument. This avoids the memory consumption and the copying time, because now only a copy of the pointer argument is made. The function will access the original structure directly through the pointer. More often than not, structures are passed to a function using a pointer, just for these reasons of efficiency. You could rewrite the siblings() function like this:

```
bool siblings(Family *pmember1, Family *pmember2)
{
  if(strcmp(pmember1->mother, pmember2->mother) == 0)
    return true;
  else
    return false;
}
```

Now, there is a downside to this. The pass-by-value mechanism provides excellent protection against accidental modification of values from within a called function. You lose this if you pass a pointer to a function. On the upside, if you don't need to modify the values pointed to by a pointer argument (you just want to access and use them, for instance), you can get a degree of protection, even though you're passing pointers to a function. It's time to dig up the const qualifier again.

Have another look at the last siblings() function. It doesn't need to modify the structures passed to it—in fact, it only needs to compare members. You could therefore rewrite it like this:

```
bool siblings(Family const *pmember1, Family const *pmember2)
{
  if(strcmp(pmember1->mother, pmember2->mother) == 0)
    return true;
  else
    return false;
}
```

You'll recall the const modifier from earlier in the book, where you used it to make a variable effectively a constant. This function declaration specifies the parameters as type pointer to constant Family structure. This implies that the structures pointed to by the pointers transferred to the function will be treated as constants within the function. Any attempt to change those structures will cause an error message during compilation. Of course, this doesn't affect their status as variables in the calling program, because the const keyword applies only to the values while the function is executing.

Note the difference between the previous definition of the function and this one:

```
bool siblings(Family *const pmember1, Family *const pmember2)
{
  if(strcmp(pmember1->mother, pmember2->mother) == 0)
    return true;
  else
    return false;
}
```

The indirection operator in each parameter definition is now in front of the const keyword, rather than in front of the parameter name as it was before. Does this make a difference? You bet it does. The parameters here are constant pointers to structures of type Family, not pointers to constant Family structures. With this version, you're free to alter the structures themselves in the function, but you must not modify the addresses stored in the pointers. It's the pointers that are protected here, not the structures to which they point. This is also pointless because the pointers are copies anyway.

Structure As a Function Return Value

There's nothing unusual about returning a structure from a function. The function prototype merely has to indicate this return value in the normal way, for example:

```
Horse my_fun(void);
```

This is a prototype for a function taking no arguments that returns a structure of type Horse.

Although you can return a structure from a function like this, it's often more convenient to return a pointer to a structure. Of course when you are returning a pointer to a structure, the structure should be created on the heap. Let's explore this in more detail through a working example.

TRY IT OUT: RETURNING A POINTER TO A STRUCTURE

To demonstrate how returning a pointer to a structure from a function works, you can rewrite the previous example in terms of humans. This example defines three functions in addition to main(). Here's the preamble followed by the definition of main():

```c
// Program 11.6 Basics of a family tree
#define __STDC_WANT_LIB_EXT1__ 1
#include <stdio.h>
#include <ctype.h>
#include <stdlib.h>
#include <stdbool.h>

typedef struct Date Date;
typedef struct Family Family;

// Function prototypes
Family *get_person(void);                                  // Input function
void show_people(bool forwards, Family *pfirst, Family *plast);  // Output function
void release_memory(Family *pfirst);                       // Release heap memory

struct Date
{
  int day;
  int month;
  int year;
};

struct Family                        // Family structure declaration
{
  Date dob;
  char name[20];
  char father[20];
  char mother[20];
  Family *next;                      // Pointer to next structure
  Family *previous;                  // Pointer to previous structure
};
```

```
int main(void)
{
  Family *first = NULL;                 // Pointer to first person
  Family *current = NULL;               // Pointer to current person
  Family *last = NULL;                  // Pointer to previous person
  char more = '\0';                     // Test value for ending input

  while(true)
  {
    printf_s("\nDo you want to enter details of a%s person (Y or N)? ",
                                    first != NULL ? "nother" : "");
    scanf_s(" %c", &more, sizeof(more));
    if(tolower(more) == 'n')
      break;

    current = get_person();

    if(first == NULL)
      first = current;                  // Set pointer to first Family
    else
    {
      last->next = current;             // Set next address for previous Family
      current->previous = last;         // Set previous address for current
    }
    last = current;                     // Remember for next iteration
  }

  show_people(true, first, last);       // Tell them what we know
  release_memory(first);
  first = last = NULL;
  return 0;
}
```

Here's the definition of the get_person() function:

```
Family *get_person(void)
{
  Family *temp = (Family*) malloc(sizeof(Family));

  printf_s("\nEnter the name of the person: ");
  scanf_s("%s", temp->name, sizeof(temp->name));

  printf_s("\nEnter %s's date of birth (day month year); ", temp->name);
  scanf_s("%d %d %d", &temp->dob.day, &temp->dob.month, &temp->dob.year);

  printf_s("\nWho is %s's father? ", temp->name);
  scanf_s("%s", temp->father, sizeof(temp->father));

  printf_s("\nWho is %s's mother? ", temp->name);
  scanf_s("%s", temp->mother, sizeof(temp->mother));

  temp->next = temp->previous = NULL;    // Set pointer members to NULL

  return temp;                           // Return address of Family structure
}
```

Here's the definition of show_people() that outputs details of the Family elements in the linked list:

```
void show_people(bool forwards, Family *pfirst, Family *plast)
{
  printf_s("\n");
  for(Family *pcurrent = forwards ? pfirst : plast ;
      pcurrent != NULL ;
      pcurrent = forwards ? pcurrent->next : pcurrent->previous)
  {
    printf_s("%s was born %d/%d/%d and has %s and %s as parents.\n",
             pcurrent->name, pcurrent->dob.day, pcurrent->dob.month,
             pcurrent->dob.year, pcurrent->father,  pcurrent->mother);
  }
}
```

Finally, here's the definition of the function that frees heap memory:

```
void release_memory(Family *pfirst)
{
  Family *pcurrent = pfirst;
  Family *temp = NULL;
  while(pcurrent)
  {
    temp = pcurrent;
    pcurrent = pcurrent->next;
    free(temp);
  }
}
```

The output is similar to previous examples, so I won't include it here.

How It Works

Although this looks like a lot of code, you should find this example quite straightforward. It operates similarly to the previous example, but it's organized as four functions instead of one.

The first structure declaration is the following:

```
struct Date
{
  int day;
  int month;
  int year;
};
```

This defines a structure type Date with three members, day, month, and year, which are all declared as integers. No instances of the structure are declared at this point. The definition precedes all the functions in the source file, so it is accessible from within any function that appears subsequently in the file.

The next structure declaration is the following:

```
struct Family
{
  Date dob;
  char name[20];
  char father[20];
  char mother[20];
  Family *next;                    // Pointer to next structure
  Family *previous;                // Pointer to previous structure
};
```

This defines a structure type Family, which has a Date type structure as its first member. It then has three conventional char arrays as members. The last two members are pointers to structures. They allow a doubly linked list to be constructed, being pointers to the next and previous structures in the list, respectively. You are able to use the structure type names without the struct keyword when defining members of Family because of the typedef statements.

The get_person() function has this prototype:

```
Family *get_person(void);                                        // Input function
```

This indicates that the function accepts no arguments but returns a pointer to a Family structure.

The output function has the prototype

```
void show_people(bool forwards, Family *pfirst, Family *plast); // Output function
```

The first argument determines whether the list members are output forward or backward, and a true argument specifies forward. The other two arguments are the addresses of the first and last Family objects in the list.

The prototype of the function to free memory is

```
void release_memory(Family *pfirst);                             // Release heap memory
```

Given the address of the first Family object in the list, the function will be able to work through all the list elements to free the memory they occupy.

The process parallels the operation of Program 11.5, with the differences that you have global structure type declarations and you input a structure within a separate function.

Input and the creation of the linked list occur in the while loop in main() that continues until the user enters 'n' or 'N' in response to the prompt. After verifying that the user wants to enter data, main() calls get_person() in the loop to create a new Family structure and obtains the data to initialize it.

The first action within the function get_person() is to allocate some heap memory:

```
  Family *temp = (Family*) malloc(sizeof(Family));
```

The temp variable is of type pointer to a Family structure, and it has local scope, so it only exists within the body of the function. This call to malloc() obtains sufficient memory to store a structure of type Family and stores the address that's returned in temp. Although temp is local and will go out of scope at the end of the function get_person(), the heap memory allocated by malloc() is more permanent. It remains allocated until you free it within the program somewhere or until you exit from the program completely.

The get_person() function reads in all the basic data for a person, just as in previous examples, and stores it in the structure pointed to by temp. As it stands, the function will accept any values for the date, but in a real situation you would include code for data validity checking. You could verify that the month value is from 1 to 12 and the day value is valid for the month entered. Because a birth date is being entered, you might verify that it isn't in the future.

The last statement in the function get_person() is the following:

```
return temp;                              // Return address of Family structure
```

This returns a *copy* of the pointer to the structure that it has created. Although temp will no longer exist after the return, the address that it contains that points to the memory block obtained from malloc() is still valid, and the copy references it.

Back in main(), the pointer that's returned is stored in the variable current and is also saved in the variable first if this is the first iteration. You do this because you must keep track of the first structure in the list. You also save current in the variable last, because for the moment at least it is the last, so on the next iteration you can fill in the backward pointer member, previous, for the current person whose data you've just obtained.

After all the input data have been read, the program outputs a summary to the screen by calling show_people() with the argument true to obtain the output in a forward sequence. The show_people() function outputs the data in a for loop:

```
for(Family *pcurrent = forwards ? pfirst : plast ;
    pcurrent != NULL ;
    pcurrent = forwards ? pcurrent->next : pcurrent->previous)
{
  printf_s("%s was born %d/%d/%d and has %s and %s as parents.\n",
           pcurrent->name, pcurrent->dob.day, pcurrent->dob.month,
           pcurrent->dob.year, pcurrent->father,  pcurrent->mother);
}
```

The first control expression initializes the control variable pcurrent to pfirst when forwards is true and plast otherwise. The second control expression determines that the loop ends when pcurrent is NULL. The third control expression sets pcurrent to the address in its next member when forwards is true or the previous member when forwards is false. In this way, the loop iterates over all the elements in the list starting with pfirst when forwards is true and with plast when it is false. The loop body is just a single output statement that calls the printf_s() function.

The last action in main() is to call release_memory() to free the memory occupied by the linked list before resetting the first and last pointers to NULL. The function does this by traversing the list forward in the while loop:

```
while(pcurrent)
  {
    temp = pcurrent;
    pcurrent = pcurrent->next;
    free(temp);
  }
```

> The local `temp` variable stores the address of the current element from `pcurrent`, and `pcurrent` is set
> to the address of the next element, which will be `NULL` if the current element is the last; `temp` is then
> passed to the `free()` function to release the memory occupied by the current element.

Binary Trees

A *binary tree* is another very useful way of organizing data because the data that you store in a binary
tree can be extracted in an ordered fashion. A binary tree is a very simple mechanism that provides an
opportunity to bring together several of the programming techniques you have learned. Implementing a
binary tree can involve recursion as well as dynamic memory allocation, and you'll use pointers to pass tree
structures around.

A binary tree consists of a set of interconnected elements called *nodes*. The starting node is the base of
the tree and is called the *root node*, as shown in Figure 11-5.

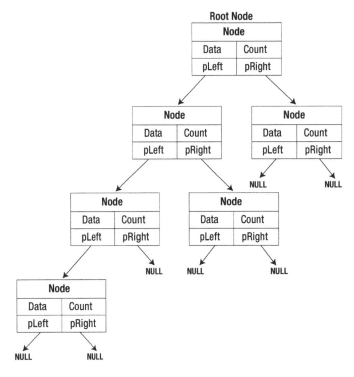

Figure 11-5. *The structure of a binary tree*

Each node typically contains an item of data, plus pointers to two subsidiary nodes, a *left node* and
a *right node*. If either subsidiary node does not exist, the corresponding pointer is `NULL`. A node may also
include a counter that records the number of duplicates of the data item that it contains.

A `struct` makes it very easy to represent a binary tree node. Here's an example of a `struct` that defines
nodes that store integers of type `long`:

```
typedef struct Node Node;
struct Node
{
  long item;                // The data item
  int count;                // Number of copies of item
  Node *pLeft;              // Pointer to left node
  Node *pRight;             // Pointer to right node
};
```

When a data item that is to be added to a binary tree already exists somewhere, a new node is not created; the count member of the existing node is simply incremented by 1. I'll use the previous definition of a struct that represents a node holding a long integer when we get to creating a binary tree in practice in Program 11.7.

Ordering Data in a Binary Tree

The way in which you construct the binary tree will determine the order of data items within the tree. Adding a data item to a tree involves comparing the item to be added with the existing items in the tree. Typically items are added so that for every node, the data item stored in the subsidiary left node is less than the data item in the current node, and the data item stored in the right node is greater than the item stored in the current node. If either subsidiary node does not exist, the pointer to it is NULL. An example of a tree containing an arbitrary sequence of integers is shown in Figure 11-6.

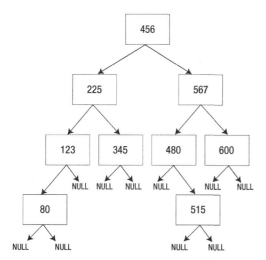

Figure 11-6. *A binary tree storing integers*

The structure of the tree will depend on the sequence in which the data items are added to the tree. Adding a new item involves comparing the data item with the values of the nodes in the tree starting with the root node. If it's less than a given node, you then inspect the left subsidiary node, whereas if it's greater, you look at the right subsidiary node. This process continues until either you find a node with an equal value, in which case you just update the count for that node, or you arrive at a left or right node pointer that is NULL. The new node becomes the left node if the data item is less than the current node or the right node if it is not.

Constructing a Binary Tree

The starting point is the creation of the root node. All nodes will be created in the same way, so the first step is to define a function that creates a node from a data item. I will assume we are creating a tree to store long integers, so the struct definition you saw earlier will apply. Here's the definition of a function that will create a node:

```
Node *create_node(long value)
{
  // Allocate memory for a new node
  Node *pNode = (Node*)malloc(sizeof(Node));

  pNode->item = value;                      // Set the value
  pNode->count = 1;                         // Set the count
  pNode->pLeft = pNode->pRight = NULL;      // No left or right nodes
  return pNode;
}
```

The function allocates memory for the new Node structure and sets the item member to value. The count member is the number of duplicates of the value in the node, so in the first instance, this has to be 1. There are no subsidiary nodes at this point, so the pLeft and pRight members are set to NULL. The function returns a pointer to the Node object that has been created.

To create the root node for a new binary tree, you can just use this function:

```
long newvalue;
printf("Enter the node value: ");
scanf_s(" %ld", &newvalue);
Node *pRoot = create_node(newvalue);
```

After reading the value to be stored from the keyboard, you call the create_node() function to create a new node on the heap. Of course, you must not forget to release the memory for the nodes when you are done.

Working with binary trees is one of the areas where recursion really pays off. The process of inserting a node involves inspecting a succession of nodes in the same way, which is a strong indicator that recursion may be helpful. You can add a node to a tree that already exists or create a root node with the following function:

```
// Add a new node to the tree
Node *add_node(long value, Node* pNode)
{
  if(!pNode)                          // If there's no node...
    return create_node(value);        // ...create one and return it

  if(value == pNode->item)
  {                                   // Value equals current node...
    ++pNode->count;                   // ...so increment count...
    return pNode;                     // ...and return the same node
  }
```

```
  if(value < pNode->item)
  {                                              // Less than current node...
    if(!pNode->pLeft)
    {                                            // ...and no left node...
      pNode->pLeft = create_node(value);         // ...so create a left node...
      return pNode->pLeft;                       // ...and return it.
    }
    else                                         // There is a left node...
      return add_node(value, pNode->pLeft);      // ...so add via the left node
  }
  else
  {                                              // Greater than current node...
    if(!pNode->pRight)
    {                                            // ...but no right node...
      pNode->pRight = create_node(value);        // ...so create one...
      return pNode->pRight;                      // ...and return it.
    }
    else                                         // There is a right node...
      return add_node(value, pNode->pRight);     // ...so add to that.
  }
}
```

The arguments to the add_node() function when you call it in the first instance are the value to be stored in the tree and the address of the root node. If you pass NULL as the second argument, it will create and return a new node, so you can also use this function to create the root node. When a root node is passed as the second argument, there are three situations to deal with:

1. If value equals the value in the current node, no new node needs to be created, so you just increment the count in the current node and return it.

2. If value is less than the value in the current node, you need to inspect the left subsidiary node. If the left node pointer is NULL, you create a new node to hold value and make it the left subsidiary node. If the left node exists, you call add_node() recursively with the pointer to the left subsidiary node as the second argument.

3. If value is greater than the value in the current node, you proceed with the right node in the same way as with the left node.

Whatever happens within the recursive function calls, the function will return a pointer to the node where value is inserted. This may be a new node or one of the existing nodes if value is already in the tree somewhere.

You could construct a complete binary tree storing an arbitrary number of integers with the following code:

```
long newvalue = 0;
Node *pRoot = NULL;
char answer = 'n';
do
{
  printf_s("Enter the node value: ");
  scanf_s(" %ld", &newvalue);
```

```
  if(!pRoot)
    pRoot = create_node(newvalue);
  else
    add_node(newvalue, pRoot);

  printf_s("Do you want to enter another (y or n)? ");
  scanf_s(" %c", &answer, sizeof(answer));
} while(tolower(answer) == 'y');
```

The do-while loop constructs the complete tree including the root node. On the first iteration, pRoot will be NULL, so the root node will be created. All subsequent iterations will add nodes to the existing tree.

Traversing a Binary Tree

You can traverse a binary tree to extract the contents in ascending or descending sequence. I'll discuss how you extract the data in ascending sequence, so you'll see how you can produce a descending sequence by analogy. At first sight, it seems a complicated problem to extract the data from the tree because of its arbitrary structure, but using recursion makes it very easy. I'll start the explanation of the process by stating the obvious: the value of the left subnode is always less than the current node, and the value of the current node is always less than that of the right subnode. You can conclude from this that the basic process is to extract the values in the following sequence: left subnode, followed by current node, followed by right subnode. Of course, where the subnodes have subnodes, the process has to be applied to those too, from left through current to right. It will be easy to see how this works if we look at some code.

There are several methods to search in a graph. A tree is a particular graph. The most common are Depth-First Search (DFS) and Breadth-First Search (BFS). As you can deduce from their names, DFS goes deep as much as it can by not considering its siblings (when returning from recursion, will go to the next sibling); on the other hand, BFS goes first by its siblings and later goes by its children (branches). Recursive DFS implementation is more natural and easy to understand (hence more elegant). There are more strategies for searching, but they are related to an advanced algorithm book.

There are different (recursive) traversals to use in DFS, pre-order, post-order, in-order, and reverse in-order, the last two methods being to fetch the ascending and descending order list of the tree's nodes, respectively.

Suppose we want to simply list the integer values contained in our binary tree in ascending sequence. The function to do that looks like this:

```
// List the node values in ascending sequence
void list_nodes_ascending (Node *pNode)
{
  if(pNode->pLeft)                        // If there's a left node...
    list_nodes_ascending(pNode->pLeft);         // ...list the left subtree.

  printf_s("%10d x %10ld\n", pNode->count, pNode->item);

  if(pNode->pRight)                       // If there's a right node...
    list_nodes_ascending(pNode->pRight);        // ...list the right subtree.
}
```

It consists of three simple steps:

1. If the left subnode exists, you call `list_nodes_ascending()` recursively for that node.

2. Write the value for the current node.

3. If the right subnode exists, call `list_nodes_ascending()` recursively for that node.

The analogy for descending order is to swap steps 1 and 3; thus, we traverse the tree by the right branch first, calling list_nodes_descending(), then the current node, and last the left node, calling list_nodes_descending().

The first step repeats the process for the left subnode of the root if it exists, so the whole subtree to the left will be written before the value of the current node. The number of times the value of the current node occurred that is recorded in count is indicated in the output. The values for the entire right subtree to the root node will be written after the value for the current node. You should be able to see that this happens for every node in the tree, so the values will be written in ascending sequence. All you have to do to output the values in ascending sequence is to call `list_nodes_ascending()` with the root node pointer as the argument, like this:

```
list_nodes(pRoot);                    // Output the contents of the tree
```

In case you find it hard to believe that such a simple function will output all the values in any binary tree of integers you care to construct, let's see it working.

TRY IT OUT: SORTING USING A BINARY TREE

This example drags together the code fragments you have already seen:

```
// Program 11.7 Sorting integers using a binary tree
#define __STDC_WANT_LIB_EXT1__ 1
#include <stdio.h>
#include <stdlib.h>
#include <ctype.h>

typedef struct Node Node;

// Defines a node in a binary tree sotring integers
struct Node
{
  long item;                          // The data item
  int count;                          // Number of copies of item
  Node *pLeft;                        // Pointer to left node
  Node *pRight;                       // Pointer to right node
};

// Function prototypes
Node *create_node(long value);        // Create a tree node
Node *add_node(long value, Node *pNode);  // Insert a new node
void list_nodes_ascending (Node *pNode);   // List all nodes
void list_nodes_descending(Node *pNode);  // List all nodes
void free_nodes(Node *pNode);         // Release memory
```

```c
// Function main - execution starts here
int main(void)
{
  long newvalue = 0;
  Node *pRoot = NULL;
  char answer = 'n';
  do
  {
    printf_s("Enter the node value: ");
    scanf_s(" %ld", &newvalue);
    if(!pRoot)
      pRoot = create_node(newvalue);
    else
      add_node(newvalue, pRoot);
    printf_s("Do you want to enter another (y or n)? ");
    scanf_s(" %c", &answer, sizeof(answer));
  } while(tolower(answer) == 'y');

  printf_s("The values in ascending sequence are:\n");
  list_nodes(pRoot);                        // Output the contents of the tree
  printf_s("The values in descending sequence are:\n");
  list_nodes_descending(pRoot);
  free_nodes(pRoot);                        // Release the heap memory

  return 0;
}

// Create a binary tree node
Node *create_node(long value)
{
  Node *pNode = (Node*)malloc(sizeof(Node));
  pNode->item = value;                      // Set the value
  pNode->count = 1;                         // Set the count
  pNode->pLeft = pNode->pRight = NULL;      // No left or right nodes
  return pNode;
}

// Add a new node to the tree
Node *add_node(long value, Node *pNode)
{
  if(!pNode)                                // If there's no node
    return create_node(value);             // ...create one and return it

  if(value == pNode->item)
  {                                         // Value equals current node...
    ++pNode->count;                         // ...so increment count ...
    return pNode;                           // ...and return the same node
  }

  if(value < pNode->item)
  {                                         // Less than current node...
    if(!pNode->pLeft)                       // ...and no left node
    {
      pNode->pLeft = create_node(value);    // ... so create a left node...
```

```
      return pNode->pLeft;                    // ...and return it.
    }
    else                                      // There is a left node...
      return add_node(value, pNode->pLeft);   // ...so add value via left node
  }
  else
  {                                           // Greater than current node...
    if(!pNode->pRight)
    {                                         // ...but no right node...
      pNode-> pRight = create_node(value);    // ...so create one...
      return pNode-> pRight;                  // ...and return it.
    }
    else                                      // There is a right node...
      return add_node(value, pNode->pRight);  // ...so add to that.
  }
}

// List the node values in ascending sequence (In-order)
void list_nodes_ascending (Node *pNode)
{
  if(pNode->pLeft)
    list_nodes_ascending (pNode->pLeft);

  printf_s("%10d x %10ld\n", pNode->count, pNode->item);

  if(pNode->pRight)
    list_nodes_ascending (pNode->pRight);
}

// List the node values in descending sequence (Reverse in-order)
void list_nodes_descending(Node *pNode)
{
  if(pNode->pRight)
    list_nodes_descending(pNode->pRight);

  printf_s("%10d x %10ld\n", pNode->count, pNode->item);

  if(pNode->pLeft)
    list_nodes_descending(pNode->pLeft);
}

// Release memory allocated to nodes
void free_nodes(Node *pNode)
{
  if(!pNode)                                  // If there's no node...
    return;                                   // ...we are done.

  if(pNode->pLeft)                            // If there's a left sub-tree...
    free_nodes(pNode->pLeft);                 // ...free memory for those nodes.

  if(pNode->pRight)                           // If there's a right sub-tree...
    free_nodes(pNode->pRight);                // ...free memory for those nodes.

  free(pNode);                                // Free current node memory
}
```

Here is some typical output from this example:

```
Enter the node value: 56
Do you want to enter another (y or n)? y
Enter the node value: 33
Do you want to enter another (y or n)? y
Enter the node value: 77
Do you want to enter another (y or n)? y
Enter the node value: -10
Do you want to enter another (y or n)? y
Enter the node value: -5
Do you want to enter another (y or n)? y
Enter the node value: 200
Do you want to enter another (y or n)? y
Enter the node value: -10
Do you want to enter another (y or n)? n
The values in ascending sequence are:
        2 x          -10
        1 x           -5
        1 x           33
        1 x           56
        1 x           77
        1 x          200
The values in descending sequence are:
        1 x          200
        1 x           77
        1 x           56
        1 x           33
        1 x           -5
        2 x          -10
```

How It Works

The do-while loop in main() constructs the binary tree from the values that are entered in the way I discussed earlier. The loop continues as long as you enter 'y' or 'Y' when prompted. Calling list_nodes_ascending() with the address of the root node as the argument outputs all the values in the tree in ascending sequence. You then call the free_nodes() function to release the memory that is allocated for the nodes for the tree.

The free_nodes() function is the only new code in the example. This is another recursive function that works in a similar way to list_nodes_ascending (). It is essential to delete the memory for the subsidiary nodes of each node before freeing the memory for the node itself, because once you have freed a memory block, it could be used immediately by some other program that is executing concurrently. This means that the addresses for the subsidiary nodes are unavailable once the memory has been released. The function therefore always calls free_nodes() for the subsidiary node pointers if they are not NULL before releasing the memory for the current node.

You can construct binary trees to store any kind of data including struct objects and strings. If you want to organize strings in a binary tree, for example, you could use a pointer in each node to refer to the string rather than making copies of the strings within the tree.

Sharing Memory

You've already seen how you can save memory through the use of bit fields, which are typically applied to logical variables. C has a further capability that allows you to define several variables that occupy the same memory area. This capability can be applied somewhat more widely than bit fields when memory is short, because circumstances frequently arise in practice in which you're working with several variables, but only one of them holds a valid value at any given moment. Another situation in which you can share memory between a number of variables to some advantage is when your program processes a number of different kinds of data records, but only one kind at a time, and the kind to be processed is determined at execution time. A further possibility is that you want to access the same data at different times, and assume that the data are of different types on different occasions. You might also have a group of variables of numeric data types that you want to treat as simply an array of char elements so that you can move them about as a single chunk of data.

The facility in C that allows the same memory area to be shared by a number of different variables is called a *union*. The syntax for declaring a union is similar to that used for structures, and a union is usually given a tag name in the same way. You use the keyword union to define a union. For example, the following statement declares a union to be shared by three variables:

```
union U_example
{
  float decval;
  int *pnum;
  double my_value;
} u1;
```

This statement declares a union with the tag name U_example, which shares memory between a floating-point value decval, a pointer to an integer pnum, and a double-precision floating-point variable my_value. The statement also defines one instance of the union with a variable name of u1. You can declare further instances of this union with a statement such as this:

```
union U_example u2, u3;
```

Members of a union are accessed in exactly the same way as members of a structure. For example, to assign values to members of u1 and u2, you can write this:

```
u1.decval = 2.5;
u2.decval = 3.5*u1.decval;
```

The size of an instance of a union is the memory required for the largest member.

Anonymous unions are similar to an anonymous struct, where no tag name is assigned and members are accessed directly, they are inside of a structure or union, and they can be wrapped recursively if the containing structure or union is also anonymous. We can see this in the next snippet code (complete example at source code repository: Program 11.8a):

```
struct Horse                    // Structure type definition
{
    char owner[9];
    union       // Anonymous union
    {
        int age;
        char height;
    };
};
// main…
    struct Horse rocinante;
    //assigning values to the members
        rocinante.age = 55;
        strcpy(rocinante.owner, "Quixote");
//accessing to the members' values:
rocinante.age, rocinante.owner
```

TRY IT OUT: USING UNIONS

Here's an example that makes use of a union:

```
// Program 11.8 The operation of a union
#define __STDC_WANT_LIB_EXT1__ 1
#include <stdio.h>

typedef union UDate UDate;
typedef struct Date Date;
typedef struct MixedDate MixedDate;
typedef struct NumericDate NumericDate;

void print_date(const Date* date);           // Prototype

enum Date_Format{numeric, text, mixed};       // Date formats

// Date in the form "day" "date month" nnnn
struct MixedDate
{
  char *day;
  char *date;
  int year;
};

// Date in the form dd mm yyyy
struct NumericDate
{
  int day;
  int month;
  int year;
};
```

```c
// Any of 3 possible date forms
union UDate
{
  char *date_str;
  MixedDate day_date;
  NumericDate nDate;
};

// A date in any form
struct Date
{
  enum Date_Format format;
  UDate date;
};

int main(void)
{
  NumericDate yesterday = { 11, 11, 2012};
  MixedDate today = {"Monday", "12th November", 2012};
  char tomorrow[] = "Tues 13th Nov 2012";

  // Create Date object with a numeric date
  UDate udate = {tomorrow};
  Date the_date;
  the_date.date = udate;
  the_date.format = text;
  print_date(&the_date);

  // Create Date object with a text date
  the_date.date.nDate = yesterday;
  the_date.format = numeric;
  print_date(&the_date);

  // Create Date object with a mixed date
  the_date.date.day_date = today;
  the_date.format = mixed;
  print_date(&the_date);

  return 0;
}

// Outputs a date
void print_date(const Date* date)
{
  switch(date->format)
  {
    case numeric:
      printf_s("The date is %d/%d/%d.\n", date->date.nDate.day,
                                          date->date.nDate.month,
                                          date->date.nDate.year);
      break;
    case text:
     printf_s("The date is %s.\n", date->date.date_str);
     break;
```

```
        case mixed:
          printf_s("The date is %s %s %d.\n", date->date.day_date.day,
                                              date->date.day_date.date,
                                              date->date.day_date.year);
          break;
        default:
          printf_s("Invalid date format.\n");
    }
  }
}
```

The output will be

```
The date is Tues 13th Nov 2012.
The date is 11/11/2012.
The date is Monday 12th November 2012.
```

How It Works

This example illustrates the use of a union as a member of a struct. It also shows that a struct can be a member of a union.

The enumerators in the enum type Date_Format identify three different ways in which a date can be represented. A date can be an instance of the MixedDate structure, an instance of the NumericDate structure, or just a string. The program assumes dates are passed around as instances of the Date structure, which has two members. One member is an instance of a union of type UDate that can contain a date in one of the three possible forms. The other is a member of type Date_Format to enable the form of date stored in the other member to be determined.

The main() function starts by defining and initializing three date representations:

```
  NumericDate yesterday = { 11, 11, 2012};
  MixedDate today = {"Monday", "12th November", 2012};
  char tomorrow[] = "Tues 13th Nov 2012";
```

The first two are structures that are initialized in the way you have seen previously.

The next four statements set up a Date structure to represent a date:

```
  UDate udate = {tomorrow};
  Date the_date;
  the_date.date = udate;
  the_date.format = text;
```

The union, udate, is initialized by the value between the braces. You can only initialize the first member of a union object when you define it. Other members must be initialized in separate statements after the object has been created. You create the structure the_date and store values in the members. The format member reflects the type of date representation stored in the date member of the_date.

The next statement calls the print_date() function to output the date represented by the_date. The argument is the address of the_date. The function determines how it should deal with the date in a switch statement:

```
switch(date->format)
{
  case numeric:
    printf_s("The date is %d/%d/%d.\n", date->date.nDate.day,
                                        date->date.nDate.month,
                                        date->date.nDate.year);

    break;
  case text:
   printf_s("The date is %s.\n", date->date.date_str);
   break;
  case mixed:
    printf_s("The date is %s %s %d.\n", date->date.day_date.day,
                                        date->date.day_date.date,
                                        date->date.day_date.year);

    break;
  default:
    printf_s("Invalid date format.\n");
}
```

The format member of the struct pointed to by date is used as the selector in the switch statement. The printf_s() function call for the numeric case shows the notation for accessing a member of a NumericDate structure that is stored in a UDate union instance that is a member of a Date structure.

Just to show that all three date representations work, the subsequent statements in main() demonstrate the two additional possibilities. This example demonstrates a union, but this is not a good approach to doing what it does. The union makes the code difficult to understand, and this representation for a date is likely to be error prone. One alternative would be to define a Date structure with a member for each of the date representations. You would just need to figure out which member was non-NULL to decide how to handle the date. A more likely solution in a practical context would be to decide on one representation for a date and provide functions to convert to whatever other representations are required.

■ **Note** You can define pointers to unions in the same way as you would define a pointer to a struct type. Accessing members of a union through a pointer works in the same way as with a structure.

Designing a Program

You've reached the end of another long chapter, and it's time to see how you can put what you've learned into practice in the context of a more substantial example.

The Problem

Numerical data are almost always easier and faster to understand when they're presented graphically. The problem that you're going to tackle is to write a program that produces a vertical bar chart from a set of data values that are suited to this kind of presentation. Average temperature by month is a typical example of data that can be usefully presented as a bar chart. Creating a bar chart is an interesting problem for several reasons. It will enable you to make use of structures in a practical context. The problem also involves working out how to place and present the bar chart within the space available, which is the kind of messy manipulation that comes up quite often in real-world applications. It will also involve several functions so you'll get some insight into this too.

The Analysis

You won't be making any assumptions about the size of the "page" that you're going to output to, or the number of columns, or even the scale of the chart. Instead, the primary function that creates the chart will accept the dimensions for the output page along with the data and make the set of bars fit the page, if possible. This will make the function useful in virtually any situation. You'll store the values in a sequence of structures organized as a linked list. You'll just need to pass the first structure to the bar chart function, and the function will be able to get at them all. You'll keep the structure very simple in this example, but you can embellish it later with other information of your own design.

Assume that the order in which the bars are to appear in the chart is going to be the same as the order in which the data values are entered, so you won't need to sort them.

Obviously the main() function will control the sequence in which things are done, and the process will be as follows:

1. Read the data to be displayed as a bar chart and create the linked list of structures.

2. Create and display the bar chart.

3. Clean up by releasing any heap memory that was allocated.

These are distinct operations that are relatively clear-cut, so it sounds like there are at least three functions for main() to call. When we get down into the detail, we may find that each of these functions can conveniently be broken down into further functions. We can start with outlining main() and the preamble for the source file.

The Solution

This section outlines the steps you'll take to solve the problem.

Step 1

Obviously you're going to use a structure in this program because that's what this chapter is about. The first stage is to design the structure you'll use throughout the program. You'll use a typedef so that you don't have to keep reusing the struct keyword when you define objects:

```
// Program 11.9 Generating a Bar chart
#define __STDC_WANT_LIB_EXT1__ 1
#include <stdio.h>

#define PAGE_HEIGHT  41
#define PAGE_WIDTH   75

typedef unsigned int uint;
typedef struct Bar Bar;
```

```
struct Bar
{
  double value;                                      // Bar value
  Bar *pNext;                                         // Pointer to next Bar
} Bar;

// Function prototypes...

int main(void)
{
  // Code for main...
}

// Definition of the other functions needed...
```

We will definitely need the input and output functions from the standard library, and we'll use the safe versions. The page width and height are defined as symbols, so they are easy to change. The units are characters across the page for the width and lines down the page for the height.

The Bar structure will define a bar in the chart simply by its value. The pointer of type Bar* in the structure will enable you to store the bars as a linked list. This has the merit that you can allocate memory as you go so none will be wasted. A singly linked list suits this situation because you'll only ever want to step through the bars forward from the first to the last.

You will need to remember the first Bar element in the linked list, and you'll need somewhere to store the title for the chart. Code in the body of main() begins like this:

```
Bar *pFirst = NULL;                                  // First Bar structure
char title[80];                                      // Chart title

printf_s("Enter the chart title: ");
gets_s(title, sizeof(title));                        // Read chart title
```

All the Bar objects will be created on the heap and added to a linked list, so you only need to store the address of the first object in main(). Using gets_s() to read the title allows spaces to be included in it.

We can take a stab at defining prototypes for the functions to be called by main(). These are, respectively, to create the linked list, to read input and create a Bar object on the heap, to create and output the bar chart, and finally to release the heap memory:

```
Bar *create_bar_list(void);
Bar *new_bar(void);
void bar_chart(Bar *pFirst, uint page_width, uint page_height, char *title);
void free_barlist_memory(Bar *pFirst);
```

The create_bar_list() function will return the address of the first Bar object in the list. It will make use of the new_bar() function that reads a value from the keyboard, creates a Bar object on the heap, stores the value in the Bar structure, and returns its address.

The bar_chart() function will create a bar chart from the linked list passed as the first argument. Passing the page dimensions and the title to the function makes it a self-contained operation. The free_barlist_memory() function only needs the address of the first object in the linked list to release all the memory that was allocated.

The implementation of main() to use these functions will look like this:

```
int main(void)
{
  Bar *pFirst = NULL;                                  // First Bar structure
  char title[80];                                      // Chart title

  printf_s("Enter the chart title: ");
  gets_s(title, sizeof(title));                        // Read chart title
  pFirst = create_bar_list();                          // Create Bar list
  bar_chart(pFirst, PAGE_WIDTH, PAGE_HEIGHT, title);   // Create Bar-chart
  free_barlist_memory(pFirst);                         // Free the memory
  return 0;
}
```

It doesn't really need further explanation, does it? In the following steps, we will implement each of these functions.

Step 2

In this step, we will implement the create_bar_list() function. Obviously we will create the linked list in a loop. The new_bar() function should create a new Bar object from keyboard input and return its address. If we make the function return NULL when there is no more input, we can use that to control the loop that will create the linked list. On that basis, here's how the implementation of create_bar_list() looks:

```
Bar* create_bar_list(void)
{
  Bar *pFirst = NULL;                     // Address of the first object
  Bar *pBar = NULL;                       // Stores address of new object
  Bar *pCurrent = NULL;                   // Address of current object
  while(pBar = new_bar())
  {
    if(pCurrent)
    { // There is a current object, so this is not the first
      pCurrent->pNext = pBar;             // New address in pNext for current
      pCurrent = pBar;                    // Make new one current
    }
    else                                  // This is the first...
      pFirst = pCurrent = pBar;           // ...so just save it.
  }
  return pFirst;
}
```

The while loop condition obtains the address of a new Bar object by calling new_bar() and storing it in pBar. When new_bar() returns NULL, the loop ends. On the first iteration, pCurrent and pFirst are NULL, so you could use either to determine whether you are dealing with the first Bar object or a subsequent one. For the first, you just store the address in both pFirst and pCurrent. For subsequent Bar objects, you store the new address in the pNext field of pCurrent, which will always point to the most recent object. You then make the new object the most recent by storing its address in pCurrent.

You can implement new_bar() like this:

```
Bar *new_bar(void)
{
  static char value[80];                      // Input buffer
  printf_s("Enter the value of the Bar, or Enter quit to end: ");
  gets_s(value, sizeof(value));               // Read a value as a string
  if(strcmp(value, "quit") == 0)              // quit entered?
    return NULL;                              // then input finished

  Bar *pBar = malloc(sizeof(Bar));
  if(!pBar)
  {
    printf_s("Oops! Couldn't allocate memory for a bar.\n");
    exit(2);
  }
  pBar->value = atof(value);
  pBar->pNext = NULL;
  return pBar;
}
```

The array that is the input buffer is declared as static. This means that it will only be created once and reused each time the function is called. If value was not declared as static, the array would be re-created each time the function is called. The input is read as a string to allow "quit" to be entered as well as a numeric value. When "quit" is read, the function returns NULL to signal that there's no more input. For any other input, a Bar object is created on the heap. If memory allocation fails, the program is terminated. The input string is converted to a numeric value by calling the atof() function that is declared in stdlib.h. There's no validation of the input so as not to bulk up the code, and I'll leave you to figure how to handle that. The converted value is stored in the value member of the structure, and the pNext member is set to NULL before returning the address.

With the linked list complete, you will create the bar chart next.

Step 3

The function to create the bar chart will need several local variables for working storage. It will also involve quite a lot of messy code because formatting text output is often a somewhat messy business, so I will explain the code for the bar_chart() function incrementally. To draw the chart within the given dimensions, the function must work out the maximum and minimum values to be plotted on the chart. It will also need to know how many samples appear in the list. Here's the initial code that will do that:

```
void bar_chart(Bar *pFirst, uint page_width, uint page_height, char *title)
{
  Bar *pLast = pFirst;                        // Pointer to previous Bar
  double max = pFirst->value;                 // Maximum Bar value - 1st to start
  double min = pFirst->value;                 // Minimum Bar value - 1st to start
  uint bar_count = 1;                         // Number of bars - at least 1
  // Plus more local variables...
```

```
  // Find maximum and minimum of all Bar values
  while(pLast = pLast->pNext)
  {
    ++bar_count;                                    // Increment Bar count
    max = (max < pLast->value) ? pLast->value : max;
    min = (min > pLast->value) ? pLast->value : min;
  }

  // Always draw chart to horizontal axis
  if(max < 0.0) max = 0.0;
  if(min > 0.0) min = 0.0;

  // Rest of the function definition...
}
```

I have not included code for it here, but you should always check pointers for NULL when they are passed as arguments to a function. The pLast is working storage that holds a Bar address while stepping through the linked list; max and min store the maximum and minimum values in the list, respectively. These are found in the while loop, along with the count of the number of Bar objects in the list, which is stored in bar_count.

Every bar on the chart must be created with its height measured from the horizontal axis, and because a value may be positive or negative, bars may appear above or below the horizontal axis. It's possible that all values may be greater than zero, so the minimum will be positive. In this case, we set min to zero to ensure the bars are full height. Similarly, all values may be less than zero, in which case we set max to 0.0 to ensure that bars below the horizontal axis are their full height.

We will use the min and max values to calculate the vertical step distance that is necessary to allow all bars to appear within page_height lines. We will use bar_count to work out the width of each bar to allow all bars to fit within page_width characters. Here's the code for that:

```
void bar_chart(Bar *pFirst, uint page_width, uint page_height, char *title)
{
  double vert_step = 0.0;                          // Unit step in vertical direction
  uint bar_count = 1;                              // Number of bars - at least 1
  uint bar_width = 0;                              // Width of a Bar
  uint space = 2;                                  // Spaces between bars
  // More local variables...

  // Code as before...

  vert_step = (max - min)/page_height;             // Calculate step length

  // Calculate and check Bar width
  if((bar_width = page_width/bar_count - space) < 1)
  {
    printf_s("\nPage width too narrow.\n");
    exit(1);
  }
  // Rest of the function definition...
}
```

You obtain the value change for a vertical step from one line to the next by dividing the difference between max and min, which are the maximum and minimum values, respectively, to appear in the bar chart, by page_height, which is the number of lines allotted to the height of the bar chart. The result is recorded in vert_step. The total width of each bar, including spaces that separate adjacent bars, is page_width characters divided by the number of bars, which you stored in bar_count. By subtracting the number of separating spaces, which is space, you obtain the width of a bar in characters and store it in bar_width. A bar has to be at least one character wide, so if the width is less than that, you don't have enough room for the chart, so you output a message and end the program.

You'll draw the vertical bars from top to bottom because that's the way the output appears. At each bar position on each output line, you'll be drawing either a series of (space + bar_width) spaces when the bar does not appear on that line or space spaces followed by bar_width bar characters ('#') when it does appear. You can create a string for each of these cases that you will be able to use repeatedly when drawing the chart. You can add the code in bar_chart() to create these next:

```
void bar_chart(Bar *pFirst, uint page_width, uint page_height, char *title)
{
  // Local variables as before...

  char *column = NULL;                        // Pointer to Bar column section
  char *blank = NULL;                         // Blank string for Bar+space
  // More local variables...

  // Code as before...

// Set up a string that will be used to build the columns
  if(!(column = chart_string(space, bar_width, '#')))
  {
    printf_s("\nFailed to allocate memory in bar_chart()"
                        " - terminating program.\n");
    exit(1);
  }

  // Set up a string that will be a blank column
  if(!(blank = chart_string(space, bar_width, ' ')))
  {
    printf_s("\nFailed to allocate memory in bar_chart()"
                        " - terminating program.\n");
    exit(1);
  }

  // Rest of the function definition...
}
```

Creating the column and blank strings is done by a new function, chart_string(), which returns the address of the string or NULL if there was a problem. You can implement the function like this:

```
char *chart_string(uint space, uint bar_width, char ch)
{
  char *str = malloc(bar_width + space + 1);          // Get memory for the string
  if(str)
  {
```

```
    uint i = 0;
    for( ; i < space ; ++i)
      str[i] =' ';                          // Blank the space between bars

    for( ; i < space + bar_width ; ++i)
      str[i] = ch;                          // Enter the Bar characters
    str[i] = '\0';                          // Add string terminator
  }
  return str;
}
```

The function allocates space for a string containing (bar_width + space) characters plus the terminating null character. The characters are only stored in the string if the malloc() call was successful. Spaces are stored in the first space characters in the string; ch is stored in the next bar_width characters in the string. Finally, the null character is stored at the last index position. When the function is called to create column, ch is '#'. When it is called to create blank, ch is a space, so in this case all characters are spaces.

We now have everything we need to draw the bar chart. The code in bar_chart() to do that is next:

```
void bar_chart(Bar *pFirst, uint page_width, uint page_height, char *title)
{
  // Local variables as before...

  double position = 0.0;                    // Current vertical position on chart
  bool axis = false;                        // Indicates axis drawn

  // Code as before...

  // Draw the Bar chart. It is drawn line by line starting at the top
  printf_s("\n^ %s\n", title);              // Output the chart title
  position = max;                           // Start at the top
  for(uint i = 0 ; i < page_height ; ++i)   // page_height lines for chart
  {
    // Check if we need to output the horizontal axis
    if(position <= 0.0 && !axis)
    {
      draw_x_axis(bar_count*(bar_width + space));
      axis = true;
    }
    printf_s("|");                          // Output vertical axis
    pLast = pFirst;                         // start with the first Bar

    // For each Bar...
    for(uint bars = 1 ; bars <= bar_count ; ++bars)
    {
      // If position is between axis and value, output column. otherwise blank
      printf_s("%s", position <= pLast->value && position > 0.0 ||
                   position >= pLast->value && position <= 0.0 ? column : blank);
      pLast = pLast->pNext;
    }
```

```
    printf_s("\n");                                    // End the line of output
    position -= vert_step;                             // Decrement position
  }
  if(!axis)                                            // Horizontal axis?
    draw_x_axis(bar_count*(bar_width + space));        // No, so draw it
  else
    printf_s("v\n");                                   // -y axis arrow head

  // Rest of the function definition...
}
```

The first output statement writes the arrow head for the top of the vertical axis followed by the title. The position variable holds the current position on the chart, and because we draw the chart from top to bottom, it starts out as max. The chart is drawn in the for loop that iterates over the horizontal lines that will form the chart. The horizontal axis is drawn if it has not been drawn previously, as soon as position is less than or equal to zero. The axis variable of type bool records whether or not the horizontal axis has been drawn, and this ensures that it is only drawn once. The draw_x_axis() function draws the axis, and I'll explain the code for that once we get through the present loop.

The first character on each line is a vertical bar that represents the vertical axis. The rest of the line consists of the output for each of the bars, and this occurs in the for loop with the bars control variable. Because we are drawing the chart from the top down, while position is above the horizontal axis and greater than the value member of the current Bar object, we output blank. When position is above the axis and less than or equal to the current value member, we output column. When position is below the horizontal axis, we output column when position is greater than or equal to the value member of the current Bar object; otherwise, we output blank. When the for loop drawing the line ends, a newline is written to move to the next line, and position is decremented by vert_step. This process repeats for all the lines.

When the for loop that iterates over all the output lines ends, it is possible that the horizontal axis may not have been drawn. This will occur when all the values are positive and axis will be false. In this case, you draw the axis after the loop. When it has been drawn in the loop, you just output a v for the down arrow on the vertical axis.

The last two statements you need to add to the function are

```
  free(blank);                                         // Free blank string memory
  free(column);                                        // Free column string memory
```

They free the memory for the strings that were allocated on the heap.

You still need the definition for the draw_x_axis() function:

```
void draw_x_axis(uint length)
{
  printf_s("+");                                       // Start of x-axis
  for(uint x = 0 ; x < length ; ++x)
    printf_s("-");
  printf_s(">\n");                                     // End of x-axis
}
```

The parameter is the length of the horizontal axis. The first character is '+' because this is where it intersects the vertical axis. The axis is drawn in a for loop, and '>' is appended to represent the arrow head marking the axis direction.

Step 4

The last piece of the program is the function to free the memory allocated to store the linked list of Bar objects:

```c
void free_barlist_memory(Bar *pBar)
{
  Bar* pTemp = NULL;
  while(pBar)
  {
    pTemp = pBar->pNext;                    // Save pointer to next
    free(pBar);                             // Free memory for current
    pBar = pTemp;                           // Make next current
  }
}
```

The process for freeing memory is carried out in the for loop that starts with the address of the first Bar object that is passed as the argument to the function. The mechanism saves the address in the pNext member of the current Bar object in pTemp. It then frees the memory for the current object and makes the address in pTemp the new current object. This continues until the address in pBar is NULL, in which case all the memory has been released.

Here's the complete program code, including the function prototypes and the #include directives that are necessary:

```c
// Program 11.9 Generating a Bar chart
#define __STDC_WANT_LIB_EXT1__  1
#include <stdio.h>
#include <string.h>                         // For strcmp()
#include <stdlib.h>                         // For atof()
#include <stdbool.h>

#define PAGE_HEIGHT   41
#define PAGE_WIDTH    75

typedef unsigned int uint;                  // Type definition
typedef struct Bar Bar;                     // Struct type definition

typedef struct Bar
{
  double value;                             // Bar value
  Bar *pNext;                               // Pointer to next Bar
};

// Function prototypes
Bar *create_bar_list(void);
Bar *new_bar(void);
void bar_chart(Bar *pFirst, uint page_width, uint page_height, char *title);
void free_barlist_memory(Bar *pFirst);
char *chart_string(uint space, uint bar_width, char ch);
void draw_x_axis(uint length);
```

```c
int main(void)
{
  Bar *pFirst = NULL;                                   // First Bar structure
  char title[80];                                       // Chart title

  printf_s("Enter the chart title: ");
  gets_s(title, sizeof(title));                         // Read chart title
  pFirst = create_bar_list();                           // Create Bar list
  bar_chart(pFirst, PAGE_WIDTH, PAGE_HEIGHT, title);    // Create Bar-chart
  free_barlist_memory(pFirst);                          // Free the memory
  return 0;
}

// Create and output the bar chart from the list
void bar_chart(Bar *pFirst, uint page_width, uint page_height, char *title)
{
  Bar *pLast = pFirst;                          // Pointer to previous Bar
  double max = pFirst->value;                   // Maximum Bar value - 1st to start
  double min = pFirst->value;                   // Minimum Bar value - 1st to start
  double vert_step = 0.0;                       // Unit step in vertical direction
  uint bar_count = 1;                           // Number of bars - at least 1
  uint bar_width = 0;                           // Width of a Bar
  uint space = 2;                               // Spaces between bars
  char *column = NULL;                           // Pointer to Bar column section
  char *blank = NULL;                           // Blank string for Bar+space
  double position = 0.0;                     // Current vertical position on chart
  bool axis = false;                            // Indicates axis drawn

  // Find maximum and minimum of all Bar values
  while(pLast = pLast->pNext)
  {
    ++bar_count;                                // Increment Bar count
    max = (max < pLast->value) ? pLast->value : max;
    min = (min > pLast->value) ? pLast->value : min;
  }

  // Always draw chart to horizontal axis
  if(max < 0.0) max = 0.0;
  if(min > 0.0) min = 0.0;
  vert_step = (max - min)/page_height;          // Calculate step length

  // Calculate and check Bar width
  if((bar_width = page_width/bar_count - space) < 1)
  {
    printf_s("\nPage width too narrow.\n");
    exit(1);
  }
```

```
// Set up a string that will be used to build the columns
if(!(column = chart_string(space, bar_width, '#')))
{
  printf_s("\nFailed to allocate memory in bar_chart()"
                        " - terminating program.\n");
  exit(1);
}

// Set up a string that will be a blank column
if(!(blank = chart_string(space, bar_width, ' ')))
{
  printf_s("\nFailed to allocate memory in bar_chart()"
                        " - terminating program.\n");
  exit(1);
}

// Draw the Bar chart. It is drawn line by line starting at the top
printf_s("\n^ %s\n", title);                    // Output the chart title
position = max;                                 // Start at the top
for(uint i = 0 ; i < page_height ; ++i)         // page_height lines for chart
{
  // Check if we need to output the horizontal axis
  if(position <= 0.0 && !axis)
  {
    draw_x_axis(bar_count*(bar_width + space));
    axis = true;
  }
  printf_s("|");                                // Output vertical axi
  pLast = pFirst;                               // start with the first Bar

  // For each Bar...
  for(uint bars = 1 ; bars <= bar_count ; ++bars)
  {
    // If position is between axis and value, output column. otherwise blank
    printf_s("%s", position <= pLast->value && position > 0.0 ||
                   position >= pLast->value && position <= 0.0 ? column : blank);
    pLast = pLast->pNext;
  }
  printf_s("\n");                               // End the line of output
  position -= vert_step;                        // Decrement position
}
if(!axis)                                        // Horizontal axis?
  draw_x_axis(bar_count*(bar_width + space));   // No, so draw it
else
  printf_s("v\n");                              // -y axis arrow head

free(blank);                                     // Free blank string memory
free(column);                                    // Free column string memory
}
```

```c
// Draw horizontal axis
void draw_x_axis(uint length)
{
  printf_s("+");                               // Start of x-axis
  for(uint x = 0 ; x < length ; ++x)
    printf_s("-");
  printf_s(">\n");                             // End of x-axis
}

// Create a bar string of ch characters
char *chart_string(uint space, uint bar_width, char ch)
{
  char *str = malloc(bar_width + space + 1);   // Get memory for the string
  if(str)
  {
    uint i = 0;
    for( ; i < space ; ++i)
      str[i] =' ';                             // Blank the space between bars

    for( ; i < space + bar_width ; ++i)
      str[i] = ch;                             // Enter the Bar characters

    str[i] = '\0';                             // Add string terminator
  }
  return str;
}

// Create list of Bar objects
Bar* create_bar_list(void)
{
  Bar *pFirst = NULL;                          // Address of the first object
  Bar *pBar = NULL;                            // Stores address of new object
  Bar *pCurrent = NULL;                        // Address of current object
  while(pBar = new_bar())
  {
    if(pCurrent)
    { // There is a current object, so this is not the first
      pCurrent->pNext = pBar;                  // New address in pNext for current
      pCurrent = pBar;                         // Make new one current
    }
    else                                       // This is the first...
      pFirst = pCurrent = pBar;                // ...so just save it.
  }
  return pFirst;
}
```

```c
// Create a new Bar object from input
Bar *new_bar(void)
{
  static char value[80];                              // Input buffer
  printf_s("Enter the value of the Bar, or Enter quit to end: ");
  gets_s(value, sizeof(value));                       // Read a value as a string
  if(strcmp(value, "quit") == 0)                      // quit entered?
    return NULL;                                       // then input finished

  Bar *pBar = malloc(sizeof(Bar));
  if(!pBar)
  {
    printf_s("Oops! Couldn't allocate memory for a bar.\n");
    exit(2);
  }
  pBar->value = atof(value);
  pBar->pNext = NULL;
  return pBar;
}

// Free memory for all Bar objects in the list
void free_barlist_memory(Bar *pBar)
{
  Bar* pTemp = NULL;
  while(pBar)
  {
    pTemp = pBar->pNext;                              // Save pointer to next
    free(pBar);                                        // Free memory for current
    pBar = pTemp;                                      // Make next current
  }
}
```

Typical output from the example is shown here:

```
Enter the chart title: Average Monthly Temperatures - Centigrade
Enter the value of the Bar, or Enter quit to end: -12
Enter the value of the Bar, or Enter quit to end: -15
Enter the value of the Bar, or Enter quit to end: 2
Enter the value of the Bar, or Enter quit to end: 5
Enter the value of the Bar, or Enter quit to end: 13
Enter the value of the Bar, or Enter quit to end: 20
Enter the value of the Bar, or Enter quit to end: 26
Enter the value of the Bar, or Enter quit to end: 32
Enter the value of the Bar, or Enter quit to end: 23
Enter the value of the Bar, or Enter quit to end: 17
Enter the value of the Bar, or Enter quit to end: -1
Enter the value of the Bar, or Enter quit to end: -4
Enter the value of the Bar, or Enter quit to end: quit
```

```
^ Average Monthly Temperatures - Centigrade
|                                         ####
|                                         ####
|                                         ####
|                                         ####
|                                         ####
|                                         ####
|                                    #### ####
|                                    #### ####
|                                    #### #### ####
|                                    #### #### ####
|                                    #### #### ####
|                               #### #### #### ####
|                               #### #### #### ####
|                               #### #### #### ####
|                               #### #### #### #### ####
|                               #### #### #### #### ####
|                               #### #### #### #### ####
|                          #### #### #### #### #### ####
|                          #### #### #### #### #### ####
|                          #### #### #### #### #### ####
|                          #### #### #### #### #### ####
|                          #### #### #### #### #### ####
|                          #### #### #### #### #### ####
|                          #### #### #### #### #### ####
|                     #### #### #### #### #### #### ####
|                     #### #### #### #### #### #### ####
|                     #### #### #### #### #### #### ####
|                #### #### #### #### #### #### #### ####
+------------------------------------------------------------------->
|  #### ####                                          #### ####
|  #### ####                                               ####
|  #### ####                                               ####
|  #### ####                                               ####
|  #### ####
|  #### ####
|  #### ####
|  #### ####
|  #### ####
|  #### ####
|  #### ####
|       ####
|       ####
```

Summary

This has been something of a marathon chapter, but the topic is extremely important. Having a good grasp of structures rates alongside understanding pointers and functions in importance, if you want to use C effectively.

Most real-world applications deal with complicated things such as people, cars, or materials, which require several different values to represent them. Structures provide a powerful tool for dealing with complex objects. Although some of the operations may seem a little complicated, remember that you're dealing with complicated entities, so the complexity of the code isn't coming from the programming language capability; rather, it's built into the problem you're tackling.

In the next chapter, you'll look at how you can store data in external files. This will, of course, include the ability to store structures.

EXERCISES

The following exercises enable you to try out what you've learned in this chapter. If you get stuck, look back over the chapter for help. If you're still stuck, you can download the solutions from the Source Code/Download area of the Apress website (www.apress.com), but that really should be a last resort.

Exercise 11-1. Define a struct type with the name Length that represents a length in yards, feet, and inches. Define an add() function that will add two Length arguments and return the sum as type Length. Define a second function, show(), that will display the value of its Length argument. Write a program that will use the Length type and the add() and show() functions to sum an arbitrary number of lengths in yards, feet, and inches that are entered from the keyboard and output the total length.

Exercise 11-2. Define a struct type that contains a person's name consisting of a first name and a second name, plus the person's phone number. Use this struct in a program that will allow one or more names and corresponding numbers to be entered and will store the entries in an array of structures. The program should allow a second name to be entered and output all the numbers corresponding to the name and optionally output all the names with their corresponding numbers.

Exercise 11-3. Modify or reimplement the program from the previous exercise to store the structures in a linked list in ascending alphabetical order of the names.

Exercise 11-4. Write a program to use a struct to count the number of occurrences of each different word in a paragraph of text that's entered from the keyboard.

Exercise 11-5. Write a program that reads an arbitrary number of names consisting of a first name followed by a last name. The program should use a binary tree to output the names in ascending alphabetical sequence ordered by first name within second name (i.e., second name takes precedence in the ordering so Ann Choosy comes after Bill Champ and before Arthur Choosy).

CHAPTER 12

Working with Files

If your computer could only ever process data stored within the main memory of the machine, the scope and variety of applications you could deal with would be severely limited. Virtually all serious business applications require more data than would fit into main memory and depend on the ability to process data that's persistent and stored on an external device such as a disk drive. In this chapter, you'll explore how you can process data stored in files.

C provides a range of functions in the header file stdio.h for writing to and reading from external devices. The external device you would use for storing and retrieving data is typically a disk drive, but not exclusively. Because, consistent with the philosophy of C, the library facilities you'll use for working with files are device independent, they apply to virtually any external storage device. However, I'll assume in the examples in this chapter that we are dealing with disk files.

In this chapter, you'll learn

- What a file is

- How files are processed

- How to write and read formatted files

- How to write and read binary files

- How to access data in a file randomly

- How to create and use temporary work files

- How to update binary files

- How to write a file viewer program

The Concept of a File

With all the examples up to now, any data that the user enters are lost once the program ends. If the user wants to run the program with the same data, he or she must enter it again each time. There are a lot of occasions when this not only is inconvenient but also makes the programming task impossible.

If you want to maintain a directory of names, addresses, and telephone numbers, for instance, a program in which you have to enter all the names, addresses, and telephone numbers each time you run it is worse than useless! The answer is to store data on permanent storage that continues to be maintained after your computer is switched off. As I'm sure you know, this storage is called a *file*, and a file is usually stored on a disk.

You're probably familiar with the basic mechanics of how a disk works. If so, this can help you recognize when a particular approach to file usage is efficient and when it isn't. On the other hand, if you know nothing about disk file mechanics, don't worry at this point. There's nothing in the concept of file processing in C that depends on any knowledge of physical storage devices.

A file is essentially a serial sequence of bytes, as illustrated in Figure 12-1.

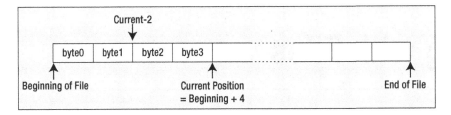

Figure 12-1. *Structure of a file*

Positions in a File

A file has a beginning and an end, and it has a *current position*, typically defined as so many bytes from the beginning, as Figure 12-1 illustrates. The current position is where any file action (a read from the file or a write to the file) will take place. You can move the current position to any point in the file. A new current position can be specified as an offset from the beginning of the file or, in some circumstances, as a positive or negative offset from the previous current position. You can also move the position to the end of the file in some situations.

File Streams

The C library provides functions for reading and writing to or from data streams. As you know from Chapter 10, a stream is an abstract representation of any external source or destination for data, so the keyboard, the command line on your display, and files on a disk are all examples of things you can work with as streams. You use the same input/output functions for reading and writing any external device that is mapped to a stream.

There are two ways of writing data to a stream that represents a file. First, you can write a file as a *text file*, in which case data are written as a sequence of characters organized as lines, where each line is terminated by a newline character. Obviously, binary data such as values of type int or type double have to be converted to characters to allow them to be written to a text file, and you have already seen how this formatting is done with the printf() and printf_s() functions. Second, you can write a file as a *binary file*. Data written to a binary file are written as a series of bytes exactly as they appear in memory, so a value of type double, for example, would be written as the 8 bytes that appear in memory.

Of course, you can write any data you like to a file, but once a file has been written, it just consists of a series of bytes. Regardless of whether you write a file as a binary file or as a text file, it ultimately ends up as just a series of bytes. This means that the program must know what sort of data the file represents to read it correctly. You've seen many times now that exactly what a series of bytes represents is dependent upon how you interpret it. A sequence of 12 bytes in a binary file could be 12 characters, 12 8-bit signed integers, 12 8-bit unsigned integers, 6 16-bit signed integers, a 32-bit integer followed by an 8-byte floating-point value, and so on. All of these will be more or less valid interpretations of the data, so it's important that a program that is reading a file has the correct assumptions about what was written.

Accessing Files

The files that are resident on your disk drive each have a name, and the rules for naming files are determined by your operating system. In the examples in this chapter, I'll use Microsoft Windows file names. If you're using a different operating system environment, you'll need to adjust the names of the files appropriately. It would not be particularly convenient if a program that processes a file would only work with a specific file with a particular name. If it did, you would need to produce a different program for each file you might want to process. For this reason, your program references a file through a *file pointer* or more accurately a *stream pointer*. You associate a stream pointer with a particular file programmatically when the program is run. A program can associate a given stream pointer with different files on different occasions, so the same program can work with a different file each time it executes. A file pointer points to a struct of type FILE that represents a stream.

The FILE structure to which a file pointer points contains information about the file. This will be such things as whether you want to read or write or update the file, the address of the buffer in memory to be used for data, and a pointer to the current position in the file for the next operation. You don't need to worry about the contents of this structure in practice. It's all taken care of by the input/output functions. However, if you really want to know all the gory details of the FILE structure, you will find them in the code for the stdio.h library header file.

I'll be referring to a stream pointer that references a file as a file pointer in this chapter, but keep in mind that all the operations I describe in the context of file pointers apply to any data source or destination that can be treated as a stream. If you want to use several files simultaneously in a program, you need a separate file pointer for each file, although as soon as you've finished using one file, you can associate the file pointer you were using with another file. So if you need to process several files, but you'll be working with them one at a time, you can do it with one file pointer.

Opening a File

You associate a specific external file name with an internal file pointer variable through a process referred to as *opening a file*. One way to open a file is by calling the fopen() function that returns the file pointer for a specific external file. There's a safer alternative function, fopen_s(), which I'll come to in a moment. The fopen() function is defined in stdio.h, and it has this prototype:

```
FILE *fopen(const char * restrict name, const char * restrict mode);
```

The first argument to the function is a pointer to a string that is the name of the external file you want to process. You can specify the name explicitly as an argument, or you can use an array or a variable of type pointer to char that contains the address of the character string that defines the file name. You would typically obtain the file name through some external means, such as from the command line when the program is started, or you could arrange to read it in from the keyboard. Of course, you can also define a file name as a constant at the beginning of a program when the program always works with the same file.

The second argument to the fopen() function is a character string that represents the file mode. The file mode specifies what you want to do with the file. As you'll see, this spans a whole range of possibilities, but for the moment, I'll introduce just three file modes (which nonetheless comprise the basic set of operations on a file). Table 12-1 lists these.

Table 12-1. *File Modes*

Mode	Description
"w"	Open a text file for *w*rite operations. If the file exists, its current contents are discarded
"a"	Open a text file for *a*ppend operations. All writes are to the end of the file
"r"	Open a text file for *r*ead operations

■ **Note** Notice that a file mode specification is a character string between double quotes, not a single character between single quotes.

These three modes only apply to text files, which are files that are written as characters. We will discuss later on "More Open Modes for Text Files" about optional parameters that make life easier. You can also work with binary files that are written as a sequence of bytes, and I'll discuss that in the section "Binary File Input and Output" later in this chapter. Assuming the call to fopen() is successful, the function returns a pointer of type FILE* that you can use to reference the file in further input/output operations using other functions in the library. If the file cannot be opened for some reason, fopen() returns NULL.

■ **Note** The pointer returned by fopen() is referred to as either a *file pointer* or a *stream pointer.*

A call to fopen() does two things: it creates a file pointer—an address—that identifies the specific file on a disk from the name argument you supply, and it determines what you can do with that file. As I mentioned earlier, when you want to have several files open at once, they must each have their own file pointer variable, and you open each of them with a separate call to fopen(). There's a limit to the number of files you can have open at one time, which will be determined by the value of the symbol FOPEN_MAX that's defined in stdio.h. The C standard requires that the value of FOPEN_MAX be at least eight, including stdin, stdout, and stderr, so as a minimum you will be able to be working with up to five files simultaneously, but typically it's many more, often 256, for example.

The safer optional alternative function for opening files, fopen_s(), has the prototype

```
errno_t fopen_s(FILE * restrict * restrict pfile, const char * restrict name,
                                             const char * restrict mode);
```

You need to define the symbol __STDC_WANT_LIB_EXT1__ as 1 to use this function. The function fopen_s() is a little different from fopen(). The first parameter is a pointer to a pointer to a FILE structure, so you pass the address of your FILE* variable that is to store the file pointer as the first argument. The function will verify that the last two arguments you pass are not NULL, and it will fail if either is. It returns a value of type errno_t, which indicates how the operation went. Type errno_t is an integer type that is defined by a typedef in stdio.h, often as equivalent to type int. The function returns 0 if everything went well and a nonzero integer if it was unable to open the file for some reason. In the latter case, the file pointer will be set to NULL.

You can use the same mode strings with this function as with fopen(), but you can optionally begin the mode strings with u, so they can be "uw" when you want to write a file or "ua" when you want to append to a file. Whether or not concurrent access to a file is permitted is controlled by your operating system, and you can influence this where your operating system allows it. With the set of modes without the u, you open a file with exclusive access; in other words, you are the only one who can access the file while it is open.

Adding the u to the file mode string causes a new file to have system default file permissions when it is closed. I'll be using fopen_s() in the examples from here on. The security issues with using fopen() are not huge, but undoubtedly it is better to use the safer version.

Write Mode

If you want to write to an existing text file with the name myfile.txt, you would use this statement:

```
FILE *pfile = NULL;
char *filename = "myfile.text";
if(!fopen_s(&pfile, filename, "w"))  // Open myfile.txt to write it
  printf_s("Failed to open %s.\n", filename);
```

This opens the file and associates the file with the name myfile.txt with your file pointer pfile. Because you've specified the mode as "w", you can only write to the file; you can't read it. The string you supply as the first argument is limited to a maximum of FILENAME_MAX characters, where FILENAME_MAX is defined in the stdio.h. This value is usually large enough that it isn't a real restriction.

If a file with the name myfile.txt does not exist, the call to fopen_s() in the previous statement will create a new file with this name. Because you have just provided the file name without any path specification as the second argument to the function, the file is assumed to be in the current directory; if the file is not found there, that's where it will be created. You can also specify a string that is the full path and name for the file, in which case the file will be assumed to be at that location and a new file will be created there if necessary. Note that if the directory that's supposed to contain the file doesn't exist when you specify the file path, neither the directory nor the file will be created, and the fopen_s() call will fail. If the call to fopen_s() does fail for any reason, a nonzero integer will be returned, and pfile will be set to NULL. If you then attempt further operations with a NULL file pointer, it will cause your program to terminate.

■ **Note**   You now know how to create a new text file. Simply call fopen_s() with mode "w" and the second argument specifying the name you want to assign to the new file.

On opening a file for writing, the file length is truncated to zero, and the position will be at the beginning of any existing data for the first operation. This means that any data that were previously written to the file will be lost and overwritten by any write operations.

Append Mode

If you want to add to an existing text file rather than overwrite it, you specify mode "a", which is the append mode of operation. This positions the file at the end of any previously written data. If the file doesn't exist, a new file will be created. If you want to reuse the file pointer you declared previously to open the file to add data to the end, use the following statement:

```
fopen_s(&pfile, "myfile.txt", "a");      // Open myfile.txt to add to it
```

I won't test the return value each time in code fragments, but don't forget that you should. When you open a file in append mode, all write operations will be at the end of the data in the file on each write operation. In other words, all write operations append data to the file, and you cannot update the existing contents in this mode.

Read Mode

If you want to read a file, open it using this statement:

```
fopen_s(&pfile, "myfile.txt", "r");
```

You have specified the mode argument as "r", indicating that you want to read the file, so you can't write to this file. The file position will be set to the beginning of the data in the file. Clearly, if you're going to read the file, it must already exist. If you inadvertently try to open a file for reading that doesn't exist, fopen_s() will set the file pointer to NULL and return a nonzero value. You should always check the value returned from fopen_s() to make sure you really are accessing the file you want.

Buffering File Operations

Once you have opened a file, you can control how input operations are buffered by calling setvbuf(), which has the following prototype:

```
int setvbuf(FILE * restrict pfile, char * restrict buffer, int mode, size_t size);
```

The first parameter is the file pointer to an open file. You can only call setvbuf() to determine the buffering before you have performed any other operation with the file pointed to by the first argument. The second parameter specifies an array that is to be used for buffering, and the fourth parameter is the size of the array. If you specify NULL as the second argument, setvbuf() will allocate a buffer for you with the size you specify as the fourth argument. Unless you have a good reason not to, I recommend always specifying the second argument as NULL because then you don't have to worry about creating the buffer or its lifetime.

The third argument specifies the buffering mode and can be one of the following:

- _IOFBF causes the file to be fully buffered. When input and output is fully buffered, data are written or read in blocks of arbitrary size.

- _IOLBF causes operations to be line buffered. When input and output is line buffered, data are written or read in blocks terminated by a newline.

- _IONBF causes input and output to be unbuffered. With unbuffered input and output, data are transferred character by character. This is extremely inefficient, so you would only use this mode when it was essential.

The setvbuf() returns 0 when everything is okay and a nonzero integer when it isn't. Here's how you might use it for a file pointed to by pfile:

```
size_t bufsize = 1024;
if(setvbuf(pfile, NULL, _IOFBF, bufsize))
  printf_s("File buffering failed!\n");
```

If you just want full buffering for input or output, you can call setbuf(), which has this prototype:

```
void setbuf(FILE * restrict pfile, char * restrict buffer);
```

The first parameter is the file pointer, and the second is the address of an array to be used as a buffer. The second argument can be NULL, which I recommend, in which case the buffer will be created for you. If you specify buffer, its length must be BUFSIZ bytes, where BUFSIZ is defined in stdio.h. Here's how you might buffer operations for a file with the pointer pfile using your own buffer:

```
char *buf = malloc(BUFSIZ);
setbuf(pfile, buf);
```

Note that you must ensure that your buffer continues to exist as long as the file is open. This implies that you must take great care when you use an automatic array that will expire at the end of the block in which you create it. If the second argument to setbuf() is NULL, the file operations will not be buffered.

Renaming a File

There are many circumstances in which you'll want to rename a file. You might be updating the contents of a file by writing a new, updated file, for instance. You'll probably want to assign a temporary name to the new file while you're creating it and then change the name to that of the old file once you've deleted it. Renaming a file is very easy. You just use the rename() function, which has the following prototype:

```
int rename(const char *oldname, const char *newname);
```

The integer that's returned will be 0 if the name change was successful and nonzero otherwise. The file must not be open when you call rename(); otherwise, the operation will fail.

Here's an example of using the rename() function:

```
if(rename( "C:\\temp\\myfile.txt", "C:\\temp\\myfile_copy.txt"))
  printf("Failed to rename file.");
else
  printf("File renamed successfully.");
```

This will change the name of myfile.txt in the temp directory on drive C to myfile_copy.txt. A message will be produced that indicates whether the name change succeeded. Obviously, if the file path is incorrect or the file doesn't exist, the renaming operation will fail.

■ **Caution**   Note the double backslash in the file path string. If you forget to use the escape sequence for a backslash when specifying a Microsoft Windows file path, you won't get the file name you want.

Closing a File

When you've finished with a file, you need to tell the operating system that this is the case and free up the file so it can be used by others. This is referred to as *closing* a file. You do this by calling the fclose() function that accepts a file pointer as an argument and returns a value of type int, which will be EOF if an error occurs and 0 otherwise. The typical usage of the fclose() function is as follows:

```
fclose(pfile);                    // Close the file associated with pfile
pfile = NULL;
```

The result of calling fclose() is that the connection between the pointer, pfile, and the physical file is broken, so pfile can no longer be used to access the file it represented. If the file was being written, the current contents of the output buffer are written to the file to ensure that data are not lost. It's good practice to always set the file pointer to NULL when you have closed a file.

■ **Note**   EOF is a special character called the *end-of-file character*. In fact, the symbol EOF is defined in stdio.h as a negative integer that is usually equivalent to the value −1. However, it isn't necessarily always this value, so you should use EOF rather than an explicit value. EOF indicates that no more data are available from a stream.

It's good programming practice to close a file as soon as you've finished with it. This protects against output data loss, which could occur if an error in another part of your program caused the execution to be stopped in an abnormal fashion. This could result in the contents of the output buffer being lost, as the file wouldn't be closed properly. You must also close a file before attempting to rename it or remove it.

■ **Note**   Another reason for closing files as soon as you've finished with them is that the operating system will usually limit the number of files you may have open at one time. Closing files as soon as you've finished with them minimizes the chances of you falling foul of the operating system in this respect.

Calling the fflush() function will force any unwritten data left in an output buffer to be written to a file. You have already used this function to flush the keyboard input buffer. With your file pointer pfile, you could force any data left in the output buffer to be written to the file by using this statement:

```
fflush(pfile);
```

The fflush() function returns a value of type int, which is normally 0 but will be EOF if an error occurs.

Deleting a File

Because you have the ability to create a file in your code, at some point you'll also want to be able to delete a file programmatically. The remove() function that's declared in stdio.h does this. You use it like this:

```
remove("myfile.txt");
```

This will delete the file that has the name myfile.txt from the current directory. Note that the file cannot be open when you try to delete it. If the file is open, the effect of calling remove() is implementation defined, so consult your library documentation. You always need to double-check any operations on files, but you need to take particular care with operations that delete files. You could wreck your system if you don't.

Writing a Text File

Once you've opened a file for writing, you can write to it anytime from anywhere in your program, provided you have access to the file pointer that has been set by fopen_s(). So if you want to be able to access a file from anywhere in a program that contains multiple functions, either you need to ensure the file pointer has global scope or you must arrange for it to be passed as an argument to any function that accesses the file.

■ **Note**   As you'll recall, to ensure that the file pointer has global scope, you place its declaration outside all of the functions, usually at the beginning of the source file.

The simplest write operation is provided by the function fputc(), which writes a single character to a text file. It has the following prototype:

```
int fputc(int ch, FILE *pfile);
```

The function writes the character specified by the first argument to the file identified by the second argument, which is a file pointer. If the write is successful, it returns the character that was written; otherwise, it returns EOF.

In practice, characters aren't usually written to a physical file one by one. This would be extremely inefficient. Hidden from your program and managed by the output routine, output characters are written to a buffer until a reasonable number have been accumulated; they are then all written to the file in one go. This mechanism is illustrated in Figure 12-2.

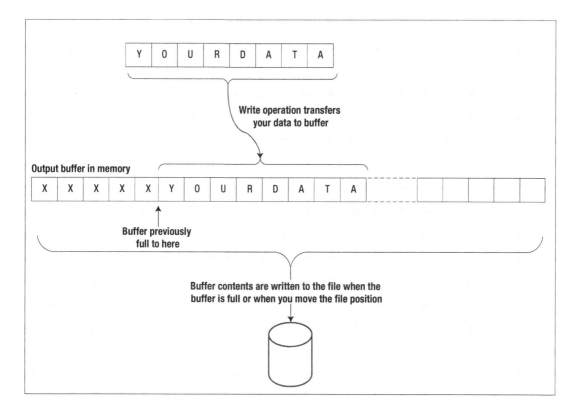

Figure 12-2. *Writing a file*

Note that the putc() function is equivalent to fputc(). It requires the same arguments, and the return type is the same. The difference between them is that putc() may be implemented in the standard library as a macro, whereas fputc() is definitely a function.

Reading a Text File

The fgetc() function is complementary to fputc() and reads a character from a text file that has been opened for reading. It takes a file pointer as its only argument and returns the character read as type int. The typical use of fgetc() is illustrated by the following statement:

```
int mchar = fgetc(pfile);                    // Reads a character into mchar
```

The mchar is type int because EOF will be returned if the end of the file has been reached. EOF is a negative integer that cannot be returned or stored as type char when char is an unsigned type. Behind the scenes, the actual mechanism for reading a file is the inverse of writing to a file. A whole block of characters is read into a buffer in one go. The characters are then handed over to your program one at a time as you request them, until the buffer is empty, whereupon another block is read. This makes the process very fast, because most fgetc() operations won't involve reading the file but simply moving a character from the buffer in main memory to the place where you want to store it.

Note that the function getc(), which is equivalent to fgetc(), is also available. It requires an argument of type FILE* and returns the character read as type int, so it's virtually identical to fgetc(). The only difference between them is that getc() may be implemented as a macro, whereas fgetc() is a function. This is a deja vu of Chapter 10, where we declared getc, getchar, and ungetc(); the last one put a character back to the stream, and this time the stream is a file that must be provided as an argument. Then the following call will retrieve that char.

You can read the contents of a file again when necessary. The rewind() function positions the file that is specified by the file pointer argument at the beginning. You use it like this:

```
rewind(pfile);
```

Of course, pfile must correspond to a file that is open.

TRY IT OUT: USING A SIMPLE FILE

You now have enough knowledge of file input/output capabilities to write a simple program that writes a file and then reads it. So let's do just that:

```
// Program 12.1 Writing a file a character at a time
#define __STDC_WANT_LIB_EXT1__ 1
#include <stdio.h>
#include <string.h>
#include <stdlib.h>

#define LENGTH 81                            // Maximum input length

int main(void)
{
  char mystr[LENGTH];                        // Input string
  int mychar = 0;                            // Character for output
  FILE *pfile = NULL;                        // File pointer
  char *filename = "myfile.txt";

  printf("Enter an interesting string of up to %d characters:\n", LENGTH - 1);
  if(!fgets(mystr, LENGTH, stdin))           // Read in a string
  {
    printf_s("Input from keyboard failed.\n");
```

```
    exit(1);
  }
  // Create a new file we can write
  if(fopen_s(&pfile, filename, "w"))
  {
    printf_s("Error opening %s for writing. Program terminated.\n", filename);
    exit(1);
  }
  setvbuf(pfile, NULL, _IOFBF, BUFSIZ);   // Buffer the file

  for(int i = strnlen_s(mystr, LENGTH) - 1 ; i >= 0 ; --i)
    fputc(mystr[i], pfile);                // Write string to file backward

  fclose(pfile);                           // Close the file

  // Open the file for reading
  if(fopen_s(&pfile, filename, "r"))
  {
    printf_s("Error opening %s for reading. Program terminated.", filename);
    exit(1);
  }
  setvbuf(pfile, NULL, _IOFBF, BUFSIZ);   // Buffer the file

  // Read a character from the file and display it
  printf_s("the data read from the file is:\n");
  while((mychar = fgetc(pfile)) != EOF)
    putchar(mychar);                       // Output character from the file
  putchar('\n');                           // Write newline

  fclose(pfile);                           // Close the file
  pfile = NULL;
  remove(filename);                        // Delete the physical file
  return 0;
}
```

Here's an example of some output from this program:

```
Enter an interesting string of up to 80 characters:
Too many cooks spoil the broth.
the data read from the file is:

.htorb eht liops skooc ynam ooT
```

How It Works

The name of the file that you're going to work with is defined by this statement:

```
    char *filename = "myfile.txt";
```

This statement defines the file with the name myfile.txt in the current directory. If you want to locate it somewhere else, add the file path. As I noted earlier, you must use the escape sequence '\\' to get a backslash character. If you forget to do this and just use a single backslash, the compiler will think that you're writing an escape sequence, which it won't recognize as valid.

Before running this program—or indeed any of the examples working with files—make sure you don't have an existing file with the same name and path. If you have a file with the same name as that used in the example, you should change the initial value for filename in the example; otherwise, your existing file will be overwritten.

After displaying a prompt, the program reads a string from the keyboard using fgets(), which you learned about in Chapter 10. It then executes the following statements:

```
if(fopen_s(&pfile, filename, "w"))
{
  printf_s("Error opening %s for writing. Program terminated.\n", filename);
  exit(1);
}
```

The condition in this if statement calls fopen_s() to create the new file myfile.txt in the current directory, opens it for writing, and stores the file pointer in pfile. The third argument determines the mode as writing the file. The block of statements will be executed if fopen_s() returns a nonzero integer, so in this case you display a message and call the exit() function that is declared in stdlib.h for an abnormal end to the program.

Next, you call setvbuf() to buffer output operations:

```
setvbuf(pfile, NULL, _IOFBF, BUFSIZ);  // Buffer the file
```

We have limited keyboard input to a total of LENGTH characters, so BUFSIZ for the size of the output buffer will be more than enough.

Next, you have the following loop:

```
for(int i = strnlen_s(mystr, LENGTH) - 1 ; i >= 0 ; --i)
    fputc(mystr[i], pfile);              // Write string to file backward
```

The loop index is varied from a value corresponding to the last character in the string back to 0. Therefore, the fputc() function call within the loop writes to the new file character by character, in reverse order. The particular file you're writing is specified by pfile as the second argument to fputc(). This is a situation where you don't want to use a control variable of type size_t, although you do use it to index an array. Ending the loop depends on the control variable being less than 0, and this is not possible with size_t because it's an unsigned type.

After closing the file with a call to fclose(), reopen it in read mode and buffer operations:

```
if(fopen_s(&pfile, filename, "r"))
{
  printf_s("Error opening %s for reading. Program terminated.", filename);
  exit(1);
}
setvbuf(pfile, NULL, _IOFBF, BUFSIZ);  // Buffer the file
```

The mode specification "r" indicates that you intend to read the file, so the file position will be set to the beginning of the file. You have the same check for a nonzero return value as when you wrote the file.

Next, you use the fgetc() function to read characters from the file within the while loop condition:

```
while((mychar = fgetc(pfile)) != EOF)
    putchar(mychar);                    // Output character from the file
```

The file is read character by character. The read operation takes place within the loop continuation condition. As each character is read, it's displayed on the screen using the function putchar() within the loop. The process stops when EOF is returned by fgetc() at the end of the file.

The last three statements before the return statement in main() are

```
fclose(pfile);                          // Close the file
pfile = NULL;
remove(filename);                       // Delete the physical file
```

These provide the necessary final tidying up, now that you've finished with the file. After closing the file and resetting the file pointer to NULL, the program calls the remove() function, which will delete the file identified by the argument. This avoids cluttering up the disk with stray files. If you want to check the contents of the file that was written using a text editor, you can remove or comment out the call to remove().

Reading and Writing Strings to a Text File

You can use the fgets() function that you have been using to read from stdin to read from any stream. It has the following prototype:

```
char *fgets(char * restrict str, int nchars, FILE * restrict pfile);
```

The function reads a string into the memory area pointed to by str, from the file specified by pfile. Characters are read until either an '\n' is read or nchars-1 characters have been read from the stream, whichever occurs first. If a newline character is read, it's retained in the string. A '\0' character will be appended to the end of the string in any event. If there is no error, fgets() returns the pointer, str; otherwise, NULL is returned. Reading EOF causes NULL to be returned.

For writing a string to a stream, you have the complementary fputs() function that has the prototype

```
int fputs(const char * restrict str, FILE * restrict pfile);
```

The first argument is a pointer to the character string that's to be written to the file, and the second argument is the file pointer. The operation of the function is slightly odd in that it continues to write characters from a string until it reaches a '\0' character, which it doesn't write to the file. This can complicate reading back variable-length strings from a file that have been written by fputs(). It works this way because it's a character-write operation, not a binary-write operation, so it's expecting to write a line of text that has a newline character at the end. A newline character isn't required by the operation of the function, but it's very helpful when you want to read the file back using fgets(), as you'll see.

The fputs() function returns EOF if an error occurs and a positive integer under normal circumstances. You use it in the same way as puts(), for example:

```
fputs("The higher the fewer.\n", pfile);
```

This will output the string appearing as the first argument to the file pointed to by pfile.

TRY IT OUT: TRANSFERRING STRINGS TO AND FROM A TEXT FILE

You can exercise the functions to transfer strings to and from a text file in an example that also uses the append mode for writing a file:

```
// Program 12.2  As the saying goes...it comes back!
#define __STDC_WANT_LIB_EXT1__ 1
#include <stdio.h>
#include <stdlib.h>
#include <stdbool.h>

#define LENGTH 81                              // Maximum input length

int main(void)
{
  char *proverbs[] =
              { "Many a mickle makes a muckle.\n",
                "Too many cooks spoil the broth.\n",
                "He who laughs last didn't get the joke in"
                                    " the first place.\n"
              };
  char more[LENGTH];                     // Stores a new proverb
  FILE *pfile = NULL;                    // File pointer
  char *filename = "myfile.txt";

  // Create a new file if myfile.txt does not exist
  if(fopen_s(&pfile, filename, "w"))          // Open the file to write it
  {
    printf_s("Error opening %s for writing. Program terminated.\n", filename);
    exit(1);
  }
  setvbuf(pfile, NULL, _IOFBF, BUFSIZ);       // Buffer file output

  // Write our locally stored proverbs to the file.
  for(size_t i = 0 ; i < sizeof proverbs/sizeof proverbs[0] ; ++i)
  {
    if(EOF == fputs(proverbs[i], pfile))
    {
      printf_s("Error writing file.\n");
      exit(1);
    }
  }
  fclose(pfile);                              // Close the file
  pfile = NULL;

  // Open the file to append more proverbs
  if(fopen_s(&pfile, filename, "a"))
  {
    printf_s("Error opening %s for appending. Program terminated.\n", filename);
    exit(1);
  }
  setvbuf(pfile, NULL, _IOFBF, BUFSIZ);       // Buffer file output
```

```
    printf_s("Enter proverbs of up to %d characters or press Enter to end:\n",
                                                        LENGTH - 1);
    while(true)
    {
      fgets(more, LENGTH, stdin);              // Read a proverb
      if(more[0] == '\n')                      // If its empty line
        break;                                 // end input operation
      if(EOF == fputs(more, pfile))            // Write the new proverb
      {
        printf_s("Error writing file.\n");
        exit(1);
      }
    }
    fclose(pfile);                             // Close the file
    pfile = NULL;

    if(fopen_s(&pfile, filename, "r"))         // Open the file to read it
    {
      printf_s("Error opening %s for reading. Program terminated.\n", filename);
      exit(1);
    }
    setvbuf(pfile, NULL, _IOFBF, BUFSIZ);      // Buffer file input

    // Read and output the file contents
    printf_s("The proverbs in the file are:\n");
    while(fgets(more, LENGTH, pfile))          // Read a proverb
     printf_s("%s", more);                     // and display it

    fclose(pfile);                             // Close the file
    remove(filename);                          // and remove it
    pfile = NULL;
    return 0;
  }
```

Here is some sample output from this program:

```
Enter proverbs of up to 80 characters or press Enter to end:
Every dog has his day.
Least said, soonest mended.
A stitch in time saves nine.
Waste not, want not.

The proverbs in the file are:
Many a mickle makes a muckle.
Too many cooks spoil the broth.
He who laughs last didn't get the joke in the first place.
Every dog has his day.
Least said, soonest mended.
A stitch in time saves nine.
Waste not, want not.
```

How It Works

You initialize the array of pointers, `proverbs[]`, in the following statement:

```
char *proverbs[] =
            {   "Many a mickle makes a muckle.\n",
                "Too many cooks spoil the broth.\n",
                "He who laughs last didn't get the joke in"
                                " the first place.\n"
            };
```

You specify the three sayings as initial values for the array elements, and this causes the compiler to allocate the space necessary to store each string. Each string is terminated with a newline character.

You have a further declaration of an array that will store a proverb and be read from the keyboard:

```
char more[LENGTH];                          // Stores a new proverb
```

After creating and opening a file for writing, the program writes the proverbs in the array to the file:

```
for(size_t i = 0 ; i < sizeof proverbs/sizeof proverbs[0] ; ++i)
{
  if(EOF == fputs(proverbs[i], pfile))
  {
    printf_s("Error writing file.\n");
    exit(1);
  }
}
```

The contents of each of the memory areas pointed to by elements of the `proverbs[]` array are written to the file in the `for` loop using `fputs()`. This function is extremely easy to use; it just requires a pointer to the string as the first argument and a pointer to the file as the second. You test the return value for `EOF` because that indicates something went wrong.

Once the local set of proverbs has been written, the file is closed and then reopened:

```
if(fopen_s(&pfile, filename, "a"))
{
  printf_s("Error opening %s for appending. Program terminated.\n", filename);
  exit(1);
}
setvbuf(pfile, NULL, _IOFBF, BUFSIZ);       // Buffer file output
```

You call `setvbuf()` to buffer output operations with an internal buffer. Because you have the open mode specified as "a", the file is opened in append mode. The current position for the file is automatically set to the end of the file in this mode, so subsequent write operations will be appended to the end of the file.

After prompting for input, you read more proverbs from the keyboard and write them to the file with the following statements:

```
while(true)
{
  fgets(more, LENGTH, stdin);               // Read a proverb
  if(more[0] == '\n')                       // If its empty line
    break;                                  // end input operation
```

```
if(EOF == fputs(more, pfile))              // Write the new proverb
{
  printf_s("Error writing file.\n");
  exit(1);
}
}
```

Each additional proverb that's stored in the more array is written to the file using fputs(). You always expect trouble with file operations, so you check for EOF being returned. Because you're in append mode, each new proverb will be added at the end of the existing data in the file. The loop terminates when an empty line is entered. An empty line will result in a string containing just '\n' followed by the string terminator.

Having written the file, you close it and then reopen it for reading using the mode specifier "r". You then have the following loop:

```
while(fgets(more, LENGTH, pfile))          // Read a proverb
  printf_s("%s", more);                    // and display it
```

You read successive strings from the file into the more array within the loop continuation condition. After each string is read, you display it on the screen by the call to printf_s() within the loop. Because more is a char array, you could write the output statement as

```
printf_s(more);
```

Here, more is used as the format string. This will work most of the time, but it is not a good idea. If the user includes a % in a proverb that is stored in more, things will go wrong.

The reading of each proverb by fgets() is terminated by detecting the '\n' character at the end of each string. The loop terminates when the function fgets() returns NULL, which will be when EOF is reached. Finally, the file is closed and then deleted using remove() in the same fashion as the previous example.

Formatted File Input and Output

Writing characters and strings to a text file is all very well as far as it goes, but you normally have many other types of data in your programs. To write numerical data to a text file, you need something more than you've seen so far, and where the contents of a file are to be human readable, you need a character representation of the numerical data. The mechanism for doing just this is provided by the functions for formatted file input and output.

Formatted Output to a File

The standard function for formatted output to a stream is fprintf(), and there is an optional safe version called fprintf_s() that works in a similar way to the printf_s() function. The prototype for fprintf_s() is

```
int fprintf_s(FILE * restrict pfile, const char * restrict format, ...);
```

The difference between this and the prototype for printf_s() is the first parameter that identifies the output stream. You specify the format string according to the same rules as for printf_s(), including the conversion specifiers. The function returns the number of characters written to the stream when everything works as it should or a negative integer when it doesn't.

Here's an example of how you might use it:

```
FILE *pfile = NULL;                          // File pointer
int num1 = 1234, num2 = 4567;
float pi = 3.1416f;
if(fopen_s(&pfile, "myfile.txt", "w"))       // Open the file to write it
{
  printf_s("Error opening file for writing. Program terminated.\n");
  exit(1);
}
if(0 > fprintf(pfile, "%12d%12d%14f", num1, num2, pi))
    printf_s("Failed to write the file.\n");
```

This example writes the values of the three variables num1, num2, and pi to the file specified by the file pointer pfile, under control of the format string specified as the second argument. The first two variables are of type int and are written with a field width of 12, and the third variable is of type float and is written with a field width of 14. Thus, this will write 38 characters to myfile.txt, overwriting any existing data that are in the file.

Formatted Input from a File

You can get formatted input from a file by using the standard fscanf() function, but I'll discuss the optional safer version fscanf_s() that has the following prototype:

```
int fscanf_s(FILE * restrict pfile, const char * restrict format, ...);
```

This function works in exactly the same way scanf_s() does with stdin, except here you're obtaining input from a stream specified by the first argument. The same rules govern the specification of the format string and the operation of the function as apply to scanf_s(). The function returns EOF when things go wrong or the end of file is reached or the number of input items assigned values when the operation is successful.

To read three variable values from the file written by the previous code fragment, you could write this:

```
if(fopen_s(&pfile, "myfile.txt", "r"))       // Open the file to read it
{
  printf_s("Error opening file for reading. Program terminated.\n");
  exit(1);
}
if(EOF == fscanf_s(pfile, "%12d%12d%14f", &num1, &num2, &pi))
    printf_s("Failed to read the file.\n");
```

The fscanf_s() function would return 3 when this works, as it should because three values are stored.

TRY IT OUT: USING FORMATTED INPUT AND OUTPUT FUNCTIONS

You can demonstrate the formatted input/output functions with an example that will also show what's happening to the data in these operations:

```c
// Program 12.3 Messing about with formatted file I/O
#define _CRT_SECURE_NO_WARNINGS
#define __STDC_WANT_LIB_EXT1__ 1
#include <stdio.h>
#include <stdlib.h>

int main(void)
{
  long num1 = 234567L;                    // Input values...
  long num2 = 345123L;
  long num3 = 789234L;

  long num4 = 0L;                         // Values read from the file...
  long num5 = 0L;
  long num6 = 0L;

  float fnum = 0.0f;                      // Value read from the file
  int   ival[6] = { 0 };                  // Values read from the file
  FILE *pfile = NULL;                     // File pointer
  char *filename = "myfile.txt";

  if(fopen_s(&pfile, filename, "w"))
  {
    printf_s("Error opening %s for writing. Program terminated.\n", filename);
    exit(1);
  }
  setbuf(pfile, NULL);

  fprintf_s(pfile, "%6ld%6ld%6ld", num1, num2, num3);     // Write file
  fclose(pfile);                                          // Close file
  printf_s(" %6ld %6ld %6ld\n", num1, num2, num3);        // Display values written

  if(fopen_s(&pfile, filename, "r"))
  {
    printf_s("Error opening %s for reading. Program terminated.\n", filename);
    exit(EXIT_FAILURE );    // 1
  }
  setbuf(pfile, NULL);

  fscanf_s(pfile, "%6ld%6ld%6ld", &num4, &num5 ,&num6); // Read back
  printf_s(" %6ld %6ld %6ld\n", num4, num5, num6);        // Display what we got

  rewind(pfile);                             // Go to the beginning of the file
  fscanf_s(pfile, "%2d%3d%3d%3d%2d%2d%3f", &ival[0], &ival[1], // Read it again
                  &ival[2], &ival[3], &ival[4] , &ival[5], &fnum);
  fclose(pfile);                             // Close the file and
  remove(filename);                          // delete physical file.
```

```
// Output the results
printf_s("\n");
for(size_t i = 0 ; i < sizeof(ival)/sizeof(ival[0]) ; ++i)
  printf_s("%sival[%zd] = %d", i == 4 ? "\n\t" : "\t", i, ival[i]);
printf_s("\nfnum = %f\n", fnum);
return 0;
}
```

The output from this example is the following:

```
234567 345123 789234
 234567 345123 789234

        ival[0] = 23    ival[1] = 456    ival[2] = 734    ival[3] = 512
        ival[4] = 37    ival[5] = 89
fnum = 234.000000
```

How It Works

This example writes the values of num1, num2, and num3 to the file myfile.txt in the current directory. You reference the file through the pointer pfile. The file is closed and reopened with mode "r" for reading, and the values are read from the file in the same format as they are written but stored in num4, num5, and num6. It's a relief that these values are identical to num1, num2, and num3.

You then have the following statement:

```
rewind(pfile);
```

This statement moves the current file position back to the beginning of the file so you can read it again. You could have achieved the same thing by closing the file and then reopening it again, but with rewind() you do it with one function call, and the operation will be a lot faster.

Having repositioned the file, you read the file again with this statement:

```
fscanf_s(pfile, "%2d%3d%3d%3d%2d%2d%3f", &ival[0], &ival[1], // Read it again
                  &ival[2], &ival[3], &ival[4] , &ival[5], &fnum);
```

This reads the same data from the file into elements of the ival array and the floating-point variable fnum, but with different formats from those used for writing the file. You can see from the output that the file contents are just a string of characters once it has been written, exactly the same as the output to the screen would be from printf_s().

■ **Note** You can lose information when you write a text file if you choose a format specifier that outputs fewer digits' precision than the stored value holds.

The values you get back from a text file when you read it will depend on both the format string you use and the variable list you specify in the fscanf_s() function.

None of the intrinsic source information that existed when you wrote the file is necessarily maintained. Once the data are in the file, it's just a sequence of bytes in which the meaning is determined by how you interpret them. This is demonstrated quite clearly by this example, in which you've converted the original three values into seven new values. To make sense of the data in a file, you must know how they were written.

Lastly, you leave everything neat and tidy in this program by closing the file and using the function `remove()` to delete it.

Dealing with Errors

The examples in this book have included minimal error checking and reporting because the code for comprehensive error checking and reporting tends to take up a lot of space and makes programs look rather more complicated than they really are. In real-world programs, however, it's essential that you do as much error checking and reporting as you can.

Generally, you should write your error messages to stderr, which is automatically available to your program and always points to your display screen. It's important to check that a file you want to read does in fact exist, which you have been doing in the examples, but there's more you can do. First, you can write error messages to stderr rather than stdin using fprintf_s(), for example:

```
char *filename = "myfile.txt";
FILE *pfile = NULL;
if(fopen_s(&pfile, filename, "r"))
{
  fprintf_s(stderr, "\nCannot open %s to read it.", filename);
  exit(1);
}
```

The merit of writing to stderr is that the output will always be directed to the command line and it will always be written immediately to the display device. This means you will always see the output directed to stderr, as long as you have not reassigned stderr to another destination. The stdin stream is buffered, so there is the risk that data could be left in the buffer and never displayed if your program crashes. Terminating a program by calling exit() ensures that output stream buffers will be flushed so output will be written to the ultimate destination.

Knowing that some kind of error occurred is useful, but you can do more than this. A stream error condition can cause an error indicator to be set that you can test by calling ferror(). The argument to ferror() is a stream pointer, and the function returns nonzero if the error indicator is set for the stream. You can then call the perror() function that outputs a string you pass as an argument plus an implementation-defined error message corresponding to the stream error that occurred. The following code tests for an error for the stream corresponding to the pointer, pfile, and outputs a message:

```
if(ferror(pfile))
{
  perror("Stream error");
  exit(EXIT_FAILURE );   //1
}
```

The output message will be

```
Stream error: Message corresponding to the error
```

As seen in Chapter 9, a good practice is to use the macros provided by stdlib.h because various operating systems may expect different return values (most are 1 or 0 based on UNIX design). Since ANSI C, macros EXIT_FAILURE and EXIT_SUCCESS were included to use with exit().

The error-specific message string will be appended to the string you supply as the argument and separated from it by a colon. If you just want the error message, you pass NULL to the function.

When an error occurs reading a file, you can check whether the error is due to reaching the end of file. The feof() function will return a nonzero integer if the end of file has been reached, so you can check for this with statements such as these:

```
if(feof(pfile))
  printf_s("End of file reached.");
```

I didn't write the message to stderr here because reaching the end of the file isn't necessarily an error.

The errno.h header file defines a value of type int with the name errno that may indicate what kind of file error has occurred. You need to read the documentation for your C implementation to find out the specifics of what the error codes are. The value of errno may be set for errors other than just file operations.

You should always include some basic error checking and reporting code in all of your programs. Once you've written a few programs, you'll find that including some standard bits of code for each type of operation warranting error checks is no hardship. With a standard approach, you can copy most of what you need from one program to another.

More Open Modes for Text Files

Text mode is the default mode of operation with the open modes you have seen up to now, but in earlier versions of C, you could specify explicitly that a file is to be opened in text mode. You could do this by adding t to the end of the existing specifiers. This gives you the mode specifiers "wt", "rt", and "at" in addition to the original three. I am only mentioning this because you may come across it in other C programs. Although some compilers support this, it's not specifically part of the current C standard, so it is best not to use this option in your code.

The complete set of mode strings for opening text files using the fopen_s() function is given in Table 12-2.

Table 12-2. *Open Modes for Use with* fopen_s()

Mode	Description
"r"	Open a text file to read it
"r+"	Open a text file to read and write it
"w"	Open or create a text file to write it. If the file exists, its length is truncated to zero so the contents will be overwritten
"wx"	Create and open a text file to write it with nonshared access
"w+"	Truncate an existing text file to zero length and open it for update. If the file does not exist, create it and open it for updating
"w+x"	Create a text file for updating with nonshared access
"a"	Open or create a text file to append to it. All writes will be to the end of the file
"a+"	Open or create a text file for update, with all writes adding data at the end of the file

Note that nonshared access can only be specified when you create a new file. Opening an existing file with a mode string that includes "x" will fail. When you open a file to append to it (a mode string containing "a"), all write operations will be to the end of the file, regardless of the current file position.

"x" is a new feature from C11 to avoid deleting existing files and throw an error instead of whether the file exists already. This means, if you use only "w", then it creates a text file (truncates it); thus, it is similar to "a" or "w", but it would be necessary to check its existence and then decide to use some of those modes; meanwhile, "wx" is more straightforward. This can be useful in many ways, by controlling concurrent access to the same file and also avoiding error-prone code that has forgotten about the file lifecycle:

```
FILE *pfile = NULL;
char *filename = "hello.txt";
pfile = fopen(filename, "wx");

if (pfile == NULL)
{
  printf("file already exists!");
  exit(EXIT_FAILURE);
}
```

When you open a file to update it (a mode string containing "+"), you can read and write to the file. However, an input operation that immediately follows an output operation must be preceded by a call to fflush() or to a function that changes the file position. This ensures that the output buffer is flushed before the read operation. When you want to write to a file immediately following a read operation, there must be a call to a file positioning function preceding the write unless the file position is at the end of the file. The functions that change the file position are rewind(), which you know about, and fseek() and fsetpos(), which you'll learn about later in this chapter.

The freopen_s() Function

The freopen_s() function is the optional safe version of freopen(). It is used most often to reassign a standard stream pointer to a file. You can reassign stdout, for example, so that all data subsequently written to the stream will be written to the file. You can also use freopen_s() to change the mode for an existing stream. The function freopen_s() has the prototype

```
errno_t freopen_s(FILE * restrict * restrict pNew,        // New stream pointer address
                  const char * restrict filename,         // Name of the file
                  const char * restrict mode,             // Open mode
                  FILE * restrict stream);                // Existing stream pointer
```

When filename is NULL, the function will attempt to change the mode for the stream specified by the fourth argument, stream, to mode. Which mode changes are possible depends on your C implementation.

When filename is not NULL, the function first tries to close the file pointed to by stream. It then opens the file and associates the existing stream passed as the fourth argument, stream, with the file. The stream pointer is stored in pNew when the operation is successful. When it fails, pNew will be set to NULL. As with fopen_s(), the return value is 0 when everything goes according to plan and a nonzero integer when an error occurs.

Here's an example of reassigning stdout to a file:

```
FILE *pOut = NULL;                        // File pointer
char *filename = "myfile.txt";
```

```
if(freopen_s(&pOut, filename, "w+", stdout))
{
  printf_s("Error assigning stdout to %s. Program terminated.\n", filename);
  exit(1);
}
printf_s("This output goes to myfile.txt\n");
```

After executing this fragment, pOut contains the stream pointer stdout, and this is now associated with myfile.txt, so all subsequent output to stdout will be written to myfile.txt. When you want to use a program that normally reads from stdin to accept input from a file, you can use freopen_s() to reassign stdin to the file in a similar way. Clearly the file must already exist and contain suitable input data when you do this.

Binary File Input and Output

The alternative to text mode operations on a file is *binary mode*. In this mode, no transformation of the data takes place, and there's no need for a format string to control input or output, so it's much simpler than text mode. The binary data as they appear in memory are transferred directly to the file. Characters such as '\n' and '\0' that have specific significance in text mode are of no consequence in binary mode.

Binary mode has the advantage that no data are transformed or precision lost, as can happen due to the conversion process with text mode. It's also faster than text mode because there's no transformation of data. The two modes are contrasted in Figure 12-3.

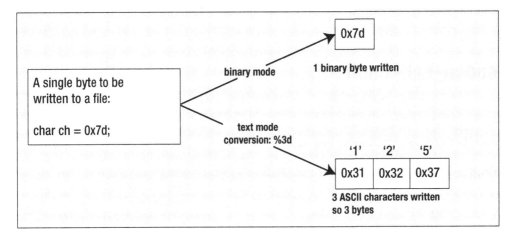

Figure 12-3. *Contrasting binary mode and text mode*

Opening a File in Binary Mode

You specify binary mode by appending b to the three basic open mode specifiers I introduced initially. Therefore, you have the open mode specifiers "wb" for writing a binary file, "rb" to read a binary file, and "ab" to append data to the end of a binary file. The complete set of mode strings for binary operations with files are given in Table 12-3.

Table 12-3. *Mode Strings for Binary Operations*

"rb"	Open a binary file to read it
"rb+" or "r+b"	Open a binary file to read and write it
"wb"	Open or create a binary file to write it. If the file exists, its length is truncated to zero so the contents will be overwritten
"wbx"	Create and open a binary file to write it with nonshared access
"wb+" or "w+b"	Truncate an existing binary file to zero length and open it for update. If the file does not exist, create it and open it for updating
"wb+x" or "w+bx"	Create a binary file for updating with nonshared access
"ab"	Open or create a binary file to append to it. All writes will be to the end of the file
"ab+" or "a+b"	Open or create a binary file for update, with all writes adding data at the end of the file

Because binary mode involves handling the data to be transferred to and from the file in a different way from text mode, you have a new set of functions to perform input and output.

Writing a Binary File

You use the fwrite() function to write a binary file. It has the following prototype:

```
size_t fwrite(const void * restrict pdata, size_t size, size_t nitems,
              FILE * restrict pfile);
```

The first parameter is the address of an array of data items to be written. With a parameter type void*, any type of array can be passed as the argument to the function. The second parameter is the size of an array element, and the third parameter is the number of array elements. The last parameter is the pointer to the file stream. The integer returned is the number of items written. This will be less than nitems if a write error occurs that prevents all of the data from being written. If size or nitems is 0, nothing is written to the file.

This is best explained with an example of its use. Suppose you open the file to be written with the following statements:

```
FILE *pfile = NULL;                      // File pointer
char *filename = "myfile.bin";
if(fopen_s(&pfile, filename, "wb"))
{
  printf_s("Error opening %s for writing. Program terminated.\n", filename);
  exit(1);
}
```

You could now write to the file myfile.bin with these statements:

```
long data[] = {2L, 3L, 4L};
size_t num_items = sizeof(data)/sizeof(long);
size_t wcount = fwrite(data, sizeof(long), num_items, pfile);
```

The fwrite() function operates on the principle of writing a specified number of binary data items to a file, where each item is a given number of bytes. This writes all of the data array to the file. Note that there is no check that you opened the file in binary mode when you call fwrite(). The write operation will write binary data to a file you open in text mode. Equally, there is nothing to prevent you from writing text data to a binary file. Of course if you do this, a considerable amount of confusion is likely to result.

Because fwrite() is geared toward writing a number of binary objects of a given length to a file, you can write in units of your own structures as easily as you can write values of type int or double or sequences of individual bytes. This doesn't mean that the data items you write in any given output operation all have to be of the same type. You might allocate some memory using malloc(), for instance, into which you assemble a sequence of data items of different types and lengths. You could then write the whole block of memory to a file in one go as a sequence of bytes. Of course, when you come to read them back, you need to know the precise sequence and types for the values in the file if you are to make sense of them.

Reading a Binary File

You use the fread() function to read a binary file once you have opened the file in read mode. The fread() has the prototype

```
size_t fread(void * restrict pdata, size_t size, size_t nitems, FILE * restrict pfile);
```

The parameters are the same as for fwrite(): pdata is the address of an array into which the data items are to be read, size is the number of bytes per item, nitems is the number of items to be read, and pfile is the file pointer.

Using the same variables as in the example of writing a binary file, you could read the file using a statement such as this:

```
size_t wcount = fread( data, sizeof(long), num_items, pfile);
```

This operates exactly inverse of the write operation. Starting at the address specified by data, the function reads num_items objects, each occupying the number of bytes specified by the second argument. The function returns the count of the number of items that were read. If the read isn't completely successful, the count will be less than the number of objects requested.

TRY IT OUT: WRITING AND READING A BINARY FILE

You can apply binary file operations in a version of Program 7.11 that calculates primes. This time, you'll use a file as a buffer to allow a much larger number of primes to be produced. You can make the program automatically spill primes into a disk file if the array assigned to store the primes is insufficient for the number of primes requested. In this version of the program to find primes, you'll improve the checking process a little.

In addition to the main() function, which will contain the prime finding loop, you'll write a function to test whether a value is prime called is_prime(), a helper function that will check a given value against a block of primes called check(), a function called list_primes() that will retrieve the primes from the file and display them, and another helper function that lists primes in the array in memory.

As this program consists of several functions and will work with variables at global scope, I'll explain it piece by piece. I'll start with the function prototypes and global data before I go into detail on the functions:

```
// Program 12.4  A prime example using binary files
#define __STDC_WANT_LIB_EXT1__ 1
#include <stdio.h>
#include <stdlib.h>
#include <stdbool.h>
#include <math.h>                               // For square root function sqrt()

#define PER_LINE     8                          // Primes per line in output
#define MEM_PRIMES 10*PER_LINE                  // Lines of primes in memory

// Function prototypes
bool is_prime(unsigned long long N);           // Check for a prime
void list_primes(void);                        // List all primes
int check(unsigned long long buffer[], size_t count, unsigned long long N);
void list_array(void);                         // List primes in memory
void write_file(void);                         // Write primes to file

// Anonymous struct type
struct
{
  char *filename;                              // File name for primes
  FILE *pfile;                                 // File stream pointer
  unsigned long long primes[MEM_PRIMES];       // Array to store primes
  size_t count;                                // Free location in primes
} global = { .filename = "myfile.bin",         // Physical file name
             .pfile = NULL,                    // File pointer value
             .primes = {2ULL, 3ULL, 5ULL},     // Initial seed primes
             .count = 3                        // Number of primes in array
           };

int main(void)
{
  // Code for main()...
}

// Definitions for other functions...
```

After the symbol definition to make optional functions accessible and the usual #include directives, you define symbols for the number of primes to be output per line and the number of primes to be stored in memory. By making the latter a multiple of the number per line, you make it easier to manage outputting the primes stored in a file.

Next, you have the prototypes for the functions used in the program. Function prototypes can be written with or without parameter names, but the parameter types must be specified. Generally, it's better to include names, because they give a clue to the purpose of the parameters. The names in the prototype can be different from the names used in the definition of the function, but you should only do this if it helps to make the code more readable. To allow the maximum range of possible prime values, you store them as values of type unsigned long long.

The prototypes are followed by the definition of an anonymous struct that contains global variables as members. The instance of the structure must be defined in the same statement as the struct type definition because this is an anonymous struct. By defining global variables as members of the global structure object, you minimize the risk of conflicts with local variable names because the global variables must be qualified with the name of the structure object to which they belong. You initialize the members of global using the notation that identifies the member names. They are in order of their appearance in the structure type definition, but they don't have to be.

The members of the struct are filename, which points to the name of the file that will store primes; the file stream pointer, pfile; the primes array, which will hold up to MEM_PRIMES values in memory; and count, which records the current number of elements in the primes array that have values.

Here's the definition for main():

```
int main(void)
{
  unsigned long long trial =
                global.primes[global.count - 1]; // Current prime candidate
  size_t num_primes = 3UL;                       // Current prime count
  size_t total = 0UL;                            // Total number required

  printf_s("How many primes would you like?  ");
  scanf_s("%zd", &total);
  total = total < 4 ? 4 : total;                 // Make sure it is at least 4

  // Prime finding and storing loop
  while(num_primes < total)                      // Loop until we get total required
  {
    trial += 2ULL;                               // Next value for checking
    if(is_prime(trial))                          // Is trial prime?
    {
      global.primes[global.count++] = trial;     // Yes, so store it
      ++num_primes;                              // Increment total primes

      if(global.count == MEM_PRIMES)             // If array is full...
        write_file();                            // ...write to file.
    }
  }
  // If there are primes in the array and there is a file, write them to the file.
  if(global.pfile && global.count > 0)
    write_file();

  list_primes();                                 // Display the file contents
  if(global.pfile)                               // If we needed a file...
  {
    if(remove(global.filename))                  // ...then delete it.
      printf_s("\nFailed to delete %s\n", global.filename); // Delete failed
    else
      printf_s("\nFile %s deleted.\n", global.filename);    // Delete OK
  }
  return 0;
}
```

How It Works

Because there are three primes defined, the number required that is entered from the keyboard must be at least 4, so you check for this and set total to 4 if necessary. Primes are found in the while loop. The is_prime() function is called in the if statement condition within the loop to check whether the current prime candidate in trial is prime. If a prime is found, then you execute these statements to store it in the array:

```
global.primes[global.count++] = trial;      // Yes, so store it
++num_primes;                                // Increment total number of primes
```

The first statement stores the prime you've found in the global.primes array. You keep track of how many primes you have so far with the variable num_primes, and this value controls the outer while loop. The struct member variable global.count records how many you have in memory at any given time so you can tell when the array is full.

Once you have stored a new prime, you check whether the array is full:

```
if(global.count == MEM_PRIMES)               // If array is full...
   write_file();                             // ...write to file.
```

If you've filled the global.primes array, the if condition will be true, and you'll call write_file(), which you'll implement to write the contents of the global.primes array to the file. The function can use global.count to determine how many elements must be written out.

When the while loop ends because the required number of primes have been found, there may be primes stored in the global.primes array. A file will only have been written if more primes were required than the capacity of the global.primes array. If this were the case and a file exists and there are primes left in the array, you call write_file() to write them to the file. You'll implement the list_primes() function to output the primes so that it will either read the primes from the file if it exists using global.primes as a buffer or just list the primes in the global.primes array.

If it is necessary to write a file, global.pfile will be non-NULL, so you can use this to determine when there is a file to delete before the program ends.

You can implement is_prime() like this:

```
bool is_prime(unsigned long long n)
{
  unsigned long long buffer[MEM_PRIMES];     // local buffer for primes from file
  size_t count = 0;                          // Number of primes in buffer
  int k = 0;

  if(global.pfile)                                      // If we have written a file...
  {                                                     // ...open it
    if(fopen_s(&global.pfile, global.filename, "rb"))
    {
      printf_s("Unable to open %s to read.\n", global.filename);
      exit(1);
    }
  }
```

```
    setvbuf(global.pfile, NULL, _IOFBF, BUFSIZ); // Buffer file input
    while(!feof(global.pfile))
    { // Check against primes in the file first
      // Read primes
      count = fread(buffer, sizeof(buffer[0]), MEM_PRIMES, global.pfile);
      if((k = check(buffer, count, n)) == 1)      // Prime?
      {
        fclose(global.pfile);                     // Yes, so close the file
        return true;                              // and return
      }
    }
    fclose(global.pfile);                         // Close the file
  }

  return 1 == check(global.primes, global.count, n); // Check primes in memory
}
```

The if statement determines whether there is a file containing primes by checking global.pfile. When this is not NULL, the file is opened, and primes are read from the file into the local array, buffer, in the while loop. The while loop condition is the negation of the value returned by feof(). The feof() returns true when the end of file has been read, so this indicates the entire file has been read and the loop will end. The check() function that is called in the loop tests n against the primes in buffer.

The last step after the loop ends is to check division by any primes that are in memory, again using check(). These are checked last because these are the latest and largest primes discovered.

You can implement the check() function like this:

```
int check(unsigned long long buffer[], size_t count, unsigned long long n)
{
  // Upper limit
  unsigned long long root_N = (unsigned long long)(1.0 + sqrt((double)n));

  for(size_t i = 0 ; i < count ; ++i)
  {
    if(n % buffer[i] == 0ULL)              // Exact division?
      return 0;                            // Then not a prime

    if(buffer[i] > root_N)                 // Divisor exceeds square root?
      return 1;                            // Then must be a prime
  }
  return -1;                               // More checks necessary...
}
```

The function returns 1 if n is prime, 0 if it is not prime, and -1 if further checks may be necessary. The function determines whether n is prime by dividing n by each of the primes in the array that are less than the square root of n. You don't need to try values greater than this because if a value greater than the square root divides into n, the result will be a factor that is less than the square root, which you will already have tried. If any existing prime divides exactly, the process ends by returning 0 because n is clearly not prime. If none of the existing primes up to the square root of n divide into n exactly, n must be prime, so 1 is returned. If all the primes in the array have been checked, the result is not determined because there may be more divisors that need to be tried, so -1 is returned.

The implementation of write_file() looks like this:

```
void write_file(void)
{
  if(fopen_s(&global.pfile, global.filename, "ab"))
  { // Failed, so explain and end the program
    printf_s("Unable to open %s to append\n", global.filename);
    exit(1);
  }
  setvbuf(global.pfile, NULL, _IOFBF, BUFSIZ); // Buffer file output
  // Write the array to file
  fwrite(global.primes, sizeof(unsigned long long), global.count, global.pfile);
  fclose(global.pfile);                         // Close the file
  global.count = 0;                             // Reset count of primes in memory
}
```

You open the file in binary mode to append data. The first time this occurs, a new file will be created. On subsequent calls of fopen_s(), the existing file will be opened with the current position set at the end of the data in the file, ready for the next block to be written. After writing a block, the file is closed, because you'll want to open it in read mode in the is_prime() function that checks prime candidates. When the contents of the array have been safely stowed in the file, the count of the number of primes in memory is reset to 0.

The code for the function that lists all the primes is

```
void list_primes(void)
{
  if(global.pfile)
  {
    if(fopen_s(&global.pfile, global.filename, "rb"))     // Open the file
    {
      printf_s("\nUnable to open %s to read primes for output\n", global.filename);
      exit(1);
    }
    setvbuf(global.pfile, NULL, _IOFBF, BUFSIZ);          // Buffer file input
    while(!feof(global.pfile))
    {
      global.count = fread(global.primes,
                    sizeof(unsigned long long), MEM_PRIMES, global.pfile);
      list_array();
    }
    printf_s("\n");
    fclose(global.pfile);
  }
  else
    list_array();
}
```

It first checks whether there is a file. If global.pfile is NULL, then there is no file, and all the primes are in the global.primes array, so you just call list_array() to list them and you are done. When there is a file, you open it in read mode. You then read primes from the file into global.primes in the while loop and call list_array() to list the contents. The fread() function returns the number of primes read, so global.count will always reflect the number of primes in the global.primes array. The loop continues until the end-of-file indicator is set, which will result in feof() returning true.

You can implement the list_array() function that list_primes() calls like this:

```
void list_array(void)
{
  for(size_t j = 0 ; j < global.count ; ++j)         // Display the primes
  {
    printf_s("%10llu", global.primes[j]);            // Output a prime
      if(((j + 1) % PER_LINE) == 0)
        printf_s("\n");
  }
}
```

This requires little explanation. The for loop lists however many primes there are in the global.primes array with PER_LINE primes on each output line.

Moving Around in a File

For many applications, you need to be able to access data in a file other than in the sequential order you've used up to now. You can always find some information that's stored in the middle of a file by reading from the beginning and continuing in sequence until you get to what you want. But if you've written a few million items to the file, this may take some time.

Of course, to access data in random sequence requires that you have some means of knowing where the data that you would like to retrieve are stored in the file. Arranging for this is a complicated topic in general. There are many different ways to construct pointers or indexes to make direct access to the data in a file faster and easier. The basic idea is similar to that of an index in a book. You have a table of keys that identify the contents of each record in the file you might want, and each key has an associated position in the file defined that records where the data are stored. Let's look at the basic tools in the library that you need to enable you to deal with this kind of file input and output.

■ **Note** You cannot update a file in append mode. Regardless of any operations you may invoke to move the file position, all writes will be to the end of the existing data.

File Positioning Operations

There are two aspects to file positioning: finding out where you are in a file and moving to a given point in a file. The former is basic to the latter: if you never know where you are, you can never decide how to get to where you want to go; this doesn't just apply to files!

You can access a file at a random position regardless of whether you opened the file concerned in binary mode or in text mode. However, accessing text mode files randomly can get rather complicated in some environments, particularly Microsoft Windows. This is because the number of characters recorded in the file can be greater than the number of characters you actually write to the file. This is because a newline ('\n' character) in memory, which is a single byte, can translate into two characters when written to a file in text mode (a carriage return character, CR, followed by a linefeed character, LF). Of course, your C library function for reading the information sorts everything out when you read the data back. A problem only arises when you think that a point in the file is 100 bytes from the beginning. When you write 100 characters to a file in text mode under Microsoft Windows, the number of bytes actually appearing in the file depends on how many newline characters it includes; it will only be 100 bytes if there are no newline characters. If you subsequently want to overwrite the data with different data that are the same length in memory as the original, it will only be the same length as the existing data in the file if it contains the same number of '\n' characters. Thus, writing to text files randomly is best avoided. For this reason, I'll sidestep the complications of moving about in text files and concentrate the examples on the much more useful—and easier—context of randomly accessing the data in binary files.

Finding Out Where You Are

You have two functions to tell you where you are in a file, which are very similar but not identical. They each complement a different positioning function. The first is the ftell() function, which has the prototype

```
long ftell(FILE *pfile);
```

This function accepts a file pointer as an argument and returns a long integer value that specifies the current position in the file. This could be used with the file that's referenced by the pointer pfile that you used previously, as in the following statement:

```
long fpos = ftell(pfile);
```

The fpos variable now holds the current position in the file; and, as you'll see, you can use this to return to this position at any subsequent time. The value is the offset in bytes from the beginning of the file.

The second function providing information on the current file position is a little more complicated. The prototype of the function is the following:

```
int fgetpos(FILE * restrict pfile, fpos_t * restrict position);
```

The first parameter is your old friend, the file pointer. The second parameter is a pointer to a type that's defined in stdio.h, fpos_t, which will be a type that is able to record every position within a file. On my system it is a structure. If you're curious about what type fpos_t is on your system, then have a look at it in stdio.h.

The fgetpos() function is designed to be used with the positioning function fsetpos(), which I'll come to shortly. The fgetpos() function stores the current position and file state information for the file in position and returns 0 if the operation is successful; otherwise, it returns a nonzero integer value. You could declare a variable here to be of type fpos_t with a statement such as this:

```
fpos_t here;
```

You could now record the current position in the file with the statement

```
fgetpos(pfile, &here);
```

This records the current file position in the variable here that you have defined. You'll be able to use this to return to this position later.

■ **Caution**   Note that you must declare a *variable* of type fpos_t. It's no good just declaring a pointer of type fpos_t* because there won't be any memory allocated to store the position data.

Setting a Position in a File

As a complement to ftell(), you have the fseek() function that has the following prototype:

```
int fseek(FILE *pfile, long offset, int origin);
```

The first parameter is a pointer to the file you're repositioning. The second and third parameters define where you want to go in the file. The second parameter is an offset from a reference point specified by the third parameter. The reference point can be one of three values that are specified by the predefined names SEEK_SET, which defines the beginning of the file; SEEK_CUR, which defines the current position in the file; and SEEK_END, which, as you might guess, defines the end of the file. SEEK_END may not be supported for binary files. Of course, all three values are defined in stdio.h.

For a text mode file, the second argument must be a value returned by ftell() if you're to avoid getting lost. The third argument for text mode files must be SEEK_SET. So for text mode files, all operations with fseek() are performed with reference to the beginning of the file.

For binary files, the offset argument is simply a relative byte count. You can therefore supply positive or negative values for the offset when the reference point is specified as SEEK_CUR.

You have the fsetpos() function to go with fgetpos(). This has the following prototype:

```
int fsetpos(FILE *pfile, const fpos_t *position);
```

The first parameter is a pointer to the open file, and the second is a pointer of the type you can see, where the position that is stored at the address was obtained by calling fgetpos().

You can't go far wrong with this one really. You could use it with a statement such as this:

```
fsetpos(pfile, &here);
```

The variable here was previously set by a call to fgetpos(). The fsetpos() returns a nonzero value on error or 0 when it succeeds. Because this function is designed to work with a value that is returned by fgetpos(), you can only use it to get to a place in a file that you've been before, whereas fseek() allows you to go to any position just by specifying the appropriate offset.

Note that the verb *seek* is used to refer to operations of moving the read and write heads of a disk drive directly to a specific position in the file. This is why the function fseek() is so named.

With a file that you've opened for update by specifying the mode as "rb+" or "wb+", for example, either a read or a write may be safely carried out on the file after executing either of the file positioning functions, fsetpos() or fseek(). This is regardless of what the previous operation on the file was.

TRY IT OUT: ACCESSING A FILE RANDOMLY

To exercise your newfound skills with files, you can create a program to keep a dossier on family members. You'll create a file containing data on all family members, and then you'll process the file to output data on each member and that member's parents. The structures used in the example only extend to a minimum range of data on family members. You can, of course, embellish these to hold any kind of scuttlebutt you like on your relatives.

Here are the structures we will use:

```
#define NAME_MAX 20
```

```
struct
{
  char *filename;                         // Physical file name
  FILE *pfile;                            // File pointer
} global = {.filename = "myfile.bin", .pfile = NULL};

// Structure types
typedef struct Date                          // Structure for a date
{
  int day;
  int month;
  int year;
} Date;

typedef struct Family                        // Structure for family member
{
  Date dob;
  char name[NAME_MAX];
  char pa_name[NAME_MAX];
  char ma_name[NAME_MAX];
} Family;
```

The first structure has no type name, so it's an anonymous structure. This contains members that store the file name that will store family data and the file pointer for use with file operations.

The second structure represents a date as a day, month, and year. The statement combines the definition of the type, struct Date, and the definition of the type name Date as equivalent to struct Date.

The third structure definition statement also incorporates the typedef. It defines struct Family with the four members you see and Family as the equivalent type name. You are able to specify dob as type Date because of the preceding typedef.

Let's look at the function prototypes and main() next:

```
// Program 12.5 Investigating the family.
#define __STDC_WANT_LIB_EXT1__ 1
#include <stdio.h>
#include <ctype.h>
#include <stdlib.h>
#include <stdbool.h>
#include <string.h>

#define NAME_MAX 20

// struct type definitions as before...

// Function prototypes
bool get_person(Family *pfamily);            // Input function for member details
void getname(char *name, size_t size);       // Read a name
void show_person_data(void);                 // Output function
void get_parent_dob(Family *pfamily);        // Function to find DOB for pa & ma
void open_file(char *mode);                  // Open the file in the given mode
inline void close_file(void);                // Close the file
```

```
int main(void)
{
  Family member;                            // Stores a family structure
  open_file("ab");                          // Open file to append to it
  while(get_person(&member))                // As long as we have input...
    fwrite(&member, sizeof member, 1, global.pfile); // ...write it away

  fclose(global.pfile);                     // Close the file now its written

  show_person_data();                       // Show what we can find out

  if(remove(global.filename))
    printf_s("Unable to delete %s.\n", global.filename);
  else
    printf_s("Deleted %s OK.\n", global.filename);
  return 0;
}
```

How It Works

There are six functions in addition to main(). The getname() function will read a name from stdin and store it in the name array that is passed as the first argument. The get_person() function will read data on a family member from stdin and store it in a Family object that is accessed through the pointer argument. The show_person_data() function will output information about all the family members in the file. The get_parent_dob() function will search the file for the dates of birth of the parents. The open_file() function packages up the code to open a file in any mode. The close_file() function just closes the file and sets the file pointer to NULL. This is a very short function, so it is inline.

The basic idea of the program is that it will read data on as many family members as you like. For each it will record a name, a date of birth, and the names of both parents. When input is complete, it will list each of the family members in the file. For each family member, it will attempt to discover the date of birth for both parents. This provides an opportunity for searching the file and leaving its position in an arbitrary state and then seeking to recover the position. Obviously, unless the family history is very strange, the data are bound to be incomplete. Thus, some members will have parents who are not in the file, and therefore their dates of birth will not be known.

After opening the file to append binary data to it, the main() function reads data on as many family members as you have stamina for in a while loop. Because you append to the file, if you delete the code at the end of main() that removes the file, you should be able to add new people to the file each time you run the program. Information on each relative is obtained by the get_person() function, which is implemented like this:

```
bool get_person(Family *temp)
{
  static char more = '\0';                  // Test value for ending input

  printf_s("\nDo you want to enter details of %s person (Y or N)? ",
                              more != '\0' ? "another" : "a" );

  scanf_s(" %c", &more, sizeof(more));
```

```
  if(tolower(more) == 'n')
         return false;

  printf_s("Enter the name of the person: ");
  getname(temp->name, sizeof(temp->name));      // Get the person's name

  printf_s("Enter %s's date of birth (day month year): ", temp->name);
  scanf_s(" %d %d %d", &temp->dob.day, &temp->dob.month, &temp->dob.year);

  printf_s("Who is %s's father? ", temp->name);
  getname(temp->pa_name, sizeof(temp->pa_name)); // Get the father's name

  printf_s("Who is %s's mother? ", temp->name);
  getname(temp->ma_name, sizeof(temp->ma_name)); // Get the mother's name

  return true;
}
```

This obtains the required data from keyboard input and uses it to populate the members of the Family object that is accessed via the pointer that is passed as the argument. Note that the parameter name is different from that in the function prototype; they don't have to be the same. The function returns false when no more input is available, and this terminates the while loop in main(). The function calls getname() to read a name, and the code for this function is

```
void getname(char *name, size_t size)
{
  fflush(stdin);                              // Skip whitespace
  //int c;
  //while (((c = getchar()) != '\n') && c != EOF);   // for visual studio 2019
  fgets(name, size, stdin);
  int len = strnlen_s(name, size);
  if(name[len-1] == '\n')                     // If last char is newline
    name[len-1] = '\0';                       // overwrite it
}
```

You use fgets() to read a name because this allows spaces to be included in the input. The first parameter is a pointer to the char array where the name is to be stored, and the second is the size of the array. If the input exceeds size characters, including the terminating null, the name will be truncated. You don't need the newline that fgets() stores, so you overwrite it with a null terminator.

We need to consider that fflush(stdin) may have different behavior depending on the compiler. The fflush function must work with output/update stream, but for input stream is undefined (from C11 standard ISO). Anyway, Pelles and Microsoft compiler (before version 2015) both clear the buffer. Since version Visual Studio 2015, this compiler does not clear the buffer, and this could be replaced with the following lines if necessary:

```
  int c;
  while(((c = getchar()) != '\n') && c != EOF);
```

When the input loop ends in main(), you close the file and call show_person_data(). This function retrieves information on the relatives you have put on file and outputs it. The implementation is like this:

```
void show_person_data(void)
{
  Family member;                        // Structure to hold data from file
  open_file("rb");                      // Open file for binary read

  // Read data on a person
  while(fread(&member, sizeof member, 1, global.pfile))
  {
    printf_s("%s's father is %s, and mother is %s.\n",
             member.name, member.pa_name, member.ma_name);
    get_parent_dob(&member);            // Get parent data
  }
  close_file();                         // Close the file
}
```

The file is opened in binary read mode. Relatives are extracted from the file in the sequence they were written in the `while` loop. After the last record has been read, `fread()` will return 0 so the loop will end. At the end of the loop, you close the file. After a record on a relative has been retrieved in the loop, you call `get_parent_dob()` to find the birth dates for both parents where possible. The `get_parent_dob()` can be implemented like this:

```
void get_parent_dob(Family *pmember)
{
  Family relative;                      // Stores a relative
  int num_found = 0;                    // Count of relatives found
  fpos_t current;                       // File position
  fgetpos(global.pfile, &current);      // Save current position
  rewind(global.pfile);                 // Set file to the beginning

  // Get the stuff on a relative
  while(fread(&relative, sizeof(Family), 1, global.pfile))
  {
    if(strcmp(pmember->pa_name, relative.name) == 0)
    { // We have found dear old dad */
      printf_s(" Pa was born on %d/%d/%d.",
            relative.dob.day, relative.dob.month, relative.dob.year);
      ++num_found;                      // Increment parent count
    }
    else if(strcmp(pmember->ma_name, relative.name) == 0)
    { // We have found dear old ma
      printf_s(" Ma was born on %d/%d/%d.",
               relative.dob.day, relative.dob.month, relative.dob.year);
      ++num_found;                      // Increment parent count
    }
    if(num_found == 2)                  // If we have both...
      break;                            // ...we are done
  }
  if(!num_found)
    printf_s("  No info on parents available.");
  printf_s("\n");
  fsetpos(global.pfile, &current);      // Restore file position file
}
```

The parameter is the address of a `Family` object for which parents' birth dates are to be found. To find the parents for a family member, the function must read records from the file starting at the beginning. Before rewinding the file, you store the current file position in `current` by calling `fgetpos()`. This will allow the file position to be restored by calling `fsetpos()` before returning to the calling function, so the calling function will never know that the file position has been moved.

The file is read from the beginning in the `while` loop. You check each record to see if it corresponds with a parent of the `Family` object pointed to by `pmember`. If it does, you output the data. As soon as both parents have been found, you exit the loop. The `printf_s()` call following the loop writes a newline if at least one parent was found or a message if no parents were found. The `fsetpos()` call restores the file to the way it was at the start. Of course, the function could be written equally well using `ftell()` and `fseek()` as positioning functions.

Note that the `fsetpos()` and `fgetpos()` functions return 0 if successful and nonzero if there's a problem. They also set a value in `errno` when an error occurs. You could check for errors like this:

```
if(fsetpos(global.pfile, &current))          // Restore file position file
{
  printf_s("Failed to set file position.\n");
  perror(global.filename);
  exit(1);
}
```

The implementation of the `open_file()` function is

```
void open_file(char *mode)
{
  if(global.pfile)
    close_file();

  if(fopen_s(&global.pfile, global.filename, mode))
  {
    printf_s("Unable to open %s with mode %s.\n", global.filename, mode);
    exit(1);
  }
  setvbuf(global.pfile, NULL, _IOFBF, BUFSIZ);
}
```

The function first checks for `global.pfile` being non-NULL, in which case `close_file()` is called to close the file and reset `global.pfile` to NULL. This ensures we won't have a file handle leak if we were to call `open_file()` more than once in the program.

The body of the `close_file()` function is just two statements:

```
inline void close_file(void)
{
  fclose(global.pfile);                       // Close the file
  global.pfile = NULL;                        // Set file pointer
}
```

That's the complete program, so it's time to try it out. You need to be clear on who is related to whom before trying to enter input. Here's some sample output—it gets a bit voluminous:

```
Do you want to enter details of a person (Y or N)? y
Enter the name of the person: Joe Bloggs
Enter Joe Bloggs's date of birth (day month year): 9 9 1950
Who is Joe Bloggs's father? Obadiah Bloggs
Who is Joe Bloggs's mother? Myrtle Muggs

Do you want to enter details of another  person (Y or N)? y
Enter the name of the person: Mary Ellen
Enter Mary Ellen's date of birth (day month year): 10 10 1952
Who is Mary Ellen's father? Hank Ellen
Who is Mary Ellen's mother? Gladys Quills

Do you want to enter details of another  person (Y or N)? y
Enter the name of the person: Mary Bloggs
Enter Mary Bloggs's date of birth (day month year): 4 4 1975
Who is Mary Bloggs's father? Joe Bloggs
Who is Mary Bloggs's mother? Mary Ellen

Do you want to enter details of another  person (Y or N)? y
Enter the name of the person: Bill Noggs
Enter Bill Noggs's date of birth (day month year): 1 2 1976
Who is Bill Noggs's father? Sam Noggs
Who is Bill Noggs's mother? Belle Biggs

Do you want to enter details of another  person (Y or N)? y
Enter the name of the person: Ned Noggs
Enter Ned Noggs's date of birth (day month year): 6 6 1995
Who is Ned Noggs's father? Bill Noggs
Who is Ned Noggs's mother? Mary Bloggs

Do you want to enter details of another  person (Y or N)? n
Joe Bloggs's father is Obadiah Bloggs, and mother is Myrtle Muggs.
  No info on parents available.
Mary Ellen's father is Hank Ellen, and mother is Gladys Quills.
  No info on parents available.
Mary Bloggs's father is Joe Bloggs, and mother is Mary Ellen.
 Pa was born on 9/9/1950. Ma was born on 10/10/1952.
Bill Noggs's father is Sam Noggs, and mother is Belle Biggs.
  No info on parents available.
Ned Noggs's father is Bill Noggs, and mother is Mary Bloggs.
 Ma was born on 4/4/1975. Pa was born on 1/2/1976.
Deleted myfile.bin OK.
```

As in the previous examples in this chapter, the program uses a specific file name, and the file is deleted at the end of the program execution.

There's a way to create temporary files that saves you the trouble of deleting files when you only need them during program execution, so let's look into that next.

Using Temporary Work Files

Very often you need a work file just for the duration of a program. You use it only to store intermediate results, and you can throw it away when the program is finished. The program that calculates primes in this chapter is a good example; you really only need the file during the calculation. You have a choice of two standard functions to help with temporary file usage, plus optional improved versions. Each has advantages and disadvantages.

Creating a Temporary Work File

This standard function will create a temporary binary file automatically. Its prototype is the following:

```
FILE *tmpfile(void);
```

The function takes no arguments and returns a pointer to the temporary file. If the file can't be created for any reason—for example, if the disk is full—the function returns NULL. The binary file is created and opened for update, so it can be written and read, but obviously it needs to be in that order because you can only ever get out what you have put in. The file is automatically deleted on exit from your program, so there's no need to worry about any mess left behind. You'll never know what the file is called, and because it doesn't last, this doesn't matter.

The optional function to create a temporary binary file and open it for update has the prototype

```
errno_t tmpfile_s(FILE * restrict * restrict pfile);
```

The function will store the stream pointer for the temporary file in pfile or NULL if the file could not be created. Obviously, the address you pass as the argument must not be NULL. The function returns 0 if the file was created and a nonzero integer if it was not. You can create multiple temporary binary files. The maximum number is TMP_MAX for the standard function or TMP_MAX_S for the optional version. Both are defined in stdio.h.

There are several disadvantages with these functions: the file will be deleted as soon as you close it, and it will be a binary file, so you can't use formatted input/output operations. You can't close the file, having written it in one part of the program, and then reopen it in another part of the program to read the data. You must keep the file open for as long as you need access to the data. A simple illustration of creating a temporary file is provided by these statements:

```
FILE *pfile = NULL;                    // File pointer
if(tmpfile_s(&pfile))                  // Get pointer to temporary file
  printf_s("Failed to create temporary file.\n");
```

Creating a Unique File Name

The second possibility is to use a function that provides you with a unique file name. Whether this ends up as the name of a temporary file is up to you. The prototype for the standard version function is

```
char *tmpnam(char *filename);
```

If the argument is NULL, the file name is generated in an internal static object, and a pointer to that object is returned. If you want the name stored in a char array that you create, it must be at least L_tmpnam characters long, where L_tmpnam is an integer constant that is defined in stdio.h. In this case, the file name is stored in the array that you specify as the argument, and a pointer to your array is also returned. If the function is unable to create a unique name, it will return NULL.

You can create a unique file with the following statements:

```
FILE *pfile = NULL;
char *filename = tmpnam(NULL);
if(!filename)
{
  printf_s("Failed to create file name.\n");
  exit(1);
}
if(fopen_s(&pfile, filename, "wb+"))
{
  printf_s("Failed to create file %s.\n", filename);
  exit(1);
}
```

Because the argument to tmpnam() is NULL, the file name will be generated as an internal static object whose address will be returned and stored in filename. As long as filename is not NULL, you call fopen_s() to create the file with the mode "wb+". Of course, you can also create temporary text files.

Don't be tempted to write this:

```
FILE *pfile = NULL;
if(fopen_s(&pfile, tmpnam(NULL), "wb+"))
{
  printf_s("Failed to create file. \n");
  exit(1);
}
```

Apart from the fact there is a possibility that tmpnam() may return NULL, you also no longer have access to the file name, so you can't use remove() to delete the file.

The optional function will verify that your array argument is large enough to store the name that it generates. It has the prototype

```
errno_t tmpnam_s(char *filename, rsize_t size);
```

The first argument is the address of the char array in which the name is to be stored, and this cannot be NULL. The second argument is the size of the filename array, which cannot be greater than RSIZE_MAX. The function creates a different name each time it is called. If the name could not be created for any reason, the function returns a nonzero integer; otherwise, it returns 0.

Here's how you might use tmpnam_s() to create a file name:

```
FILE *pfile = NULL;
char filename[20] = {'\0'};
if(tmpnam_s(filename, sizeof(filename)))
{
  printf_s("Failed to create file name.\n");
  exit(1);
}
```

```
if(fopen_s(&pfile, filename, "w+x"))
{
  printf_s("Failed to create file %s.\n", filename);
  exit(1);
}
```

I chose the maximum file name length I am prepared to work with as 20. This could prevent tmpnam_s()
from creating the name. If I want to be sure the array size will not be a constraint, I must define it with
L_tmpnam_s elements. This time I created the file as a text file for update.

It is much better to use tmpfile_s() to create a temporary file, rather than tmpnam() or tmpnam_s(),
and to create the file yourself. One reason is that it is possible that a file could be created by another program
that is executing concurrently after you obtain a unique file name using tmpnam_s() but before you have
created a file using the name. You also have to take care of removing the file at the end of the program
when you create it. Of course, if you need a temporary text file, you have to create and manage it yourself.
Remember, the assistance you've obtained from the standard library is just to provide a unique name. It's
your responsibility to delete any files created.

Updating Binary Files

As you saw earlier, you have three open modes that provide for updating binary files:

- The mode "r+b" or "rb+" opens an existing binary file for both reading and writing.
  With this open mode, you can read or write anywhere in the file.

- The mode "w+b" or "wb+" truncates the length of an existing binary file to zero so
  the contents will be lost; you can then carry out both read and write operations
  but, obviously, because the file length is zero, you must write something before you
  can read the file. If the file does not exist, a new file will be created when you call
  fopen_s() with mode "wb+" or "w+b".

- The mode "a+b" or "ab+" opens an existing file for update. This mode only allows
  write operations at the end of the file.

Although you can write each of the open modes for updating binary files in two ways, I prefer to always
put the + at the end because for me it is more obvious that the + is significant and means update. We can
first put together an example that uses mode "wb+" to create a new file, which we can then update using the
other modes.

TRY IT OUT: WRITING A BINARY FILE WITH AN UPDATE MODE

The file will contain names of people and their ages, with the data being read from the keyboard. A
name will be stored as a single string containing a first name and a second name:

```
// Program 12.6 Writing a binary file with an update mode
#define __STDC_WANT_LIB_EXT1__ 1
#include <stdio.h>
#include <ctype.h>
#include <string.h>
#include <stdlib.h>
```

```
#define MAXLEN   50                               // Size of name buffer

void listfile(const char *filename);             // List the file contents

int main(void)
{
  const char *filename = "mypeople.bin";
  char name[MAXLEN];                             // Stores a name
  size_t length = 0;                            // Length of a name
  int age = 0;                                  // Person's age
  char answer = 'y';
  FILE *pfile = NULL;
  if(fopen_s(&pfile, filename, "wb+"))
  {
    printf_s("Failed to create file %s.\n", filename);
    exit(1);
  }

  do
  {
    fflush(stdin);                              // Remove whitespace
    //int c;
    //while (((c = getchar()) != '\n') && c != EOF);   // for visual studio 2019
    printf_s("Enter a name less than %d characters: ", MAXLEN);
    gets_s(name, sizeof(name));                 // Read the name

    printf_s("Enter the age of %s: ", name);
    scanf_s(" %d", &age);                       // Read the age

    // Write the name & age to file
    length = strnlen_s(name, sizeof(name));     // Get name length
    fwrite(&length, sizeof(length), 1, pfile);  // Write name length
    fwrite(name, sizeof(char), length, pfile);  // then the name
    fwrite(&age, sizeof(age), 1, pfile);        // then the age

    printf_s("Do you want to enter another(y or n)?  " );
    scanf_s("\n%c", &answer, sizeof(answer));
  } while(tolower(answer) == 'y');

  fclose(pfile);                                // Close the file

  listfile(filename);                           // List the contents
  return 0;
}

// List the contents of the binary file
void listfile(const char *filename)
{
  size_t length = 0;                            // Name length
  char name[MAXLEN];                            // Stores a name
  int age = 0;
  char format[20];                              // Format string
  FILE *pfile = NULL;
```

```
    // Create format string for names up to MAXLEN characters
    sprintf_s(format, sizeof(format), "%%-%ds Age:%%4d\n", MAXLEN);

    if(fopen_s(&pfile, filename, "rb"))              // Open to read
    {
      printf_s("Failed to open file %s to read it.\n", filename);
      exit(1);
    }
    printf_s("\nThe folks recorded in the %s file are:\n", filename);

    // Read records as long as we read a length value
    while(fread(&length, sizeof(length), 1, pfile) == 1)
    {
      if(length + 1 > MAXLEN)
      {
        printf_s("Name too long.\n");
        exit(1);
      }
      fread(name, sizeof(char), length, pfile);      // Read the name
      name[length] = '\0';                           // Append terminator
      fread(&age, sizeof(age), 1, pfile);            // Read the age
      printf_s(format, name, age);                   // Output the record
    }
    fclose(pfile);
}
```

Here's some sample output from this program:

```
Enter a name less than 50 characters: Emma Chizit
Enter the age of Emma Chizit: 23
Do you want to enter another(y or n)?  y
Enter a name less than 50 characters: Fred Bear
Enter the age of Fred Bear: 32
Do you want to enter another(y or n)?  y
Enter a name less than 50 characters: Eva Brick
Enter the age of Eva Brick: 18
Do you want to enter another(y or n)?  y
Enter a name less than 50 characters: Ella Mentry
Enter the age of Ella Mentry: 28
Do you want to enter another(y or n)?  n

The folks recorded in the mypeople.bin file are:
Emma Chizit                              Age:  23
Fred Bear                                Age:  32
Eva Brick                                Age:  18
Ella Mentry                              Age:  28
```

How It Works

Names and ages are read from the keyboard in a do-while loop. The loop ends when n or N is entered in response the prompt. The \n in the format string to scanf_s() causes whitespace to be skipped, so it ensures that a whitespace character is not read into answer.

The file is opened for binary update operations with the mode specified as "wb+". In this mode, the file contents will be overwritten because the file length is truncated to zero. If the file does not exist, a file will be created. The data are read from the keyboard, and the file is written in the do-while loop. The first statement in the loop flushes stdin:

```
fflush(stdin);                              // Remove whitespace
//int c;
//while (((c = getchar()) != '\n') && c != EOF);   // for visual studio 2019
```

This is necessary because the read operation for a single character that appears in the loop condition will leave a newline character in stdin on all loop iterations after the first. If you don't get rid of this character, the read operation for the name will not work correctly because the newline will be read as an empty name string. As mentioned before, certain compilers may behave differently, and a while(((c = getchar()) != '\n') && c != EOF); should be used instead.

After reading a name and an age from the keyboard, the information is written to the file as binary data with these statements:

```
length = strnlen_s(name, sizeof(name));    // Get name length
fwrite(&length, sizeof(length), 1, pfile); // Write name length
fwrite(name, sizeof(char), length, pfile); // then the name
fwrite(&age, sizeof(age), 1, pfile);       // then the age
```

The names will vary in length, and you have basically two ways to deal with this. You can write the entire name array to the file each time and not worry about the length of a name string. This is simpler to code but means that there would be a lot of spurious data in the file. The alternative is to adopt the approach used in the example. The length of each name string is written preceding the name, so to read the file, you will first read the length and then read that number of characters from the file as the name. Note that the '\0' string terminator is not written to the file, so you must add this at the end of each name string when you read the file back.

The loop allows as many records as you want to be added to the file because it continues as long as you enter 'y' or 'Y' when prompted. When the loop ends, you close the file and call the listfile() function, which lists the contents of the file on stdout. The listfile() function opens the file for binary read operations with the mode "rb". In this mode, the file pointer will be positioned at the beginning of the file, and you can only read it.

The maximum length of a name is specified by the MAXLEN symbol, so it would be helpful to use the format %-MAXLENs for outputting names. This would output a name left justified in a field that has a width that is the maximum name length, so the names would line up nicely and they would always fit in the field. Of course, you can't write this as part of the format string because the letters in the MAXLEN symbol name would be interpreted as just that, a sequence of letters, and not the value of the symbol. To achieve the required result, the listfile() function uses the sprintf_s() function to write to the format array to create a format string:

```
sprintf_s(format, sizeof(format), "%%-%ds Age:%%4d\n", MAXLEN);
```

As you saw in Chapter 10, the sprintf_s() function works just like printf_s() except that the output is written to an array of char elements that you specify as the first argument. This operation therefore writes the value of MAXLEN to the format array, using the format string:

```
"%%-%ds Age:%%4d\n"
```

The %% specifies a single % symbol in the output. The - will appear next in the output followed by the value of MAXLEN formatted using the %d specification. This will be followed by s, then a space followed by Age:. Finally, the output will contain %4d followed by a newline. Because the MAXLEN symbol is defined as 50, after executing the sprintf_s() function, the format array will contain the following string:

```
"%-50s Age:%d\n"
```

The file is read and the contents listed on stdout in the while loop that is controlled by the value of an expression that reads the name length from the file:

```
while(fread(&length, sizeof(length), 1, pfile) == 1)
{
...
}
```

The call to fread() reads one item of sizeof(length) bytes into the location specified by &length. When the operation is successful, the fread() function returns the number of items read, but when the end of file is reached, the function will return less than the number requested because there are no more data to be read. Thus, when we reach the end of file, the loop will end.

An alternative way of recognizing when the end of file is reached is to code the loop like this:

```
while(true)
{
  fread(&length, sizeof(length), 1, pfile);
  // Now check for end of file
  if(feof(pfile))
    break;
...
}
```

The feof() function tests the end-of-file indicator for the stream specified by the argument and returns true if the indicator is set. Thus, when the end of file is reached, the break statement will be executed, and the loop will end.

After reading the length value from the file, you check that you have space to accommodate the name that follows with the following statements:

```
if(length + 1 > MAXLEN)
{
  printf_s("Name too long.\n");
  exit(1);
}
```

Remember that the name in the file does not have a terminating '\0' character, so you have to allow for that in the name array. Hence, you compare length + 1 with MAXLEN.

You read the name and age from the file with these statements:

```
fread(name, sizeof(char), length, pfile);    // Read the name
name[length] = '\0';                          // Append terminator
fread(&age, sizeof(age), 1, pfile);           // Read the age
```

Finally, in the loop, you write the name and age to stdout using the format string you created using sprintf_s():

```
printf_s(format, name, age);                   // Output the record
```

Changing the Contents of a File

You can overwrite existing data in a file with new data provided the existing data are the same number of bytes. When the new data are shorter or longer, you can't write in place, and you need to take special care to deal with this. We can revise and extend the previous example so that it uses the other two binary update modes. Let's add the capability to update the existing records in the file as well as add new records or delete the file. We will still write the file so the names are recorded as they are, so the records consisting of a name and an age will vary in length. This will provide an opportunity for you to see some of the complications this introduces when we want to change the contents of the file. We can use a structure to pass data between functions, but we won't write structure objects to the file. Here's the struct definition:

```
typedef struct Record
{
  char name[MAXLEN];
  int age;
} Record;
```

This defines the struct and Record as a type name for struct Record. A Record object packages the name and age for a person. If we wrote Record objects to the file, the entire name array would be written, including unused elements, so a lot of space would be wasted in the file. We also would not encounter the problem of dealing with file records that vary in length, which is one of the things this example is about.

We can define the name of the file at global scope with this statement:

```
const char *filename = "my-people.bin";                        // File name
```

The file will be created in the current directory when the program executes. If you want to locate the file in a specific directory, change the string to include the file path, for example:

```
const char *filename = "C:\\Beginning C Files\\my-people.bin";        // File name
```

Make sure the directory exists before you run the example; otherwise, it will fail.

To give you an idea of where we are headed, let's look at the program in outline. The program will consist of the following functions:

> main(): Controls overall operation of the program and allows the user to select from a range of operations on the file.
>
> list_file(): Outputs the contents of the file to stdout.
>
> update_file(): Updates an existing record in the file.
>
> write_file(): Operates in two modes: either writes a new file with records read from stdin or appends a record to the existing file.

get_person(): Reads data on a person from stdin and stores it in a Record object.

get_name(): Reads a name from stdin.

write_record(): Writes a record to the file at the current file position.

read_record(): Reads a record from the file at the current file position.

find_record(): Finds the record in the file with a name that matches input.

duplicate_file(): Reproduces the file replacing a single updated record. This function is used to update a record when the new record will be a different length from the record being replaced.

Figure 12-4 shows the call hierarchy for the functions in the application. The three functions called by main() implement the basic functionality of the program. The functions to the right of these in Figure 12-4 provide functionality that helps to simplify the three primary functions.

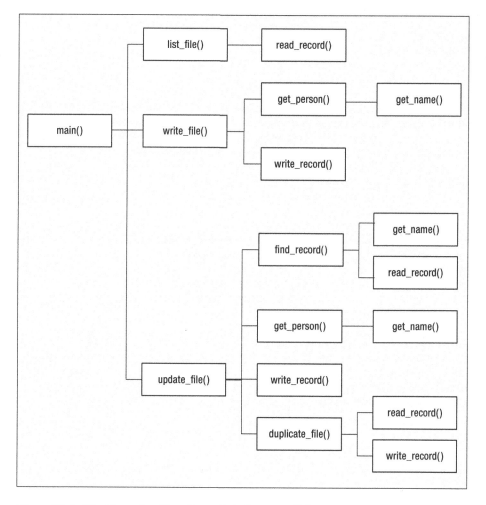

Figure 12-4. *The hierarchy of function calls in Program 12.7*

Creating a Record from Keyboard Input

We can write a function that will read a name string and age value from `stdin` and store them in a `Record` object. The prototype of the function will be the following:

```
Record *get_person(Record *precord);
```

The parameter is a pointer to an existing `Record` structure object, and it returns the address of the same object. By returning the address of the `Record` object, you make it possible to call this function as an argument to another function that expects an argument of type `Record *`. Here's how the implementation of the function looks:

```
Record *get_person(Record *precord)
{
  printf_s("Enter a name less than %d characters: ", MAXLEN);
  get_name(precord->name, MAXLEN);                   // read the name

  printf_s("Enter the age of %s: ", precord->name);
  scanf_s(" %d", &precord->age);                     // Read the age
  return precord;
}
```

I haven't checked whether the argument to the function is `NULL`, but in production code, you should always do this. The function implements a straightforward operation where the name and age that are read from `stdin` are stored in the appropriate members of the `Record` object that is pointed to by `precord`. The name is read by the auxiliary function `get_name()`, which you can implement like this:

```
void get_name(char *pname, size_t size)
{
  fflush(stdin);
    //int c;
    //while (((c = getchar()) != '\n') && c != EOF);    // for visual studio 2019
  fgets(pname, size, stdin);                          // Read the name
  size_t len = strnlen_s(pname, size);
  if(pname[len - 1] == '\n')                          // if there's a newline...
    pname[len - 1] = '\0';                            // overwrite it...
}
```

The only slight complication is the need to deal with the `'\n'` that is stored by the `fgets()` function. If the input exceeds `size` characters, then the `'\n'` will still be in the input buffer and not stored in the array pointed to by pname, so you must check that it's there. You'll need to read a name at more than one location in the program, so packaging the operation in the `get_name()` function is convenient. Specifying the size of the pname array by the second parameter makes the `get_name()` function more general.

Writing a Record to a File

You can now define a function that will write the members of a record object to a file identified by a file pointer. The prototype would look like this:

```
void write_record(const Record *precord, FILE *pfile);
```

The first parameter is a pointer to a Record structure that has the name and age that are to be written to the file as members. The second argument is the file pointer.

The implementation looks like this:

```
void write_record(const Record *precord, FILE *pfile)
{
  // Write the name & age to file
  size_t length = strnlen_s(precord->name, sizeof(precord->name));
  fwrite(&length, sizeof(length), 1, pfile);              // Write name length
  fwrite(precord->name, sizeof(char), length, pfile);     // ...then the name
  fwrite(&precord->age, sizeof(precord->age), 1, pfile);  // ...then the age
}
```

It is the responsibility of the calling function to ensure that the file has been opened in the correct mode and the file position has been set appropriately. The function writes the length of the string to the file, followed by the string itself, excluding the terminating '\0'. This is to enable the code that will read the file to determine first how many characters are in the name string. Finally, the age value is written to the file.

Reading a Record from a File

Here's the prototype of a function to read a single record from a file:

```
Record *read_record(Record *precord, FILE *pfile);
```

The file to be read is identified by the second parameter, a file pointer. Purely as a convenience, the return value is the address that is passed as the first argument.

You can implement the read_record() function like this:

```
Record *read_record(Record *precord, FILE *pfile)
{
  size_t length = 0;                                // Name length
  fread(&length, sizeof(length), 1, pfile);         // Read the length
  if(feof(pfile))                                   // If it's end file
    return NULL;

  fread(precord->name, sizeof(char), length, pfile); // Read the name
  precord->name[length] = '\0';                      // Append terminator
  fread(&precord->age, sizeof(precord->age), 1, pfile); // Read the age

  return precord;
}
```

Like the write_record() function, read_record() assumes the file has been opened with the correct mode specified and attempts to read a record from the current position. Each record starts with a length value that is read first. Of course the file position could be at the end of the file, so you check for EOF by calling feof() with the file pointer as the argument after the read operation. If it is the end of file, the feof() function returns a nonzero integer value, so in this case you return NULL to signal the calling function that EOF has been reached.

If all is well, the name and age are read from the file and stored in the members of the record object. A '\0' is appended to the name string to avoid disastrous consequences when working with the string subsequently.

Writing a File

Here's the prototype of a function that will write an arbitrary number of records to a file, where the records are entered from the keyboard:

```
void write_file(const char *mode);
```

The parameter is the file open mode to be used. With "wb+" as the mode, the function will write to a file discarding any existing contents or create a new file if it does not already exist. If the mode is "ab+", records will be appended to an existing file, or a new file will be created if there isn't one already.

Here's the implementation of the function:

```
void write_file(const char *mode)
{
  char answer = 'y';

  FILE *pfile = NULL;
  if(fopen_s(&pfile, filename, mode))
  {
    fprintf_s(stderr, "File open failed.\n");
    exit(1);
  }

  do
  {
    Record record;                             // Stores a record name & age
    write_record(get_person(&record), pfile);  // Get record & write the file

    printf_s("Do you want to enter another(y or n)?  " );
    scanf_s(" %c", &answer, sizeof(answer));
    fflush(stdin);                             // Remove whitespace
  } while(tolower(answer) == 'y');

  fclose(pfile);                               // Close the file
}
```

After opening the file with the mode passed as the argument, the function writes the file in the do-while loop. Reading from stdin and writing to the file are done in the single statement that calls write_record() with a call to get_person() as the first argument. The get_person() returns the address that is passed to it, and this is passed directly as the first argument to the write_record() function. The operation ends when the user enters anything other than 'y' or 'Y' to indicate that no more data are to be entered. The file is closed before returning from the function.

Listing the File Contents

The prototype of a function that will list the records in a file on the standard output stream looks like this:

```
void list_file(void);
```

The function will take care of opening the file initially and then closing it when the operation is complete. The file name is accessible at global scope, so no parameters are needed.

Here's the implementation:

```
void list_file(void)
{
  // Create the format string for names up to MAXLEN long
  // format array length allows up to 5 digits for MAXLEN
  char format[18];                          // Format string
  sprintf_s(format, sizeof(format), "%%-%ds Age:%%4d\n", MAXLEN);

  FILE *pfile = NULL;
  if(fopen_s(&pfile, filename, "rb"))
  {
    fprintf_s(stderr, "Unable to open %s. Verify it exists.\n", filename);
    return;
  }

  Record record;                            // Stores a record
  printf_s("The folks recorded in the %s file are:\n", filename);

  while(read_record(&record, pfile))        // As long as we have records
    printf_s(format, record.name, record.age); // Output them

  printf_s("\n");                           // Move to next line
  fclose(pfile);                            // Close the file
}
```

The function generates a format string that will adjust the field width for the output specifier for the name string to be MAXLEN characters, where MAXLEN is a symbol that we'll define. The sprintf_s() function writes the format string to the format array.

The file is opened in binary read mode, so the initial position will be at the beginning of the file. If the file is opened successfully, records are read from the file in the while loop by calling the read_record() function, which was defined earlier. The read_record() is called in the loop condition, so when NULL is returned, signaling the end of file has been detected, the loop ends. Within the loop you write the members of the Record object that was initialized by read_record() to stdout using the string in the format array that was created initially. When all the records have been read, the file is closed by calling fclose() with the file pointer as the argument.

Updating the Existing File Contents

Updating existing records in the file adds a complication because of the variable length of the names in the file. You can't just arbitrarily overwrite an existing record because the chances are it won't fit in the space occupied by the record to be replaced. If the length of the new record is the same as the original, you can overwrite it. If they are different, the only solution is to write a new file. Here's the prototype of the function to update the file:

```
void update_file(void);
```

The function will handle finding out which record is to be changed, as well as opening and closing the file. Here's the code:

```
void update_file(void)
{
  FILE *pfile = NULL;
  if(fopen_s(&pfile, filename, "rb+"))
  {
    fprintf_s(stderr, " File open for updating records failed."
                      " Maybe file does not exist.\n");
    return;
  }

  Record record;                           // Stores a record
  int index = find_record(&record, pfile); // Find the record for a name
  if(index < 0)                            // If the record isn't there
  {
    printf_s("Record not found.\n");       // Output a message
    fclose(pfile);
    pfile = NULL;
    return;                                // and we are done.
  }

  printf_s("%s is aged %d.\n", record.name, record.age);
  Record newrecord;                        // Stores replacement record
  printf_s("You can now enter the new name and age for %s.\n", record.name);
  get_person(&newrecord);                  // Get the new record

  // Check if we can update in place
  if(strnlen_s(record.name, sizeof(record.name)) ==
    strnlen_s(newrecord.name, sizeof(record.name)))
  { // Name lengths are the same so we can update in place
    fseek(pfile,                           // Move to start of old record
        -(long)(sizeof(size_t) +
            strnlen_s(record.name, sizeof(record.name)) + sizeof(record.age)),
            SEEK_CUR);
    write_record(&newrecord, pfile);       // Write the new record
    fflush(pfile);                         // Force the write
    fclose(pfile);                         // Close the file
    pfile = NULL;
  }
  else
    duplicate_file(&newrecord, index, pfile);

  printf_s("File update complete.\n");
}
```

There's quite a lot of code in this function, but it consists of a sequence of fairly simple steps:

1. Open the file for update.

2. Find the index (first record is at index 0) for the record to be updated.

3. Get the data for the record to replace the old record.

4. Check if the record can be updated in place. This is possible when the lengths of the names are the same. If so, move the current position back by the length of the old record and write the new record to the old file.

5. If the names are different lengths, duplicate the file with the new record replacing the old in the duplicate file.

After opening the file for update, the function calls the find_record() function, which I'll get to in a moment. The find_record() will read the name for the record to be updated from the keyboard and then return the index value for that record if it exists. It will return –1 if the record is not found.

If the old and new names are the same length, you move the file position back by the length of the old record by calling fseek(). You then write the new record to the file and flush the output buffer. Calling fflush() for the file forces the new record to be transferred to the file.

If the old and new records are different lengths, call duplicate_file() to copy the file with the new record replacing the old in the copy. The duplicate_file() function has this prototype:

```
void duplicate_file(const Record *pnewrecord, int index, FILE *pfile);
```

You can implement the function like this:

```
void duplicate_file(const Record *pnewrecord, int index, FILE *pfile)
{
  // Create and open a new file
  char tempname[L_tmpnam_s];
  if(tmpnam_s(tempname, sizeof(tempname))
  {
    fprintf_s(stderr, "Temporary file name creation failed.\n");
    exit(1);
  }
  FILE *ptempfile = NULL;
  if(fopen_s(&ptempfile, tempname, "wb+"))
  {
    fprintf_s(stderr, "Temporary file creation failed.\n");
    exit(1);
  }

  // Copy first index records from old file to new file
  rewind(pfile);                            // Old file back to start
  Record record;                           // Store for a record
  for(int i = 0 ; i < index ; ++i)
    write_record(read_record(&record, pfile), ptempfile);

  write_record(pnewrecord, ptempfile);     // Write the new record
  read_record(&record,pfile);              // Skip the old record

  // Copy the rest of the old file to the new file
  while(read_record(&record, pfile))
    write_record(&record, ptempfile);
```

```
  // close the files
  fclose(pfile);
  fclose(ptempfile);

  if(remove(filename))                          // Delete the old file
  {
    fprintf_s(stderr, "Failed to remove the old file.\n");
    exit(1);
  }

  // Rename the new file same as original
  if(rename(tempname, filename))
  {
    fprintf_s(stderr, "Renaming the file copy failed.\n");
    exit(1);
  }
}
```

This is an even longer function but also is composed of the following straightforward discrete steps:

1. Create a new file with a unique name.

2. Copy all records preceding the record to be changed from the old file to the new file.

3. Write the new record to the new file and skip over the record to be updated in the old file.

4. Write all the remaining records from the old file to the new file.

5. Close both files.

6. Delete the old file and rename the new file with the name of the old file.

Once the new file is created using the name generated by tmpnam_s(), records are copied from the original file to the new file, with the exception that the record to be updated is replaced with the new record in the new file. The copying of the first index records is done in the for loop where the pointer that is returned by read_record() reading the old file is passed as the argument to write_record() for the new file. The copying of the records that follow the updated record is done in the while loop. Here you have to continue copying records until the end of the file is reached in the old file. Finally, after closing both files, delete the old file to free up its name and then rename the new file to the old. If you want to do this more safely, you can rename the old file in some way rather than deleting it, perhaps by appending "_old" to the existing file name or generating another temporary name. You can then rename the new file as you do here. This would leave a backup file in the directory that would be useful if the update goes awry.

The implementation of the find_record() function that is called by update_file() to find the index for the record that matches the name that is entered looks like this:

```
int find_record(Record* precord, FILE* pfile)
{
  char name[MAXLEN];
  printf_s("Enter the name for the record you wish to find: ");
  get_name(name, MAXLEN);

  rewind(pfile);                      // Make sure we are at the start
  int index = 0;                      // Index of current record
```

```
  while(true)
  {
    if(!read_record(precord, pfile))      // If NULL returned
      return -1;                          // record not found

    if(!strcmp(name, precord->name))
      break;
    ++index;
  }
  return index;                           // Return record index
}
```

This function reads a name for the record that is to be changed and then reads successive records from the file starting at the beginning, looking for a name that matches the name that was entered. If read_record() returns NULL, –1 is returned by find_record() to signal to the calling function that the record is not in the file. If a name match is found, the function returns the index value of the matching record.

You can now assemble the complete working example.

TRY IT OUT: READING, WRITING, AND UPDATING A BINARY FILE

I won't repeat all the functions I have just described. You can add the code for them following main() in a source file containing this code:

```
// Program 12.7 Writing, reading and updating a binary file
#define __STDC_WANT_LIB_EXT1__ 1
#include <stdio.h>
#include <ctype.h>
#include <string.h>
#include <stdlib.h>
#include <stdbool.h>

#define MAXLEN 50                              // Size of name buffer
const char *filename = "my-people.bin";        // File name

// Structure encapsulating a name and age
typedef struct Record
{
  char name[MAXLEN];
  int age;
} Record;

void list_file(void);                          // List the file contents
void update_file(void);                        // Update the file contents
Record *get_person(Record *precord);      // Create a record from keyboard input
void get_name(char *pname, size_t size);       // Read a name from stdin
void write_file(const char *mode);             // Write records to a file
void write_record(const Record *precord, FILE *pfile);// Write a file record
Record *read_record(Record *precord, FILE *pfile);    // Read a file record
int find_record(Record *precord, FILE *pfile);
void duplicate_file(const Record *pnewrecord, int index, FILE *pfile);
```

```c
int main(void)
{
  // Choose activity
  char answer = 'q';
  while(true)
  {
    printf_s("Choose from the following options:\n"
            "    To list the file contents enter  L\n"
            "    To create a new file enter       C\n"
            "    To add new records enter         A\n"
            "    To update existing records enter U\n"
            "    To delete the file enter         D\n"
            "    To end the program enter         Q\n : ");
    scanf_s("\n%c", &answer, sizeof(answer));

    switch(toupper(answer))
    {
      case 'L':                                      // List file contents
        list_file();
        break;
      case 'C':                                      // Create new file
        write_file("wb+");
        printf_s("\nFile creation complete.\n");
        break;
      case 'A':                                      // Append new record
        write_file("ab+");
        printf_s("\nFile append complete.\n");
        break;
      case 'U':                                      // Update existing records
        update_file();
        break;
      case 'D':
        printf_s("Are you sure you want to delete %s (y or n)? ", filename);
        scanf_s("\n%c", &answer, sizeof(answer));
        if(tolower(answer) == 'y')
          remove(filename);
        break;
      case 'Q':                                      // Quit the program
        printf_s("Ending the program.\n");
        exit(0);
      default:
        printf_s("Invalid selection. Try again.\n");
        break;
    }
  }
  return 0;
}
```

Here's some sample output from a session entering some data and updating with a name of a different length:

```
Choose from the following options:
   To list the file contents enter  L
   To create a new file enter       C
   To add new records enter         A
   To update existing records enter U
   To delete the file enter         D
   To end the program enter         Q
 : c
Enter a name less than 50 characters: Fred Bear
Enter the age of Fred Bear: 23
Do you want to enter another(y or n)?  y
Enter a name less than 50 characters: Mary Christmas
Enter the age of Mary Christmas: 35
Do you want to enter another(y or n)?  y
Enter a name less than 50 characters: Ella Mentry
Enter the age of Ella Mentry: 22
Do you want to enter another(y or n)?  y
Enter a name less than 50 characters: Neil Down
Enter the age of Neil Down: 44
Do you want to enter another(y or n)?  n

File creation complete.
Choose from the following options:
   To list the file contents enter  L
   To create a new file enter       C
   To add new records enter         A
   To update existing records enter U
   To delete the file enter         D
   To end the program enter         Q
 : L
The folks recorded in the my-people.bin file are:
Fred Bear                                   Age:  23
Mary Christmas                              Age:  35
Ella Mentry                                 Age:  22
Neil Down                                   Age:  44

Choose from the following options:
   To list the file contents enter  L
   To create a new file enter       C
   To add new records enter         A
   To update existing records enter U
   To delete the file enter         D
   To end the program enter         Q
 : u
Enter the name for the record you wish to find: Mary Christmas
Mary Christmas is aged 35.
You can now enter the new name and age for Mary Christmas.
Enter a name less than 50 characters: Mary Noel
Enter the age of Mary Noel: 35
File update complete.
```

```
Choose from the following options:
   To list the file contents enter   L
   To create a new file enter        C
   To add new records enter          A
   To update existing records enter U
   To delete the file enter          D
   To end the program enter          Q
 : l
The folks recorded in the my-people.bin file are:
Fred Bear                                    Age:  23
Mary Noel                                    Age:  35
Ella Mentry                                  Age:  22
Neil Down                                    Age:  44

Choose from the following options:
   To list the file contents enter   L
   To create a new file enter        C
   To add new records enter          A
   To update existing records enter U
   To delete the file enter          D
   To end the program enter          Q
 : q
Ending the program.
```

How It Works

The code in main() is very simple. The indefinite while loop offers a series of choices of action, and the choice entered is determined in the switch statement. Depending on the character entered, one of the functions you developed for the program is called. Execution continues until the option 'Q' or 'q' is entered to end the program.

File Open Modes Summary

You probably will need a little practice before the file open mode strings come immediately to mind, so Table 12-4 contains a summary you can refer to when necessary.

Table 12-4. *File Modes for fopen_s()*

Mode	Description
"w"	Open a text file and truncate to zero length or create a text file for **w**rite operations. "uw" is the same but with default permissions
"wx"	Create a text file for **w**rite operations. "uwx" is the same but with default permissions
"a"	Open a text file for *a*ppend operations, adding to the end of the file. "ua" is the same but with default permissions
"r"	Open a text file for *r*ead operations
"wb"	Open a binary file and truncate to zero length or create a *b*inary file for *w*rite operations. "uwb" is the same but with default permissions
"wbx"	Create a *b*inary file for *w*rite operations. "uwbx" is the same but with default permissions
"ab"	Open a *b*inary file for *a*ppend operations. "uab" is the same but with default permissions
"rb"	Open a *b*inary file for *r*ead operations
"w+"	Open or create a text file for update operations. An existing file will be truncated to zero length. "uw+" is the same but with default permissions
"a+"	Open or create a text file for update operations, adding to the end of the file
"r+"	Open a text file for update operations (read and write anywhere)
"w+x"	Create a text file for updating. "uw+x" is the same but with default permissions
"w+b" or "wb+"	Open or create a binary file for update operations. An existing file will be truncated to zero length. "uw+b" or "uwb+" is the same but with default permissions
"w+bx" or "wb+x"	Create a binary file for update operations. "uw+bx" or "uwb+x" is the same but with default permissions
"a+b" or "ab+"	Open a binary file for update operations, adding to the end of the file. "ua+b" or "uab+" is the same but with default permissions
"r+b" or "rb+"	Open a binary file for update operations (read and write anywhere)

Note that opening a file with 'r' as the first character in the mode fails if the file does not exist, and opening a file with 'x' as the last character in the mode fails if the file already exists.

Designing a Program

Now that you've come to the end of this chapter, you can put what you've learned into practice with a final program. This program will be shorter than the previous example, but nonetheless it's an interesting program you may find useful.

The Problem

The problem you're going to solve is to write a file viewer program. This will display any file in hexadecimal representation and as characters.

The Analysis

The program will open the file as binary read-only and then display the information in two columns, the first being the hexadecimal representation of the bytes in the file and the second being the bytes represented as characters. The file name will be supplied as a command-line argument, or if there's no command-line argument for the file name, the program will ask for it.

The stages are as follows:

1. If the file name isn't supplied, get it from the user.

2. Open the file.

3. Read and display the contents of the file.

The Solution

This section outlines the steps you'll take to solve the problem.

Step 1

You need to specify parameters for the function `main()` to retrieve command-line arguments. You'll recall from Chapter 9 that when `main()` is called, two arguments may be passed to it. The first argument is an integer indicating the number of parameters in the command line, and the second is an array of pointers to strings. The first string in the array will be the name you use to start the program at the command line, and the remaining strings will be the command-line arguments that follow at the `.exe` file name. This mechanism allows an arbitrary number of values to be entered at the command line and passed to `main()`.

If the value of the first argument to `main()` is 1, there's only the program name on the command line, so in this case you'll have to prompt for the file name to be entered:

```
// Program 12.8 Viewing the contents of a file
#define _CRT_SECURE_NO_WARNINGS
#define __STDC_WANT_LIB_EXT1__ 1
#include <stdio.h>
#include <ctype.h>
#include <string.h>

int main(int argc, char *argv[])
{
  char filename[FILENAME_MAX];          // Stores the file path
  FILE *pfile = NULL;                   // File pointer
  // More variables...

  if(argc == 1)                         // No file name on command line?
  {
    printf_s("Please enter a filename: "); // Prompt for input
    fgets(filename, MAXLEN, stdin);     // Get the file name entered

    // Remove the newline if it's there
    int len = strnlen_s(filename, sizeof(filename));
    if(filename[len - 1] == '\n')
      filename[len - 1] = '\0';
  }
```

```
  else
    strcpy(filename, argv[1]);              // Get 2nd command line string
  // Rest of the code for the program...
}
```

FILENAME_MAX is a macro defined in stdio.h that expands to an integer specifying the maximum number of characters in a file name string that is guaranteed to be opened within the current implementation, so we use this to specify the size of the filename array. If argv is 1, you prompt for entry of the file name. If the first argument to main() isn't 1, then you have at least one more argument, which you assume is the file name. You therefore copy the string pointed to by argv[1] to the filename array.

Step 2

Assuming that you have a valid file name, you can open the file in binary read mode, so you can add the following after the code that obtains the file name:

```
  if(fopen_s(&pfile, filename, "rb"))       // Open for binary read
  {
    printf_s("Sorry, can't open %s.\n", filename);
    return -1;
  }
  setvbuf(pfile, NULL, _IOFBF, BUFSIZ);      // Buffer file input
```

You have no idea what is in the file and whether or not it is a text file, but by opening it in binary mode, you can read anything—it's all just bytes. You create an internal buffer for input operations on the file by passing NULL as the second argument to setvbuf().

Step 3

You can now output the file contents. You'll do this by reading the file 1 byte at a time and saving these data in a char array. Of course, you won't be accessing the file 1 byte at a time because it is buffered. The host environment will read a buffer full of data at a time, and your read operations will extract from the file buffer. Once the buffer is full or the end of file has been reached, you'll output the buffer in the format you want.

You can add two symbol definitions at the beginning of the source file:

```
#define DISPLAY     80                       // Length of display line
#define PAGE_LENGTH 20                       // Lines per page
```

You can place the characters that you read from the file in a local buffer, so add the following variable definitions following the pfile definition in main():

```
  unsigned char buffer[DISPLAY/4 - 1];       // File input buffer
  size_t count = 0;                          // Count of characters in buffer
  int lines = 0;                             // Number of lines displayed
```

You'll output the hexadecimal values for a sequence of bytes from the file on a line with a field width of two and a following space. You'll output the sequence of character equivalents to the hexadecimal on the same line occupying one character each. Thus, each character read from the file occupies four characters on a line. If the output line length is DISPLAY, the size of buffer needs to be DISPLAY/4 - 1. You subtract 1 to allow four characters for a separator string between the hexadecimal output and the corresponding characters.

You'll read the file in a while loop. Here's the code for that:

```
while(!feof(pfile))                              // Continue until end of file
{
  count = fread(buffer, 1, sizeof(buffer), pfile);
  // Output the buffer contents, first as hexadecimal
  for(size_t i = 0 ; i < sizeof(buffer) ; ++i)
  {
    if(i < count)
      printf_s("%02X ", buffer[i]);
    else
      printf_s("   ");
  }
  printf_s("| ");                                // Output separator

  // Now display buffer contents as characters
  for(size_t i = 0 ; i < count ; ++i)
    printf_s("%c", isprint(buffer[i]) ? buffer[i]:'.');
  printf_s("\n");                                // End the line

  if(!(++lines % PAGE_LENGTH))                    // End of page?
   if(toupper(getchar())=='E')                   // Wait for Enter
      continue;
}
```

The loop condition tests for the EOF indicator for the file being set by calling feof(). When it is, the end of file has been reached, so the loop ends. The read operation tries to read a buffer full of data at a time, which corresponds to one line of output. This will be the case for every line except the last, when less than a buffer full of data may be available from the file. The fread() function returns the number of characters read, and you store this in count.

After a block has been read, the contents of the buffer array are first written to the current line as hexadecimal values in the first for loop. When the last block of data is read from the file, it is likely that the buffer array will not be full, and in this case you'll write three spaces for each of the buffer elements that were not filled by the read operation. This ensures that on the last line of output, the text to the right of the line remains aligned. You then write a vertical bar as a separator and write the contents of buffer as characters to the line in the second for loop.

When you output the data as characters, you must first check that the character is printable; otherwise, strange things may start happening on the screen. You use the isprint() function that is declared in ctype.h for this. If the character isn't printable, you output a period instead. After buffer has been written out, you write a newline to move to the next line. The if statement at the end of the loop tests for 'e' or 'E' being entered after each PAGE_LENGTH lines of output. If you just press Enter after a page of output, the output for the next page will be displayed. If you enter 'e' or 'E', this terminates the output and the program. This is desirable because you could conceivably be listing a very large file, and you don't necessarily want to see the entire 10 million lines. The EOF indicator will be set when the last block of data is read, and the while loop and the program will end.

Here's the complete code for the program:

```
// Program 12.8 Viewing the contents of a file
#define __STDC_WANT_LIB_EXT1__ 1
#include <stdio.h>
#include <ctype.h>
#include <string.h>
```

```c
#define DISPLAY     80                          // Length of display line
#define PAGE_LENGTH 20                          // Lines per page

int main(int argc, char *argv[])
{
  char filename[FILENAME_MAX];                  // Stores the file path
  FILE *pfile = NULL;                           // File pointer
  unsigned char buffer[DISPLAY/4 - 1];          // File input buffer
  size_t count = 0;                             // Count of characters in buffer
  int lines = 0;                                // Number of lines displayed

  if(argc == 1)                                 // No file name on command line?
  {
    printf_s("Please enter a filename: ");      // Prompt for input
    fgets(filename, FILENAME_MAX, stdin);       // Get the file name entered

    // Remove the newline if it's there
    int len = strnlen_s(filename, sizeof(filename));
    if(filename[len - 1] == '\n')
      filename[len - 1] = '\0';
  }
  else
    strcpy(filename, argv[1]);                   // Get 2nd command line string

  if(fopen_s(&pfile, filename, "rb"))            // Open for binary read
  {
    printf_s("Sorry, can't open %s.\n", filename);
    return -1;
  }
  setvbuf(pfile, NULL, _IOFBF, BUFSIZ);          // Buffer file input

  while(!feof(pfile))                            // Continue until end of file
  {
    count = fread(buffer, 1, sizeof(buffer), pfile);
   // Output the buffer contents, first as hexadecimal
    for(size_t i = 0 ; i < sizeof(buffer) ; ++i)
    {
      if(i < count)
        printf_s("%02X ", buffer[i]);
      else
        printf_s("   ");
    }
    printf_s("| ");                              // Output separator

    // Now display buffer contents as characters
    for(size_t i = 0 ; i < count ; ++i)
      printf_s("%c", isprint(buffer[i]) ? buffer[i]:'.');

    printf_s("\n");                              // End the line
```

```
  if(!(++lines % PAGE_LENGTH))                    // End of page?
    if(toupper(getchar())=='E')                   // Wait for Enter
      break;
}

fclose(pfile);                                    // Close the file
pfile = NULL;
return 0;
}
```

Here's some sample output:

```
Please enter a filename: program12_08.c
2F 2F 20 50 72 6F 67 72 61 6D 20 31 32 2E 38 20 56 69 65 | // Program 12.8 Vie
77 69 6E 67 20 74 68 65 20 63 6F 6E 74 65 6E 74 73 20 6F | wing the contents of
66 20 61 20 66 69 6C 65 0D 0A 23 64 65 66 69 6E 65 20 5F | a file..#define _
5F 53 54 44 43 5F 57 41 4E 54 5F 4C 49 42 5F 45 58 54 31 | _STDC_WANT_LIB_EXT1
5F 5F 20 31 0D 0A 23 69 6E 63 6C 75 64 65 20 3C 73 74 64 | __ 1..#include
69 6F 2E 68 3E 0D 0A 23 69 6E 63 6C 75 64 65 20 3C 63 74 | <stdio.h>..#include
79 70 65 2E 68 3E 0D 0A 23 69 6E 63 6C 75 64 65 20 3C 73 | <ctype.h>..#include
74 72 69 6E 67 2E 68 3E 0D 0A 0D 0A 23 64 65 66 69 6E 65 | <string.h>....#define
20 44 49 53 50 4C 41 59 20 20 20 20 20 38 30 20 20 20 20 |  DISPLAY       80
20 20 20 20 20 20 20 20 20 20 20 20 20 20 20 20 20 20 20 |
20 20 20 20 20 20 20 20 2F 2F 20 4C 65 6E 67 74 68 20 6F |           // Length o
66 20 64 69 73 70 6C 61 79 20 6C 69 6E 65 0D 0A 23 64 65 | f display line..#de
66 69 6E 65 20 50 41 47 45 5F 4C 45 4E 47 54 48 20 32 30 | fine PAGE_LENGTH 20
20 20 20 20 20 20 20 20 20 20 20 20 20 20 20 20 20 20 20 |
20 20 20 20 20 20 20 20 20 20 20 20 2F 2F 20 4C 69 6E 65 |            // Line
73 20 70 65 72 20 70 61 67 65 0D 0A 0D 0A 69 6E 74 20 6D | s per page....int m
61 69 6E 28 69 6E 74 20 61 72 67 63 2C 20 63 68 61 72 20 | ain(int argc, char
2A 61 72 67 76 5B 5D 29 0D 0A 7B 0D 0A 20 20 63 68 61 72 | *argv[])..{..  char
20 66 69 6C 65 6E 61 6D 65 5B 46 49 4C 45 4E 41 4D 45 5F |  filename[FILENAME_
4D 41 58 5D 3B 20 20 20 20 20 20 20 20 20 20 20 20 20 20 | MAX];

20 20 20 20 20 20 20 20 20 20 2F 2F 20 53 74 6F 72 65 73 |           // Stores
20 74 68 65 20 66 69 6C 65 20 70 61 74 68 0D 0A 20 20 46 |  the file path..  F
49 4C 45 20 2A 70 66 69 6C 65 20 3D 20 4E 55 4C 4C 3B 20 | ILE *pfile = NULL;
20 20 20 20 20 20 20 20 20 20 20 20 20 20 20 20 20 20 20 |
20 20 20 20 20 20 20 20 20 20 20 20 20 2F 2F 20 46 69 6C |               // Fil
65 20 70 6F 69 6E 74 65 72 0D 0A 20 20 75 6E 73 69 67 6E | e pointer..  unsign
65 64 20 63 68 61 72 20 62 75 66 66 65 72 5B 44 49 53 50 | ed char buffer[DISP
4C 41 59 2F 34 20 2D 20 31 5D 3B 20 20 20 20 20 20 20 20 | LAY/4 - 1];
20 20 20 20 20 20 20 20 2F 2F 20 46 69 6C 65 20 69 6E 70 |         // File inp
75 74 20 62 75 66 66 65 72 0D 0A 20 20 73 69 7A 65 5F 74 | ut buffer..  size_t
20 63 6F 75 6E 74 20 3D 20 30 3B 20 20 20 20 20 20 20 20 |  count = 0;
20 20 20 20 20 20 20 20 20 20 20 20 20 20 20 20 20 20 20 |
20 20 20 20 20 20 20 20 2F 2F 20 43 6F 75 6E 74 20 6F 66 |         // Count of
20 63 68 61 72 61 63 74 65 72 73 20 69 6E 20 62 75 66 66 |  characters in buff
65 72 0D 0A 20 20 69 6E 74 20 6C 69 6E 65 73 20 3D 20 30 | er..  int lines = 0
3B 20 20 20 20 20 20 20 20 20 20 20 20 20 20 20 20 20 20 | ;
20 20 20 20 20 20 20 20 20 20 20 20 20 20 20 20 20 20 20 |
```

```
20 2F 2F 20 4E 75 6D 62 65 72 20 6F 66 20 6C 69 6E 65 73 |   // Number of lines
20 64 69 73 70 6C 61 79 65 64 0D 0A 0D 0A 20 20 69 66 28 |   displayed....  if
61 72 67 63 20 3D 3D 20 31 29 20 20 20 20 20 20 20 20 20 |   (argc == 1)
e
```

I didn't show the entire file. I just entered 'e' after the first two blocks.

Summary

Within this chapter, I've covered all of the basic tools necessary to enable you to program the complete spectrum of file operations in C. The degree to which these have been demonstrated in examples has been, of necessity, relatively limited. There are many ways of applying these tools to provide more sophisticated ways of managing and retrieving information in a file. For example, it's possible to write index information into the file, either as a specific index at a known place in the file, often the beginning, or as position pointers within the blocks of data, rather like the pointers in a linked list. You should experiment with file operations until you feel confident that you understand the mechanisms involved.

Although the functions I discussed in this chapter cover most of the abilities you're likely to need in C programming, you'll find that the input and output library provided with your compiler offers quite a few additional functions that give you even more options for handling your file operations. For example, the C library does not provide any way to create or delete folders or directories, but it is more than likely that the library that comes with your compiler will provide functions for such operations.

EXERCISES

The following exercises enable you to try out what you've learned in this chapter. If you get stuck, look back over the chapter for help. If you're still stuck, you can download the solutions from the Source Code/Download area of the Apress website (www.apress.com), but that really should be a last resort.

Exercise 12-1. Write a program that will write an arbitrary number of strings to a file. The strings should be entered from the keyboard, and the program shouldn't delete the file, as it will be used in the next exercise.

Exercise 12-2. Write a program that will read the file that was created by the previous exercise, and retrieve the strings one at a time in reverse sequence and then write them to a new file in the sequence in which they were retrieved. For example, the program will retrieve the last string and write that to the new file, then retrieve the second to last and write that to the file, and so on, for each string in the original file.

Exercise 12-3. Write a program that will read names consisting of a first name and a second name and associated telephone numbers from the keyboard and write them to a new file if a file doesn't already exist and add them if the file does exist. The program should optionally list all the entries.

Exercise 12-4. Extend the program from the previous exercise to implement retrieval of all the numbers corresponding to a given second name. The program should allow further inquiries, adding new name/number entries and deleting existing entries.

CHAPTER 13

The Preprocessor and Debugging

In this chapter, you'll delve deeper into the capabilities of the preprocessor, and I'll explain how you can use it to help find bugs in your code. You'll also explore some library functions that complement some of the standard capabilities of the preprocessor.

In this chapter, you'll learn

- More about the preprocessor and its operation

- How to write preprocessor macros

- What standard preprocessor macros are available

- What logical preprocessor directives are and how you can use them

- What conditional compilation is and how you can apply it

- More about the debugging methods that are available to you

- How you get the current date and time at runtime

Preprocessing

As you are certainly aware by now, preprocessing of your source code occurs before it's compiled to machine instructions. The preprocessing phase can execute a range of service operations specified by preprocessing directives, which are identified by the # symbol as the first character of each preprocessor directive. The preprocessing phase provides an opportunity for manipulating and modifying your C source code prior to compilation. Once the preprocessing phase is complete and all directives have been analyzed and executed, all such preprocessing directives will no longer appear in the source code. The compiler begins the compile phase proper, which generates the machine code equivalent of your program.

You've already used preprocessor directives in all the examples so far, and you're familiar with both the #include and #define directives. There are other directives that add considerable flexibility to the way in which you write your programs. Keep in mind as you proceed that all these are preprocessing operations that occur before your program is compiled. They modify the set of statements that constitute your program. They aren't involved in the execution of your program at all.

Including Header Files

You're completely familiar with statements such as this:

```
#include <stdio.h>
```

© German Gonzalez-Morris and Ivor Horton 2020
G. Gonzalez-Morris and I. Horton, *Beginning C*, https://doi.org/10.1007/978-1-4842-5976-4_13

This brings the contents of the standard library header file that supports input/output operations into your program. This is a particular case of the general statement for including standard library headers into a file:

```
#include <standard_library_file_name>
```

Any standard library header file name can appear between the angled brackets. If you include a header file that you don't use, the only effect, apart from slightly confusing anyone reading the program, is to extend the compilation time.

■ **Note**   A file introduced into your program by an #include directive may also contain #include directives. If so, preprocessing will deal with these #include directives in the same way and continue replacing such directives with the contents of the corresponding file until there are no #include directives in the program.

Defining Your Own Header Files

You can define your own header files, usually with the extension .h. You can give the file whatever name you like within the constraints of the operating system. In theory you don't have to use the extension .h for your header files, although it's a convention commonly adhered to by most programmers in C, so I strongly recommend you stick to it too.

Header files should not include implementation, by which I mean executable code. You create header files to contain declarations, not function definitions or initialized global data. All your function definitions and initialized global variables are placed in source files with the extension .c. You can place function prototypes, struct type definitions, symbol definitions, extern statements, and typedefs in a header file. A very common practice is to create a header file containing the function prototypes and type declarations for a program. These can then be managed as a separate unit and included at the beginning of any source file for the program. You need to avoid duplicating information if you include more than one header file in a source file. Duplicate code will often cause compilation errors. You'll see later in this chapter in the "Conditional Compilation" section how you can ensure that any given block of code will appear only once in your program, even if you inadvertently include it several times.

You can include your own files into a program source with a slightly different #include statement. A typical example might be this:

```
#include "myfile.h"
```

This statement will introduce the contents of the file named between double quotes into the program in place of the #include directive. The contents of any file can be included in your program by this means, not just header files. You simply specify the name of the file between quotes, as shown in the example.

The difference between enclosing the file name between double quotes and using angled brackets lies in the process used to find the file. The precise operation is compiler dependent and will be described in your compiler documentation, but usually the angled brackets form will search a default header file directory that is the repository for standard header files for the required file, whereas the double quotes form will search the current source directory first and then search the default header file directory if the file was not in the current directory.

Managing Multiple Source Files

A complex program is invariably comprised of multiple source files and header files. In theory you can use an #include directive to add the contents of another .c source file to the current .c file, but it's not usually necessary or even desirable. You should only use #include directives in a .c file to include header files. Of course, header files can and often do contain #include directives to include other header files into them.

Each .c file in a complex program will typically contain a set of related functions. The preprocessor inserts the contents of each header identified in an #include directive before compilation starts. The compiler creates an object file from each .c source file. When all the .c files have been compiled, the object files are combined into an executable module by the linker.

If your C compiler has an interactive development environment with it, it will typically provide a project capability, where a project contains and manages all the source and header files that make up the program. This usually means you don't have to worry too much about where files are stored for the stages involved in creating an executable. The development environment takes care of it. For larger applications though, it's better still if you create a decent folder structure yourself instead of letting the IDE put all the files in the same folder.

External Variables

With a program that's made up of several source files, you'll often want to use a global variable that's defined in another file. You can do this by declaring the variable as external to the current source file using the extern keyword. For example, suppose you have global variables defined in another file (which means outside of any of the functions) by these statements:

```
int number = 0;
double in_to_mm = 2.54;
```

In a source file in which you want to access these, you can specify that these variable names are external by using these statements:

```
extern int number;
extern double in_to_mm;
```

These statements don't create these variables—they just identify to the compiler that these names are defined elsewhere, and this assumption about these names should apply to the rest of this source file. The variables you specify as extern must be declared and defined somewhere else in the program, usually in another source file. If you want to make these external variables accessible to all functions within the current file, you should declare them as external at the very beginning of the file, prior to any of the function definitions. With programs consisting of several files, you could place all initialized global variables at the beginning of one file and all the extern statements in a header file. The extern statements can then be incorporated into any program file that needs access to these variables by using an #include statement for the header file.

■ **Note** Only one definition of each global variable is allowed. Of course, global variables may be declared as external in as many files as necessary.

Static Functions

By default, all the functions in a source file are implicitly extern, which means they are visible in all object files when they are processed by the linker. This is essential for the linker to be able to bind all the code in several object files into an executable module. However, sometimes you may not want this to be the case. You can ensure that a function is only visible within the source file in which you define it by declaring it as static, for example:

```
static double average(double x, double y) { return (x + y) / 2.0; }
```

This function can only be called in the .c file in which this definition appears. Without the static keyword, the function could be called from any function in any of the source files that make up the program.

■ **Note** You can apply the static keyword in a function prototype, and the effect is the same.

Substitutions in Your Program Source Code

You are familiar with preprocessor directives for replacing symbols in your source code before it is compiled. The simplest kind of symbol substitution is one you've already seen. For example, the preprocessor directive to substitute the string for a specified numeric value, wherever the character string PI occurs, is as follows:

```
#define PI 3.14159265
```

Although the identifier PI *looks* like a variable, it is not a variable and has nothing to do with variables. PI is a token, rather like a voucher, that is exchanged for the sequence of characters specified in the #define directive during the preprocessing phase. When your program is ready to be compiled after preprocessing has been completed, the string PI will no longer appear, having been replaced by its definition wherever it occurs in the source file. The general form of this sort of preprocessor directive is the following:

```
#define identifier sequence_of_characters
```

Here, identifier conforms to the usual definition of an identifier in C: any sequence of letters and digits, the first of which is a letter, and underline characters count as letters. Note that sequence_of_characters, which is the replacement for identifier, is any sequence of characters, not just digits. It's easy to make this sort of typographical error:

```
#define PI 3,14159265
```

This is perfectly correct as a preprocessor directive but is sure to result in compiler errors here.

A very common use of the #define directive is to define array dimensions by way of a substitution to allow a number of array dimensions to be determined by a single token. Only one directive in the program then needs to be modified to alter the dimensions of a number of arrays in the program. This helps considerably in minimizing errors when such changes are necessary, as shown in the following example:

```
#define MAXLEN 256
char *buffer[MAXLEN];
char *str[MAXLEN];
```

The dimensions of both arrays can be changed by modifying the single #define directive, and of course the array declarations that are affected can be anywhere in the program file. The advantages of this approach in a large program involving dozens or even hundreds of functions should be obvious. Not only is it easy to make a change but using this approach also ensures that the same value is being used throughout a program. This is especially important with large projects involving several programmers working together to produce the final product.

Of course, you can also define a value such as MAXLEN as a const variable:

```
const size_t MAXLEN = 256;
```

The difference between this approach and using the #define directive is that MAXLEN here is no longer a token but is a variable of a specific type with the name MAXLEN. The MAXLEN in the #define directive does not exist once the source file has been preprocessed because all occurrences of MAXLEN in the code will be replaced by 256. You will find that the preprocessor #define directive is often a better way of specifying array dimensions because an array with a dimension specified by a variable, even a const variable, is likely to be interpreted as a variable-length array by the compiler.

I used numerical substitutions in the previous two examples, but as I said, you're in no way limited to this. You could, for example, write the following:

```
#define Black White
```

This will cause any occurrence of Black in your program to be replaced with White. The sequence of characters that is to replace the token identifier can be anything at all. The preprocessor will not make substitutions inside string literals though.

Macros

A *macro* is another preprocessor capability that is based on the ideas implicit in the #define directive examples you've seen so far, but it provides greater flexibility by allowing what might be called *multiple parameterized substitutions*. This involves substitution of a sequence of characters for a token identifier, where the substitution string can contain parameters that may be replaced by argument values wherever the parameters appear in the substitution sequence. An example will make this easier to understand:

```
#define Print(My_var) printf_s("%d", My_var)
```

My_var is a parameter name, for which you can specify a string. This directive provides for two levels of substitution. An occurrence of Print(My_var) in your code will be replaced by the string immediately following it and with whatever argument you specify for My_var. You could, for example, write the following:

```
Print(ival);
```

This will be converted during preprocessing to this statement:

```
printf_s("%d", ival);
```

You could use this directive to specify a printf_s() function call to output the value of an integer at various points in your program. A common use for this kind of macro is to provide a simple representation of a complicated function call in order to enhance the readability of a program.

Macros That Look Like Functions

The general form of the kind of substitution directive just discussed is the following:

```
#define macro_name( list_of_identifiers ) substitution_string
```

The list of identifiers separated by commas appears between parentheses following `macro_name`, and each of these identifiers can appear one or more times in the substitution string. This enables you to define more complex substitutions. To illustrate how you use this, you can define a macro for producing a maximum of two values with the following directive:

```
#define max(x, y) x>y ? x : y
```

You can then put the statement in the program:

```
int result = max(myval, 99);
```

This will be expanded during preprocessing to produce the following code:

```
int result = myval>99 ? myval : 99;
```

It's important to be conscious of the substitution that is taking place and not to assume that this is a function. You can get some strange results otherwise, particularly if your substitution identifiers include an explicit or implicit assignment. For example, the following modest extension of the previous example can produce an erroneous result:

```
int result = max(++myval, 99);
```

The substitution process will generate this statement:

```
int result = ++myval>99 ? ++myval : 99;
```

The consequence of this is that if the value of `myval` is larger than or equal to 99, `myval` will be incremented twice. Note that it does *not* help to use parentheses in this situation. Suppose you write this statement:

```
int result = max((++myval), 99);
```

Preprocessing will convert this to

```
int result = (++myval)>99 ? (++myval) : 99;
```

The way to get the correct result for `result` is to write

```
++myval;
int result = max(myval, 99);
```

You need to be very cautious if you're writing macros that generate expressions of any kind. In addition to the multiple substitution trap you've just seen, precedence rules can also catch you out. A simple example will illustrate this. Suppose you write a macro for the product of two parameters:

```
#define product(m, n)   m*n
```

You then try to use this macro with the following statement:

```
int result = product(x, y + 1);
```

Of course everything works fine so far as the macro substitution is concerned, but you don't get the result you want, as the macro expands to this:

```
int result = x*y + 1;
```

It could take a long time to discover that you aren't getting the product of the two arguments because there's no external indication of an error. There's just a more or less erroneous value propagating through the program. The solution is very simple. If you use macros to generate expressions, put parentheses around every parameter occurrence and the whole substitution string. So you should rewrite the example as follows:

```
#define product(m, n)  ((m)*(n))
```

Now everything will work as it should. The inclusion of the outer parentheses may seem excessive, but because you don't know the context in which the macro expansion will be placed, it's better to include them. If you write a macro to sum its parameters, you will easily see that without the outer parentheses, there are many contexts in which you will get a result that's different from what you expect. Even with parentheses, expanded expressions that repeat a parameter, such as the one you saw earlier that uses the conditional operator, will still not work properly when the argument involves the increment or decrement operator.

Strings As Macro Arguments

String constants are a potential source of confusion when they are used with macros. The simplest string substitution is a single-level definition such as the following:

```
#define MYSTR "This string"
```

Suppose you now write the statement

```
printf_s("%s", MYSTR);
```

This will be converted during preprocessing into the statement

```
printf_s("%s", "This string");
```

This should be what you are expecting. You couldn't use the #define directive without the quotes in the substitution sequence and expect to be able to put the quotes in your program text instead. For example, suppose you write the following:

```
#define  MYSTR  This string
  ...
printf_s("%s", "MYSTR");
```

There will be no substitution for MYSTR in the printf_s() function argument in this case. Anything in quotes in your program is assumed to be a literal string, so it won't be analyzed during preprocessing.

There's a special way of specifying that the substitution for a macro argument is to be implemented as a string. For example, you could specify a macro to display a string using the function printf_s() as follows:

```
#define PrintStr(arg) printf_s("%s", #arg)
```

The # character preceding the appearance of the arg parameter in the macro expansion indicates that the argument is to be surrounded by double quotes when the substitution is generated. Suppose you write the following statement in your program:

```
PrintStr(Output);
```

This will be converted during preprocessing to

```
printf_s("%s", "Output");
```

You may be wondering why this apparent complication has been introduced into preprocessing. Well, without this facility, you wouldn't be able to include a variable string in a macro definition at all. If you were to put the double quotes around the macro parameter, it wouldn't be interpreted as a variable; it would be merely a string with quotes around it. On the other hand, if you put the quotes in the macro expansion, the string between the quotes wouldn't be interpreted as an identifier for a parameter; it would be just a string constant. So what might appear to be an unnecessary complication at first sight is actually an essential tool for creating macros that allows strings between quotes to be created.

A common use of this mechanism is for converting a variable name to a string, such as in this directive:

```
#define show(var) printf_s(#var" = %d\n", var);
```

If you now write

```
show(number);
```

this will generate the statement

```
printf_s("number"" = %d\n", number);
```

The strings "number" and " = %d\n" will be joined by the compiler to form the format string that will be used for the output:

```
"number = %d\n"
```

You can also generate a substitution that would allow you to display a string with double quotes included. Assuming you've defined the macro PrintStr as shown previously and you write the statement

```
PrintStr("Output");
```

this will be preprocessed into the statement

```
printf_s("%s", "\"Output\"");
```

This is possible because the preprocessing phase is clever enough to recognize the need to put \" at each end to get a string that includes double quotes to be displayed correctly.

Joining Two Arguments in a Macro Expansion

There are times when you may wish to join two or more macro arguments together in a macro expansion with no spaces between them. Suppose you try to define a macro to do this as follows:

```
#define join(a, b) ab
```

This can't work in the way you need it to. The definition of the expansion will be interpreted as ab, not as the parameter a followed by the parameter b. If you separate them with a space, the result will be separated with a space, which isn't what you want either. The preprocessor provides another operator to solve this problem. The solution is to specify the macro like this:

```
#define join(a, b) a##b
```

The presence of the operator that consists of two hash characters, ##, serves to separate the parameters and to indicate that the arguments for the parameters are to be joined. For example, suppose you write this:

```
strnlen_s(join(var, 123), sizeof(join(var,123)));
```

This will result in the following statement:

```
strnlen_s(var123, sizeof(var123));
```

This might be applied to synthesizing a variable name for some reason or when generating a format control string from two or more macro parameters.

Preprocessor Directives on Multiple Lines

A preprocessor directive must be a single logical line, but this doesn't prevent you from using the statement continuation character, which is just a backslash, \. In doing so, you can span a directive across multiple *physical* lines, using the continuation character to designate those physical lines as a single, *logical* line.
You could write the following:

```
#define min(x, y) \
            ((x)<(y) ? (x) : (y))
```

Here, the directive definition continues on the second physical line with the first nonblank character found, so you can position the text on the second line to wherever you feel looks like the nicest arrangement. Note that the \ must be the last character on the line, immediately before you press Enter. The result is seen by the compiler as a single, logical line.

Logical Preprocessor Directives

The previous example you looked at appears to be of limited value, because it's hard to envision when you would want to simply join var to 123. After all, you could always use one parameter and write var123 as the argument. One aspect of preprocessing that adds considerably more potential to the previous example is the possibility for multiple macro substitutions where the arguments for one macro are derived from substitutions defined in another. In the previous example, both arguments to the join() macro could be generated by other #define substitutions or macros. Preprocessing also supports directives that provide a logical if capability, which vastly expands the scope of what you can do during the preprocessing phase.

Conditional Compilation

The first logical directive I'll discuss allows you to test whether an identifier exists as a result of having been created in a previous #define directive. It takes the following form:

```
#if defined identifier
// Statements...
#endif
```

If the specified identifier is defined by a #define directive prior to this point, statements that follow the #if are included in the program code until the directive #endif is reached. If the identifier isn't defined, the statements between the #if and the #endif will be skipped. This is the same logical process you use in C programming, except that here you're applying it to the inclusion or exclusion of program statements in the source file.

You can also test for the absence of an identifier. In fact, this tends to be used more frequently than the form you've just seen. The general form of this directive is

```
#if !defined identifier
// Statements...
#endif
```

Here the statements following the #if down to the #endif will be included if identifier hasn't previously been defined. This provides you with a method of avoiding duplicating functions, or other blocks of code and directives, in a program consisting of several files or ensuring bits of code that may occur repeatedly in different libraries aren't repeated when the #include statements in your program are processed.

The mechanism is simply to top and tail the block of code you want to avoid duplicating as follows:

```
#if !defined block1
  #define block1
  /* Statements you do not        */
  /* want to occur more than once. */
#endif
```

If the identifier block1 hasn't been defined, the sequence of statements following the #define directive for block1 will be included and processed, and the identifier block1 will be defined. Any subsequent occurrence of this directive to include the same group of statements won't include the code because the identifier block1 now exists.

The #define directive for block1 doesn't need to specify a substitution value in this case. For the conditional directives to operate, it's sufficient for block1 to appear in a #define directive without a substitution string. You can now include this block of code anywhere you think you might need it, with the assurance that it will never be duplicated within a program. The preprocessing directives ensure this can't happen.

This is how you ensure that the contents of a header file cannot be included more than once into a source file. You just structure all your header files like this:

```
// MyHeader.h
#if !defined MYHEADER_H
  #define MYHEADER_H
  // All the statements in the file...
#endif
```

With this arrangement, it is impossible for the contents of MyHeader.h to appear more than once in a source file.

■ **Note**   You should always protect code in your own header files in this way.

Testing for Multiple Conditions

You aren't limited to testing for the existence of just one identifier with the #if preprocessor directive. You can use logical operators to test if multiple identifiers have been defined, for example:

```
#if defined block1 && defined block2
  // Statements...
#endif
```

This will evaluate to true if both block1 and block2 have previously been defined, so the code that follows such a directive won't be included unless this is the case. You can use the || and ! operators in combination with && if you really want to go to town.

Undefining Identifiers

A further flexibility you have with preprocessor directives is the ability to undefine an identifier you've previously defined. This is achieved using a directive such as

```
#undef block1
```

If block1 was previously defined, it is no longer defined after this directive. The ways in which these directives can all be combined to useful effect are only limited by your own ingenuity.

There are alternative ways of writing these directives that are slightly more concise. You can use whichever of the following forms you prefer. The directive #ifdef block is the same as the #if defined block. And the directive #ifndef block is the same as the #if !defined block.

Testing for Specific Values for Identifiers

You can use a form of the #if directive to test the value of a constant expression. If the value of the constant expression is nonzero, the following statements down to the next #endif are included in the program code. If the constant expression evaluates to zero, the following statements down to the next #endif are skipped. The general form of the #if directive is:

```
#if constant_expression
```

This is most frequently applied to test for a specific value being assigned to an identifier by a previous preprocessing directive. You might have the following sequence of statements, for example:

```
#if CPU == Intel_i7
  printf_s("Performance should be good.\n" );
#endif
```

The printf_s() statement will be included in the program here only if the identifier CPU has been defined as Intel_i7 in a previous #define directive.

Multiple-Choice Selections

To complement the #if directives, you have the #else directive. This works exactly the same way as the else statement does in that it identifies a group of directives to be executed or statements to be included if the #if condition fails, for example:

```
#if CPU == Intel_i7
  printf_s("Performance should be good.\n" );
#else
  printf_s("Performance may not be so good.\n" );
#endif
```

In this case, one or the other of the printf_s() statements will be included, depending on whether or not CPU has been defined as Intel_i7.

The preprocessing phase also supports a special form of the #if for multiple-choice selections, in which only one of several choices of statements for inclusion in the program is required. This is the #elif directive, which has the general form:

```
#elif constant_expression
```

Here's an example using this:

```
#define US 0
#define UK 1
#define France 2
#define Germany 3
#define Country US
#if Country == US || Country == UK
  #define Greeting "Hello."
#elif Country == France
  #define Greeting "Bonjour."
#elif Country == Germany
  #define Greeting "Guten Tag."
#endif
printf_s("%s\n", Greeting );

        #if Country == US
            #define Currency "Dollar."
        #elif Country =WrongExpression= UK
            #define Currency "Pound."
        #elif Country == France
            #define Currency "Euro."
        #elif Country == Germany
            #define Currency "Euro."
        #endif
    printf_s("%s\n", Currency);
```

With this sequence of directives, the output of the `printf_s()` statement will depend on the value assigned to the identifier Country, in this case US.

We need to be careful about these evaluations that if the first expression evaluates to true, then the rest of expressions will not be evaluated at all; therefore, we may have invalid expressions in our source code, but it will compile successfully. This behavior was clarified in C17. We can see in the preceding example, the second expression is wrong on purpose, and currency will be printed as Dollar.

Standard Preprocessing Macros

There are usually a considerable number of standard preprocessing macros defined, which you'll find described in your compiler documentation. I'll mention those that are of general interest and that are available in a conforming implementation.

You can always obtain the name of any function in the code that represents the function body by using the identifier __func__, for example:

```
#include <stdio.h>
void print_the_name(void)
{
  printf("%s was called.\n", __func__);
}
```

This function just outputs its own name within the format string, so the output will be

```
print_the_name was called.
```

The __DATE__ macro generates a string representation of the date in the form Mmm dd yyyy when it's invoked in your program. Here Mmm is the month in characters, such as Jan, Feb, and so on. The pair of characters dd is the day in the form of a pair of digits 1–31, where single-digit days are preceded by a space. Finally, yyyy is the year as four digits—2012, for example.

A similar macro, __TIME__, provides a string containing the value of the time when it's invoked, in the form hh:mm:ss, which is evidently a string containing pairs of digits for hours, minutes, and seconds, separated by colons. Note that the time is when the compiler is executed, not when the program is run.

You could use this macro to record in the output when your program was last compiled with this statement:

```
printf_s("Program last compiled at %s on %s\n", __TIME__, __DATE__ );
```

Executing this statement will produce output similar to the following:

```
Program last compiled at 13:47:02 on Nov 24 2012
```

Note that both __DATE__ and __TIME__ have two underscore characters at the beginning and the end. Once the program containing this statement is compiled, the values that will be output are fixed until you compile it again. On each execution of the program, the time and date that it was last compiled will be output. Don't confuse these macros with the `time()` function, which I'll discuss later in this chapter in the section "Date and Time Functions."

The __FILE__ macro represents the name of the current source file as a string literal. This is typically a string literal comprising the entire file path, such as `"C:\\Projects\\Test\\MyFile.c"`.

The __LINE__ macro results in an integer constant corresponding to the current line number. You can use this in combination with the __FILE__ macro to identify where in the source code a particular event or error has been detected, for example:

```
if(fopen_s(&pfile, filename, "rb"))              // Open for binary read
{
    fprintf_s(stderr, "Failed to open file in %s line %d\n", __FILE__, __LINE__);
    return -1;
}
```

If fopen_s() fails, there will be a message specifying the source file name and the line number within the source file where the failure occurred.

_Generic Macro

Since C11, _Generic was added; thus, it can have dynamic type macros at compilation time. Hence it is being introduced a more flexible typing (that is new in C) for macros. This new feature behaves like a function. Well, here there is another vision about macros vs. functions and the trade-off between both approaches).

In the signature, we can find the expression and then several comma-separated associations with the corresponding value and last a default value. We can see more clearly in the following example:

```
// Program 13.1b _Generic macro example
#include <stdio.h>
#include <math.h>

#define custom_exp(x) _Generic((x), \
    double: exp, \
    float: expf, \
    long double: expl, \
    default: clone \
)(x)

//for default type:
int clone(int a) {
    return a;
}

int main(void)
{
    int i = 2;
    double d = 1;
    float f = 1;
    long double ld = 1;

    printf("double %f\n", custom_exp(d));
    printf("float %f\n", custom_exp(f));
    printf("long double %Lf\n", custom_exp(ld));
    printf("default %d\n", custom_exp(i));

    return 0;
}
```

As you can see, the macro can return a function from your code or from a standard library (math.h). _Generic is not supported by Visual Studio 2019 yet; please use GCC or Pelles for this example. The output is

```
double 2.718282
float 2.718282
long double 2.718282
default 2
```

Debugging Methods

Most of your programs will contain errors, or *bugs*, when you first complete them. Removing such bugs from a program can represent a substantial proportion of the time required to write the program. The larger and more complex the program, the more bugs it's likely to contain and the more time it will take to get the program to run properly. Very large programs, such as those typified by operating systems, or complex applications, such as word processing systems or even C program development systems, can be so involved that all the bugs can never be eliminated. You may already have experience of this in practice with some of the systems on your own computer. Usually these kinds of residual bugs are relatively minor, with ways in the system to work around them.

Your approach to writing a program can significantly affect how difficult it will be to test. A well-structured program consisting of compact functions, each with a well-defined purpose, is much easier to test than one without these attributes. Finding bugs will also be easier in a program that has extensive comments documenting the operation and purpose of its component functions and has well-chosen variable and function names. Good use of indentation and statement layout also makes testing and fault finding simpler. It's beyond the scope of this book to deal with debugging comprehensively, but in this section I'll introduce the basic ideas that you need to be aware of.

Integrated Debuggers

Many compilers are supplied with extensive debugging tools built into the program development environment. These can be very powerful facilities that can dramatically reduce the time required to get a program working. They typically provide a varied range of aids to testing a program that include the following:

> *Tracing program flow*: This capability allows you to execute your program one source statement at a time. It operates by pausing execution after each statement and continuing with the next statement after you press a designated key. Other provisions of the debug environment will usually allow you to display information easily, pausing to show you what's happening to the data in your program.

> *Setting breakpoints*: Executing a large or complex program one statement at a time can be very tedious. It may even be impossible in a reasonable period of time. All you need is a loop that executes 10,000 times to make it an unrealistic proposition. Breakpoints provide an excellent alternative. With breakpoints, you define specific selected statements in your program at which a pause should occur to allow you to check what's happening. Execution continues to the next breakpoint when you press a specified key.

Setting watches: This sort of facility allows you to identify variables that you want to track the value of as execution progresses. The values of the variables you select are displayed at each pause point in your program. If you step through your program statement by statement, you can see the exact point at which values are changed or perhaps not changed when you expect them to be.

Inspecting program elements: It may also be possible to examine a wide variety of program components. For example, at breakpoints the inspection can show details of a function such as its return type and its arguments. You can also see details of a pointer in terms of its address, the address it contains, and the data stored at the address contained in the pointer. Seeing the values of expressions and modifying variables may also be provided for. Modifying variables can help to bypass problem areas to allow other areas to be executed with correct data, even though an earlier part of the program may not be working properly.

The Preprocessor in Debugging

By using conditional preprocessor directives, you can arrange for blocks of code to be included in your program to assist in testing. In spite of the power of the debug facilities included with many C development systems, the addition of tracing code of your own can still be very useful. You have complete control of the formatting of data to be displayed for debugging purposes, and you can even arrange for the kind of output to vary according to conditions or relationships within the program.

TRY IT OUT: USING PREPROCESSOR DIRECTIVES

I can illustrate how you can use preprocessor directives to control execution and switch debugging output on and off through a program that calls functions at random through an array of function pointers:

```c
// Program 13.1 Debugging using preprocessing directives
#define __STDC_WANT_LIB_EXT1__ 1
#include <stdio.h>
#include <stdlib.h>
#include <time.h>

// Macro to generate pseudo-random number from 0 to NumValues */
#define random(NumValues) ((int)(((double)(rand())*(NumValues))/(RAND_MAX+1.0)))

#define iterations 6
#define test            // Select testing output
#define testf           // Select function call trace
#define repeatable      // Select repeatable execution

// Function prototypes
int sum(int, int);
int product(int, int);
int difference(int, int);
```

```
int main(void)
{
  int funsel = 0;                      // Index for function selection
  int a = 10, b = 5;                   // Starting values
  int result = 0;                      // Storage for results

  // Function pointer array declaration
  int (*pfun[])(int, int) = {sum, product, difference};

#ifdef repeatable                      // Conditional code for repeatable execution
  srand(1);
#else
  srand((unsigned int)time(NULL));     // Seed random number generation
#endif

  // Execute random function selections
  int element_count = sizeof(pfun)/sizeof(pfun[0]);
  for(int i = 0 ; i < iterations ; ++i)
  {
    funsel = random(element_count);    // Generate random index to pfun array
    if( funsel > element_count - 1 )
    {
      printf_s("Invalid array index = %d\n", funsel);
      exit(1);
    }
 #ifdef test
    printf_s("Random index = %d\n", funsel);
 #endif

    result = pfun[funsel](a , b);      // Call random function
    printf_s("result = %d\n", result );
  }
  return 0;
}

// Definition of the function sum
int sum(int x, int y)
{
#ifdef testf
  printf_s("Function sum called args %d and %d.\n", x, y);
#endif

  return x + y;
}

// Definition of the function product
int product( int x, int y )
{
  #ifdef testf
  printf_s("Function product called args %d and %d.\n", x, y);
  #endif

  return x * y;
}
```

```
// Definition of the function difference
int difference(int x, int y)
{
  #ifdef testf
  printf_s("Function difference called args %d and %d.\n", x, y);
  #endif

  return x - y;
}
```

How It Works

You have a macro defined at the beginning of the program:

```
#define random(NumValues) ((int)(((double)(rand())*(NumValues))/(RAND_MAX+1.0)))
```

This defines the `random()` macro in terms of the `rand()` function that's declared in `stdlib.h`. The `rand()` function generates random numbers in the range 0–RAND_MAX, which is a constant defined in `stdlib.h`. The macro maps values from this range to produce values from 0 to `NumValues-1`. You cast the value from `rand()` to `double` to ensure that computation will be carried out as type `double`, and you cast the overall result back to `int` because you want an integer in the program.

I defined `random()` as a macro to show you how, but it would be better defined as a function because this would eliminate any potential problems that might arise with argument values to the macro.

You then have four directives that define symbols:

```
#define iterations 6
#define test                        // Select testing output
#define testf                       // Select function call trace
#define repeatable                  // Select repeatable execution
```

The first defines a symbol that specifies the number of iterations in the loop that executes one of three functions at random. The other three are symbols that control the selection of code to be included in the program. Defining the `test` symbol causes code to be included that will output the value of the index that selects a function. Defining `testf` causes code that traces function calls to be included in the function definitions. When the `repeatable` symbol is defined, the `srand()` function is called with a fixed seed value, so the `rand()` function will always generate the same pseudo-random sequence, and the same output will be produced on successive runs of the program. Having repeatable output during test runs of the program obviously makes the testing process somewhat easier. If you remove the directive that defines the `repeatable` symbol, `srand()` will be called with the current time value as the argument, so the seed will be different each time the program executes, and you will get a different output on each execution of the program.

After setting up the initial variables used in `main()`, you have the following statement declaring and initializing the `pfun` array:

```
int (*pfun[])(int, int) = {sum, product, difference};
```

This defines an array of pointers to functions that have two parameters of type `int` and a return value of type `int`. The array is initialized using the names of three functions, so the array will contain three elements.

Next, you have a directive that includes one of two alternative statements in the source, depending on whether or not the repeatable symbol is defined:

```
#ifdef repeatable                    // Conditional code for repeatable execution
  srand(1);
#else
  srand((unsigned int)time(NULL));   // Seed random number generation
#endif
```

If repeatable is defined, the statement that calls srand() with the argument value 1 will be included in the source for compilation. This will result in the same output each time you execute the program. Otherwise, the statement with the result of the time() function as the argument will be included, and you will get a different output each time you run the program.

In the loop in main(), the number of iterations is determined by the value of the iterations symbol; in this case it is 6. The first action in the loop is

```
    funsel = random(element_count);    // Generate random index to pfun array
    if( funsel > element_count - 1 )
    {
      printf_s("Invalid array index = %d\n", funsel);
      exit(1);
    }
```

This executes the random() macro with element_count as the argument. This is the number of elements in the pfun array and is calculated immediately before the loop. The preprocessor will substitute element_count in the macro expansion before the code is compiled. For safety, there is a check that we do indeed get a valid index value for the pfun array.

The next three lines are the following:

```
#ifdef test
    printf_s("Random index = %d\n", funsel);
 #endif
```

These include the printf_s() statement in the code when the test symbol is defined. If you remove the directive that defines test, the printf_s() call will not be included in the program that is compiled.

The last two statements in the loop call a function through one of the pointers in the pfun array and output the result of the call:

```
    result = pfun[funsel](a , b);      // Call random function
    printf_s("result = %d\n", result );
```

Let's look at just one of the functions that may be called because they are all similar, product(), for example:

```
int product( int x, int y )
{
  #ifdef testf
  printf_s("Function product called args %d and %d.\n", x, y);
  #endif

  return x * y;
}
```

The function definition includes an output statement if the testf symbol is defined. You can therefore control whether the statements in the #ifdef block are included here independently from the output block in main() that is controlled by test. With the program as written with both test and testf defined, you'll get trace output for the random index values generated and a message from each function as it's called, so you can follow the sequence of calls in the program exactly.

You can have as many different symbolic constants defined as you wish. As you've seen previously in this chapter, you can combine them into logical expressions using the #ifdef form of the conditional directive.

Assertions

An assertion is an error message that is output when some condition is met. There are two kinds of assertions: compile-time assertions and runtime assertions. I'll discuss the latter first because they are used more widely.

Runtime Assertions

The assert() macro is defined in the standard library header file assert.h. This macro enables you to insert tests of arbitrary expressions in your program that will cause the program to be terminated with a diagnostic message if a specified expression is false (i.e., evaluates to 0) during execution. The argument to the assert() macro is an expression that results in a scalar value, for example:

```
assert(a == b);
```

The expression will be true (nonzero) if a is equal to b. If a and b are unequal, the argument to the macro will be false, and the program will be terminated with a message relating to the assertion that includes the text of the argument to the macro, the source file name, the line number, and the name of the function in which the assert() appears. Termination is achieved by calling abort(), so it's an abnormal end to the program. When abort() is called, the program terminates immediately. Whether stream output buffers are flushed, open streams are closed, or temporary files are removed, it is implementation dependent, so consult your compiler documentation on this.

In Program 13.1 I could have used an assertion to verify that funsel is valid:

```
assert(funsel < element_count);
```

If funsel is not less than element_count, the expression will be false, so the program will assert. Typical output from the assertion looks like this:

```
Assertion failed: file  d:\examples\program13_01.c, func main line 44, funsel<element_
count abort -- terminating
```

You can see that the function name and the line number of the code are identified as well as the condition that was not met.

Also, there is a #line directive with two possible arguments that will reset the line number and change file name, of course, with a debugging purpose. The following lines will be adding to the set number, and it must be greater than zero and less than or equal to 2147483647:

```
#line linenumber "filename"

// Program 13.1c Debugging using preprocessing directives
#include <stdio.h>
#include <assert.h>

int main(void)
{
#line 314 "qux.c"
    assert( 3 < 2 );
    printf("Hello World!");
    return 0;
}
```

The output is

```
qux.c(315): warning #2154: Unreachable code.
```

Switching Off Assertions

Runtime assertions can be switched off by defining the symbol NDEBUG before the #include directive for assert.h, like this:

```
#define NDEBUG                       // Switch off runtime assertions
#include <assert.h>
```

This code snippet will cause all assert() macros in your code to be ignored.

With some nonstandard systems, assertions are disabled by default, in which case you can enable them by undefining NDEBUG:

```
#undef NDEBUG                        // Switch on assertions
#include <assert.h>
```

By including the directive to undefine NDEBUG, you ensure that assertions are enabled for your source file. The #undef directive must appear before the #include directive for assert.h to be effective.

Compile-Time Assertions

The static_assert() macro enables you to output an error message during compilation. The message includes a string literal that you specify, and whether or not the output is produced depends on the value of an expression that is a compile-time constant. The macro is of the form

```
static_assert(constant_expression, string_literal);
```

When the constant expression evaluates to zero, compilation stops, and the error message is output.

The static_assert() enables you to build checks into your code about your implementation. For example, suppose your code assumes that type char is an unsigned type. You could include this static assertion in the source file:

```
static_assert(CHAR_MIN == 0, "Type char is a signed type. Code won't work.");
```

CHAR_MIN is defined in limits.h and is the minimum value for type char. When char is an unsigned type, CHAR_MIN will be zero, and when it is a signed type, it will be negative. Thus, this will cause compilation to be halted and an error message that includes your string to be produced when type char is signed.

■ **Note** The static_assert is defined in assert.h as _Static_assert, which is a keyword. You can use _Static_assert instead of static_assert without including assert.h into your source file.

I can demonstrate runtime assertions in operation with a simple example.

```
┌─────────────────────────────────────────────────────────────────────────┐
│         TRY IT OUT: DEMONSTRATING THE ASSERT() MACRO                     │
└─────────────────────────────────────────────────────────────────────────┘
```

Here's the code for a program that uses the assert() macro:

```c
// Program 13.2 Demonstrating assertions
#define __STDC_WANT_LIB_EXT1__ 1
#include <stdio.h>
#include <assert.h>

int main(void)
{
  int y = 5;
  for(int x = 0 ; x < 20 ; ++x)
  {
    printf("x = %d   y = %d\n", x, y);
    assert(x < y);
  }
  return 0;
}
```

Compiling and executing this with my compiler produces the following output:

```
x = 0    y = 5
x = 1    y = 5
x = 2    y = 5
x = 3    y = 5
x = 4    y = 5
x = 5    y = 5
Assertion failed: file C:\Projects\program13_02.c, func main, line 13, x < y
abort -- terminating
*** Process returned 1 ***
```

How It Works

Apart from the assert() statement, the program doesn't need much explanation because it simply displays the values of x and y in the for loop. The program is terminated by the assert() macro as soon as the condition x < y becomes false. As you can see from the output, this is when x reaches the value 5. The macro displays the output on stderr. Not only do you get the condition that failed displayed but you also get the file name and line number in the file where the failure occurred. This is particularly useful with multifile programs in which the source of the error is pinpointed exactly.

Assertions are often used for critical conditions in a program in which, if certain conditions aren't met, disaster will surely ensue. You would want to be sure that the program wouldn't continue if such errors arise.

You could switch off the assertion mechanism in the example by adding the following directive:

```
#define NDEBUG
```

This must be placed before the #include directive for assert.h to be effective. With this #define at the beginning of Program 13.2, you'll see that you get output for all the values of x from 0 to 19 and no diagnostic message.

Date and Time Functions

The preprocessor macros for the date and the time produce values that are fixed at compile time. The time.h header declares functions that produce the time and date when you call them. They provide output in various forms from the hardware timer in your PC. You can use these functions to obtain the current time and date, to calculate the time elapsed between two events, and to measure how long the processor has been occupied performing a calculation.

Getting Time Values

The simplest function returning a time value has the following prototype:

```
clock_t clock(void);
```

This function returns the processor time (not the elapsed time) used by the program since some implementation-defined reference point, often since execution began. You typically call the clock() function at the start and end of some process in a program, and the difference is a measure of the processor time consumed by the process. The return value is of type clock_t, which is an integer type that is defined in time.h. Your computer will typically be executing multiple processes at any given moment. The processor time is the total time the processor has been executing on behalf of the process that called the clock() function. The value that is returned by the clock() function is measured in *clock ticks*. To convert this value to seconds, you divide it by the value that is produced by the macro CLOCKS_PER_SEC, which is also defined in time.h. The value produced by CLOCKS_PER_SEC is the number of clock ticks in 1 second. The clock() function returns –1 if an error occurs. In C17, it was clarified and added that if the value cannot be represented, the function returns an unspecified value; this may be due to *overflow* of the clock_t type.

As I said, to determine the processor time used in executing a process, you need to record the time when the process starts executing and subtract this from the time returned when the process finishes, for example:

```
clock_t start = 0, end = 0;
double cpu_time = 0.0;
start = clock();

// Execute the process for which you want the processor time...

end = clock();
cpu_time = (double)(end-start)/CLOCKS_PER_SEC;        // Processor time in seconds
```

This fragment stores the total processor time used by the process in cpu_time. The cast to type double is necessary in the last statement to get the correct result.

As you've seen, the time() function returns the calendar time as a value of type time_t. The calendar time is the current time usually measured in seconds since a fixed time on a particular date. The fixed time and date is often 00:00:00GMT on January 1, 1970, and this is typical of how time values are defined. However, the reference point is implementation defined, so check your compiler and library documentation to verify this.

The prototype of the time() function is

```
time_t time(time_t *timer);
```

If the argument isn't NULL, the current calendar time is also stored in timer. The type time_t is defined in the header file and is often equivalent to type long.

To calculate the elapsed time in seconds between two successive time_t values returned by time(), you can use the function difftime(), which has this prototype:

```
double difftime(time_t T2, time_t T1);
```

The function will return the value of T2 - T1 expressed in seconds as a value of type double. This value is the time elapsed between the two time() function calls that produce the time_t values, T1 and T2.

TRY IT OUT: USING TIME FUNCTIONS

You could log the elapsed time and processor time used for a computation by using functions from time.h as follows:

```
// Program 13.3 Test our timer function
#define __STDC_WANT_LIB_EXT1__ 1
#include <stdio.h>
#include <time.h>
#include <math.h>
#include <ctype.h>

int main(void)
{
  time_t calendar_start = time(NULL);         // Initial calendar time
  clock_t cpu_start = clock();                // Initial processor time
  int count = 0;                              // Count of number of loops
```

```
  const long long iterations = 1000000000LL;   // Loop iterations
  char answer = 'y';
  double x = 0.0;
  printf_s("Initial clock time = %lld Initial calendar time = %lld\n",
                        (long long)cpu_start, (long long)calendar_start);
  while(tolower(answer) == 'y')
  {
    for(long long i = 0LL ; i < iterations ; ++i)
      x = sqrt(3.14159265);

    printf_s("%lld square roots completed.\n", iterations*(++count));
    printf_s("Do you want to run some more(y or n)? \n");
    scanf_s("\n%c", &answer, sizeof(answer));
  }

  clock_t cpu_end = clock();                   // Final cpu time
  time_t calendar_end = time(NULL);            // Final calendar time

  printf_s("Final clock time = %lld Final calendar time = %lld\n",
                        (long long)cpu_end, (long long)calendar_end);
  printf_s("CPU time for %lld iterations is %.2lf seconds\n",
              count*iterations, ((double)(cpu_end-cpu_start))/CLOCKS_PER_SEC);
  printf_s("Elapsed calendar time to execute the program is %8.2lf seconds.\n",
                              difftime(calendar_end, calendar_start));

  return 0;
}
```

On my machine I get the following output:

```
Initial clock time = 0 Initial calendar time = 1354017916
1000000000 square roots completed.
Do you want to run some more(y or n)?
y
2000000000 square roots completed.
Do you want to run some more(y or n)?
y
3000000000 square roots completed.
Do you want to run some more(y or n)?
n
Final clock time = 24772 Final calendar time = 1354017941
CPU time for 3000000000 iterations is 24.77 seconds
Elapsed calendar time to execute the program is    25.00 seconds.
```

How It Works

This program illustrates the use of the functions `clock()`, `time()`, and `difftime()`. The `time()` function usually returns the current time in seconds, and when this is the case, you may not get values less than 1 second. Depending on the speed of your machine, you may want to adjust the number of iterations in the loop to reduce or increase the time required to execute this program. Note that the `clock()` function may not be a very accurate way of determining the processor time used in the program. You also need to keep in mind that measuring elapsed time using the time() function can be a second out.

You record and display the initial values for the processor time and the calendar time and set up the controls for the loop that follows with these statements:

```
time_t calendar_start = time(NULL);        // Initial calendar time
clock_t cpu_start = clock();               // Initial processor time
int count = 0;                             // Count of number of loops
const long long iterations = 1000000000LL; // Loop iterations
char answer = 'y';
double x = 0.0;
printf_s("Initial clock time = %lld Initial calendar time = %lld\n",
                          (long long)cpu_start, (long long)calendar_start);
```

Casting the values of cpu_start and calendar_start to type long long obviates any formatting problems that might arise because of the types that clock_t and time_t are implemented as.

You then have a loop controlled by the character stored in answer, so the loop will execute as long as you want it to continue:

```
while(tolower(answer) == 'y')
{
  for(long long i = 0LL ; i < iterations ; ++i)
    x = sqrt(3.14159265);

  printf_s("%lld square roots completed.\n", iterations*(++count));
  printf_s("Do you want to run some more(y or n)? \n");
  scanf_s("\n%c", &answer, sizeof(answer));
}
```

The inner loop calls the sqrt() function that is declared in the math.h header iterations times, so this is just to occupy some processor time. If you are leisurely in your entry of a response to the prompt for input, this should extend the elapsed time. Note the newline escape sequence in the beginning of the first argument to scanf_s(). If you leave this out, your program will loop indefinitely, because scanf_s() will not ignore whitespace characters in the input stream buffer.

Finally, you output the final values returned by clock() and time() and calculate the processor and calendar time intervals. The library that comes with your C compiler may well have additional nonstandard functions for obtaining processor time that are more accurate than the clock() function.

▪ **Caution**   Note that the processor clock can wrap around, and the resolution with which processor time is measured can vary between different hardware platforms. For example, if the processor clock is a 32-bit value that has a microsecond resolution, the clock will wrap back to zero roughly every 72 minutes.

Getting the Date

Having the time in seconds dating to a date over a quarter of a century ago is interesting, but it's often more convenient to get today's date as a string. You can do this with the function ctime(), which has this prototype:

```
char *ctime(const time_t *timer);
```

The function accepts a pointer to a time_t variable as an argument that contains a calendar time value returned by the time() function. It returns a pointer to a 26-character string containing the day, the date, the time, and the year, which is terminated by a newline and '\0'.

A typical string returned might be the following:

```
"Mon Aug 25 10:45:56 2003\n\0"
```

The ctime() function has no knowledge of the length of the string you have allocated to store the result, which makes this an unsafe operation. There is an optional safer version of the function that has this prototype:

```
errno_t ctime_s(char * str, rsize_t size, const time_t *timer);
```

The first parameter is the address of the array where the result is to be stored, and the second parameter is the size of the str array. The function returns 0 if the conversion was successful and a nonzero value otherwise. The str array should have at least 26 elements but not more than RSIZE_MAX elements. Remember RSIZE_MAX is data type size_t, and it is runtime constraint for several _s functions. It is a good practice, for instance, if large numbers appeared when handling unsigned int (by being negative by error). It will depend on your machine (i.e., 9223372036854775807):

```
#define __STDC_WANT_LIB_EXT1__ 1
#include <stdio.h>
#include <stdint.h>
int main(void)
{
        printf("rsize_max=%zu\n", RSIZE_MAX);
        return 0;
}
```

You might use the ctime_s() function like this:char time_str[30] = {'\0'};
```
time_t calendar = time(NULL);
if(!ctime_s(time_str, sizeof(time_str), &calendar))
   printf_s("%s", time_str);                    // Output calendar time as date string
else
   fprintf_s(stderr, "Error converting time_t value\n");
```

You can also get at the various components of the time and date from a calendar time value by using the localtime() function. This has the prototype

```
struct tm *localtime(const time_t *timer);
```

This function accepts a pointer to a time_t value and returns a pointer to a structure of type tm, which is defined in time.h. It returns NULL if timer cannot be converted. The optional version has the prototype

```
struct tm *localtime_s(const time_t * restrict timer, struct tm * restrict result);
```

Both arguments must be non-NULL. The structure contains at least the members listed in Table 13-1.

We need to do a highlight that this function is from the standard C17 (since C11). Meanwhile, Microsoft compiler has a very different signature (these differences can be seen in Program 13.04, where the arguments are reversed and the function's return is opposed):

```
errno_t localtime_s(
    struct tm* const tmDest,
    time_t const* const sourceTime
);
```

Table 13-1. *Members of the tm Structure*

Member	Description
tm_sec	Seconds (0-60) after the minute on 24-hour clock. This value goes up to 60 for positive leap-second support
tm_min	Minutes after the hour on 24-hour clock (0-59)
tm_hour	The hour on 24-hour clock (0-23)
tm_mday	Day of the month (1-31)
tm_mon	Month (0-11)
tm_year	Year (current year minus 1900)
tm_wday	Weekday (Sunday is 0; Saturday is 6)
tm_yday	Day of year (0-365)
tm_isdst	Daylight saving flag. Positive for daylight saving time, 0 for not daylight saving time, and negative for not known

All the members are of type int. The localtime() function returns a pointer to the same structure each time you call it, and the structure members are overwritten on each call. If you want to keep any of the member values, you need to copy them elsewhere before the next call to localtime(), or you could create your own tm structure and save the whole lot if you really need to. You supply the structure as an argument to localtime_s() so you control whether you reuse a structure object. This makes operations simpler and less error prone.

The time that localtime() and localtime_s() produce is local to where you are. If you want to get the time in a tm structure that reflects UTC (Coordinated Universal Time), you can use the gmtime() function or, better, the optional gmtime_s() function. These expect the same arguments as the localtime() and localtime_s() functions and return a pointer to a tm structure.

TIME_UTC and timespec_get are new in C11; TIME_UTC can be as argument to function timespec_get(&ts, TIME_UTC).

The timespec_get function sets the interval pointed to by ts to hold the current calendar time based on the specified time base.

Here's a code fragment that will output the day and the date from the members of the tm structure:

```
time_t calendar = time(NULL);                    // Current calendar time
struct tm time_data;
const char *days[] =    {"Sunday",    "Monday", "Tuesday", "Wednesday",
                        "Thursday", "Friday", "Saturday"            };
const char *months[] = {"January", "February", "March",
                        "April",    "May",     "June",
                        "July",     "August",  "September",
                        "October", "November", "December"  };

if(localtime_s(&calendar, &time_data))
  printf_s("Today is %s %s %d %d\n",
                    days[time_data.tm_wday], months[time_data.tm_mon],
                    time_data.tm_mday,       time_data.tm_year+1900);
```

You've defined arrays of strings to hold the days of the week and the months. You use the appropriate member of the structure that has been set up by the call to the localtime_s() function. You use the day in the month and the year values from the structure directly. You can easily extend this to output the time.

Typical output from executing this is

```
Today is Tuesday November 27 2012
```

The asctime() and its optional safer partner asctime_s() generate a string representation of a tm structure. Their prototypes are

```
char *asctime(const struct tm *time_data);
errno_t asctime_s(char *str, rsize_t size, const struct tm *time_data);
```

The asctime_s() stores the string in str, which must be an array with at least 26 elements and smaller than RSIZE_MAX; size is the number of elements in str. The function returns 0 when everything works and a nonzero integer when it does not. The function works for tm structures where the year is from 1000 to 9999, so it should be okay for a while yet! The string that results is of the same form as that produced by ctime().

TRY IT OUT: GETTING THE DATE

It's very easy to pick out the members you want from the structure of type tm populated by the localtime_s() function. You can demonstrate this with the following example:

```
// Program 13.4       Getting date data with ease
#define __STDC_WANT_LIB_EXT1__ 1
#include <stdio.h>
#include <time.h>

int main(void)
{
  const char *day[7] = {
                    "Sunday"  , "Monday", "Tuesday", "Wednesday",
                    "Thursday", "Friday", "Saturday"
                        };
```

```
const char *month[12] = {
                    "January",   "February", "March",    "April",
                    "May",       "June",     "July",     "August",
                    "September", "October",  "November", "December"
                   };
const char *suffix[] = { "st", "nd", "rd", "th" };
enum sufindex { st, nd, rd, th } sufsel = th;   // Suffix selector

struct tm ourT;                                 // The time structure
time_t tVal = time(NULL);                       // Calendar time

//if(localtime_s(&ourT , &tVal))                // VS 2019 - Populate time structure
if(!localtime_s(&tVal, &ourT))                  // C11 standard - Populate time
structure  {
  fprintf_s(stderr, "Failed to populate tm struct.\n");
  return -1;
}

switch(ourT.tm_mday)
{
  case 1: case 21: case 31:
    sufsel= st;
    break;
  case 2: case 22:
    sufsel= nd;
    break;
  case 3: case 23:
    sufsel= rd;
    break;
  default:
    sufsel= th;
    break;
}

printf_s("Today is %s the %d%s %s %d. ", day[ourT.tm_wday],
    ourT.tm_mday, suffix[sufsel], month[ourT.tm_mon], 1900 + ourT.tm_year);
printf_s("The time is %d : %d : %d.\n",
    ourT.tm_hour, ourT.tm_min, ourT.tm_sec );
return 0;
}
```

Here's an example of output from this program:

```
Today is Tuesday the 27th November 2012. The time is 15 : 42 : 44.
```

How It Works

You define arrays of strings in main() for the days of the week, the months in the year, and the suffix to be applied to a date value. Each statement defines an array of pointers to char. You could omit the array dimensions in the first two declarations, and the compiler would compute them for you, but in this case you're reasonably confident about both these numbers, so this is an instance in which putting them in helps to avoid an error. The const qualifier specifies that the strings pointed to are constants and should not be altered in the code.

The enumeration provides a mechanism for selecting an element from the suffix array:

```
enum sufindex { st, nd, rd, th } sufsel = th;       // Suffix selector
```

The enumeration constants, st, nd, rd, and th, will be assigned values 0–3 by default, so we can use the sufsel variable as an index to access elements in the suffix array. The names for the enumeration constants make the code a little more readable.

You also declare a structure variable in the following declaration:

```
struct tm ourT;                                     // The time structure
```

The values for the members of this structure will be set by the localtime_s() function.

You initialize tVal with the current time using the time() function. You pass the address of tVal as the first argument to localtime_s() to generate the values of the members of the ourT structure whose address you pass as the second argument. If the call to localtime_s() is successful, you execute the switch:

```
switch(ourT.tm_mday)
{
  case 1: case 21: case 31:
    sufsel= st;
    break;
  case 2: case 22:
    sufsel= nd;
    break;
  case 3: case 23:
    sufsel= rd;
    break;
  default:
    sufsel= th;
    break;
}
```

The sole purpose of this is to select what to append to the date value. Based on the member tm_mday, the switch selects an index to the suffix array for use when outputting the date by setting the sufsel variable to the appropriate enumeration constant value.

The day, the date, and the time are displayed, with the day and month strings obtained by indexing the appropriate array with the corresponding structure member value. You add 1900 to the value of the tm_year member because this value is measured relative to the year 1900.

Getting the Day for a Date

You can use the mktime() function to determine the day of the week for a given date. The function has the prototype

```
time_t mktime(struct tm *ptime);
```

You pass the address of a tm structure object to the function with the tm_mon, tm_mday, and tm_year members set to values corresponding to the date you are interested in. The values of the tm_wday and tm_yday members of the structure will be ignored, and if the operation is successful, the values will be replaced with the values that are correct for the date you have supplied. The function returns the calendar time as a value of type time_t if the operation is successful or –1 if the date cannot be represented as a time_t value, causing the operation to fail. Let's see it working in an example.

TRY IT OUT: GETTING THE DAY FOR A DATE

You can demonstrate the mktime() function with the following invaluable example:

```
// Program 13.5        Getting the day for a given date
#define __STDC_WANT_LIB_EXT1__ 1
#include <stdio.h>
#include <time.h>

int main(void)
{
  const char *day[7] = {
                  "Sunday"  , "Monday", "Tuesday", "Wednesday",
                  "Thursday", "Friday", "Saturday"
                };
  const char *month[12] = {
                  "January",   "February", "March",    "April",
                  "May",       "June",     "July",     "August",
                  "September", "October",  "November", "December"
                };
  const char *suffix[] = { "st", "nd", "rd", "th" };
  enum sufindex { st, nd, rd, th } sufsel = th;   // Suffix selector

  struct tm birthday = {0};                        // A birthday time structure
  char name[30] = {'\0'};

  printf_s("Enter a name: ");
  gets_s(name, sizeof(name));

  printf_s("Enter the birthday for %s as day month year integers separated by
spaces."
          "\ne.g. Enter 1st February 1985 as 1 2 1985 : ", name);
  scanf_s(" %d %d %d", &birthday.tm_mday, &birthday.tm_mon, &birthday.tm_year);

  birthday.tm_mon -= 1;                            // Month zero-based
  birthday.tm_year -= 1900;                        // Year relative to 1900

  if(mktime(&birthday) == - 1)
  {
    fprintf_s(stderr, "Operation failed.\n");
    return -1;
  }
```

```
  switch(birthday.tm_mday)
  {
    case 1: case 21: case 31:
      sufsel= st;
      break;
    case 2: case 22:
      sufsel= nd;
      break;
    case 3: case 23:
      sufsel= rd;
      break;
    default:
      sufsel= th;
      break;
  }
  printf_s("%s was born on the %d%s %s %d, which was a %s.\n", name,
                  birthday.tm_mday, suffix[sufsel], month[birthday.tm_mon],
                          1900 + birthday.tm_year, day[birthday.tm_wday]);
  return 0;
}
```

Here's a sample of the output:

```
Enter a name: Kate Middleton
Enter the birthday for Kate Middleton as day month year integers separated by spaces.
e.g. Enter 1st February 1985 as 1 2 1985 : 9 1 1982
Kate Middleton was born on the 9th January 1982, which was a Saturday.
```

How It Works

You create arrays of constant strings for the day, month, and date suffixes as you did in Program 13.4. You then create a tm structure and an array to store a name:

```
struct tm birthday = {0};                       // A birthday time structure
char name[30] = {'\0'};
```

You prompt for and read a name and values for the day, month, and year of a birthday date for the person named:

```
printf_s("Enter a name: ");
gets_s(name, sizeof(name));

printf_s("Enter the birthday for %s as day month year integers separated by
spaces."
          "\ne.g. Enter 1st February 1985 as 1 2 1985 : ", name);
scanf_s(" %d %d %d", &birthday.tm_mday, &birthday.tm_mon, &birthday.tm_year);
```

The date values are read directly into the members of the birthday structure. The month should be zero based and the year relative to 1900, so you adjust the values stored accordingly.

With the date set, you get the values for `tm_wday` and `tm_yday` members set by calling the `mktime()` function:

```
if(mktime(&birthday) == - 1)
{
  fprintf_s(stderr, "Operation failed.\n");
  return -1;
}
```

The `if` statement checks whether the function returns –1, indicating that the operation has failed. In this case, you simply output a message and terminate the program. Finally, you display the day corresponding to the birth date that was entered in the same way as in the previous example.

Summary

In this chapter, I discussed the preprocessor directives that you use to manipulate and transform the code in a source file before it is compiled. Because the chapter is primarily about preprocessing, there is no "Designing a Program" section. Your standard library header files are an excellent source of examples of coding preprocessing directives. You can view these examples with any text editor. Virtually all of the capabilities of the preprocessor are used in the libraries, and you'll find a lot of other interesting code there too. It's also useful to familiarize yourself with the contents of the libraries, as you can find many things not necessarily described in the library documentation. If you want to know what the type `clock_t` is, for example, just look in `time.h`.

The debugging capability that the preprocessor provides is useful, but you will find that the debugging tools provided with many C programming systems are much more powerful. For serious program development, the debugging tools are as important as the efficiency of the compiler. We will wrap up our discussion in the next chapter on advanced and specialized areas of programming.

EXERCISES

The following exercises enable you to try out what you learned in this chapter. If you get stuck, look back over the chapter for help. If you're still stuck, you can download the solutions from the Source Code/Download area of the Apress website (www.apress.com), but that really should be a last resort.

Exercise 13-1. Define a macro, `COMPARE(x, y)`, that will result in the value –1 if x < y, 0 if x == y, and 1 if x > y. Write an example to demonstrate that your macro works as it should. Can you see any advantage that your macro has over a function that does the same thing?

Exercise 13-2. Define a function that will return a string containing the current time in 12-hour format (a.m./p.m.) if the argument is 0 and in 24-hour format if the argument is 1. Demonstrate that your function works with a suitable program.

Exercise 13-3. Define a macro, `print_value(expr)`, that will output on a new line `expr = result` where `result` is the value that results from evaluating `expr`. Demonstrate the operation of your macro with a suitable program.

CHAPTER 14

Advanced and Specialized Topics

This last chapter is a summary of the more advanced capabilities in C. The preceding chapters cover what you need for the majority of programming tasks. Whether you need the stuff in this chapter depends on the kinds of applications you are developing.

In this chapter, you will learn

- What facilities there are to support international character sets and working with several national languages

- What Unicode is and how the encodings are represented

- What locales are and how they help with international data representations

- Which C data types store Unicode characters

- The integer data types you can use to ensure your code is portable

- How you can work with complex numbers

- What threads are, how you create them, and what joining them does

- What a mutex is and how you use it

Working with International Character Sets

Unicode is the standard character representation for encoding characters for most of the world's languages. Unicode also defines codes for a large number of special character sets, such as punctuation characters, mathematical symbols, and many others. Unicode is fundamental to writing applications that will be used internationally. Such a program must present its user interface and output in the language and conventions of the environment in which it is to be used.

Understanding Unicode

Unicode characters are represented by code values from 0 to 0x10ffff. This range of code values provides for representing more than a million characters, which is more than enough to accommodate the character sets for all the languages in the world. The codes are divided into 17 code planes, each of which contains 65,536 code values. Code plane 0 contains code values from 0 to 0xffff, code plane 1 contains codes from 0x10000 to 0x1ffff, code plane 2 contains codes from 0x20000 to 0x2ffff, and so on, with code plane 17 containing codes from 0x100000 to 0x10ffff. Character codes for most of the national languages are contained within code plane 0, which contains code values from 0 to 0xffff, so strings in the majority of languages can be represented as a sequence of single 16-bit Unicode codes.

© German Gonzalez-Morris and Ivor Horton 2020
G. Gonzalez-Morris and I. Horton, *Beginning C*, https://doi.org/10.1007/978-1-4842-5976-4_14

One aspect of Unicode that can be confusing at first sight is that it provides more than one character encoding method. The most commonly used encodings are referred to as **U**niversal Character Set Transformation **F**ormat (UTF)-8 and UTF-16, either of which can represent all the characters in the Unicode set. The difference between UTF-8 and UTF-16 is only in how a given character code value is presented; the numerical code value for any given character is the same in either representation. Here's how these encodings represent characters:

- *UTF-8* is a character encoding that represents a character as a variable-length sequence of between 1 and 4 bytes. I'll explain how these are distinguished later in this chapter. The ASCII character set appears in UTF-8 as single-byte codes that have the same code values as ASCII (ASCII code values are shown in Appendix B). Most web pages use UTF-8 to encode the text they contain. Code plane 0 is accommodated by 1-byte and 2-byte codes in UTF-8.

- *UTF-16* represents Unicode characters as one or two 16-bit values. UTF-16 includes UTF-8. Because a single 16-bit value accommodates all of code plane 0, UTF-16 covers most situations in programming for a multilingual context.

You have three integer types that store Unicode characters. Type wchar_t has been available in the C standard library for some time, but it has been augmented by types char16_t and char32_t. The problem with wchar_t is that its size is implementation defined, and this uncertainty and variability reduces its usability when code needs to be ported between different systems. Types char16_t and char32_t have fixed sizes of 2 and 4 bytes, respectively, which removes this uncertainty. I'll describe all three data types so you know about the complete set, but first I'll introduce you to locales.

Setting the Locale

A *locale* identifies a country or territory. Selecting a locale for a program selects a national language, and consequently a character set, and determines how formatted data will be presented. You set the locale for an application by calling the setlocale() function that is declared in locale.h. The function has the prototype

```
char *setlocale(int category, const char *locale);
```

The locale is specified by the string you pass as the second argument. This is usually a name from the ISO 3166 standard for identifying countries. This standard includes codes of two letters, three letters, and three digits, but the two-letter codes are used most often. For example, the codes "US", "USA", and "840" all identify the United States, the codes "GB", "GBR", and "826" all identify the United Kingdom, and the codes "FR", "FRA", and "250" all identify France. The string "C" represents the minimum environment for compiling C code, and an empty string, "", specifies the native environment. The locale that is set can determine the representation of many things, including the character set, numerical values, and monetary symbols. The first argument to setlocale() enables you to control which value representations are affected by the call. You can use any of the following as the first argument to select what should be affected by the locale string value:

- LC_ALL causes everything to be set.

- LC_COLLATE affects how the strcoll() and strxfrm() functions in string.h behave.

- LC_CTYPE affects the character classification functions in ctype.h and the multibyte and wide character functions in wchar.h and wctype.h.

- LC_MONETARY affects the representation of monetary values and the currency symbols used.

- LC_NUMERIC affects the decimal point symbol and the thousands separator in the representation of numeric data.

- LC_TIME affects how strftime() and wcsftime() in time.h behave.

The default locale for your program if you don't call setlocale() is as if you had called setlocale (LC_ALL, "C").

If you pass NULL as the second argument in a setlocale() call, the function will return a pointer to the locale string that is currently in effect. This enables you to check the current locale, which is useful when your program operates with multiple locales.

It is often helpful to be able to access the formatting symbols, such as the currency denotation, that are used with the current locale. The localeconv() function that is declared in locale.h allows you to do this. Its prototype is

```
struct lconv *localeconv(void);
```

The function returns the address of a structure of type lconv that contains members specifying components used in formatting numeric and monetary values. I'll just mention a few of the more interesting members that are all of type char*:

- decimal_point is a pointer to the decimal point character for numeric values that are not monetary values.

- thousands_sep is a pointer to the thousands separator character for numeric values that are not monetary values. This applies to digits to the left of the decimal point.

- mon_decimal_point is a pointer to the decimal point character for monetary values.

- mon_thousands_sep is a pointer to the thousands separator character for monetary values and applies to groups of digits to the left of the decimal point.

- currency_symbol is a pointer to the currency symbol.

Here's how you might access one of these members:

```
setlocale(LC_ALL, "US");
struct lconv *pconventions = localeconv();
printf_s(" The currency symbol in use is %c.\n", *(pconventions->currency_symbol));
```

Executing this code will result in output indication that $ is the currency symbol in use.

The Wide Character Type wchar_t

Type wchar_t is an integer type defined in the stddef.h header file that stores a multibyte character code. The size of wchar_t is typically 2 bytes, although its size is implementation defined and can vary between different compilers. This is because type wchar_t is defined as an integer type that can accommodate the largest extended character set in any of the locales that are supported. If the macro __STDC_ISO_10646__ is defined, then type wchar_t can store all characters in the Unicode required set (also called the Universal Character Set or UCS), which is defined by the standard ISO/IEC 10646. Under Microsoft Windows, wchar_t is 2 bytes and stores characters represented in the UTF-16 encoding.

Type wchar_t has an advantage over the fixed size types for storing Unicode characters because there is specific formatted input/output (I/O) support for it in the standard library. This is not a significant advantage in real-world applications for phones or PCs though because communication with the user will be through a graphical user interface that will not be supported by standard library functions. The absence of standard routines for formatted file I/O is not a problem because you can always store data in files in binary form, and this has the advantage that there's no potential for losing information when you write numerical values to a file.

Storing Wide Characters

You define a wide character constant by preceding what would otherwise be a character constant of type char with the modifier L. For example, here's how you would declare a variable of type wchar_t and initialize it with the code for an uppercase A:

```
wchar_t w_ch = L'A';
```

Operations with type wchar_t work in much the same way as operations with type char. Type wchar_t is an integer type, so you can perform arithmetic operations with values of this type.

To read a character from the keyboard into a variable of type wchar_t, use the %lc format specification. You use the same format specifier to output a value. Here's how you could read a character from the keyboard and then display it on the next line:

```
wchar_t wch = 0;
scanf_s("%lc", &wch, sizeof(wch));
printf_s("You entered %lc", wch);
```

Of course you need #include directives for stdio.h and stddef.h for this fragment to compile correctly.

The wchar.h header includes specific functions for formatted I/O of wide character data. The functions fwscanf_s() and fwprintf_s() are the wide character equivalents of the fscanf_s() and fprintf_s() functions that you saw in Chapter 12, and they work in essentially the same way. The format string that is the second argument to these functions must be a wide character string. There are also the old standard unsafe versions that have names without _s at the end.

Operations on Wide Characters

In addition to towlower() and towupper(), which offer the equivalent of tolower() and toupper() for wide characters, wctype.h also declares a set of wide character classification functions that complement those for single-byte ASCII characters in ctype.h. The names for the wide character classification functions are derived from the names of the functions in ctype.h by inserting w. For example, you have iswdigit() and iswalpha() in wctype.h, which correspond to the isdigit() and isalpha() functions in ctype.h. You can see some of these working in an example.

TRY IT OUT: WORKING WITH WIDE CHARACTERS

Here's an elementary example of using some of the wide character classification functions:

```
// Program 14.1 Classifying wide characters
#define __STDC_WANT_LIB_EXT1__ 1
#include <stdio.h>
#include <wchar.h>
#include <wctype.h>
```

```
int main(void)
{
  wchar_t ch = 0;                                // Stores a character

  fwprintf_s(stdout, L"Enter a character: ");
  fwscanf_s(stdin, L" %lc", &ch, sizeof(ch));    // Read a non-whitespace character

  if(iswalnum(ch))                               // Is it a letter or a digit?
  {
    if(iswdigit(ch))                             // Is it a digit?
      fwprintf_s(stdout, L"You entered the digit %lc\n", ch);
    else if(iswlower(ch))                        // Is a lowercase letter?
      fwprintf_s(stdout, L"You entered a lowercase %lc\n", towupper(ch));
    else
      fwprintf_s(stdout, L"You entered an uppercase %lc\n", towlower(ch));
  }
  else if(iswpunct(ch))                          // Is it punctuation?
    fwprintf_s(stdout, L"You entered the punctuation character %lc.\n", ch);
  else
    fwprintf_s(stdout, L"You entered %lc, but I don't know what it is!\n", ch);
  return 0;
}
```

How It Works

This example doesn't need much explanation. The variable ch is type wchar_t, so it stores a wide character. The iswalnum() function returns true if the argument is a wide letter or digit. The fwprintf_s() function call writes to stdout, which is the standard output stream, and fwscanf_s() reads from stdin, which is the standard input stream. The format specifications for input and output of wide characters are %lc instead of %c, which applies to char values.

Of course the wide character input and output functions used in this example work with files too. For reading wide characters from the keyboard, I could have used wscanf_s() in the example, and for writing to stdout, I could have used wprintf_s().

Working with Wide Character Strings

Working with wide character strings is just as easy as working with the strings you have been using up to now. You store a wide character string in an array of elements of type wchar_t, and a wide character string constant just needs the L modifier in front of it. Thus, you can declare and initialize a wide character string like this:

```
wchar_t proverb[] = L"A nod is as good as a wink to a blind horse.";
```

The proverb string contains 44 characters plus the terminating null character, so if a wchar_t character occupies 2 bytes, the string will occupy 90 bytes.

To write the proverb string to the command line using printf_s(), you use the %ls format specifier rather than the %s specifier you would use for an ASCII string. The following statement will output the wide character string correctly:

```
printf_s("The proverb is:\n  %ls\n", proverb);
```

If you use %s for a wide character string, the printf_s() function will assume the string consists of single-byte characters, so the output will not be correct.

Operations on Wide Character Strings

The wchar.h header declares a range of functions for operating on wide character strings that parallel the functions you have been working with that apply to ordinary strings. Table 14-1 shows some of the functions that are the wide character equivalents to the ASCII string functions. The optional bounds checking versions of standard functions have names ending in _s, and they follow the equivalent standard functions listed in Table 14-1.

Table 14-1. *Functions That Operate on Wide Character Strings*

Function	Description
wcslen(const wchar_t *ws)	Returns a value of type size_t that is the number of characters in the wide character string ws that you pass as the argument, excluding the termination L'\0' character
wcsnlen_s(const wchar_t *ws, size_t max_size)	The optional safe version works as wcslen() except that it will not reference beyond the end of the array. The second argument is the size of the ws array. If the null character is not found by the end of ws, then max_size is returned
wcscpy(wchar_t *dest, const wchar_t *source)	Copies the wide character string source to the wide character string dest. The function returns dest
wcscpy_s(wchar_t *dest, rsize_t dest_max, const wchar_t *source)	The optional safe version works as wcscpy() except that it will not reference beyond the end of the dest array. It returns 0 if everything works as it should and nonzero if it doesn't
wcsncpy(wchar_t* dest, const wchar_t *source, size_t n)	Copies n characters from the wide character string, source, to the wide character string, dest. If source contains less than n characters, dest is padded with L'\0' characters. The function returns dest
wcsncpy_s(wchar_t* dest, rsize_t dest_max, const wchar_t *source, rsize_t n)	Works as wcsncpy() except that it will not copy to locations beyond the end of the dest array. It returns 0 if everything works as it should and nonzero if it doesn't
wcscat(wchar_t* ws1, wchar_t* ws2)	Appends a copy of ws2 to ws1. The first character of ws2 overwrites the terminating null at the end of ws1. The function returns ws1
wcscat_s(whar_t* ws1, rsize_t ws1_max, const whar_t* ws2)	Appends a copy of ws2 to ws1 and will not copy beyond the end of ws1. It will not copy if ws1 and ws2 overlap. The first character of ws2 overwrites the terminating null at the end of ws1. The function returns 0 if everything works as it should and nonzero if it doesn't

(continued)

Table 14-1. (*continued*)

Function	Description
wmemmove(wchar_t *dest, const wchar_t *source, size_t n)	Copies n characters from source to dest and returns dest. The copy operates as though source is first copied to a temporary array of n wide characters and then the contents of this array are copied to dest. This effectively moves the contents of source to dest and allows copying when source and dest overlap
wcscmp(const wchar_t* ws1, const wchar_t* ws2)	Compares the wide character string pointed to by ws1 with the wide character string pointed to by ws2 and returns a value of type int that is less than, equal to, or greater than 0 if the string ws1 is less than, equal to, or greater than the string ws2
wcsncmp(const wchar_t* ws1, const wchar_t* ws2, size_t n)	Compares up to n characters from the wide character string pointed to by ws1 with the wide character string pointed to by ws2. The function returns a value of type int that is less than, equal to, or greater than 0 if the string of up to n characters from ws1 is less than, equal to, or greater than the string of up to n characters from ws2.
wcscoll(const wchar_t* ws1, const wchar_t* ws2)	Compares the wide character string pointed to by ws1 with the wide character string pointed to by ws2 and returns a value of type int that is less than, equal to, or greater than 0 if the string ws1 is less than, equal to, or greater than the string ws2. The comparison is made taking account of the LC_COLLATE category of the current locale
wcschr(const wchar_t* ws, wchar_t wc)	Returns a pointer to the first occurrence of the wide character, wc, in the wide character string pointed to by ws. If wc is not found in ws, NULL is returned
wcsstr(const wchar_t* ws1, const wchar_t* ws2)	Returns a pointer to the first occurrence of the wide character string ws2 in the wide character string ws1. If ws2 is not found in ws1, the NULL pointer value is returned
wcstod(const wchar_t * restrict nptr, wchar_t ** restrict endptr)	Converts the initial part of the string nptr to a value of type double. The character following the last character making up the string representation of the value is stored in endptr. There are versions with the d in the function name replaced by f and ld that convert to type float and type long double, respectively

All these functions work in essentially the same way as the string functions you have already seen. Among others, the wchar.h header also declares the fgetws() function that reads a wide character string from a stream such as stdin, which by default corresponds to the keyboard. You must supply three arguments to the fgetws() function, just like the fgets() function you use for reading for single-byte strings:

- The first argument is a pointer to an array of wchar_t elements that is to store the string.

- The second argument is a value n of type int that is the maximum number of characters that can be stored in the array.

- The third argument is the stream from which the data are to be read, which will be stdin when you are reading a string from the keyboard.

The function reads up to n-1 characters from the stream and stores them in the array with an L'\0' appended. Reading a newline in less than n-1 characters from the stream signals the end of input. The function returns a pointer to the array containing the string. You can see some of the wide character functions in action in another simple example.

A necessary clarification was done in C17: RSIZE_MAX is pretended to be the maximum size, in bytes, permitted by an implementation for an object; however, the allowed size is smaller because wchar_t has a bigger size. All the constraints for the largest size for rsize_t arguments must be less than RSIZE_MAX/ sizeof(wchar_t)

TRY IT OUT: CONVERTING WIDE CHARACTERS

This example uses the wide character equivalents of `fgets()`, `toupper()`, and `strstr()`:

```c
// Program 14.2 Finding occurrences of one wide character string in another
#define __STDC_WANT_LIB_EXT1__ 1
#include <stdio.h>
#include <wchar.h>
#include <wctype.h>

#define TEXT_SIZE    100
#define SUBSTR_SIZE  40

wchar_t *wstr_towupper(wchar_t *wstr, size_t size);    // Wide string to uppercase

int main(void)
{
  wchar_t text[TEXT_SIZE];                             // Input buffer for string to
                                                       // be searched
  wchar_t substr[SUBSTR_SIZE];                         // Input buffer for string
                                                       // sought

  wprintf_s(L"Enter the string to be searched (less than %d characters):\n", TEXT_SIZE);
  fgetws(text, TEXT_SIZE, stdin);
  wprintf_s(L"\nEnter the string sought (less than %d characters):\n", SUBSTR_SIZE);
  fgetws(substr, SUBSTR_SIZE, stdin);

  // Overwrite the newline character in each string
  int textlen = wcsnlen_s(text, sizeof(text)/sizeof(wchar_t));
  int substrlen = wcsnlen_s(substr, sizeof(substr)/sizeof(wchar_t));
  text[--textlen] = L'\0';
  substr[--substrlen] = L'\0';

  fwprintf_s(stdout, L"\nFirst string entered:\n%ls\n", text);
  fwprintf_s(stdout, L"Second string entered:\n%ls\n", substr);

  // Convert both strings to uppercase
  wstr_towupper(text, sizeof(text)/sizeof(wchar_t));
  wstr_towupper(substr, sizeof(substr)/sizeof(wchar_t));

  // Count the appearances of substr in text
  wchar_t *pwstr = text;
  int count = 0;
  while((pwstr < text + textlen - substrlen) && (pwstr = wcsstr(pwstr, substr)))
```

```
  {
    ++count;
    pwstr += substrlen;
  }
  wprintf_s(L"The second string %ls found in the first%ls",
              count ? L"was" : L"was not", count ? L" " : L".\n");
  if(count)
    wprintf_s(L"%d times.\n",count);
  return 0;
}

// Convert a wide string to uppercase
wchar_t *wstr_towupper(wchar_t *wstr, size_t size)
{
  for(size_t i = 0 ; i < wcsnlen_s(wstr, size) ; ++i)
    wstr[i] = towupper(wstr[i]);
  return wstr;
}
```

Here's some sample output:

```
Enter the string to be searched (less than 100 characters):
Smith, where Jones had had, "had", had had "had had".

Enter the string sought (less than 40 characters):
Had

First string entered:
Smith, where Jones had had, "had", had had "had had".
Second string entered:
Had
The second string was found in the first 7 times.
```

How It Works

This example defines a helper function that converts a wide string to uppercase using the towupper() function, which converts a wide character. You enter two strings that are read as wide strings using fgetws(). All strings in the example are wide strings, including the format strings passed to the wprintf_s() output function. The objective of the program is to determine how many times the second string occurs in the first.

String searching happens in the while loop:

```
while((pwstr < text + textlen - substrlen) && (pwstr = wcsstr(pwstr, substr)))
{
  ++count;
  pwstr += substrlen;
}
```

The `wcsstr()` function returns `NULL` when the string that is the second argument is not found in the first, so when `substr` is not found in `pwstr`, the loop ends; `pwstr` starts out as `text`, the address of the first character in the string, so this is where the `wcsstr()` search begins. The pointer that `wcsstr()` returns is either `NULL` or the address of where `substr` was found in `pwstr`, and this is stored in `pwstr`. Within the loop body, this is incremented by the length of `substr`, so the next search starts at the character following the previous occurrence of `substr`. The first logical expression in the loop condition ensures that the loop ends if the address in `pwstr` is such that there are insufficient characters to the end of the string to accommodate another instance of `substr`. This ensures that you don't search beyond the end of `text`. The loop body also increments `count` to accumulate the number of occurrences of `substr` in `text`.

File Stream Operations with Wide Characters

Writing wide characters to a stream is just as easy as writing regular byte characters, but you should not mix file stream operations for wide characters with operations for normal characters. When you first open a stream, it has no *orientation*, which means that it can be used for either wide characters or normal characters. However, the first I/O operation sets the stream orientation. If you use a normal character I/O function immediately after opening a stream, the stream will be a normal stream with *byte orientation*, so using wide character I/O functions is prohibited. There will be no error indication if you do this; things just won't work as they should.

Similarly, using a wide character I/O function immediately after opening the stream will cause the stream to have *wide orientation*, and subsequently using normal I/O functions such as `fread()` and `fwrite()` will cause problems. You can test whether an open stream has wide orientation by calling the `fwide()` function that is declared in `wchar.h`. It has two parameters, a stream pointer and a value of type `int`. When the second argument is 0, it queries the orientation of the stream pointed to by the first argument. Here's an example using the stream pointer `pstream`:

```
int mode = fwide(pstream, 0);
if(mode > 0)
{
   printf_s("We have a wide stream.\n");
   ...
} else if(mode < 0)
{
   printf_s("We have a byte-oriented stream.\n");
   ...
} else
   printf_s("The stream has no orientation.\n");
```

The integer that is returned is positive if the stream has wide orientation, negative if it has byte orientation, and 0 if the orientation is not set. You can also call `fwide()` to set the orientation for a stream, but only if the orientation was not set before. If you call `fwide()` with a positive second argument, the function tries to set the stream identified by the first argument to have wide orientation, for example:

```
fwide(pstream, +1);                 // Set wide orientation
```

A negative value for the second argument attempts to set the stream to have byte orientation. If the stream orientation has already been set, calling `fwide()` will not change it.

Fixed Size Types That Store Unicode Characters

I'll discuss the char16_t and char32_t types together. Both are unsigned types defined by the uchar.h header with 16 and 32 bits, respectively. The char16_t type usually stores characters in UTF-16 encoding, and the char32_t type usually stores characters with UTF-32 encoding. The __STDC_UTF_16__ symbol is defined to be 1 when char16_t characters are UTF-16 encoded, and __STDC_UTF_32__ is defined to be 1 when char32_t characters are UTF-32 encoded. Don't forget that all Unicode encodings store all Unicode characters with the same code values, and some characters in UTF-16 will occupy two 16-bit words.

You define Unicode character literals by prefixing a character between single quotes by u or U, u for UTF-16 and U for UTF-32. Here's how:

```
char16_t ch16 = u'Z';
char32_t ch32 = U'!';
```

There will be many characters you cannot enter from the keyboard. If you have a US English keyboard, then entering Cyrillic characters or French characters with accents or German with umlauts is difficult to say the least. There is a solution. If you know the Unicode code, you can specify a character by its *universal character name*. There are two forms of universal character names: \u followed by a character code consisting of four hexadecimal digits or \U followed by eight hexadecimal digits for the code, although you'll rarely need the latter. Here are a couple of examples:

```
char16_t  ch1 = u'\u00e9';       // French 'e' with acute accent é
char32_t  ch2 = U'\u20ac';       // Euro currency symbol €
```

As you can see, you use a universal character name prefixed with \u to specify a UTF-32 character.

You define UTF-16 string literals by prefixing the string with u and UTF-32 string literals with U. Thus, you can declare and initialize variables to store Unicode strings like this:

```
char16_t *str16   = u"This is a Unicode string using UTF-16 encoding.";
char32_t *str32   = U"This is a Unicode string using UTF-32 encoding.";
```

Unicode arrays are just like char arrays. Here you define two arrays: one of char16_t elements and the other of char32_t elements. Don't forget that the Unicode code for a given character is the same in any encoding. The difference will be in the number of array elements necessary to store a given character. Codes for the majority of national language character sets fit within 16 bits, so only one array element per character is necessary with a char16_t array and, of course, the same goes for a char32_t array.

You can use universal character names in string literals too:

```
char16_t *str16   = u"Un charact\u00e8re agr\u00e9able."; // Un charactère agréable.
```

An array of char elements can store multibyte characters in UTF-8 encoding. You define string literals with UTF-8 encoding by prefixing the string with u8. Here's an example:

```
char *str8 = u8"This is a Unicode string using UTF-8 encoding.";
```

Each Unicode code will require from 1 to 6 bytes to store it. Unicode codes for ASCII characters are stored in a single byte, so strings of ASCII characters occupy the same space as a regular char array. You may be wondering how it is possible to interpret a string of Unicode characters where the number of bytes required per character can vary. It is very simple. Here's how it works:

- Single-byte UTF-8 character codes have 0 as the first bit in the byte, so the character codes are of the form 0xxxxxxx. The x's are the bits in the code value. Thus, the code values are from 0 to 0x7F.

- For 2-byte UTF-8 character codes, the first byte has 110 as the first three bits, and the second byte has 10 as the first two bits, so 2-byte codes are of the form 110xxxxx 10xxxxxx. Thus, these codes are 11-bit code values and can be from 0x080 to 0x7FF.

- For 3-byte UTF-8 character codes, the first byte has 1110 as the first four bits, and the subsequent 2 bytes have 10 as the first two bits, so 3-byte codes are of the form 1110xxxx 10xxxxxx 10xxxxxx. The code values are 16 bits and will have values from 0x800 to 0xFFFF.

- In 4-byte UTF-8 character codes, the first byte has 11110 as the first five bits, and the subsequent bytes have 10 as the first two bits, so 4-byte codes are of the form 11110xxx 10xxxxxx 10xxxxxx 10xxxxxx. These codes are 21 bits and represent code values from 0x10000 to 0x1FFFFF.

- In 5-byte UTF-8 character codes, the first byte has 111110 as the first six bits, and the subsequent bytes have 10 as the first two bits, so 5-byte codes are of the form 111110xx 10xxxxxx 10xxxxxx 10xxxxxx 10xxxxxx. The codes in this block are 26 bits and store codes from 0x200000 to 0x3FFFFFF.

- In 6-byte UTF-8 character codes, the first byte has 1111110 as the first seven bits, and the subsequent bytes have 10 as the first two bits, so 6-byte codes are of the form 1111110x 10xxxxxx 10xxxxxx 10xxxxxx 10xxxxxx 10xxxxxx. The last block contains codes that require 31 bits and have values from 0x4000000 to 0x7FFFFFFF.

As I mentioned earlier, the x's are the bits in the Unicode code in each case. The explicit leading bits are markers that enable a multibyte UTF-8 string to be interpreted. You should be able to see how the initial bits in the first byte of each multibyte code enable the number of bytes that follow in the representation of a code value to be determined.

The uchar.h header provides functions to convert between multibyte Unicode characters and type char16_t or char32_t. There are four functions: two for converting to and from a char16_t character and two that convert to and from a char32_t character. These functions are described as *restartable* (indicated by r in the function names), because although each call processes a single character, these functions remember what went before, so you can use them to convert character strings. The function that converts a multibyte character stored in an array of char elements to a char16_t character has the following prototype:

```
size_t mbrtoc16(char16_t * restrict pch16, const char * restrict pchmb, size_t n,
                                                  mbstate_t * restrict pstate)
```

This converts the multibyte character starting at address pchmb to a char16_t character that will be stored at the location pointed to by pch16. The function can determine how many bytes define the multibyte character by inspecting the leftmost bits in the first byte. A maximum of n bytes in pchmb will be processed. The pstate parameter is used by the function to record the shift state, and mbstate_t is a struct type defined in uchar.h. The need for this arises because Unicode allows a locking shift character to appear in a string, and this affects the interpretation of characters that follow until the shift is reset. If you pass NULL as the fourth argument, the function will use an internal variable to record the conversion state. The significance of the integer value returned by mbrtoc16() is as follows:

- 0 means that a wide null character marking the end of the string was stored. The state is reset to the initial state when this occurs.

- A value between 1 and n (the third argument value) is the number of bytes in pchmb occupied by the multibyte character that was converted and stored. You can use this value to increment pchmb when you are calling mbrtoc16() repeatedly to convert successive characters in a multibyte string.

- (size_t)-1 indicates that an encoding error occurred and nothing is stored in pch16.

- (size_t)-2 indicates that the next n bytes are not a complete multibyte character and nothing is stored in pch16.

- (size_t)-3 indicates that the next character from the previous call of the function has been stored. This occurs when the multibyte character requires two char16_t characters to accommodate it. No bytes of the input will be consumed.

Note that size_t is an unsigned integral type, so the return value cannot be negative. Casting values -1, -2, and -3 to size_t produces very large positive values. For example, on my system (size_t)-3 is 18446744073709551613.

You might use this function to convert a multibyte string, str, to a char16_t string, str16, like this:

```
char *str = u8"This is a multibyte string.";
char *pstr = str;                    // Pointer to multibyte string
size_t n = 0;                        // Return value from conversion
char16_t str16[100];
char16_t *pstr16 = str16;            // Pointer to char16_t string
mbstate_t state;                     // Struct that records conversion state

while((pstr < str + sizeof(str)) &&                          // Before source string end
      (pstr16 < str16 + sizeof(str16)/sizeof(char16_t)) &&   // and before destination string
                                                             // end
      (n = mbrtoc16(pstr16, pstr, MB_CUR_MAX, &state)))
{
  if(n == (size_t)-1)
  {
    printf_s("Encoding error.\n");
    break;
  }
  else if(n == (size_t)-2)
  {
    printf_s("Incomplete multibyte character.\n");
    break;
  }
  else if(n == (size_t)-3)
  { // Second character so no new conversion
    printf_s("Second UTF-16 stored.\n");
    ++pstr16;                        // Increment destination pointer
  }
  else
  { //Increment source and destination string pointers
    ++pstr16;
    pstr += n;
  }
}
```

The stdlib.h header defines the MBR_CUR_MAX macro that evaluates to the maximum number of bytes in a multibyte character for the current locale. The value can vary between different locales.

The c16rtomb() function that converts characters in the opposite direction has this prototype:

```
size_t c16rtomb(char * restrict pchmb, char16_t ch16, mbstate * restrict pstate);
```

This converts the character stored in ch16 to a multibyte character, which is stored in the char array starting at location pchmb. The function returns the number of bytes stored in pchmb, so you can use this to increment the array when converting successive characters in a string of char16_t characters. If the char16_t character is invalid, the function returns (size_t)-1. When a Unicode code that occupies two char16_t elements is processed, no bytes are stored when the first element is passed as the second argument to the function, so 0 will be returned. You can use this to detect when this occurs and call the function again with the next char16_t character as the second argument.

Here's how you might use c16rtomb() to convert a char16_t string to a multibyte string:

```
char16_t str16[] = u"This is a UTF-16 string.";
char strmb[100];
char *pstrmb = strmb;
size_t n = 0;                          // Return value from conversion
size_t i = 0;                          // char16_t array index

while(true)
{
  n = c16rtomb(pstrmb, str16[i++], NULL);
  if(n == (size_t)-1)
  {
    printf_s("Encoding error.\n");
    break;
  }
  else if(n == 0)
    continue;                          // 1st of two elements for code processed
  else if(str16[i-1] == u'\0')
    break;                             // Null string terminator so we are done
  else
    pstrmb += n;                       // n bytes stored
}
```

When 0 is returned by c16rtomb(), we go straight to the next loop iteration to process the second char16_t element of a pair. When the element processed in the current loop iteration is the null terminator for a string, the loop ends.

The corresponding functions for converting between multibyte characters and char32_t characters are mbrtoc32() and c32rtomb(). These work in essentially the same way as the two functions I have just described.

Specialized Integer Types for Portability

The compiler writer can decide how many bits each basic integer type has. This creates a problem if you want to run your program on different systems that have different C compilers because the range of values you can store may not be the same on all systems. C provides a number of integer types that are designed to address this difficulty.

Fixed-Width Integer Types

The stdint.h header defines signed and unsigned integer types that have a fixed number of bits and uses 2's to complement representation for a negative value. The idea of these types is to provide portability between machines that may differ in the way that integers are represented. Obviously, an integer of 16 bits will be the same on any machine.

The fixed-width signed type names are of the form intN_t, where N is an integer that specifies the number of bits. Thus, int8_t is an 8-bit signed integer type, and int32_t is a 32-bit signed integer type. Here's an example:

```
int8_t b = 8;                    // 8-bit signed integer variable
int16_t a = 5;                   // 16-bit signed integer variable
int32_t product = a*b;           // 32-bit signed integer variable
```

The corresponding unsigned integer type names are the signed types prefixed with u, so, for example, you could write

```
uint8_t b = 8u;                  // 8-bit unsigned integer variable
uint16_t a = 5u;                 // 16-bit unsigned integer variable
uint32_t product = a*b;          // 32-bit unsigned integer variable
```

These types are nominally optional in the C11 standard, but if your compiler supports integer types with widths of 8, 16, 32, or 64 bits, it must support the fixed-width integer types in stdint.h that correspond to these bit lengths if it is to conform to the C11 standard. Thus, any C11-conforming compiler should support some of these types.

Minimum-Width Integer Types

The minimum-width integer types are another aid to portability, and these are also defined in stdint.h. The type of the form int_leastN_t is a signed integer type with at least N bits. Thus, the int_least16_t type will result in a 16-bit type if 16-bit integers are supported; otherwise, it will correspond to a type with more bits, a 32-bit type, for example. The idea here is that if you know the range of values that your code will use, you can choose a type that is guaranteed to support at least that range. This removes the uncertainty inherent in the basic integer types such as short and int where it is up to the compiler writer how many bits they represent. You also have types of the form uint_leastN_t that correspond to unsigned integer types with at least N bits. Here's an example:

```
uint_least8_t a = 5u;
uint_least16_t b = 330u;
int_least32_t product = a*b;
```

The value of a can be accommodated in 8 bits, so the type specification is for at least that. The value of b requires more than 8 bits, so here at least 16 bits are specified. The result of multiplying a by b is stored in a variable with at least 32 bits.

When you have computation-intensive integer operations, you would want to be sure that the operations type you are using to store the integers is fast. The stdint.h header defines integer types with a minimum number of bits that correspond to the type to accommodate the minimum number of bits and provides the fastest integer operations. A type of the form int_fastN_t is the fastest signed integer type accommodating N bits, and `uint_fastN_t` is the fastest unsigned integer type that holds at least N bits. Fast types with at least 8, 16, 32, or 64 bits are supported by a C11-conforming compiler. Types with other values for N are optional. Here are some examples:

```
uint_fast8_t a = 5;
uint_fast16_t b = 130;
int_fast32_t product = a*b;
```

With the `uint_least8_t` type, the type will be 8 bits if that is available. With the `uint_fast8_t` type, the type will be an unsigned 16-bit type if operations with that are faster than those with the 8-bit type.

Maximum-Width Integer Types

When you want to be sure you are able to store integers with the maximum possible range in any given environment, you can use the type `intmax_t` for signed integer variables and the type `uintmax_t` for unsigned integer variables. If you are concerned about the range of integers that can be stored, you are likely to be interested in what the range is. `INTMAX_MIN` and `INTMAX_MAX` provide the minimum and maximum values, respectively, for variables of type `intmax_t`. Variables of type `uintmax_t` will store values from 0 to `UINTMAX_MAX`.

The Complex Number Types

This section assumes you have learned about complex numbers at some point. I'll just briefly introduce the idea of the types that store complex numbers because the applications for these are very specialized. In case you are a little rusty on complex numbers, I'll first remind you of their basic characteristics.

Complex Number Basics

A *complex number* is a number of the form `a + bi` (or `a + bj` if you are an electrical engineer), where `i` is the square root of minus one and a and b are real numbers; a is called the *real part*, and bi is called the *imaginary part* of the complex number. A complex number can also be regarded as an ordered pair of real numbers (a, b).

Complex numbers can be represented in the complex plane, as illustrated in Figure 14-1.

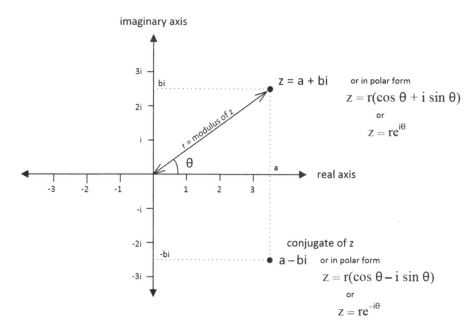

Figure 14-1. *Representing a complex number in the complex plane*

You can apply the following operations to complex numbers:

- *Modulus*: The modulus of a complex number a + bi is $\sqrt{(a^2 + b^2)}$.

- *Equality*: The complex numbers a + bi and c + di are equal if a equals c and b equals d.

- *Addition*: The sum of the complex numbers a + bi and c + di is $(a + c) + (b + d)i$.

- *Subtraction*: The subtraction of the complex numbers a + bi and c + di is $(a - c) + (b - d)i$.

- *Multiplication*: The product of the complex numbers a + bi and c + di is $(ac - bd) + (ad + bc)i$.

- *Division*: The result of dividing the complex number a + bi by c + di is $(ac + bd)/(c2 + d2) + ((bc - ad)/(c2 + d2))i$.

- *Conjugate*: The conjugate of a complex number a + bi is a - bi. Note that the product of a complex number a + bi and its conjugate is $(a^2 + b^2)$.

Complex numbers also have a polar representation: a complex number can be written in polar form as $r(\cos \theta + i \sin \theta)$ or as the ordered pair of real numbers (r, θ), where r and θ are as shown in Figure 14-1. From Euler's formula, a complex number can also be represented as $re^{i\theta}$.

Complex Types and Operations

A C11-conforming compiler is not obliged to implement complex arithmetic. If it does not, it must implement the macro __STDC_NO_COMPLEX__.

Not all compilers support _Imaginary (imaginary); it is highly expected to have only complex numbers implemented. It can be confirmed whether the __STDC_IEC_559_COMPLEX__ macro, in particular, is not implemented in most popular compilers we have been working in this book.

This means you can test whether your compiler supports complex arithmetic using preprocessor directives:

```
#ifdef __STDC_NO_COMPLEX__
printf_s("Complex arithmetic is not supported.\n");
#else
printf_s("Complex arithmetic is supported.\n");
#endif
#ifdef __STDC_IEC_559_COMPLEX__
    printf("Complex and Imaginary arithmetic is supported with IEC 60559.\n");
#else
    printf("Complex and Imaginary arithmetic is NOT supported with IEC 60559.\n");
#endif
```

The first printf_s() statement will be included in the code if __STDC_NO_COMPLEX__ is defined; otherwise, the second printf_s() statement will be included. Thus, when the code executes, you'll see output telling you whether complex arithmetic is supported. The types that store complex data are shown in Table 14-2.

Table 14-2. *Complex Types*

Type	Description
float _Complex	Stores a complex number with real and imaginary parts as type float
double _Complex	Stores a complex number with real and imaginary parts as type double
long double _Complex	Stores a complex number with real and imaginary parts as type long double
float _Imaginary	Stores an imaginary number as type float
double _Imaginary	Stores an imaginary number as type double
long double _Imaginary	Stores an imaginary number as type long double

The complex.h header file defines complex and imaginary as alternatives to the keywords _Complex and _Imaginary, and it defines I to represent i, the square root of -1. You could declare a variable to store complex numbers like this:

```
double _Complex z1;                      // Real and imaginary parts are type double
```

The somewhat cumbersome _Complex keyword was chosen for the complex number types for the same reasons as type _Bool—to avoid breaking existing code. The complex.h header defines complex as being equivalent to _Complex, as well as many other functions and macros for working with complex numbers. With the complex.h header included in the source file, you can declare the variable z1 like this:

```
double complex z1;                       // Real and imaginary parts are type double
```

The imaginary unit, which is the square root of -1, is represented by the keyword _Complex_I, notionally as a value of type float. Thus, you can write a complex number with the real part as 2.0 and the imaginary part as 3.0, such as 2.0 + 3.0*_Complex_I. The complex.h header defines I to be the equivalent of _Complex_I, so you can use this much simpler representation as long as you have included the header in your source file. Thus, you can write the previous example of a complex number as 2.0 + 3.0*I. You could therefore declare and initialize the variable z1 with this statement:

```
double complex z1 = 2.0 + 3.0*I;          // Real and imaginary parts are type double
```

The creal() function returns the real part of a value of type double complex that is passed as the argument, and cimag() returns the imaginary part, for example:

```
double real_part = creal(z1);             // Get the real part of z1
double imag_part = cimag(z1);             // Get the imaginary part of z1
```

You append an f to these function names when you are working with float complex values (crealf() and cimagf()) and a lowercase l when you are working with long double complex values (creall() and cimagl()). The conj() function returns the complex conjugate of its double complex argument, and you have the conjf() and conjl() functions for the other two complex types.

You use the _Imaginary keyword to define variables that store purely imaginary numbers; in other words, there is no real component. There are three types for imaginary numbers: using the keywords float, double, and long double, analogous to the three complex types. The complex.h header defines imaginary as a more readable equivalent of _Imaginary, so you could declare a variable that stores imaginary numbers like this:

```
double imaginary ix = 2.4*I;
```

Casting an imaginary value to a complex type produces a complex number with a zero real part and a complex part the same as the imaginary number. Casting a value of an imaginary type to a real type other than _Bool results in 0. Casting a value of an imaginary type to type _Bool results in 0 for a zero imaginary value and 1 otherwise.

We need to remember (as already established) that most compilers do not implement Imaginary types and only complex. You can write arithmetic expressions involving complex and imaginary values using the arithmetic operators +, -, *, and /. Let's see them at work.

```
There are macros since C11 that can be used to create complex numbers too: CMPLX, CMPLXF,
CMPLXL. They are for double, float, and long double arguments, respectively: double complex
CMPLX(double x, double y);
float complex CMPLXF(float x, float y);
long double complex CMPLXL(long double x, long double y);
```

TRY IT OUT: WORKING WITH COMPLEX NUMBERS

Here's a simple example that creates a couple of complex variables and performs some simple arithmetic operations:

```
// Program 14.3 Working with complex numbers
#define __STDC_WANT_LIB_EXT1__ 1
#include <complex.h>
#include <stdio.h>
```

```
int main(void)
{
#ifdef __STDC_NO_COMPLEX__
  printf_s("Complex numbers are not supported.\n");
  exit(1);
#else
  printf_s("Complex numbers are supported.\n");
#endif
#ifdef __STDC_IEC_559_COMPLEX__
    printf("Complex and Imaginary arithmetic is supported with IEC 60559.\n");
#else
    printf("Complex and Imaginary arithmetic is NOT supported with IEC 60559.\n");
#endif
  double complex cx = 1.0 + 3.0*I;
  double complex cy =  CMPLX(1.0, -4.0);  printf_s("Working with complex
  numbers:\n");
  printf_s("Starting values: cx = %.2f%+.2fi   cy = %.2f%+.2fi\n",
                                      creal(cx), cimag(cx), creal(cy), cimag(cy));

  double complex  sum = cx+cy;
  printf_s("\nThe sum cx + cy = %.2f%+.2fi\n", creal(sum),cimag(sum));

  double complex  difference = cx-cy;
  printf_s("The difference cx - cy = %.2f%+.2fi\n", creal(difference),cimag(difference));

  double complex product = cx*cy;
  printf_s("The product    cx * cy = %.2f%+.2fi\n",
                                      creal(product),cimag(product));

  double complex quotient = cx/cy;
  printf_s("The quotient    cx / cy = %.2f%+.2fi\n", creal(quotient),cimag(quotient));

  double complex conjugate = conj(cx);
  printf_s("\nThe conjugate of cx =  %.2f%+.2fi\n",
                                      creal(conjugate) ,cimag(conjugate));

    return 0;
}
```

You should get the following output from this example if your compiler and library support complex numbers:

```
Complex numbers are supported.
Working with complex numbers:
Starting values: cx = 1.00+3.00i   cy = 1.00-4.00i

The sum cx + cy = 2.00-1.00i
The difference cx - cy = 0.00+7.00i
The product    cx * cy = 13.00-1.00i
The quotient    cx / cy = -0.65+0.41i
The conjugate of cx =  1.00-3.00i
```

<u>How It Works</u>

The code is fairly self-explanatory. After defining and initializing the variables cx and cy, you use the four arithmetic operators with these and output the result in each case. You could equally well use the keyword _Complex instead of complex.

The output specification used for the imaginary part of each complex value is %+.2f. The + following the % specifies that the sign should always be output. If the + had been omitted, you would only get the sign in the output when the value is negative. The 2 following the decimal point specifies that two places after the decimal point are to be output.

If you explore the contents of the complex.h header that is supplied with your compiler, you'll find it provides a wide range of other functions that operate on complex values.

Programming with Threads

Programming with threads allows you to write an application so that several computations can execute concurrently. Each independently executing process is called a *thread of execution*. All the examples up to now have had a single thread of execution in which main() executes. Thread programming provides the potential for greatly increased execution performance for many applications, particularly if your computer has multiple cores. However, there are many difficulties that go with the territory.

Thread programming is difficult because it's so easy to overlook the consequences of interactions between concurrently executing threads. There is considerable potential for very obscure errors in your code. An obvious problem that must be managed is the potential for two or more threads attempting to access the same data at the same time. The kind of difficulty this can cause is easy to visualize. Imagine a program with several threads that may access a variable containing salary data. Suppose that two independent threads can modify the value. If one thread accesses the value to change it and the second thread does the same before the first thread has stored the modified value, you have a recipe for totally incorrect results. This is just one example of complications among many others that can arise when using threads.

The threads.h standard header provides types and tools for creating multiple threads of execution and managing the complications that can arise with them. In the following sections, I'm going to outline some of the facilities that threads.h offers, but if you intend to use threads extensively, I recommend that you obtain a book dedicated to the subject. There are a multitude of pitfalls and programming techniques in this area that it really does require another book.

threads.h is not implemented in Microsoft C/C++ compiler; their approach is very different. There are some similar libraries to handle threads with Microsoft compiler, but they are out of the scope of this book that will keep working with the C17 standard. Pelles compiler has threads.h implemented.

Creating a Thread

The code that you want to execute in a new thread consists of a function that you define. Of course when the function executes, it can call other functions. The function that represents a thread must be of a particular form. It must have exactly one parameter of type void* and must return a value of type int. A single pointer argument might seem at first sight to be a limitation, but it's not. Any type of pointer can be passed, so you could pass a struct to the function that could contain many members of different types, including other structs.

Suppose you define a function that will perform a particular thread task like this:

```
int get_data(void *data)
{
  // code to be executed in a thread...
}
```

You can start the execution of this function in a new thread by calling the thrd_create() function that has this prototype:

```
int thrd_create(thrd_t *thr, thrd_start_t func, void *arg);
```

Type thrd_t stores an identifier for a thread. The first argument to the function is the address of a variable that you create in which the function will store the thread identifier. The second argument to the function is a pointer to your function that will execute in the thread. The thrd_start_t is a function pointer type that is defined as int(*)(void*), so your function definition must be consistent with this. The third argument is the address of the argument that is to be passed to your function when it is called. The value returned by thrd_create() is thrd_success if everything worked, thrd_nomem if memory could not be allocated for the thread, or thrd_error if things didn't otherwise work out.

The following code will start a thread executing the get_data() function:

```
thrd_t id;                          // Stores thread identifier
struct MyData mydata;               // Data for the function executing in the thread
switch(thrd_create(&id, get_data, &mydata))
{
  case thrd_success:
    printf_s("Thread started.\n");
    break;
  case thrd_nomem:
    fprintf_s(stderr, "Failed to allocate thread memory.\n");
  case thrd_error:
    fprintf_s(stderr, "Failed to start thread.\n");
    exit(1);
}
// Join the current thread to id...
```

The comment at the end of the code fragment indicates that you should join the current thread to the new thread, id. I'll explain why a little later in this chapter. Passing the address of mydata as the third argument to thrd_create() causes the same pointer to be passed to get_data() when it is called. The get_data() function can then access the members of mydata through the pointer and perhaps set their values. When the call is successful, the new thread is created, and get_data() starts executing when thrd_create() returns. It is most important that the data that are passed to a thread are not destroyed before the thread ends. This means in the example code that the mydata object must continue to exist as long as the thread identifier is executing.

A thread can always obtain its own identifier by calling thrd_current(). No argument is required, and the function returns the thrd_t value that uniquely identifies the thread, for example:

```
thrd_t this_thrd = thrd_current();    // Store the ID for the current thread
```

Exiting a Thread

You exit a thread by calling `thrd_exit()` anywhere in code that is executing on the thread. The argument of type `int` that you pass to the function represents the result code for the thread, and you can then use this value in whatever way you want, perhaps to indicate whether or not there were problems. Here's how you call the function:

```
int get_data(void *data)
{
  // code to be executed in a thread...
  thrd_exit(0);                      // Success!
}
```

You can call `thrd_exit()` from any executing thread to end it, including the thread executing `main()`.

Joining One Thread to Another

The `thrd_join()` function creates a dependency between the thread that calls the function and another thread. Its prototype is

```
int thrd_join(thrd_t thr, int *res);
```

Calling the function joins the thread identified by `thr` with the current thread. This causes the current thread to block until the thread identified by `thr` terminates. *Blocking* just means that execution of the current thread will not continue, so `thrd_join()` provides a way to make the current thread wait for the completion of another thread. It is important to do this, particularly when you start a thread from the main thread. If you don't, the main thread can end, thus terminating all the subsidiary threads.

If the second argument to `thrd_join()` is not `NULL`, `thrd_join()` will store the result code for the other thread in `res`; `thrd_join()` returns `thrd_success()` when the operation is successful and `thrd_error` when it is not.

Suppose you have created a thread executing the `get_data()` function and you start this thread by calling `thrd_create()`, as in the previous section. Suppose you also have a `process_data()` function that works with the data acquired by `get_data()`. You can implement `process_data()` like this:

```
int process_data(void * pdata)
{
  int result = 0;
  if(thrd_error == thrd_join(id, &result))
  {
    fprintf_s(stderr, "Thread join failed.\n");
    thrd_exit(-1);                        // Terminate this thread with error results code
  }
  if(result == -1)
  {
    fprintf_s(stderr, "Thread reading data failed.\n");
    thrd_exit(-2);                        // Terminate this thread with error results
                                          // code
  }
  // Code to process the data passed as the argument...

  thrd_exit(0);                           // Terminate with success results code
}
```

The thrd_join() function is called with the id of the thread executing get_data() as the first argument, so this will block until the get_data() thread ends. The id variable would need to be accessible here, possibly defined at global scope, or it could be a member of the struct object that is passed to process_data(). When the get_data() thread ends, its result code will be stored in result, so you can use this to determine whether the data were obtained. The result code of -1 indicates there was a problem, so you output an error message and terminate this thread with -2 as the result code. All result codes are arbitrary; you can use any integer value for whatever purpose you choose.

Let's try an example showing how joining threads works.

TRY IT OUT: JOINING THREADS

This program starts two threads from the main thread. One thread gets some data, and the other thread processes the data when the first thread has gotten it:

```
// Program 14.4 Joining threads
#define __STDC_WANT_LIB_EXT1__ 1
#include <stdio.h>
#include <stdlib.h>
#include <threads.h>
// please use Pelles C compiler for this example.

typedef struct MyData
{
  thrd_t id;                                // get_data thread ID
  int a;
  int b;
}MyData;

// Get data function
int get_data(void *pdata)
{
  MyData* pd = (MyData*)pdata;
  printf_s("The get_data thread received: data.a=%d and data.b=%d\n", pd->a, pd->b);

  int mult = 0;
  printf_s("Enter an integer multiplier:\n");
  scanf_s("%d", &mult);
  pd->a *= mult;

  printf_s("The get_data thread makes it: data.a=%d and data.b=%d\n", pd->a, pd->b);

  return 0;
}

// Process data function
int process_data(void * pdata)
{
  MyData* pd = (MyData*)pdata;
  int result = 0;
  if(thrd_error == thrd_join(pd->id, &result))
```

```c
  {
    fprintf_s(stderr, "get_data thread join by process_data failed.\n");
    thrd_exit(-1);                            // Terminate this thread with error results
                                                 code
  }
  if(result == -1)
  {
    fprintf_s(stderr, "process_data thread reading data failed.\n");
    thrd_exit(-2);                            // Terminate this thread with error results
                                                 code
  }
  printf_s("The process_data thread received: data.a=%d and data.b=%d\n", pd->a, pd->b);

  thrd_exit(0);                              // Terminate with success results code
}

int main(void)
{
  thrd_t process_id;
  MyData mydata = { .a = 123, .b = 345};
  printf_s("Before starting the get_data thread: mydata.a=%d and mydata. b=%d\n",
                                                     mydata.a, mydata.b);
  switch(thrd_create(&mydata.id, get_data, &mydata))
  {
   case thrd_success:
    printf_s("get_data thread started.\n");
    break;
   case thrd_nomem:
    fprintf_s(stderr, "Failed to allocate get_data thread memory.\n");
   case thrd_error:
    fprintf_s(stderr, "Failed to start get_data thread.\n");
    exit(1);
  }
  switch(thrd_create(&process_id, process_data, &mydata))
  {
   case thrd_success:
    printf_s("process_data thread started.\n");
    break;
   case thrd_nomem:
    fprintf_s(stderr, "Failed to allocate process_data thread memory.\n");
   case thrd_error:
    fprintf_s(stderr, "Failed to start process_data thread.\n");
    exit(1);
  }

  thrd_join(process_id, NULL);

  printf_s("After both threads finish executing: mydata.a=%d and mydata. b=%d\n",
                                                     mydata.a, mydata.b);

  return 0;
}
```

Here's an example of output:

```
Before starting the get_data thread: mydata.a=123 and mydata. b=345
get_data thread started.
The get_data thread received: data.a=123 and data.b=345
Enter an integer multiplier:
process_data thread started.
3
The get_data thread makes it: data.a=369 and data.b=345
The process_data thread received: data.a=369 and data.b=345
After both threads finish executing: mydata.a=369 and mydata. b=345
```

How It Works

The main() function starts get_data() in a new thread and then starts process_data() in another new thread. The thread ID for get_data() is recorded in a member of the mydata structure. The process_data() thread starts executing before the get_data() thread has finished, so at this point there are three threads running concurrently. The process_data() thread joins the get_data() thread by calling thrd_join() using the ID stored in the struct, which it can access through the pointer that is passed to it. The process_data() thread will block at this point until a result code is available from the get_data() thread, which will be when the get_data() thread finishes. Joining the thread ensures that the process_data() thread does not attempt to process the data before get_data() has finished its job.

The main() function joins the process_data() thread, but not the get_data() thread because we know that process_data() will be the last of the two to finish executing. The output shows that the data are processed properly. It also shows that get_data() and process_data() are executing concurrently, because output from process_data() appears within the get_data() output.

Suspending a Thread

A thread can suspend execution for a time by calling the thrd_sleep() function. One use for this is in a thread that only checks at intervals for data, a thread that checks for the availability of mail, for example. The prototype is

```
int thrd_sleep(const struct timespec *period, struct timespec *remaining);
```

Calling the function suspends the current thread for the period specified by the first argument. The second argument is used by the function to store the time remaining of the sleep interval when the thread resumes in less time than that specified in period. I'll get to how this can occur a little later. You can use the same pointer for both arguments, and the second argument can be NULL. The timespec type is defined in time.h as

```
struct timespec
{
  time_t tv_sec;      // Whole seconds
long tv_nsec;       // nanoseconds
};
```

Thus, you can define any time interval as tv_sec (seconds) or tv_nsec (nanoseconds). The tv_nsec value must be a nonnegative integer less than 1 billion. Note that although you can specify an interval with nanosecond resolution, the actual resolution will depend on your system. The threads.h header includes time.h, so you don't have to include time.h explicitly in your source file to use timespec. The thrd_sleep() returns 0 if the requested time period has elapsed, -1 if the sleep period was interrupted, and some other negative integer if the operation failed.

You could use the following statements to suspend a thread for 4.5 minutes:

```
struct timespec interval = { .tv_sec = 270, .tv_nsec = 0};
thrd_sleep(&interval, NULL);
```

The sleep interval is defined by setting the tv_sec member of interval to 270. Here we don't expect the sleep interval to be interrupted, so the second argument to thrd_sleep() is NULL.

Managing Thread Access to Data

A *mutex* (from *mu*tual *ex*clusion) provides a signaling mechanism for locking data from within a thread to prevent other threads from accessing them while they are being updated. A mutex is an object of type mtx_t that can be owned by only one thread at a time. Each data element or block that needs to be protected against concurrent updating or access would have its own mutex object. Each thread would only access a given protected data element when it had successfully acquired ownership of the appropriate mutex.

Creating a Mutex

You create a mutex like this:

```
mtx_t mutex1;
if(thrd_error  == mtx_init(&mutex1, mtx_plain))
{
  fprintf_s(stderr, "Mutex creation failed.\n");
  thrd_exit(-3);                                              // Terminate this
                                                              thread
}
```

The first argument is the address of where the mutex is to be stored, so if all goes well, mtx_init() will store the mutex object in mutex1 and return thrd_success. If the operation fails, it returns thrd_error. The mutex that is created will be unique. The second argument is an integer constant that specifies the type of mutex and can be any of the following:

- mtx_plain specifies a simple nonrecursive mutex.

- mtx_timed specifies a nonrecursive mutex that supports timeout.

- mtx_plain|mtx_recursive specifies a simple recursive mutex.

- mtx_timed|mtx_recursive specifies a recursive mutex that supports timeout.

Creating a mutex does not gain ownership of the mutex.

Acquiring a Mutex

When a mutex has been created, a thread can obtain ownership of a mutex or *lock* the mutex by calling the mtx_lock() function, with the address of the required mutex as the argument. For a *nonrecursive mutex*, the function blocks until the mutex is acquired. A *recursive mutex* is one for which a thread may call mtx_lock() repeatedly. An obvious situation where this may be required is in a direct or indirect recursive function call on a given thread. Attempting to acquire a mutex that is nonrecursive more than once using mtx_lock() in such a situation will result in a *deadlock*, where execution is locked and cannot be unlocked. A mutex that supports timeout allows a time to be specified in a request for ownership, in which case you need to use mtx_timedlock() instead of mtx_lock(). Without a timeout, the request will block indefinitely if the request is not granted, so a mutex supporting timeout enables an indefinite block to be avoided. The mtx_lock() function returns thrd_success when ownership is granted or thrd_error if there is an error.

You can specify a timeout period for acquiring a mutex that supports a timeout with mtx_timedlock(). This avoids blocking the thread indefinitely when the mutex cannot be acquired. You could create a mutex supporting timeout like this:

```
mtx_t mtx;
if(thrd_error  == mtx_init(&mtx, mtx_timed))
{
  fprintf_s(stderr, "Mutex creation failed.\n");
  thrd_exit(-3);                                              // Terminate this thread
}
```

This creates mtx as a nonrecursive mutex supporting timeout. For a recursive mutex supporting timeout, the second argument to mtx_init() would be mtx_timed|mtx_recursive.

The function to acquire a mutex subject to a timeout has the prototype

```
int mtx_timedlock(mtx_t * restrict mtx, const struct timespec * restrict period);
```

The timeout period is specified by the second argument. This function will block for a maximum of the timeout period if the mutex cannot be acquired, and it will return thrd_timedout. If the mutex can be acquired in less than the timeout period, the function returns thrd_success. An error will result in thrd_error being returned.

You may have code in a thread that can deal with several blocks of data, each controlled by its own mutex. You won't want to block the thread requesting a mutex for one data block when you could be processing another block that is free. The mtx_trylock() function provides for this situation. Its prototype is

```
int mtx_trylock(mtx_t *mtx);
```

If the mutex can be acquired, the function returns thrd_success. If the mutex is owned by another thread and thus cannot be acquired, the function does not block but returns thrd_busy; besides, it returns thrd_busy, if it may *spuriously fail* to lock an unused resource (since C17). If an error occurs, thrd_error is returned. The function never blocks, so you have the possibility of trying several mutexes until you find one that is available, perhaps like this:

```
struct timespec interval = { .tv_sec = 1, .tv_nsec = 0};
while(...)
{
  if(thrd_success == mtx_trylock(&mutex1))
  {
    // Deal with data corresponding to mutex1...
  }
```

```
else if(thrd_success == mtx_trylock(&mutex2))
{
  // Deal with data corresponding to mutex2...
}
else
  thrd_sleep(&interval, NULL);                // Nothing available so wait a while...
}
```

Releasing a Mutex

To release a mutex that you have acquired, you call mtx_unlock() with the address of the mutex object as the argument. This releases and unlocks the mutex so it is available to other threads. The possible return values are the same as those for mtx_lock(). One typical pattern for acquiring and releasing a mutex that has been created is

```
// Create a mutex object to manage access to specific data, possibly at global scope...
...
mtx_lock(&mutex1);                           // Request the mutex - blocks until we get it
// Process and update the data...
mtx_unlock(&mutex1);                         // Release the mutex
```

As long as all threads only access the data after acquiring the appropriate mutex, there is no possibility of problems arising due to concurrent access to the data.

Let's try a simple example that uses some of the thread capabilities I have described.

TRY IT OUT: WORKING WITH THREADS

This is a simple example that creates and starts some threads. Note that the initial version won't work correctly, but we will fix it eventually:

```
// Program 14.5 Thread operations
#define __STDC_WANT_LIB_EXT1__ 1
#include <stdio.h>
#include <threads.h>
#include <math.h>
// please use Pelles C compiler for this example.

#define thread_count 5                       // Number of task threads

thrd_t thread_id[thread_count];              // Array of thread identifiers
size_t task = 0;                             // Integer identifying a task
struct timespec duration = {.tv_sec = 1, .tv_nsec = 0};   // Task work period

// Function to carry out a task
int execute_task(void *arg)
{
  printf_s("Task %zd started.\n", ++task);

  thrd_sleep(&duration, NULL);               // Just to make things take longer...
  double x = 0;
  for(int i = 0 ; i< 1000000000 ; ++i)
    x = sqrt(3.1415926);
```

```
    printf_s("  Task %zd finished\n", task);
    return 0;
}

int main(void)
{
    // Create the threads to carry out the tasks concurrently
    for(size_t i = 0 ; i<thread_count ; ++i)
    {
        if(thrd_error == thrd_create(&(thread_id[i]), execute_task, NULL))
        {
            fprintf_s(stderr, "Thread creation failed.\n");
            thrd_exit(-1);
        }
    }

    // Join the additional threads to the main thread
    for(size_t j = 0 ; j <thread_count ; ++j)
        thrd_join(thread_id[j], NULL);

    return 0;
}
```

Here's the output:

```
Task 1 started.
Task 2 started.
Task 3 started.
Task 4 started.
Task 5 started.
  Task 5 finished
  Task 5 finished
  Task 5 finished
  Task 5 finished
  Task 5 finished
```

How It Works

The output shows that something is not quite right, but we will return to that later. The thread_id array will store the identifier for the thread_count threads that will be created in main(). The global task variable represents an identifier for a thread task that will be incremented each time a new task executes. The timespec variable, duration, that is defined at global scope is a sleep period for a task. The call to sleep() is not necessary and is just there to show it at work. Here it also serves to make the thread execution time even longer than it otherwise would be.

The execute_task() function carries out the arduous task of calculating a billion square roots. When it begins executing, it outputs a message identifying the task that has started. Tasks are numbered starting at 1, so the value of task is incremented by each new task to identify it uniquely. Because it's such a heavyweight task, the thread takes a nap for 1 second by calling thrd_sleep() before starting the task. When the task is complete, it outputs a message to that effect.

The main() function creates thread_count threads that each perform a similar task. Each task is carried out by execute_task() because a pointer to the function is passed as the second argument to thrd_create(). The second for loop in main() joins all the new threads to the main thread using thrd_join(). This causes main() to wait for all the threads that it created to end before it ends too. If you don't do this, main() will end immediately, and the threads it created will also end, so you won't get much in the way of output. You can comment out the second for loop if you want to see what happens.

The output shows that five tasks are started, and the task ending messages show that task 5 ends five times and the others not at all. Obviously, tasks 1–4 are outputting the value identifying the last task, and it's easy to see why this is the case. All the tasks start in succession, and the task identifier is incremented to five before any of the tasks can output a completion message. This is because they all access the same data item, task. We could prevent concurrent access to task by using a mutex. Add the following statement at global scope:

```
mtx_t task_mtx;                              // Mutex for access to task
```

You can create the mutex by adding the following code to the beginning of main():

```
  if(thrd_error == mtx_init(&task_mtx, mtx_plain))
  {
    fprintf_s(stderr, "Mutex creation failed.\n");
    thrd_exit(-2);
  }
```

The execute_task() function can use the mutex to gain exclusive access to the task variable:

```
int execute_task(void *arg)
{
  mtx_lock(&task_mtx);                        // mutex lock - blocks until acquired
  printf_s("Task %zd started.\n", ++task);

  thrd_sleep(&duration, NULL);
  double x = 0;
  for(int i = 0 ; i< 1000000000 ; ++i)
    x = sqrt(3.1415926);

  printf_s("  Task %zd finished\n", task);
  mtx_unlock(&task_mtx);                       // mutex unlock - for use by other
                                               //                threads

  return 0;
}
```

If you recompile and run the example with these changes, you should see the following output:

```
Task 1 started.
  Task 1 finished
Task 2 started.
  Task 2 finished
Task 3 started.
  Task 3 finished
```

```
Task 4 started.
  Task 4 finished
Task 5 started.
  Task 5 finished
```

It all works swimmingly, but there's still a problem. I'm sure you will notice how slow it runs. The reason is that none of the tasks can execute concurrently. The mutex lock applies throughout the duration of a task, so there is only ever one thread executing. They run end to end. There's an obvious solution in this case. We could store the task identity in a local automatic variable in execute_task(). Then we don't need to use the mutex:

```
int execute_task(void *arg)
{
  size_t local_task = ++task;
//  mtx_lock(&task_mtx);                              // mutex lock - blocks until acquired
  printf_s("Task %zd started.\n", local_task);

  thrd_sleep(&duration, NULL);                        // Just to make things take
                                                      //   longer...

  double x = 0;
  for(int i = 0 ; i< 1000000000 ; ++i)
    x = sqrt(3.1415926);

  printf_s("  Task %zd finished\n", local_task);
//  mtx_unlock(&task_mtx);                             // mutex unlock - for use by other
                                                      //   threads

  return 0;
}
```

Now we get overlapped thread execution and output something like this:

```
Task 1 started.
Task 2 started.
Task 3 started.
Task 4 started.
Task 5 started.
  Task 3 finished
  Task 2 finished
  Task 1 finished
  Task 5 finished
  Task 4 finished
```

The results show that concurrent execution is happening and each thread has its own copy of local_task in execute_task(). The sequence in which the tasks complete will depend on the scheduling model implemented by your operating system and how many cores your processor has. We have eliminated the use of a mutex; although everything seems to work correctly, there is still a problem with the code. Look at this statement at the beginning of execute_task():

```
size_t local_task = ++task;
```

This is not thread safe because it introduces a data race. Executing ++tasks requires the following steps:

1. Retrieve the current value.

2. Increment the value.

3. Store the value.

Another thread could start anywhere in the middle of this operation and access and modify task. One way of dealing with this is to use a mutex:

```
mtx_lock(&task_mtx);
size_t local_task = ++task;
mtx_unlock(&task_mtx);
```

This gives the thread exclusive access to task until mtx_unlock() is called, and thus task is incremented safely.

Another interesting approach for concurrent programming is to use fork(); this is from POSIX. As described in Chapter 1, POSIX is a standard that was born by the necessity to have several useful libraries with features that C didn't have in that time, aiming to UNIX platform.

Many of these libraries are already in the C standard today, or have a similar solution, of course, it includes libraries like features from threads.h (others still are remaining).

Operating systems have processes (where a process can have multiple threads). With unistd.h API, we can create child processes using the fork() function. fork() spawns a new process (child) by cloning the parent and shares resources (especially memory); this way, we can have exponential numbers of child processes from there.

I want to emphasize that the target is the UNIX platform; it does not work in Windows native API. Nevertheless, we can use MinGW GCC to emulate the fork() creation process function in Windows. (Windows API uses CreateProcess()):

```
//Example 14.6 simple fork

// it does not work in Windows, unless MinGW gcc is used
#include <stdio.h>
#include <unistd.h>
int main(void)
{
    printf("parent-getpid: %d\n", getpid());

        for (int j = 0; j < 4; j++)
        {
                int c = fork();
                if(c==0) // if fork() return 0 then it is a child
                        // 1, 4, 7, 15,... children processes
                        printf("%d* child spawned -  child-getpid():%d\n", j,
                        getpid());
```

```
                else
                        printf("%d. child created-fork(): %d  parent-getpid():%d\n",
                        j, c, getpid());
        }
    return 0;
}
```

Mentioning fork() was only to have a broader horizon in concurrency. More in-depth details on fork() can be found at `https://pubs.opengroup.org/onlinepubs/9699919799/functions/fork.html`.

Summary

If you've reached this point and are confident that you understand and can apply what you've read in the book, you should now be very comfortable with programming in C. All you need is more practice to improve your expertise. To get better at programming, there's no alternative to practice, and the more varied the types of programs you write, the better. You can always improve your skills, but, fortunately—or unfortunately, depending on your point of view—it's unlikely that you'll ever reach perfection in programming. It's almost impossible to sit down and write a bug-free program of any significant size from the outset. However, every time you get a new piece of code to work as it should, it will always generate a thrill and a feeling of satisfaction. Enjoy your programming!

APPENDIX A

Computer Arithmetic

I have deliberately kept discussion of number bases and arithmetic to a minimum in the chapters of this book. However, it's important to have some understanding of this, so I'm summarizing the subject in this appendix. If you feel confident in your math skills, this review will be old hat for you. If you think the math parts are going to be tough, then this section should show you how easy it really is.

Binary Numbers

First, let's consider exactly what you intend when you write a common, everyday decimal number, such as 324 or 911. Obviously, what you mean is "300 and 24" or "900 and 11." These are a shorthand way of saying "300" plus "two 10s" plus "4" and "900" plus "one 10" plus "1." Put more numerically and more precisely, you really mean

$$324 \text{ is } 3 \times 10^2 + 2 \times 10^1 + 4 \times 10^0, \text{ which is } 3 \times 10 \times 10 + 2 \times 10 + 4$$

$$911 \text{ is } 9 \times 10^2 + 1 \times 10^1 + 1 \times 10^0, \text{ which is } 9 \times 10 \times 10 + 1 \times 10 + 1$$

We call this *decimal notation* because it's built around powers of 10. (This is derived from the Latin word *decimal*, meaning "of tithes," which was a tax of 10 percent. Ah, those were the days!) We also say that we are representing numbers to *base 10* here because each digit position is a power of 10.

Representing numbers in this way is very handy for people with ten fingers and ten toes, or indeed ten of any kind of appendage. However, your PC is rather less handy, being built mainly of switches that are either on or off. It's okay for counting up to two, but not spectacular at counting to ten. I'm sure you're aware that this is the primary reason why your computer represents numbers using base 2 rather than base 10. Representing numbers using base 2 is called the *binary system* of counting. With numbers expressed using base 10, digits can be from zero to nine inclusive. In general, if you are representing numbers in an arbitrary base, n, the digit in each position in a number can be from 0 to n-1. Thus, with binary numbers, digits can only be zero or one, which is ideal when you only have on and off switches to represent them. In an exact analogy to the system of counting in base 10, the binary number 1101, for example, breaks down like this:

$$1 \times 2^3 + 1 \times 2^2 + 0 \times 2^1 + 1 \times 2^0, \text{ which is } 1 \times 2 \times 2 \times 2 + 1 \times 2 \times 2 + 0 \times 2 + 1$$

This amounts to 13 in the decimal system. In Table A-1, you can see the decimal equivalents of all the possible numbers you can represent using eight binary digits (a **bi**nary digit is more commonly known as a *bit*).

© German Gonzalez-Morris and Ivor Horton 2020

G. Gonzalez-Morris and I. Horton, *Beginning C*, https://doi.org/10.1007/978-1-4842-5976-4

Table A-1. *Decimal Equivalents of 8-Bit Binary Values*

Binary	Decimal	Binary	Decimal
0000 0000	0	1000 0000	128
0000 0001	1	1000 0001	129
0000 0010	2	1000 0010	130
. . .	. . .	. . .	. . .
0001 0000	16	1001 0000	144
0001 0001	17	1001 0001	145
. . .	. . .	. . .	. . .
0111 1100	124	1111 1100	252
0111 1101	125	1111 1101	253
0111 1110	126	1111 1110	254
0111 1111	127	1111 1111	255

Notice that using the first 7 bits, you can represent numbers from 0 to 127, which is a total of 128 numbers, and that using all 8 bits, you get 256 or 2^8 numbers. In general, if you have n bits available, you can represent 2^n integers, with values from 0 to 2^n-1.

Adding binary numbers inside your computer is a piece of cake, because the "carry" from adding corresponding digits can only be zero or one. This means that very simple circuitry can handle the process. Figure A-1 shows how the addition of two 8-bit binary values would work.

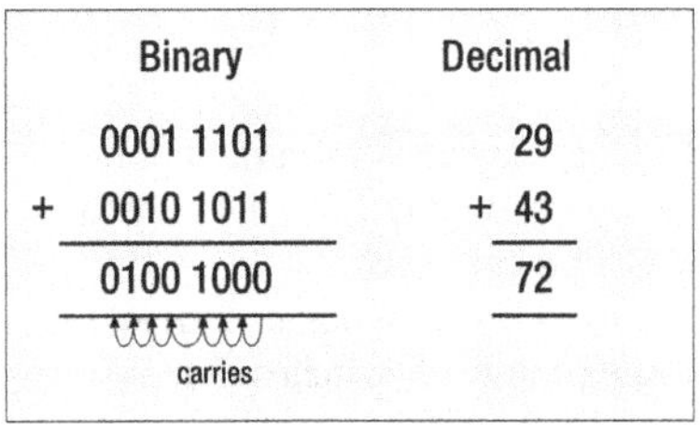

Binary	Decimal
0001 1101	29
+ 0010 1011	+ 43
0100 1000	72
carries	

Figure A-1. *Adding binary values*

The addition operation starts with adding the rightmost bits in the numbers. Figure A-1 shows that there is a "carry" of 1 to the next bit position for each of the first six bit positions. This is because each digit can only be zero or one. When you add $1 + 1$, the result cannot be stored in the current bit position and is equivalent to one in the next bit position to the left.

Hexadecimal Numbers

When you start dealing with larger binary numbers, a small problem arises when you want to write them down. Look at this one:

1111 0101 1011 1001 1110 0001

Binary notation here starts to be more than a little cumbersome for practical use, particularly when you consider that if you work out what this is in decimal, it's only 16,103,905—a miserable eight decimal digits. You can sit more angels on the head of a pin than that! Clearly, you need a more economical way of writing this, but decimal isn't always appropriate. Sometimes you might need to be able to specify that the 10th and 24th bits from the right are set to one, but without the overhead of writing out all the bits in binary notation. To figure out the decimal integer required to do this sort of thing is hard work, and there's a good chance you'll get it wrong anyway. A much easier solution is to use *hexadecimal notation*, in which the numbers are represented using base 16.

Arithmetic to base 16 is a much more convenient option, and it fits rather well with binary. Each hexadecimal digit can have values from 0 to 15, and the digits from 10 to 15 are represented by the letters A–F (or a–f), as shown in Table A-2. Values from 0 to 15 happen to correspond nicely with the range of values that four binary digits can represent.

Table A-2. *Hexadecimal Digits and Their Values in Decimal and Binary*

Hexadecimal	Decimal	Binary
0	0	0000
1	1	0001
2	2	0010
3	3	0011
4	4	0100
5	5	0101
6	6	0110
7	7	0111
8	8	1000
9	9	1001
A	10	1010
B	11	1011
C	12	1100
D	13	1101
E	14	1110
F	15	1111

Because a hexadecimal digit corresponds to four binary digits, you can represent any large binary number as a hexadecimal number simply by taking groups of four binary digits, starting from the right, and writing the equivalent hexadecimal digit for each group. Look at the following binary number:

1111 0101 1011 1001 1110 0001

Taking each group of 4 bits in turn and replacing it with the corresponding hexadecimal digit from the table, this number expressed in hexadecimal notation will come out as follows:

F 5 B 9 E 1

You have six hexadecimal digits corresponding to the six groups of four binary digits. Just to prove that it all works out with no cheating, you can convert this number directly from hexadecimal to decimal by again using the analogy with the meaning of a decimal number. The value of this hexadecimal number therefore works out as follows.

F5B9E1 as a decimal value is given by

$$15 \times 16^5 + 5 \times 16^4 + 11 \times 16^3 + 9 \times 16^2 + 14 \times 16^1 + 1 \times 16^0$$

This turns out to be

$$15{,}728{,}640 + 327{,}680 + 45{,}056 + 2{,}304 + 224 + 1$$

Thankfully, this adds up to the same number you got when converting the equivalent binary number to a decimal value: 16,103,905.

The other very handy coincidence with hexadecimal numbers is that modern computers store integers in words that are even numbers of bytes, typically 2, 4, 8, or 16 bytes. A byte is 8 bits, which is exactly two hexadecimal digits, so any binary integer word in memory always corresponds to an exact number of hexadecimal digits.

Negative Binary Numbers

There's another aspect to binary arithmetic that you need to understand: negative numbers. So far, you've assumed that everything is positive—the optimist's view, if you will—and so the glass is still half full. But you can't avoid the negative side of life—the pessimist's perspective—that the glass is already half empty. How can a negative number be represented inside a computer? Well, you have only binary digits at your disposal, so the solution has to be to use at least one of those to indicate whether the number is negative or positive.

For numbers that you want to allow to have negative values (referred to as *signed numbers*), you must first decide on a fixed length (in other words, the number of binary digits) and then designate the leftmost binary digit as a sign bit. You have to fix the length to avoid any confusion about which bit is the sign bit.

As you know, your computer's memory consists of 8-bit bytes, so the binary numbers are going to be stored in some multiple (usually a power of 2) of 8 bits. Thus, you can have some numbers with 8 bits, some with 16 bits, and some with 32 bits or whatever. As long as you know what the length is in each case, you can find the sign bit—it's just the leftmost bit. If the sign bit is zero, the number is positive, and if it's one, the number is negative.

This seems to solve the problem, and in some computers it does. Each number consists of a sign bit that is zero for positive values and one for negative values, plus a given number of bits that specify the absolute value of the number—unsigned, in other words. Changing +6 to –6 then just involves flipping the sign bit from zero to one. Unfortunately, this representation carries a lot of overhead with it in terms of the complexity of the circuits that are needed to perform arithmetic. For this reason, most computers take a different approach. You can get the idea of how this approach works by considering how the computer would handle arithmetic with positive and negative values so that operations are as simple as possible.

Ideally, when two integers are added, you don't want the computer to be searching about, checking whether either or both of the numbers are negative. You just want to use simple "add" circuitry regardless of the signs of the operands. The add operation will combine corresponding binary digits to produce the appropriate bit as a result, with a carry to the next digit along where this is necessary. If you add –8 in binary to +12, you would really like to get the answer +4 using the same circuitry that would apply if you were adding +3 and +8.

If you try this with the simplistic solution, which is just to set the sign bit of the positive value to one to make it negative, and then perform the arithmetic with conventional carries, it doesn't quite work:

12 in binary is	0000 1100
–8 in binary (you suppose) is	1000 1000
If you now add these together, you get	1001 0100

This seems to be –20, which isn't what you wanted at all. It's definitely not +4, which you know is 0000 0100. "Ah," I hear you say, "you can't treat a sign just like another digit." But that is just what you *do* want to do.

You can see how the computer would like to represent –8 by subtracting +12 from +4 and seeing what the result is:

+4 in binary is	0000 0100
+12 in binary is	0000 1100
Subtract the latter from the former and you get	1111 1000

For each digit from the fourth from the right onward, you had to "borrow" 1 to do the subtraction, just as you would when performing ordinary decimal arithmetic. This result is supposed to be –8, and even though it doesn't look like it, that's exactly what it is. Just try adding it to +12 or +15 in binary, and you'll see that it works! Of course, if you want to produce –8, you can always do so by subtracting +8 from 0.

What exactly did you get when you subtracted 12 from 4 or +8 from 0, for that matter? It turns out that what you have here is called the *two's complement representation* of a negative binary number, and you can produce this from any positive binary number by a simple procedure you can perform in your head. At this point, I need to ask a little faith on your part and avoid getting into explanations of why it works. I'll just show you how the two's complement form of a negative number can be constructed from a positive value, and you can prove to yourself that it does work. Let's return to the previous example, in which you need the two's complement binary representation for –8.

You start with +8 in binary:

0000 1000

You now "flip" each binary digit, changing 0s to 1s and vice versa:

1111 0111

This is called the *one's complement* form, and if you now add 1 to this, you'll get the two's complement form:

1111 1000

This is exactly the same as the representation of –8 you got by subtracting +12 from +4. Just to make absolutely sure, let's try the original sum of adding –8 to +12:

+12 in binary is 0000 1100

Your version of –8 is   1111 1000

If you add *these* together, you get   0000 0100

The answer is 4—magic. It works! The "carry" propagates through all the leftmost ones, setting them back to zero. One fell off the end, but you shouldn't worry about that—it's probably compensating for the one you borrowed from the end in the subtraction sum you did to get –8. In fact, what's happening is that you're implicitly assuming that the sign bit, one or zero, repeats forever to the left. Try a few examples of your own; you'll find it always works, automatically. The really great thing about the two's complement representation of negative numbers is that it makes arithmetic very easy (and fast) for your computer.

Big-Endian and Little-Endian Systems

As I have discussed, integers generally are stored in memory as binary values in a contiguous sequence of bytes, commonly groups of 2, 4, 8, or 16 bytes. The question of the sequence in which the bytes appear can be very important—it's one of those things that doesn't matter until it matters, and then it *really* matters.

Let's consider the decimal value 262,657 stored as a 4-byte binary value. I chose this value because in binary it happens to be

0000 0000 0000 0100 0000 0010 0000 0001

So each byte has a pattern of bits that is easily distinguished from the others.

If you're using a PC with an Intel processor, the number will be stored as follows:

Byte address:	00	01	02	03
Data bits:	0000 0001	0000 0010	0000 0100	0000 0000

As you can see, the most significant 8 bits of the value—the one that's all zeros—are stored in the byte with the highest address (last, in other words), and the least significant 8 bits are stored in the byte with the lowest address, which is the leftmost byte. This arrangement is described as a *little-endian system*.

If you're using a mainframe computer, a workstation, a Mac machine based on a Motorola processor (nevertheless, current Mac machines are Intel), or networking protocols (ICMP/TCP/UDP commonly uses big endian), the same data are likely to be arranged in memory like this:

Byte address:	00	01	02	03
Data bits:	0000 0000	0000 0100	0000 0010	0000 0001

Now the bytes are in reverse sequence with the most significant 8 bits stored in the leftmost byte, which is the one with the lowest address. This arrangement is described as a *big-endian system*.

■ **Note** Regardless of whether the byte order is big endian or little endian, the bits within each byte are arranged with the most significant bit on the left and the least significant bit on the right.

This is all very interesting, you might say, but why should it matter? Most of the time, it doesn't. More often than not, you can happily write your C program without knowing whether the computer on which the code will execute is big endian or little endian. It does matter, however, when you're processing binary data that come from another machine. Binary data will be written to a file or transmitted over a network as a sequence of bytes. It's up to you how you interpret these data. If the source of the data is a machine with a different endianness from the machine on which your code is running, you must reverse the order of the bytes in each binary value. If you don't, you will have garbage.

For those who collect curious background information, the terms big endian and little endian are drawn from the book *Gulliver's Travels* by Jonathan Swift. In the story, the emperor of Lilliput commanded all his subjects to always crack their eggs at the smaller end. This was a consequence of the emperor's son having cut his finger following the traditional approach of cracking his egg at the big end. Ordinary, law-abiding Lilliputian subjects who cracked their eggs at the smaller end were described as Little Endians. The Big Endians were a rebellious group of traditionalists in the Lilliputian kingdom who insisted on continuing to crack their eggs at the big end. Many were put to death as a result.

Continuing with the number 262,657 about little- and big-endian representations, we can test it against the following code. As you can perceive, it examines the number itself. Besides, there is a simple integer (int e) to see the architecture endianness (depending on the order, it will return a one if it is little endian or a zero if it's big endian):

```c
// Program a.1 Checking endianness
#include <stdio.h>

int main(void)
{
        int n = 0x40201;  // 0x40201 = 262657
        char* p = (char*) &n;
        int e = 0x1;
        char *q = (char*)&e;

    //4 bytes an integer:
        for (int i = 0; i < 4; i++)
        {
                printf("memory address: %p: value: %d\n", p, *p++);
        }

        if(q[0] == 1)  // checking endianness
        {
                printf("\nIt's Little-Endian.\n");
        }
        else
        {
                printf("\nIt's Big-Endian.\n");
        }
        return 0;
}
```

Here's an example of some output from this program on my machine:

```
memory address: 00000000002df785: value: 1
memory address: 00000000002df786: value: 2
memory address: 00000000002df787: value: 4
memory address: 00000000002df788: value: 0

It's Little-Endian..
```

Floating-Point Numbers

We often have to deal with very large numbers—the number of protons in the universe, for example—which need around 79 decimal digits. Clearly there are lots of situations in which you'll need more than the ten decimal digits you get from a 4-byte binary number. Equally, there are lots of very small numbers, for example, the amount of time in minutes it takes the typical car salesperson to accept your generous offer on a 2001 Honda (which has covered only 480,000 miles…). A mechanism for handling both these kinds of numbers is, as you may have guessed, *floating-point* numbers.

A floating-point representation of a number in decimal notation is a decimal value, called the *mantissa*, which is greater than or equal to 0.0 and less than 1.0 with a fixed number of digits, with this value multiplied by a power of 10 to produce the actual value. This power of 10 is called the *exponent*. It's easier to demonstrate this than to describe it, so let's look at some examples. The number 365 in normal decimal notation could be written in floating-point form as follows:

    0.3650000E03

The E stands for "exponent" and precedes the power of 10 that the 0.3650000 (the mantissa) part is multiplied by to get the required value. That is

0.3650000 × 10 × 10 × 10

This is clearly 365.

The mantissa in the number here has seven decimal digits. The number of digits of precision in a floating-point number will depend on how much memory it is allocated. A single-precision floating-point value occupies 4 bytes where the 32 bits are allocated like this:

> bit 0: The sign bit
>
> bits 1–8: The binary exponent
>
> bits 9–31: The binary mantissa

Thus, a single-precision floating-point value will provide approximately seven decimal digits' accuracy. I say "approximately" because a binary fraction with 23 bits doesn't exactly correspond to a decimal fraction with seven decimal digits.

■ **Note**   To be more precise, the mantissa in a single-precision binary floating-point number is 24 bits because the leading bit in regular values is 1 and therefore implied. It's still approximately seven decimal digits though.

A double-precision binary floating-point value occupies 8 bytes with the exponent using 11 bits after the sign bit and the mantissa occupying the remaining 52 bits with an implied leading binary digit that is 1.

Now let's look at a small number:

0.3650000E-04

This is evaluated as 0.365×10^{-4}, which is 0.0000365—exactly the time in minutes required by the car salesperson to accept your cash.

Suppose you have a large number such as 2,134,311,179. How does this look as a floating-point number? Well, it would look like this:

0.2134311E10

It's not quite the same. You've lost three low-order digits, and you've approximated your original value as 2,134,311,000. This is a small price to pay for being able to handle such a vast range of numbers, typically from 10^{-38} to 10^{+38} either positive or negative, as well as having an extended representation that goes from a minute 10^{-308} to a mighty 10^{+308}. They're called floating-point numbers for the fairly obvious reason that the decimal point "floats" and its position depends on the exponent value.

Aside from the fixed precision limitation in terms of accuracy, there's another aspect of which you may need to be conscious. You need to take great care when adding or subtracting numbers of significantly different magnitudes. A simple example will demonstrate the problem. You can first consider adding 0.365E-3 to 0.365E+7. You can write this as a decimal sum:

0.000365 + 3,650,000.0

This produces this result:

3,650,000.000365

When converted back to a floating-point value with seven digits of precision, this becomes

0.3650000E+7

Adding 0.365E-3 to 0.365E+7 has had no effect whatsoever, so you might as well not have bothered. The problem lies directly with the fact that you carry only six or seven digits of precision. The digits of the larger number aren't affected by any of the digits of the smaller number because they're all farther to the right. Oddly enough, you must also take care when the numbers are nearly equal. If you compute the difference between such numbers, you may end up with a result that has only one or two digits of precision. It's quite easy in such circumstances to end up computing with numbers that are totally garbage.

While floating-point numbers enable you to carry out calculations that would be impossible without them, you must always keep their limitations in mind if you want to be sure your results are valid. This means considering the range of values you are likely to be working with and their relative values.

APPENDIX B

▦ ▦ ▦

ASCII Character Code Definitions

The first 32 American Standard Code for Information Interchange (ASCII) characters provide control functions for peripheral devices such as printers and do not have a specific printable representation. Many of these haven't been referenced in this book but are included here for completeness. In Table B-1, only the first 128 characters are included. The remaining 128 characters include further special symbols and letters for national character sets.

Table B-1. *ASCII Character Code Values*

Decimal	Hexadecimal	Character	Control
000	00		NUL: Null character
001	01		SOH: Start of Heading
002	02		STX: Start of Text
003	03		ETX: End of Text
004	04		EOT: End of Transmission
005	05		ENQ: Enquiry
006	06		ACK: Acknowledgement
007	07		BEL: (audible bell)
008	08		BS: Backspace
009	09		HT: Horizontal Tab
010	0A		LF: Line Feed
011	0B		VT: Vertical Tab
012	0C		FF: Form-Feed
013	0D		CR: Carriage Return
014	0E		SO: Shift Out/X-On
015	0F		SI: Shift In/X-Off
016	10		DLE: Data Line Escape
017	11		DC1: Device Control 1
018	12		DC2: Device Control 2
019	13		DC3: Device Control 3

(continued)

© German Gonzalez-Morris and Ivor Horton 2020
G. Gonzalez-Morris and I. Horton, *Beginning C*, https://doi.org/10.1007/978-1-4842-5976-4

Table B-1. (*continued*)

Decimal	Hexadecimal	Character	Control
020	14		DC4: Device Control 4
021	15		NAK: Negative Acknowledgment
022	16		SYN: Synchronous Idle
023	17		ETB: End of Transmission Block
024	18		CAN: Cancel
025	19		EM: End of Medium
026	1A		SUB: Substitute
027	1B		ESC: Escape
028	1C		FS: File Separator
029	1D		GS: Group Separator
030	1E		RS: Record Separator
031	1F		US: Unit Separator
032	20		Space
033	21	!	—
034	22	"	—
035	23	#	—
036	24	$	—
037	25	%	—
038	26	&	—
039	27	'	—
040	28	(	—
041	29	)	—
042	2A	*	—
043	2B	+	—
044	2C	,	—
045	2D	-	—
046	2E	.	—
047	2F	/	—
048	30	0	—
049	31	1	—
050	32	2	—
051	33	3	—
052	34	4	—
053	35	5	—

(*continued*)

Table B-1. (*continued*)

Decimal	Hexadecimal	Character	Control
054	36	6	—
055	37	7	—
056	38	8	—
057	39	9	—
058	3A	:	—
059	3B	;	—
060	3C	<	—
061	3D	=	—
062	3E	>	—
063	3F	?	—
064	40	@	—
065	41	A	—
066	42	B	—
067	43	C	—
068	44	D	—
069	45	E	—
070	46	F	—
071	47	G	—
072	48	H	—
073	49	I	—
074	4A	J	—
075	4B	K	—
076	4C	L	—
077	4D	M	—
078	4E	N	—
079	4F	O	—
080	50	P	—
081	51	Q	—
082	52	R	—
083	53	S	—
084	54	T	—
085	55	U	—
086	56	V	—
087	57	W	—

(*continued*)

Table B-1. (*continued*)

Decimal	Hexadecimal	Character	Control
088	58	X	—
089	59	Y	—
090	5A	Z	—
091	5B	[	—
092	5C	\	—
093	5D	]	—
094	5E	^	—
095	5F	_	—
096	60	`	—
097	61	a	—
098	62	b	—
099	63	c	—
100	64	d	—
101	65	e	—
102	66	f	—
103	67	g	—
104	68	h	—
105	69	i	—
106	6A	j	—
107	6B	k	—
108	6C	l	—
109	6D	m	—
110	6E	n	—
111	6F	o	—
112	70	p	—
113	71	q	—
114	72	r	—
115	73	s	—
116	74	t	—
117	75	u	—
118	76	v	—
119	77	w	—
120	78	x	—
121	79	y	—

(*continued*)

Table B-1. (*continued*)

Decimal	Hexadecimal	Character	Control
122	7A	z	—
123	7B	{	—
124	7C	|	—
125	7D	}	—
126	7E	~	—
127	7F		Delete

APPENDIX C

Reserved Words in C

The words in the following list are **keywords** in C, so you must not use them for other purposes such as variable names or function names.

auto	break	case	char
const	continue	default	do
double	else	enum	extern
float	for	goto	if
inline	int	long	register
restrict	return	short	signed
sizeof	static	struct	switch
typedef	union	unsigned	void
volatile	while	_Alignas	_Alignof
_Atomic	_Bool	_Complex	_Generic
_Imaginary	_Noreturn	_Static_assert	_Thread_local

© German Gonzalez-Morris and Ivor Horton 2020
G. Gonzalez-Morris and I. Horton, *Beginning C*, https://doi.org/10.1007/978-1-4842-5976-4

Input and Output Format Specifications

Output Format Specifications

There are 16 standard library functions for formatted output that have the following prototypes:

```
int printf(const char * restrict format, ...);
int printf_s(const char * restrict format, ...);
int sprintf(char * restrict str, const char* restrict format, ...);
int sprintf_s(char * restrict str, rsize_t n, const char* restrict format, ...);
int snprintf(char * restrict, size_t, const char * restrict, ...);
int snprintf_s(char * restrict str, rsize_t n, const char* restrict format, ...);
int fprintf(FILE * restrict stream, const char* restrict format, ...);
int fprintf_s(FILE * restrict stream, const char* restrict format, ...);
int vfprintf(FILE * restrict, const char * restrict, va_list);
int vsprintf(char * restrict, const char * restrict, va_list);
int vprintf(const char * restrict, va_list);
int vsnprintf(char * restrict, size_t, const char * restrict, va_list);
int vfprintf_s(FILE * restrict, const char * restrict, va_list);
int vprintf_s(const char * restrict, va_list);
int vsnprintf_s(char * restrict, rsize_t, const char * restrict, va_list);
int vsprintf_s(char * restrict, rsize_t, const char * restrict, va_list);
```

The functions with names ending in _s are optional and require that __STDC_WANT_LIB_EXT1__ be defined as 1. The ellipsis at the end of the parameter list indicates that there can be zero or more arguments supplied. These functions return the number of bytes written or a negative value if an error occurred. The format string can contain ordinary characters (including escape sequences) that are written to the output together with format specifications for outputting the values of succeeding arguments.

An output format specification always begins with a % character and has the following general form:

```
%[flags][width][.precision][size_flag]type
```

The items between square brackets are all optional, so the only mandatory bits are the % character at the beginning and the type specifier for the type of conversion to be used.

The possible choices for each of the optional parts are as follows:

G. Gonzalez-Morris and I. Horton, *Beginning C*, https://doi.org/10.1007/978-1-4842-5976-4

- [flags] are zero or more conversion flags that control how the output is presented. The flags you can use are as follows:

  - +: Include the sign in the output, + or -. For example, %+d will output a decimal integer with the sign always included.

  - space: Use space or - for the sign (i.e., a positive value is preceded by a space). This is useful for aligning output when there may be positive and negative values in a column of output. For example, % d will output a decimal integer with a space for the sign with positive values.

  - -: Left justify the output in the field width with spaces padding to the right if necessary. For example, %-10d will output an integer as a decimal value left justified in a field width of ten characters. The %-+10d specification will output a decimal integer with the sign always appearing and left justified in a field width of ten characters.

  - #: Prefix hexadecimal output values with 0x or 0X (corresponding to x and X conversion type specifications, respectively) and octal values with 0. Always include a decimal point in floating-point values. Do not remove trailing zeros for g and G specifications.

  - 0: Use 0 as the pad character to the left in a right-justified numerical output value. For example, %012d will output a decimal integer right justified in a field width of 12 characters, padded to the left with zeros as necessary. If precision is specified for an integer output, the 0 flag is ignored.

- [width] specifies the minimum field width for the output value. The width you specify will be exceeded if the value does not fit within the specified minimum width. For example, %15u outputs an unsigned integer value right justified in a field width of 15 characters padded to the left with spaces as necessary.

- [.precision] specifies the number of places following the decimal point in the output for a floating-point value. For example, %15.6f outputs a floating-point value in a minimum field width of 15 characters with six places after the decimal point. For integer conversions, it specifies the minimum number of digits.

- [size_flag] is a size specification for the value that modifies the meaning of the type specification. Possible size specifications are as follows:

  - l (lowercase l) specifies that a d, i, u, o, x, or X conversion type applies to an argument of type long or unsigned long. When applied to a type n conversion, the argument is type long*. When applied to a type c conversion, the argument is type wint_t. When applied to a type s conversion, the argument is type wchar_t*.

  - L specifies that a following floating-point conversion specifier applies to a long double argument.

  - ll (two lowercase Ls) specifies that a d, i, u, o, x, or X conversion type applies to an argument of type long long or unsigned long long. When applied to a type n conversion, the argument is type long long*.

  - h specifies that a d, i, u, o, x, or X conversion type applies to an argument of type short or unsigned short. When applied to a type n conversion, the argument is type short*.

- hh specifies that a d, i, u, o, x, or X conversion type applies to an argument of type signed char or unsigned char. When applied to a type n conversion, the argument is type signed char*.

- j specifies that a following d, i, u, o, x, or X conversion type applies to an argument of type intmax_t or uintmax_t. When applied to an n conversion, the argument is of type intmax_t*.

- z specifies that a following d, i, u, o, x, or X conversion type applies to an argument of type size_t. When applied to an n conversion, the argument is of type size_t*.

- t specifies that a following d, i, u, o, x, or X conversion type applies to an argument of type ptrdiff_t. When applied to an n conversion, the argument is of type ptrdiff_t*.

- type is a character specifying the type of conversion to be applied to a value as output:

  - d, i: The value is assumed to be of type int, and the output is as a signed decimal integer.

  - u: The value is assumed to be of type unsigned int, and the output is as an unsigned decimal integer.

  - o: The value is assumed to be of type unsigned int, and the output is as an unsigned octal value.

  - x: or X The value is assumed to be of type unsigned int, and the output is as an unsigned hexadecimal value. The hexadecimal digits a-f are used if the lowercase type conversion specification is used and A-F otherwise.

  - c: The value is assumed to be of type char, and the output is as a character.

  - a or A: The value is assumed to be of type double, and the output is as a floating-point value in hexadecimal scientific notation (with an exponent). The exponent value in the output will be preceded by p when you use the lowercase type conversion and P otherwise. Uppercase hexadecimal digits are used for output with A and lowercase with a.

  - e or E: The value is assumed to be of type double, and the output is as a floating-point value in decimal scientific notation (with an exponent). The exponent value in the output will be preceded by e when you use the lowercase type conversion and E otherwise.

  - f or F: The value is assumed to be of type double, and the output is as a floating-point value in ordinary notation (without an exponent).

  - g or G: The value is assumed to be of type double, and the output is as a floating-point value in ordinary notation (without an exponent) unless the exponent value is greater than the precision (default value 6) or is less than –4, in which case the output will be in scientific notation.

  - s: The argument is assumed to be a null-terminated string of characters of type char, and characters are output until the null character is found or until the precision specification is reached if it is present. The optional precision specification represents the maximum number of characters that may be output.

- p: The argument is assumed to be a pointer, and because the output is an address, it will be a hexadecimal value.

- n: The argument is assumed to be a pointer of type int*, and the number of characters in the output so far is stored at the address pointed to by the argument. You cannot use this with the optional library functions for formatted output.

- %: No argument is expected, and the output is the % character.

Input Format Specifications

C supports a number of input specifications, which are described in this section. These apply to the input functions that have the following prototypes:

```
int scanf(const char * restrict format, ...);
int scanf_s(const char * restrict format, ...);
int vscanf(const char * restrict format, va_list arg);
int vscanf_s(const char * restrict format, va_list arg);
int sscanf(const char * restrict source, const char * restrict format, ...);
int sscanf_s(const char * restrict source, const char * restrict format, ...);
int vsscanf(const char * restrict source, const char * restrict format, va_list arg);
int vsscanf_s(const char * restrict source, const char * restrict format, va_list arg);
int fscanf(FILE * restrict stream, const char * restrict format, ...);
int fscanf_s(FILE * restrict stream, const char * restrict format, ...);
int vfscanf(FILE * restrict stream, const char * restrict format, va_list arg);
int vfscanf_s(FILE * restrict stream, const char * restrict format, va_list arg);
```

The first eight functions read from stdin, and the last four read from a stream. The functions with names ending in _s are optional safe bounds checking versions of standard functions and require that __STDC_WANT_LIB_EXT1__ be defined as 1. Each of these functions returns a count of the number of data items read by the operation. The ellipsis at the end of the parameter list indicates that there can be zero or more arguments here. Don't forget single arguments corresponding to a format specification that follow the format string must always be pointers. It is a common error to use a variable that is not a pointer as an argument to one of these input functions. The secure functions require that two arguments are supplied for c, s, and [type specifiers, in which case the first must be a pointer and the second must be a value of type size_t.

The format string controlling how the input is processed can contain spaces, other characters, and format specifications for data items, each format specification beginning with a % character.

A single whitespace character in the format string causes the function to ignore successive whitespace characters in the input. The first nonwhitespace character found will be interpreted as the first character of the next data item. When a newline character in the input follows a value that has been read (e.g., when you are reading a single character from the keyboard using the %c format specification), any newline, tab, or space character that is entered will be read as the input character. This will be particularly apparent when you are reading a single character repeatedly, where the newline from the Enter key press will be left in the buffer. If you want the function to ignore the whitespace in such situations, you can force the function to skip whitespace by including at least one whitespace character preceding the %c in the format string.

You can also include nonwhitespace characters in the input format string that are not part of a format specification. Any nonwhitespace character in the format string that is not part of a format specification must be matched by the same character in the input; otherwise, the input operation ends.

The format specification for an item of data is of the form:

%[*][width][size_flag]type

The items enclosed between square brackets are optional. The mandatory parts of the format specification are the % character marking the start of the format specification and the conversion type specification at the end. The choices for the optional parts are as follows:

- [*] indicates that the input data item corresponding to this format specification should be scanned but not stored. For example, %*d will scan an integer value and discard it.

- [width] specifies the maximum number of characters to be scanned for this input value. If a whitespace character is found before width characters have been scanned, then that is the end of the input for the current data item. For example, %2d reads up to two characters as an integer value. The width specification is useful for reading multiple inputs that are not separated by whitespace characters. You could read 12131415 and interpret it as the values 12, 13, 14, and 15 by using "%2d%2d%2d%2d" as the format string.

- [size_flag] modifies the input type specified by the type part of the specification. Possible size_flag specifications are as follows:

  - l (lowercase L) specifies that a d, i, u, o, x, X, or n conversion type applies to an argument of type long* or unsigned long*. When applied to a type a, A, e, E, f, F, g, or G conversion, the argument is type double*. When applied to a type c, s, or [conversion, the argument is type wchar_t*.

  - L specifies that a following floating-point conversion specifier applies to a long double* argument.

  - ll (two lowercase Ls) specifies that a d, i, u, o, x, X, or n conversion type applies to an argument of type long long* or unsigned long long*.

  - h specifies that a d, i, u, o, x, X, or n conversion type applies to an argument of type short* or unsigned short*.

  - hh specifies that a d, i, u, o, x, X, or n conversion type applies to an argument of type signed char* or unsigned char*.

  - j specifies that a following d, i, u, o, x, X, or n conversion type applies to an argument of type intmax_t* or uintmax_t*.

  - z specifies that a following d, i, u, o, x, X, or n conversion type applies to an argument of type size_t*.

  - t specifies that a following d, i, u, o, x, X, or n conversion type applies to an argument of type ptrdiff_t*.

- type specifies the type of data conversion and can be any of the following:

  - c reads a single character as type char.

  - d or i reads successive decimal digits as a value of type int.

  - u reads successive decimal digits as a value of type unsigned int.

  - o reads successive octal digits as a value of type unsigned int.

- x or X reads successive hexadecimal digits as a value of type unsigned int.

- a, A, e, E, f, F, g, or G reads an optionally signed floating-point value as a value of type float.

- s reads successive characters until a whitespace is reached and stores the characters read in the buffer pointed to by the corresponding argument.

- p reads the input as a pointer value. The corresponding argument must be of type void**.

- % matches a single % character in the input that is not stored.

- n: No input is read, but the number of characters that have been read from the input source up to this point is stored in the corresponding argument, which should be of type int*.

To read a string that includes whitespace characters, you have the %[set_of_characters] form of specification available. This specification reads successive characters from the input source as long as they appear in the set you supply between the square brackets. Thus, the specification %[abcdefghijklmnopqrstuvwxyz] will read any sequence of lowercase letters and spaces as a single string. A more useful variation on this is to precede the set of characters with a caret, ^, as in %[^set_of_characters], in which case the set_of_characters represents the characters that will be interpreted as ending the string input. For example, the specification %[^,!] will read a sequence of characters until either a comma or an exclamation point is found, which will end the string input.

APPENDIX E

Standard Library Header Files

The following table lists the standard header files that may be implemented by a compiler that conforms to the C11 language standard. Some of these are optional and so may not be provided by a conforming implementation.

Header file name	Contents
assert.h	Defines the assert and static_assert macros
complex.h	An optional header in the C11 standard. It defines functions and macros that support operations with complex numbers
ctype.h	Defines functions for classifying and mapping characters:
	isalpha() isalnum() isupper() islower()
	isblank() isspace() iscntrl() isdigit()
	ispunct() isgraph() isprint() isxdigit()
	tolower() toupper()
errno.h	Defines macros for the reporting of errors:
	errno EDOM ERANGE EILSEQ
fenv.h	Defines types, functions, and macros for setting up the floating-point environment
float.h	Defines macros that define limits and properties for floating-point values.
inttypes.h	Extends stdint.h to provide macros for format specifiers for input and output using fprintf() and fscanf(). Each macro expands to a string literal containing a format specifier. The header also contains functions for greatest-width integer types
iso646.h	Defines macros such as bitand, and, and bitor, or, that expand to tokens that represent logical operations such as &, &&, |, and ||. These are for use in circumstances where the bitwise and logical operators cannot otherwise be entered from the keyboard
limits.h	Defines macros that expand to values defining limits for the standard integer types

(continued)

© German Gonzalez-Morris and Ivor Horton 2020
G. Gonzalez-Morris and I. Horton, *Beginning C*, https://doi.org/10.1007/978-1-4842-5976-4

Header file name	Contents
locale.h	Defines functions and macros to assist with formatting data such as monetary units for different countries
math.h	Defines functions for common mathematical operations
setjmp.h	Defines facilities that enable you to bypass the normal function call and return mechanism
signal.h	Defines facilities for dealing with conditions that arise during program execution, including error conditions
stdalign.h	Defines macros for determining and setting the alignment of variables in memory. Alignment can be important for the efficient execution of computationally intensive operations
stdarg.h	Defines facilities that enable a variable number of arguments to be passed to a function
stdatomic.h	An optional header that defines facilities for managing multithreaded program execution
stdbool.h	Defines the macros bool, true, and false: bool expands to _Bool, and true and false expand to 1 and 0, respectively. These provide more readable alternatives to the formal language representations that were chosen so as not to break existing code
stddef.h	Declares standard types size_t, max_align_t, ptrdiff_t, and wchar_t: size_t is an unsigned integer type that is the type for the value returned by the sizeof operator, max_align_t is a type whose alignment is as large as any other supported scalar type, wchar_t is an integer type that accommodates a complete set of character codes for any supported locale, and ptrdiff_t is a signed integer type that is the type for the value that results from subtracting one pointer from another. The header also defines the macros NULL and offsetof(type, member). NULL is a constant that corresponds to a pointer value that does not point to anything. And offsetof(type, member) expands to a value of size_t that is the offset in bytes of member in a type structure
stdint.h	Defines integer types with specified widths and macros, specifying the limits for these types
stdio.h	Defines macros and functions for input and output. Reading data from the keyboard and writing output to the command line require this header to be included
stdlib.h	Defines a large number of general-purpose functions and macros. It includes functions to convert strings to numerical values, the rand() function that generates pseudo-random numbers, functions for dynamically allocating and deallocating memory for your data, searching and sorting routines, integer arithmetic functions, and functions for converting multibyte and wide character strings
stdnoreturn.h	Defines the macro noreturn that expands to _Noreturn. Specifying a return type as _Noreturn indicates to the compiler that the function does not return a value. This allows the compiler to perform code optimization while taking this into account
string.h	Defines functions for processing strings

(continued)

Header file name	Contents
tgmath.h	A header that includes math.h and complex.h and defines macros for type generic mathematical operations
threads.h	An optional header that defines macros, types, and functions that support programming with multiple threads of execution
time.h	Defines macros and functions supporting operations with dates and times, including the ability to determine elapsed times during program execution
uchar.h	Defines types and functions for working with Unicode characters
wchar.h	Defines types and functions for working with wide character data
wctype.h	Defines functions for classifying and mapping wide characters. These include towupper() and towlower() for converting to uppercase and lowercase, respectively, and iswupper() and iswlower() functions for testing wide characters

Index

■ D

Q

R

■ T